Clement J. Lambert, Sm.

Jung Institute

or

Apartmenthouse
Zeltweg
Beustweg 3
Zürich

Danke sehr!

BOLLINGEN SERIES XX

THE COLLECTED WORKS

OF

C. G. JUNG

VOLUME 8

EDITORS

SIR HERBERT READ

MICHAEL FORDHAM, M.D., M.R.C.P.

GERHARD ADLER, PH.D.

The Dream of Nebuchadnezzar

From the "Speculum humanae salvationis," Codex Palatinus Latinus 413, Vatican, 15th cent. (see pp. 80, 251, 293)

THE STRUCTURE
AND DYNAMICS
OF THE PSYCHE

C. G. JUNG

TRANSLATED BY R. F. C. HULL

BOLLINGEN SERIES XX

PANTHEON BOOKS

THIS EDITION IS BEING PUBLISHED IN THE
UNITED STATES OF AMERICA FOR THE BOL-
LINGEN FOUNDATION BY PANTHEON BOOKS
INC., AND IN ENGLAND BY ROUTLEDGE AND
KEGAN PAUL, LTD. IN THE AMERICAN EDI-
TION, ALL THE VOLUMES COMPRISING THE
COLLECTED WORKS CONSTITUTE NUMBER
XX IN BOLLINGEN SERIES. THE PRESENT
VOLUME IS NUMBER 8 OF THE COLLECTED
WORKS, AND IS THE NINTH TO APPEAR.

LIBRARY OF CONGRESS CATALOG CARD NUMBER: 52-8757
MANUFACTURED IN THE UNITED STATES OF AMERICA BY H. WOLFF
NEW YORK, N. Y.

EDITORIAL NOTE

This volume of the Collected Works contains essays which reveal the main dynamic models Jung has used and developed over a period that began when he broke away from psychoanalysis and formulated his own concepts as distinct from those of Freud.

The first work, "On Psychic Energy," was written by Jung in answer to criticisms of his libido theory as it had been expounded in *Wandlungen und Symbole der Libido* (trans. as *Psychology of the Unconscious*) and *The Theory of Psychoanalysis*. Originally entitled "The Theory of Libido," it was begun *circa* 1912 but not completed till many years later (1928). Its importance lies in the clarity of its argument and the comprehensiveness of its subject-matter.

Another and longer essay, "On the Nature of the Psyche" (first version, 1946), presents an extensive review of Jung's theoretical position many years later and covers almost the whole field of his endeavour. In it the author thoroughly examines the concepts of consciousness and the unconscious against their historical background, particularly in relation to instinct, and elaborates his theory of archetypes, a subject first broached more than twenty-five years earlier in "Instinct and the Unconscious" (1919).

Of the first importance for understanding Jung's thinking is "Synchronicity: An Acausal Connecting Principle" (1952). Here he advocates the inclusion of "meaningful coincidence" as a dimension of understanding over and above causality. This more specialized essay is truly revolutionary in nature, and Jung hesitated for many years before writing it; the subject was first broached in 1930, and eventually he published the developed work in a volume to which Professor Pauli also contributed. It contains hints for linking physics with psychology, as indeed the two aforementioned essays do also.

Round these three works the remaining papers are grouped thematically. From among them two may be singled out: "The Stages of Life," because of the influence of the ideas it contains on individuation as a phenomenon of the second half of life, and "The Transcendent Function," written in 1916 but not brought to light for forty years. The latter develops Jung's earliest researches into the prospective character of unconscious processes and contains the first and, indeed, one of the most comprehensive accounts of "active imagination," though his later writings refer to and exemplify this technique again and again.

The papers in Section V may also be of particular interest, as showing how the entities "soul," "mind," "spirit," and "life" are reduced to an empirical basis and replaced by the phenomenological concept of "psychic reality" as the subject of psychological investigation.

TRANSLATOR'S NOTE

As indicated in the editorial footnotes appended to these papers, previous translations have been consulted whenever possible in the preparation of this volume. Grateful acknowledgment is here made, in particular, to Mr. A. R. Pope, for help derived from his version of "The Transcendent Function," issued by the Students Association of the C. G. Jung Institute, Zurich; to Dr. Robert A. Clark, for reference to his translation of "General Aspects of Dream Psychology," privately published by the Analytical Psychology Club of New York, in *Spring*, 1956; to Miss Ethel Kirkham, for reference to her translation of "On the Nature of Dreams," *Spring*, 1948; and to Dr. Eugene H. Henley, whose translation of "The Soul and Death" in *Spring*, 1945, forms the basis of the present version.

TABLE OF CONTENTS

Translated from "Über die Energetik der Seele," in *Über psychische Energetik und das Wesen der Träume* (Zurich: Rascher, 1948).

I. General Remarks on the Energic Point of View in Psychology, 3 (*a*. Introduction, 3; *b*. The Possibility of Quantitative Measurement in Psychology, 6).—II. Application of the Energic Standpoint, 14 (*a*. The Psychological Concept of Energy, 14; *b*. The Conservation of Energy, 18; *c*. Entropy, 25; *d*. Energism and Dynamism, 28).—III. Fundamental Concepts of the Libido Theory, 32 (*a*. Progression and Regression, 32; *b*. Extraversion and Introversion, 40; *c*. The Canalization of Libido, 41; *d*. Symbol Formation, 45).—IV. The Primitive Conception of Libido, 61

Translated from an unpublished ms., "Die Transzendente Funktion," written in 1916, later published in *Geist und Werk* (Zurich: Rhein-Verlag, 1958).

Translated from "Allgemeines zur Komplextheorie," *Über psychische Energetik und das Wesen der Träume* (Zurich: Rascher, 1948).

IV

V

I

ON PSYCHIC ENERGY

THE TRANSCENDENT FUNCTION

A REVIEW OF THE COMPLEX THEORY

ON PSYCHIC ENERGY [1]

I. GENERAL REMARKS ON THE ENERGIC
POINT OF VIEW IN PSYCHOLOGY

a. Introduction

1   The concept of libido which I have advanced [2] has met with many misunderstandings and, in some quarters, complete repudiation; it may therefore not be amiss if I examine once more the bases of this concept.

2   It is a generally recognized truth that physical events can be looked at in two ways: from the mechanistic and from the energic standpoint.[3] The mechanistic view is purely causal; it

[1] [First published as "Über die Energetik der Seele" in a volume of the same title (Zurich, 1928), which version was translated by H. G. and C. F. Baynes as "On Psychical Energy" in *Contributions to Analytical Psychology* (London and New York, 1928). The translators' foreword to the latter volume states that this paper "was framed soon after the author had finished the *Psychology of the Unconscious* [i.e., *Wandlungen und Symbole der Libido*, pub. 1912]. It was, however, pressed aside by the greater importance of the type-problem . . . , and, originally entitled 'The Theory of the Libido,' was taken up again only last summer." The original version was republished, under the same title, in *Über psychische Energetik und das Wesen der Träume* (Zurich, 1948). Both Swiss volumes are no. II of the Psychologische Abhandlungen.—EDITORS.]

[2] Cf. *Symbols of Transformation*, pp. 190ff.

[3] Cf. Wundt, *Grundzüge der physiologischen Psychologie*, III, 692ff. For the dynamistic standpoint see von Hartmann, *Weltanschauung der modernen Physik*, pp. 202ff.

conceives an event as the effect of a cause, in the sense that unchanging substances change their relations to one another according to fixed laws.

3 The energic point of view on the other hand is in essence final; [4] the event is traced back from effect to cause on the assumption that some kind of energy underlies the changes in phenomena, that it maintains itself as a constant throughout these changes and finally leads to entropy, a condition of general equilibrium. The flow of energy has a definite direction (goal) in that it follows the gradient of potential in a way that cannot be reversed. The idea of energy is not that of a substance moved in space; it is a concept abstracted from relations of movement. The concept, therefore, is founded not on the substances themselves but on their relations, whereas the moving substance itself is the basis of the mechanistic view.

4 Both points of view are indispensable for understanding physical events and consequently enjoy general recognition. Meanwhile, their continued existence side by side has gradually given rise to a third conception which is mechanistic as well as energic—although, logically speaking, the advance from cause to effect, the progressive action of the cause, cannot at the same time be the retrogressive selection of a means to an end.[5] It is not possible to conceive that one and the same combination of events could be simultaneously causal and final, for

---

[4] I use the word "final" rather than "teleological" in order to avoid the misunderstanding that attaches to the common conception of teleology, namely that it contains the idea of an anticipated end or goal.

[5] "Final causes and mechanical causes are mutually exclusive, because a function having one meaning cannot at the same time be one with many meanings" (Wundt, p. 728). It seems to me inadmissible to speak of "final causes," since this is a hybrid concept born of the mixing of the causal and final points of view. For Wundt the causal sequence has two terms and one meaning, i.e., cause M and effect E, whereas the final sequence has three terms and several meanings, i.e., the positing of a goal A, the means M', and the achievement of the goal E'. This construction I hold also to be a hybrid product, in that the positing of a goal is a causally conceived complement of the real final sequence M'–E', which likewise has two terms and one meaning. In so far as the final standpoint is only the reverse of the causal (Wundt), M'–E' is simply the causal sequence M–E seen in reverse. The principle of finality recognizes no cause posited at the beginning, for the final standpoint is not a causal one and therefore has no concept of a cause, just as the causal standpoint has no concept of a goal or of an end to be achieved.

the one determination excludes the other. There are in fact two different points of view, the one reversing the other; for the principle of finality is the logical reverse of the principle of causality. Finality is not only logically possible, it is also an indispensable explanatory principle, since no explanation of nature can be mechanistic only. If indeed our concepts were exclusively those of moving bodies in space, there would be only causal explanation; but we have also to deal conceptually with relations of movement, which require the energic standpoint.[6] If this were not so, there would have been no need to invent the concept of energy.

5   The predominance of one or the other point of view depends less upon the objective behaviour of things than upon the psychological attitude of the investigator and thinker. Empathy leads to the mechanistic view, abstraction to the energic view. Both these types are liable to commit the error of hypostatizing their principles because of the so-called objective facts of experience. They make the mistake of assuming that the subjective concept is identical with the behaviour of the thing itself; that, for example, causality as we experience it is also to be found objectively in the behaviour of things. This error is very common and leads to incessant conflicts with the opposing principle; for, as was said, it is impossible to think of the determining factor being both causal and final at the same time. But this intolerable contradiction only comes about through the illegitimate and thoughtless projection into the object of what is a mere point of view. Our points of view remain without contradiction only when they are restricted to the sphere of the psychological and are projected merely as hypotheses into the objective behaviour of things. The causality principle can suffer without contradiction its logical reversal, but the facts cannot; hence causality and finality must preclude one another in the object. On the well-known principle of minimizing differences, it is customary to effect a theoretically inadmissible

6 The conflict between energism and mechanism is a parallel of the old problem of universals. Certainly it is true that the individual thing is all that is "given" in sense perception, and to that extent a universal is only a *nomen*, a word. But at the same time the similarities, the relations between things, are also given, and to that extent a universal is a reality (Abelard's "relative realism").

compromise by regarding a process as partly causal, partly final [7]—a compromise which gives rise to all sorts of theoretical hybrids but which yields, it cannot be denied, a relatively faithful picture of reality.[8] We must always bear in mind that despite the most beautiful agreement between the facts and our ideas, explanatory principles are only points of view, that is, manifestations of the psychological attitude and of the *a priori* conditions under which all thinking takes place.

b. *The Possibility of Quantitative Measurement in Psychology*

6   From what has been said it should be sufficiently clear that every event requires the mechanistic-causal as well as the energic-final point of view. Expediency, that is to say, the possibility of obtaining results, alone decides whether the one or the other view is to be preferred. If, for example, the qualitative side of the event comes into question, then the energic point of view takes second place, because it has nothing to do with the things themselves but only with their quantitative relations of movement.

7   It has been much disputed whether or not mental and psychic events can be subjected to an energic view. *A priori* there is no reason why this should not be possible, since there are no grounds for excluding psychic events from the field of objective experience. The psyche itself can very well be an object of experience. Yet, as Wundt's example shows,[9] one can question in good faith whether the energic point of view is applicable to psychic phenomena at all, and if it is applicable, whether the psyche can be looked upon as a relatively closed system.

---

[7] Finality and causality are two possible ways of understanding which form an antinomy. They are progressive and regressive "interpretants" (Wundt) and as such are contradictory. Naturally this statement is correct only if it is assumed that the concept of energy is an abstraction that expresses relation. ("Energy is relation": von Hartmann, p. 196). But the statement is not correct if an hypostatized concept of energy is assumed, as in Ostwald's *Die Philosophie der Werte.*

[8] "The difference between the teleological and the causal view of things is not a real one dividing the contents of experience into two disparate realms. The sole difference between the two views is the formal one that a causal connection belongs as a complement to every final relationship, and conversely, every causal connection can be given, if need be, a teleological form." Wundt, p. 737.

[9] [Cf. n. 5.—EDITORS.]

8   As to the first point, I am in entire agreement with von Grot —one of the first to propose the concept of psychic energy—when he says: "The concept of psychic energy is as much justified in science as that of physical energy, and psychic energy has just as many quantitative measurements and different forms as has physical energy." [10]

9   As to the second point, I differ from previous investigators in that I am not concerned in the least in fitting psychic energy processes into the physical system. I am not interested in such a classification because we have at best only the vaguest conjectures to go on and no real point of departure. Although it seems certain to me that psychic energy is in some way or other closely connected with physical processes, yet, in order to speak with any authority about this connection, we would need quite different experiences and insights. As to the philosophical side of the question, I entirely endorse the views of Busse.[11] I must also support Külpe when he says: "It would thus make no difference whether a quantum of mental energy inserts itself into the course of the material process or not: the law of the conservation of energy as formulated hitherto would not be impaired." [12]

10   In my view the psychophysical relation is a problem in itself, which perhaps will be solved some day. In the meantime, however, the psychologist need not be held up by this difficulty, but can regard the psyche as a *relatively* closed system. In that case we must certainly break with what seems to me the untenable "psychophysical" hypothesis, since its epiphenomenalist point of view is simply a legacy from the old-fashioned scientific materialism. Thus, as Lasswitz, von Grot, and others think, the phenomena of consciousness have no functional connections with one another, for they are *only* (!) "phenomena, expressions, symptoms of certain deeper functional relationships." The causal connections existing between psychic facts, which we can observe at any time, contradict the epiphenomenon theory, which has a fatal similarity to the materialistic belief that the psyche is secreted by the brain as the gall is by the liver. A

[10] "Die Begriffe der Seele und der psychischen Energie in der Psychologie," *Archiv für systematische Philosophie*, IV.
[11] Busse, *Geist und Körper, Seele und Leib*.
[12] Külpe, *Einleitung in die Philosophie*, p. 150.

psychology that treats the psyche as an epiphenomenon would better call itself brain-psychology, and remain satisfied with the meagre results that such a psycho-physiology can yield. The psyche deserves to be taken as a phenomenon in its own right; there are no grounds at all for regarding it as a mere epiphenomenon, dependent though it may be on the functioning of the brain. One would be as little justified in regarding life as an epiphenomenon of the chemistry of carbon compounds.

11 The immediate experience of quantitative psychic relations on the one hand, and the unfathomable nature of a psychophysical connection on the other, justify at least a provisional view of the psyche as a relatively closed system. Here I find myself in direct opposition to von Grot's psychophysical energetics. In my view he is moving here on very uncertain ground, so that his further remarks have little plausibility. Nevertheless, I would like to put von Grot's formulations before the reader in his own words, as they represent the opinions of a pioneer in this difficult field:

(1) Psychic energies possess quantity and mass, just like physical energies.

(2) As different forms of psychic work and psychic potentiality, they can be transformed into one another.

(3) They can be converted into physical energies and vice versa, by means of physiological processes.[13]

12 I need scarcely add that statement three seems to require a significant question mark. In the last analysis it is only expediency that can decide, not whether the energic view is possible in itself, but whether it promises results in practice.[14]

13 The possibility of exact quantitative measurement of physical energy has *proved* that the energic standpoint does yield results when applied to physical events. But it would still be possible to consider physical events as forms of energy even if there were no exact quantitative measurement but merely the possibility of *estimating quantities*.[15] If, however, even that

13 Ibid., p. 323.
14 Von Grot goes so far as to say (p. 324): "The burden of proof falls on those who deny psychic energy, not on those who acknowledge it."
15 This was actually the case with Descartes, who first formulated the principle of the conservation of the quantity of movement, but had not at his disposal the methods of physical measurement which were discovered only in recent times.

proved to be impossible, then the energic point of view would have to be abandoned, since if there is not at least a possibility of a quantitative estimate the energic standpoint is quite superfluous.

(i) THE SUBJECTIVE SYSTEM OF VALUES

14   The applicability of the energic standpoint to psychology rests, then, exclusively on the question whether a quantitative estimate of psychic energy is possible or not. This question can be met with an unconditional affirmative, since our psyche actually possesses an extraordinarily well-developed evaluating system, namely the *system of psychological values*. Values are quantitative estimates of energy. Here it should be remarked that in our collective moral and aesthetic values we have at our disposal not merely an objective system of value but an objective system of measurement. This system of measurement is not, however, directly available for our purpose, since it is a general scale of values which takes account only indirectly of subjective, that is to say individual, psychological conditions.

15   What we must first of all consider, therefore, is the *subjective value system*, the subjective estimates of the single individual. We can, as a matter of fact, estimate the subjective values of our psychic contents up to a certain point, even though it is at times extraordinarily difficult to measure them with objective accuracy against the generally established values. However, this comparison is superfluous for our purpose, as already said. We can weigh our subjective evaluations against one another and determine their *relative* strength. Their measurement is nevertheless relative to the value of other contents and therefore not absolute and objective, but it is sufficient for our purpose inasmuch as different intensities of value in relation to similar qualities can be recognized with certainty, while equal values under the same conditions plainly maintain themselves in equilibrium.

16   The difficulty begins only when we have to compare the value intensities of different qualities, say the value of a scientific idea compared with a feeling impression. Here the subjective estimate becomes uncertain and therefore unreliable. In the same way, the subjective estimate is restricted to the contents

of consciousness; hence it is useless with respect to unconscious influences, where we are concerned with valuations that go beyond the boundaries of consciousness.

17 In view of the compensatory relationship known to exist between the conscious and the unconscious,[16] however, it is of great importance to find a way of determining the value of unconscious products. If we want to carry through the energic approach to psychic events, we must bear in mind the exceedingly important fact that conscious values can apparently disappear without showing themselves again in an equivalent conscious achievement. In this case we should theoretically expect their appearance in the unconscious. But since the unconscious is not directly accessible either in ourselves or in others, the evaluation can only be an indirect one, so we must have recourse to auxiliary methods in order to arrive at our estimates of value. In the case of subjective evaluation, feeling and insight come to our aid immediately, because these are functions which have been developing over long periods of time and have become very finely differentiated. Even the child practises very early the differentiation of his scale of values; he weighs up whether he likes his father or mother better, who comes in the second and third place, who is most hated, etc. This conscious evaluation not only breaks down in regard to the manifestations of the unconscious but is actually twisted into the most obvious false estimates, also described as "repressions" or the "displacement of affect." Subjective evaluation is therefore completely out of the question in estimating unconscious value intensities. Consequently we need an objective point of departure that will make an indirect but objective estimate possible.

(ii) OBJECTIVE ESTIMATE OF QUANTITY

18 In my study of the phenomena of association [17] I have shown that there are certain constellations of psychic elements grouped

[16] The one-sidedness of consciousness is compensated by a counterposition in the unconscious. It is chiefly the facts of psychopathology that show the compensatory attitude of the unconscious most clearly. Evidence for this may be found in the writings of Freud and Adler, also in my "Psychology of Dementia Praecox." For a theoretical discussion see my "Instinct and the Unconscious," pars. 263ff., infra. On the general significance of psychological compensation see Maeder, "Régulation psychique et guérison."

[17] [Cf. Vol. 2, *Collected Works* (1918 edn.: *Studies in Word Association*).—EDITORS.]

round feeling-toned [18] contents, which I have called "complexes." The feeling-toned content, the complex, consists of a nuclear element and a large number of secondarily constellated associations. The nuclear element consists of two components: first, a factor determined by experience and causally related to the environment; second, a factor innate in the individual's character and determined by his disposition.

19   The nuclear element is characterized by its feeling-tone, the emphasis resulting from the intensity of affect. This emphasis, expressed in terms of energy, is a value quantity. In so far as the nuclear element is conscious, the quantity can be subjectively estimated, at least relatively. But if, as frequently happens, the nuclear element is unconscious,[19] at any rate in its psychological significance, then a subjective estimate becomes impossible, and one must substitute the indirect method of evaluation. This is based, in principle, on the following fact:

18 [Cf. *Psychiatric Studies*, p. 97, n. 2a.—EDITORS.]

19 That a complex or its essential nucleus can be unconscious is not a self-evident fact. A complex would not be a complex at all if it did not possess a certain, even a considerable, affective intensity. One would expect that this energic value would automatically force the complex into consciousness, that the power of attraction inherent within it would compel conscious attention. (Fields of power attract one another mutually!) That this, as experience shows, is frequently not the case requires a special explanation. The readiest and simplest explanation is given by Freud's theory of repression. This theory presupposes a counterposition in the conscious mind: the conscious attitude is, so to speak, hostile to the unconscious complex and does not allow it to reach consciousness. This theory certainly explains very many cases, but in my experience there are some cases that cannot be so explained. Actually, the repression theory takes account only of those cases in which a content, in itself perfectly capable of becoming conscious, is either quite consciously repressed and made unconscious, or has right from the beginning never reached consciousness. It does not take into account those other cases in which a content of high energic intensity is formed out of unconscious material that is not in itself capable of becoming conscious, and so cannot be made conscious at all, or only with the greatest difficulty. In these cases the conscious attitude, far from being hostile to the unconscious content, would be most favourably disposed towards it, as in the case of creative products, which, as we know, almost always have their first beginnings in the unconscious. Just as a mother awaits her child with longing and yet brings it into the world only with effort and pain, so a new, creative content, despite the willingness of the conscious mind, can remain for a long time in the unconscious without being "repressed." Though it has a high energic value it still does not become conscious. Cases of this sort are not too difficult to explain. Because the content is new and therefore strange to consciousness, there are no existing

11

that the nuclear element automatically creates a complex to the degree that it is affectively toned and possesses energic value, as I have shown in detail in the second and third chapters of my "Psychology of Dementia Praecox." The nuclear element has a constellating power corresponding to its energic value. It produces a specific constellation of psychic contents, thus giving rise to the complex, which is a constellation of psychic contents dynamically conditioned by the energic value. The resultant constellation, however, is not just an irradiation of the psychic stimulus, but a selection of the stimulated psychic contents which is conditioned by the *quality* of the nuclear element. This selection cannot, of course, be explained in terms of energy, because the energic explanation is quantitative and not qualitative. For a qualitative explanation we must have recourse to the causal view.[20] The proposition upon which the objective estimate of psychological value intensities is based therefore runs as follows: *the constellating power of the nuclear element corresponds to its value intensity, i.e., to its energy.*

20   But what means have we of estimating the energic value of the constellating power which enriches the complex with associations? We can estimate this quantum of energy in various ways: (1) from the relative number of constellations effected by the nuclear element; (2) from the relative frequency and intensity of the reactions indicating a disturbance or complex; (3) from the intensity of the accompanying affects.

21   1. The data required to determine the relative number of constellations may be obtained partly by direct observation and partly by analytical deduction. That is to say, the more frequent the constellations conditioned by one and the same complex, the greater must be its psychological valency.

22   2. The reactions indicating a disturbance or complex do not

associations and connecting bridges to the conscious contents. All these connections must first be laid down with considerable effort, for without them no consciousness is possible. Two main grounds must therefore be considered in explaining the unconsciousness of a complex: (1) the repression of a content capable of becoming conscious, and (2) the strangeness of a content not yet capable of reaching consciousness.

20 Or to an hypostatized concept of energy, such as Ostwald holds. But the concept of substance needed for a causal-mechanistic mode of explanation can hardly be circumvented in this fashion, since "energy" is at bottom always a concept concerned with quantity alone.

include only the symptoms that appear in the course of the association experiment. These are really nothing but the effects of the complex, and their form is determined by the particular type of experiment. We are more concerned here with those phenomena that are peculiar to psychological processes outside experimental conditions. Freud has described the greater part of them under the head of lapses of speech, mistakes in writing, slips of memory, misunderstandings, and other symptomatic actions. To these we must add the automatisms described by me, "thought-deprivation," "interdiction," "irrelevant talk," [21] etc. As I have shown in my association experiments, the intensity of these phenomena can be directly determined by a time record, and the same thing is possible also in the case of an unrestricted psychological procedures, when, watch in hand, we can easily determine the value intensity from the time taken by the patient to speak about certain things. It might be objected that patients very often waste the better part of their time talking about irrelevancies in order to evade the main issue, but that only shows how much more important these so-called irrelevancies are to them. The observer must guard against arbitrary judgments that explain the real interests of the patient as irrelevant, in accordance with some subjective, theoretical assumption of the analyst's. In determining values, he must hold strictly to objective criteria. Thus, if a patient wastes hours complaining about her servants instead of coming to the main conflict, which may have been gauged quite correctly by the analyst, this only means that the servant-complex has in fact a higher energic value than the still unconscious conflict, which will perhaps reveal itself as the nuclear element only during the further course of treatment, or that the inhibition exercised by the highly valued conscious position keeps the nuclear element in the unconscious through overcompensation.

23   3. In order to determine the intensity of affective phenomena we have objective methods which, while not measuring the quantity of affect, nevertheless permit an estimate. Experimental psychology has furnished us with a number of such methods. Apart from time measurements, which determine the inhibition

21 [Cf. "The Psychology of Dementia Praecox," pars. 175ff.—EDITORS.]

of the association process rather than the actual affects, we have the following devices in particular:

    (a) the pulse curve; [22]

    (b) the respiration curve; [23]

    (c) the psycho-galvanic phenomenon.[24]

[24]   The easily recognizable changes in these curves permit inferential estimates to be made concerning the intensity of the disturbing cause. It is also possible, as experience has shown to our satisfaction, deliberately to induce affective phenomena in the subject by means of psychological stimuli which one knows to be especially charged with affect for this particular individual in relation to the experimenter.[25]

[25]   Besides these experimental methods we have a highly differentiated subjective system for recognizing and evaluating affective phenomena in others. There is present in each of us a direct instinct for registering this, which animals also possess in high degree, with respect not only to their own species but also to other animals and human beings. We can perceive the slightest emotional fluctuations in others and have a very fine feeling for the quality and quantity of affects in our fellow-men.

II. APPLICATION OF THE ENERGIC STANDPOINT

a. The Psychological Concept of Energy

[26]   The term "psychic energy" has long been in use. We find it, for example, as early as Schiller,[26] and the energic point of view

---

[22] Cf. Berger, *Über die körperlichen Aeusserungen psychischer Zustände;* Lehmann, *Die körperlichen Äusserungen psychischer Zustände,* trans. (into German) by Bendixen.

[23] Peterson and Jung, "Psycho-physical Investigations with the Galvanometer and Pneumograph in Normal and Insane Individuals"; Nunberg, "On the Physical Accompaniments of Association Processes," in Jung, *Studies in Word Association;* Ricksher and Jung, "Further Investigations on the Galvanic Phenomenon."

[24] Veraguth, *Das psycho-galvanische Reflexphänomen;* Binswanger, "On the Psycho-galvanic Phenomenon in Association Experiments," in Jung, *Studies in Word Association.*

[25] Cf. *Studies in Word Association* and "The Association Method."

[26] Schiller thinks in terms of energy, so to speak. He operates with ideas like "transfer of intensity," etc. Cf. *On the Aesthetic Education of Man,* trans. by Snell.

14

was also used by von Grot [27] and Theodor Lipps.[28] Lipps distinguishes psychic energy from physical energy, while Stern [29] leaves the question of their connection open. We have to thank Lipps for the distinction between psychic *energy* and psychic *force*. For Lipps, psychic force is the possibility of processes arising in the psyche at all and of attaining a certain degree of efficiency. Psychic energy, on the other hand, is defined by Lipps as the "inherent capacity of these processes to actualize this force in themselves." [30] Elsewhere Lipps speaks of "psychic quantities." The distinction between force and energy is a conceptual necessity, for energy is really a concept and, as such, does not exist objectively in the phenomena themselves but only in the specific data of experience. In other words, energy is always experienced specifically as motion and force when actual, and as a state or condition when potential. Psychic energy appears, when actual, in the specific, dynamic phenomena of the psyche, such as instinct, wishing, willing, affect, attention, capacity for work, etc., which make up the psychic forces. When potential, energy shows itself in specific achievements, possibilities, aptitudes, attitudes, etc., which are its various states.

27   The differentiation of specific energies, such as pleasure energy, sensation energy, contrary energy, etc., proposed by Lipps, seems to me theoretically inadmissible as the specific forms of energy are the above-mentioned forces and states. Energy is a quantitative concept which includes them all. It is only these forces and states that are determined qualitatively, for they are concepts that express qualities brought into action through energy. The concept of quantity should never be qualitative at the same time, otherwise it would never enable us to expound the relations between forces, which is after all its real function.

28   Since, unfortunately, we cannot prove scientifically that a relation of equivalence exists between physical and psychic energy,[31] we have no alternative except either to drop the

27 "Die Begriffe der Seele und der psychischen Energie in der Psychologie."
28 *Leitfaden der Psychologie*, pp. 62, 66f.
29 Stern, *Über Psychologie der individuellen Differenzen*, pp. 119ff.
30 *Leitfaden der Psychologie*, p. 36 (1903 edn.).
31 Maeder is of the opinion that the "creative activity" of the organism, and particularly that of the psyche, "exceeds the energy consumed." He also holds that

energetic viewpoint altogether, or else to postulate a special psychic energy—which would be entirely possible as a hypothetical operation. Psychology as much as physics may avail itself of the right to build its own concepts, as Lipps has already remarked, but only in so far as the energic view proves its value and is not just a summing-up under a vague general concept—an objection justly enough raised by Wundt. We are of the opinion, however, that the energic view of psychic phenomena is a valuable one because it enables us to recognize just those quantitative relations whose existence in the psyche cannot possibly be denied but which are easily overlooked from a purely qualitative standpoint.

29   Now if the psyche consisted, as the psychologists of the conscious mind maintain, of conscious processes alone (admittedly somewhat "dark" now and then), we might rest content with the postulate of a "special psychic energy." But since we are persuaded that the unconscious processes also belong to psychology, and not merely to the physiology of the brain (as substratum processes), we are obliged to put our concept of energy on a rather broader basis. We fully agree with Wundt that there are things of which we are dimly conscious. We accept, as he does, a scale of clarity for conscious contents, but for us the psyche does not stop where the blackness begins but is continued right into the unconscious. We also leave brain-psychology its share, since we assume that the unconscious functions ultimately go over into substratum processes to which no psychic quality can be assigned, except by way of the philosophical hypothesis of pan-psychism.

30   In delimiting a concept of psychic energy we are thus faced with certain difficulties, because we have absolutely no means of dividing what is psychic from the biological process as such. Biology as much as psychology can be approached from the energic standpoint, in so far as the biologist feels it to be useful and valuable. Like the psyche, the life-process in general does not stand in any exactly demonstrable relationship of equivalence to physical energy.

---

in regard to the psyche, together with the principle of conservation and the principle of entropy, one must make use of yet a third principle, that of integration. Cf. *Heilung und Entwicklung im Seelenleben,* pp. 50 and 69f.

31   If we take our stand on the basis of scientific common sense and avoid philosophical considerations which would carry us too far, we would probably do best to regard the psychic process simply as a life-process. In this way we enlarge the narrower concept of psychic energy to a broader one of life-energy, which includes "psychic energy" as a specific part. We thus gain the advantage of being able to follow quantitative relations beyond the narrow confines of the psychic into the sphere of biological functions in general, and so can do justice, if need be, to the long discussed and ever-present problem of "mind and body."

32   The concept of life-energy has nothing to do with a so-called life-force, for this, *qua* force, would be nothing more than a specific form of universal energy. To regard life-energy thus, and so bridge over the still yawning gulf between physical processes and life-processes, would be to do away with the special claims of bio-energetics as opposed to physical energetics. I have therefore suggested that, in view of the psychological use we intend to make of it, we call our hypothetical life-energy "libido." To this extent I have differentiated it from a concept of universal energy, so maintaining the right of biology and psychology to form their own concepts. In adopting this usage I do not in any way wish to forestall workers in the field of bio-energetics, but freely admit that I have adopted the term libido with the intention of using it for *our* purposes: for theirs, some such term as "bio-energy" or "vital energy" may be preferred.

33   I must at this point guard against a possible misunderstanding. I have not the smallest intention, in the present paper, of letting myself in for a discussion of the controversial question of psychophysical parallelism and reciprocal action. These theories are speculations concerning the possibility of mind and body functioning together or side by side, and they touch on the very point I am purposely leaving out of account here, namely whether the psychic energy process exists independently of, or is included in, the physical process. In my view we know practically nothing about this. Like Busse,[32] I consider the idea of reciprocal action tenable, and can see no reason to prejudice its credibility with the hypothesis of psychophysical parallelism. To the psychotherapist, whose special field lies just in this crucial

32 *Geist und Körper, Seele und Leib.*

17

sphere of the interaction of mind and body, it seems highly probable that the psychic and the physical are not two independent parallel processes, but are essentially connected through reciprocal action, although the actual nature of this relationship is still completely outside our experience. Exhaustive discussions of this question may be all very well for philosophers, but empirical psychology should confine itself to empirically accessible facts. Even though we have not yet succeeded in proving that the processes of psychic energy are included in the physical process, the opponents of such a possibility have been equally unsuccessful in separating the psychic from the physical with any certainty.

b. The Conservation of Energy

34   If we undertake to view the psychic life-process from the energic standpoint, we must not rest content with the mere concept, but must accept the obligation to test its applicability to empirical material. An energic standpoint is otiose if its main principle, the conservation of energy, proves to be inapplicable. Here we must follow Busse's suggestion and distinguish between the principle of equivalence and the principle of constancy.[33] The principle of equivalence states that "for a given quantity of energy expended or consumed in bringing about a certain condition, an equal quantity of the same or another form of energy will appear elsewhere"; while the principle of constancy states that "the sum total of energy remains constant, and is susceptible neither of increase nor of decrease." Hence the principle of constancy is a logically necessary but generalized conclusion from the principle of equivalence and is not so important in practice, since our experience is always concerned with partial systems only.

35   For our purpose, the principle of equivalence is the only one of immediate concern. In my book *Symbols of Transformation*,[34] I have demonstrated the possibility of considering certain developmental processes and other transformations of the kind under the principle of equivalence. I will not repeat *in extenso* what I have said there, but will only emphasize once again that

33 Ibid.   34 Cf. particularly Part II, ch. III.

Freud's investigation of sexuality has made many valuable contributions to our problem. Nowhere can we see more clearly
than in the relation of sexuality to the total psyche how the
disappearance of a given quantum of libido is followed by the
appearance of an equivalent value in another form. Unfortunately Freud's very understandable over-valuation of sexuality
led him to reduce transformations of other specific psychic
forces co-ordinated with sexuality to sexuality pure and simple,
thus bringing upon himself the not unjustified charge of pan-
sexualism. The defect of the Freudian view lies in the one-
sidedness to which the mechanistic-causal standpoint always
inclines, that is to say in the all-simplifying *reductio ad causam*,
which, the truer, the simpler, the more inclusive it is, does the
less justice to the product thus analysed and reduced. Anyone
who reads Freud's works with attention will see what an important role the equivalence principle plays in the structure of
his theories. This can be seen particularly clearly in his investigations of case material, where he gives an account of repressions and their substitute formations.[35] Anyone who has had
practical experience of this field knows that the equivalence
principle is of great heuristic value in the treatment of neuroses.
Even if its application is not always conscious, you nevertheless
apply it instinctively or by feeling. For instance, when a conscious value, say a transference, decreases or actually disappears,
you immediately look for the substitute formation, expecting
to see an equivalent value spring up somewhere else. It is not
difficult to find the substitute if the substitute formation is a
conscious content, but there are frequent cases where a sum of
libido disappears apparently without forming a substitute. In
that case the substitute is unconscious, or, as usually happens,
the patient is unaware that some new psychic fact is the corresponding substitute formation. But it may also happen that
a considerable sum of libido disappears as though completely
swallowed up by the unconscious, with no new value appearing
in its stead. In such cases it is advisable to cling firmly to the
principle of equivalence, for careful observation of the patient
will soon reveal signs of unconscious activity, for instance an
intensification of certain symptoms, or a new symptom, or

[35] *Sammlung kleiner Schriften zur Neurosenlehre* [cf. *Collected Papers*, I–IV].

peculiar dreams, or strange, fleeting fragments of fantasy, etc. If the analyst succeeds in bringing these hidden contents into consciousness, it can usually be shown that the libido which disappeared from consciousness generated a product in the unconscious which, despite all differences, has not a few features in common with the conscious contents that lost their energy. It is as if the libido dragged with it into the unconscious certain qualities which are often so distinct that one can recognize from their character the source of the libido now activating the unconscious.

36   There are many striking and well-known examples of these transformations. For instance, when a child begins to separate himself subjectively from his parents, fantasies of substitute parents arise, and these fantasies are almost always transferred to real people. Transferences of this sort prove untenable in the long run, because the maturing personality must assimilate the parental complex and achieve authority, responsibility, and independence. He or she must become a father or mother. Another field rich in striking examples is the psychology of Christianity, where the repression of instincts (i.e., of primitive instinctuality) leads to religious substitute formations, such as the medieval *Gottesminne*, 'love of God,' the sexual character of which only the blind could fail to see.

37   These reflections lead us to a further analogy with the theory of physical energy. As we know, the theory of energy recognizes not only a factor of *intensity*, but also a factor of *extensity*, the latter being a necessary addition in practice to the pure concept of energy. It combines the concept of pure intensity with the concept of quantity (e.g., the quantity of light as opposed to its strength). "The quantity, or the extensity factor, of energy is attached to one structure and cannot be transferred to another structure without carrying with it parts of the first; but the intensity factor can pass from one structure to another." [36] The extensity factor, therefore, shows the dynamic measure of energy present at any time in a given phenomenon.[37]

38   Similarly, there is a psychological extensity factor which cannot pass into a new structure without carrying over parts or characteristics of the previous structure with which it was con-

[36] Hartmann, *Weltanschauung der modernen Physik*, p. 6.

[37] Physics today equates energy with mass, but this is irrelevant for our purpose.

nected. In my earlier work, I have drawn particular attention to this peculiarity of energy transformation, and have shown that libido does not leave a structure as pure intensity and pass without trace into another, but that it takes the character of the old function over into the new.[38] This peculiarity is so striking that it gives rise to false conclusions—not only to wrong theories, but to self-deceptions fraught with unfortunate consequences. For instance, say a sum of libido having a certain sexual form passes over into another structure, taking with it some of the peculiarities of its previous application. It is then very tempting to think that the dynamism of the new structure will be sexual too.[39] Or it may be that the libido of some spiritual activity goes over into an essentially material interest, whereupon the individual erroneously believes that the new structure is equally spiritual in character. These conclusions are false in principle because they take only the relative similarities of the two structures into account while ignoring their equally essential differences.

39   Practical experience teaches us as a general rule that a psychic activity can find a substitute only on the basis of equivalence. A pathological interest, for example, an intense attachment to a symptom, can be replaced only by an equally intense attachment to another interest, which is why a release of libido from the symptom never takes place without this substitute. If the substitute is of less energic value, we know at once that a part of the energy is to be sought elsewhere—if not in the conscious mind, then in unconscious fantasy formations or in a disturbance of the "parties supérieures" of the psychological functions (to borrow an apt expression of Janet's).

40   Apart from these practical experiences which have long been at our disposal, the energic point of view also enables us to

38 *Symbols of Transformation,* par. 226.
39 The reduction of a complex structure to sexuality is a valid causal explanation only if it is agreed beforehand that we are interested in explaining solely the function of the sexual components in complex structures. But if we accept the reduction to sexuality as valid, this can only be done on the tacit assumption that we are dealing with an exclusively sexual structure. To assume this, however, is to assert *a priori* that a complex psychic structure can only be a sexual structure, a manifest *petitio principii!* It cannot be asserted that sexuality is the only fundamental psychic instinct, hence every explanation on a sexual basis can be only a partial explanation, never an all-sufficing psychological theory.

build up another side of our theory. According to the causal standpoint of Freud, there exists only this same immutable substance, the sexual component, to whose activity every interpretation is led back with monotonous regularity, a fact which Freud himself once pointed out. It is obvious that the spirit of the *reductio ad causam* or *reductio in primam figuram* can never do justice to the idea of final development, of such paramount importance in psychology, because each change in the conditions is seen as nothing but a "sublimation" of the basic substance and therefore as a masked expression of the same old thing.

41   The idea of development is possible only if the concept of an immutable substance is not hypostatized by appeals to a so-called "objective reality"—that is to say, if causality is not assumed to be identical with the behaviour of things. The idea of development requires the possibility of change in substances, which, from the energic standpoint, appear as systems of energy capable of theoretically unlimited interchangeability and modulation under the principle of equivalence, and on the obvious assumption of a difference in potential. Here again, just as in examining the relations between causality and finality, we come upon an insoluble antinomy resulting from an illegitimate projection of the energic hypothesis, for an immutable substance cannot at the same time be a system of energy.[40] According to the mechanistic view, energy is attached to substance, so that Wundt can speak of an "energy of the psychic" which has increased in the course of time and therefore does not permit the application of the principles of energy. From the energic standpoint, on the other hand, substance is nothing more than the expression or sign of an energic system. This antinomy is insoluble only so long as it is forgotten that points of view correspond to fundamental psychological attitudes, which obviously coincide to some extent with the conditions and behaviour of objects—a coincidence that renders the points of view applicable in practice. It is therefore quite understandable that causalists and finalists alike should fight desperately for the objective validity of their principles, since the principle each is defending is also that of his personal attitude to life and the

40 This applies only to the macrophysical realm, where "absolute" laws hold good.

22

world, and no one will allow without protest that his attitude may have only a conditional validity. This unwelcome admission feels somewhat like a suicidal attempt to saw off the branch upon which one is sitting. But the unavoidable antinomies to which the projection of logically justified principles gives rise force us to a fundamental examination of our own psychological attitudes, for only in this way can we avoid doing violence to the other logically valid principle. The antinomy must resolve itself in an *antinomian postulate,* however unsatisfactory this may be to our concretistic thinking, and however sorely it afflicts the spirit of natural science to admit that the essence of so-called reality is of a mysterious irrationality. This, however, necessarily follows from an acceptance of the antinomian postulate.[41]

42   The theory of development cannot do without the final point of view. Even Darwin, as Wundt points out, worked with final concepts, such as adaptation. The palpable fact of differentiation and development can never be explained exhaustively by causality; it requires also the final point of view, which man produced in the course of his psychic evolution, as he also produced the causal.

43   According to the concept of finality, causes are understood as means to an end. A simple example is the process of regression. Regarded causally, regression is determined, say, by a "mother fixation." But from the final standpoint the libido regresses to the *imago* of the mother in order to find there the memory associations by means of which further development can take place, for instance from a sexual system into an intellectual or spiritual system.

44   The first explanation exhausts itself in stressing the importance of the cause and completely overlooks the final significance of the regressive process. From this angle the whole edifice of civilization becomes a mere substitute for the impossibility of incest. But the second explanation allows us to foresee what will follow from the regression, and at the same time it helps us to understand the significance of the memory-images that have been reactivated by the regressive libido. To the causalist the latter interpretation naturally seems unbelievably hypothetical,

---

41 Cf. *Psychological Types* (1923 edn., pp. 372ff.).

while to the finalist the "mother fixation" is an arbitrary assumption. This assumption, he objects, entirely fails to take note of the aim, which alone can be made responsible for the reactivation of the mother imago. Adler, for instance, raises numerous objections of this sort against Freud's theory. In my *Symbols of Transformation* I tried to do justice to both views, and met for my pains the accusation from both sides of holding an obscurantist and dubious position. In this I share the fate of neutrals in wartime, to whom even good faith is often denied.

45   What to the causal view is *fact* to the final view is *symbol,* and vice versa. Everything that is real and essential to the one is unreal and inessential to the other. We are therefore forced to resort to the antinomian postulate and must view the world, too, as a psychic phenomenon. Certainly it is necessary for science to know how things are "in themselves," but even science cannot escape the psychological conditions of knowledge, and psychology must be peculiarly alive to these conditions. Since the psyche also possesses the final point of view, it is psychologically inadmissible to adopt the purely causal attitude to psychic phenomena, not to mention the all too familiar monotony of its one-sided interpretations.

46   The symbolic interpretation of causes by means of the energic standpoint is necessary for the differentiation of the psyche, since unless the facts are symbolically interpreted, the causes remain immutable substances which go on operating continuously, as in the case of Freud's old trauma theory. Cause alone does not make development possible. For the psyche the *reductio ad causam* is the very reverse of development; it binds the libido to the elementary facts. From the standpoint of rationalism this is all that can be desired, but from the standpoint of the psyche it is lifeless and comfortless boredom—though it should never be forgotten that for many people it is absolutely necessary to keep their libido close to the basic facts. But, in so far as this requirement is fulfilled, the psyche cannot always remain on this level but must go on developing, the causes transforming themselves into means to an end, into symbolical expressions for the way that lies ahead. The exclusive importance of the cause, i.e., its energic value, thus disappears and emerges again in the symbol, whose power of attraction represents the equivalent quantum of libido. The energic value of

a cause is never abolished by positing an arbitrary and rational goal: that is always a makeshift.

47   Psychic development cannot be accomplished by intention and will alone; it needs the attraction of the symbol, whose value quantum exceeds that of the cause. But the formation of a symbol cannot take place until the mind has dwelt long enough on the elementary facts, that is to say until the inner or outer necessities of the life-process have brought about a transformation of energy. If man lived altogether instinctively and automatically, the transformation could come about in accordance with purely biological laws. We can still see something of the sort in the psychic life of primitives, which is entirely concretistic and entirely symbolical at once. In civilized man the rationalism of consciousness, otherwise so useful to him, proves to be a most formidable obstacle to the frictionless transformation of energy. Reason, always seeking to avoid what to it is an unbearable antinomy, takes its stand exclusively on one side or the other, and convulsively seeks to hold fast to the values it has once chosen. It will continue to do this so long as human reason passes for an "immutable substance," thereby precluding any symbolical view of itself. But reason is only relative, and eventually checks itself in its own antinomies. It too is only a means to an end, a symbolical expression for a transitional stage in the path of development.

c. Entropy

48   The principle of equivalence is one proposition of practical importance in the theory of energy; the other proposition, necessary and complementary, is the principle of entropy. Transformations of energy are possible only as a result of differences in intensity. According to Carnot's law, heat can be converted into work only by passing from a warmer to a colder body. But mechanical work is continually being converted into heat, which on account of its reduced intensity cannot be converted back into work. In this way a closed energic system gradually reduces its differences in intensity to an even temperature, whereby any further change is prohibited.

49   So far as our experience goes, the principle of entropy is known to us only as a principle of partial processes which make

up a relatively closed system. The psyche, too, can be regarded as such a relatively closed system, in which transformations of energy lead to an equalization of differences. According to Boltzmann's formulation,[42] this levelling process corresponds to a transition from an improbable to a probable state, whereby the possibility of further change is increasingly limited. Psychologically, we can see this process at work in the development of a lasting and relatively unchanging attitude. After violent oscillations at the beginning the opposites equalize one another, and gradually a new attitude develops, the final stability of which is the greater in proportion to the magnitude of the initial differences. The greater the tension between the pairs of opposites, the greater will be the energy that comes from them; and the greater the energy, the stronger will be its constellating, attracting power. This increased power of attraction corresponds to a wider range of constellated psychic material, and the further this range extends, the less chance is there of subsequent disturbances which might arise from friction with material not previously constellated. For this reason an attitude that has been formed out of a far-reaching process of equalization is an especially lasting one.

50   Daily psychological experience affords proof of this statement. The most intense conflicts, if overcome, leave behind a sense of security and calm which is not easily disturbed, or else a brokenness that can hardly be healed. Conversely, it is just these intense conflicts and their conflagration which are needed in order to produce valuable and lasting results. Since our experience is confined to relatively closed systems, we are never in a position to observe an absolute psychological entropy; but the more the psychological system is closed off, the more clearly is the phenomenon of entropy manifested.[43] We see this particularly well in those mental disturbances which are characterized by intense seclusion from the environment. The so-called "dulling of affect" in dementia praecox or schizophrenia may well be understood as a phenomenon of entropy. The same applies to all those so-called degenerative phenomena which develop in psychological attitudes that permanently ex-

[42] *Populäre Schriften,* p. 33.
[43] A system is absolutely closed when no energy from outside can be fed into it. Only in such a system can entropy occur.

26

clude all connection with the environment. Similarly, such voluntarily directed processes as directed thinking and directed feeling can be viewed as relatively closed psychological systems. These functions are based on the principle of the exclusion of the inappropriate, or unsuitable, which might bring about a deviation from the chosen path. The elements that "belong" are left to a process of mutual equalization, and meanwhile are protected from disturbing influences from outside. Thus after some time they reach their "probable" state, which shows its stability in, say, a "lasting" conviction or a "deeply ingrained" point of view, etc. How firmly such things are rooted can be tested by anyone who has attempted to dissolve such a structure, for instance to uproot a prejudice or change a habit of thought. In the history of nations these changes have cost rivers of blood. But in so far as absolute insulation is impossible (except, maybe, in pathological cases), the energic process continues as development, though, because of "loss by friction," with lessening intensity and decreased potential.

51   This way of looking at things has long been familiar. Everyone speaks of the "storms of youth" which yield to the "tranquillity of age." We speak, too, of a "confirmed belief" after "battling with doubts," of "relief from inner tension," and so on. This is the involuntary energic standpoint shared by everyone. For the scientific psychologist, of course, it remains valueless so long as he feels no need to estimate psychological values, while for physiological psychology this problem does not arise at all. Psychiatry, as opposed to psychology, is purely descriptive, and until recently it has not concerned itself at all about psychological causality, has in fact even denied it. Analytical psychology, however, was obliged to take the energic standpoint into account, since the causal-mechanistic standpoint of Freudian psychoanalysis was not sufficient to do justice to psychological values. Value requires for its explanation a quantitative concept, and a qualitative concept like sexuality can never serve as a substitute. A qualitative concept is always the description of a thing, a substance; whereas a quantitative concept deals with relations of intensity and never with a substance or a thing. A qualitative concept that does not designate a substance, a thing, or a fact is a more or less arbitrary exception, and as such I must count a qualitative, hypostatized concept of energy. A scientific

27

causal explanation now and then needs assumptions of this kind, yet they must not be taken over merely for the purpose of making an energic standpoint superfluous. The same is true of the theory of energy, which at times shows a tendency to deny substance in order to become purely teleological or finalistic. To substitute a qualitative concept for energy is inadmissible, for that would be a specification of energy, which is in fact a force. This would be in biology vitalism, in psychology sexualism (Freud), or some other "ism," in so far as it could be shown that the investigators reduced the energy of the total psyche to one definite force or drive. But drives, as we have shown, are specific forms of energy. Energy includes these in a higher concept of relation, and it cannot express anything else than the relations between psychological values.

d. Energism and Dynamism

52   What has been said above refers to a *pure* concept of energy. The concept of energy, like its correlate, the concept of time, is on the one hand an immediate, *a priori*, intuitive idea,[44] and on the other a concrete, applied, or empirical concept abstracted from experience, like all scientific explanatory concepts.[45] The *applied* concept of energy always deals with the behaviour of forces, with substances in motion; for energy is accessible to experience in no other way than through the observation of moving bodies. Hence, in practice, we speak of electrical energy and the like, as if energy were a definite force. This merging of

[44] Therefore the idea of it is as old as humanity. We meet it in the fundamental ideas of primitives. Cf. Lehmann, *Mana, der Begriff des 'ausserordentlich Wirkungsvollen' bei Südseevölkern,* and my remarks in *Two Essays on Analytical Psychology,* par. 108. Hubert and Mauss (*Mélanges d'histoire des religions,* preface, p. xxix) also call *mana* a "category" of the understanding. I quote their words verbatim: "[The categories] constantly manifested in language, though not necessarily explicit in it, exist as a rule rather in the form of habits that govern consciousness, while themselves unconscious. The notion of mana is one of these principles. It is a datum of language; it is implied in a whole series of judgements and reasonings concerned with attributes which are those of mana. We have called mana a category. But it is not only a category peculiar to primitive thought, and today, by reduction, it is still the first form taken on by other categories which are always operative in our minds, those of substance and cause," etc.

[45] For further discussion see *Psychological Types* (1923 edn., pp. 382ff. and 547).

the applied or empirical concept with the intuitive idea of the event gives rise to those constant confusions of "energy" with "force." Similarly, the psychological concept of energy is not a pure concept, but a concrete and applied concept that appears to us in the form of sexual, vital, mental, moral "energy," and so on. In other words, it appears in the form of a drive, the unmistakably dynamic nature of which justifies us in making a conceptual parallel with physical forces.

53   The application of the pure concept to the stuff of experience necessarily brings about a concretization or visualization of the concept, so that it looks as if a substance had been posited. This is the case, for instance, with the physicist's concept of ether, which, although a concept, is treated exactly as if it were a substance. This confusion is unavoidable, since we are incapable of imagining a quantum unless it be a quantum of something. This something is the substance. Therefore every applied concept is unavoidably hypostatized, even against our will, though we must never forget that what we are dealing with is still a concept.

54   I have suggested calling the energy concept used in analytical psychology by the name "libido." The choice of this term may not be ideal in some respects, yet it seemed to me that this concept merited the name libido if only for reasons of historical justice. Freud was the first to follow out these really dynamic, psychological relationships and to present them coherently, making use of the convenient term "libido," albeit with a specifically sexual connotation in keeping with his general starting-point, which was sexuality. Together with "libido" Freud used the expressions "drive" or "instinct" (e.g., "ego-instincts") [46] and "psychic energy." Since Freud confines himself almost exclusively to sexuality and its manifold ramifications in the psyche, the sexual definition of energy as a specific driving force is quite sufficient for his purpose. In a general psychological theory, however, it is impossible to use purely sexual energy, that is, one specific drive, as an explanatory concept, since psychic energy transformation is not merely a matter of sexual

46 [Jung here uses the terms *Trieb* and *Ichtriebe* (lit. "drive," "ego-drives") following Freud's German terminology. Freud's terms have been trans. into English as "instinct" and "ego-instincts." Cf., e.g., Freud, *Introductory Lectures*, pp. 294ff.—EDITORS.]

dynamics. Sexual dynamics is only one particular instance in the total field of the psyche. This is not to deny its existence, but merely to put it in its proper place.

55   Since, for our concretistic thinking, the applied concept of energy immediately hypostatizes itself as the psychic forces (drives, affects, and other dynamic processes), its concrete character is in my view aptly expressed by the term "libido." Similar conceptions have always made use of designations of this kind, for instance Schopenhauer's "Will," Aristotle's ὁρμή, Plato's Eros, Empedocles' "love and hate of the elements," or the *élan vital* of Bergson. From these concepts I have borrowed only the concrete character of the term, not the definition of the concept. The omission of a detailed explanation of this in my earlier book is responsible for numerous misunderstandings, such as the accusation that I have built up a kind of vitalistic concept.

56   While I do not connect any specifically sexual definition with the word "libido," [47] this is not to deny the existence of a sexual dynamism any more than any other dynamism, for instance that of the hunger-drive, etc. As early as 1912 I pointed out that my conception of a general life instinct, named libido, takes the place of the concept of "psychic energy" which I used in "The Psychology of Dementia Praecox." I was, however, guilty of a sin of omission in presenting the concept only in its psychological concreteness and leaving out of account its metaphysical aspect, which is the subject of the present discussion. But, by leaving the libido concept wholly in its concrete form, I treated it as though it were hypostatized. Thus far I am to blame for the misunderstandings. I therefore expressly declared, in my "Theory of Psychoanalysis," [48] published in 1913, that "the libido with which we operate is not only not concrete or known, but is a complete X, a pure hypothesis, a model or counter, and is no more concretely conceivable than the energy known to the world of physics." Libido, therefore, is nothing but an abbreviated expression for the "energic standpoint." In a concrete presentation we shall never be able to operate with pure concepts unless we succeed in expressing the phenomenon mathe-

[47] The Latin word *libido* has by no means an exclusively sexual connotation, but the general meaning of desire, longing, urge. Cf. *Symbols of Transformation*, pars. 185ff.   [48] *Freud and Psychoanalysis*, par. 281.

matically. So long as this is impossible, the applied concept will automatically become hypostatized through the data of experience.

57 We must note yet another obscurity arising out of the concrete use of the libido-concept and of the concept of energy in general, namely the confusion, unavoidable in practical experience, of energy with the causal concept of effect, which is a dynamic and not an energic concept at all.

58 The causal-mechanistic view sees the sequence of facts, *a-b-c-d*, as follows: *a* causes *b*, *b* causes *c*, and so on. Here the concept of effect appears as the designation of a quality, as a "virtue" of the cause, in other words, as a dynamism. The final-energic view, on the other hand, sees the sequence thus: *a-b-c* are means towards the transformation of energy, which flows causelessly from *a*, the improbable state, entropically to *b-c* and so to the probable state *d*. Here a causal effect is totally disregarded, since only intensities of effect are taken into account. In so far as the intensities are the same, we could just as well put *w-x-y-z* instead of *a-b-c-d*.

59 The datum of experience is in both cases the sequence *a-b-c-d*, with the difference that the mechanistic view infers a dynamism from the causal effect observed, while the energic view observes the equivalence of the transformed effect rather than the effect of a cause. That is to say, both observe the sequence *a-b-c-d*, the one qualitatively, the other quantitatively. The causal mode of thought abstracts the dynamic concept from the datum of experience, while the final view applies its pure concept of energy to the field of observation and allows it, as it were, to become a dynamism. Despite their epistemological differences, which are as absolute as could be wished, the two modes of observation are unavoidably blended in the concept of force, the causal view abstracting its pure perception of the operative quality into a concept of dynamism, and the final view allowing its pure concept to become concretized through application. Thus the mechanist speaks of the "energy of *the psychic*," while the energist speaks of "psychic *energy*." From what has been said it should be evident that one and the same process takes on different aspects according to the different standpoints from which it is viewed.

III. FUNDAMENTAL CONCEPTS OF THE LIBIDO THEORY

a. Progression and Regression

60   One of the most important energic phenomena of psychic life is the progression and regression of libido. Progression could be defined as the daily advance of the process of psychological adaptation. We know that adaptation is not something that is achieved once and for all, though there is a tendency to believe the contrary. This is due to mistaking a person's psychic attitude for actual adaptation. We can satisfy the demands of adaptation only by means of a suitably directed attitude. Consequently, the achievement of adaptation is completed in two stages: (1) attainment of attitude, (2) completion of adaptation by means of the attitude. A man's attitude to reality is something extraordinarily persistent, but the more persistent his mental habitus is, the less permanent will be his effective achievement of adaptation. This is the necessary consequence of the continual changes in the environment and the new adaptations demanded by them.

61   The progression of libido might therefore be said to consist in a continual satisfaction of the demands of environmental conditions. This is possible only by means of an attitude, which as such is necessarily directed and therefore characterized by a certain one-sidedness. Thus it may easily happen that an attitude can no longer satisfy the demands of adaptation because changes have occurred in the environmental conditions which require a different attitude. For example, a feeling-attitude that seeks to fulfil the demands of reality by means of empathy may easily encounter a situation that can only be solved through thinking. In this case the feeling-attitude breaks down and the progression of libido also ceases. The vital feeling that was present before disappears, and in its place the psychic value of certain conscious contents increases in an unpleasant way; subjective contents and reactions press to the fore and the situation becomes full of affect and ripe for explosions. These symptoms indicate a damming up of libido, and the stoppage is always marked by the breaking up of the pairs of opposites. During the progression of libido the pairs of opposites are united in the co-ordinated flow of psychic processes. Their working together makes possible the

32

balanced regularity of these processes, which without this inner polarity would become one-sided and unreasonable. We are therefore justified in regarding all extravagant and exaggerated behaviour as a loss of balance, because the co-ordinating effect of the opposite impulse is obviously lacking. Hence it is essential for progression, which is the successful achievement of adaptation, that impulse and counter-impulse, positive and negative, should reach a state of regular interaction and mutual influence. This balancing and combining of pairs of opposites can be seen, for instance, in the process of reflection that precedes a difficult decision. But in the stoppage of libido that occurs when progression has become impossible, positive and negative can no longer unite in co-ordinated action, because both have attained an equal value which keeps the scales balanced. The longer the stoppage lasts, the more the value of the opposed positions increases; they become enriched with more and more associations and attach to themselves an ever-widening range of psychic material. The tension leads to conflict, the conflict leads to attempts at mutual repression, and if one of the opposing forces is successfully repressed a dissociation ensues, a splitting of the personality, or disunion with oneself. The stage is then set for a neurosis. The acts that follow from such a condition are unco-ordinated, sometimes pathological, having the appearance of symptomatic actions. Although in part normal, they are based partly on the repressed opposite which, instead of working as an equilibrating force, has an obstructive effect, thus hindering the possibility of further progress.

62   The struggle between the opposites would persist in this fruitless way if the process of regression, the backward movement of libido, did not set in with the outbreak of the conflict. Through their collision the opposites are gradually deprived of value and depotentiated. This loss of value steadily increases and is the only thing perceived by consciousness. It is synonymous with regression, for in proportion to the decrease in value of the conscious opposites there is an increase in the value of all those psychic processes which are not concerned with outward adaptation and therefore are seldom or never employed consciously. These psychic factors are for the most part unconscious. As the value of the subliminal elements and of the unconscious increases, it is to be expected that they will gain influence over

33

the conscious mind. On account of the inhibiting influence which the conscious exercises over the unconscious, the unconscious values assert themselves at first only indirectly. The inhibition to which they are subjected is a result of the exclusive directedness of conscious contents. (This inhibition is identical with what Freud calls the "censor.") The indirect manifestation of the unconscious takes the form of disturbances of conscious behaviour. In the association experiment they appear as complex-indicators, in daily life as the "symptomatic actions" first described by Freud, and in neurotic conditions they appear as symptoms.

63   Since regression raises the value of contents that were previously excluded from the conscious process of adaptation, and hence are either totally unconscious or only "dimly conscious," the psychic elements now being forced over the threshold are momentarily useless from the standpoint of adaptation, and for this reason are invariably kept at a distance by the directed psychic function. The nature of these contents is for all the world to read in Freudian literature. They are not only of an infantile-sexual character, but are altogether incompatible contents and tendencies, partly immoral, partly unaesthetic, partly again of an irrational, imaginary nature. The obviously inferior character of these contents as regards adaptation has given rise to that depreciatory view of the psychic background which is habitual in psychoanalytic writings.[49] What the regression brings to the surface certainly seems at first sight to be slime from the depths; but if one does not stop short at a superficial evaluation and refrains from passing judgment on the basis of a preconceived dogma, it will be found that this "slime" contains not merely incompatible and rejected remnants of every-

[49] Somewhat after the manner of Hudibras, whose opinion is quoted by Kant (*Träume eines Geistersehers*, III): "When a hypochondriacal wind is roaring in the bowels, everything depends on the direction it takes. If it goes downwards, it turns into a fart, but if it mounts upwards, it is a vision or a divine inspiration." [For a much bowdlerized version see *Dreams of a Spirit-Seer*, trans. by Emanuel Goerwitz, p. 84. Kant's version is presumably based on Samuel Butler's *Hudibras*, Part II, Canto iii, lines 773–76:

> "As wind i' th' *Hypochondrias* pent
> Is but a blast if downward sent;
> But if it upwards chance to fly
> Becomes new *Light* and *Prophecy*."—TRANS.]

day life, or inconvenient and objectionable animal tendencies, but also germs of new life and vital possibilities for the future.[50] This is one of the great merits of psychoanalysis, that it is not afraid to dredge up the incompatible elements, which would be a thoroughly useless and indeed reprehensible undertaking were it not for the possibilities of new life that lie in the repressed contents. That this is and must be so is not only proved by a wealth of practical experience but can also be deduced from the following considerations.

64   The process of adaptation requires a directed conscious function characterized by inner consistency and logical coherence. Because it is directed, everything unsuitable must be excluded in order to maintain the integrity of direction. The unsuitable elements are subjected to inhibition and thereby escape attention. Now experience shows that there is only *one* consciously directed function of adaptation. If, for example, I have a thinking orientation I cannot at the same time orient myself by feeling, because thinking and feeling are two quite different functions. In fact, I must carefully exclude feeling if I am to satisfy the logical laws of thinking, so that the thought-process will not be disturbed by feeling. In this case I withdraw as much libido as possible from the feeling process, with the result that this function becomes relatively unconscious. Experience shows, again, that the orientation is largely habitual; accordingly the other unsuitable functions, so far as they are incompatible with the prevailing attitude, are relatively unconscious, and hence unused, untrained, and undifferentiated. Moreover, on the principle of coexistence they necessarily become associated with other contents of the unconscious, the inferior and incompatible quality of which I have already pointed out. Consequently, when these functions are activated by regression and so reach consciousness, they appear in a somewhat incompatible form, disguised and covered up with the slime of the deep.

65   If we remember that the stoppage of libido was due to the failure of the conscious attitude, we can now understand what valuable seeds lie in the unconscious contents activated by regression. They contain the elements of that other function

50 Though professional satiety with neurotic unrealities makes the analyst sceptical, a generalized judgment from the pathological angle has the disadvantage of being always biased.

which was excluded by the conscious attitude and which would be capable of effectively complementing or even of replacing the inadequate conscious attitude. If thinking fails as the adapted function, because it is dealing with a situation to which one can adapt only by feeling, then the unconscious material activated by regression will contain the missing feeling function, although still in embryonic form, archaic and undeveloped. Similarly, in the opposite type, regression would activate a thinking function that would effectively compensate the inadequate feeling.

66   By activating an unconscious factor, regression confronts consciousness with the problem of the psyche as opposed to the problem of outward adaptation. It is natural that the conscious mind should fight against accepting the regressive contents, yet it is finally compelled by the impossibility of further progress to submit to the regressive values. In other words, regression leads to the necessity of adapting to the inner world of the psyche.

67   Just as adaptation to the environment may fail because of the one-sidedness of the adapted function, so adaptation to the inner world may fail because of the one-sidedness of the function in question. For instance, if the stoppage of libido was due to the failure of the thinking attitude to cope with the demands of outward adaptation, and if the unconscious feeling function is activated by regression, there is only a feeling attitude towards the inner world. This may be sufficient at first, but in the long run it will cease to be adequate, and the thinking function will have to be enlisted too, just as the reverse was necessary when dealing with the outer world. Thus a complete orientation towards the inner world becomes necessary until such time as inner adaptation is attained. Once the adaptation is achieved, progression can begin again.

68   The principle of progression and regression is portrayed in the myth of the whale-dragon worked out by Frobenius,[51] as I have shown in detail in my book *Symbols of Transformation* (pars. 307ff.). The hero is the symbolical exponent of the movement of libido. Entry into the dragon is the regressive direction, and the journey to the East (the "night sea journey") with its attendant events symbolizes the effort to adapt to the conditions

[51] *Das Zeitalter des Sonnengottes.*

36

of the psychic inner world. The complete swallowing up and disappearance of the hero in the belly of the dragon represents the complete withdrawal of interest from the outer world. The overcoming of the monster from within is the achievement of adaptation to the conditions of the inner world, and the emergence ("slipping out") of the hero from the monster's belly with the help of a bird, which happens at the moment of sunrise, symbolizes the recommencement of progression.

69   It is characteristic that the monster begins the night sea journey to the East, i.e., towards sunrise, while the hero is engulfed in its belly. This seems to me to indicate that regression is not necessarily a retrograde step in the sense of a backwards development or degeneration, but rather represents a necessary phase of development. The individual is, however, not consciously aware that he is developing; he feels himself to be in a compulsive situation that resembles an early infantile state or even an embryonic condition within the womb. It is only if he remains stuck in this condition that we can speak of involution or degeneration.

70   Again, *progression* should not be confused with *development,* for the continuous flow or current of life is not necessarily development and differentiation. From primeval times certain plant and animal species have remained at a standstill without further differentiation, and yet have continued in existence. In the same way the psychic life of man can be progressive without evolution and regressive without involution. Evolution and involution have as a matter of fact no immediate connection with progression and regression, since the latter are mere life-movements which, notwithstanding their direction, actually have a static character. They correspond to what Goethe has aptly described as systole and diastole.[52]

71   Many objections have been raised against the view that myths represent psychological facts. People are very loath to

[52] Diastole is an extraversion of libido spreading through the entire universe; systole is its contraction into the individual, the monad. ("Systole, the conscious, powerful contraction that brings forth the individual, and diastole, the longing to embrace the All." Chamberlain, *Goethe,* p. 571.) To remain in either of these attitudes means death (p. 571), hence the one type is insufficient and needs complementing by the opposite function. ("If a man holds himself exclusively in the receptive attitude, if diastole persists indefinitely, then there enters into his psychic life, as into his bodily life, crippling and finally death. Only action can

give up the idea that the myth is some kind of explanatory allegory of astronomical, meteorological, or vegetative processes. The coexistence of explanatory tendencies is certainly not to be denied, since there is abundant proof that myths also have an explanatory significance, but we are still faced with the question: why should myths explain things in this allegorical way? It is essential to understand where the primitive gets this explanatory material from, for it should not be forgotten that the primitive's need of causal explanations is not nearly so great as it is with us. He is far less interested in explaining things than in weaving fables. We can see almost daily in our patients how mythical fantasies arise: they are not thought up, but present themselves as images or chains of ideas that force their way out of the unconscious, and when they are recounted they often have the character of connected episodes resembling mythical dramas. That is how myths arise, and that is the reason why the fantasies from the unconscious have so much in common with primitive myths. But in so far as the myth is nothing but a projection from the unconscious and not a conscious invention at all, it is quite understandable that we should everywhere come upon the same myth-motifs, and that myths actually represent typical psychic phenomena.

72   We must now consider how the processes of progression and regression are to be understood energically. That they are essentially dynamic processes should by now be sufficiently clear. Progression might be compared to a watercourse that flows from a mountain into a valley. The damming up of libido is analogous to a specific obstruction in the direction of the flow, such as a dike, which transforms the kinetic energy of the flow into the potential energy of a reservoir. Thus dammed back, the water is forced into another channel, if as a result of the damming it reaches a level that permits it to flow off in another direction. Perhaps it will flow into a channel where the energy arising from the difference in potential is transformed into electricity by means of a turbine. This transformation might serve as a model for the new progression brought about by the dam-

---

animate, and its first condition is limitation, i.e., systole, which creates a firmly bounded measure. The more energetic the act, the more resolute must be the enforcing of the limitation."—p. 581.)

ming up and regression, its changed character being indicated by the new way in which the energy now manifests itself. In this process of transformation the principle of equivalence has a special heuristic value: the intensity of progression reappears in the intensity of regression.

73   It is not an essential postulate of the energic standpoint that there must be progression and regression of libido, only that there must be equivalent transformations, for energetics is concerned only with quantity and makes no attempt to explain quality. Thus progression and regression are specific processes which must be conceived as dynamic, and which as such are conditioned by the qualities of matter. They cannot in any sense be derived from the essential nature of the concept of energy, though in their reciprocal relations they can only be understood energically. Why progression and regression should exist at all can only be explained by the qualities of matter, that is by means of a mechanistic-causal hypothesis.

74   Progression as a continuous process of adaptation to environmental conditions springs from the vital need for such adaptation. Necessity enforces complete orientation to these conditions and the suppression of all those tendencies and possibilities which subserve individuation.

75   Regression, on the other hand, as an adaptation to the conditions of the inner world, springs from the vital need to satisfy the demands of individuation. Man is not a machine in the sense that he can consistently maintain the same output of work. He can meet the demands of outer necessity in an ideal way only if he is also adapted to his own inner world, that is, if he is in harmony with himself. Conversely, he can only adapt to his inner world and achieve harmony with himself when he is adapted to the environmental conditions. As experience shows, the one or the other function can be neglected only for a time. If, for example, there is only one-sided adaptation to the outer world while the inner one is neglected, the value of the inner world will gradually increase, and this shows itself in the irruption of personal elements into the sphere of outer adaptation. I once saw a drastic instance of this: A manufacturer who had worked his way up to a high level of success and prosperity began to remember a certain phase of his youth when he took great pleasure in art. He felt the need to return to these pursuits,

and began making artistic designs for the wares he manufactured. The result was that nobody wanted to buy these artistic products, and the man became bankrupt after a few years. His mistake lay in carrying over into the outer world what belonged to the inner, because he misunderstood the demands of individuation. So striking a failure of a function that was adequately adapted before can only be explained by this typical misunderstanding of the inner demands.

76   Although progression and regression are causally grounded in the nature of the life-processes on the one hand and in environmental conditions on the other, yet, if we look at them energically, we must think of them only as a means, as transitional stages in the flow of energy. Looked at from this angle, progression and the adaptation resulting therefrom are a means to regression, to a manifestation of the inner world in the outer. In this way a new means is created for a changed mode of progression, bringing better adaptation to environmental conditions.

b. Extraversion and Introversion

77   Progression and regression can be brought into relationship with extraversion and introversion: progression, as adaptation to outer conditions, could be regarded as extraversion; regression, as adaptation to inner conditions, could be regarded as introversion. But this parallel would give rise to a great deal of conceptual confusion, since progression and regression are at best only vague analogies of extraversion and introversion. In reality the latter two concepts represent dynamisms of a different kind from progression and regression. These are dynamic forms of a specifically determined transformation of energy, whereas extraversion and introversion, as their names suggest, are the forms taken both by progression and by regression. Progression is a forwards movement of life in the same sense that time moves forwards. This movement can occur in two different forms: either extraverted, when the progression is predominantly influenced by objects and environmental conditions, or introverted, when it has to adapt itself to the conditions of the ego (or, more accurately, of the "subjective factor"). Similarly, regression can proceed along two lines: either as a retreat from

the outside world (introversion), or as a flight into extravagant experience of the outside world (extraversion). Failure in the first case drives a man into a state of dull brooding, and in the second case into leading the life of a wastrel. These two different ways of reacting, which I have called introversion and extraversion, correspond to two opposite types of attitude and are described in detail in my book *Psychological Types*.

78   Libido moves not only forwards and backwards, but also outwards and inwards. The psychology of the latter movement is described at some length in my book on types, so I can refrain from further elaboration here.

c. The Canalization of Libido

79   In my *Symbols of Transformation* (pars. 203f.) I used the expression "canalization of libido" to characterize the process of energic transformation or conversion. I mean by this a transfer of psychic intensities or values from one content to another, a process corresponding to the physical transformation of energy; for example, in the steam-engine the conversion of heat into the pressure of steam and then into the energy of motion. Similarly, the energy of certain psychological phenomena is converted by suitable means into other dynamisms. In the above-mentioned book I have given examples of these transformation processes and need not elaborate them here.

80   When Nature is left to herself, energy is transformed along the line of its natural "gradient." In this way natural phenomena are produced, but not "work." So also man when left to himself lives as a natural phenomenon, and, in the proper meaning of the word, produces no work. It is culture that provides the machine whereby the natural gradient is exploited for the performance of work. That man should ever have invented this machine must be due to something rooted deep in his nature, indeed in the nature of the living organism as such. For living matter is itself a transformer of energy, and in some way as yet unknown life participates in the transformation process. Life proceeds, as it were, by making use of natural physical and chemical conditions as a means to its own existence. The living body is a machine for converting the energies it uses into other dynamic manifestations that are their

41

equivalents. We cannot say that physical energy is transformed into life, only that its transformation is the expression of life.

81   In the same way that the living body as a whole is a machine, other adaptations to physical and chemical conditions have the value of machines that make other forms of transformation possible. Thus all the means an animal employs for safeguarding and furthering its existence—apart from the direct nourishment of its body—can be regarded as machines that exploit the natural gradient for the performance of work. When the beaver fells trees and dams up a river, this is a performance conditioned by its differentiation. Its differentiation is a product of what one might call "natural culture," which functions as a transformer of energy, as a machine. Similarly human culture, as a natural product of differentiation, is a machine; first of all a technical one that utilizes natural conditions for the transformation of physical and chemical energy, but also a psychic machine that utilizes psychic conditions for the transformation of libido.

82   Just as man has succeeded in inventing a turbine, and, by conducting a flow of water to it, in transforming the latter's kinetic energy into electricity capable of manifold applications, so he has succeeded, with the help of a psychic mechanism, in converting natural instincts, which would otherwise follow their gradient without performing work, into other dynamic forms that are productive of work.

83   The transformation of instinctual energy is achieved by its canalization into an *analogue of the object of instinct.* Just as a power-station imitates a waterfall and thereby gains possession of its energy, so the psychic mechanism imitates the instinct and is thereby enabled to apply its energy for special purposes. A good example of this is the spring ceremony performed by the Wachandi, of Australia.[53] They dig a hole in the ground, oval in shape and set about with bushes so that it looks like a woman's genitals. Then they dance round this hole, holding their spears in front of them in imitation of an erect penis. As they dance round, they thrust their spears into the hole, shouting: "Pulli nira, pulli nira, wataka!" (not a pit, not a pit, but a c——!). During the ceremony none of the participants is allowed to look at a woman.

53 Preuss, "Der Ursprung der Religion und Kunst," p. 388; Schultze, *Psychologie der Naturvölker,* p. 168; *Symbols of Transformation,* pars. 213f.

84   By means of the hole the Wachandi make an analogue of the female genitals, the object of natural instinct. By the reiterated shouting and the ecstasy of the dance they suggest to themselves that the hole is really a vulva, and in order not to have this illusion disturbed by the real object of instinct, none may look at a woman. There can be no doubt that this is a canalization of energy and its transference to an analogue of the original object by means of the dance (which is really a mating-play, as with birds and other animals) and by imitating the sexual act.[54]

85   This dance has a special significance as an earth-impregnation ceremony and therefore takes place in the spring. It is a magical act for the purpose of transferring libido to the earth, whereby the earth acquires a special psychic value and becomes an object of expectation. The mind then busies itself with the earth, and in turn is affected by it, so that there is a possibility and even a probability that man will give it his attention, which is the psychological prerequisite for cultivation. Agriculture did in fact arise, though not exclusively, from the formation of sexual analogies. The "bridal bed in the field" is a canalization ceremony of this kind: on a spring night the farmer takes his wife into the field and has intercourse with her there, in order to make the earth fruitful. In this way a very close analogy is established, which acts like a channel that conducts water from a river to a power-station. The instinctual energy becomes closely associated with the field, so that the cultivation of it acquires the value of a sexual act. This association assures a permanent flow of interest to the field, which accordingly exerts an attraction on the cultivator. He is thus induced to occupy himself with the field in a way that is obviously beneficial to fertility.

86   As Meringer has convincingly shown, the association of libido (also in the sexual sense) and agriculture is expressed in linguistic usage.[55] The putting of libido into the earth is achieved not by sexual analogy alone, but by the "magic touch," as in the custom of rolling (*wälzen, walen*) in the field.[56]

---

54 Cf. the observation in Pechuël-Loesche, *Volkskunde von Loango*, p. 38: the dancers scrape the ground with one foot and at the same time carry out specific abdominal movements.

55 "Wörter und Sachen." Cf. *Symbols of Transformation*, p. 150, n. 21.

56 Mannhardt, *Wald- und Feldkulte*, I, pp. 480ff.

To primitive man the canalization of libido is so concrete a thing that he even feels fatigue from work as a state of being "sucked dry" by the daemon of the field.[57] All major undertakings and efforts, such as tilling the soil, hunting, war, etc., are entered upon with ceremonies of magical analogy or with preparatory incantations which quite obviously have the psychological aim of canalizing libido into the necessary activity. In the buffalo-dances of the Taos Pueblo Indians the dancers represent both the hunters and the game. Through the excitement and pleasure of the dance the libido is channelled into the form of hunting activity. The pleasure required for this is produced by rhythmic drumming and the stirring chants of the old men who direct the whole ceremony. It is well known that old people live in their memories and love to speak of their former deeds; this "warms" them. Warmth "kindles," and thus the old men in a sense give the first impulse to the dance, to the mimetic ceremony whose aim is to accustom the young men and boys to the hunt and to prepare them for it psychologically. Similar *rites d'entrée* are reported of many primitive tribes.[58] A classic example of this is the *atninga* ceremony of the Aruntas, of Australia. It consists in first stirring to anger the members of a tribe who are summoned for an expedition of revenge. This is done by the leader tying the hair of the dead man to be avenged to the mouth and penis of the man who is to be made angry. Then the leader kneels on the man and embraces him as if performing the sexual act with him.[59] It is supposed that in this way "the bowels of the man will begin to burn with desire to avenge the murder." The point of the ceremony is obviously to bring about an intimate acquaintance of each individual with the murdered man, so that each is made ready to avenge the dead.

87   The enormous complexity of such ceremonies shows how much is needed to divert the libido from its natural river-bed of everyday habit into some unaccustomed activity. The modern mind thinks this can be done by a mere decision of the will and

[57] Ibid., p. 483.
[58] A comprehensive survey in Lévy-Bruhl, *How Natives Think*, trans. by Clare, pp. 228ff.
[59] See illustration in Spencer and Gillen, *The Northern Tribes of Central Australia*, p. 560.

that it can dispense with all magical ceremonies—which explains why it was so long at a loss to understand them properly. But when we remember that primitive man is much more unconscious, much more of a "natural phenomenon" than we are, and has next to no knowledge of what we call "will," then it is easy to understand why he needs complicated ceremonies where a simple act of will is sufficient for us. We are more conscious, that is to say more domesticated. In the course of the millennia we have succeeded not only in conquering the wild nature all round us, but in subduing our own wildness—at least temporarily and up to a point. At all events we have been acquiring "will," i.e., disposable energy, and though it may not amount to much it is nevertheless more than the primitive possesses. We no longer need magical dances to make us "strong" for whatever we want to do, at least not in ordinary cases. But when we have to do something that exceeds our powers, something that might easily go wrong, then we solemnly lay a foundation-stone with the blessing of the Church, or we "christen" a ship as she slips from the docks; in time of war we assure ourselves of the help of a patriotic God, the sweat of fear forcing a fervent prayer from the lips of the stoutest. So it only needs slightly insecure conditions for the "magical" formalities to be resuscitated in the most natural way. Through these ceremonies the deeper emotional forces are released; conviction becomes blind auto-suggestion, and the psychic field of vision is narrowed to one fixed point on which the whole weight of the unconscious forces is concentrated. And it is, indeed, an objective fact that success attends the sure rather than the unsure.

d. Symbol Formation

88   The psychological mechanism that transforms energy is the symbol. I mean by this a real symbol and not a sign. The Wachandi's hole in the earth is not a sign for the genitals of a woman, but a symbol that stands for the idea of the earth woman who is to be made fruitful. To mistake it for a human woman would be to interpret the symbol semiotically, and this would fatally disturb the value of the ceremony. It is for this reason that none of the dancers may look at a woman. The mechanism would be destroyed by a semiotic interpretation—it would be like

45

smashing the supply-pipe of a turbine on the ground that it was a very unnatural waterfall that owed its existence to the repression of natural conditions. I am far from suggesting that the semiotic interpretation is meaningless; it is not only a possible interpretation but also a very true one. Its usefulness is undisputed in all those cases where nature is merely thwarted without any effective work resulting from it. But the semiotic interpretation becomes meaningless when it is applied exclusively and schematically—when, in short, it ignores the real nature of the symbol and debases it to a mere sign.

89   The first achievement wrested by primitive man from instinctual energy, through analogy-building, is magic. A ceremony is magical so long as it does not result in effective work but preserves the state of expectancy. In that case the energy is canalized into a new object and produces a new dynamism, which in turn remains magical so long as it does not create effective work. The advantage accruing from a magical ceremony is that the newly invested object acquires a working potential in relation to the psyche. Because of its value it has a determining and stimulating effect on the imagination, so that for a long time the mind is fascinated and possessed by it. This gives rise to actions that are performed in a half-playful way on the magical object, most of them rhythmical in character. A good example is those South American rock-drawings which consist of furrows deeply engraved in the hard stone. They were made by the Indians playfully retracing the furrows again and again with stones, over hundreds of years. The content of the drawings is difficult to interpret, but the activity bound up with them is incomparably more significant.[60]

90   The influence exerted on the mind by the magically effective object has other possible consequences. Through a sustained playful interest in the object, a man may make all sorts of discoveries about it which would otherwise have escaped him. As we know, many discoveries have actually been made in this way. Not for nothing is magic called the "mother of science." Until late in the Middle Ages what we today call science was nothing other than magic. A striking example of this is alchemy, whose symbolism shows quite unmistakably the principle of

[60] Koch-Grünberg, *Südamerikanische Felszeichnungen.*

46

transformation of energy described above, and indeed the later alchemists were fully conscious of this fact.[61] But only through the development of magic into science, that is, through the advance from the stage of mere expectation to real technical work on the object, have we acquired that mastery over the forces of nature of which the age of magic dreamed. Even the alchemist's dream of the transmutation of the elements has been fulfilled, and magical action at a distance has been realized by the discovery of electricity. So we have every reason to value symbol-formation and to render homage to the symbol as an inestimable means of utilizing the mere instinctual flow of energy for effective work. A waterfall is certainly more beautiful than a power-station, but dire necessity teaches us to value electric light and electrified industry more highly than the superb wastefulness of a waterfall that delights us for a quarter of an hour on a holiday walk.

91   Just as in physical nature only a very small portion of natural energy can be converted into a usable form, and by far the greater part must be left to work itself out unused in natural phenomena, so in our psychic nature only a small part of the total energy can be diverted from its natural flow. An incomparably greater part cannot be utilized by us, but goes to sustain the regular course of life. Hence the libido is apportioned by nature to the various functional systems, from which it cannot be wholly withdrawn. The libido is invested in these functions as a specific force that cannot be transformed. Only where a symbol offers a steeper gradient than nature is it possible to canalize libido into other forms. The history of civilization has amply demonstrated that man possesses a relative surplus of energy that is capable of application apart from the natural flow. The fact that the symbol makes this deflection possible proves that not all the libido is bound up in a form that enforces the natural flow, but that a certain amount of energy remains over, which could be called excess libido. It is conceivable that this excess may be due to failure of the firmly organized functions to equalize differences in intensity. They might be compared to a system of water-pipes whose diameter is too small to draw off the water that is being steadily supplied. The water would then

61 Silberer, *Problems of Mysticism and Its Symbolism;* also Rosencreutz, *Chymische Hochzeit* (1616).

47

have to flow off in one way or another. From this excess libido certain psychic processes arise which cannot be explained—or only very inadequately—as the result of merely natural conditions. How are we to explain religious processes, for instance, whose nature is essentially symbolical? In abstract form, symbols are religious ideas; in the form of action, they are rites or ceremonies. They are the manifestation and expression of excess libido. At the same time they are stepping-stones to new activities, which must be called cultural in order to distinguish them from the instinctual functions that run their regular course according to natural law.

92   I have called a symbol that converts energy a "libido analogue." [62] By this I mean an idea that can give equivalent expression to the libido and canalize it into a form different from the original one. Mythology offers numerous equivalents of this kind, ranging from sacred objects such as *churingas,* fetishes, etc., to the figures of gods. The rites with which the sacred objects are surrounded often reveal very clearly their nature as transformers of energy. Thus the primitive rubs his *churinga* rhythmically and takes the magic power of the fetish into himself, at the same time giving it a fresh "charge." [63] A higher stage of the same line of thought is the idea of the totem, which is closely bound up with the beginnings of tribal life and leads straight to the idea of the palladium, the tutelary tribal deity, and to the idea of an organized human community in general. The transformation of libido through the symbol is a process that has been going on ever since the beginnings of humanity and continues still. Symbols were never devised consciously, but were always produced out of the unconscious by way of revelation or intuition.[64] In view of the close connection between mythological symbols and dream-symbols, and of the fact that the dream is "le dieu des sauvages," it is more than probable that most of the historical symbols derive directly from dreams

62 *Symbols of Transformation,* par. 146.   63 Spencer and Gillen, p. 277.
64 "Man, of course, has always been trying to understand and to control his environment, but in the early stages this process was unconscious. The matters which are problems for us existed latent in the primitive brain; there, undefined, lay both problem and answer; through many ages of savagery, first one and then another partial answer emerged into consciousness; at the end of the series, hardly completed today, there will be a new synthesis in which riddle and answer are one." Crawley, *The Idea of the Soul,* p. 11.

or are at least influenced by them.[65] We know that this is true of the choice of totem, and there is similar evidence regarding the choice of gods. This age-old function of the symbol is still present today, despite the fact that for many centuries the trend of mental development has been towards the suppression of individual symbol-formation. One of the first steps in this direction was the setting up of an official state religion, a further step was the extermination of polytheism, first attempted in the reforms of Amenophis IV. We know the extraordinary part played by Christianity in the suppression of individual symbol-formation. But as the intensity of the Christian idea begins to fade, a recrudescence of individual symbol-formation may be expected. The prodigious increase of Christian sects since the eighteenth century, the century of "enlightenment," bears eloquent witness to this. Christian Science, theosophy, anthroposophy, and "Mazdaznan" are further steps along the same path.

93   In practical work with our patients we come upon symbol-formations at every turn, the purpose of which is the transformation of libido. At the beginning of treatment we find the symbol-forming process at work, but in an unsuitable form that offers the libido too low a gradient. Instead of being converted into effective work, the libido flows off unconsciously along the old channels, that is, into archaic sexual fantasies and fantasy activities. Accordingly the patient remains at war with himself, in other words, neurotic. In such cases analysis in the strict sense is indicated, i.e., the reductive psychoanalytic method inaugurated by Freud, which breaks down all inappropriate symbol-formations and reduces them to their natural elements. The power-station, situated too high and unsuitably constructed, is dismantled and separated into its original components, so that the natural flow is restored. The unconscious continues to produce symbols which one could obviously go on reducing to their elements *ad infinitum*.

94   But man can never rest content with the natural course of things, because he always has an excess of libido that can be offered a more favourable gradient than the merely natural one. For this reason he will inevitably seek it, no matter how often

[65] "Dreams are to the savage man what the Bible is to us—the source of divine revelation." Gatschet, "The Klamath Indians of South-Western Oregon," cited in Lévy-Bruhl, p. 57.

he may be forced back by reduction to the natural gradient. We have therefore reached the conclusion that when the unsuitable structures have been reduced and the natural course of things is restored, so that there is some possibility of the patient living a normal life, the reductive process should not be continued further. Instead, symbol-formation should be reinforced in a synthetic direction until a more favourable gradient for the excess libido is found. Reduction to the natural condition is neither an ideal state nor a panacea. If the natural state were really the ideal one, then the primitive would be leading an enviable existence. But that is by no means so, for aside from all the other sorrows and hardships of human life the primitive is tormented by superstitions, fears, and compulsions to such a degree that, if he lived in our civilization, he could not be described as other than profoundly neurotic, if not mad. What would one say of a European who conducted himself as follows? —A Negro dreamt that he was pursued by his enemies, caught, and burned alive. The next day he got his relatives to make a fire and told them to hold his feet in it, in order, by this apotropaic ceremony, to avert the misfortune of which he had dreamed. He was so badly burned that for many months he was unable to walk.[66]

95   Mankind was freed from these fears by a continual process of symbol-formation that leads to culture. Reversion to nature must therefore be followed by a synthetic reconstruction of the symbol. Reduction leads down to the primitive natural man and his peculiar mentality. Freud directed his attention mainly to the ruthless desire for pleasure, Adler to the "psychology of prestige." These are certainly two quite essential peculiarities of the primitive psyche, but they are far from being the only ones. For the sake of completeness we would have to mention other characteristics of the primitive, such as his playful, mystical, or "heroic" tendencies, but above all that outstanding quality of the primitive mind, which is its subjection to suprapersonal "powers," be they instincts, affects, superstitions, fantasies, magicians, witches, spirits, demons, or gods. Reduction leads back to the subjection of the primitive, which civilized man hopes he had escaped. And just as reduction makes a man

66 Lévy-Bruhl, p. 57.

aware of his subjection to these "powers" and thus confronts him with a rather dangerous problem, so the synthetic treatment of the symbol brings him to the religious question, not so much to the problem of present-day religious creeds as to the religious problem of primitive man. In the face of the very real powers that dominate him, only an equally real fact can offer help and protection. No intellectual system, but direct experience only, can counterbalance the blind power of the instincts.

96   Over against the polymorphism of the primitive's instinctual nature there stands the regulating principle of individuation. Multiplicity and inner division are opposed by an integrative unity whose power is as great as that of the instincts. Together they form a pair of opposites necessary for self-regulation, often spoken of as nature and spirit. These conceptions are rooted in psychic conditions between which human consciousness fluctuates like the pointer on the scales.

97   The primitive mentality can be directly experienced by us only in the form of the infantile psyche that still lives in our memories. The peculiarities of this psyche are conceived by Freud, justly enough, as infantile sexuality, for out of this germinal state there develops the later, mature sexual being. Freud, however, derives all sorts of other mental peculiarities from this infantile germinal state, so that it begins to look as if the mind itself came from a preliminary sexual stage and were consequently nothing more than an offshoot of sexuality. Freud overlooks the fact that the infantile, polyvalent germinal state is not just a singularly perverse preliminary stage of normal and mature sexuality; it seems perverse because it is a preliminary stage not only of adult sexuality but also of the whole mental make-up of the individual. Out of the infantile germinal state there develops the complete adult man; hence the germinal state is no more exclusively sexual than is the mind of the grown man. In it are hidden not merely the beginnings of adult life, but also the whole ancestral heritage, which is of unlimited extent. This heritage includes not only instincts from the animal stage, but all those differentiations that have left hereditary traces behind them. Thus every child is born with an immense split in his make-up: on one side he is more or less like an animal, on the other side he is the final embodiment of an age-old and endlessly complicated sum of hereditary factors. This

51

split accounts for the tension of the germinal state and does much to explain the many puzzles of child psychology, which certainly has no lack of them.

98   If now, by means of a reductive procedure, we uncover the infantile stages of the adult psyche, we find as its ultimate basis germs containing on the one hand the later sexual being *in statu nascendi,* and on the other all those complicated preconditions of the civilized being. This is reflected most beautifully in children's dreams. Many of them are very simple "childish" dreams and are immediately understandable, but others contain possibilities of meaning that almost make one's head spin, and things that reveal their profound significance only in the light of primitive parallels. This other side is the mind *in nuce.* Childhood, therefore, is important not only because various warpings of instinct have their origin there, but because this is the time when, terrifying or encouraging, those far-seeing dreams and images appear before the soul of the child, shaping his whole destiny, as well as those retrospective intuitions which reach back far beyond the range of childhood experience into the life of our ancestors. Thus in the child-psyche the natural condition is already opposed by a "spiritual" one. It is recognized that man living in the state of nature is in no sense merely "natural" like an animal, but sees, believes, fears, worships things whose meaning is not at all discoverable from the conditions of his natural environment. Their underlying meaning leads us in fact far away from all that is natural, obvious, and easily intelligible, and quite often contrasts most sharply with the natural instincts. We have only to think of all those gruesome rites and customs against which every natural feeling rises in revolt, or of all those beliefs and ideas which stand in insuperable contradiction to the evidence of the facts. All this drives us to the assumption that the spiritual principle (whatever that may be) asserts itself against the merely natural conditions with incredible strength. One can say that this too is "natural," and that both have their origin in one and the same "nature." I do not in the least doubt this origin, but must point out that this "natural" something consists of a conflict between two principles, to which you can give this or that name according to taste, and that this opposition is the expression, and perhaps also the basis, of the tension we call psychic energy.

99   For theoretical reasons as well there must be some such tension of opposites in the child, otherwise no energy would be possible, for, as Heraclitus has said, "war is the father of all things." As I have remarked, this conflict can be understood as an opposition between the profoundly primitive nature of the newborn infant and his highly differentiated inheritance. The natural man is characterized by unmitigated instinctuality, by his being completely at the mercy of his instincts. The inheritance that opposes this condition consists of mnemonic deposits accruing from all the experience of his ancestors. People are inclined to view this hypothesis with scepticism, thinking that "inherited ideas" are meant. There is naturally no question of that. It is rather a question of inherited *possibilities* of ideas, "paths" that have gradually been traced out through the cumulative experience of our ancestors. To deny the inheritance of these paths would be tantamount to denying the inheritance of the brain. To be consistent, such sceptics would have to assert that the child is born with the brain of an ape. But since it is born with a human brain, this must sooner or later begin to function in a human way, and it will necessarily begin at the level of the most recent ancestors. Naturally this functioning remains profoundly unconscious to the child. At first he is conscious only of the instincts and of what opposes these instincts— namely, his parents. For this reason the child has no notion that what stands in his way may be within himself. Rightly or wrongly it is projected on to the parents. This infantile prejudice is so tenacious that we doctors often have the greatest difficulty in persuading our patients that the wicked father who forbade everything is far more inside than outside themselves. Everything that works from the unconscious appears projected on others. Not that these others are wholly without blame, for even the worst projection is at least hung on a hook, perhaps a very small one, but still a hook offered by the other person.

100   Although our inheritance consists of psychological paths, it was nevertheless mental processes in our ancestors that traced these paths. If they came to consciousness again in the individual, they can do so only in the form of other mental processes; and although these processes can become conscious only through individual experience and consequently appear as individual acquisitions, they are nevertheless pre-existent traces which are

53

merely "filled out" by individual experience. Probably every "impressive" experience is just such a break-through into an old, previously unconscious river-bed.

101   These pre-existent paths are hard facts, as indisputable as the historical fact of man having built a city out of his original cave. This development was made possible only by the formation of a community, and the latter only by the curbing of instinct. The curbing of instinct by mental and spiritual processes is carried through with the same force and the same results in the individual as in the history of mankind. It is a normative or, more accurately, a "nomothetical" [67] process, and it derives its power from the unconscious fact of the inherited disposition. The mind, as the active principle in the inheritance, consists of the sum of the ancestral minds, the "unseen fathers" [68] whose authority is born anew with the child.

102   The philosophical concept of mind as "spirit" has still not been able to free itself, as a term in its own right, from the overpowering bond of identity with the other connotation of spirit, namely "ghost." Religion, on the other hand, has succeeded in getting over the linguistic association with "spirits" by calling the supreme spiritual authority "God." In the course of the centuries this conception came to formulate a spiritual principle which is opposed to mere instinctuality. What is especially significant here is that God is conceived at the same time as the Creator of nature. He is seen as the maker of those imperfect creatures who err and sin, and at the same time he is their judge and taskmaster. Simple logic would say: if I make a creature who falls into error and sin, and is practically worthless because of his blind instinctuality, then I am manifestly a bad creator and have not even completed my apprenticeship. (As we know, this argument played an important role in Gnosticism.) But the religious point of view is not perturbed by this criticism; it asserts that the ways and intentions of God are inscrutable. Actually the Gnostic argument found little favour in history, because the unassailability of the God-concept obviously answers a vital need before which all logic pales. (It should be understood that we are speaking here not of God as a

[67] ["Ordained by law."—EDITORS.]
[68] Söderblom, *Das Werden des Gottesglaubens*, pp. 88ff. and 175ff.

Ding an sich, but only of a human conception which as such is a legitimate object of science.)

103   Although the God-concept is a spiritual principle *par excellence,* the collective metaphysical need nevertheless insists that it is at the same time a conception of the First Cause, from which proceed all those instinctual forces that are opposed to the spiritual principle. God would thus be not only the essence of spiritual light, appearing as the latest flower on the tree of evolution, not only the spiritual goal of salvation in which all creation culminates, not only the end and aim, but also the darkest, nethermost cause of Nature's blackest deeps. This is a tremendous paradox which obviously reflects a profound psychological truth. For it asserts the essential contradictoriness of one and the same being, a being whose innermost nature is a tension of opposites. Science calls this "being" energy, for energy is like a living balance between opposites. For this reason the God-concept, in itself impossibly paradoxical, may be so satisfying to human needs that no logic however justified can stand against it. Indeed the subtlest cogitation could scarcely have found a more suitable formula for this fundamental fact of inner experience.

104   It is not, I believe, superfluous to have discussed in considerable detail the nature of the opposites that underlie psychic energy.[69] Freudian theory consists in a causal explanation of the psychology of instinct. From this standpoint the spiritual principle is bound to appear only as an appendage, a by-product of the instincts. Since its inhibiting and restrictive power cannot be denied, it is traced back to the influence of education, moral authorities, convention and tradition. These authorities in their turn derive their power, according to the theory, from repression in the manner of a vicious circle. The spiritual principle is not recognized as an equivalent counterpart of the instincts.

105   The spiritual standpoint, on the other hand, is embodied in religious views which I can take as being sufficiently known. Freudian psychology appears threatening to this standpoint, but it is not more of a threat than materialism in general, whether scientific or practical. The one-sidedness of Freud's sexual

69 I have treated this same problem under other aspects and in another way in *Symbols of Transformation,* pars. 253, 680; and *Psychological Types* (1923 edn., p. 240).

theory is significant at least as a symptom. Even if it has no scientific justification, it has a moral one. It is undoubtedly true that instinctuality conflicts with our moral views most frequently and most conspicuously in the realm of sex. The conflict between infantile instinctuality and ethics can never be avoided. It is, it seems to me, the *sine qua non* of psychic energy. While we are all agreed that murder, stealing, and ruthlessness of any kind are obviously inadmissible, there is nevertheless what we call a "sexual question." We hear nothing of a murder question or a rage question; social reform is never invoked against those who wreak their bad tempers on their fellow men. Yet these things are all examples of instinctual behaviour, and the necessity for their suppression seems to us self-evident. Only in regard to sex do we feel the need of a question mark. This points to a doubt—the doubt whether our existing moral concepts and the legal institutions founded on them are really adequate and suited to their purpose. No intelligent person will deny that in this field opinion is sharply divided. Indeed, there would be no problem at all if public opinion were united about it. It is obviously a reaction against a too rigorous morality. It is not simply an outbreak of primitive instinctuality; such outbreaks, as we know, have never yet bothered themselves with moral laws and moral problems. There are, rather, serious misgivings as to whether our existing moral views have dealt fairly with the nature of sex. From this doubt there naturally arises a legitimate interest in any attempt to understand the nature of sex more truly and deeply, and this interest is answered not only by Freudian psychology but by numerous other researches of the kind. The special emphasis, therefore, that Freud has laid on sex could be taken as a more or less conscious answer to the question of the hour, and conversely, the acceptance that Freud has found with the public proves how well-timed his answer was.

106   An attentive and critical reader of Freud's writings cannot fail to remark how wide and flexible his concept of sexuality is. In fact it covers so much that one often wonders why in certain places the author uses a sexual terminology at all. His concept of sexuality includes not only the physiological sexual processes but practically every stage, phase, and kind of feeling or desire. This enormous flexibility makes his concept universally applicable, though not always to the advantage of the resulting

explanations. By means of this inclusive concept you can explain a work of art or a religious experience in exactly the same terms as an hysterical symptom. The absolute difference between these three things then drops right out of the picture. The explanation can therefore be only an apparent one for at least two of them. Apart from these inconveniences, however, it is psychologically correct to tackle the problem first from the sexual side, for it is just there that the unprejudiced person will find something to think about.

107   The conflict between ethics and sex today is not just a collision between instinctuality and morality, but a struggle to give an instinct its rightful place in our lives, and to recognize in this instinct a power which seeks expression and evidently may not be trifled with, and therefore cannot be made to fit in with our well-meaning moral laws. Sexuality is not mere instinctuality; it is an indisputably creative power that is not only the basic cause of our individual lives, but a very serious factor in our psychic life as well. Today we know only too well the grave consequences that sexual disturbances can bring in their train. We could call sexuality the spokesman of the instincts, which is why from the spiritual standpoint sex is the chief antagonist, not because sexual indulgence is in itself more immoral than excessive eating and drinking, avarice, tyranny, and other extravagances, but because the spirit senses in sexuality a counterpart equal and indeed akin to itself. For just as the spirit would press sexuality, like every other instinct, into its service, so sexuality has an ancient claim upon the spirit, which it once—in procreation, pregnancy, birth, and childhood—contained within itself, and whose passion the spirit can never dispense with in its creations. Where would the spirit be if it had no peer among the instincts to oppose it? It would be nothing but an empty form. A reasonable regard for the other instincts has become for us a self-evident necessity, but with sex it is different. For us sex is still problematical, which means that on this point we have not reached a degree of consciousness that would enable us to do full justice to the instinct without appreciable moral injury. Freud is not only a scientific investigator of sexuality, but also its champion; therefore, having regard to the great importance of the sexual problem, I recognize the moral justifica-

tion of his concept of sexuality even though I cannot accept it scientifically.

108   This is not the place to discuss the possible reasons for the present attitude to sex. It is sufficient to point out that sexuality seems to us the strongest and most immediate instinct,[70] standing out as *the* instinct above all others. On the other hand, I must also emphasize that the spiritual principle does not, strictly speaking, conflict with instinct as such but only with blind instinctuality, which really amounts to an unjustified preponderance of the instinctual nature over the spiritual. The spiritual appears in the psyche also as an instinct, indeed as a real passion, a "consuming fire," as Nietzsche once expressed it. It is not derived from any other instinct, as the psychologists of instinct would have us believe, but is a principle *sui generis,* a specific and necessary form of instinctual power. I have gone into this problem in a special study, to which I would refer the reader.[71]

109   Symbol-formation follows the road offered by these two possibilities in the human mind. Reduction breaks down all inappropriate and useless symbols and leads back to the merely natural course, and this causes a damming up of libido. Most of the alleged "sublimations" are compulsory products of this situation, activities cultivated for the purpose of using up the unbearable surplus of libido. But the really primitive demands are not satisfied by this procedure. If the psychology of this dammed-up condition is studied carefully and without prejudice, it is easy to discover in it the beginnings of a primitive form of religion, a religion of an individual kind altogether different from a dogmatic, collective religion.

110   Since the making of a religion or the formation of symbols is just as important an interest of the primitive mind as the satisfaction of instinct, the way to further development is logically given: escape from the state of reduction lies in evolving a religion of an individual character. One's true individuality then emerges from behind the veil of the collective personality, which would be quite impossible in the state of reduction since our instinctual nature is essentially collective. The development

70 This is not the case with primitives, for whom the food question plays a far greater role.
71 See "Instinct and the Unconscious," infra.

of individuality is also impossible, or at any rate seriously
impeded, if the state of reduction gives rise to forced sublimations in the shape of various cultural activities, since these are
in their essence equally collective. But, as human beings are for
the most part collective, these forced sublimations are therapeutic products that should not be underestimated, because they
help many people to bring a certain amount of useful activity
into their lives. Among these cultural activities we must include
the practice of a religion within the framework of an existing
collective religion. The astonishing range of Catholic symbolism, for instance, has an emotional appeal which for many
natures is absolutely satisfying. The immediacy of the relationship to God in Protestantism satisfies the mystic's passion for
independence, while theosophy with its unlimited speculative
possibilities meets the need for pseudo-Gnostic intuitions and
caters to lazy thinking.

111   These organizations or systems are "symbola" (σύμβολον =
confession of faith) which enable man to set up a spiritual
counterpole to his primitive instinctual nature, a cultural attitude as opposed to sheer instinctuality. This has been the function of all religions. For a long time and for the great majority
of mankind the symbol of a collective religion will suffice. It is
perhaps only temporarily and for relatively few individuals that
the existing collective religions have become inadequate. Wherever the cultural process is moving forward, whether in single individuals or in groups, we find a shaking off of collective beliefs.
Every advance in culture is, psychologically, an extension of
consciousness, a coming to consciousness that can take place
only through discrimination. Therefore an advance always
begins with individuation, that is to say with the individual,
conscious of his isolation, cutting a new path through hitherto
untrodden territory. To do this he must first return to the
fundamental facts of his own being, irrespective of all authority
and tradition, and allow himself to become conscious of his
distinctiveness. If he succeeds in giving collective validity to his
widened consciousness, he creates a tension of opposites that
provides the stimulation which culture needs for its further
progress.

112   This is not to say that the development of individuality is
in all circumstances necessary or even opportune. Yet one may

well believe, as Goethe has said, that "the highest joy of man should be the growth of personality." There are large numbers of people for whom the development of individuality is the prime necessity, especially in a cultural epoch like ours, which is literally flattened out by collective norms, and where the newspaper is the real monarch of the earth. In my naturally limited experience there are, among people of maturer age, very many for whom the development of individuality is an indispensable requirement. Hence I am privately of the opinion that it is just the mature person who, in our times, has the greatest need of some further education in individual culture after his youthful education in school or university has moulded him on exclusively collective lines and thoroughly imbued him with the collective mentality. I have often found that people of riper years are in this respect capable of education to a most unexpected degree, although it is just those matured and strengthened by the experience of life who resist most vigorously the purely reductive standpoint.

113   Obviously it is in the youthful period of life that we have most to gain from a thorough recognition of the instinctual side. A timely recognition of sexuality, for instance, can prevent that neurotic suppression of it which keeps a man unduly withdrawn from life, or else forces him into a wretched and unsuitable way of living with which he is bound to come into conflict. Proper recognition and appreciation of normal instincts leads the young person into life and entangles him with fate, thus involving him in life's necessities and the consequent sacrifices and efforts through which his character is developed and his experience matured. For the mature person, however, the continued expansion of life is obviously not the right principle, because the descent towards life's afternoon demands simplification, limitation, and intensification—in other words, individual culture. A man in the first half of life with its biological orientation can usually, thanks to the youthfulness of his whole organism, afford to expand his life and make something of value out of it. But the man in the second half of life is oriented towards culture, the diminishing powers of his organism allowing him to subordinate his instincts to cultural goals. Not a few are wrecked during the transition from the biological to the cultural sphere.

Our collective education makes practically no provision for this transitional period. Concerned solely with the education of the young, we disregard the education of the adult, of whom it is always assumed—on what grounds who can say?—that he needs no more education. There is an almost total lack of guidance for this extraordinarily important transition from the biological to the cultural attitude, for the transformation of energy from the biological form into the cultural form. This transformation process is an individual one and cannot be enforced by general rules and maxims. It is achieved by means of the symbol. Symbol-formation is a fundamental problem that cannot be discussed here. I must refer the reader to Chapter V in my *Psychological Types*, where I have dealt with this question in detail.

IV. THE PRIMITIVE CONCEPTION OF LIBIDO

114   How intimately the beginnings of religious symbol-formation are bound up with a concept of energy is shown by the most primitive ideas concerning a magical potency, which is regarded both as an objective force and as a subjective state of intensity.

115   I will give some examples to illustrate this. According to the report of McGee, the Dakota Indians have the following conception of this "power." The sun is *wakonda*, not *the wakonda*, or *a wakonda*, but simply *wakonda*. The moon is *wakonda*, and so are thunder, lightning, stars, wind, etc. Men too, especially the shaman, are *wakonda*, also the demons of the elemental forces, fetishes, and other ritual objects, as well as many animals and localities of an especially impressive character. McGee says: "The expression [*wakonda*] can perhaps be rendered by the word 'mystery' better than any other, but even this concept is too narrow, because *wakonda* can equally well mean power, holy, old, greatness, alive, immortal." [72]

116   Similar to the use of *wakonda* by the Dakotas is that of *oki* by the Iroquois and of *manitu* by the Algonquins, with the abstract meaning of power or productive energy. *Wakonda* is the conception of a "diffused, all-pervasive, invisible, manipu-

[72] "The Siouan Indians—A Preliminary Sketch," p. 182; Lovejoy, "The Fundamental Concept of the Primitive Philosophy," p. 363.

lable and transferable life-energy and universal force." [73] The life of the primitive with all its interests is centred upon the possession of this power in sufficient amount.

117   Especially valuable is the observation that a concept like *manitu* occurs also as an exclamation when anything astonishing happens. Hetherwick [74] reports the same thing of the Yaos of central Africa, who cry *mulungu!* when they see something astonishing or incomprehensible. *Mulungu* means: (1) the soul of a man, which is called *lisoka* in life and becomes *mulungu* after death; (2) the entire spirit world; (3) the magically effective property or power inherent in any kind of object, such as the life and health of the body; (4) the active principle in everything magical, mysterious, inexplicable, and unexpected; and (5) the great spiritual power that has created the world and all life.

118   Similar to this is the *wong* concept of the Gold Coast. *Wong* can be a river, a tree, an amulet, or a lake, a spring, an area of land, a termite hill, crocodiles, monkeys, snakes, birds, etc. Tylor [75] erroneously interprets the *wong* force animistically as spirit or soul. But the way in which *wong* is used shows that it is a dynamic relation between man and objects.

119   The *churinga* [76] of the Australian aborigines is a similar energic concept. It means: (1) the ritual object; (2) the body of an individual ancestor (from whom the life force comes); (3) the mystical property of any object.

120   Much the same is the *zogo* concept of the Australian tribesmen of the Torres Strait, the word being used both as a noun

[73] Lovejoy, p. 365.
[74] "Some Animistic Beliefs among the Yaos of Central Africa."
[75] Tylor, *Primitive Culture*, II, pp. 176, 205.
[76] Spencer and Gillen, pp. 277f., where the following is reported of the *churinga* as a ritual object: "The native has a vague and undefined but still a very strong idea that any sacred object such as a Churinga, which has been handed down from generation to generation, is not only endowed with the magic power put into it when first it was made, but has gained some kind of virtue from every individual to whom it has belonged. A man who owns such a Churinga as this snake one will constantly rub it over with his hand, singing as he does so the Alcheringa history of the snake, and gradually comes to feel that there is some special association between him and the sacred object—that a virtue of some kind passes from it to him and also from him to it." Fetishes become charged with new power if left standing for some weeks or months near another strong fetish. Cf. Pechuël-Loesche, p. 366.

and an adjective. The Australian *arunquiltha* is a parallel concept of similar meaning, only it is the word for bad magic and for the evil spirit who likes to swallow the sun in an eclipse.[77] Of similar character is the Malayan *badi*, which also includes evil magical relationships.

121   The investigations of Lumholtz[78] have shown that the Mexican Huichols likewise have a fundamental conception of a power that circulates through men, ritual animals and plants (deer, mescal, corn, plumes, etc.).[79]

122   From the researches of Alice Fletcher among North American Indians it appears that the *wakan* concept is one of energic relationship similar to those already discussed. A man may become *wakan* through fasting, prayer, or visions. The weapons of a young man are *wakan;* they may not be touched by a woman (otherwise the libido runs backwards). For this reason the weapons are prayed to before battle (in order to make them powerful by charging them with libido). *Wakan* establishes the connection between the visible and the invisible, between the living and the dead, between the part and the whole of an object.

123   Codrington says of the Melanesian concept of *mana:* "The Melanesian mind is entirely possessed by the belief in a supernatural power or influence, called almost universally *mana.* This is what works to effect everything which is beyond the power of the ordinary man, outside the common processes of nature; it is present in the atmosphere of life, attaches itself to persons and to things, and is manifested by results which can only be ascribed to its operation. . . . It is a power or influence, not physical, and in a way supernatural; but it shows itself in physical force, or in any kind of power or influence which a man possesses. This *mana* is not fixed in anything, and can be conveyed in almost anything; but spirits, whether disembodied souls or supernatural beings, have it and can impart it; and it essentially belongs to personal beings to originate it, though it

[77] Spencer and Gillen, p. 458.   [78] *Unknown Mexico.*
[79] "When the Huichols, influenced by the law of participation, affirm the identity of corn, deer, *hikuli* [= mescal], and plumes, a classification has been established between their representatives. the governing principle of which is a common presence in these entities, or rather the circulation among them of a mystic power which is of supreme importance to the tribe." Lévy-Bruhl, p. 128.

may act through the medium of water, or a stone, or a bone." [80]

124   This description shows clearly that in the case of *mana,* as with the other concepts, we are dealing with a concept of energy which alone enables us to explain the remarkable fact of these primitive ideas. This is not to suggest that the primitive has an abstract idea of energy, but there can be no doubt that his concept is the preliminary concretistic stage of the abstract idea.

125   We find similar views in the *tondi* concept of the Bataks,[81] in the *atua* of the Maoris, in the *ani* or *han* of Ponape, the *kasinge* or *kalit* of Palau, the *anut* of Kusaie, the *yaris* of Tobi, the *ngai* of the Masai, the *andriamanitra* of the Malagasy, the *njom* of the Ekoi, etc. A complete survey is given by Söderblom in his book *Das Werden des Gottesglaubens.*

126   Lovejoy is of the opinion—with which I am in full agreement—that these concepts "are not primarily names for the 'supernormal' or the astonishing and certainly not for that which evokes awe, respect and love—but rather for the efficacious, the powerful, the productive." The concept in question really concerns the idea of "a diffused substance or energy upon the possession of which all exceptional power or ability or fecundity depends. The energy *is,* to be sure, terrible (under certain circumstances) and it is mysterious and incomprehensible; but it is so because it is vastly powerful, not because the things that manifest it are unusual and 'supernatural' or such as 'defeat reasonable expectation.'" The pre-animistic principle is the belief in "a force which is conceived as working according to quite regular and intelligible laws, a force which can be studied and controlled." [82] For these concepts Lovejoy suggests the term "primitive energetics."

127   Much that was taken by investigators animistically as spirit, demon, or numen really belongs to the primitive concept of energy. As I have already remarked, it is, in the strict sense, incorrect to speak of a "concept." "A concept of primitive philosophy," as Lovejoy calls it, is an idea obviously born of our own mentality; that is to say, for us *mana* would be a psy-

---

[80] Codrington, *The Melanesians,* p. 118. Seligmann, in his book *The Melanesians of British New Guinea,* so rich in valuable observations, speaks of *bariaua* (p. 446), which likewise belongs to the *mana* concept.
[81] Warnecke, *Die Religion der Batak.*
[82] Lovejoy, pp. 380f.

chological concept of energy, but for the primitive it is a psychic *phenomenon* that is perceived as something inseparable from the object. There are no abstract ideas to be found among primitives, not even, as a rule, simple concrete concepts, but only "representations." All primitive languages offer abundant proof of this. Thus *mana* is not a concept but a representation based on the perception of a "phenomenal" relationship. It is the essence of Lévy-Bruhl's *participation mystique*. In primitive speech only the fact of the relationship and the experience it evokes are indicated, as some of the above examples clearly show, not the nature or essence of that relationship, or of the principle determining it. The discovery of a suitable designation for the nature and essence of the unifying principle was reserved for a later level of culture, which substituted symbolic expressions.

128   In his classic study of *mana* Lehmann defines it as something "extraordinarily effective." The psychic nature of *mana* is especially emphasized by Preuss [83] and Röhr.[84] We cannot escape the impression that the primitive view of *mana* is a forerunner of our concept of psychic energy and, most probably, of energy in general.[85]

129   The basic conception of *mana* crops up again on the animistic level in personified form.[86] Here it is souls, demons, gods, who produce the extraordinary effect. As Lehmann rightly points out, nothing "divine" attaches to *mana,* so that one cannot see in *mana* the original form of an idea of God. Nonetheless, it cannot be denied that *mana* is a necessary or at least a very important precondition for the development of an idea of God, even though it may not be the most primitive of all

83 "Der Ursprung der Religion und Kunst."
84 "Das Wesen des Mana."
85 Cf. my discussion of the way in which Robert Mayer discovered the concept of energy: *Two Essays on Analytical Psychology,* pars. 106ff.
86 Seligmann (pp. 640ff.) reports observations which in my view show transitions of *mana* into animistic personifications. Such are the *labuni* of the Gelaria people of New Guinea. *Labuni* means "sending." It has to do with dynamic (magical) effects which emanate, or can be sent out, from the ovaries (?) of women who have borne children. *Labuni* look like "shadows," they use bridges to cross streams, change into animals, but otherwise possess no personality or definable form. Similar to this is the conception of the *ayik* which I observed among the Elgonyi, in northern Kenya.

preconditions. Another essential precondition is personification, for whose explanation other psychological factors must be adduced.

130   The almost universal incidence of the primitive concept of energy is a clear expression of the fact that even at early levels of human consciousness man felt the need to represent the sensed dynamism of psychic events in a concrete way. If, therefore, in our psychology we lay stress on the energic point of view, this is in accord with the psychic facts which have been graven on the mind of man since primordial times.

THE TRANSCENDENT FUNCTION [1]

Prefatory Note

This essay was written in 1916. Recently it was discovered by students of the C. G. Jung Institute, Zurich, and was brought out in a private edition in its first, provisional form, in an English translation. In order to prepare it for publication, I have worked over the manuscript, while preserving the main trend of thought and the unavoidable limitedness of its horizon. After forty-two years, the problem has lost nothing of its topicality, though its presentation is still in need of extensive improvement, as anyone can see who knows the material. The essay may therefore stand, with all its imperfections, as an historical document. It may give the reader some idea of the efforts of understanding which were needed for the first attempts at a synthetic view of the psychic process in analytical treatment. As its basic argument is still valid today, it may stimulate the reader to a broader and deeper understanding of the problem. This problem is identical with the universal question: How does one come to terms in practice with the unconscious?

[1] [Written in 1916 under the title "Die Transzendente Funktion," the ms. lay in Professor Jung's files until 1953. First published in 1957 by the Students Association, C. G. Jung Institute, Zurich, in an English translation by A. R. Pope. The German original, considerably revised by the author, was published in *Geist und Werk . . . zum 75. Geburtstag von Dr. Daniel Brody* (Zurich, 1958), together with a prefatory note of more general import specially written for that volume. The author has partially rewritten the note for publication here. The present translation is based on the revised German version, and Mr. Pope's translation has been consulted.—EDITORS.]

67

This is the question posed by the philosophy of India, and particularly by Buddhism and Zen. Indirectly, it is the fundamental question, in practice, of all religions and all philosophies. For the unconscious is not this thing or that; it is the Unknown as it immediately affects us.

The method of "active imagination," hereinafter described, is the most important auxiliary for the production of those contents of the unconscious which lie, as it were, immediately below the threshold of consciousness and, when intensified, are the most likely to irrupt spontaneously into the conscious mind. The method, therefore, is not without its dangers and should, if possible, not be employed except under expert supervision. One of the lesser dangers is that the procedure may not lead to any positive result, since it easily passes over into the so-called "free association" of Freud, whereupon the patient gets caught in the sterile circle of his own complexes, from which he is in any case unable to escape. A further danger, in itself harmless, is that, though authentic contents may be produced, the patient evinces an exclusively aesthetic interest in them and consequently remains stuck in an all-enveloping phantasmagoria, so that once more nothing is gained. The meaning and value of these fantasies are revealed only through their integration into the personality as a whole—that is to say, at the moment when one is confronted not only with what they mean but also with their moral demands.

Finally, a third danger—and this may in certain circumstances be a very serious matter—is that the subliminal contents already possess such a high energy charge that, when afforded an outlet by active imagination, they may overpower the conscious mind and take possession of the personality. This gives rise to a condition which—temporarily, at least—cannot easily be distinguished from schizophrenia, and may even lead to a genuine "psychotic interval." The method of active imagination, therefore, is not a plaything for children. The prevailing undervaluation of the unconscious adds considerably to the dangers of this method. On the other hand, there can be no doubt that it is an invaluable auxiliary for the psychotherapist.

C. G. J.

Küsnacht, July 1958 / September 1959

131   There is nothing mysterious or metaphysical about the term "transcendent function." It means a psychological function comparable in its way to a mathematical function of the same name, which is a function of real and imaginary numbers. The psychological "transcendent function" arises from the union of conscious and unconscious contents.

132   Experience in analytical psychology has amply shown that the conscious and the unconscious seldom agree as to their contents and their tendencies. This lack of parallelism is not just accidental or purposeless, but is due to the fact that the unconscious behaves in a compensatory or complementary manner towards the conscious. We can also put it the other way round and say that the conscious behaves in a complementary manner towards the unconscious. The reasons for this relationship are:

(1) Consciousness possesses a threshold intensity which its contents must have attained, so that all elements that are too weak remain in the unconscious.

(2) Consciousness, because of its directed functions, exercises an inhibition (which Freud calls censorship) on all incompatible material, with the result that it sinks into the unconscious.

(3) Consciousness constitutes the momentary process of adaptation, whereas the unconscious contains not only all the forgotten material of the individual's own past, but all the inherited behaviour traces constituting the structure of the mind.

(4) The unconscious contains all the fantasy combinations which have not yet attained the threshold intensity, but which in the course of time and under suitable conditions will enter the light of consciousness.

133   This readily explains the complementary attitude of the unconscious towards the conscious.

134   The definiteness and directedness of the conscious mind are qualities that have been acquired relatively late in the history of the human race, and are for instance largely lacking among primitives today. These qualities are often impaired in the neurotic patient, who differs from the normal person in that his threshold of consciousness gets shifted more easily; in other words, the partition between conscious and unconscious is much more permeable. The psychotic, on the other hand, is under the direct influence of the unconscious.

135   The definiteness and directedness of the conscious mind are

69

extremely important acquisitions which humanity has bought at a very heavy sacrifice, and which in turn have rendered humanity the highest service. Without them science, technology, and civilization would be impossible, for they all presuppose the reliable continuity and directedness of the conscious process. For the statesman, doctor, and engineer as well as for the simplest labourer, these qualities are absolutely indispensable. We may say in general that social worthlessness increases to the degree that these qualities are impaired by the unconscious. Great artists and others distinguished by creative gifts are, of course, exceptions to this rule. The very advantage that such individuals enjoy consists precisely in the permeability of the partition separating the conscious and the unconscious. But, for those professions and social activities which require just this continuity and reliability, these exceptional human beings are as a rule of little value.

136   It is therefore understandable, and even necessary, that in each individual the psychic process should be as stable and definite as possible, since the exigencies of life demand it. But this involves a certain disadvantage: the quality of directedness makes for the inhibition or exclusion of all those psychic elements which appear to be, or really are, incompatible with it, i.e., likely to bias the intended direction to suit their purpose and so lead to an undesired goal. But how do we know that the concurrent psychic material is "incompatible"? We know it by an act of judgment which determines the direction of the path that is chosen and desired. This judgment is partial and prejudiced, since it chooses one particular possibility at the cost of all the others. The judgment in its turn is always based on experience, i.e., on what is already known. As a rule it is never based on what is new, what is still unknown, and what under certain conditions might considerably enrich the directed process. It is evident that it cannot be, for the very reason that the unconscious contents are excluded from consciousness.

137   Through such acts of judgment the directed process necessarily becomes one-sided, even though the rational judgment may appear many-sided and unprejudiced. The very rationality of the judgment may even be the worst prejudice, since we call reasonable what appears reasonable to us. What appears to us unreasonable is therefore doomed to be excluded because of its

irrational character. It may really be irrational, but may equally well merely appear irrational without actually being so when seen from another standpoint.

138   One-sidedness is an unavoidable and necessary characteristic of the directed process, for direction implies one-sidedness. It is an advantage and a drawback at the same time. Even when no outwardly visible drawback seems to be present, there is always an equally pronounced counter-position in the unconscious, unless it happens to be the ideal case where all the psychic components are tending in one and the same direction. This possibility cannot be disputed in theory, but in practice it very rarely happens. The counter-position in the unconscious is not dangerous so long as it does not possess any high energy-value. But if the tension increases as a result of too great one-sidedness, the counter-tendency breaks through into consciousness, usually just at the moment when it is most important to maintain the conscious direction. Thus the speaker makes a slip of the tongue just when he particularly wishes not to say anything stupid. This moment is critical because it possesses a high energy tension which, when the unconscious is already charged, may easily "spark" and release the unconscious content.

139   Civilized life today demands concentrated, directed conscious functioning, and this entails the risk of a considerable dissociation from the unconscious. The further we are able to remove ourselves from the unconscious through directed functioning, the more readily a powerful counter-position can build up in the unconscious, and when this breaks out it may have disagreeable consequences.

140   Analysis has given us a profound insight into the importance of unconscious influences, and we have learnt so much from this for our practical life that we deem it unwise to expect an elimination or standstill of the unconscious after the so-called completion of the treatment. Many patients, obscurely recognizing this state of affairs, have great difficulty in deciding to give up the analysis, although both they and the analyst find the feeling of dependency irksome. Often they are afraid to risk standing on their own feet, because they know from experience that the unconscious can intervene again and again in their lives in a disturbing and apparently unpredictable manner.

141   It was formerly assumed that patients were ready to cope

71

with normal life as soon as they had acquired enough practical self-knowledge to understand their own dreams. Experience has shown, however, that even professional analysts, who might be expected to have mastered the art of dream interpretation, often capitulate before their own dreams and have to call in the help of a colleague. If even one who purports to be an expert in the method proves unable to interpret his own dreams satisfactorily, how much less can this be expected of the patient. Freud's hope that the unconscious could be "exhausted" has not been fulfilled. Dream-life and intrusions from the unconscious continue—*mutatis mutandis*—unimpeded.

142   There is a widespread prejudice that analysis is something like a "cure," to which one submits for a time and is then discharged healed. That is a layman's error left over from the early days of psychoanalysis. Analytical treatment could be described as a readjustment of psychological attitude achieved with the help of the doctor. Naturally this newly won attitude, which is better suited to the inner and outer conditions, can last a considerable time, but there are very few cases where a single "cure" is permanently successful. It is true that medical optimism has never stinted itself of publicity and has always been able to report definitive cures. We must, however, not let ourselves be deceived by the all-too-human attitude of the practitioner, but should always remember that the life of the unconscious goes on and continually produces problematical situations. There is no need for pessimism; we have seen too many excellent results achieved with good luck and honest work for that. But this need not prevent us from recognizing that analysis is no once-and-for-all "cure"; it is no more, at first, than a more or less thorough readjustment. There is no change that is unconditionally valid over a long period of time. Life has always to be tackled anew. There are, of course, extremely durable collective attitudes which permit the solution of typical conflicts. A collective attitude enables the individual to fit into society without friction, since it acts upon him like any other condition of life. But the patient's difficulty consists precisely in the fact that his individual problem cannot be fitted without friction into a collective norm; it requires the solution of an individual conflict if the whole of his personality is to remain viable. No rational solution can do justice to this task, and there is abso-

lutely no collective norm that could replace an individual solution without loss.

143   The new attitude gained in the course of analysis tends sooner or later to become inadequate in one way or another, and necessarily so, because the constant flow of life again and again demands fresh adaptation. Adaptation is never achieved once and for all. One might certainly demand of analysis that it should enable the patient to gain new orientations in later life, too, without undue difficulty. And experience shows that this is true up to a point. We often find that patients who have gone through a thorough analysis have considerably less difficulty with new adjustments later on. Nevertheless, these difficulties prove to be fairly frequent and may at times be really troublesome. That is why even patients who have had a thorough analysis often turn to their old analyst for help at some later period. In the light of medical practice in general there is nothing very unusual about this, but it does contradict a certain misplaced enthusiasm on the part of the therapist as well as the view that analysis constitutes a unique "cure." In the last resort it is highly improbable that there could ever be a therapy that got rid of all difficulties. Man needs difficulties; they are necessary for health. What concerns us here is only an excessive amount of them.

144   The basic question for the therapist is not how to get rid of the momentary difficulty, but how future difficulties may be successfully countered. The question is: what kind of mental and moral attitude is it necessary to have towards the disturbing influences of the unconscious, and how can it be conveyed to the patient?

145   The answer obviously consists in getting rid of the separation between conscious and unconscious. This cannot be done by condemning the contents of the unconscious in a one-sided way, but rather by recognizing their significance in compensating the one-sidedness of consciousness and by taking this significance into account. The tendencies of the conscious and the unconscious are the two factors that together make up the transcendent function. It is called "transcendent" because it makes the transition from one attitude to another organically possible, without loss of the unconscious. The constructive or synthetic method of treatment presupposes insights which are at least potentially present in the patient and can therefore be

73

made conscious. If the analyst knows nothing of these potentialities he cannot help the patient to develop them either, unless analyst and patient together devote proper scientific study
to this problem, which as a rule is out of the question.

146   In actual practice, therefore, the suitably trained analyst
mediates the transcendent function for the patient, i.e., helps
him to bring conscious and unconscious together and so arrive
at a new attitude. In this function of the analyst lies one of the
many important meanings of the *transference*. The patient
clings by means of the transference to the person who seems to
promise him a renewal of attitude; through it he seeks this
change, which is vital to him, even though he may not be conscious of doing so. For the patient, therefore, the analyst has
the character of an indispensable figure absolutely necessary for
life. However infantile this dependence may appear to be, it
expresses an extremely important demand which, if disappointed, often turns to bitter hatred of the analyst. It is therefore
important to know what this demand concealed in the transference is really aiming at; there is a tendency to understand it
in the reductive sense only, as an erotic infantile fantasy. But
that would mean taking this fantasy, which is usually concerned with the parents, literally, as though the patient, or
rather his unconscious, still had the expectations the child once
had towards the parents. Outwardly it still is the same expectation of the child for the help and protection of the parents, but
in the meantime the child has become an adult, and what was
normal for a child is improper in an adult. It has become a
metaphorical expression of the not consciously realized need
for help in a crisis. Historically it is correct to explain the erotic
character of the transference in terms of the infantile *eros*. But
in that way the meaning and purpose of the transference are not
understood, and its interpretation as an infantile sexual fantasy
leads away from the real problem. The understanding of the
transference is to be sought not in its historical antecedents but
in its purpose. The one-sided, reductive explanation becomes
in the end nonsensical, especially when absolutely nothing new
comes out of it except the increased resistances of the patient.
The sense of boredom which then appears in the analysis is
simply an expression of the monotony and poverty of ideas—not
of the unconscious, as is sometimes supposed, but of the analyst,

who does not understand that these fantasies should not be taken merely in a concretistic-reductive sense, but rather in a constructive one. When this is realized, the standstill is often overcome at a single stroke.

147   Constructive treatment of the unconscious, that is, the question of meaning and purpose, paves the way for the patient's insight into that process which I call the transcendent function.

148   It may not be superfluous, at this point, to say a few words about the frequently heard objection that the constructive method is simply "suggestion." The method is based, rather, on evaluating the symbol (i.e., dream-image or fantasy) not *semiotically*, as a sign for elementary instinctual processes, but symbolically in the true sense, the word "symbol" being taken to mean the best possible expression for a complex fact not yet clearly apprehended by consciousness. Through reductive analysis of this expression nothing is gained but a clearer view of the elements originally composing it, and though I would not deny that increased insight into these elements may have its advantages, it nevertheless bypasses the question of purpose. Dissolution of the symbol at this stage of analysis is therefore a mistake. To begin with, however, the method for working out the complex meanings suggested by the symbol is the same as in reductive analysis. The associations of the patient are obtained, and as a rule they are plentiful enough to be used in the synthetic method. Here again they are evaluated not semiotically but symbolically. The question we must ask is: to what meaning do the individual associations A, B, C point, when taken in conjunction with the manifest dream-content?

149   An unmarried woman patient dreamt that *someone gave her a wonderful, richly ornamented, antique sword dug up out of a tumulus.* [For interpretation, see p. 76.]

150   In this case there was no need of any supplementary analogies on the part of the analyst. The patient's associations provided all that was necessary. It might be objected that this treatment of the dream involves suggestion. But this ignores the fact that a suggestion is never accepted without an inner readiness for it, or if after great insistence it is accepted, it is immediately lost again. A suggestion that is accepted for any length of time always presupposes a marked psychological readiness which is merely brought into play by the so-called suggestion.

This objection is therefore thoughtless and credits suggestion with a magical power it in no way possesses, otherwise suggestion therapy would have an enormous effect and would render analytical procedures quite superfluous. But this is far from being the case. Furthermore, the charge of suggestion does not take account of the fact that the patient's own associations point to the cultural significance of the sword.

151   After this digression, let us return to the question of the transcendent function. We have seen that during treatment the transcendent function is, in a sense, an "artificial" product because it is largely supported by the analyst. But if the patient is

ASSOCIATIONS	ANALYTICAL INTERPRETATION	CONSTRUCTIVE INTERPRETATION
Her *father's* dagger, which he once flashed in the sun in front of her. It made a great impression on her. Her father was in every respect an energetic, strong-willed man, with an impetuous temperament, and adventurous in love affairs. A *Celtic* bronze sword: Patient is proud of her Celtic ancestry. The Celts are full of temperament, impetuous, passionate. The ornamentation has a mysterious look about it, ancient tradition, runes, signs of ancient wisdom, ancient civilizations, heritage of mankind, brought to light again out of the grave.	Patient has a pronounced father complex and a rich tissue of sexual fantasies about her father, whom she lost early. She always put herself in her mother's place, although with strong resistances towards her father. She has never been able to accept a man like her father and has therefore chosen weakly, neurotic men against her will. Also in the analysis a violent resistance towards the physician-father. The dream digs up her wish for her father's "weapon." The rest is clear. In theory, this would immediately point to a phallic fantasy.	It is as if the patient needed such a weapon. Her father had the weapon. He was energetic, lived accordingly, and also took upon himself the difficulties inherent in his temperament. Therefore, though living a passionate, exciting life he was not neurotic. This weapon is a very ancient heritage of mankind, which lay buried in the patient and was brought to light through excavation (analysis). The weapon has to do with insight, with wisdom. It is a means of attack and defence. Her father's weapon was a passionate, unbending will, with which he made his way through life.

Up till now the patient has been the opposite in every respect. She is just on the point of realizing that a person can also will something and need not merely be driven, as she had always believed. The will based on a knowledge of life and on insight is an ancient heritage of the human race, which also is in her, but till now lay buried, for in this respect, too, she is her father's daughter. But she had not appreciated this till now, because her character had been that of a perpetually whining, pampered, spoilt child. She was extremely passive and completely given to sexual fantasies.

Interpretation of dream (see par. 149)

76

to stand on his own feet he must not depend permanently on outside help. The interpretation of dreams would be an ideal method for synthesizing the conscious and unconscious data, but in practice the difficulties of analyzing one's own dreams are too great.

152   We must now make clear what is required to produce the transcendent function. First and foremost, we need the unconscious material. The most readily accessible expression of unconscious processes is undoubtedly dreams. The dream is, so to speak, a pure product of the unconscious. The alterations which the dream undergoes in the process of reaching consciousness, although undeniable, can be considered irrelevant, since they too derive from the unconscious and are not intentional distortions. Possible modifications of the original dream-image derive from a more superficial layer of the unconscious and therefore contain valuable material too. They are further fantasy-products following the general trend of the dream. The same applies to the subsequent images and ideas which frequently occur while dozing or rise up spontaneously on waking. Since the dream originates in sleep, it bears all the characteristics of an "abaissement du niveau mental" (Janet), or of low energy-tension: logical discontinuity, fragmentary character, analogy formations, superficial associations of the verbal, clang, or visual type, condensations, irrational expressions, confusion, etc. With an increase of energy-tension, the dreams acquire a more ordered character; they become dramatically composed and reveal clear sense-connections, and the valency of the associations increases.

153   Since the energy-tension in sleep is usually very low, dreams, compared with conscious material, are inferior expressions of unconscious contents and are very difficult to understand from a constructive point of view, but are usually easier to understand reductively. In general, dreams are unsuitable or difficult to make use of in developing the transcendent function, because they make too great demands on the subject.

154   We must therefore look to other sources for the unconscious material. There are, for instance, the unconscious interferences in the waking state, ideas "out of the blue," slips, deceptions and lapses of memory, symptomatic actions, etc. This material is generally more useful for the reductive method than for the

constructive one; it is too fragmentary and lacks continuity, which is indispensable for a meaningful synthesis.

155   Another source is spontaneous fantasies. They usually have a more composed and coherent character and often contain much that is obviously significant. Some patients are able to produce fantasies at any time, allowing them to rise up freely simply by eliminating critical attention. Such fantasies can be used, though this particular talent is none too common. The capacity to produce free fantasies can, however, be developed with practice. The training consists first of all in systematic exercises for eliminating critical attention, thus producing a vacuum in consciousness. This encourages the emergence of any fantasies that are lying in readiness. A prerequisite, of course, is that fantasies with a high libido-charge are actually lying ready. This is naturally not always the case. Where this is not so, special measures are required.

156   Before entering upon a discussion of these, I must yield to an uncomfortable feeling which tells me that the reader may be asking dubiously, what really is the point of all this? And why is it so absolutely necessary to bring up the unconscious contents? Is it not sufficient if from time to time they come up of their own accord and make themselves unpleasantly felt? Does one have to drag the unconscious to the surface by force? On the contrary, should it not be the job of analysis to empty the unconscious of fantasies and in this way render it ineffective?

157   It may be as well to consider these misgivings in somewhat more detail, since the methods for bringing the unconscious to consciousness may strike the reader as novel, unusual, and perhaps even rather weird. We must therefore first discuss these natural objections, so that they shall not hold us up when we begin demonstrating the methods in question.

158   As we have seen, we need the unconscious contents to supplement the conscious attitude. If the conscious attitude were only to a slight degree "directed," the unconscious could flow in quite of its own accord. This is what does in fact happen with all those people who have a low level of conscious tension, as for instance primitives. Among primitives, no special measures are required to bring up the unconscious. Nowhere, really, are special measures required for this, because those people who are least aware of their unconscious side are the most influenced

by it. But they are unconscious of what is happening. The secret participation of the unconscious is everywhere present without our having to search for it, but as it remains unconscious we never really know what is going on or what to expect. What we are searching for is a way to make conscious those contents which are about to influence our actions, so that the secret interference of the unconscious and its unpleasant consequences can be avoided.

159   The reader will no doubt ask: why cannot the unconscious be left to its own devices? Those who have not already had a few bad experiences in this respect will naturally see no reason to control the unconscious. But anyone with sufficiently bad experience will eagerly welcome the bare possibility of doing so. Directedness is absolutely necessary for the conscious process, but as we have seen it entails an unavoidable one-sidedness. Since the psyche is a self-regulating system, just as the body is, the regulating counteraction will always develop in the unconscious. Were it not for the directedness of the conscious function, the counteracting influences of the unconscious could set in unhindered. It is just this directedness that excludes them. This, of course, does not inhibit the counteraction, which goes on in spite of everything. Its regulating influence, however, is eliminated by critical attention and the directed will, because the counteraction as such seems incompatible with the conscious direction. To this extent the psyche of civilized man is no longer a self-regulating system but could rather be compared to a machine whose speed-regulation is so insensitive that it can continue to function to the point of self-injury, while on the other hand it is subject to the arbitrary manipulations of a one-sided will.

160   Now it is a peculiarity of psychic functioning that when the unconscious counteraction is suppressed it loses its regulating influence. It then begins to have an accelerating and intensifying effect on the conscious process. It is as though the counteraction had lost its regulating influence, and hence its energy, altogether, for a condition then arises in which not only no inhibiting counteraction takes place, but in which its energy seems to add itself to that of the conscious direction. To begin with, this naturally facilitates the execution of the conscious intentions, but because they are unchecked, they may easily assert them-

79

selves at the cost of the whole. For instance, when someone makes a rather bold assertion and suppresses the counteraction, namely a well-placed doubt, he will insist on it all the more, to his own detriment.

161   The ease with which the counteraction can be eliminated is proportional to the degree of dissociability of the psyche and leads to loss of instinct. This is characteristic of, as well as very necessary for, civilized man, since instincts in their original strength can render social adaptation almost impossible. It is not a real atrophy of instinct but, in most cases, only a relatively lasting product of education, and would never have struck such deep roots had it not served the interests of the individual.

162   Apart from the everyday cases met with in practice, a good example of the suppression of the unconscious regulating influence can be found in Nietzsche's *Zarathustra*. The discovery of the "higher" man, and also of the "ugliest" man, expresses the regulating influence, for the "higher" men want to drag Zarathustra down to the collective sphere of average humanity as it always has been, while the "ugliest" man is actually the personification of the counteraction. But the roaring lion of Zarathustra's moral conviction forces all these influences, above all the feeling of pity, back again into the cave of the unconscious. Thus the regulating influence is suppressed, but not the secret counteraction of the unconscious, which from now on becomes clearly noticeable in Nietzsche's writings. First he seeks his adversary in Wagner, whom he cannot forgive for *Parsifal,* but soon his whole wrath turns against Christianity and in particular against St. Paul, who in some ways suffered a fate similar to Nietzsche's. As is well known, Nietzsche's psychosis first produced an identification with the "Crucified Christ" and then with the dismembered Dionysus. With this catastrophe the counteraction at last broke through to the surface.

163   Another example is the classic case of megalomania preserved for us in the fourth chapter of the Book of Daniel. Nebuchadnezzar at the height of his power had a dream which foretold disaster if he did not humble himself. Daniel interpreted the dream quite expertly, but without getting a hearing. Subsequent events showed that his interpretation was correct, for Nebuchadnezzar, after suppressing the unconscious regulating influence, fell victim to a psychosis that contained the very

counteraction he had sought to escape: he, the lord of the earth, was degraded to an animal.

164   An acquaintance of mine once told me a dream in which *he stepped out into space from the top of a mountain.* I explained to him something of the influence of the unconscious and warned him against dangerous mountaineering expeditions, for which he had a regular passion. But he laughed at such ideas. A few months later while climbing a mountain he actually did step off into space and was killed.

165   Anyone who has seen these things happen over and over again in every conceivable shade of dramatic intensity is bound to ponder. He becomes aware how easy it is to overlook the regulating influences, and that he should endeavour to pay attention to the unconscious regulation which is so necessary for our mental and physical health. Accordingly he will try to help himself by practising self-observation and self-criticism. But mere self-observation and intellectual self-analysis are entirely inadequate as a means to establishing contact with the unconscious. Although no human being can be spared bad experiences, everyone shrinks from risking them, especially if he sees any way by which they might be circumvented. Knowledge of the regulating influences of the unconscious offers just such a possibility and actually does render much bad experience unnecessary. We can avoid a great many detours that are distinguished by no particular attraction but only by tiresome conflicts. It is bad enough to make detours and painful mistakes in unknown and unexplored territory, but to get lost in inhabited country on broad highways is merely exasperating. What, then, are the means at our disposal of obtaining knowledge of the regulating factors?

166   If there is no capacity to produce fantasies freely, we have to resort to artificial aid. The reason for invoking such aid is generally a depressed or disturbed state of mind for which no adequate cause can be found. Naturally the patient can give any number of rationalistic reasons—the bad weather alone suffices as a reason. But none of them is really satisfying as an explanation, for a causal explanation of these states is usually satisfying only to an outsider, and then only up to a point. The outsider is content if his causal requirements are more or less satisfied; it is sufficient for him to know where the thing comes

from; he does not feel the challenge which, for the patient, lies in the depression. The patient would like to know what it is all for and how to gain relief. *In the intensity of the emotional disturbance itself lies the value, the energy which he should have at his disposal in order to remedy the state of reduced adaptation.* Nothing is achieved by repressing this state or devaluing it rationally.

167   In order, therefore, to gain possession of the energy that is in the wrong place, he must make the emotional state the basis or starting point of the procedure. He must make himself as conscious as possible of the mood he is in, sinking himself in it without reserve and noting down on paper all the fantasies and other associations that come up. Fantasy must be allowed the freest possible play, yet not in such a manner that it leaves the orbit of its object, namely the affect, by setting off a kind of "chain-reaction" association process. This "free association," as Freud called it, leads away from the object to all sorts of complexes, and one can never be sure that they relate to the affect and are not displacements which have appeared in its stead. Out of this preoccupation with the object there comes a more or less complete expression of the mood, which reproduces the content of the depression in some way, either concretely or symbolically. Since the depression was not manufactured by the conscious mind but is an unwelcome intrusion from the unconscious, the elaboration of the mood is, as it were, a picture of the contents and tendencies of the unconscious that were massed together in the depression. The whole procedure is a kind of enrichment and clarification of the affect, whereby the affect and its contents are brought nearer to consciousness, becoming at the same time more impressive and more understandable. This work by itself can have a favourable and vitalizing influence. At all events, it creates a new situation, since the previously unrelated affect has become a more or less clear and articulate idea, thanks to the assistance and co-operation of the conscious mind. This is the beginning of the transcendent function, i.e., of the collaboration of conscious and unconscious data.

168   The emotional disturbance can also be dealt with in another way, not by clarifying it intellectually but by giving it visible shape. Patients who possess some talent for drawing or painting can give expression to their mood by means of a picture. It is

not important for the picture to be technically or aesthetically satisfying, but merely for the fantasy to have free play and for the whole thing to be done as well as possible. In principle this procedure agrees with the one first described. Here too a product is created which is influenced by both conscious and unconscious, embodying the striving of the unconscious for the light and the striving of the conscious for substance.

169   Often, however, we find cases where there is no tangible mood or depression at all, but just a general, dull discontent, a feeling of resistance to everything, a sort of boredom or vague disgust, an indefinable but excruciating emptiness. In these cases no definite starting point exists—it would first have to be created. Here a special introversion of libido is necessary, supported perhaps by favourable external conditions, such as complete rest, especially at night, when the libido has in any case a tendency to introversion. ("'Tis night: now do all fountains speak louder. And my soul also is a bubbling fountain." [2])

170   Critical attention must be eliminated. Visual types should concentrate on the expectation that an inner image will be produced. As a rule such a fantasy-picture will actually appear—perhaps hypnagogically—and should be carefully observed and noted down in writing. Audio-verbal types usually hear inner words, perhaps mere fragments of apparently meaningless sentences to begin with, which however should be carefully noted down too. Others at such times simply hear their "other" voice. There are, indeed, not a few people who are well aware that they possess a sort of inner critic or judge who immediately comments on everything they say or do. Insane people hear this voice directly as auditory hallucinations. But normal people too, if their inner life is fairly well developed, are able to reproduce this inaudible voice without difficulty, though as it is notoriously irritating and refractory it is almost always repressed. Such persons have little difficulty in procuring the unconscious material and thus laying the foundation of the transcendent function.

171   There are others, again, who neither see nor hear anything inside themselves, but whose hands have the knack of giving expression to the contents of the unconscious. Such people can

2 [Nietzsche, *Thus Spake Zarathustra*, XXXI; Common trans., p. 156.—EDITORS.]

profitably work with plastic materials. Those who are able to express the unconscious by means of bodily movements are rather rare. The disadvantage that movements cannot easily be fixed in the mind must be met by making careful drawings of the movements afterwards, so that they shall not be lost to the memory. Still rarer, but equally valuable, is automatic writing, direct or with the planchette. This, too, yields useful results.

172   We now come to the next question: what is to be done with the material obtained in one of the manners described. To this question there is no *a priori* answer; it is only when the conscious mind confronts the products of the unconscious that a provisional reaction will ensue which determines the subsequent procedure. Practical experience alone can give us a clue. So far as my experience goes, there appear to be two main tendencies. One is the way of *creative formulation,* the other the way of *understanding.*

173   Where the principle of creative formulation predominates, the material is continually varied and increased until a kind of condensation of motifs into more or less stereotyped symbols takes place. These stimulate the creative fantasy and serve chiefly as aesthetic motifs. This tendency leads to the aesthetic problem of artistic formulation.

174   Where, on the other hand, the principle of understanding predominates, the aesthetic aspect is of relatively little interest and may occasionally even be felt as a hindrance. Instead, there is an intensive struggle to understand the *meaning* of the unconscious product.

175   Whereas aesthetic formulation tends to concentrate on the formal aspect of the motif, an intuitive understanding often tries to catch the meaning from barely adequate hints in the material, without considering those elements which would come to light in a more careful formulation.

176   Neither of these tendencies can be brought about by an arbitrary effort of will; they are far more the result of the peculiar make-up of the individual personality. Both have their typical dangers and may lead one astray. The danger of the aesthetic tendency is overvaluation of the formal or "artistic" worth of the fantasy-productions; the libido is diverted from the real goal of the transcendent function and sidetracked into purely aesthetic problems of artistic expression. The danger of

wanting to understand the meaning is overvaluation of the content, which is subjected to intellectual analysis and interpretation, so that the essentially symbolic character of the product is lost. Up to a point these bypaths must be followed in order to satisfy aesthetic or intellectual requirements, whichever predominate in the individual case. But the danger of both these bypaths is worth stressing, for, after a certain point of psychic development has been reached, the products of the unconscious are greatly overvalued precisely because they were boundlessly undervalued before. This undervaluation is one of the greatest obstacles in formulating the unconscious material. It reveals the collective standards by which anything individual is judged: nothing is considered good or beautiful that does not fit into the collective schema, though it is true that contemporary art is beginning to make compensatory efforts in this respect. What is lacking is not the collective recognition of the individual product but its subjective appreciation, the understanding of its meaning and value for the *subject*. This feeling of inferiority for one's own product is of course not the rule everywhere. Sometimes we find the exact opposite: a naïve and uncritical overvaluation coupled with the demand for collective recognition once the initial feeling of inferiority has been overcome. Conversely, an initial overvaluation can easily turn into depreciatory scepticism. These erroneous judgments are due to the individual's unconsciousness and lack of self-reliance: either he is able to judge only by collective standards, or else, owing to ego-inflation, he loses his capacity for judgment altogether.

177   *One tendency seems to be the regulating principle of the other;* both are bound together in a compensatory relationship. Experience bears out this formula. So far as it is possible at this stage to draw more general conclusions, we could say that aesthetic formulation needs understanding of the meaning, and understanding needs aesthetic formulation. The two supplement each other to form the transcendent function.

178   The first steps along both paths follow the same principle: consciousness puts its media of expression at the disposal of the unconscious content. It must not do more than this at first, so as not to exert undue influence. In giving the content form, the lead must be left as far as possible to the chance ideas and associations thrown up by the unconscious. This is naturally some-

thing of a setback for the conscious standpoint and is often felt as painful. It is not difficult to understand this when we remember how the contents of the unconscious usually present themselves: as things which are too weak by nature to cross the threshold, or as incompatible elements that were repressed for a variety of reasons. Mostly they are unwelcome, unexpected, irrational contents, disregard or repression of which seems altogether understandable. Only a small part of them has any unusual value, either from the collective or from the subjective standpoint. But contents that are collectively valueless may be exceedingly valuable when seen from the standpoint of the individual. This fact expresses itself in their affective tone, no matter whether the subject feels it as negative or positive. Society, too, is divided in its acceptance of new and unknown ideas which obtrude their emotionality. The purpose of the initial procedure is to discover the feeling-toned contents, for in these cases we are always dealing with situations where the one-sidedness of consciousness meets with the resistance of the instinctual sphere.

179   The two ways do not divide until the aesthetic problem becomes decisive for the one type of person and the intellectual-moral problem for the other. The ideal case would be if these two aspects could exist side by side or rhythmically succeed each other; that is, if there were an alternation of creation and understanding. It hardly seems possible for the one to exist without the other, though it sometimes does happen in practice: the creative urge seizes possession of the object at the cost of its meaning, or the urge to understand overrides the necessity of giving it form. The unconscious contents want first of all to be seen clearly, which can only be done by giving them shape, and to be judged only when everything they have to say is tangibly present. It was for this reason that Freud got the dream-contents, as it were, to express themselves in the form of "free associations" before he began interpreting them.

180   It does not suffice in all cases to elucidate only the conceptual context of a dream-content. Often it is necessary to clarify a vague content by giving it a visible form. This can be done by drawing, painting, or modelling. Often the hands know how to solve a riddle with which the intellect has wrestled in vain. By shaping it, one goes on dreaming the dream in greater detail

in the waking state, and the initially incomprehensible, isolated event is integrated into the sphere of the total personality, even though it remains at first unconscious to the subject. Aesthetic formulation leaves it at that and gives up any idea of discovering a meaning. This sometimes leads patients to fancy themselves artists—misunderstood ones, naturally. The desire to understand, if it dispenses with careful formulation, starts with the chance idea or association and therefore lacks an adequate basis. It has better prospects of success if it begins only with the formulated product. The less the initial material is shaped and developed, the greater is the danger that understanding will be governed not by the empirical facts but by theoretical and moral considerations. The kind of understanding with which we are concerned at this stage consists in a reconstruction of the meaning that seems to be immanent in the original "chance" idea.

181   It is evident that such a procedure can legitimately take place only when there is a sufficient motive for it. Equally, the lead can be left to the unconscious only if it already contains the will to lead. This naturally happens only when the conscious mind finds itself in a critical situation. Once the unconscious content has been given form and the meaning of the formulation is understood, the question arises as to how the ego will relate to this position, and how the ego and the unconscious are to come to terms. This is the second and more important stage of the procedure, the bringing together of opposites for the production of a third: the transcendent function. At this stage it is no longer the unconscious that takes the lead, but the ego.

182   We shall not define the individual ego here, but shall leave it in its banal reality as that continuous centre of consciousness whose presence has made itself felt since the days of childhood. It is confronted with a psychic product that owes its existence mainly to an unconscious process and is therefore in some degree opposed to the ego and its tendencies.

183   This standpoint is essential in coming to terms with the unconscious. The position of the ego must be maintained as being of equal value to the counter-position of the unconscious, and vice versa. This amounts to a very necessary warning: for just as the conscious mind of civilized man has a restrictive effect on the unconscious, so the rediscovered unconscious often has a really dangerous effect on the ego. In the same way that the

ego suppressed the unconscious before, a liberated unconscious can thrust the ego aside and overwhelm it. There is a danger of the ego losing its head, so to speak, that it will not be able to defend itself against the pressure of affective factors—a situation often encountered at the beginning of schizophrenia. This danger would not exist, or would not be so acute, if the process of having it out with the unconscious could somehow divest the affects of their dynamism. And this is what does in fact happen when the counter-position is aestheticized or intellectualized. But the confrontation with the unconscious must be a many-sided one, for the transcendent function is not a partial process running a conditioned course; it is a total and integral event in which all aspects are, or should be, included. The affect must therefore be deployed in its full strength. Aestheticization and intellectualization are excellent weapons against dangerous affects, but they should be used only when there is a vital threat, and not for the purpose of avoiding a necessary task.

184   Thanks to the fundamental insight of Freud, we know that emotional factors must be given full consideration in the treatment of the neuroses. The personality *as a whole* must be taken seriously into account, and this applies to both parties, the patient as well as the analyst. How far the latter may hide behind the shield of theory remains a delicate question, to be left to his discretion. At all events, the treatment of neurosis is not a kind of psychological water-cure, but a renewal of the personality, working in every direction and penetrating every sphere of life. Coming to terms with the counter-position is a serious matter on which sometimes a very great deal depends. Taking the other side seriously is an essential prerequisite of the process, for only in that way can the regulating factors exert an influence on our actions. Taking it seriously does not mean taking it literally, but it does mean giving the unconscious credit, so that it has a chance to co-operate with consciousness instead of automatically disturbing it.

185   Thus, in coming to terms with the unconscious, not only is the standpoint of the ego justified, but the unconscious is granted the same authority. The ego takes the lead, but the unconscious must be allowed to have its say too—*audiatur et altera pars.*

186   The way this can be done is best shown by those cases in which the "other" voice is more or less distinctly heard. For

such people it is technically very simple to note down the "other" voice in writing and to answer its statements from the standpoint of the ego. It is exactly as if a dialogue were taking place between two human beings with equal rights, each of whom gives the other credit for a valid argument and considers it worth while to modify the conflicting standpoints by means of thorough comparison and discussion or else to distinguish them clearly from one another. Since the way to agreement seldom stands open, in most cases a long conflict will have to be borne, demanding sacrifices from both sides. Such a rapprochement could just as well take place between patient and analyst, the role of devil's advocate easily falling to the latter.

187   The present day shows with appalling clarity how little able people are to let the other man's argument count, although this capacity is a fundamental and indispensable condition for any human community. Everyone who proposes to come to terms with himself must reckon with this basic problem. For, to the degree that he does not admit the validity of the other person, he denies the "other" within himself the right to exist—and vice versa. The capacity for inner dialogue is a touchstone for outer objectivity.

188   Simple as the process of coming to terms may be in the case of the inner dialogue, it is undoubtedly more complicated in other cases where only visual products are available, speaking a language which is eloquent enough for one who understands it, but which seems like deaf-and-dumb language to one who does not. Faced with such products, the ego must seize the initiative and ask: "How am I affected by this sign?" [3] This Faustian question can call forth an illuminating answer. The more direct and natural the answer is, the more valuable it will be, for directness and naturalness guarantee a more or less total reaction. It is not absolutely necessary for the process of confrontation itself to become conscious in every detail. Very often a total reaction does not have at its disposal those theoretical assumptions, views, and concepts which would make clear apprehension possible. In such cases one must be content with the

3 [Cf. *Faust: Part I*, Wayne trans., p. 46.]

wordless but suggestive feelings which appear in their stead and are more valuable than clever talk.

189   The shuttling to and fro of arguments and affects represents the transcendent function of opposites. The confrontation of the two positions generates a tension charged with energy and creates a living, third thing—not a logical stillbirth in accordance with the principle *tertium non datur* but a movement out of the suspension between opposites, a living birth that leads to a new level of being, a new situation. The transcendent function manifests itself as a quality of conjoined opposites. So long as these are kept apart—naturally for the purpose of avoiding conflict—they do not function and remain inert.

190   In whatever form the opposites appear in the individual, at bottom it is always a matter of a consciousness lost and obstinately stuck in one-sidedness, confronted with the image of instinctive wholeness and freedom. This presents a picture of the anthropoid and archaic man with, on the one hand, his supposedly uninhibited world of instinct and, on the other, his often misunderstood world of spiritual ideas, who, compensating and correcting our one-sidedness, emerges from the darkness and shows us how and where we have deviated from the basic pattern and crippled ourselves psychically.

191   I must content myself here with a description of the outward forms and possibilities of the transcendent function. Another task of greater importance would be the description of its *contents*. There is already a mass of material on this subject, but not all the difficulties in the way of exposition have yet been overcome. A number of preparatory studies are still needed before the conceptual foundation is laid which would enable us to give a clear and intelligible account of the contents of the transcendent function. I have unfortunately had the experience that the scientific public are not everywhere in a position to follow a purely psychological argument, since they either take it too personally or are bedevilled by philosophical or intellectual prejudices. This renders any meaningful appreciation of the psychological factors quite impossible. If people take it personally their judgment is always subjective, and they declare everything to be impossible which seems not to apply in their case or which they prefer not to acknowledge. They are quite incapable of realizing that what is valid for them may not be

valid at all for another person with a different psychology. We are still very far from possessing a general valid scheme of explanation in all cases.

192   One of the greatest obstacles to psychological understanding is the inquisitive desire to know whether the psychological factor adduced is "true" or "correct." If the description of it is not erroneous or false, then the factor is valid in itself and proves its validity by its very existence. One might just as well ask if the duck-billed platypus is a "true" or "correct" invention of the Creator's will. Equally childish is the prejudice against the role which mythological assumptions play in the life of the psyche. Since they are not "true," it is argued, they have no place in a scientific explanation. But mythologems *exist,* even though their statements do not coincide with our incommensurable idea of "truth."

193   As the process of coming to terms with the counter-position has a total character, nothing is excluded. Everything takes part in the discussion, even if only fragments become conscious. Consciousness is continually widened through the confrontation with previously unconscious contents, or—to be more accurate— could be widened if it took the trouble to integrate them. That is naturally not always the case. Even if there is sufficient intelligence to understand the procedure, there may yet be a lack of courage and self-confidence, or one is too lazy, mentally and morally, or too cowardly, to make an effort. But where the necessary premises exist, the transcendent function not only forms a valuable addition to psychotherapeutic treatment, but gives the patient the inestimable advantage of assisting the analyst on his own resources, and of breaking a dependence which is often felt as humiliating. It is a way of attaining liberation by one's own efforts and of finding the courage to be oneself.

A REVIEW OF THE COMPLEX THEORY [1]

194   Modern psychology has one thing in common with modern physics, that its method enjoys greater intellectual recognition than its subject. Its subject, the psyche, is so infinitely diverse in its manifestations, so indefinite and so unbounded, that the definitions given of it are difficult if not impossible to interpret, whereas the definitions based on the mode of observation and on the method derived from it are—or at least should be—known quantities. Psychological research proceeds from these empirically or arbitrarily defined factors and observes the psyche in terms of their alteration. The psyche therefore appears as the *disturbance* of a probable mode of behaviour postulated by one or other of these methods. This procedure is, *cum grano salis,* that of natural science in general.

195   It goes without saying that in these circumstances almost everything depends on the method and its presuppositions and that they largely determine the result. The actual object of investigation does, of course, have some say in the matter, yet it does not behave as an autonomous being would behave if left

[1] Inaugural lecture delivered at the Federal Polytechnic Institute, Zurich, May 5, 1934. [First published as *Allgemeines zur Komplextheorie* (Kultur- und staatswissenschaftliche Schriften der Eidgenössischen Technischen Hochschule, 12; Aarau, 1934). Republished with slight revisions in *Über psychische Energetik und das Wesen der Träume* (Psychologische Abhandlungen, II; Zurich, 1948).— EDITORS.]

undisturbed in its natural conditions. It has therefore long been recognized in experimental psychology, and above all in psychopathology, that a particular experimental procedure does not apprehend the psychic process directly, but that a certain psychic condition interpolates itself between it and the experiment, which one could call the "experimental situation." This psychic "situation" can sometimes jeopardize the whole experiment by *assimilating* not only the experimental procedure but the purpose underlying it. By "assimilation" we mean an attitude on the part of the subject, who misinterprets the experiment because he has at first an insuperable tendency to assume that it is, shall we say, an intelligence test or an attempt to take an indiscreet look behind the scenes. Such an attitude disguises the process which the experimenter is struggling to observe.

196   Experiences of this kind were very common in the association tests, and it was discovered on these occasions that what the method was aiming at, namely to establish the average speed of the reactions and their qualities, was a relatively subsidiary result compared with the way in which the method was *disturbed* by the autonomous behaviour of the psyche, that is, by assimilation. It was then that I discovered the feeling-toned complexes, which had always been registered before as *failures to react*.

197   The discovery of complexes, and of the phenomena of assimilation caused by them, showed very clearly on what a weak footing the old view—dating back to Condillac—stood, that it was possible to investigate *isolated* psychic processes. There are no isolated psychic processes, just as there are no isolated life-processes; at any rate, no means have yet been found of isolating them experimentally.[2] Only with the help of specially trained attention and concentration can the subject isolate a process so that it appears to meet the requirements of the experiment. But this is yet another "experimental situation," which differs from the one previously described only because this time the role of the assimilating complex is taken over by the conscious mind, whereas before this was done by more or less unconscious inferiority complexes.

198   Now this does not mean that the *value* of the experiment is

2 Exceptions to this rule are the processes of growth in tissues that can be kept alive in a nutrient medium.

93

put in question in any fundamental sense, only that it is critically limited. In the realm of psychophysiological processes—for instance, sense perceptions or motor reactions, where the purpose of the experiment is obviously harmless—pure reflex mechanisms predominate, and there are few if any assimilations, so that the experiment is not appreciably disturbed. It is very different in the realm of complicated psychic processes, where the experimental procedure cannot be restricted to certain definite possibilities. Here, where the safeguards afforded by specific aims fall away, unlimited possibilities emerge, and these sometimes give rise right at the beginning to an experimental situation which we call a "constellation." This term simply expresses the fact that the outward situation releases a psychic process in which certain contents gather together and prepare for action. When we say that a person is "constellated" we mean that he has taken up a position from which he can be expected to react in a quite definite way. But the constellation is an automatic process which happens involuntarily and which no one can stop of his own accord. The constellated contents are definite complexes possessing their own specific energy. If the experiment in question is an association test, the complexes will influence its course in high degree by provoking disturbed reactions or—more rarely—by hiding behind a definite mode of reaction which, however, can be recognized by the fact that it no longer corresponds to the meaning of the stimulus word. Educated subjects with strong wills can, through verbal-motor facility, screen off the meaning of a stimulus word by short reaction times in such a way that it does not reach them at all. But this only works when really important personal secrets have to be protected. Talleyrand's art of using words to conceal thoughts is given only to a few. Unintelligent people, and particularly women, protect themselves with the help of *value predicates*. This often presents a very comical picture. Value predicates are attributes of feeling, such as *beautiful, good, dear, sweet, friendly,* etc. One often notices, in conversation, how certain people find everything *interesting, charming, good, lovely,* or—if they are English—*fine, marvellous, grand, splendid,* and (a great favourite!) *fascinating,* all of which serve either to cover up their total lack of interest or to hold the object at arm's length. But the great majority of subjects cannot prevent their com-

94

plexes from picking on certain stimulus words and furnishing them with various symptoms of disturbance, the chief of these being delayed reaction time. One can also combine these experiments with the electrical measurement of resistance, first used by Veraguth,[3] where the so-called psychogalvanic reflex phenomenon provides further indications of reactions disturbed by complexes.

199   The association test is of general interest in that, like no other psychological experiment of comparable simplicity, it reproduces the psychic situation of the *dialogue,* and at the same time makes fairly accurate quantitative and qualitative evaluation possible. Instead of questions in the form of definite sentences, the subject is confronted with the vague, ambiguous, and therefore disconcerting stimulus word, and instead of an answer he has to react with a *single* word. Through accurate observation of the reaction disturbances, facts are revealed and registered which are often assiduously overlooked in ordinary discussion, and this enables us to discover things that point to the unspoken background, to those states of readiness, or constellations, which I mentioned before. What happens in the association test also happens in every discussion between two people. In both cases there is an experimental situation which constellates complexes that assimilate the topic discussed or the situation as a whole, including the parties concerned. The discussion loses its objective character and its real purpose, since the constellated complexes frustrate the intentions of the speakers and may even put answers into their mouths which they can no longer remember afterwards. This fact has been put to practical use in the cross-examination of witnesses. Its place in psychology is taken by the so-called repetition experiment, which discovers and localizes the gaps in the memory. After, say, a hundred reactions, the subject is asked what answers he gave to the individual stimulus words. Gaps or falsifications of memory occur with average regularity in all spheres of association disturbed by complexes.

200   So far, I have purposely avoided discussing the nature of complexes, on the tacit assumption that their nature is generally known. The word "complex" in its psychological sense has

---

[3] *Das psycho-galvanische Reflexphänomen.*

passed into common speech both in German and in English. Everyone knows nowadays that people "have complexes." What is not so well known, though far more important theoretically, is that complexes can *have us*. The existence of complexes throws serious doubt on the naïve assumption of the unity of consciousness, which is equated with "psyche," and on the supremacy of the will. Every constellation of a complex postulates a disturbed state of consciousness. The unity of consciousness is disrupted and the intentions of the will are impeded or made impossible. Even memory is often noticeably affected, as we have seen. The complex must therefore be a psychic factor which, in terms of energy, possesses a value that sometimes exceeds that of our conscious intentions, otherwise such disruptions of the conscious order would not be possible at all. And in fact, an active complex puts us momentarily under a state of duress, of compulsive thinking and acting, for which under certain conditions the only appropriate term would be the judicial concept of diminished responsibility.

201 What then, scientifically speaking, is a "feeling-toned complex"? It is the *image* of a certain psychic situation which is strongly accentuated emotionally and is, moreover, incompatible with the habitual attitude of consciousness. This image has a powerful inner coherence, it has its own wholeness and, in addition, a relatively high degree of autonomy, so that it is subject to the control of the conscious mind to only a limited extent, and therefore behaves like an animated foreign body in the sphere of consciousness. The complex can usually be suppressed with an effort of will, but not argued out of existence, and at the first suitable opportunity it reappears in all its original strength. Certain experimental investigations seem to indicate that its intensity or activity curve has a wavelike character, with a "wave-length" of hours, days, or weeks. This very complicated question remains as yet unclarified.

202 We have to thank the French psychopathologists, Pierre Janet in particular, for our knowledge today of the extreme *dissociability* of consciousness. Janet and Morton Prince both succeeded in producing four to five splittings of the personality, and it turned out that each fragment of personality had its own peculiar character and its own separate memory. These fragments subsist relatively independently of one another and can

96

take one another's place at any time, which means that each fragment possesses a high degree of autonomy. My findings in regard to complexes corroborate this somewhat disquieting picture of the possibilities of psychic disintegration, for fundamentally there is no difference in principle between a fragmentary personality and a complex. They have all the essential features in common, until we come to the delicate question of fragmented consciousness. Personality fragments undoubtedly have their own consciousness, but whether such small psychic fragments as complexes are also capable of a consciousness of their own is a still unanswered question. I must confess that this question has often occupied my thoughts, for complexes behave like Descartes' devils and seem to delight in playing impish tricks. They slip just the wrong word into one's mouth, they make one forget the name of the person one is about to introduce, they cause a tickle in the throat just when the softest passage is being played on the piano at a concert, they make the tiptoeing latecomer trip over a chair with a resounding crash. They bid us congratulate the mourners at a burial instead of condoling with them, they are the instigators of all those maddening things which F. T. Vischer attributed to the "mischievousness of the object." [4] They are the actors in our dreams, whom we confront so powerlessly; they are the elfin beings so aptly characterized in Danish folklore by the story of the clergyman who tried to teach the Lord's prayer to two elves. They took the greatest pains to repeat the words after him correctly, but at the very first sentence they could not avoid saying: "Our Father, who art not in heaven." As one might expect on theoretical grounds, these impish complexes are unteachable.

203   I hope that, taking it with a very large grain of salt, no one will mind this metaphorical paraphrase of a scientific problem. But even the soberest formulation of the phenomenology of complexes cannot get round the impressive fact of their autonomy, and the deeper one penetrates into their nature—I might almost say into their biology—the more clearly do they reveal their character as *splinter psyches*. Dream psychology shows us as plainly as could be wished how complexes appear in personified form when there is no inhibiting consciousness to

4 Cf. *Auch Einer*. [Also cf. *Psychological Types* (1923 edn., p. 369, n. 1).—EDITORS.]

suppress them, exactly like the hobgoblins of folklore who go crashing round the house at night. We observe the same phenomenon in certain psychoses when the complexes get "loud" and appear as "voices" having a thoroughly personal character.

204   Today we can take it as moderately certain that complexes are in fact "splinter psyches." The aetiology of their origin is frequently a so-called trauma, an emotional shock or some such thing, that splits off a bit of the psyche. Certainly one of the commonest causes is a moral conflict, which ultimately derives from the apparent impossibility of affirming the whole of one's nature. This impossibility presupposes a direct split, no matter whether the conscious mind is aware of it or not. As a rule there is a marked unconsciousness of any complexes, and this naturally guarantees them all the more freedom of action. In such cases their powers of assimilation become especially pronounced, since unconsciousness helps the complex to assimilate even the ego, the result being a momentary and unconscious alteration of personality known as identification with the complex. In the Middle Ages it went by another name: it was called possession. Probably no one imagines this state as being particularly harmless, and there is in fact no difference in principle between a slip of the tongue caused by a complex and the wildest blasphemies; it is only a difference of degree. The history of language provides innumerable illustrations of this. When some one is in the throes of a violent emotion we exclaim: "What's got into him today?" "He is driven by the devil," "hag-ridden," etc. In using these somewhat worn metaphors we naturally do not think of their original meaning, although it is easily recognizable and points without a doubt to the fact that naïver and more primitive people did not "psychologize" disturbing complexes as we do, but regarded them as beings in their own right, that is, as demons. Later levels of conscious development created such an intense ego-complex or ego-consciousness that the complexes were deprived of their original autonomy, at least in ordinary speech. As a rule a person says: "*I* have a complex," or the admonishing voice of the doctor says to the hysterical patient: "Your pain is not real, you merely imagine it hurts you." Fear of infection is, apparently, an arbitrary fancy of the patient's, at any rate everybody tries to convince him that he is cooking up a delusional idea.

98

205   It is not difficult to see that the ordinary modern conception of the problem treats it as though it were certain beyond all doubt that the complex was invented and "imagined" by the patient, and that it would not exist at all had the patient not gone to the trouble of deliberately bringing it to life. As against this, it has now been firmly established that complexes possess a remarkable degree of autonomy, that organically unfounded, so-called "imaginary" pains hurt just as much as legitimate ones, and that a phobia of illness has not the slightest inclination to disappear even if the patient himself, his doctor, and common speech-usage all unite in asseverating that it is nothing but "imagination."

206   Here we have an interesting example of "apotropaic" thinking, which is quite on a par with the euphemistic names bestowed by the ancients, a classic example of which is the πόντος εὔξεινος, the 'hospitable sea.' Just as the Erinyes ("Furies") were called, cautiously and propitiatingly, the Eumenides ("Kindly Ones"), so the modern mind conceives all inner disturbances as its own activity: it simply assimilates them. This is not done, of course, with an open avowal of apotropaic euphemism, but with an equally unconscious tendency to make the autonomy of the complex *unreal* by giving it a different name. Consciousness behaves like some one who hears a suspicious noise in the attic and thereupon dashes down into the cellar, in order to assure himself that no burglar has broken in and that the noise was mere imagination. In reality he has simply not dared to go up into the attic.

207   It is not immediately apparent that fear could be the motive which prompts consciousness to explain complexes as its own activity. Complexes appear to be such trivial things, such ridiculous "nothings," in fact, that we are positively ashamed of them and do everything possible to conceal them. But if they were really "nothing" they could not be so painful. Painful is what causes pain—something decidedly unpleasant, therefore, which for that reason is important in itself and deserves to be taken seriously. But we are only too ready to make anything unpleasant *unreal*—so long as we possibly can. The outbreak of neurosis signalizes the moment when this can no longer be done by the primitive magical means of apotropaic gestures and euphemisms. From this moment the complex establishes itself

99

on the conscious surface; it can no longer be circumvented and proceeds to assimilate the ego-consciousness step by step, just as, previously, the ego-consciousness tried to assimilate it. This eventually leads to a neurotic dissociation of the personality.

208   Such a development reveals the complex in its original strength, which, as I said, sometimes exceeds even that of the ego-complex. Only then can one understand that the ego had every reason for practising the magic of names on complexes, for it is obvious enough that what I fear is something sinister that threatens to swallow me up. There are, among people who generally pass for normal, a large number who have a "skeleton in the cupboard," the existence of which must not be mentioned in their presence on pain of death, so great is their fear of the lurking spectre. All those people who are still in the stage of making their complexes unreal use any reference to neurosis as proving that this obviously applies only to positively morbid natures, to which category, of course, they do not belong. As though it were the privilege only of the sick person to become sick!

209   The tendency to make complexes unreal by assimilation does not prove their nugatoriness but, on the contrary, their importance. It is a negative admission of the instinctive fear which primitive man has of invisible things that move in the dark. With primitives, this fear does in fact set in with the fall of darkness, just as, with us, complexes are swamped by day, but at night raise their voices all the more clamorously, driving away sleep or filling it with bad dreams. Complexes are objects of inner experience and are not to be met in the street and in public places. It is on them that the weal and woe of personal life depends; they are the *lares* and *penates* who await us at the fireside and whose peaceableness it is dangerous to extol; they are the "little people" whose pranks disturb our nights. Naturally, so long as the evil falls only on our neighbours, it counts for nothing; but when it attacks us—then one must be a doctor in order to appreciate what an appalling menace a complex can be. Only when you have seen whole families destroyed by them, morally and physically, and the unexampled tragedy and hopeless misery that follow in their train, do you feel the full impact of the reality of complexes. You then understand how idle and unscientific it is to think that a person can

"imagine" a complex. Casting about for a medical comparison, one could best compare them with infections or with malign tumours, both of which arise without the least assistance from the conscious mind. This comparison is not altogether satisfactory because complexes are not entirely morbid by nature but are *characteristic expressions of the psyche,* irrespective of whether this psyche is differentiated or primitive. Consequently we find unmistakable traces of them in all peoples and in all epochs. The oldest literary records bear witness to them; thus the Gilgamesh Epic describes in masterly fashion the psychology of the power-complex, and the Book of Tobit in the Old Testament gives the history of an erotic complex together with its cure.

210   The universal belief in spirits is a direct expression of the complex structure of the unconscious. Complexes are in truth the living units of the unconscious psyche, and it is only through them that we are able to deduce its existence and its constitution. The unconscious would in fact be—as it is in Wundt's psychology—nothing but a vestige of dim or "obscure" representations, or a "fringe of consciousness," as William James calls it, were it not for the existence of complexes. That is why Freud became the real discoverer of the unconscious in psychology, because he examined those dark places and did not simply dismiss them, with a disparaging euphemism, as "parapraxes." The *via regia* to the unconscious, however, is not the dream, as he thought, but the complex, which is the architect of dreams and of symptoms. Nor is this *via* so very "royal," either, since the way pointed out by the complex is more like a rough and uncommonly devious footpath that often loses itself in the undergrowth and generally leads not into the heart of the unconscious but past it.

211   Fear of complexes is a bad signpost, however, because it always points away from the unconscious and back into consciousness. Complexes are something so unpleasant that nobody in his right senses can be persuaded that the motive forces which maintain them could betoken anything good. The conscious mind is invariably convinced that complexes are something unseemly and should therefore be eliminated somehow or other. Despite overwhelming evidence of all kinds that complexes have always existed and are ubiquitous, people cannot bring them-

selves to regard them as normal phenomena of life. The fear of complexes is a rooted prejudice, for the superstitious fear of anything unfavourable has remained untouched by our vaunted enlightenment. This fear provokes violent resistance whenever complexes are examined, and considerable determination is needed to overcome it.

212   Fear and resistance are the signposts that stand beside the *via regia* to the unconscious, and it is obvious that what they primarily signify is a preconceived opinion of the thing they are pointing at. It is only natural that from the feeling of fear one should infer something dangerous, and from the feeling of resistance something repellent. The patient does so, the public does so, and in the end the analyst does so too, which is why the first medical theory about the unconscious was, logically, the theory of repression worked out by Freud. By drawing conclusions *a posteriori* from the nature of complexes, this view naturally conceives the unconscious as consisting essentially of incompatible tendencies which are repressed on account of their immorality. Nothing could offer a more striking proof that the author of this view proceeded purely empirically, without being in the least influenced by philosophical considerations. There had been talk of the unconscious long before Freud. It was Leibniz who first introduced the idea into philosophy; Kant and Schelling expressed opinions about it, and Carus elaborated it into a system, on whose foundations Eduard von Hartmann built his portentous *Philosophy of the Unconscious*. The first medico-psychological theory of the unconscious has as little to do with these antecedents as it has with Nietzsche.

213   Freud's theory is a faithful account of his actual experiences during the investigation of complexes. But since such an investigation is always a dialogue between two people, in building up the theory one has to consider not only the complexes of the one partner, but also those of the other. Every dialogue that pushes forward into territory hedged about by fear and resistance is aiming at something vital, and by impelling the one partner to integrate his wholeness it forces the other to take up a broader position. He too is impelled towards wholeness, for without this he would not be able to push the dialogue deeper and deeper into those fear-bound regions. No investi-

gator, however unprejudiced and objective he is, can afford to disregard his own complexes, for they enjoy the same autonomy as those of other people. As a matter of fact, he *cannot* disregard them, because they do not disregard *him*. Complexes are very much a part of the psychic constitution, which is the most absolutely prejudiced thing in every individual. His constitution will therefore inexorably decide *what* psychological view a given observer will have. Herein lies the unavoidable limitation of psychological observation: its validity is contingent upon the personal equation of the observer.

214   Psychological theory therefore formulates, first and foremost, a psychic situation that has come about through a dialogue between one particular observer and a number of observed persons. As the dialogue moves mainly in the sphere of resistances set up by complexes, the character of these complexes will necessarily become attached to the theory, that is to say it will be, in the most general sense of the word, offensive, because it works on the complexes of the public. That is why all the views of modern psychology are not only controversial in the objective sense, but provocative. They force the public to react violently either for or against and, in scientific discussions, give rise to emotional debates, outbursts of dogmatism, personal vituperation, and so forth.

215   It can easily be seen from all this that modern psychology with its investigation of complexes has opened up a psychic taboo area riddled with hopes and fears. Complexes are the real focus of psychic unrest, and its repercussions are so far-reaching that psychological investigators have no immediate hope of pursuing their work in peace, for this presupposes some consensus of scientific opinion. But complex psychology is, at present, far indeed from any such agreement, much further, it seems to me, than even the pessimists suppose. For, with the discovery of incompatible tendencies, only *one* sector of the unconscious has come under review, and only *one* source of fear has been revealed.

216   It will no doubt be remembered what a storm of indignation was unleashed on all sides when Freud's works became generally known. This violent reaction of public complexes drove Freud into an isolation which has brought the charge of dogmatism upon him and his school. All psychological theoreticians in this

field run the same risk, for they are playing with something that directly affects all that is uncontrolled in man—the *numinosum,* to use an apt expression of Rudolf Otto's. Where the realm of complexes begins the freedom of the ego comes to an end, for complexes are psychic agencies whose deepest nature is still unfathomed. Every time the researcher succeeds in advancing a little further towards the psychic *tremendum,* then, as before, reactions are let loose in the public, just as with patients who, for therapeutic reasons, are urged to take up arms against the inviolability of their complexes.

217   To the uninitiated ear, my presentation of the complex theory may sound like a description of primitive demonology or of the psychology of taboos. This peculiar note is due simply to the fact that the existence of complexes, of split-off psychic fragments, is a quite perceptible vestige of the primitive state of mind. The primitive mind is marked by a high degree of dissociability, which expresses itself in the fact, for instance, that primitives assume the existence of several souls—in one case, even six—besides an immense number of gods and spirits, who are not just talked about, as with us, but are very often highly impressive psychic experiences.

218   I would like to take this opportunity to remark that I use the term "primitive" in the sense of "primordial," and that I do not imply any kind of value judgment. Also, when I speak of a "vestige" of a primitive state, I do not necessarily mean that this state will sooner or later come to an end. On the contrary, I see no reason why it should not endure as long as humanity lasts. So far, at any rate, it has not changed very much, and with the World War and its aftermath there has even been a considerable increase in its strength. I am therefore inclined to think that autonomous complexes are among the normal phenomena of life and that they make up the structure of the unconscious psyche.

219   As can be seen, I have contented myself with describing only the essential features of the complex theory. I must refrain, however, from filling in this incomplete picture by a description of the problems arising out of the existence of autonomous complexes. Three important problems would have to be dealt with: the therapeutic, the philosophical, and the moral. All three still await discussion.

II

THE SIGNIFICANCE OF CONSTITUTION AND HEREDITY IN PSYCHOLOGY   *f adler*

PSYCHOLOGICAL FACTORS DETERMINING HUMAN BEHAVIOUR

THE SIGNIFICANCE OF CONSTITUTION AND HEREDITY IN PSYCHOLOGY [1]

220 In the opinion of scientists today, there is no doubt that the individual psyche is in large measure dependent on the physiological constitution; indeed, there are not a few who consider this dependence absolute. I would not like to go as far as that myself, but would regard it as more appropriate in the circumstances to grant the psyche a *relative* independence of the physiological constitution. It is true that there are no rigorous proofs of this, but then there is no proof of the psyche's total dependence on the constitution either. We should never forget that if the psyche is the X, constitution is its complementary Y. Both, at bottom, are unknown factors, which have only recently begun to take on clearer form. But we are still far from having anything approaching a real understanding of their nature.

221 Although it is impossible to determine, in individual cases, the relations between constitution and psyche, such attempts have frequently been made, but the results are nothing more than unproven opinions. The only method that could lead to fairly reliable results at present is the *typological* method, applied by Kretschmer to the constitution and by me to the psychological attitude. In both cases the method is based on a large

1 ["Die Bedeutung von Konstitution und Vererbung für die Psychologie," *Die medizinische Welt* (Berlin), III : 47 (Nov., 1929), 1677–79.—Editors.]

amount of empirical material, and though the individual variations cancel one another out to a large extent, certain typical basic features emerge all the more clearly and enable us to construct a number of ideal types. These ideal types, of course, never occur in reality in their pure form, but only as individual variations of the principle underlying them, just as crystals are usually individual variations of the same isometric system. Physiological typology endeavours first and foremost to ascertain the outward physical features by means of which individuals can be classified and their residual qualities examined. Kretschmer's researches have shown that the physiological peculiarities may determine the psychic conditions.

222   Psychological typology proceeds in exactly the same way in principle, but its starting point is not, so to speak, outside, but inside. It does not try to enumerate the outward characteristics; it seeks, rather, to discover the inner principles governing typical psychological attitudes. While physiological typology is bound to employ essentially scientific methods in order to obtain results, the invisible and non-measurable nature of psychic processes compels us to employ methods derived from the humane sciences, above all an analytical critique. There is, as I have said, no difference of principle but only of the nuance given by the different point of departure. The present state of research justifies us in hoping that the results obtained on both sides will show a substantial measure of agreement with regard to certain basic facts. I personally have the impression that some of Kretschmer's main types are not so far removed from certain of the basic psychological types I have enumerated. It is conceivable that at these points a bridge might be established between the physiological constitution and the psychological attitude. That this has not been done already may well be due to the fact that the physiological findings are still very recent, while on the other hand investigation from the psychological side is very much more difficult and therefore less easy to understand.

223   We can readily agree that physiological characteristics are something that can be seen, touched, measured. But in psychology not even the meanings of words are fixed. There are hardly two psychologies that could agree, for instance, about the concept of "feeling." Yet the verb "to feel" and the noun "feeling" refer to psychic facts, otherwise a word for them would

never have been invented. In psychology we have to do with facts which are definite enough in themselves but have not been defined scientifically. The state of our knowledge might be compared with natural philosophy in the Middle Ages—that is to say, everybody in psychology knows better than everybody else. There are only opinions about unknown facts. Hence the psychologist has an almost invincible tendency to cling to the physiological facts, because there he feels safe, in the security of things that appear to be known and defined. As science is dependent on the definiteness of verbal concepts, it is incumbent upon the psychologist to make conceptual distinctions and to attach definite names to certain groups of psychic facts, regardless of whether somebody else has a different conception of the meaning of this term or not. The only thing he has to consider is whether the name he uses agrees, in its ordinary usage, with the psychic facts designated by it. At the same time he must rid himself of the common notion that the name *explains* the psychic fact it denotes. The name should mean to him no more than a mere cipher, and his whole conceptual system should be to him no more than a trigonometrical survey of a certain geographical area, in which the fixed points of reference are indispensable in practice but irrelevant in theory.

224   Psychology has still to invent its own specific language. When I first started giving names to the attitude-types I had discovered empirically, I found this question of language the greatest obstacle. I was driven, whether I would or no, to fix definite boundaries to my concepts and give these areas names which were taken, as far as possible, from common usage. In so doing, I inevitably exposed myself to the danger I have already mentioned—the common prejudice that the name explains the thing. Although this is an undoubted survival left over from the old belief in the magic of words, it does not prevent misunderstandings, and I have repeatedly heard the objection, "But feeling is something quite different."

225   I mention this apparently trivial fact only because its very triviality is one of the greatest obstacles to psychological research. Psychology, being the youngest of all the sciences, is still afflicted with a medieval mentality in which no distinction is made between words and things. I must lay stress on these difficulties in order to explain to a wider scientific public

unacquainted with it the apparent inadequacies as well as the peculiar nature of psychological research.

226   The typological method sets up what it is pleased to call "natural" classifications—no classification is natural!—which are of the greatest heuristic value because they bring together individuals who have outward features in common, or common psychic attitudes, and enable us to submit them to a closer and more accurate scrutiny. Research into constitution gives the psychologist an extremely valuable criterion with which he can either eliminate the organic factor when investigating the psychic context, or take it into his calculations.

227   This is one of the most important points at which pure psychology comes into collision with the X represented by the organic disposition. But it is not the only point where this happens. There is still another factor, of which those who are engaged in investigating the constitution take no account at present. This is the fact that the psychic process does not start from scratch with the individual consciousness, but is rather a repetition of functions which have been ages in the making and which are inherited with the brain structure. Psychic processes antedate, accompany, and outlive consciousness. Consciousness is an interval in a continuous psychic process; it is probably a climax requiring a special physiological effort, therefore it disappears again for a period each day. The psychic process underlying consciousness is, so far as we are concerned, automatic and its coming and going are unknown to us. We only know that the nervous system, and particularly its centres, condition and express the psychic function, and that these inherited structures start functioning in every new individual exactly as they have always done. Only the climaxes of this activity appear in our consciousness, which is periodically extinguished. However infinitely varied individual consciousnesses may be, the basic substrate of the unconscious psyche remains uniform. So far as it is possible to understand the nature of unconscious processes, they manifest themselves everywhere in astonishingly identical forms, although their expressions, filtered through the individual consciousness, may assume a diversity that is just as great. It is only because of this fundamental uniformity of the unconscious psyche that human beings are able to communicate

with one another and to transcend the differences of individual consciousness.

228   There is nothing strange about these observations, at least to begin with; they become perplexing only when we discover how far even the individual consciousness is infected by this uniformity. Astounding cases of mental similarity can be found in families. Fürst published a case of a mother and daughter with a concordance of associations amounting to thirty per cent.[2] A large measure of psychic concordance between peoples and races separated from one another in space and time is generally regarded as flatly impossible. In actual fact, however, the most astonishing concordances can be found in the realm of so-called fantastic ideas. Every endeavour has been made to explain the concordance of myth-motifs and -symbols as due to migration and tradition; Goblet d'Almellas' *Migration of Symbols* is an excellent example of this. But this explanation, which naturally has some value, is contradicted by the fact that a mythologem can arise anywhere, at any time, without there being the slightest possibility of any such transmission. For instance, I once had under my observation an insane patient who produced, almost word for word, a long symbolic passage which can be read in a papyrus published by Dieterich a few years later.[3] After I had seen a sufficient number of such cases, my original idea that such things could only happen to people belonging to the same race was shattered, and I accordingly investigated the dreams of pure-bred Negroes living in the southern United States. I found in these dreams, among other things, motifs from Greek mythology, and this dispelled any doubt I had that it might be a question of racial inheritance.

229   I have frequently been accused of a superstitious belief in "inherited ideas"—quite unjustly, because I have expressly emphasized that these concordances are not produced by "ideas" but rather by the inherited disposition to react in the same way as people have always reacted. Again, the concordance has been denied on the ground that the redeemer-figure is in one case a hare, in another a bird, and in another a human being. But this is to forget something which so much impressed a pious Hindu visiting an English church that, when he got home, he told the

2 Cf. *Studies in Word Association* (1918 edn., p. 435).
3 [Cf. infra, "The Structure of the Psyche," pars. 318ff.—EDITORS.]

story that the Christians worshipped animals, because he had seen so many lambs about. The names matter little; everything depends on the connection between them. Thus it does not matter if the "treasure" is in one case a golden ring, in another a crown, in a third a pearl, and in a fourth a hidden hoard. The essential thing is the idea of an exceedingly precious treasure hard to attain, no matter what it is called locally. And the essential thing, psychologically, is that in dreams, fantasies, and other exceptional states of mind the most far-fetched mythological motifs and symbols can appear autochthonously at any time, often, apparently, as the result of particular influences, traditions, and excitations working on the individual, but more often without any sign of them. These "primordial images," or "archetypes," as I have called them, belong to the basic stock of the unconscious psyche and cannot be explained as personal acquisitions. Together they make up that psychic stratum which I have called the collective unconscious.

230   The existence of the collective unconscious means that individual consciousness is anything but a *tabula rasa* and is not immune to predetermining influences. On the contrary, it is in the highest degree influenced by inherited presuppositions, quite apart from the unavoidable influences exerted upon it by the environment. The collective unconscious comprises in itself the psychic life of our ancestors right back to the earliest beginnings. It is the matrix of all conscious psychic occurrences, and hence it exerts an influence that compromises the freedom of consciousness in the highest degree, since it is continually striving to lead all conscious processes back into the old paths. This positive danger explains the extraordinary resistance which the conscious puts up against the unconscious. It is not a question here of resistance to sexuality, but of something far more general—the instinctive fear of losing one's freedom of consciousness and of succumbing to the automatism of the unconscious psyche. For certain types of people the danger seems to lie in sex, because it is there that they are afraid of losing their freedom. For others it lies in very different regions, but it is always where a certain weakness is felt, and where, therefore, a high threshold cannot be opposed to the unconscious.

231   The collective unconscious is another of those points at which pure psychology comes up against organic factors, where

it has, in all probability, to recognize a non-psychological fact resting on a physiological foundation. Just as the most inveterate psychologist will never succeed in reducing the physiological constitution to the common denominator of individual psychic causation, so it will not be possible to dismiss the physiologically necessary postulate of the collective unconscious as an individual acquisition. The constitutional type and the collective unconscious are both factors which are outside the control of the conscious mind. The constitutional conditions and the immaterial forms in the collective unconscious are thus realities, and this, in the case of the unconscious, means nothing less than that its symbols and motifs are factors quite as real as the constitution, which can be neither dismissed nor denied. Neglect of the constitution leads to pathological disturbances, and disregard of the collective unconscious does the same. In my therapeutic work I therefore direct my attention chiefly to the patient's relation to occurrences in the collective unconscious, for ample experience has taught me that it is just as important for him to live in harmony with the unconscious as with his individual disposition.

PSYCHOLOGICAL FACTORS DETERMINING
HUMAN BEHAVIOUR [1]

232   The separation of psychology from the basic assumptions of
biology is purely artificial, because the human psyche lives in
indissoluble union with the body. And since these biological
assumptions hold good not only for man but for the whole world
of living things, the scientific foundation on which they rest
obtains a validity far exceeding that of a psychological judgment, which is valid only in the realm of consciousness. It is
therefore no matter for surprise if the psychologist is often inclined to fall back on the security of the biological standpoint
and to borrow freely from physiology and the theory of instinct.
Nor is it astonishing to find a widely accepted point of view
which regards psychology as merely a chapter in physiology.
Although psychology rightly claims autonomy in its own special
field of research, it must recognize a far-reaching correspondence
between its facts and the data of biology.

233   Among the psychological factors determining human be-

1 [Originally delivered (in English) as a lecture at the Harvard (University)
Tercentenary Conference of Arts and Sciences, Cambridge, Mass., 1936, and published in a symposium, *Factors Determining Human Behavior* (Cambridge, 1937).
With slight alterations it was republished as "Human Behaviour" in another
symposium, *Science and Man*, edited by Ruth Nanda Anshen (New York, 1942).
The latter version is here published, with further slight alterations based on the
original German typescript.—EDITORS.]

haviour, the instincts are the chief motivating forces of psychic events. In view of the controversy which has raged around the nature of the instincts, I should like to establish clearly what seems to me to be the relation between instincts and the psyche, and why I call instincts psychological factors. If we started with the hypothesis that the psyche is absolutely identical with the state of being alive, then we should have to accept the existence of a psychic function even in unicellular organisms. In that case, instinct would be a kind of psychic organ, and the hormone-producing activity of the glands would have a psychic causation.

234   But if we look upon the appearance of the psyche as a relatively recent event in evolutionary history, and assume that the psychic function is a phenomenon accompanying a nervous system which in some way or other has become centralized, then it would be difficult to believe that the instincts were originally psychic in nature. And since the connection of the psyche with the brain is a more probable conjecture than the psychic nature of life in general, I regard the characteristic *compulsiveness* of instinct as an ectopsychic factor. None the less, it is psychologically important because it leads to the formation of structures or patterns which may be regarded as determinants of human behaviour. Under these circumstances the immediate determining factor is not the ectopsychic instinct but the structure resulting from the interaction of instinct and the psychic situation of the moment. The determining factor would thus be a *modified* instinct. The change undergone by the instinct is as significant as the difference between the colour we see and the objective wave-length producing it. Instinct as an ectopsychic factor would play the role of a stimulus merely, while instinct as a psychic phenomenon would be an assimilation of this stimulus to a pre-existent psychic pattern. A name is needed for this process. I should term it *psychization*. Thus, what we call instinct offhand would be a datum already psychized, but of ectopsychic origin.

1. General Phenomenology

235   The view outlined above makes it possible for us to understand the variability of instinct within the framework of its general phenomenology. The psychized instinct forfeits its

uniqueness to a certain extent, at times actually losing its most essential characteristic—compulsiveness. It is no longer an ecto-psychic, unequivocal fact, but has become instead a modification conditioned by its encounter with a psychic datum. As a determining factor, instinct is variable and therefore lends itself to different applications. Whatever the nature of the psyche may be, it is endowed with an extraordinary capacity for variation and transformation.

236   For example, no matter how unequivocal the physical state of excitation called hunger may be, the psychic consequences resulting from it can be manifold. Not only can the reactions to ordinary hunger vary widely, but the hunger itself can be "de-natured," and can even appear as something metaphorical. It is not only that we use the word hunger in different senses, but in combination with other factors hunger can assume the most varied forms. The originally simple and unequivocal determinant can appear transformed into pure greed, or into many aspects of boundless desire or insatiability, as for instance the lust for gain or inordinate ambition.

237   *Hunger,* as a characteristic expression of the instinct of self-preservation, is without doubt one of the primary and most powerful factors influencing behaviour; in fact, the lives of primitives are more strongly affected by it than by sexuality. At this level, hunger is the alpha and omega—existence itself.

238   The importance of the instinct for preservation of the species is obvious. However, the growth of culture having brought with it so many restrictions of a moral and a social nature, sexuality has been lent, temporarily at least, an excess value comparable to that of water in a desert. Because of the premium of intense sensuous enjoyment which nature has set upon the business of reproduction, the urge for sexual satisfaction appears in man—no longer conditioned by a mating season—almost as a separate instinct. The sexual instinct enters into combination with many different feelings, emotions, affects, with spiritual and material interests, to such a degree that, as is well known, the attempt has even been made to trace the whole of culture to these combinations.

239   *Sexuality,* like hunger, undergoes a radical psychization which makes it possible for the originally purely instinctive energy to be diverted from its biological application and turned

116

into other channels. The fact that the energy can be deployed in various fields indicates the existence of still other drives strong enough to change the direction of the sexual instinct and to deflect it, at least in part, from its immediate goal.

240   I should like, then, to differentiate as a third group of instincts the *drive to activity*. This urge starts functioning when the other urges are satisfied; indeed, it is perhaps only called into being after this has occurred. Under this heading would come the urge to travel, love of change, restlessness, and the play-instinct.

241   There is another instinct, different from the drive to activity and so far as we know specifically human, which might be called the *reflective instinct*. Ordinarily we do not think of "reflection" as ever having been instinctive, but associate it with a conscious state of mind. *Reflexio* means 'bending back' and, used psychologically, would denote the fact that the reflex which carries the stimulus over into its instinctive discharge is interfered with by psychization. Owing to this interference, the psychic processes exert an attraction on the impulse to act excited by the stimulus. Therefore, before having discharged itself into the external world, the impulse is deflected into an endopsychic activity. *Reflexio* is a turning inwards, with the result that, instead of an instinctive action, there ensues a succession of derivative contents or states which may be termed reflection or deliberation. Thus in place of the compulsive act there appears a certain degree of freedom, and in place of predictability a relative unpredictability as to the effect of the impulse.

242   The richness of the human psyche and its essential character are probably determined by this reflective instinct. Reflection re-enacts the process of excitation and carries the stimulus over into a series of images which, if the impetus is strong enough, are reproduced in some form of expression. This may take place directly, for instance in speech, or may appear in the form of abstract thought, dramatic representation, or ethical conduct; or again, in a scientific achievement or a work of art.

243   Through the reflective instinct, the stimulus is more or less wholly transformed into a psychic content, that is, it becomes an experience: a natural process is transformed into a conscious content. Reflection is the cultural instinct *par excellence,* and

its strength is shown in the power of culture to maintain itself in the face of untamed nature.

244   Instincts are not creative in themselves; they have become stably organized and are therefore largely automatic. The reflective instinct is no exception to this rule, for the production of consciousness is not of itself a creative act but may under certain conditions be a merely automatic process. It is a fact of great importance that this compulsiveness of instinct, so feared by civilized man, also produces that characteristic fear of becoming conscious, best observed in neurotic persons, but not in them alone.

245   Although, in general, instinct is a system of stably organized tracts and consequently tends towards unlimited repetition, man nevertheless has the distinctive power of creating something new in the real sense of the word, just as nature, in the course of long periods of time, succeeds in creating new forms. Though we cannot classify it with a high degree of accuracy, the *creative instinct* is something that deserves special mention. I do not know if "instinct" is the correct word. We use the term "creative instinct" because this factor behaves at least dynamically, like an instinct. Like instinct it is compulsive, but it is not common, and it is not a fixed and invariably inherited organization. Therefore I prefer to designate the creative impulse as a psychic factor similar in nature to instinct, having indeed a very close connection with the instincts, but without being identical with any one of them. Its connections with sexuality are a much discussed problem and, furthermore, it has much in common with the drive to activity and the reflective instinct. But it can also suppress them, or make them serve it to the point of the self-destruction of the individual. Creation is as much destruction as construction.

246   To recapitulate, I would like to emphasize that from the psychological standpoint five main groups of instinctive factors can be distinguished: hunger, sexuality, activity, reflection, and creativity. In the last analysis, instincts are ectopsychic determinants.

247   A discussion of the dynamic factors determining human behaviour is obviously incomplete without mention of the *will*. The part that will plays, however, is a matter for dispute, and the whole problem is bound up with philosophical considera-

tions, which in turn depend on the view one takes of the world. If the will is posited as free, then it is not tied to causality and there is nothing more to be said about it. But if it is regarded as predetermined and causally dependent upon the instincts, it is an epiphenomenon of secondary importance.

248   Different from the dynamic factors are the *modalities* of psychic functioning which influence human behaviour in other ways. Among these I would mention especially the sex, age, and hereditary disposition of the individual. These three factors are understood primarily as physiological data, but they are also psychological inasmuch as, like the instincts, they are subject to psychization. Anatomical masculinity, for instance, is far from being proof of the psychic masculinity of the individual. Similarly, physiological age does not always correspond with the psychological age. As regards the hereditary disposition, the determining factor of race or family may be overlaid by a psychological superstructure. Much that is interpreted as heredity in the narrow sense is rather a sort of psychic contagion, which consists in an adaptation of the child psyche to the unconscious of the parents.

249   To these three semi-physiological modalities I should like to add three that are psychological. Among these I wish to stress the conscious and the unconscious. It makes a great deal of difference to the behaviour of the individual whether his psyche is functioning mainly consciously or unconsciously. Naturally it is only a question of a greater or lesser degree of consciousness, because total consciousness is empirically impossible. An extreme state of unconsciousness is characterized by the predominance of compulsive instinctual processes, the result of which is either uncontrolled inhibition or a lack of inhibition throughout. The happenings within the psyche are then contradictory and proceed in terms of alternating, non-logical antitheses. In such a case the level of consciousness is essentially that of a dream-state. A high degree of consciousness, on the other hand, is characterized by a heightened awareness, a preponderance of will, directed, rational behaviour, and an almost total absence of instinctual determinants. The unconscious is then found to be at a definitely animal level. The first state is lacking in intellectual and ethical achievement, the second lacks naturalness.

250   The second modality is extraversion and introversion. It

119

determines the direction of psychic activity, that is, it decides whether the conscious contents refer to external objects or to the subject. Therefore, it also decides whether the value stressed lies outside or inside the individual. This modality operates so persistently that it builds up habitual attitudes, that is, types with recognizable outward traits.

251   The third modality points, to use a metaphor, upward and downward, because it has to do with spirit and matter. It is true that matter is in general the subject of physics, but it is also a psychic category, as the history of religion and philosophy clearly shows. And just as matter is ultimately to be conceived of merely as a working hypothesis of physics, so also spirit, the subject of religion and philosophy, is a hypothetical category in constant need of reinterpretation. The so-called reality of matter is attested primarily by our sense-perceptions, while belief in the existence of spirit is supported by psychic experience. Psychologically, we cannot establish anything more final with respect to either matter or spirit than the presence of certain conscious contents, some of which are labelled as having a material, and others a spiritual, origin. In the consciousness of civilized peoples, it is true, there seems to exist a sharp division between the two categories, but on the primitive level the boundaries become so blurred that matter often seems endowed with "soul" while spirit appears to be material. However, from the existence of these two categories ethical, aesthetic, intellectual, social, and religious systems of value arise which in the end determine how the dynamic factors in the psyche are to be used. Perhaps it would not be too much to say that the most crucial problems of the individual and of society turn upon the way the psyche functions in regard to spirit and matter.

2. *Special Phenomenology*

252   Let us now turn to the special phenomenology. In the first section we distinguished five principal groups of instincts and six modalities. The concepts described, however, have only an academic value as general categories. In reality the psyche is a complicated interplay of all these factors. Moreover, in conformity with its peculiar structure, it shows endless individual variation on the one hand, and on the other an equally great

capacity for change and differentiation. The variability is due to the fact that the psyche is not a homogeneous structure but apparently consists of hereditary units only loosely bound together, and therefore it shows a very marked tendency to split into parts. The tendency to change is conditioned by influences coming both from within and from without. Functionally speaking, these tendencies are closely related to one another.

253   1. Let us turn first to the question of the psyche's tendency to split. Although this peculiarity is most clearly observable in psychopathology, fundamentally it is a normal phenomenon, which can be recognized with the greatest ease in the projections made by the primitive psyche. The tendency to split means that parts of the psyche detach themselves from consciousness to such an extent that they not only appear foreign but lead an autonomous life of their own. It need not be a question of hysterical multiple personality, or schizophrenic alterations of personality, but merely of so-called "complexes" that come entirely within the scope of the normal. Complexes are psychic fragments which have split off owing to traumatic influences or certain incompatible tendencies. As the association experiments prove, complexes interfere with the intentions of the will and disturb the conscious performance; they produce disturbances of memory and blockages in the flow of associations; they appear and disappear according to their own laws; they can temporarily obsess consciousness, or influence speech and action in an unconscious way. In a word, complexes behave like independent beings, a fact especially evident in abnormal states of mind. In the voices heard by the insane they even take on a personal ego-character like that of the spirits who manifest themselves through automatic writing and similar techniques. An intensification of complexes leads to morbid states, which are extensive multiple dissociations endowed with an indomitable life of their own.

254   The behaviour of *new* contents that have been constellated in the unconscious but are not yet assimilated to consciousness is similar to that of complexes. These contents may be based on subliminal perceptions, or they may be creative in character. Like complexes, they lead a life of their own so long as they are not made conscious and integrated with the life of the personality. In the realm of artistic and religious phenomena, these

contents may likewise appear in personified form, especially as archetypal figures. Mythological research designates them as "motifs," to Lévy-Bruhl they are *représentations collectives*, Hubert and Mauss call them "categories of the imagination." I have employed the concept of the collective unconscious to embrace all these archetypes. They are psychic forms which, like the instincts, are common to all mankind, and their presence can be proved wherever the relevant literary records have been preserved. As factors influencing human behaviour, archetypes play no small role. The total personality can be affected by them through a process of identification. This effect is best explained by the fact that archetypes probably represent typical situations in life. Abundant proof of identification with archetypes can be found in the psychological and psychopathological case material. The psychology of Nietzsche's *Zarathustra* also furnishes a good example. The difference between archetypes and the dissociated products of schizophrenia is that the former are entities endowed with personality and charged with meaning, whereas the latter are only fragments with vestiges of meaning—in reality, they are products of disintegration. Both, however, possess to a high degree the capacity to influence, control, and even to suppress the ego-personality, so that a temporary or lasting transformation of personality ensues.

255   2. As we have seen, the inherent tendency of the psyche to split means on the one hand dissociation into multiple structural units, but on the other hand the possibility of change and differentiation. It allows certain parts of the psychic structure to be singled out so that, by concentration of the will, they can be trained and brought to their maximum development. In this way certain capacities, especially those that promise to be socially useful, can be fostered to the neglect of others. This produces an unbalanced state similar to that caused by a dominant complex—a change of personality. It is true that we do not refer to this as obsession by a complex, but as one-sidedness. Still, the actual state is approximately the same, with this difference, that the one-sidedness is intended by the individual and is fostered by all the means in his power, whereas the complex is felt to be injurious and disturbing. People often fail to see that consciously willed one-sidedness is one of the most important causes of an undesirable complex, and that, conversely,

certain complexes cause a one-sided differentiation of doubtful value. Some degree of one-sidedness is unavoidable, and, in the same measure, complexes are unavoidable too. Looked at in this light, complexes might be compared to modified instincts. An instinct which has undergone too much psychization can take its revenge in the form of an autonomous complex. This is one of the chief causes of neurosis.

256   It is well known that very many faculties in man can become differentiated. I do not wish to lose myself in the details of case histories and must limit myself to the normal faculties that are always present in consciousness. Consciousness is primarily an organ of orientation in a world of outer and inner facts. First, and foremost, it establishes the fact that something is there. I call this faculty *sensation*. By this I do not mean the specific activity of any one of the senses, but perception in general. Another faculty interprets what is perceived; this I call *thinking*. By means of this function, the object perceived is assimilated and its transformation into a psychic content proceeds much further than in mere sensation. A third faculty establishes the value of the object. This function of evaluation I call *feeling*. The pain-pleasure reaction of feeling marks the highest degree of subjectivation of the object. Feeling brings subject and object into such a close relationship that the subject must choose between acceptance and rejection.

257   These three functions would be quite sufficient for orientation if the object in question were isolated in space and time. But, in space, every object is in endless connection with a multiplicity of other objects; and, in time, the object represents merely a transition from a former state to a succeeding one. Most of the spatial relationships and temporal changes are unavoidably unconscious at the moment of orientation, and yet, in order to determine the meaning of an object, space-time relationships are necessary. It is the fourth faculty of consciousness, *intuition*, which makes possible, at least approximately, the determination of space-time relationships. This is a function of perception which includes subliminal factors, that is, the possible relationship to objects not appearing in the field of vision, and the possible changes, past and future, about which the object gives no clue. Intuition is an immediate awareness of

relationships that could not be established by the other three functions at the moment of orientation.

258   I mention the orienting functions of consciousness because they can be singled out for empirical observation and are subject to differentiation. At the very outset, nature has established marked differences in their importance for different individuals. As a rule, one of the four functions is especially developed, thus giving the mentality as a whole its characteristic stamp. The predominance of one or the other function gives rise to typical attitudes, which may be designated thinking types, feeling types, and so on. A type of this kind is a bias like a vocation with which a person has identified himself. Anything that has been elevated into a principle or a virtue, whether from inclination or because of its usefulness, always results in one-sidedness and a compulsion to one-sidedness which excludes all other possibilities, and this applies to men of will and action just as much as to those whose object in life is the constant training of memory. Whatever we persistently exclude from conscious training and adaptation necessarily remains in an untrained, undeveloped, infantile, or archaic condition, ranging from partial to complete unconsciousness. Hence, besides the motives of consciousness and reason, unconscious influences of a primitive character are always normally present in ample measure and disturb the intentions of consciousness. For it is by no means to be assumed that all those forms of activity latent in the psyche, which are suppressed or neglected by the individual, are thereby robbed of their specific energy. For instance, if a man relied wholly on the data of vision, this would not mean that he would cease to hear. Even if he could be transplanted to a soundless world, he would in all probability soon satisfy his need to hear by indulging in auditory hallucinations.

259   The fact that the natural functions of the psyche cannot be deprived of their specific energy gives rise to characteristic antitheses, which can best be observed wherever these four orienting functions of consciousness come into play. The chief contrasts are those between thinking and feeling on the one hand, and sensation and intuition on the other. The opposition between the first two is an old story and needs no comment. The opposition between the second pair becomes clearer when it is understood as the opposition between objective fact and mere

124

possibility. Obviously anyone on the look-out for new possibilities does not rest content with the actual situation of the moment, but will pass beyond it as soon as ever he can. These polarities have a markedly irritating nature, and this remains true whether the conflict occurs within the individual psyche or between individuals of opposite temperament.

260   It is my belief that the problem of opposites, here merely hinted at, should be made the basis for a critical psychology. A critique of this sort would be of the utmost value not only in the narrower field of psychology, but also in the wider field of the cultural sciences in general.

261   In this paper I have gathered together all those factors which, from the standpoint of a purely empirical psychology, play a leading role in determining human behaviour. The multiplicity of aspects claiming attention is due to the nature of the psyche, reflecting itself in innumerable facets, and they are a measure of the difficulties confronting the investigator. The tremendous complexity of psychic phenomena is borne in upon us only after we see that all attempts to formulate a comprehensive theory are foredoomed to failure. The premises are always far too simple. The psyche is the starting-point of all human experience, and all the knowledge we have gained eventually leads back to it. The psyche is the beginning and end of all cognition. It is not only the object of its science, but the subject also. This gives psychology a unique place among all the other sciences: on the one hand there is a constant doubt as to the possibility of its being a science at all, while on the other hand psychology acquires the right to state a theoretical problem the solution of which will be one of the most difficult tasks for a future philosophy.

262   In my survey, far too condensed, I fear, I have left unmentioned many illustrious names. Yet there is one which I should not like to omit. It is that of William James, whose psychological vision and pragmatic philosophy have on more than one occasion been my guides. It was his far-ranging mind which made me realize that the horizons of human psychology widen into the immeasurable.

III

INSTINCT AND THE UNCONSCIOUS

———

THE STRUCTURE OF THE PSYCHE

———

ON THE NATURE OF THE PSYCHE

INSTINCT AND THE UNCONSCIOUS [1]

263   The theme of this symposium concerns a problem that is of great importance for biology as well as for psychology and philosophy. But if we are to discuss the relation between instinct and the unconscious, it is essential that we start out with a clear definition of our terms.

264   With regard to the definition of instinct, I would like to stress the significance of the "all-or-none" reaction formulated by Rivers; indeed, it seems to me that this peculiarity of instinctive activity is of special importance for the psychological side of the problem. I must naturally confine myself to this aspect of the question, because I do not feel competent to treat the problem of instinct under its biological aspect. But when I attempt to give a psychological definition of instinctive activity, I find I cannot rely solely on Rivers' criterion of the "all-or-none" reaction, and for the following reason: Rivers defines this reaction as a process that shows no gradation of intensity in respect of the circumstances which provoke it. It is a

[1] A contribution to the symposium of the same name, presented, in an English translation by C. F. and H. G. Baynes, at a joint meeting of the Aristotelian Society, the Mind Association, and the British Psychological Society, at Bedford College, London University, July, 1919. [First published in the *British Journal of Psychology* (General Section) (London), X (1919) : 1, 15–26; republished in *Contributions to Analytical Psychology* (London and New York, 1928). The original ms. was subsequently published as "Instinkt und Unbewusstes" in *Über die Energetik der Seele* (Psychologische Abhandlungen, II; Zurich, 1928); republished, with a short concluding note, in *Über psychische Energetik und das Wesen der Träume* (Zurich, 1948). The Baynes version has been consulted in the preparation of the present translation.—EDITORS.]

reaction that takes place with its own specific intensity under all circumstances and is not proportional to the precipitating stimulus. But when we examine the psychological processes of consciousness in order to determine whether there are any whose intensity is out of all proportion to the stimulus, we can easily find a great many of them in everybody, for instance disproportionate affects, impressions, exaggerated impulses, intentions that go too far, and others of the kind. It follows that all these processes cannot possibly be classed as instinctive processes, and we must therefore look round for another criterion.

265   We use the word "instinct" very frequently in ordinary speech. We speak of "instinctive actions," meaning by that a mode of behaviour of which neither the motive nor the aim is fully conscious and which is prompted only by obscure inner necessity. This peculiarity has already been stressed by an older English writer, Thomas Reid, who says: "By instinct, I mean a natural impulse to certain actions, without having any end in view, without deliberation and without any conception of what we do." [2] Thus instinctive action is characterized by an *unconsciousness* of the psychological motive behind it, in contrast to the strictly conscious processes which are distinguished by the conscious continuity of their motives. Instinctive action appears to be a more or less abrupt psychic occurrence, a sort of interruption of the continuity of consciousness. On this account, it is felt as an inner necessity—which is, in fact, the definition of instinct given by Kant.[3]

266   Accordingly, instinctive activity would have to be included among the specifically unconscious processes, which are accessible to consciousness only through their results. But were we to rest content with this conception of instinct, we should soon discover its insufficiency: it merely marks off instinct from the conscious processes and characterizes it as unconscious. If, on the other hand, we survey the unconscious processes as a whole, we find it impossible to class them all as instinctive, even though no differentiation is made between them in ordinary speech. If you suddenly meet a snake and get a violent fright, you can legitimately call this impulse instinctive because it is no different from the instinctive fear of snakes in monkeys. It is just

[2] *Essays on the Active Powers of Man* (1788), p. 103.
[3] *Anthropologie,* in *Werke,* ed. by Cassirer, VIII, p. 156.

the uniformity of the phenomenon and the regularity of its recurrence which are the most characteristic qualities of instinctive action. As Lloyd Morgan aptly remarks, it would be as uninteresting to bet on an instinctive reaction as on the rising of the sun tomorrow. On the other hand, it may also happen that someone is regularly seized with fright whenever he meets a perfectly harmless hen. Although the mechanism of fright in this case is just as much an unconscious impulse as the instinct, we must nevertheless distinguish between the two processes. In the former case the fear of snakes is a purposive process of general occurrence; the latter, when habitual, is a phobia and not an instinct, since it occurs only in isolation and is not a general peculiarity. There are many other unconscious compulsions of this kind—for instance, obsessive thoughts, musical obsessions, sudden ideas and moods, impulsive affects, depressions, anxiety states, etc. These phenomena are met with in normal as well as abnormal individuals. In so far as they occur only in isolation and are not repeated regularly they must be distinguished from instinctive processes, even though their psychological mechanism seems to correspond to that of an instinct. They may even be characterized by the all-or-none reaction, as can easily be observed in pathological cases. In psychopathology there are many such cases where a given stimulus is followed by a definite and relatively disproportionate reaction comparable to an instinctive reaction.

267   All these processes must be distinguished from instinctive ones. Only those unconscious processes which are inherited, and occur uniformly and regularly, can be called instinctive. At the same time they must show the mark of compelling necessity, a reflex character of the kind pointed out by Herbert Spencer. Such a process differs from a mere sensory-motor reflex only because it is more complicated. William James therefore calls instinct, not unjustly, "a mere excito-motor impulse, due to the pre-existence of a certain 'reflex-arc' in the nerve-centres." [4] Instincts share with reflexes their uniformity and regularity as well as the unconsciousness of their motivations.

268   The question of where instincts come from and how they were acquired is extraordinarily complicated. The fact that they

[4] *Principles of Psychology*, II, p. 391.

are invariably inherited does nothing to explain their origin; it merely shifts the problem back to our ancestors. The view is widely held that instincts originated in individual, and then general, acts of will that were frequently repeated. This explanation is plausible in so far as we can observe every day how certain laboriously learnt activities gradually become automatic through constant practice. But if we consider the marvellous instincts to be found in the animal world, we must admit that the element of learning is sometimes totally absent. In certain cases it is impossible to conceive how any learning and practice could ever have come about. Let us take as an example the incredibly refined instinct of propagation in the yucca moth (*Pronuba yuccasella*).[5] The flowers of the yucca plant open for one night only. The moth takes the pollen from one of the flowers and kneads it into a little pellet. Then it visits a second flower, cuts open the pistil, lays its eggs between the ovules and then stuffs the pellet into the funnel-shaped opening of the pistil. Only once in its life does the moth carry out this complicated operation.

269   Such cases are difficult to explain on the hypothesis of learning and practice. Hence other ways of explanation, deriving from Bergson's philosophy, have recently been put forward, laying stress on the factor of intuition. Intuition is an unconscious process in that its result is the irruption into consciousness of an unconscious content, a sudden idea or "hunch."[6] It resembles a process of perception, but unlike the conscious activity of the senses and introspection the perception is unconscious. That is why we speak of intuition as an "instinctive" act of comprehension. It is a process analogous to instinct, with the difference that whereas instinct is a purposive impulse to carry out some highly complicated action, intuition is the unconscious, purposive apprehension of a highly complicated situation. In a sense, therefore, intuition is the reverse of instinct, neither more nor less wonderful than it. But we should never forget that what we call complicated or even wonderful is not at all wonderful for Nature, but quite ordinary. We always tend to project into things our own difficulties of understanding and to call them

[5] Kerner von Marilaun, *The Natural History of Plants*, II, p. 156.
[6] Cf. the definition of intuition in *Psychological Types*.

complicated, when in reality they are very simple and know nothing of our intellectual problems.

270   A discussion of the problem of instinct without reference to the concept of the unconscious would be incomplete, because it is just the instinctive processes which make the supplementary concept of the unconscious necessary. I define the unconscious as the totality of all psychic phenomena that lack the quality of consciousness. These psychic contents might fittingly be called "subliminal," on the assumption that every psychic content must possess a certain energy value in order to become conscious at all. The lower the value of a conscious content falls, the more easily it disappears below the threshold. From this it follows that the unconscious is the receptacle of all lost memories and of all contents that are still too weak to become conscious. These contents are products of an unconscious associative activity which also gives rise to dreams. Besides these we must include all more or less intentional repressions of painful thoughts and feelings. I call the sum of all these contents the "personal unconscious." But, over and above that, we also find in the unconscious qualities that are not individually acquired but are inherited, e.g., instincts as impulses to carry out actions from necessity, without conscious motivation. In this "deeper" stratum we also find the *a priori*, inborn forms of "intuition," namely the *archetypes* [7] of perception and apprehension, which are the necessary *a priori* determinants of all psychic processes. Just as his instincts compel man to a specifically human mode of existence, so the archetypes force his ways of perception and apprehension into specifically human patterns. The instincts and the archetypes together form the "collective

---

[7] [This is the first occasion on which Jung uses the term "archetype" (*Archetypus*). Previously, in his publications, he had discussed the same concept under the term "primordial image" (*Urbild*), which he derived from Burckhardt (cf. *Symbols of Transformation*, p. 32, n. 45; *Two Essays*, p. 64). The primordial image, it will be observed, is here and elsewhere used as the equivalent of the archetype; this has given rise to some confusion and to the belief that Jung's theory of hereditary elements involves the inheritance of representations (ideas or images), a view against which Jung repeatedly protests. The primordial image is, however, in the present text, clearly understood as a more graphic term for the archetype, an essentially unconscious entity which, as Jung states elsewhere, is an *a priori* form—the inherited component of the representational image perceived in consciousness.—EDITORS.]

unconscious." I call it "collective" because, unlike the personal unconscious, it is not made up of individual and more or less unique contents but of those which are universal and of regular occurrence. Instinct is an essentially collective, i.e., universal and regularly occurring phenomenon which has nothing to do with individuality. Archetypes have this quality in common with the instincts and are likewise collective phenomena.

271   In my view the question of instinct cannot be dealt with psychologically without considering the archetypes, because at bottom they determine one another. It is, however, extremely difficult to discuss this problem, as opinions about the role of instinct in human psychology are extraordinarily divided. Thus William James is of the opinion that man is swarming with instincts, while others restrict them to a very few processes barely distinguishable from reflexes, namely to certain movements executed by the infant, to particular reactions of its arms and legs, of the larynx, the use of the right hand, and the formation of syllabized sounds. In my opinion, this restriction goes too far, though it is very characteristic of human psychology in general. Above all, we should always remember that in discussing human instincts we are speaking of ourselves and, therefore, are doubtless prejudiced.

272   We are in a far better position to observe instincts in animals or in primitives than in ourselves. This is due to the fact that we have grown accustomed to scrutinizing our own actions and to seeking rational explanations for them. But it is by no means certain that our explanations will hold water, indeed it is highly unlikely. No superhuman intellect is needed to see through the shallowness of many of our rationalizations and to detect the real motive, the compelling instinct behind them. As a result of our artificial rationalizations it may seem to us that we were actuated not by instinct but by conscious motives. Naturally I do not mean to say that by careful training man has not succeeded in partially converting his instincts into acts of the will. Instinct has been domesticated, but the basic motive still remains instinct. There is no doubt that we have succeeded in enveloping a large number of instincts in rational explanations to the point where we can no longer recognize the original motive behind so many veils. In this way it seems as though we possessed practically no instincts any more. But if we apply the

towards the regions westward it is as though there were an infinite east wind. But if the other wind should prevail towards the regions of the east, you will in like manner see the vision veering in that direction." The Greek word for 'tube,' αὐλός, means a wind-instrument, and the combination αὐλὸς παχύς in Homer means 'a thick jet of blood.' So evidently a stream of wind is blowing through the tube out of the sun.

319   The vision of my patient in 1906, and the Greek text first edited in 1910, should be sufficiently far apart to rule out the possibility of cryptomnesia on his side and of thought-transference on mine. The obvious parallelism of the two visions cannot be disputed, though one might object that the similarity is purely fortuitous. In that case we should expect the vision to have no connections with analogous ideas, nor any inner meaning. But this expectation is not fulfilled, for in certain medieval paintings this tube is actually depicted as a sort of hose-pipe reaching down from heaven under the robe of Mary. In it the Holy Ghost flies down in the form of a dove to impregnate the Virgin. As we know from the miracle of Pentecost, the Holy Ghost was originally conceived as a mighty rushing wind, the πνεῦμα, "the wind that bloweth where it listeth." In a Latin text we read: "Animo descensus per orbem solis tribuitur" (They say that the spirit descends through the disc of the sun). This conception is common to the whole of late classical and medieval philosophy.

320   I cannot, therefore, discover anything fortuitous in these visions, but simply the revival of possibilities of ideas that have always existed, that can be found again in the most diverse minds and in all epochs, and are therefore not to be mistaken for inherited ideas.

321   I have purposely gone into the details of this case in order to give you a concrete picture of that deeper psychic activity which I call the collective unconscious. Summing up, I would like to emphasize that we must distinguish three psychic levels: (1) consciousness, (2) the personal unconscious, and (3) the collective unconscious. The personal unconscious consists firstly of all those contents that became unconscious either because they lost their intensity and were forgotten or because consciousness was withdrawn from them (repression), and secondly of contents, some of them sense-impressions, which never had sufficient

intensity to reach consciousness but have somehow entered the psyche. The collective unconscious, however, as the ancestral heritage of possibilities of representation, is not individual but common to all men, and perhaps even to all animals, and is the true basis of the individual psyche.

322   This whole psychic organism corresponds exactly to the body, which, though individually varied, is in all essential features the specifically human body which all men have. In its development and structure, it still preserves elements that connect it with the invertebrates and ultimately with the protozoa. Theoretically it should be possible to "peel" the collective unconscious, layer by layer, until we came to the psychology of the worm, and even of the amoeba.

323   We are all agreed that it would be quite impossible to understand the living organism apart from its relation to the environment. There are countless biological facts that can only be explained as reactions to environmental conditions, e.g., the blindness of *Proteus anguinus,* the peculiarities of intestinal parasites, the anatomy of vertebrates that have reverted to aquatic life.

324   The same is true of the psyche. Its peculiar organization must be intimately connected with environmental conditions. We should expect consciousness to react and adapt itself to the present, because it is that part of the psyche which is concerned chiefly with events of the moment. But from the collective unconscious, as a timeless and universal psyche, we should expect reactions to universal and constant conditions, whether psychological, physiological, or physical.

325   The collective unconscious—so far as we can say anything about it at all—appears to consist of mythological motifs or primordial images, for which reason the myths of all nations are its real exponents. In fact, the whole of mythology could be taken as a sort of projection of the collective unconscious. We can see this most clearly if we look at the heavenly constellations, whose originally chaotic forms were organized through the projection of images. This explains the influence of the stars as asserted by astrologers. These influences are nothing but unconscious, introspective perceptions of the activity of the collective unconscious. Just as the constellations were projected into the heavens, similar figures were projected into legends and fairy-

tales or upon historical persons. We can therefore study the collective unconscious in two ways, either in mythology or in the analysis of the individual. As I cannot make the latter material available here, I must confine myself to mythology. This is such a wide field that we can select from it only a few types. Similarly, environmental conditions are endlessly varied, so here too only a few of the more typical can be discussed.

326   Just as the living body with its special characteristics is a system of functions for adapting to environmental conditions, so the psyche must exhibit organs or functional systems that correspond to regular physical events. By this I do not mean sense-functions dependent on organs, but rather a sort of psychic parallel to regular physical occurrences. To take an example, the daily course of the sun and the regular alternation of day and night must have imprinted themselves on the psyche in the form of an image from primordial times. We cannot demonstrate the existence of this image, but we find instead more or less fantastic analogies of the physical process. Every morning a divine hero is born from the sea and mounts the chariot of the sun. In the West a Great Mother awaits him, and he is devoured by her in the evening. In the belly of a dragon he traverses the depths of the midnight sea. After a frightful combat with the serpent of night he is born again in the morning.

327   This conglomerate myth undoubtedly contains a reflection of the physical process. Indeed this is so obvious that many investigators assume that primitives invent such myths merely to explain physical processes. There can be no doubt that science and philosophy have grown from this matrix, but that primitives think up such things merely from a need for explanation, as a sort of physical or astronomical theory, seems to me highly improbable.

328   What we can safely say about mythical images is that the physical process imprinted itself on the psyche in this fantastic, distorted form and was preserved there, so that the unconscious still reproduces similar images today. Naturally the question now arises: why does the psyche not register the actual process, instead of mere fantasies about the physical process?

329   If you can put yourself in the mind of the primitive, you will at once understand why this is so. He lives in such "participation mystique" with his world, as Lévy-Bruhl calls it, that there

153

is nothing like that absolute distinction between subject and object which exists in our minds. What happens outside also happens in him, and what happens in him also happens outside. I witnessed a very fine example of this when I was with the Elgonyi, a primitive tribe living on Mount Elgon, in East Africa. At sunrise they spit on their hands and then hold the palms towards the sun as it comes over the horizon. "We are happy that the night is past," they say. Since the word for sun, *adhista*, also means God, I asked: "Is the sun God?" They said "No" to this and laughed, as if I had said something especially stupid. As the sun was just then high in the heavens, I pointed to it and asked: "When the sun is there you say it is not God, but when it is in the east you say it is God. How is that?" There was an embarrassed silence till an old chief began to explain. "It is so," he said. "When the sun is up there it is not God, but when it rises, that is God [or: then it is God]." To the primitive mind it is immaterial which of these two versions is correct. Sunrise and his own feeling of deliverance are for him the same divine experience, just as night and his fear are the same thing. Naturally his emotions are more important to him than physics; therefore what he registers is his emotional fantasies. For him night means snakes and the cold breath of spirits, whereas morning means the birth of a beautiful god.

330   There are mythological theories that explain everything as coming from the sun and lunar theories that do the same for the moon. This is due to the simple fact that there are countless myths about the moon, among them a whole host in which the moon is the wife of the sun. The moon is the changing experience of the night, and thus coincides with the primitive's sexual experience of woman, who for him is also the experience of the night. But the moon can equally well be the injured brother of the sun, for at night affect-laden and evil thoughts of power and revenge may disturb sleep. The moon, too, is a disturber of sleep, and is also the abode of departed souls, for at night the dead return in dreams and the phantoms of the past terrify the sleepless. Thus the moon also signifies madness ("lunacy"). It is such experiences as these that have impressed themselves on the mind, rather than the changing image of the moon.

331   It is not storms, not thunder and lightning, not rain and cloud that remain as images in the psyche, but the fantasies

154

caused by the affects they arouse. I once experienced a violent earthquake, and my first, immediate feeling was that I no longer stood on the solid and familiar earth, but on the skin of a gigantic animal that was heaving under my feet. It was this image that impressed itself on me, not the physical fact. Man's curses against devastating thunderstorms, his terror of the unchained elements—these affects anthropomorphize the passion of nature, and the purely physical element becomes an angry god.

332   Like the physical conditions of his environment, the physiological conditions, glandular secretions, etc., also can arouse fantasies charged with affect. Sexuality appears as a god of fertility, as a fiercely sensual, feminine daemon, as the devil himself with Dionysian goat's legs and obscene gestures, or as a terrifying serpent that squeezes its victims to death.

333   Hunger makes food into gods. Certain Mexican tribes even give their food-gods an annual holiday to allow them to recuperate, and during this time the staple food is not eaten. The ancient Pharaohs were worshipped as eaters of gods. Osiris is the wheat, the son of the earth, and to this day the Host must be made of wheat-meal, i.e., a god to be eaten, as also was Iacchos, the mysterious god of the Eleusinian mysteries. The bull of Mithras is the edible fruitfulness of the earth.

334   The psychological conditions of the environment naturally leave similar mythical traces behind them. Dangerous situations, be they dangers to the body or to the soul, arouse affect-laden fantasies, and, in so far as such situations typically repeat themselves, they give rise to *archetypes,* as I have termed myth-motifs in general.

335   Dragons make their lairs by watercourses, preferably near a ford or some such dangerous crossing; jinn and other devils are to be found in waterless deserts or in dangerous gorges; spirits of the dead haunt the eerie thickets of the bamboo forest; treacherous nixies and sea-serpents live in the depths of the ocean and its whirlpools. Mighty ancestor-spirits or gods dwell in the man of importance; deadly fetish-power resides in anyone strange or extraordinary. Sickness and death are never due to natural causes, but are invariably caused by spirits, witches, or wizards. Even the weapon that has killed a man is *mana,* endowed with extraordinary power.

336   How is it then, you may ask, with the most ordinary everyday

events, with immediate realities like husband, wife, father, mother, child? These ordinary everyday facts, which are eternally repeated, create the mightiest archetypes of all, whose ceaseless activity is everywhere apparent even in a rationalistic age like ours. Let us take as an example the Christian dogma. The Trinity consists of Father, Son, and Holy Ghost, who is represented by the bird of Astarte, the dove, and who in early Christian times was called Sophia and thought of as feminine. The worship of Mary in the later Church is an obvious substitute for this. Here we have the archetype of the family ἐν ὑπερουρανίῳ τόπῳ, 'in a supracelestial place,' as Plato expresses it, enthroned as a formulation of the ultimate mystery. Christ is the bridegroom, the Church is the bride, the baptismal font is the womb of the Church, as it is still called in the text of the *Benedictio fontis*. The holy water has salt put into it, with the idea of making it like the amniotic fluid, or like sea-water. A *hieros gamos* or sacred wedding is performed on Holy Saturday before Easter, which I have just mentioned, and a burning candle as a phallic symbol is plunged three times into the font, in order to fertilize it and lend it the power to bear the baptized child anew (*quasimodo genitus*). The *mana* personality, the medicine-man, is the *pontifex maximus, the Papa;* the Church is *mater ecclesia,* the *magna mater* of magical power, and mankind are children in need of help and grace.

337   The deposit of mankind's whole ancestral experience—so rich in emotional imagery—of father, mother, child, husband and wife, of the magic personality, of dangers to body and soul, has exalted this group of archetypes into the supreme regulating principles of religious and even of political life, in unconscious recognition of their tremendous psychic power.

338   I have found that a rational understanding of these things in no way detracts from their value; on the contrary, it helps us not only to feel but to gain insight into their immense significance. These mighty projections enable the Catholic to experience large tracts of his collective unconscious in tangible reality. He has no need to go in search of authority, superior power, revelation, or something that would link him with the eternal and the timeless. These are always present and available for him: there, in the Holy of Holies on every altar, dwells the presence of God. It is the Protestant and the Jew who have to

seek, the one because he has, in a manner of speaking, destroyed the earthly body of the Deity, the other because he can never find it. For both of them the archetypes, which to the Catholic world have become a visible and living reality, lie in the unconscious. Unfortunately I cannot enter here into the remarkable differences of attitude towards the unconscious in our culture, but would only point out that this question is one of the greatest problems confronting humanity.

339   That this is so is immediately understandable when we consider that the unconscious, as the totality of all archetypes, is the deposit of all human experience right back to its remotest beginnings. Not, indeed, a dead deposit, a sort of abandoned rubbish-heap, but a living system of reactions and aptitudes that determine the individual's life in invisible ways—all the more effective because invisible. It is not just a gigantic historical prejudice, so to speak, an *a priori* historical condition; it is also the source of the instincts, for the archetypes are simply the forms which the instincts assume. From the living fountain of instinct flows everything that is creative; hence the unconscious is not merely conditioned by history, but is the very source of the creative impulse. It is like Nature herself—prodigiously conservative, and yet transcending her own historical conditions in her acts of creation. No wonder, then, that it has always been a burning question for humanity how best to adapt to these invisible determinants. If consciousness had never split off from the unconscious—an eternally repeated event symbolized as the fall of the angels and the disobedience of the first parents—this problem would never have arisen, any more than would the question of environmental adaptation.

340   The existence of an individual consciousness makes man aware of the difficulties of his inner as well as his outer life. Just as the world about him takes on a friendly or a hostile aspect to the eyes of primitive man, so the influences of his unconscious seem to him like an opposing power, with which he has to come to terms just as with the visible world. His countless magical practices serve this end. On higher levels of civilization, religion and philosophy fulfil the same purpose. Whenever such a system of adaptation breaks down a general unrest begins to appear, and attempts are made to find a suitable new form of relationship to the unconscious.

341 These things seem very remote to our modern, "enlightened" eyes. When I speak of this hinterland of the mind, the unconscious, and compare its reality with that of the visible world, I often meet with an incredulous smile. But then I must ask how many people there are in our civilized world who still believe in *mana* and spirits and suchlike theories—in other words, how many millions of Christian Scientists and spiritualists are there? I will not add to this list of questions. They are merely intended to illustrate the fact that the problem of invisible psychic determinants is as alive today as ever it was.

342 The collective unconscious contains the whole spiritual heritage of mankind's evolution, born anew in the brain structure of every individual. His conscious mind is an ephemeral phenomenon that accomplishes all provisional adaptations and orientations, for which reason one can best compare its function to orientation in space. The unconscious, on the other hand, is the source of the instinctual forces of the psyche and of the forms or categories that regulate them, namely the archetypes. All the most powerful ideas in history go back to archetypes. This is particularly true of religious ideas, but the central concepts of science, philosophy, and ethics are no exception to this rule. In their present form they are variants of archetypal ideas, created by consciously applying and adapting these ideas to reality. For it is the function of consciousness not only to recognize and assimilate the external world through the gateway of the senses, but to translate into visible reality the world within us.

ON THE NATURE OF THE PSYCHE [1]

1. The Unconscious in Historical Perspective

343　　More clearly, perhaps, than any other science, psychology demonstrates the spiritual transition from the classical age to the modern. The history of psychology [2] up to the seventeenth century consists essentially in the enumeration of doctrines concerning the soul, but the soul was never able to get a word in as the object investigated. As the immediate datum of experience, it seemed so completely known to every thinker that he was convinced there could be no need of any further, let alone objective, experience. This attitude is totally alien to the modern standpoint, for today we are of the opinion that, over and above all subjective certainty, objective experience is needed to substantiate an opinion that lays claim to be scientific. Notwithstanding

[1] [Originally published as "Der Geist der Psychologie," *Eranos-Jahrbuch 1946* (Zurich, 1947), pp. 385–490. This essay, revised and augmented, was republished as "Theoretische Überlegungen zum Wesen des Psychischen" in *Von den Wurzeln des Bewusstseins* (Psychologische Abhandlungen, IX; Zurich, 1954), pp. 497–608. The former version was translated by R. F. C. Hull as "The Spirit of Psychology" and published in *Spirit and Nature* (Papers from the Eranos Yearbooks, 1; New York, 1954; London, 1955), pp. 371–444. That translation is now further revised to bring it into conformity with the 1954 German version.—EDITORS.]
[2] Hermann Siebeck, *Geschichte der Psychologie.*

this it is still difficult, even today, to apply the purely empirical or phenomenological standpoint consistently in psychology, because the original naïve idea that the soul, being the immediate datum of experience, was the best known of all knowables is one of our most deeply rooted convictions. Not only does every layman presume to an opinion, but every psychologist too—and not merely with reference to the subject but, what is of greater consequence, with reference to the object. He knows, or rather he thinks he knows, what is going on in another individual, and what is good for him. This is due less to a sovereign disregard of differences than to a tacit assumption that all individuals are alike. As a result, people incline unconsciously to a belief in the universal validity of subjective opinions. I mention this fact only to show that, in spite of the growing empiricism of the last three hundred years, the original attitude has by no means disappeared. Its continued existence only goes to prove how difficult is the transition from the old philosophical view to the modern empirical one.

344 Naturally it never occurred to the representatives of the old view that their doctrines were nothing but psychic phenomena, for it was naïvely assumed that with the help of intelligence or reason man could, as it were, climb out of his psychic condition and remove himself to one that was suprapsychic and rational. Even now, the doubt as to whether the statements of the human mind might not in the end be symptoms of certain psychic conditions is one that few people would consider seriously.[3] This question would be very much to the point, but it has such far-reaching and revolutionary consequences that we can understand only too well why both past and present have done their best to ignore it. We are still very far today from Nietzsche's view of philosophy, and indeed of theology, as an "ancilla psychologiae," for not even the psychologist is prepared to regard his statements, at least in part, as a subjectively conditioned confession. We can say that individuals are equal only in so far as they are in large measure unconscious—unconscious, that is, of their actual differences. The more unconscious a man is, the more he will conform to the general canon of psychic behaviour. But the more conscious he becomes of his individuality, the

[3] Actually this is true only of the old psychology. In recent times there has been a considerable change of standpoint.

more pronounced will be his difference from other subjects and the less he will come up to common expectations. Further, his reactions are much less predictable. This is due to the fact that an individual consciousness is always more highly differentiated and more extensive. But the more extensive it becomes the more differences it will perceive and the more it will emancipate itself from the collective rules, for the empirical freedom of the will grows in proportion to the extension of consciousness.

345   As the individual differentiation of consciousness proceeds, the objective validity of its views decreases and their subjectivity increases, at least in the eyes of the environment, if not in actual fact. For if a view is to be valid, it must have the acclaim of the greatest possible number, regardless of the arguments put forward in its favour. "True" and "valid" describe what the majority believe, for this confirms the equality of all. But a differentiated consciousness no longer takes it for granted that one's own preconceptions are applicable to others, and vice versa. This logical development had the consequence that in the seventeenth century—a century of great importance for the growth of science—psychology began to rise up by the side of philosophy, and it was Christian von Wolf (1679–1754) who was the first to speak of "empirical" or "experimental" psychology,[4] thus acknowledging the need to put psychology on a new footing. Psychology had to forgo the philosopher's rational definition of truth, because it gradually became clear that no philosophy had sufficient general validity to be uniformly fair to the diversity of individual subjects. And since on questions of principle, too, an indefinitely large number of different subjective statements was possible, whose validity in their turn could be maintained only subjectively, it naturally became necessary to abandon philosophical argument and to replace it by experience. Psychology thereupon turned into a natural science.

346   For the time being, however, philosophy retained its grip on the wide field of "rational" or "speculative" psychology, and only with the passage of the centuries could the latter gradually develop into a natural science. This process of change is not complete even today. Psychology, as a subject, still comes under

[4] *Psychologia empirica* (1732).

the Philosophical Faculty in most universities and remains in the hands of professional philosophers, while "medical" psychology has still to seek refuge with the Medical Faculty. So officially the situation is still largely medieval, since even the natural sciences are only admitted as "Phil. II," under the cloak of Natural Philosophy.[5] Although it has been obvious for at least two hundred years that philosophy above all is dependent on psychological premises, everything possible was done to obscure the autonomy of the empirical sciences after it became clear that the discovery of the earth's rotation and the moons of Jupiter could no longer be suppressed. Of all the natural sciences, psychology has been the least able to win its independence.

347   This backwardness seems to me significant. The position of psychology is comparable with that of a psychic function which is inhibited by the conscious mind: only such components of it are admitted to exist as accord with the prevailing trend of consciousness. Whatever fails to accord is actually denied existence, in defiance of the fact that there are numerous phenomena or symptoms to prove the contrary. Anyone acquainted with these psychic processes knows with what subterfuges and self-deceiving manoeuvres one sets about splitting off the inconvenience. It is precisely the same with empirical psychology: as the discipline subordinate to a general philosophical psychology, experimental psychology is admitted as a concession to the empiricism of natural science, but is cluttered up with technical philosophical terms. As for psychopathology, it stays put in the Medical Faculty as a curious appendix to psychiatry. "Medical" psychology, as might be expected, finds little or no recognition in the universities.[6]

348   If I express myself somewhat drastically in this matter, it is with intent to throw into relief the position of psychology at the turn of the nineteenth and the beginning of the twentieth century. Wundt's standpoint is entirely representative of the situation as it then was—representative also because there emerged from his school a succession of notable psychologists who set the tone at the beginning of the twentieth century. In his *Outlines*

5 In Anglo-Saxon countries there is the degree of "Doctor Scientiae," and psychology too enjoys greater independence.
6 Recently these conditions have somewhat improved.

of Psychology, Wundt says: "Any psychical element that has disappeared from consciousness is to be called unconscious in the sense that we assume the possibility of its renewal, that is, its reappearance in the actual interconnection of psychical processes. Our knowledge of an element that has become unconscious does not extend beyond this possibility of its renewal. . . . For psychology, therefore, it has no meaning except as a disposition for the inception of future components. . . . Assumptions as to the state of the 'unconscious' or as to 'unconscious processes' of any kind . . . are *entirely unproductive for psychology*. There are, of course, physical concomitants of the psychical dispositions mentioned, of which some can be directly demonstrated, some inferred from various experiences." [7]

349   A representative of the Wundt school opines that "a psychic state cannot be described as psychic unless it has reached at least the threshold of consciousness." This argument assumes, or rather asserts, that only the conscious is psychic and that therefore everything psychic is conscious. The author happens to say a "psychic" state: logically he should have said a "state," for whether such a state is psychic is precisely the point at issue. Another argument runs: the simplest psychic fact is sensation, since it cannot be analysed into simpler facts. Consequently, that which precedes or underlies a sensation is never psychic, but only physiological. *Ergo*, there is no unconscious.

350   J. F. Herbart once said: "When a representation [idea] falls below the threshold of consciousness it goes on living in a latent way, continually striving to recross the threshold and to displace the other representations." As it stands, the proposition is undoubtedly incorrect, for unfortunately anything genuinely forgotten has no tendency to recross the threshold. Had Herbart said "complex" in the modern sense of the word instead of "representation," his proposition would have been absolutely right. We shall hardly be wrong in assuming that he really did mean something of the sort. In this connection, a philosophical opponent of the unconscious makes the very illuminating remark: "Once this be admitted, one finds oneself at the mercy of all manner of hypotheses concerning this unconscious life,

---

[7] Trans. by C. H. Judd, pp. 227-28, from *Grundriss der Psychologie*. (My italics.)

hypotheses which cannot be controlled by any observation." [8]
It is evident that this thinker is not out to recognize facts, but
that for him the fear of running into difficulties is decisive. And
how does he know that these hypotheses cannot be controlled by
observation? For him this is simply an *a priori*. But with
Herbart's observation he does not deal at all.

351   I mention this incident not because of its positive significance but only because it is so thoroughly characteristic of the
antiquated philosophical attitude towards empirical psychology.
Wundt himself is of the opinion that, as regards the "so-called
unconscious processes, it is not a question of unconscious psychic
elements, but only of *more dimly conscious* ones," and that "for
hypothetical unconscious processes we could substitute actually
demonstrable or at any rate less hypothetical conscious processes." [9] This attitude implies a clear rejection of the unconscious as a psychological hypothesis. The cases of "double
consciousness" he explains as "modifications of individual consciousness which very often occur continuously, in steady succession, and for which, by a violent misinterpretation of the
facts, a plurality of individual consciousnesses is substituted."
The latter, so Wundt argues, "would have to be simultaneously
present in one and the same individual." This, he says, "is
admittedly not the case." Doubtless it is hardly possible for two
consciousnesses to express themselves simultaneously in a single
individual in a blatantly recognizable way. That is why these
states usually alternate. Janet has shown that while the one
consciousness controls the head, so to speak, the other simultaneously puts itself into communication with the observer by
means of a code of expressive manual movements. [10] Double
consciousness may therefore very well be simultaneous.

352   Wundt thinks that the idea of a double consciousness, and
hence of a "superconsciousness" and "subconsciousness" in
Fechner's sense, [11] is a "survival from the psychological mysti-

8 Guido Villa, *Einleitung in die Psychologie der Gegenwart*, p. 339.

9 Wilhelm Wundt, *Grundzüge der physiologischen Psychologie*, III, p. 327.

10 Pierre Janet, *Automatisme psychologique*, pp. 243, 238ff.

11 Gustav Theodor Fechner, *Elemente der Psychophysik*, II, p. 438: ". . . the idea
of a psychophysical threshold . . . gives a firm foundation to that of the unconscious generally. Psychology cannot abstract representations from unconscious
perceptions, nor even from the effects of unconscious perceptions."

cism" of the Schelling school. He obviously boggles at an unconscious representation being one which nobody "has." [12] In that case the word "representation" would naturally be obsolete too, since it suggests a subject to whom something is present or "presented." That is the basic reason for Wundt's rejection of the unconscious. But we can easily get round this difficulty by speaking, not of "representations" or "perceptions," but of *contents*, as I usually do. Here I must anticipate a point with which I shall be dealing at some length later on, namely the fact that something very like "representedness" or consciousness does attach to unconscious contents, so that the possibility of an unconscious subject becomes a serious question. Such a subject, however, is not identical with the ego. That it was principally the "representations" which were Wundt's *bête noire* is clear also from his emphatic rejection of "inborn ideas." How literally he takes this can be seen from the following: "If the new-born animal really had an idea beforehand of all the actions it purposes to do, what a wealth of anticipated life-experiences would lie stored in the human and animal instincts, and how incomprehensible it would seem that not man alone, but animals too, acquire most things only through experience and practice!" [13] There is, nevertheless, an inborn "pattern of behaviour" and just such a treasure-house, not indeed of anticipated, but of accumulated, life-experiences; only, it is not a question of "representations" but of sketches, plans, or images which, though not actually "presented" to the ego, are yet just as real as Kant's hundred thalers, which had been sewn into the lining of a jacket and forgotten by the owner. Wundt might have remembered Christian von Wolf, whom he himself mentions, and his distinction with regard to "unconscious" states which "can be inferred only from what we find in our consciousness." [14]

353   To the category of "inborn ideas" also belong Adolf Bastian's "elementary ideas," [15] by which we are to understand the fundamentally analogous forms of perception that are to be found everywhere, therefore more or less what we know today as

---

[12] Ibid., p. 439.   [13] *Grundzüge der physiologischen Psychologie*, III, p. 328.
[14] Ibid., p. 326. Cited from Wolf's *Vernünftige Gedanken von Gott, der Welt, und der Seele des Menschen* (1719), §193.
[15] *Ethnische Elementargedanken in der Lehre vom Menschen* and *Der Mensch in der Geschichte*, I, pp. 166ff., 213ff.; II, pp. 24ff.

"archetypes." Wundt, of course, rejects this notion, under the
delusion that he is dealing here with "representations" and not
with "dispositions." He says: "The origination of one and the
same phenomenon in different places is not absolutely impossible, but, from the standpoint of empirical psychology, it is in
the highest degree unlikely." [16] He denies a "common psychic
heritage of humanity" in this sense and repudiates the very idea
of an intelligible myth-symbolism with the characteristic pro-
nouncement that the supposition of a "system of ideas" hiding
behind the myth is impossible.[17] The pedantic assumption that
the unconscious is, of all things, a system of ideas would not hold
water even in Wundt's day, let alone before or afterwards.

354   It would be incorrect to assume that the rejection of the idea
of the unconscious in academic psychology at the turn of the
century was anything like universal. That is by no means the
case, for Fechner,[18] and after him Theodor Lipps, had given
the unconscious a place of decisive importance.[19] Although for
Lipps psychology is a "science of consciousness," he nevertheless
speaks of "unconscious" perceptions and representations, which
he regards as processes. "The nature or, more accurately, the
idea of a 'psychic' process is not so much a conscious content or
conscious experience as the psychic reality which must necessarily be thought to underlie the existence of such a process." [20]
"Observation of conscious life persuades us that not only are
unconscious perceptions and representations . . . at times to be
found in us, but that psychic life *proceeds in that form most of
the time, and only occasionally, at special points, does the agent
within us reveal its presence directly, in appropriate images.*" [21]

---

[16] *Völkerpsychologie*, V, Part II, p. 459.   [17] Ibid., IV, Part I, p. 41.

[18] Cf. Fechner's remark that "the idea of a psychophysical threshold is of the utmost importance because it gives a firm foundation to that of the unconscious
generally." He goes on: "Perceptions and representations in the state of unconsciousness have, of course, ceased to exist as real ones . . . but something continues in us, psychophysical activity," etc. (II, pp. 438f.). This conclusion is a
little incautious, because the psychic process remains more or less the same
whether conscious or not. A "representation" exists not only through its "representedness," but—and this is the main point—it also exists in its own psychic
right.

[19] Cf. Lipps, "Der Begriff des Unbewussten," pp. 146ff.; and *Grundtatsachen des
Seelenlebens*, pp. 125ff.

[20] *Leitfaden der Psychologie*, p. 64.   [21] Ibid., pp. 65f. (My italics.)

"Thus psychic life always goes far beyond the bounds of what is or may be present in us in the form of conscious contents or images."

355   Theodor Lipps' remarks in no wise conflict with our modern views, on the contrary they form the theoretical basis for the psychology of the unconscious in general. Nevertheless resistance to the hypothesis of the unconscious persisted for a long time afterwards. For instance it is characteristic that Max Dessoir, in his history of modern German psychology,[22] does not even mention C. G. Carus and Eduard von Hartmann.

2. The Significance of the Unconscious in Psychology

356   The hypothesis of the unconscious puts a large question-mark after the idea of the psyche. The soul, as hitherto postulated by the philosophical intellect and equipped with all the necessary faculties, threatened to emerge from its chrysalis as something with unexpected and uninvestigated properties. It no longer represented anything immediately known, about which nothing more remained to be discovered except a few more or less satisfying definitions. Rather it now appeared in strangely double guise, as both known and unknown. In consequence, the old psychology was thoroughly unseated and as much revolutionized [23] as classical physics had been by the discovery of radioactivity. These first experimental psychologists were in the same predicament as the mythical discoverer of the numerical sequence, who strung peas together in a row and

22 *Geschichte der neueren deutschen Psychologie.*
23 I reproduce here what William James says about the importance of the discovery of the unconscious psyche (*Varieties of Religious Experience*, p. 233): "I cannot but think that the most important step forward that has occurred in psychology since I have been a student of that science is the discovery, first made in 1886, that . . . there is not only the consciousness of the ordinary field, with its usual center and margin, but an addition thereto in the shape of a set of memories, thoughts, and feelings which are extramarginal and outside of the primary consciousness altogether, but yet must be classed as conscious facts of some sort, able to reveal their presence by unmistakable signs. I call this the most important step forward because, unlike the other advances which psychology has made, this discovery has revealed to us an entirely unsuspected peculiarity in the constitution of human nature. No other step forward which psychology has made can proffer any such claim as this." The discovery of 1886 to which James refers is the positing of a "subliminal consciousness" by Frederic W. H. Myers. See n. 47, infra.

simply went on adding another unit to those already present. When he contemplated the result, it looked as if there were nothing but a hundred identical units; but the numbers he had thought of only as names unexpectedly turned out to be peculiar entities with irreducible properties. For instance, there were even, uneven, and primary numbers; positive, negative, irrational, and imaginary numbers, etc.[24] So it is with psychology: if the soul is really only an idea, this idea has an alarming air of unpredictability about it—something with qualities no one would ever have imagined. One can go on asserting that the psyche is consciousness and its contents, but that does not prevent, in fact it hastens, the discovery of a background not previously suspected, a true matrix of all conscious phenomena, a preconsciousness and a postconsciousness, a superconsciousness and a subconsciousness. The moment one forms an idea of a thing and successfully catches one of its aspects, one invariably succumbs to the illusion of having caught the whole. One never considers that a total apprehension is right out of the question. Not even an idea posited as total is total, for it is still an entity on its own with unpredictable qualities. This self-deception certainly promotes peace of mind: the unknown is named, the far has been brought near, so that one can lay one's finger on it. One has taken possession of it, and it has become an inalienable piece of property, like a slain creature of the wild that can no longer run away. It is a magical procedure such as the primitive practises upon objects and the psychologist upon the psyche. He is no longer at its mercy, but he never suspects that the very fact of grasping the object conceptually gives it a golden opportunity to display all those qualities which would never have made their appearance had it not been imprisoned in a concept (remember the numbers!).

357   The attempts that have been made, during the last three hundred years, to grasp the psyche are all part and parcel of that tremendous expansion of knowledge which has brought the universe nearer to us in a way that staggers the imagination. The thousandfold magnifications made possible by the electron-microscope vie with the five hundred million light-year distances which the telescope travels. Psychology is still a long way from

[24] A mathematician once remarked that everything in science was man-made except numbers, which had been created by God himself.

a development similar to that which the other natural sciences have undergone; also, as we have seen, it has been much less able to shake off the trammels of philosophy. All the same, every science is a function of the psyche, and all knowledge is rooted in it. The psyche is the greatest of all cosmic wonders and the *sine qua non* of the world as an object. It is in the highest degree odd that Western man, with but very few—and ever fewer—exceptions, apparently pays so little regard to this fact. Swamped by the knowledge of external objects, the subject of all knowledge has been temporarily eclipsed to the point of seeming non-existence.

358   The soul was a tacit assumption that seemed to be known in every detail. With the discovery of a possible unconscious psychic realm, man had the opportunity to embark upon a great adventure of the spirit, and one might have expected that a passionate interest would be turned in this direction. Not only was this not the case at all, but there arose on all sides an outcry against such an hypothesis. Nobody drew the conclusion that if the subject of knowledge, the psyche, were in fact a veiled form of existence not immediately accessible to consciousness, then all our knowledge must be incomplete, and moreover to a degree that we cannot determine. The validity of conscious knowledge was questioned in an altogether different and more menacing way than it had ever been by the critical procedures of epistemology. The latter put certain bounds to human knowledge in general, from which post-Kantian German Idealism struggled to emancipate itself; but natural science and common sense accommodated themselves to it without much difficulty, if they condescended to notice it at all. Philosophy fought against it in the interests of an antiquated pretension of the human mind to be able to pull itself up by its own bootstraps and know things that were right outside the range of human understanding. The victory of Hegel over Kant dealt the gravest blow to reason and to the further development of the German and, ultimately, of the European mind, all the more dangerous as Hegel was a psychologist in disguise who projected great truths out of the subjective sphere into a cosmos he himself had created. We know how far Hegel's influence extends today. The forces compensating this calamitous development personified themselves partly in the later Schelling, partly in Schopenhauer and Carus,

while on the other hand that unbridled "bacchantic God" whom Hegel had already scented in nature finally burst upon us in Nietzsche.

359   Carus' hypothesis of the unconscious was bound to hit the then prevailing trend of German philosophy all the harder, as the latter had apparently just got the better of Kantian criticism and had restored, or rather reinstated, the well-nigh godlike sovereignty of the human spirit—Spirit with a capital S. The spirit of medieval man was, in good and bad alike, still the spirit of the God whom he served. Epistemological criticism was on the one hand an expression of the modesty of medieval man, and on the other a renunciation of, or abdication from, the spirit of God, and consequently a modern extension and reinforcement of human consciousness within the limits of reason. Wherever the spirit of God is extruded from our human calculations, an unconscious substitute takes its place. In Schopenhauer we find the unconscious Will as the new definition of God, in Carus the unconscious, and in Hegel identification and inflation, the practical equation of philosophical reason with Spirit, thus making possible that intellectual juggling with the object which achieved such a horrid brilliance in his philosophy of the State. Hegel offered a solution of the problem raised by epistemological criticism in that he gave ideas a chance to prove their unknown power of autonomy. They induced that hybris of reason which led to Nietzsche's superman and hence to the catastrophe that bears the name of Germany. Not only artists, but philosophers too, are sometimes prophets.

360   I think it is obvious that all philosophical statements which transgress the bounds of reason are anthropomorphic and have no validity beyond that which falls to psychically conditioned statements. A philosophy like Hegel's is a self-revelation of the psychic background and, philosophically, a presumption. Psychologically, it amounts to an invasion by the unconscious. The peculiar high-flown language Hegel uses bears out this view: it is reminiscent of the megalomanic language of schizophrenics, who use terrific spellbinding words to reduce the transcendent to subjective form, to give banalities the charm of novelty, or pass off commonplaces as searching wisdom. So bombastic a terminology is a symptom of weakness, ineptitude, and lack of substance. But that does not prevent the latest German philos-

ophy from using the same crackpot power-words and pretending
that it is not unintentional psychology.

361   In the face of this elemental inrush of the unconscious into
the Western sphere of human reason, Schopenhauer and Carus
had no solid ground under them from which to develop and
apply their compensatory effect. Man's salutary submission to a
benevolent Deity, and the *cordon sanitaire* between him and
the demon of darkness—the great legacy of the past—remained
unimpaired with Schopenhauer, at any rate in principle, while
with Carus it was hardly touched at all, since he sought to tackle
the problem at the root by leading it away from the over-pre-
sumptuous philosophical standpoint towards that of psychology.
We have to close our eyes to his philosophical allure if we wish
to give full weight to his essentially psychological hypothesis.
He had at least come a step nearer to the conclusion we mentioned earlier, by trying to construct a world-picture that included the dark part of the soul. This structure still lacked
something whose unprecedented importance I would like to
bring home to the reader.

362   For this purpose we must first make it quite clear to ourselves
that all knowledge is the result of imposing some kind of order
upon the reactions of the psychic system as they flow into our
consciousness—an order which reflects the behaviour of a *meta-
psychic* reality, of that which is in itself real. If, as certain modern points of view, too, would have it, the psychic system
coincides and is identical with our conscious mind, then, in
principle, we are in a position to know everything that is capable
of being known, i.e., everything that lies within the limits of
the theory of knowledge. In that case there is no cause for
disquiet, beyond that felt by anatomists and physiologists when
contemplating the function of the eye or the organ of hearing.
But should it turn out that the psyche does *not* coincide with
consciousness, and, what is more, that it functions unconsciously
in a way similar to, or *different* from, the conscious portion of
it, then our disquiet must rise to the point of agitation. For it is
then no longer a question of general epistemological limits, but
of a flimsy threshold that separates us from the unconscious contents of the psyche. The hypothesis of the threshold and of the
unconscious means that the indispensable raw material of all
knowledge—namely psychic reactions—and perhaps even uncon-

171

scious "thoughts" and "insights" lie close beside, above, or below consciousness, separated from us by the merest "threshold" and yet apparently unattainable. We have no knowledge of how this unconscious functions, but since it is conjectured to be a psychic system it may possibly have everything that consciousness has, including perception, apperception, memory, imagination, will, affectivity, feeling, reflection, judgment, etc., all in subliminal form.[25]

363   Here we are faced with Wundt's objection that one cannot possibly speak of unconscious "perceptions," "representations," "feelings," much less of "volitional actions," seeing that none of these phenomena can be represented without an experiencing subject. Moreover, the idea of a threshold presupposes a mode of observation in terms of energy, according to which consciousness of psychic contents is essentially dependent upon their intensity, that is, their energy. Just as only a stimulus of a certain intensity is powerful enough to cross the threshold, so it may with some justice be assumed that other psychic contents too must possess a higher energy-potential if they are to get across. If they possess only a small amount of energy they remain subliminal, like the corresponding sense-perceptions.

364   As Lipps has already pointed out, the first objection is nullified by the fact that the psychic process remains essentially the same whether it is "represented" or not. Anyone who takes the view that the phenomena of consciousness comprise the whole psyche must go a step further and say that "representations which we do not have" [26] can hardly be described as "representa-

25 G. H. Lewes in *The Physical Basis of Mind* takes all this for granted. For instance, on p. 358, he says: "Sentience has various modes and degrees, such as Perception, Ideation, Emotion, Volition, which may be conscious, subconscious, or unconscious." On p. 363: "Consciousness and Unconsciousness are correlatives, both belonging to the sphere of Sentience. Every one of the unconscious processes is operant, changes the general state of the organism, and is capable of at once issuing in a discriminated sensation when the force which balances it is disturbed." On p. 367: "There are many involuntary actions of which we are distinctly conscious, and many voluntary actions of which we are at times subconscious and unconscious. . . . Just as the thought which at one moment passes unconsciously, at another consciously, is in itself the same thought . . . so the action which at one moment is voluntary, and at another involuntary, is itself the same action." Lewes certainly goes too far when he says (p. 373): "There is no real and essential distinction between voluntary and involuntary actions." Occasionally there is a world of difference.   26 Fechner, II, pp. 438f.

tions." He must also deny any psychic quality to what is left over. For this rigorous point of view the psyche can only have the phantasmagoric existence that pertains to the ephemeral phenomena of consciousness. This view does not square with common experience, which speaks in favour of a possible psychic activity without consciousness. Lipps' idea of the existence of psychic processes *an sich* does more justice to the facts. I do not wish to waste time in proving this point, but will content myself with saying that never yet has any reasonable person doubted the existence of psychic processes in a dog, although no dog has, to our knowledge, ever expressed consciousness of its psychic contents.[27]

3. *The Dissociability of the Psyche*

365   There is no *a priori* reason for assuming that unconscious processes must inevitably have a subject, any more than there is for doubting the reality of psychic processes. Admittedly the problem becomes difficult when we suppose unconscious acts of the will. If this is not to be just a matter of "instincts" and "inclinations," but rather of considered "choice" and "decision" which are peculiar to the will, then one cannot very well get round the need for a controlling subject to whom something is "represented." But that, by definition, would be to lodge a consciousness in the unconscious, though this is a conceptual operation which presents no great difficulties to the psychopathologist. He is familiar with a psychic phenomenon that seems to be quite unknown to "academic" psychology, namely the dissociation or dissociability of the psyche. This peculiarity arises from the fact that the connecting link between the psychic processes themselves is a very conditional one. Not only are unconscious processes sometimes strangely independent of the experiences of the conscious mind, but the conscious processes, too, show a distinct loosening or discreteness. We all know of the absurdities which are caused by complexes and are to be observed with the greatest accuracy in the association experiment. Just as the cases of double consciousness doubted by Wundt really do happen, so the cases where not the whole personality is split in half, but

27 I am not counting "Clever Hans" [but cf. D. Katz, *Animals and Men*, 13ff.—Editors] and the dog who talked about the "primordial soul."

only smaller fragments are broken off, are much more probable and in fact more common. This is an age-old experience of mankind which is reflected in the universal supposition of a plurality of souls in one and the same individual. As the plurality of psychic components at the primitive level shows, the original state is one in which the psychic processes are very loosely knit and by no means form a self-contained unity. Moreover, psychiatric experience indicates that it often takes only a little to shatter the unity of consciousness so laboriously built up in the course of development and to resolve it back into its original elements.

366   This dissociability also enables us to set aside the difficulties that flow from the logically necessary assumption of a threshold of consciousness. If it is correct to say that conscious contents become subliminal, and therefore unconscious, through loss of energy, and conversely that unconscious processes become conscious through accretion of energy, then, if unconscious acts of volition are to be possible, it follows that these must possess an energy which enables them to achieve consciousness, or at any rate to achieve a state of secondary consciousness which consists in the unconscious process being "represented" to a subliminal subject who chooses and decides. This process must necessarily possess the amount of energy required for it to achieve such a consciousness; in other words, it is bound eventually to reach its "bursting point." [28] If that is so, the question arises as to why the unconscious process does not go right over the threshold and become perceptible to the ego. Since it obviously does not do this, but apparently remains suspended in the domain of a subliminal secondary subject, we must now explain why this subject, which is *ex hypothesi* charged with sufficient energy to become conscious, does not in its turn push over the threshold and articulate with the primary ego-consciousness. Psychopathology has the material needed to answer this question. This secondary consciousness represents a personality-component which has not been separated from ego-consciousness by mere accident, but which owes its separation to definite causes. Such a dissociation has two distinct aspects: in the one case, there is

28 James, *Varieties of Religious Experience*, p. 232.

an originally conscious content that became subliminal because
it was repressed on account of its incompatible nature: in the
other case, the secondary subject consists essentially in a process
that never entered into consciousness at all because no possibilities exist there of apperceiving it. That is to say, ego-consciousness cannot accept it for lack of understanding, and in
consequence it remains for the most part subliminal, although,
from the energy point of view, it is quite capable of becoming
conscious. It owes its existence not to repression, but to subliminal processes that were never themselves conscious. Yet
because there is in both cases sufficient energy to make it potentially conscious, the secondary subject does in fact have an effect
upon ego-consciousness—indirectly or, as we say, "symbolically,"
though the expression is not a particularly happy one. The point
is that the contents that appear in consciousness are at first
symptomatic. In so far as we know, or think we know, what they
refer to or are based on, they are *semiotic,* even though Freudian
literature constantly uses the term "symbolic," regardless of the
fact that in reality symbols always express something we do *not*
know. The symptomatic contents are in part truly symbolic,
being the indirect representatives of unconscious states or processes whose nature can be only imperfectly inferred and realized
from the contents that appear in consciousness. It is therefore
possible that the unconscious harbours contents so powered
with energy that under other conditions they would be bound
to become perceptible to the ego. In the majority of cases they
are not repressed contents, but simply contents that are *not yet
conscious* and have not been subjectively realized, like the
demons and gods of the primitives or the "isms" so fanatically
believed in by modern man. This state is neither pathological
nor in any way peculiar; it is on the contrary the original norm,
whereas the psychic wholeness comprehended in the unity of
consciousness is an ideal goal that has never yet been reached.

367   Not without justice we connect consciousness, by analogy,
with the sense functions, from the physiology of which the whole
idea of a "threshold" is derived. The sound-frequencies perceptible to the human ear range from 20 to 20,000 vibrations
per second; the wave-lengths of light visible to the eye range
from 7700 to 3900 angstrom-units. This analogy makes it

conceivable that there is a lower as well as an upper threshold for psychic events, and that consciousness, the perceptual system par excellence, may therefore be compared with the perceptible scale of sound or light, having like them a lower and upper limit. Maybe this comparison could be extended to the psyche in general, which would not be an impossibility if there were "psychoid" processes at both ends of the psychic scale. In accordance with the principle "natura non facit saltus," such an hypothesis would not be altogether out of place.

368 In using the term "psychoid" I am aware that it comes into collision with the concept of the same name postulated by Driesch. By "the psychoid" he understands the directing principle, the "reaction determinant," the "prospective potency" of the germinal element. It is "the elemental agent discovered in action," [29] the "entelechy of real acting." [30] As Eugen Bleuler has aptly pointed out, Driesch's concept is more philosophical than scientific. Bleuler, on the other hand, uses the expression "die Psychoide" [31] as a collective term chiefly for the subcortical processes, so far as they are concerned with biological "adaptive functions." Among these Bleuler lists "reflexes and the development of species." He defines it as follows: "The *Psychoide* is the sum of all the purposive, mnemonic, and life-preserving functions of the body and central nervous system, with the exception of those cortical functions which we have always been accustomed to regard as psychic." [32] Elsewhere he says: "The body-psyche of the individual and the phylo-psyche together form a unity which, for the purposes of our present study, can most usefully be designated by the name *Psychoide*. Common to both *Psychoide* and psyche are . . . conation and the utilization of previous experiences . . . in order to reach the goal. This would include memory (engraphy and ecphoria) and association, hence something analogous to thinking." [33] Although it is clear what is meant by the "Psychoide," in practice it often gets confused with "psyche," as the above passage shows. But it is not at all clear why the subcortical functions it is supposed to

29 Hans A. E. Driesch, *The Science and Philosophy of the Organism*, 1929, p. 221.
30 Ibid., p. 281.
31 In *Die Psychoide als Prinzip der organischen Entwicklung*, p. 11. A fem. sing. noun derived from *Psyche* ($\psi\nu\chi o\varepsilon\iota\delta\eta s$ = 'soul-like').
32 Ibid., p. 11.   33 Ibid., p. 33.

designate should then be described as "quasi-psychic." The confusion obviously springs from the organological standpoint, still observable in Bleuler, which operates with concepts like "cortical soul" and "medullary soul" and has a distinct tendency to derive the corresponding psychic functions from these parts of the brain, although it is always the function that creates its own organ, and maintains or modifies it. The organological standpoint has the disadvantage that all the purposeful activities inherent in living matter ultimately count as "psychic," with the result that "life" and "psyche" are equated, as in Bleuler's use of the words "phylo-psyche" and "reflexes." It is extremely difficult, if not impossible, to think of a psychic function as independent of its organ, although in actual fact we experience the psychic process apart from its relation to the organic substrate. For the psychologist, however, it is the totality of these experiences that constitutes the object of investigation, and for this reason he must abjure a terminology borrowed from the anatomist. If I make use of the term "psychoid" [34] I do so with three reservations: firstly, I use it as an adjective, not as a noun; secondly, no psychic quality in the proper sense of the word is implied, but only a "quasi-psychic" one such as the reflex-processes possess; and thirdly, it is meant to distinguish a category of events from merely vitalistic phenomena on the one hand and from specifically psychic processes on the other. The latter distinction also obliges us to define more closely the nature and extent of the psyche, and of the unconscious psyche in particular.

369   If the unconscious can contain everything that is known to be a function of consciousness, then we are faced with the possibility that it too, like consciousness, possesses a subject, a sort of ego. This conclusion finds expression in the common and ever-recurring use of the term "subconsciousness." The latter term is certainly open to misunderstanding, as either it means what is "below consciousness," or it postulates a "lower" and

---

[34] I can avail myself of the word "psychoid" all the more legitimately because, although my use of the term derives from a different field of perception, it nevertheless seeks to delineate roughly the same group of phenomena that Bleuler had in mind. A. Busemann, in his book *Die Einheit der Psychologie* (p. 31), calls this non-differentiated psyche the "micropsychic."

secondary consciousness. At the same time this hypothetical "subconsciousness," which immediately becomes associated with a "superconsciousness," [35] brings out the real point of my argument: the fact, namely, that a second psychic system coexisting with consciousness—no matter what qualities we suspect it of possessing—is of absolutely revolutionary significance in that it could radically alter our view of the world. Even if no more than the perceptions taking place in such a second psychic system were carried over into ego-consciousness, we should have the possibility of enormously extending the bounds of our mental horizon.

370   Once we give serious consideration to the hypothesis of the unconscious, it follows that our view of the world can be but a provisional one; for if we effect so radical an alteration in the subject of perception and cognition as this dual focus implies, the result must be a world view very different from any known before. This holds true only if the hypothesis of the unconscious holds true, which in turn can be verified only if unconscious contents can be changed into conscious ones—if, that is to say, the disturbances emanating from the unconscious, the effects of spontaneous manifestations, of dreams, fantasies, and complexes, can successfully be integrated into consciousness by the interpretative method.

4. Instinct and Will

371   Whereas, in the course of the nineteenth century, the main concern was to put the unconscious on a philosophical footing,[36] towards the end of the century various attempts were made in different parts of Europe, more or less simultaneously and independently of one another, to understand the unconscious experimentally or empirically. The pioneers in this field were

---

35 Especial exception is taken to this "superconsciousness" by people who have come under the influence of Indian philosophy. They usually fail to appreciate that their objection only applies to the hypothesis of a "subconsciousness," which ambiguous term I avoid using. On the other hand my concept of the *unconscious* leaves the question of "above" or "below" completely open, as it embraces both aspects of the psyche.

36 Cf. in particular Eduard von Hartmann, *Philosophie des Unbewussten* (1869).

Pierre Janet [37] in France and Sigmund Freud [38] in the old Austria. Janet made himself famous for his investigation of the formal aspect, Freud for his researches into the content of psychogenic symptoms.

372   I am not in a position here to describe in detail the transformation of unconscious contents into conscious ones, so must content myself with hints. In the first place, the structure of psychogenic symptoms was successfully explained on the hypothesis of unconscious processes. Freud, starting from the symptomatology of the neuroses, also made out a plausible case for dreams as the mediators of unconscious contents. What he elicited as contents of the unconscious seemed, on the face of it, to consist of elements of a personal nature that were quite capable of consciousness and had therefore been conscious under other conditions. It seemed to him that they had "got repressed" on account of their morally incompatible nature. Hence, like forgotten contents, they had once been conscious and had become subliminal, and more or less irrecoverable, owing to a counter-effect exerted by the attitude of the conscious mind. By suitably concentrating the attention and letting oneself be guided by associations—that is, by the pointers still existing in consciousness—the associative recovery of lost contents went forward as in a mnemo-technical exercise. But whereas forgotten contents were irrecoverable because of their lowered threshold-value, repressed contents owed their relative irrecoverability to a check exercised by the conscious mind.

373   This initial discovery logically led to the interpretation of the unconscious as a phenomenon of repression which could be understood in personalistic terms. Its contents were lost elements that had once been conscious. Freud later acknowledged the continued existence of archaic vestiges in the form of primitive modes of functioning, though even these were explained personalistically. On this view the unconscious psyche appears as a subliminal appendix to the conscious mind.

[37] An appreciation of his work is to be found in Jean Paulus, *Le Problème de l'hallucination et l'évolution de la psychologie d'Esquirol à Pierre Janet.*
[38] In this connection we should also mention the important Swiss psychologist Théodore Flournoy and his chef d'œuvre *Des Indes à la Planète Mars* (1900). Other pioneers were W. B. Carpenter (*Principles of Mental Physiology*, 1874) and G. H. Lewes (*Problems of Life and Mind*, 1873–79). For Frederic W. H. Myers see nn. 23 and 47.

374   The contents that Freud raised to consciousness are those which are the most easily recoverable because they have the capacity to become conscious and were originally conscious. The only thing they prove with respect to the unconscious psyche is that there is a psychic limbo somewhere beyond consciousness. Forgotten contents which are still recoverable prove the same. This would tell us next to nothing about the nature of the unconscious psyche did there not exist an undoubted link between these contents and the instinctual sphere. We think of the latter as physiological, as in the main a function of the glands. The modern theory of internal secretions and hormones lends the strongest support to this view. But the theory of human instincts finds itself in a rather delicate situation, because it is uncommonly difficult not only to define the instincts conceptually, but even to establish their number and their limitations.[39] In this matter opinions diverge. All that can be ascertained with any certainty is that the instincts have a physiological and a psychological aspect.[40] Of great use for descriptive purposes is Pierre Janet's view of the "partie supérieure et inférieure d'une fonction." [41]

375   The fact that all the psychic processes accessible to our observation and experience are somehow bound to an organic substrate indicates that they are articulated with the life of the organism as a whole and therefore partake of its dynamism—in other words, they must have a share in its instincts or be in a certain sense the results of the action of those instincts. This is not to say that the psyche derives exclusively from the instinctual sphere and hence from its organic substrate. The psyche as such cannot be explained in terms of physiological chemistry, if only because, together with "life" itself, it is the only "natural factor" capable of converting statistical organizations which are

---

[39] This indistinctness and blurring of the instincts may, as E. N. Marais has shown in his experiments with apes (*The Soul of the White Ant,* p. 429), have something to do with the superior learning-capacity prevailing over the instincts, as is obviously the case with man too. On the question of instincts see L. Szondi, *Experimentelle Triebdiagnostik* and *Triebpathologie.*

[40] "The instincts are physiological and psychic dispositions which . . . cause the organism to move in a clearly defined direction" (W. Jerusalem, *Lehrbuch der Psychologie,* p. 188). From another point of view Oswald Külpe describes instinct as "a fusion of feelings and organ sensations" (*Outlines of Psychology,* p. 322, modified).   [41] *Les Névroses,* pp. 384ff.

subject to natural law into "higher" or "unnatural" states, in opposition to the rule of entropy that runs throughout the inorganic realm. How life produces complex organic systems from the inorganic we do not know, though we have direct experience of how the psyche does it. Life therefore has a specific law of its own which cannot be deduced from the known physical laws of nature. Even so, the psyche is to some extent dependent upon processes in the organic substrate. At all events, it is highly probable that this is so. The instinctual base governs the *partie inférieure* of the function, while the *partie supérieure* corresponds to its predominantly "psychic" component. The *partie inférieure* proves to be the relatively unalterable, automatic part of the function, and the *partie supérieure* the voluntary and alterable part.[42]

376   The question now arises: when are we entitled to speak of "psychic" and how in general do we define the "psychic" as distinct from the "physiological"? Both are life-phenomena, but they differ in that the functional component characterized as the *partie inférieure* has an unmistakably physiological aspect. Its existence or nonexistence seems to be bound up with the hormones. Its functioning has a compulsive character: hence the designation "drive." Rivers asserts that the "all-or-none reaction"[43] is natural to it, i.e., the function acts altogether or not at all, which is specific of compulsion. On the other hand the *partie supérieure,* which is best described as psychic and is moreover sensed as such, has lost its compulsive character, can be subjected to the will[44] and even applied in a manner contrary to the original instinct.

377   From these reflections it appears that the psychic is an

---

[42] Janet says (p. 384): "It seems that we must distinguish in every function inferior and superior parts. When a function has been in use for a long time it contains parts which are very old, work very easily, and are represented by very distinct and specialized organs. . . . these are the inferior parts of the function. But it is my opinion that in every function there are also superior parts which consist in the function's adaptation to more recent and much less usual circumstances, and are represented by organs which are differentiated in a markedly lesser degree." But the highest part of the function consists "in its adaptation to the particular circumstances of the present moment, the moment at which we have to use it."   [43] W. H. R. Rivers, "Instinct and the Unconscious."
[44] This formulation is purely psychological and has nothing to do with the philosophical problem of indeterminism.

emancipation of function from its instinctual form and so from the compulsiveness which, as sole determinant of the function, causes it to harden into a mechanism. The psychic condition or quality begins where the function loses its outer and inner determinism and becomes capable of more extensive and freer application, that is, where it begins to show itself accessible to a will motivated from other sources. At the risk of anticipating my programme, I cannot refrain from pointing out that if we delimit the psyche from the physiological sphere of instinct at the bottom, so to speak, a similar delimitation imposes itself at the top. For, with increasing freedom from sheer instinct the *partie supérieure* will ultimately reach a point at which the intrinsic energy of the function ceases altogether to be oriented by instinct in the original sense, and attains a so-called "spiritual" form. This does not imply a substantial alteration of the motive power of instinct, but merely a different mode of its application. The meaning or purpose of the instinct is not unambiguous, as the instinct may easily mask a sense of direction other than biological, which only becomes apparent in the course of development.

378   Within the psychic sphere the function can be deflected through the action of the will and modified in a great variety of ways. This is possible because the system of instincts is not truly harmonious in composition and is exposed to numerous internal collisions. One instinct disturbs and displaces the other, and, although taken as a whole it is the instincts that make individual life possible, their blind compulsive character affords frequent occasion for mutual injury. Differentiation of function from compulsive instinctuality, and its voluntary application, are of paramount importance in the maintenance of life. But this increases the possibility of collision and produces cleavages—the very dissociations which are forever putting the unity of consciousness in jeopardy.

379   In the psychic sphere, as we have seen, the will influences the function. It does this by virtue of the fact that it is itself a form of energy and has the power to overcome another form. In this sphere which I define as psychic, the will is in the last resort motivated by instincts—not, of course, absolutely, otherwise it would not be a will, which by definition must have a certain freedom of choice. "Will" implies a certain amount of energy

freely disposable by the psyche. There must be such amounts of disposable libido (or energy), or modifications of the functions would be impossible, since the latter would then be chained to the instincts—which are in themselves extremely conservative and correspondingly unalterable—so exclusively that no variations could take place, unless it were organic variations. As we have already said, the motivation of the will must in the first place be regarded as essentially biological. But at the (permitting such an expression) upper limit of the psyche, where the function breaks free from its original goal, the instincts lose their influence as movers of the will. Through having its form altered, the function is pressed into the service of other determinants or motivations, which apparently have nothing further to do with the instincts. What I am trying to make clear is the remarkable fact that the will cannot transgress the bounds of the psychic sphere: it cannot coerce the instinct, nor has it power over the spirit, in so far as we understand by this something more than the intellect. Spirit and instinct are by nature autonomous and both limit in equal measure the applied field of the will. Later I shall show what seems to me to constitute the relation of spirit to instinct.

380   Just as, in its lower reaches, the psyche loses itself in the organic-material substrate, so in its upper reaches it resolves itself into a "spiritual" form about which we know as little as we do about the functional basis of instinct. What I would call the psyche proper extends to all functions which can be brought under the influence of a will. Pure instinctuality allows no consciousness to be conjectured and needs none. But because of its empirical freedom of choice, the will needs a supraordinate authority, something like a consciousness of itself, in order to modify the function. It must "know" of a goal different from the goal of the function. Otherwise it would coincide with the driving force of the function. Driesch rightly emphasizes: "There is no willing without knowing." [45] Volition presupposes a choosing subject who envisages different possibilities. Looked at from this angle, psyche is essentially conflict between blind instinct and will (freedom of choice). Where instinct predominates, *psychoid*

[45] *Die "Seele" als elementarer Naturfaktor*, p. 80. "Individualized stimuli inform . . . the 'primary knower' of the abnormal state, and now this 'knower' not only *wants* a remedy but *knows* what it is" (p. 82).

processes set in which pertain to the sphere of the unconscious as elements incapable of consciousness. The psychoid process is not the unconscious as such, for this has a far greater extension. Apart from psychoid processes, there are in the unconscious ideas and volitional acts, hence something akin to conscious processes; [46] but in the instinctual sphere these phenomena retire so far into the background that the term "psychoid" is probably justified. If, however, we restrict the psyche to acts of the will, we arrive at the conclusion that psyche is more or less identical with consciousness, for we can hardly conceive of will and freedom of choice without consciousness. This apparently brings us back to where we always stood, to the axiom *psyche = consciousness*. What, then, has happened to the postulated psychic nature of the unconscious?

5. *Conscious and Unconscious*

381   This question, regarding the nature of the unconscious, brings with it the extraordinary intellectual difficulties with which the psychology of the unconscious confronts us. Such difficulties must inevitably arise whenever the mind launches forth boldly into the unknown and invisible. Our philosopher sets about it very cleverly, since, by his flat denial of the unconscious, he clears all complications out of his way at one sweep. A similar quandary faced the physicist of the old school, who believed exclusively in the wave theory of light and was then led to the discovery that there are phenomena which can be explained only by the particle theory. Happily, modern physics has shown the psychologist that it can cope with an apparent *contradictio in adiecto*. Encouraged by this example, the psychologist may be emboldened to tackle this controversial problem without having the feeling that he has dropped out of the world of natural science altogether. It is not a question of his *asserting* anything, but of constructing a *model* which opens up a promising and useful field of inquiry. A model does not assert that something *is* so, it simply illustrates a particular mode of observation.

382   Before we scrutinize our dilemma more closely, I would like

---

[46] Cf. sec. 6 below, "The Unconscious as a Multiple Consciousness."

to clarify one aspect of the concept of the unconscious. The unconscious is not simply the unknown, it is rather the *unknown psychic;* and this we define on the one hand as all those things in us which, if they came to consciousness, would presumably differ in no respect from the known psychic contents, with the addition, on the other hand, of the psychoid system, of which nothing is known directly. So defined, the unconscious depicts an extremely fluid state of affairs: everything of which I know, but of which I am not at the moment thinking; everything of which I was once conscious but have now forgotten; everything perceived by my senses, but not noted by my conscious mind; everything which, involuntarily and without paying attention to it, I feel, think, remember, want, and do; all the future things that are taking shape in me and will sometime come to consciousness: all this is the content of the unconscious. These contents are all more or less capable, so to speak, of consciousness, or were once conscious and may become conscious again the next moment. Thus far the unconscious is "a fringe of consciousness," as William James put it.[47] To this marginal phenomenon, which is born of alternating shades of light and darkness, there also belong the Freudian findings we have already noted. But, as I say, we must also include in the unconscious the psychoid functions that are not capable of consciousness and of whose existence we have only indirect knowledge.

383   We now come to the question: in what state do psychic

---

47 James speaks also of a "transmarginal field" of consciousness and identifies it with the "subliminal consciousness" of F. W. H. Myers, one of the founders of the British Society for Psychical Research (cf. *Proceedings S.P.R.,* VII, 1892, pp. 298ff., and William James, "Frederic Myers' Service to Psychology," ibid., XVII, 1901, pp. 13ff.). Concerning the "field of consciousness" James says (*Varieties of Religious Experience,* p. 232): "The important fact which this 'field' formula commemorates is the indetermination of the margin. Inattentively realized as is the matter which the margin contains, it is nevertheless there, and helps both to guide our behavior and to determine the next movement of our attention. It lies around us like a 'magnetic field' inside of which our center of energy turns like a compass needle as the present phase of consciousness alters into its successor. Our whole past store of memories floats beyond this margin, ready at a touch to come in; and the entire mass of residual powers, impulses, and knowledges that constitute our empirical self stretches continuously beyond it. So vaguely drawn are the outlines between what is actual and what is only potential at any moment of our conscious life, that it is always hard to say of certain mental elements whether we are conscious of them or not."

contents find themselves when not related to the conscious ego? (This relation constitutes all that can be called consciousness.) In accordance with "Occam's razor," *entia praeter necessitatem non sunt multiplicanda* ("principles are not to be multiplied beyond the necessary"), the most cautious conclusion would be that, except for the relation to the conscious ego, nothing is changed when a content becomes unconscious. For this reason I reject the view that momentarily unconscious contents are only physiological. The evidence is lacking, and apart from that the psychology of neurosis provides striking proofs to the contrary. One has only to think of the cases of double personality, *automatisme ambulatoire*, etc. Both Janet's and Freud's findings indicate that everything goes on functioning in the unconscious state just as though it were conscious. There is perception, thinking, feeling, volition, and intention, just as though a subject were present; indeed, there are not a few cases—e.g., the double personality above mentioned—where a second ego actually appears and vies with the first. Such findings seem to show that the unconscious is in fact a "subconscious." But from certain experiences—some of them known already to Freud—it is clear that the state of unconscious contents is not quite the same as the conscious state. For instance, feeling-toned complexes in the unconscious do not change in the same way that they do in consciousness. Although they may be enriched by associations, they are not corrected, but are conserved in their original form, as can easily be ascertained from the continuous and uniform effect they have upon the conscious mind. Similarly, they take on the uninfluenceable and compulsive character of an automatism, of which they can be divested only if they are made conscious. This latter procedure is rightly regarded as one of the most important therapeutic factors. In the end such complexes—presumably in proportion to their distance from consciousness—assume, by self-amplification, an archaic and mythological character and hence a certain numinosity, as is perfectly clear in schizophrenic dissociations. Numinosity, however, is wholly outside conscious volition, for it transports the subject into the state of rapture, which is a state of will-less surrender.

384   These peculiarities of the unconscious state contrast very strongly with the way complexes behave in the conscious mind. Here they can be corrected: they lose their automatic character

and can be substantially transformed. They slough off their mythological envelope, and, by entering into the adaptive process going forward in consciousness, they personalize and rationalize themselves to the point where a dialectical discussion becomes possible.[48] Evidently the unconscious state is different after all from the conscious. Although at first sight the process continues in the unconscious as though it were conscious, it seems, with increasing dissociation, to sink back to a more primitive (archaic-mythological) level, to approximate in character to the underlying instinctual pattern, and to assume the qualities which are the hallmarks of instinct: automatism, non-susceptibility to influence, all-or-none reaction, and so forth. Using the analogy of the spectrum, we could compare the lowering of unconscious contents to a displacement towards the red end of the colour band, a comparison which is especially edifying in that red, the blood colour, has always signified emotion and instinct.[49]

385   The unconscious is accordingly a different medium from the conscious. In the near-conscious areas there is not much change, because here the alternation of light and shadow is too rapid. But it is just this no man's land which is of the greatest value in supplying the answer to the burning question of whether psyche = consciousness. It shows us how relative the unconscious state is, so relative, indeed, that one feels tempted to make use of a concept like "the subconscious" in order to define the darker part of the psyche. But consciousness is equally relative, for it embraces not only consciousness as such, but a whole scale of intensities of consciousness. Between "I do this" and "I am conscious of doing this" there is a world of difference, amounting sometimes to outright contradiction. Consequently there is a consciousness in which unconsciousness predominates, as well as a consciousness in which self-consciousness predominates. This paradox becomes immediately intelligible when we realize that there is no conscious content which can with absolute certainty

48 In schizophrenic dissociation there is no such change in the conscious state, because the complexes are received not into a complete but into a fragmentary consciousness. That is why they so often appear in the original archaic state.

49 Red had a *spiritual* significance for Goethe, but that was in accord with his creed of feeling. Here we may conjecture the alchemical and Rosicrucian background, e.g., the red tincture and the carbuncle. Cf. *Psychology and Alchemy*, p. 449.

be said to be totally conscious,[50] for that would necessitate an unimaginable totality of consciousness, and that in turn would presuppose an equally unimaginable wholeness and perfection of the human mind. So we come to the paradoxical conclusion that there is no conscious content which is not in some other respect unconscious. Maybe, too, there is no unconscious psychism which is not at the same time conscious.[51] The latter proposition is more difficult to prove than the first, because our ego, which alone could verify such an assertion, is the point of reference for all consciousness and has no such association with unconscious contents as would enable it to say anything about their nature. So far as the ego is concerned, they are, for all practical purposes, unconscious: which is not to say that they are not conscious to it in another respect, for the ego may know these contents under one aspect but not know them under another aspect, when they cause disturbances of consciousness. Besides, there are processes with regard to which no relation to the conscious ego can be demonstrated and which yet seem to be "represented" or "quasi-conscious." Finally, there are cases where an unconscious ego and hence a second consciousness are present, as we have already seen, though these are the exceptions.[52]

386   In the psychic sphere, the compulsive pattern of behaviour gives way to variations of behaviour which are conditioned by experience and by volitional acts, that is, by conscious processes. With respect to the psychoid, reflex-instinctual state, therefore, the psyche implies a loosening of bonds and a steady recession of mechanical processes in favour of "selected" modifications. This selective activity takes place partly inside consciousness and

[50] As already pointed out by E. Bleuler: *Naturgeschichte der Seele und ihres Bewusstwerdens*, pp. 300f.

[51] With the explicit exception of the psychoid unconscious, as this includes things which are not capable of consciousness and are only "quasi-psychic."

[52] In this connection I would mention that C. A. Meier associates observations of this kind with similar phenomena in physics. He says: "The relationship of complementarity between conscious and unconscious urges upon us yet another physical parallel, namely the need for a strict application of the 'principle of correspondence.' This might provide the key to the 'strict logic' of the unconscious (the logic of probability) which we so often experience in analytical psychology and which makes us think of an 'extended state of consciousness.' "— "Moderne Physik—Moderne Psychologie," p. 360.

partly outside it, i.e., without reference to the conscious ego, and hence unconsciously. In the latter case the process is "quasi-conscious," *as if* it were "represented" and conscious.

387 As there are no sufficient grounds for assuming that a second ego exists in every individual or that everyone suffers from dissociation of personality, we have to discount the idea of a second ego-consciousness as a source of voluntary decisions. But since the existence of highly complex, quasi-conscious processes in the unconscious has been shown, by the study of psychopathology and dream psychology, to be uncommonly probable, we are for better or worse driven to the conclusion that although the state of unconscious contents is not identical with that of conscious ones, it is somehow very "like" it. In these circumstances there is nothing for it but to suppose something midway between the conscious and unconscious state, namely an approximative consciousness. As we have immediate experience only of a reflected state, which is *ipso facto* conscious and known because it consists essentially in relating ideas or other contents to an ego-complex that represents our empirical personality, it follows that any other kind of consciousness—either without an ego or without contents—is virtually unthinkable. But there is no need to frame the question so absolutely. On a somewhat more primitive human level, ego-consciousness loses much of its meaning, and consciousness is accordingly modified in a characteristic way. Above all, it ceases to be reflected. And when we observe the psychic processes in the higher vertebrates and particularly in domestic animals, we find phenomena resembling consciousness which nevertheless do not allow us to conjecture the existence of an ego. As we know from direct experience, the light of consciousness has many degrees of brightness, and the ego-complex many gradations of emphasis. On the animal and primitive level there is a mere "luminosity," differing hardly at all from the glancing fragments of a dissociated ego. Here, as on the infantile level, consciousness is not a unity, being as yet uncentred by a firmly-knit ego-complex, and just flickering into life here and there wherever outer or inner events, instincts, and affects happen to call it awake. At this stage it is still like a chain of islands or an archipelago. Nor is it a fully integrated whole even at the higher and highest stages; rather, it is capable of indefinite expansion. Gleaming islands, indeed whole continents,

can still add themselves to our modern consciousness—a phenomenon that has become the daily experience of the psychotherapist. Therefore we would do well to think of ego-consciousness as being surrounded by a multitude of little luminosities.

6. The Unconscious as a Multiple Consciousness

388   The hypothesis of multiple luminosities rests partly, as we have seen, on the quasi-conscious state of unconscious contents and partly on the incidence of certain images which must be regarded as symbolical. These are to be found in the dreams and visual fantasies of modern individuals, and can also be traced in historical records. As the reader may be aware, one of the most important sources for symbolical ideas in the past is alchemy. From this I take, first and foremost, the idea of the *scintillae*—sparks—which appear as visual illusions in the "arcane substance."[53] Thus the *Aurora consurgens*, Part II, says: "Scito quod terra foetida cito recipit scintillulas albas" (Know that the foul earth quickly receives white sparks).[54] These sparks Khunrath explains as "radii atque scintillae" of the "anima catholica," the world-soul, which is identical with the spirit of God.[55] From this interpretation it is clear that certain of the alchemists had already divined the psychic nature of these luminosities. They were seeds of light broadcast in the chaos, which Khunrath calls "mundi futuri seminarium" (the seed plot of a world to come).[56]

[53] *Psychology and Alchemy*, p. 126.

[54] *Artis auriferae* (1593), I, p. 208. Said to be a quotation from Morienus (cf. infra, par. 394), repeated by Mylius, *Philosophia reformata* (1622), p. 146. On p. 149 he adds "scintillas aureas."

[55] "Variae eius radii atque scintillae, per totius ingentem materiei primae massae molem hinc inde dispersae ac dissipatae: inque mundi partibus disiunctis etiam et loco et corporis mole, necnon circumscriptione, postea separatis . . . unius Animae universalis scintillae nunc etiam inhabitantes" (Its divers rays and sparks are dispersed and dissipated throughout the immense bulk of the whole mass of the *prima materia*: the sparks of the one universal soul now inhabiting those disunited parts of the world which were later separated from the place and mass of the body, and even from its circumference). Khunrath, *Amphitheatrum sapientiae aeternae solius verae* (1604), pp. 195f., 198.

[56] Ibid., p. 197. Cf. the Gnostic doctrine of the Seeds of Light harvested by the Virgin of Light, and the Manichaean doctrine of the light-particles which have to

One such spark is the human mind.[57] The arcane substance—the watery earth or earthy water (*limus:* mud) of the World Essence —is "universally animated" by the "fiery spark of the soul of the world," in accordance with the Wisdom of Solomon 1 : 7: "For the Spirit of the Lord filleth the world." [58] In the "Water of the Art," in "our Water," which is also the chaos,[59] there are to be found the "fiery sparks of the soul of the world as pure *Formae Rerum essentiales.*" [60] These *formae* [61] correspond to the Platonic Ideas, from which one could equate the *scintillae* with the archetypes on the assumption that the Forms "stored up in a supracelestial place" are a philosophical version of the latter. One would have to conclude from these alchemical visions that the archetypes have about them a certain effulgence or quasi-consciousness, and that numinosity entails luminosity. Paracelsus seems to have had an inkling of this. The following is taken from his *Philosophia sagax:* "And as little as aught can exist in man without the divine numen, so little can aught exist in man without the natural lumen. A man is made perfect by numen and lumen and these two alone. Everything springs from these two, and these two are in man, but without them man is nothing, though they can be without man." [62] In confirmation of this Khunrath writes: "There be . . . *Scintillae Animae Mundi igneae, Luminis nimirum Naturae,* fiery sparks of the world soul, i.e., of the light of nature . . . dispersed or sprinkled in and throughout the structure of the great world

be taken into one's body as ritual food, at a sort of Eucharist when melons were eaten. The earliest mention of this idea seems to be the καρπιστής (Irenaeus, *Contra haereses,* I, 2, 4). Concerning the melons see M.-L. von Franz, "Der Traum des Descartes."

57 "Mens humani animi scintilla altior et lucidior" (The mind of the human soul is a higher and more luminous spark). *Amphitheatrum,* p. 63.

58 Khunrath, *Von hylealischen . . . Chaos* (1597), p. 63.

59 As synonyms, Khunrath mentions (p. 216) "forma aquina, pontica, limus terrae Adamae, Azoth, Mercurius" (a form watery and sea-like, the slime of the earth of Adama, etc.). [*Adama* is Hebrew for 'earth.'—EDITORS.]   60 Ibid., p. 216.

61 The "formae scintillaeve Animae Mundi" (forms or sparks of the world soul) are also called by Khunrath (p. 189) "rationes seminariae Naturae specificae" (the seed-ideas of Nature, the origin of species), thus reproducing an ancient idea. In the same way he calls the *scintilla "Entelechia"* (p. 65).

62 *Paracelsus: Sämtliche Werke,* ed. by Karl Sudhoff, XII, p. 231; *Bücher und Schrifften . . . Paracelsi . . . ,* ed. by Johannes Huser, X, p. 206.

into all fruits of the elements everywhere." [63] The sparks come from the "Ruach Elohim," the Spirit of God.[64] Among the *scintillae* he distinguishes a "scintilla perfecta Unici Potentis ac Fortis," which is the elixir and hence the arcane substance itself.[65] If we may compare the sparks to the archetypes, it is evident that Khunrath lays particular stress on one of them. This One is also described as the Monad and the Sun, and they both indicate the Deity. A similar image is to be found in the letter of Ignatius of Antioch to the Ephesians, where he writes of the coming of Christ: "How, then, was he manifested to the world? A star shone in heaven beyond the stars, and its light was unspeakable, and its newness caused astonishment, and all the other stars, with the sun and moon, gathered in chorus round this star. . . ." [66] Psychologically, the One Scintilla or Monad is to be regarded as a symbol of the self—an aspect I mention only in passing.

389   The sparks have a clear psychological meaning for Dorn. He says: "Thus little by little he will come to see with his mental eyes a number of sparks shining day by day and more and more and growing into such a great light that thereafter all things needful to him will be made known." [67] This light is the *lumen naturae* which illuminates consciousness, and the *scintillae* are germinal luminosities shining forth from the darkness of the unconscious. Dorn, like Khunrath, owes much to Paracelsus, with whom he concurs when he supposes an "invisibilem solem plurimis incognitum" in man (an invisible sun unknown to many).[68] Of this natural light innate in man Dorn says: "For the life, the light of men,[69] shineth in us, albeit dimly, and as

63 *Von hylealischen Chaos*, p. 94.   64 Ibid., p. 249.

65 Ibid., p. 54. In this he agrees with Paracelsus, who calls the *lumen naturae* the Quintessence, extracted from the four elements by God himself. (Sudhoff, XII, pp. 36, 304.)

66 Ch. XIX, 1ff. (trans. by Lake in *The Apostolic Fathers*, I, p. 193).

67 "Sic paulatim scintillas aliquot magis ac magis indies perlucere suis oculis mentalibus percipiet, ac in tantam excrescere lucem, ut successivo tempore quaevis innotescant, quae sibi necessaria fuerint." Gerhard Dorn, "Speculativae philosophiae," in *Theatrum chemicum*, I (1602), p. 275.

68 "Sol est invisibilis in hominibus, in terra vero visibilis, tamen ex uno et eodem sole sunt ambo" (The sun is invisible in men, but visible in the world, yet both are of one and the same sun). Ibid., p. 308.

69 "Et vita erat lux hominum. Et lux in tenebris lucet" (And the life was the light of men. And the light shineth in the darkness). John 1 : 4, 5.

though in darkness. It is not to be extracted from us, yet it is in us and not of us, but of Him to Whom it belongs, Who deigns to make us his dwelling-place. . . . He has implanted that light in us that we may see in its light the light of Him Who dwells in inaccessible light, and that we may excel His other creatures; in this wise we are made like unto Him, that He has given us a spark of His light. Thus the truth is to be sought not in ourselves, but in the image of God which is within us." [70]

390   Thus the one archetype emphasized by Khunrath is known also to Dorn as the *sol invisibilis* or *imago Dei*. In Paracelsus the *lumen naturae* comes primarily from the "astrum" or "sydus," the "star" in man.[71] The "firmament" (a synonym for the star) is the natural light.[72] Hence the "corner-stone" of all truth is "Astronomia," which is "a mother to all the other arts. . . . After her beginneth the divine wisdom, after her beginneth the light of nature," [73] even the "most excellent Religiones" hang upon Astronomia.[74] For the star "desireth to drive man toward great wisdom . . . that he may appear wondrous in the light of nature, and the mysteria of God's wondrous work be discovered and revealed in their grandeur." [75] Indeed, man himself is an "Astrum": "not by himself alone, but for ever and ever with all apostles and saints; each and every one is an astrum, the heaven a star . . . therefore saith also the Scripture: ye are lights of the world." [76] "Now as in the star lieth the whole natural light, and from it man taketh the same like food from the earth into which he is born, so too must he be born into the star." [77] Also the

---

[70] "Lucet in nobis licet obscure vita lux hominum tanquam in tenebris, quae non ex nobis quaerenda, tamen in et non a nobis, sed ab eo cuius est, qui etiam in nobis habitationem facere dignatur. . . . Hic eam lucem plantavit in nobis, ut in eius lumine qui lucem inaccessibilem inhabitat, videremus lumen; hoc ipso quoque caeteras eius praecelleremus creaturas; illi nimirum similes hac ratione facti, quod scintillam sui luminis dederit nobis. Est igitur veritas non in nobis quaerenda, sed in imagine Dei quae in nobis est." "Philosophia meditativa," *Theatrum chemicum*, I, p. 460.

[71] Sudhoff, XII, p. 23: "That which is in the light of nature, the same is the working of the star." (Huser, X, p. 19.)

[72] *Philosophia sagax*, Huser, X, p. 1 (Sudhoff, XII, p. 3).

[73] Ibid., pp. 3f. (pp. 5f.).

[74] The apostles are "Astrologi": ibid., p. 23 (p. 27).   [75] Ibid., p. 54 (p. 62).

[76] Ibid., p. 344 (p. 386). The last sentence refers to Matthew 5 : 14: "Vos estis lux mundi."   [77] Ibid., p. 409 (pp. 456f.).

animals have the natural light which is an "inborn spirit." [78]
Man at his birth is "endowed with the perfect light of nature." [79]
Paracelsus calls it "primum ac optimum thesaurum, quem
naturae Monarchia in se claudit" [80] (the first and best treasure
which the monarchy of nature hides within itself), in this con-
curring with the world-wide descriptions of the One as the pearl
of great price, the hidden treasure, the "treasure hard to attain,"
etc. The light is given to the "inner man" or the inner body
(*corpus subtile,* breath-body), as the following passage makes
clear:

A man may come forth with sublimity and wisdom from his outer
body, because the same wisdom and understanding which he
needeth for this are coaeval with this body and are the inner man; [81]
thus he may live and not as an outer man. For such an inner man is
eternally transfigured and true, and if in the mortal body he appeareth not perfect, yet he appeareth perfect after the separation of the
same. That which we now tell of is called *lumen naturae* and is
eternal. God hath given it to the inner body, that it may be ruled by
the inner body and in accordance with reason . . . for the light of
nature alone is reason and no other thing . . . the light is that
which giveth faith . . . to each man God hath given sufficient predestined light that he err not. . . . But if we are to describe the
origin of the inner man or body, mark that all inner bodies be but
one body and one single thing in all men, albeit divided in accordance with the well-disposed numbers of the body, each one different.
And should they all come together, it is but one light, and one
reason.[82]

391   "Moreover, the light of nature is a light that is lit from the
Holy Ghost and goeth not out, for it is well lit . . . and the
light is of a kind that desireth to burn,[83] and the longer [it burns]

[78] ". . . like the cocks which crow the coming weather and the peacocks the death
of their master . . . all this is of the inborn spirit and is the light of nature."
Fragmenta medica, cap. "De morbis somnii," Huser, V, p. 130 (Sudhoff, IX, p. 361).
[79] *Liber de generatione hominis,* VIII, p. 172 (I, p. 300).
[80] *De vita longa,* ed. by Adam von Bodenstein (1562), Lib. V, c. ii.
[81] *Philosophia sagax,* X, p. 341 (XII, p. 382): "Now it is clear that all the human
wisdom of the earthly body lieth in the light of nature." It is "man's light of
eternal wisdom": ibid., p. 395 (p. 441).
[82] *Liber de generatione hominis,* VIII, pp. 171f. (I, pp. 299f.).
[83] "I am come to send fire on the earth; and what will I, if it be already kindled?"
Luke (AV) 12 : 49.

to shine the more, and the longer the greater . . . therefore in the light of nature is a fiery longing to enkindle." [84] It is an "invisible" light: "Now it follows that in the invisible alone hath man his wisdom, his art from the light of nature." [85] Man is "a prophet of the natural light." [86] He "learns" the *lumen naturae* through dreams,[87] among other things. "As the light of nature cannot speak, it buildeth shapes in sleep from the power of the word" (of God).[88]

392   I have allowed myself to dwell at some length on Paracelsus and to cite a number of authentic texts, because I wanted to give the reader a rough idea of the way in which this author conceives the *lumen naturae*. It strikes me as significant, particularly in regard to our hypothesis of a multiple consciousness and its phenomena, that the characteristic alchemical vision of sparks scintillating in the blackness of the arcane substance should, for Paracelsus, change into the spectacle of the "interior firmament" and its stars. He beholds the darksome psyche as a star-strewn night sky, whose planets and fixed constellations represent the archetypes in all their luminosity and numinosity.[89] The starry vault of heaven is in truth the open book of cosmic projection, in which are reflected the mythologems, i.e., the archetypes. In this vision astrology and alchemy, the two classical functionaries of the psychology of the collective unconscious, join hands.

393   Paracelsus was directly influenced by Agrippa von Nettesheim,[90] who supposes a "luminositas sensus naturae." From this "gleams of prophecy came down to the four-footed beasts, the birds, and other living creatures," and enabled them to foretell future things.[91] He bases the *sensus naturae* on the authority of

84 *Fragmenta cum libro de fundamento sapientiae*, IX, p. 448 (XIII, pp. 325f.).
85 *Philosophia sagax*, X, p. 46 (XII, p. 53).   86 Ibid., p. 79 (p. 94).
87 *Practica in scientiam divinationis*, X, p. 438 (XII, p. 488).
88 *Liber de Caducis*, IV, p. 274 (VIII, p. 298).
89 In the *Hieroglyphica* of Horapollo the starry sky signifies God as ultimate Fate, symbolized by a "5," presumably a quincunx. [Trans. by George Boas, p. 66.—Editors.]   90 Cf. my "Paracelsus as a Spiritual Phenomenon" (Swiss edn.. pp. 47ff.).
91 Cornelius Heinrich Agrippa von Nettesheim, *De occulta philosophia* (1533), p. lxix: "Nam iuxta Platonicorum doctrinam, est rebus inferioribus vis quaedam insita, per quam magna ex parte cum superioribus conveniunt, unde etiam animalium taciti consensus cum divinis corporibus consentire videntur, atque his viribus eorum corpora et affectus affici." (For according to the doctrine of the

Gulielmus Parisiensis, who is none other than William of Auvergne (G. Alvernus; d. 1249), bishop of Paris from about 1228, author of many works, which influenced Albertus Magnus among others. Alvernus says that the *sensus naturae* is superior to the perceptive faculty in man, and he insists that animals also possess it.[92] The doctrine of the *sensus naturae* is developed from the idea of the all-pervading world-soul with which another Gulielmus Parisiensis was much concerned, a predecessor of Alvernus by name of Guillaume de Conches [93] (1080–1154), a Platonist scholastic who taught in Paris. He identified the *anima mundi*, this same *sensus naturae*, with the Holy Ghost, just as Abelard did. The world-soul is a natural force which is responsible for all the phenomena of life and the psyche. As I have shown elsewhere, this view of the *anima mundi* ran through the whole tradition of alchemy in so far as Mercurius was interpreted now as *anima mundi* and now as the Holy Ghost.[94] In view of the importance of alchemical ideas for the psychology of the unconscious, it may be worth our while to devote a little time to a very illuminating variant of this spark symbolism.

394   Even more common than the spark-motif is that of the fish's eyes, which have the same significance. I said above that a Morienus passage is given by the authors as the source for the "doctrine" of the *scintillae*. This passage is, indeed, to be found in the treatise of Morienus Romanus. But it reads: ". . . Purus laton tamdiu decoquitur, donec veluti oculi piscium elucescat . . ."[95] Here too the saying seems to be a citation from a still earlier source. In later authors these fish's eyes are always cropping up. There is a variant in Sir George Ripley, stating that on the "desiccation of the sea" a substance is left behind

---

Platonists there is in the lower things a certain virtue through which they agree in large measure with the higher; whence it would seem that the tacit consent of animals is in agreement with divine bodies, and that their bodies and affections are touched by these virtues), etc.

92 Lynn Thorndike, *History of Magic and Experimental Science*, II, pp. 348f.

93 François Picavet, *Essais sur l'histoire générale et comparée des théologies et des philosophies médiévales*, p. 207.

94 Cf. *Psychology and Alchemy*, pp. 126, 178f., 405, and pp. 330f., 416f.

95 "Liber de compositione Alchemiae," in *Artis auriferae*, II, p. 32: "The pure lato is cooked until it has the lustre of fish's eyes." Thus, by the authors themselves, the *oculi piscium* are interpreted as *scintillae*.

which "glitters like a fish's eye" [96]—an obvious allusion to the gold and the sun (God's eye). Hence it is not to be wondered at if an alchemist [97] of the seventeenth century uses the words of Zacharias 4 : 10 as a motto for his edition of Nicholas Flamel: "Et videbunt lapidem stanneum in manu Zorobabel. Septem isti oculi sunt Domini, qui discurrunt in universam terram" (And . . . they shall see the tin plummet in the hand of Zorobabel. These are the seven eyes of the Lord that run to and fro through the whole earth).[98] These seven eyes are evidently the seven planets which, like the sun and moon, are the eyes of God, never resting, ubiquitous and all-seeing. The same motif is probably at the bottom of the many-eyed giant Argus. He is nicknamed Πανόπτης, 'the All-Seeing,' and is supposed to symbolize the starry heavens. Sometimes he is one-eyed, sometimes four-eyed, sometimes hundred-eyed, and even myriad-eyed (μυριωπός). Besides which he never sleeps. Hera transferred the eyes of Argus Panoptes to the peacock's tail.[99] Like the guardian Argus, the constellation of the Dragon is also given an all-surveying position in the Aratus citations of Hippolytus. He is there described as the one "who from the height of the Pole looks down upon all things and sees all things, so that nothing that happens shall be hidden from him." [100] This dragon is sleepless, because the Pole "never sets." Often he appears to be confused with the sun's serpentine passage through the sky: "C'est pour ce motif qu'on dispose parfois les signes du zodiaque entre les circonvolutions du reptile," says Cumont.[101] Sometimes the serpent bears six signs of the zodiac upon his back.[102] As Eisler has remarked, on account of the time symbolism the all-seeing quality of the dragon

96 *Opera omnia chemica* (1649), p. 159.

97 Eirenaeus Orandus, *Nicholas Flamel: His Exposition of the Hieroglyphicall Figures etc.* (1624).

98 Zach. 3 : 9 is also relevant: ". . . upon one stone there are seven eyes." (Both DV.)

99 This mythologem is of importance in interpreting the "cauda pavonis."

100 "Τετάχθαι γὰρ νομίζουσι κατὰ τὸν ἀρκτικὸν πόλον τὸν Δράκοντα, τὸν ὄφιν, ἀπὸ τοῦ ὑψηλοτάτου πόλου πάντα ἐπιβλέποντα καὶ πάντα ἐφορῶντα, ἵνα μηδὲν τῶν πραττομένων αὐτὸν λάθῃ." *Elenchos*, IV, 47, 2, 3. Cf. Legge, I, p. 109.

101 F. Cumont, *Textes et monuments figurés relatifs aux mystères de Mithra*, I, p. 80.

102 "Προσέταξε τὸν αὐτὸν δράκοντα βαστάζειν ἐξ ζῴδια ἐπὶ τοῦ νώτου αὐτοῦ."—Pitra, ed., *Analecta sacra*, V, p. 300. Quoted in Robert Eisler, *Weltenmantel und Himmelszelt* (1910), II, p. 389, 5.

is transferred to Chronos, whom Sophocles names "ὁ πάντ' ὁρῶν Χρόνος," while in the memorial tablet for those who fell at Chaeronea he is called "πανεπίσκοπος δαίμων." [103] The Uroboros has the meaning of eternity (αἰών) and cosmos in Horapollo. The identification of the All-Seeing with Time probably explains the eyes on the wheels in Ezekiel's vision (A.V., 1 : 18: "As for their rings, they were so high that they were dreadful; and their rings were full of eyes round about them four"). We mention this identification because of its special importance: it indicates the relation between the *mundus archetypus* of the unconscious and the "phenomenon" of Time—in other words, it points to the *synchronicity* of archetypal events, of which I shall have more to say towards the end of this paper.

395   From Ignatius Loyola's autobiography, which he dictated to Loys Gonzales,[104] we learn that he used to see a bright light, and sometimes this apparition seemed to him to have the form of a serpent. It appeared to be full of shining eyes, which were yet no eyes. At first he was greatly comforted by the beauty of the vision, but later he recognized it to be an evil spirit.[105] This vision sums up all the aspects of our optic theme and presents a most impressive picture of the unconscious with its disseminated luminosities. One can easily imagine the perplexity which a medieval man would be bound to feel when confronted by such an eminently "psychological" intuition, especially as he had no dogmatic symbol and no adequate patristic allegory to come to his rescue. But, as a matter of fact, Ignatius was not so very wide of the mark, for multiple eyes are also a characteristic of Purusha, the Hindu Cosmic Man. The Rig-Veda (10. 90) says: "Thousand-headed is Purusha, thousand-eyed, thousand-footed. He encompasses the earth on every side and rules over the ten-finger space." [106] Monoïmos the Arabian, according to Hip-

---

103 Eisler, p. 388. "The All-seeing Chronos" and "the all-beholding daemon."
104 *The Testament of Ignatius Loyola*, trans. by E. M. Rix, p. 72.
105 Ignatius also had the vision of a "res quaedam rotunda tanquam ex auro et magna" that floated before his eyes: a thing round, as if made of gold, and great. He interpreted it as Christ appearing to him like a *sun*. Philipp Funk, *Ignatius von Loyola*, pp. 57, 65, 74, 112.
106 [Trans. derived from various sources. As Coomaraswamy explains in the *Journal of the American Oriental Society*, LVI (1946), 145–61, "the ten-finger space" (lit. "the ten-fingered") refers "macrocosmically to the distance between sky and earth and microcosmically to the space between the top of the head and

polytus, taught that the First Man (Ἄνθρωπος) was a single Monad (μία μονάς), not composed (ἀσύνθετος), indivisible (ἀδιαίρετος), and at the same time composed (συνθετή) and divisible (διαιρετή). This Monad is the iota or dot (μία κεραία), and this tiniest of units which corresponds to Khunrath's one *scintilla* has "many faces" (πολυπρόσωπος) and "many eyes'" (πολυόμματος).[107] Monoïmos bases himself here mainly on the prologue to the Gospel of St. John! Like Purusha, his First Man is the universe (ἄνθρωπος εἶναι τὸ πᾶν).[108]

396   Such visions must be understood as introspective intuitions that somehow capture the state of the unconscious and, at the same time, as assimilations of the central Christian idea. Naturally enough, the motif has the same meaning in modern dreams and fantasies, where it appears as the star-strewn heavens, as stars reflected in dark water, as nuggets of gold or golden sand scattered in black earth,[109] as a regatta at night, with lanterns on the dark surface of the sea, as a solitary eye in the depths of the sea or earth, as a parapsychic vision of luminous globes, and so on. Since consciousness has always been described in terms derived from the behaviour of light, it is in my view not too much to assume that these multiple luminosities correspond to tiny conscious phenomena. If the luminosity appears in monadic form as a single star, sun, or eye, it readily assumes the shape of a mandala and must then be interpreted as the self. It has nothing whatever to do with "double consciousness," because there is no indication of a dissociated personality. On the contrary, the symbols of the self have a "uniting" character.[110]

---

the chin" of a man. He continues: "I therefore consider it shown that what RV 10. 90. 1 . . . means is that Purusha, making the whole earth his footstool, fills the entire universe, and rules over it by means of the powers of vision, etc., that proceed from his face, and to which man's own powers of vision, etc., are analogous; this face, whether of God or man, being . . . itself an image of the whole threefold universe."—TRANS.]

[107] *Elenchos*, VIII, 12, 5. [Cf. *Aion*, pars. 340ff.—EDITORS.]

[108] Ibid., VIII, 12, 2.

[109] Cf. the alchemical dictum: "Seminate aurum in terram albam foliatam" (Sow the gold in white foliated earth).

[110] Cf. my remarks on the "uniting symbol" in *Psychological Types*, s.v., Definitions.

7. *Patterns of Behaviour and Archetypes*

397   We have stated that the lower reaches of the psyche begin where the function emancipates itself from the compulsive force of instinct and becomes amenable to the will, and we have defined the will as disposable energy. But that, as said, presupposes a disposing subject, capable of judgment and endowed with consciousness. In this way we arrived at the position of proving, as it were, the very thing that we started by rejecting, namely the identification of psyche with consciousness. This dilemma resolves itself once we realize how very relative consciousness is, since its contents are conscious and unconscious at the same time, i.e., conscious under one aspect and unconscious under another. As is the way of paradoxes, this statement is not immediately comprehensible.[111] We must, however, accustom ourselves to the thought that conscious and unconscious have no clear demarcations, the one beginning where the other leaves off. It is rather the case that the psyche is a conscious-unconscious whole. As to the no man's land which I have called the "personal unconscious," it is fairly easy to prove that its contents correspond exactly to our definition of the psychic. But—as we define "psychic"—is there a psychic unconscious that is not a "fringe of consciousness" and not personal?

398   I have already mentioned that Freud established the existence of archaic vestiges and primitive modes of functioning in the unconscious. Subsequent investigations have confirmed this result and brought together a wealth of observational material. In view of the structure of the body, it would be astonishing if the psyche were the only biological phenomenon not to show clear traces of its evolutionary history, and it is altogether probable that these marks are closely connected with the instinctual base. Instinct and the archaic mode meet in the bio-

[111] Freud also arrived at similar paradoxical conclusions. Thus, in his article "The Unconscious" (p. 177): he says: "An instinct can never become an object of consciousness—only the idea that represents the instinct can. *Even in the unconscious, moreover, an instinct cannot be represented otherwise than by an idea.*" (My italics.) As in my above account we were left asking, "Who is the subject of the unconscious will?" so we must ask here, "Exactly *who* has the idea of the instinct in the unconscious state?" For "unconscious" ideation is a *contradictio in adjecto.*

logical conception of the "pattern of behaviour." There are, in fact, no amorphous instincts, as every instinct bears in itself the pattern of its situation. Always it fulfils an image, and the image has fixed qualities. The instinct of the leaf-cutting ant fulfils the image of ant, tree, leaf, cutting, transport, and the little ant-garden of fungi.[112] If any one of these conditions is lacking, the instinct does not function, because it cannot exist without its total pattern, without its image. Such an image is an *a priori* type. It is inborn in the ant prior to any activity, for there can be no activity at all unless an instinct of corresponding pattern initiates and makes it possible. This schema holds true of all instincts and is found in identical form in all individuals of the same species. The same is true also of man: he has in him these *a priori* instinct-types which provide the occasion and the pattern for his activities, in so far as he functions instinctively. As a biological being he has no choice but to act in a specifically human way and fulfil his pattern of behaviour. This sets narrow limits to his possible range of volition, the more narrow the more primitive he is, and the more his consciousness is dependent upon the instinctual sphere. Although from one point of view it is quite correct to speak of the pattern of behaviour as a still-existing archaic vestige, as Nietzsche did in respect of the function of dreams, such an attitude does scant justice to the biological and psychological meaning of these types. They are not just relics or vestiges of earlier modes of functioning; they are the ever-present and biologically necessary regulators of the instinctual sphere, whose range of action covers the whole realm of the psyche and only loses its absoluteness when limited by the relative freedom of the will. We may say that the image represents the *meaning* of the instinct.

399   Although the existence of an instinctual pattern in human biology is probable, it seems very difficult to prove the existence of distinct types empirically. For the organ with which we might apprehend them—consciousness—is not only itself a transformation of the original instinctual image, but also its transformer. It is therefore not surprising that the human mind finds it impossible to specify precise types for man similar to those we know in the animal kingdom. I must confess that I can see no

112 For details see C. Lloyd Morgan, *Habit and Instinct*.

direct way to solve this problem. And yet I have succeeded, or so I believe, in finding at least an indirect way of approach to the instinctual image.

400   In what follows, I would like to give a brief description of how this discovery took place. I had often observed patients whose dreams pointed to a rich store of fantasy-material. Equally, from the patients themselves, I got the impression that they were stuffed full of fantasies, without their being able to tell me just where the inner pressure lay. I therefore took up a dream-image or an association of the patient's, and, with this as a point of departure, set him the task of elaborating or developing his theme by giving free rein to his fantasy. This, according to individual taste and talent, could be done in any number of ways, dramatic, dialectic, visual, acoustic, or in the form of dancing, painting, drawing, or modelling. The result of this technique was a vast number of complicated designs whose diversity puzzled me for years, until I was able to recognize that in this method I was witnessing the spontaneous manifestation of an unconscious process which was merely assisted by the technical ability of the patient, and to which I later gave the name "individuation process." But, long before this recognition dawned upon me, I had made the discovery that this method often diminished, to a considerable degree, the frequency and intensity of the dreams, thus reducing the inexplicable pressure exerted by the unconscious. In many cases, this brought a large measure of therapeutic success, which encouraged both myself and the patient to press forward despite the baffling nature of the results.[113] I felt bound to insist that they were baffling, if only to stop myself from framing, on the basis of certain theoretical assumptions, interpretations which I felt were not only inadequate but liable to prejudice the ingenuous productions of the patient. The more I suspected these configurations of harbouring a certain purposefulness, the less inclined I was to risk any theories about them. This reticence was not made easy for me, since in many cases I was dealing with patients who needed an intellectual *point d'appui* if they were not to get totally lost in the darkness. I had to try to give provisional interpretations at least, so far as I was able, interspersing them with innumer-

113 Cf. "The Aims of Psychotherapy," pars. 101ff.; and *Two Essays on Analytical Psychology*, pars. 343ff.

able "perhapses" and "ifs" and "buts" and never stepping beyond the bounds of the picture lying before me. I always took good care to let the interpretation of each image tail off into a question whose answer was left to the free fantasy-activity of the patient.

401   The chaotic assortment of images that at first confronted me reduced itself in the course of the work to certain well-defined themes and formal elements, which repeated themselves in identical or analogous form with the most varied individuals. I mention, as the most salient characteristics, chaotic multiplicity and order; duality; the opposition of light and dark, upper and lower, right and left; the union of opposites in a third; the quaternity (square, cross); rotation (circle, sphere); and finally the centring process and a radial arrangement that usually followed some quaternary system. Triadic formations, apart from the *complexio oppositorum* in a third, were relatively rare and formed notable exceptions which could be explained by special conditions.[114] The centring process is, in my experience, the never-to-be-surpassed climax of the whole development,[115] and is characterized as such by the fact that it brings with it the greatest possible therapeutic effect. The typical features listed above go to the limits of abstraction, yet at the same time they are the simplest expressions of the formative principles here at work. In actual reality, the patterns are infinitely more variegated and far more concrete than this would suggest. Their variety defies description. I can only say that there is probably no motif in any known mythology that does not at some time appear in these configurations. If there was any conscious knowledge of mythological motifs worth mentioning in my patients, it is left far behind by the ingenuities of creative fantasy. In general, my patients had only a minimal knowledge of mythology.

402   These facts show in an unmistakable manner how fantasies guided by unconscious regulators coincide with the records of man's mental activity as known to us from tradition and ethnological research. All the abstract features I have mentioned are in a certain sense conscious: everyone can count up to four and knows what a circle is and a square; but, as formative principles, they are unconscious, and by the same token their psychological

114 The same applies to the pentadic figures.
115 So far as the development can be ascertained from the objective material.

meaning is not conscious either. My most fundamental views and ideas derive from these experiences. First I made the observations, and only then did I hammer out my views. And so it is with the hand that guides the crayon or brush, the foot that executes the dance-step, with the eye and the ear, with the word and the thought: a dark impulse is the ultimate arbiter of the pattern, an unconscious *a priori* precipitates itself into plastic form, and one has no inkling that another person's consciousness is being guided by these same principles at the very point where one feels utterly exposed to the boundless subjective vagaries of chance. Over the whole procedure there seems to reign a dim foreknowledge not only of the pattern but of its meaning.[116] Image and meaning are identical; and as the first takes shape, so the latter becomes clear. Actually, the pattern needs no interpretation: it portrays its own meaning. There are cases where I can let interpretation go as a therapeutic requirement. Scientific knowledge, of course, is another matter. Here we have to elicit from the sum total of our experience certain concepts of the greatest possible general validity, which are not given *a priori*. This particular work entails a translation of the timeless, ever-present operative archetype into the scientific language of the present.

403   These experiences and reflections lead me to believe that there are certain collective unconscious conditions which act as regulators and stimulators of creative fantasy-activity and call forth corresponding formations by availing themselves of the existing conscious material. They behave exactly like the motive forces of dreams, for which reason active imagination, as I have called this method, to some extent takes the place of dreams. The existence of these unconscious regulators—I sometimes refer to them as "dominants" [117] because of their mode of functioning—seemed to me so important that I based upon it my hypothesis of an impersonal collective unconscious. The most remarkable thing about this method, I felt, was that it did not involve a *reductio in primam figuram*, but rather a synthesis—supported by an attitude voluntarily adopted, though for the rest wholly natural—of passive conscious material and unconscious influences, hence a kind of spontaneous amplification of

116 Cf. *Psychology and Alchemy*, pp. 211f.
117 Cf. *Two Essays on Analytical Psychology*, par. 151.

the archetypes. The images are not to be thought of as a reduction of conscious contents to their simplest denominator, as this would be the direct road to the primordial images which I said previously was unimaginable; they make their appearance only in the course of amplification.

404　　On this natural amplification process I also base my method of eliciting the meaning of dreams, for dreams behave in exactly the same way as active imagination; only the support of conscious contents is lacking. To the extent that the archetypes intervene in the shaping of conscious contents by regulating, modifying, and motivating them, they act like the instincts. It is therefore very natural to suppose that these factors are connected with the instincts and to inquire whether the typical situational patterns which these collective form-principles apparently represent are not in the end identical with the instinctual patterns, namely, with the patterns of behaviour. I must admit that up to the present I have not laid hold of any argument that would finally refute this possibility.

405　　Before I pursue my reflections further, I must stress one aspect of the archetypes which will be obvious to anybody who has practical experience of these matters. That is, the archetypes have, when they appear, a distinctly numinous character which can only be described as "spiritual," if "magical" is too strong a word. Consequently this phenomenon is of the utmost significance for the psychology of religion. In its effects it is anything but unambiguous. It can be healing or destructive, but never indifferent, provided of course that it has attained a certain degree of clarity.[118] This aspect deserves the epithet "spiritual" above all else. It not infrequently happens that the archetype appears in the form of a *spirit* in dreams or fantasy-products, or even comports itself like a ghost. There is a mystical aura about

[118] Occasionally it is associated with synchronistic or parapsychic effects. I mean by synchronicity, as I have explained elsewhere, the not uncommonly observed "coincidence" of subjective and objective happenings, which just cannot be explained causally, at least in the present state of our knowledge. On this premise astrology is based and the methods of the *I Ching*. These observations, like the astrological findings, are not generally accepted, though as we know this has never hurt the facts. I mention these special effects solely for the sake of completeness and solely for the benefit of those readers who have had occasion to convince themselves of the reality of parapsychic phenomena. For a detailed discussion, see the final paper in this volume.

its numinosity, and it has a corresponding effect upon the emotions. It mobilizes philosophical and religious convictions in the very people who deemed themselves miles above any such fits of weakness. Often it drives with unexampled passion and remorseless logic towards its goal and draws the subject under its spell, from which despite the most desperate resistance he is unable, and finally no longer even willing, to break free, because the experience brings with it a depth and fulness of meaning that was unthinkable before. I fully appreciate the resistance that all rooted convictions are bound to put up against psychological discoveries of this kind. With more foreboding than real knowledge, most people feel afraid of the menacing power that lies fettered in each of us, only waiting for the magic word to release it from the spell. This magic word, which always ends in "ism," works most successfully with those who have the least access to their interior selves and have strayed the furthest from their instinctual roots into the truly chaotic world of *collective consciousness*.

406   In spite or perhaps because of its affinity with instinct, the archetype represents the authentic element of spirit, but a spirit which is not to be identified with the human intellect, since it is the latter's *spiritus rector*. The essential content of all mythologies and all religions and all isms is archetypal. The archetype is spirit or pseudo-spirit: what it ultimately proves to be depends on the attitude of the human mind. Archetype and instinct are the most polar opposites imaginable, as can easily be seen when one compares a man who is ruled by his instinctual drives with a man who is seized by the spirit. But, just as between all opposites there obtains so close a bond that no position can be established or even thought of without its corresponding negation, so in this case also "les extrêmes se touchent." They belong together as correspondences, which is not to say that the one is derivable from the other, but that they subsist side by side as reflections in our own minds of the opposition that underlies all psychic energy. Man finds himself simultaneously driven to act and free to reflect. This contrariety in his nature has no moral significance, for instinct is not in itself bad any more than spirit is good. Both can be both. Negative electricity is as good as positive electricity: first and foremost it is electricity. The psychological opposites, too, must be regarded from a scientific

standpoint. True opposites are never incommensurables; if they were they could never unite. All contrariety notwithstanding, they do show a constant propensity to union, and Nicholas of Cusa defined God himself as a *complexio oppositorum*.

407   Opposites are extreme qualities in any state, by virtue of which that state is perceived to be real, for they form a potential. The psyche is made up of processes whose energy springs from the equilibration of all kinds of opposites. The spirit / instinct antithesis is only one of the commonest formulations, but it has the advantage of reducing the greatest number of the most important and most complex psychic processes to a common denominator. So regarded, psychic processes seem to be balances of energy flowing between spirit and instinct, though the question of whether a process is to be described as spiritual or as instinctual remains shrouded in darkness. Such evaluation or interpretation depends entirely upon the standpoint or state of the conscious mind. A poorly developed consciousness, for instance, which because of massed projections is inordinately impressed by concrete or apparently concrete things and states, will naturally see in the instinctual drives the source of all reality. It remains blissfully unaware of the spirituality of such a philosophical surmise, and is convinced that with this opinion it has established the essential instinctuality of all psychic processes. Conversely, a consciousness that finds itself in opposition to the instincts can, in consequence of the enormous influence then exerted by the archetypes, so subordinate instinct to spirit that the most grotesque "spiritual" complications may arise out of what are undoubtedly biological happenings. Here the instinctuality of the fanaticism needed for such an operation is ignored.

408   Psychic processes therefore behave like a scale along which consciousness "slides." At one moment it finds itself in the vicinity of instinct, and falls under its influence; at another, it slides along to the other end where spirit predominates and even assimilates the instinctual processes most opposed to it. These counter-positions, so fruitful of illusion, are by no means symptoms of the abnormal; on the contrary, they form the twin poles of that psychic one-sidedness which is typical of the normal man of today. Naturally this does not manifest itself only in the

spirit / instinct antithesis; it assumes many other forms, as I have shown in my *Psychological Types*.

409 This "sliding" consciousness is thoroughly characteristic of modern man. But the one-sidedness it causes can be removed by what I have called the "realization of the shadow." A less "poetic" and more scientific-looking Greco-Latin neologism could easily have been coined for this operation. In psychology, however, one is to be dissuaded from ventures of this sort, at least when dealing with eminently practical problems. Among these is the "realization of the shadow," the growing awareness of the inferior part of the personality, which should not be twisted into an intellectual activity, for it has far more the meaning of a suffering and a passion that implicate the whole man. The essence of that which has to be realized and assimilated has been expressed so trenchantly and so plastically in poetic language by the word "shadow" that it would be almost presumptuous not to avail oneself of this linguistic heritage. Even the term "inferior part of the personality" is inadequate and misleading, whereas "shadow" presumes nothing that would rigidly fix its content. The "man without a shadow" is statistically the commonest human type, one who imagines he actually *is* only what he cares to know about himself. Unfortunately neither the so-called religious man nor the man of scientific pretensions forms any exception to this rule.

410 Confrontation with an archetype or instinct is an *ethical* problem of the first magnitude, the urgency of which is felt only by people who find themselves faced with the need to assimilate the unconscious and integrate their personalities. This only falls to the lot of the man who realizes that he has a neurosis or that all is not well with his psychic constitution. These are certainly not the majority. The "common man," who is preponderantly a mass man, acts on the principle of realizing nothing, nor does he need to, because for him the only thing that commits mistakes is that vast anonymity conventionally known as "State" or "Society." But once a man knows that he is, or should be, responsible, he feels responsible also for his psychic constitution, the more so the more clearly he sees what he would have to be in order to become healthier, more stable, and more efficient. Once he is on the way to assimilating the unconscious he can be certain that he will escape no difficulty that is an integral part of

his nature. The mass man, on the other hand, has the privilege of being at all times "not guilty" of the social and political catastrophes in which the whole world is engulfed. His final calculation is thrown out accordingly; whereas the other at least has the possibility of finding a spiritual point of vantage, a kingdom that "is not of this world."

411   It would be an unpardonable sin of omission were one to overlook the *feeling-value* of the archetype. This is extremely important both theoretically and therapeutically. As a numinous factor, the archetype determines the nature of the configurational process and the course it will follow, with seeming foreknowledge, or as though it were already in possession of the goal to be circumscribed by the centring process.[119] I would like to make the way in which the archetype functions clear from this simple example. While sojourning in equatorial east Africa, on the southern slopes of Mount Elgon, I found that the natives used to step out of their huts at sunrise, hold their hands before their mouths, and spit or blow into them vigorously. Then they lifted their arms and held their hands with the palms toward the sun. I asked them the meaning of what they did, but nobody could give me an explanation. They had always done it like that, they said, and had learnt it from their parents. The medicine-man, he would know what it meant. So I asked the medicine-man. He knew as little as the others, but assured me that his grandfather had still known. It was just what people did at every sunrise, and at the first phase of the new moon. For these people, as I was able to show, the moment when the sun or the new moon appeared was "mungu," which corresponds to the Melanesian words "mana" or "mulungu" [120] and is translated by the missionaries as "God." Actually the word *athista* in Elgonyi means sun as well as God, although they deny that the sun is God. Only the moment when it rises is *mungu* or *athista*. Spittle and breath mean soul-substance. Hence they offer their soul to God, but do not know what they are doing and never have known. They do it, motivated by the same preconscious archetype which the ancient Egyptians, on their monuments, also ascribed to the sun-worshipping dog-headed baboon, albeit in

119 Cf. *Psychology and Alchemy*, Part II, for evidence of this.
120 [*Mulungu* = 'spirit, soul, daemonism, magic, prestige': *Two Essays*, par. 108, and the first paper in this volume, pars. 117, 123f.—EDITORS.]

full knowledge that this ritual gesture was in honour of God. The behaviour of the Elgonyi certainly strikes us as exceedingly primitive, but we forget that the educated Westerner behaves no differently. What the meaning of the Christmas-tree might be our forefathers knew even less than ourselves, and it is only quite recently that we have bothered to find out at all.

412   The archetype is pure, unvitiated nature,[121] and it is nature that causes man to utter words and perform actions whose meaning is unconscious to him, so unconscious that he no longer gives it a thought. A later, more conscious humanity, faced with such meaningful things whose meaning none could declare, hit upon the idea that these must be the last vestiges of a Golden Age, when there were men who knew all things and taught wisdom to the nations. In the degenerate days that followed, these teachings were forgotten and were now only repeated as mindless mechanical gestures. In view of the findings of modern psychology it cannot be doubted that there are preconscious archetypes which were never conscious and can be established only indirectly through their effects upon the conscious contents. There is in my opinion no tenable argument against the hypothesis that all the psychic functions which today seem conscious to us were once unconscious and yet worked as if they *were* conscious. We could also say that all the psychic phenomena to be found in man were already present in the natural unconscious state. To this it might be objected that it would then be far from clear why there is such a thing as consciousness at all. I would, however, remind the reader that, as we have already seen, all unconscious functioning has the automatic character of an instinct, and that the instincts are always coming into collision or, because of their compulsiveness, pursuing their courses unaltered by any influence even under conditions that may positively endanger the life of the individual. As against this, consciousness enables him to adapt in an orderly way and to check the instincts, and consequently it cannot be dispensed with. Man's capacity for consciousness alone makes him man.

413   The achievement of a synthesis of conscious and unconscious contents, and the conscious realization of the archetype's effects upon the conscious contents, represents the climax of a con-

---

[121] "Nature" here means simply that which is, and always was, given.

centrated spiritual and psychic effort, in so far as this is undertaken consciously and of set purpose. That is to say, the synthesis can also be prepared in advance and brought to a certain point—James's "bursting point"—unconsciously, whereupon it irrupts into consciousness of its own volition and confronts the latter with the formidable task of assimilating the contents that have burst in upon it, yet without damaging the viability of the two systems, i.e., of ego-consciousness on the one hand and the irrupted complex on the other. Classical examples of this process are Paul's conversion and the Trinity vision of Nicholas of Flüe.

414   By means of "active imagination" we are put in a position of advantage, for we can then make the discovery of the archetype without sinking back into the instinctual sphere, which would only lead to blank unconsciousness or, worse still, to some kind of intellectual substitute for instinct. This means—to employ once more the simile of the spectrum—that the instinctual image is to be located not at the red end but at the violet end of the colour band. The dynamism of instinct is lodged as it were in the infra-red part of the spectrum, whereas the instinctual image lies in the ultra-violet part. If we remember our colour symbolism, then, as I have said, red is not such a bad match for instinct. But for spirit, as might be expected,[122] blue would be a better match than violet. Violet is the "mystic" colour, and it certainly reflects the indubitably "mystic" or paradoxical quality of the archetype in a most satisfactory way. Violet is a compound of blue and red, although in the spectrum it is a colour in its own right. Now, it is, as it happens, rather more than just an edifying thought if we feel bound to emphasize that the archetype is more accurately characterized by violet, for, as well as being an image in its own right, it is at the same time a *dynamism* which makes itself felt in the numinosity and fascinating power of the archetypal image. The realization and assimilation of instinct never take place at the red end, i.e., by absorption into the instinctual sphere, but only through integration of the image which signifies and at the same time evokes the instinct, although in a form quite different from the one we meet on the

122 This expectation is based on the experience that blue, the colour of air and sky, is most readily used for depicting spiritual contents, whereas red, the "warm" colour, is used for feelings and emotions.

biological level. When Faust remarks to Wagner: "You are conscious only of the single urge / O may you never learn to know the other!" this is a saying that could equally well be applied to instinct in general. It has two aspects: on the one hand it is experienced as physiological dynamism, while on the other hand its multitudinous forms enter into consciousness as images and groups of images, where they develop numinous effects which offer, or appear to offer, the strictest possible contrast to instinct physiologically regarded. For anyone acquainted with religious phenomenology it is an open secret that although physical and spiritual passion are deadly enemies, they are nevertheless brothers-in-arms, for which reason it often needs the merest touch to convert the one into the other. Both are real, and together they form a pair of opposites, which is one of the most fruitful sources of psychic energy. There is no point in deriving one from the other in order to give primacy to one of them. Even if we know only one at first, and do not notice the other until much later, that does not prove that the other was not there all the time. Hot cannot be derived from cold, nor high from low. An opposition either exists in its binary form or it does not exist at all, and a being without opposites is completely unthinkable, as it would be impossible to establish its existence.

415   Absorption into the instinctual sphere, therefore, does not and cannot lead to conscious realization and assimilation of instinct, because consciousness struggles in a regular panic against being swallowed up in the primitivity and unconsciousness of sheer instinctuality. This fear is the eternal burden of the hero-myth and the theme of countless taboos. The closer one comes to the instinct-world, the more violent is the urge to shy away from it and to rescue the light of consciousness from the murks of the sultry abyss. Psychologically, however, the archetype as an image of instinct is a spiritual goal toward which the whole nature of man strives; it is the sea to which all rivers wend their way, the prize which the hero wrests from the fight with the dragon.

416   Because the archetype is a formative principle of instinctual power, its blue is contaminated with red: it appears to be violet, or again, we could interpret the simile as an apocatastasis of instinct raised to a higher frequency, just as we could easily

derive instinct from a latent (i.e., transcendent) archetype that manifests itself on a longer wave-length.[123] Although it can admittedly be no more than an analogy, I nevertheless feel tempted to recommend this violet image to my reader as an illustrative hint of the archetype's affinity with its own opposite. The creative fantasy of the alchemists sought to express this abstruse secret of nature by means of another, no less concrete, symbol: the Uroboros, or tail-eating serpent.

417   I do not want to work this simile to death, but, as the reader will understand, one is always delighted, when discussing difficult problems, to find support in a helpful analogy. In addition this simile helps to throw light on a question we have not yet asked ourselves, much less answered, the question regarding the *nature* of the archetype. The archetypal representations (images and ideas) mediated to us by the unconscious should not be confused with the archetype as such. They are very varied structures which all point back to one essentially "irrepresentable" basic form. The latter is characterized by certain formal elements and by certain fundamental meanings, although these can be grasped only approximately. The archetype as such is a psychoid factor that belongs, as it were, to the invisible, ultraviolet end of the psychic spectrum. It does not appear, in itself, to be capable of reaching consciousness. I venture this hypothesis because everything archetypal which is perceived by consciousness seems to represent a set of variations on a ground theme. One is most impressed by this act when one studies the endless variations of the mandala motif. This is a relatively simple ground form whose meaning can be said to be "central." But although it looks like the structure of a centre, it is still uncertain whether within that structure the centre or the periphery, division or non-division, is the more accentuated. Since other archetypes give rise to similar doubts, it seems to me probable that the real nature of the archetype is not capable of being made conscious, that it is transcendent, on which account I call it psychoid. Moreover every archetype, when represented to the mind, is already conscious and therefore differs to an indeterminable extent from that which caused the representation. As

123 Sir James Jeans (*Physics and Philosophy*, p. 193) points out that the shadows on the wall of Plato's cave are just as real as the invisible figures that cast them and whose existence can only be inferred mathematically.

Theodor Lipps has stressed, the nature of the psychic is unconscious. Anything conscious is part of the phenomenal world which—so modern physics teaches—does not supply explanations of the kind that objective reality requires. Objective reality requires a mathematical model, and experience shows that this is based on invisible and irrepresentable factors. Psychology cannot evade the universal validity of this fact, the less so as the observing psyche is already included in any formulation of objective reality. Nor can psychological theory be formulated mathematically, because we have no measuring rod with which to measure psychic quantities. We have to rely solely upon qualities, that is, upon perceptible phenomena. Consequently psychology is incapacitated from making any valid statement about unconscious states, or to put it another way, there is no hope that the validity of any statement about unconscious states or processes will ever be verified scientifically. Whatever we say about the archetypes, they remain visualizations or concretizations which pertain to the field of consciousness. But—we cannot speak about archetypes in any other way. We must, however, constantly bear in mind that what we mean by "archetype" is in itself irrepresentable, but has effects which make visualizations of it possible, namely, the archetypal images and ideas. We meet with a similar situation in physics: there the smallest particles are themselves irrepresentable but have effects from the nature of which we can build up a model. The archetypal image, the motif or mythologem, is a construction of this kind. When the existence of two or more irrepresentables is assumed, there is always the possibility—which we tend to overlook—that it may not be a question of two or more factors but of one only. The identity or non-identity of two irrepresentable quantities is something that cannot be proved. If on the basis of its observations psychology assumes the existence of certain irrepresentable psychoid factors, it is doing the same thing in principle as physics does when the physicist constructs an atomic model. And it is not only psychology that suffers from the misfortune of having to give its object, the unconscious, a name that has often been criticized because it is merely negative; the same thing happened in physics, since it could not avoid using the ancient term "atom" (meaning "indivisible") for the smallest particle of matter. Just as the atom is not indivisible, so, as we shall see, the unconscious is not merely unconscious. And just as physics in its psychological aspect can do no more than establish the existence of an observer without being able to assert anything about the nature of that observer, so psychology can only indicate the relation of psyche to matter without being able to make out the least thing about its nature.

418   Since psyche and matter are contained in one and the same world, and moreover are in continuous contact with one another and ultimately rest on irrepresentable, transcendental factors, it is not only possible but fairly probable, even, that psyche and matter are two different aspects of one and the same thing. The synchronicity phenomena point, it seems to me, in this direction, for they show that the nonpsychic can behave like the psychic, and vice versa, without there being any causal connection between them. Our present knowledge does not allow us to do much more than compare the relation of the psychic to the material world with two cones, whose apices, meeting in a point without extension—a real zero-point—touch and do not touch.

419   In my previous writings I have always treated archetypal phenomena as psychic, because the material to be expounded or investigated was concerned solely with ideas and images. The psychoid nature of the archetype, as put forward here, does not contradict these earlier formulations; it only means a further degree of conceptual differentiation, which became inevitable as soon as I saw myself obliged to undertake a more general analysis of the nature of the psyche and to clarify the empirical concepts concerning it, and their relation to one another.

420   Just as the "psychic infra-red," the biological instinctual psyche, gradually passes over into the physiology of the organism and thus merges with its chemical and physical conditions, so the "psychic ultra-violet," the archetype, describes a field which exhibits none of the peculiarities of the physiological and yet, in the last analysis, can no longer be regarded as psychic, although it manifests itself psychically. But physiological processes behave in the same way, without on that account being declared psychic. Although there is no form of existence that is not mediated to us psychically and only psychically, it would hardly do to say that everything is merely psychic. We must apply this argument logically to the archetypes as well. Since their essential being is unconscious to us, and still they are

experienced as spontaneous agencies, there is probably no alternative now but to describe their nature, in accordance with their chiefest effect, as "spirit," in the sense which I attempted to make plain in my paper "The Phenomenology of the Spirit in Fairytales." If so, the position of the archetype would be located beyond the psychic sphere, analogous to the position of physiological instinct, which is immediately rooted in the stuff of the organism and, with its psychoid nature, forms the bridge to matter in general. In archetypal conceptions and instinctual perceptions, spirit and matter confront one another on the psychic plane. Matter and spirit both appear in the psychic realm as distinctive qualities of conscious contents. The ultimate nature of both is transcendental, that is, irrepresentable, since the psyche and its contents are the only reality which is given to us *without a medium.*

8. *General Considerations and Prospects*

421   The problems of analytical psychology, as I have tried to outline them here, led to conclusions that astonished even me. I fancied I was working along the best scientific lines, establishing facts, observing, classifying, describing causal and functional relations, only to discover in the end that I had involved myself in a net of reflections which extend far beyond natural science and ramify into the fields of philosophy, theology, comparative religion, and the humane sciences in general. This transgression, as inevitable as it was suspect, has caused me no little worry. Quite apart from my personal incompetence in these fields, it seemed to me that my reflections were suspect also in principle, because I am profoundly convinced that the "personal equation" has a telling effect upon the results of psychological observation. The tragic thing is that psychology has no self-consistent mathematics at its disposal, but only a calculus of subjective prejudices. Also, it lacks the immense advantage of an Archimedean point such as physics enjoys. The latter observes the physical world from the psychic standpoint and can translate it into psychic terms. The psyche, on the other hand, observes itself and can only translate the psychic back into the psychic. Were physics in this position, it could do nothing except leave the physical process to its own devices, because in that way

it would be most plainly itself. There is no medium for psychology to reflect itself in: it can only portray itself in itself, and describe itself. That, logically, is also the principle of my own method: it is, at bottom, a purely experiential process in which hit and miss, interpretation and error, theory and speculation, doctor and patient, form a *symptosis* (σύμπτωσις) or a *symptoma* (σύμπτωμα)—a coming together—and at the same time are symptoms of a certain process or run of events. What I am describing, therefore, is basically no more than an outline of psychic happenings which exhibit a certain statistical frequency. We have not, scientifically speaking, removed ourselves to a plane in any way "above" the psychic process, nor have we translated it into another medium. Physics, on the other hand, is in a position to detonate mathematical formulae—the product of pure psychic activity—and kill seventy-eight thousand persons at one blow.

422   This literally "devastating" argument is calculated to reduce psychology to silence. But we can, in all modesty, point out that mathematical thinking is also a psychic function, thanks to which matter can be organized in such a way as to burst asunder the mighty forces that bind the atoms together—which it would never occur to them to do in the natural course of things, at least not upon this earth. The psyche is a disturber of the natural laws of the cosmos, and should we ever succeed in doing something to Mars with the aid of atomic fission, this too will have been brought to pass by the psyche.

423   The psyche is the world's pivot: not only is it the one great condition for the existence of a world at all, it is also an intervention in the existing natural order, and no one can say with certainty where this intervention will finally end. It is hardly necessary to stress the dignity of the psyche as an object of natural science. With all the more urgency, then, we must emphasize that the smallest alteration in the psychic factor, if it be an alteration of principle, is of the utmost significance as regards our knowledge of the world and the picture we make of it. The integration of unconscious contents into consciousness, which is the main endeavour of analytical psychology, is just such an alteration of principle, in that it does away with the sovereignty of the subjective ego-consciousness and confronts it with unconscious collective contents. Accordingly ego-consciousness seems to be dependent on two factors: firstly, on the

conditions of the collective, i.e., the social, consciousness; and secondly, on the archetypes, or dominants, of the collective unconscious. The latter fall phenomenologically into two categories: instinctual and archetypal. The first includes the natural impulses, the second the dominants that emerge into consciousness as universal ideas. Between the contents of collective consciousness, which purport to be generally accepted truths, and those of the collective unconscious there is so pronounced a contrast that the latter are rejected as totally irrational, not to say meaningless, and are most unjustifiably excluded from the scientific purview as though they did not exist. However, psychic phenomena of this kind exist with a vengeance, and if they appear nonsensical to us, that only proves that we do not understand them. Once their existence is recognized they can no longer be banished from our world-picture, even though the prevailing conscious *Weltanschauung* proves to be incapable of grasping the phenomena in question. A conscientious study of these phenomena quickly reveals their uncommon significance, and we can hardly avoid the conclusion that between collective consciousness and the collective unconscious there is an almost unbridgeable gulf over which the subject finds himself suspended.

424   As a rule, collective consciousness wins hands down with its "reasonable" generalities that cause the average intelligence no difficulty whatever. It still believes in the necessary connection of cause and effect and has scarcely taken note of the fact that causality has become relative. The shortest distance between two points is still, for it, a straight line, although physics has to reckon with innumerable shortest distances, which strikes the educated Philistine of today as exquisitely absurd. Nevertheless the impressive explosion at Hiroshima has induced an awestruck respect for even the most abstruse alembications of modern physics. The explosion which we recently had occasion to witness in Europe, though far more terrible in its repercussions, was recognized as an unmitigated psychic disaster only by the few. Rather than do this, people prefer the most preposterous political and economic theories, which are about as useful as explaining the Hiroshima explosion as the chance hit of a large meteorite.

425   If the subjective consciousness prefers the ideas and opinions of collective consciousness and identifies with them, then the contents of the collective unconscious are repressed. The repression has typical consequences: the energy-charge of the repressed contents adds itself, in some measure,[124] to that of the repressing factor, whose effectiveness is increased accordingly. The higher its charge mounts, the more the repressive attitude acquires a fanatical character and the nearer it comes to conversion into its opposite, i.e., an enantiodromia. And the more highly charged the collective consciousness, the more the ego forfeits its practical importance. It is, as it were, absorbed by the opinions and tendencies of collective consciousness, and the result of that is the mass man, the ever-ready victim of some wretched "ism." The ego keeps its integrity only if it does not identify with one of the opposites, and if it understands how to hold the balance between them. This is possible only if it remains conscious of both at once. However, the necessary insight is made exceedingly difficult not by one's social and political leaders alone, but also by one's religious mentors. They all want decision in favour of one thing, and therefore the utter identification of the individual with a necessarily one-sided "truth." Even if it were a question of some great truth, identification with it would still be a catastrophe, as it arrests all further spiritual development. Instead of knowledge one then has only belief, and sometimes that is more convenient and therefore more attractive.

426   If, on the other hand, the content of the collective unconscious is realized, if the existence and efficacy of archetypal representations are acknowledged, then a violent conflict usually breaks out between what Fechner has called the "day-time and the night-time view." Medieval man (and modern man too, in so far as he has kept the attitude of the past) lived fully conscious of the discord between worldliness, which was subject to

124 It is very probable that the archetypes, as instincts, possess a specific energy which cannot be taken away from them in the long run. The energy peculiar to the archetype is normally not sufficient to raise it into consciousness. For this it needs a definite quantum of energy flowing into the unconscious from consciousness, whether because consciousness is not using this energy or because the archetype attracts it to itself. The archetype can be deprived of its supplementary charge, but not of its specific energy.

the *princeps huius mundi* (St. John 12 : 31 and 16 : 11 [125]), and the will of God. For centuries this contradiction was demonstrated before his very eyes by the struggle between imperial and papal power. On the moral plane the conflict swelled to the everlasting cosmic tug of war between good and evil in which man was implicated on account of original sin. The medieval man had not yet fallen such a helpless victim to worldliness as the contemporary mass man, for, to offset the notorious and, so to speak, tangible powers of this world, he still acknowledged the equally influential metaphysical potencies which demanded to be taken into account. Although in one respect he was politically and socially unfree and without rights—e.g., as a serf—and also found himself in the extremely disagreeable situation of being tyrannized over by black superstition, he was at least biologically nearer to that unconscious wholeness which primitive man enjoys in even larger measure, and the wild animal possesses to perfection. Looked at from the standpoint of modern consciousness, the position of medieval man seems as deplorable as it is in need of improvement. But the much needed broadening of the mind by science has only replaced medieval one-sidedness—namely, that age-old unconsciousness which once predominated and has gradually become defunctive—by a new one-sidedness, the overvaluation of "scientifically" attested views. These each and all relate to knowledge of the external object and in a chronically one-sided way, so that nowadays the backwardness of psychic development in general and of self-knowledge in particular has become one of the most pressing contemporary problems. As a result of the prevailing one-sidedness, and in spite of the terrifying optical demonstration of an unconscious that has become alienated from the conscious, there are still vast numbers of people who are the blind and helpless victims of these conflicts, and who apply their scientific scrupulosity only to external objects, never to their own psychic condition. Yet the psychic facts are as much in need of objective scrutiny and acknowledgment. There are objective psychic factors which are every bit as important as radios and automobiles. Ultimately everything (particularly in the case of the atom-

[125] Although both passages hint that the devil was cast out during the life-time of Jesus, in the Apocalypse the business of rendering him harmless is deferred until Doomsday (Rev. 20 : 2ff.).

bomb) depends on the uses to which these factors are put, and that is always conditioned by one's state of mind. The current "isms" are the most serious threat in this respect, because they are nothing but dangerous identifications of the subjective with the collective consciousness. Such an identity infallibly produces a mass psyche with its irresistible urge to catastrophe. Subjective consciousness must, in order to escape this doom, avoid identification with collective consciousness by recognizing its shadow as well as the existence and the importance of the archetypes. These latter are an effective defence against the brute force of collective consciousness and the mass psyche that goes with it. In point of effectiveness, the religious outlook of medieval man corresponds roughly to the attitude induced in the ego by the integration of unconscious contents, with the difference that in the latter case susceptibility to environmental influences and unconsciousness are replaced by scientific objectivity and conscious knowledge. But so far as religion, for the contemporary consciousness, still means, if anything, a creed, and hence a collectively accepted system of religious statements neatly codified as dogmatic precepts, it has closer affinities with collective consciousness even though its symbols express the once-operative archetypes. So long as the communal consciousness presided over by the Church is objectively present, the psyche, as said, continues to enjoy a certain equilibrium. At all events, it constitutes a sufficiently effective defence against inflation of the ego. But once Mother Church and her motherly Eros fall into abeyance, the individual is at the mercy of any passing collectivism and the attendant mass psyche. He succumbs to social or national inflation, and the tragedy is that he does so with the same psychic attitude which had once bound him to a church.

427   But if he is independent enough to recognize the bigotedness of the social "ism," he may then be threatened with subjective inflation, for usually he is not capable of seeing that religious ideas do not, in psychological reality, rest solely upon tradition and faith, but originate with the archetypes, the "careful consideration" of which—*religere!*—constitutes the essence of religion. The archetypes are continuously present and active; as such they need no believing in, but only an intuition of their meaning and a certain sapient awe, a δεισιδαιμονία, which never

loses sight of their import. A consciousness sharpened by experience knows the catastrophic consequences that disregard of this entails for the individual as well as for society. Just as the archetype is partly a spiritual factor, and partly like a hidden meaning immanent in the instincts, so the spirit, as I have shown,[126] is two-faced and paradoxical: a great help and an equally great danger.[127] It seems as if man were destined to play a decisive role in solving this uncertainty, and to solve it moreover by virtue of his consciousness, which once started up like a light in the murk of the primeval world. Nowhere do we know for sure about these matters, but least of all where "isms" flourish, for they are only a sophisticated substitute for the lost link with psychic reality. The mass psyche that infallibly results destroys the meaning of the individual and of culture generally.

428   From this it is clear that the psyche not only disturbs the natural order but, if it loses its balance, actually destroys its own creation. Therefore the careful consideration of psychic factors is of importance in restoring not merely the individual's balance, but society's as well, otherwise the destructive tendencies easily gain the upper hand. In the same way that the atom-bomb is an unparalleled means of physical mass destruction, so the misguided development of the soul must lead to psychic mass destruction. The present situation is so sinister that one cannot suppress the suspicion that the Creator is planning another deluge that will finally exterminate the existing race of men. But if anyone imagines that a healthy belief in the existence of archetypes can be inculcated from outside, he is as simple as the people who want to outlaw war or the atom-bomb. Such measures remind one of the bishop who excommunicated the cockchafers for their unseemly proliferation. Change of consciousness begins at home; it is a secular matter that depends entirely on how far the psyche's capacity for development extends. All we know at present is that there are single individuals who are capable of developing. How great their total number is we do not know, just as we do not know what the suggestive power of an extended consciousness may be, or what influence it may

126 Cf. "The Phenomenology of the Spirit in Fairytales."
127 Aptly expressed in the logion cited by Origen (*Homiliae in Jeremiam*, XX, 3): "He who is near unto me is near unto the fire. He who is far from me is far from the kingdom." This "unclaimed saying of the Master" refers to Isaiah 33 : 14.

have upon the world at large. Effects of this kind never depend on the reasonableness of an idea, but far more on the question (which can only be answered *ex effectu*): is the time ripe for change, or not?

*

429   As I have said, the psychology of complex phenomena finds itself in an uncomfortable situation compared with the other natural sciences because it lacks a base outside its object. It can only translate itself back into its own language, or fashion itself in its own image. The more it extends its field of research and the more complicated its objects become, the more it feels the lack of a point which is distinct from those objects. And once the complexity has reached that of the empirical man, his psychology inevitably merges with the psychic process itself. It can no longer be distinguished from the latter, and so turns into it. But the effect of this is that the process attains to consciousness. In this way, psychology actualizes the unconscious urge to consciousness. It is, in fact, the coming to consciousness of the psychic process, but it is not, in the deeper sense, an explanation of this process, for no explanation of the psychic can be anything other than the living process of the psyche itself. Psychology is doomed to cancel itself out as a science and therein precisely it reaches its scientific goal. Every other science has so to speak an outside; not so psychology, whose object is the inside subject of all science.

430   Psychology therefore culminates of necessity in a developmental process which is peculiar to the psyche and consists in integrating the unconscious contents into consciousness. This means that the psychic human being becomes a whole, and becoming whole has remarkable effects on ego-consciousness which are extremely difficult to describe. I doubt my ability to give a proper account of the change that comes over the subject under the influence of the individuation process; it is a relatively rare occurrence, which is experienced only by those who have gone through the wearisome but, if the unconscious is to be integrated, indispensable business of coming to terms with the unconscious components of the personality. Once these unconscious components are made conscious, it results not only in

their assimilation to the already existing ego-personality, but in a transformation of the latter. The main difficulty is to describe the manner of this transformation. Generally speaking the ego is a hard-and-fast complex which, because tied to consciousness and its continuity, cannot easily be altered, and should not be altered unless one wants to bring on pathological disturbances. The closest analogies to an alteration of the ego are to be found in the field of psychopathology, where we meet not only with neurotic dissociations but also with the schizophrenic fragmentation, or even dissolution, of the ego. In this field, too, we can observe pathological attempts at integration— if such an expression be permitted. These consist in more or less violent irruptions of unconscious contents into consciousness, the ego proving itself incapable of assimilating the intruders. But if the structure of the ego-complex is strong enough to withstand their assault without having its framework fatally dislocated, then assimilation can take place. In that event there is an alteration of the ego as well as of the unconscious contents. Although it is able to preserve its structure, the ego is ousted from its central and dominating position and thus finds itself in the role of a passive observer who lacks the power to assert his will under all circumstances, not so much because it has been weakened in any way, as because certain considerations give it pause. That is, the ego cannot help discovering that the afflux of unconscious contents has vitalized the personality, enriched it and created a figure that somehow dwarfs the ego in scope and intensity. This experience paralyzes an over-egocentric will and convinces the ego that in spite of all difficulties it is better to be taken down a peg than to get involved in a hopeless struggle in which one is invariably handed the dirty end of the stick. In this way the will, as disposable energy, gradually subordinates itself to the stronger factor, namely to the new totality-figure I call the *self*. Naturally, in these circumstances there is the greatest temptation simply to follow the power-instinct and to identify the ego with the self outright, in order to keep up the illusion of the ego's mastery. In other cases the ego proves too weak to offer the necessary resistance to the influx of unconscious contents and is thereupon assimilated by the unconscious, which produces a blurring or darkening of ego-consciousness and its identification with a preconscious wholeness.[128] Both these developments make the realization of the self impossible, and at the same time are fatal to the maintenance of ego-consciousness. They amount, therefore, to pathological effects. The psychic phenomena recently observable in Germany fall into this category. It is abundantly clear that such an *abaissement du niveau mental,* i.e., the overpowering of the ego by unconscious contents and the consequent identification with a preconscious wholeness, possesses a prodigious psychic virulence, or power of contagion, and is capable of the most disastrous results. Developments of this kind should, therefore, be watched very carefully; they require the closest control. I would recommend anyone who feels himself threatened by such tendencies to hang a picture of St. Christopher on the wall and to meditate upon it. For the self has a functional meaning only when it can act compensatorily to ego-consciousness. If the ego is dissolved in identification with the self, it gives rise to a sort of nebulous superman with a puffed-up ego and a deflated self. Such a personage, however saviourlike or baleful his demeanour, lacks the *scintilla,* the soul-spark, the little wisp of divine light that never burns more brightly than when it has to struggle against the invading darkness. What would the rainbow be were it not limned against the lowering cloud?

431   This simile is intended to remind the reader that pathological analogies of the individuation process are not the only ones. There are spiritual monuments of quite another kind, and they are positive illustrations of our process. Above all I would mention the *koans* of Zen Buddhism, those sublime paradoxes that light up, as with a flash of lightning, the inscrutable interrelations between ego and self. In very different language, St. John of the Cross has made the same problem more readily accessible to the Westerner in his account of the "dark night of the soul." That we find it needful to draw analogies from psychopathology and from both Eastern and Western mysticism is only to be expected: the individuation process is, psychically, a border-line

128 Conscious wholeness consists in a successful union of ego and self, so that both preserve their intrinsic qualities. If, instead of this union, the ego is overpowered by the self, then the self too does not attain the form it ought to have, but remains fixed on a primitive level and can express itself only through archaic symbols.

phenomenon which needs special conditions in order to become conscious. Perhaps it is the first step along a path of development to be trodden by the men of the future—a path which, for the time being, has taken a pathological turn and landed Europe in catastrophe.

432   To one familiar with our psychology, it may seem a waste of time to keep harping on the long-established difference between becoming conscious and the coming-to-be of the self (individuation). But again and again I note that the individuation process is confused with the coming of the ego into consciousness and that the ego is in consequence identified with the self, which naturally produces a hopeless conceptual muddle. Individuation is then nothing but ego-centredness and autoeroticism. But the self comprises infinitely more than a mere ego, as the symbolism has shown from of old. It is as much one's self, and all other selves, as the ego. Individuation does not shut one out from the world, but gathers the world to oneself.

433   With this I would like to bring my exposition to an end. I have tried to sketch out the development and basic problems of our psychology and to communicate the quintessence, the very spirit, of this science. In view of the unusual difficulties of my theme, the reader may pardon the undue demands I have made upon his good-will and attention. Fundamental discussions are among the things that mould a science into shape, but they are seldom entertaining.

Supplement

434   As the points of view that have to be considered in elucidating the unconscious are often misunderstood, I would like, in connection with the foregoing discussions of principle, to examine at least two of the main prejudices somewhat more closely.

435   What above all stultifies understanding is the arrant assumption that "archetype" means an inborn idea. No biologist would ever dream of assuming that each individual acquires his general mode of behaviour afresh each time. It is much more probable that the young weaver-bird builds his characteristic nest because he is a weaver-bird and not a rabbit. Similarly, it is more probable that man is born with a specifically human mode

of behaviour and not with that of a hippopotamus or with none at all. Integral to his characteristic behaviour is his psychic phenomenology, which differs from that of a bird or quadruped. Archetypes are typical forms of behaviour which, once they become conscious, naturally present themselves *as ideas and images,* like everything else that becomes a content of consciousness. Because it is a question of characteristically human modes, it is hardly to be wondered at that we can find psychic forms in the individual which occur not only at the antipodes but also in other epochs with which archaeology provides the only link.

436   Now if we wish to prove that a certain psychic form is not a unique but a typical occurrence, this can be done only if I myself testify that, having taken the necessary precautions, I have observed the same thing in different individuals. Then other observers, too, must confirm that they have made the same or similar observations. Finally we have to establish that the same or similar phenomena can be shown to occur in the folklore of other peoples and races and in the texts that have come down to us from earlier centuries and epochs. My method and whole outlook, therefore, begin with individual psychic facts which not I alone have established, but other observers as well. The material brought forward—folkloristic, mythological, or historical—serves in the first place to demonstrate the uniformity of psychic events in time and space. But, since the meaning and substance of the typical individual forms are of the utmost importance in practice, and knowledge of them plays a considerable role in each individual case, it is inevitable that the mythologem and its content will also be drawn into the limelight. This is not to say that the purpose of the investigation is to interpret the mythologem. But, precisely in this connection, a widespread prejudice reigns that the psychology of unconscious processes is a sort of *philosophy* designed to explain mythologems. This unfortunately rather common prejudice assiduously overlooks the crucial point, namely, that our psychology starts with observable facts and not with philosophical speculations. If, for instance, we study the mandala structures that are always cropping up in dreams and fantasies, ill-considered criticism might raise, and indeed has raised, the objection that we are reading Indian or Chinese philosophy into the psyche. But in reality all we have done is to compare individual

psychic occurrences with obviously related collective phenomena. The introspective trend of Eastern philosophy has brought to light material which all introspective attitudes bring to light all over the world, at all times and places. The great snag so far as the critic is concerned is that he has no personal experience of the facts in question, any more than he has of the state of mind of a lama engaged in "constructing" a mandala. These two prejudices render any access to modern psychology impossible for not a few heads with scientific pretensions. There are in addition many other stumbling-blocks that cannot be overcome by reason. We shall therefore refrain from discussing them.

437   Inability to understand, or the ignorance of the public, cannot however prevent the scientist from employing certain calculations of probability, of whose treacherous nature he is sufficiently well informed. We are fully aware that we have no more knowledge of the various states and processes of the unconscious as such than the physicist has of the process underlying physical phenomena. Of what lies beyond the phenomenal world we can have absolutely no idea, for there is no idea that could have any other source than the phenomenal world. If we are to engage in fundamental reflections about the nature of the psychic, we need an Archimedean point which alone makes a judgment possible. This can only be the nonpsychic, for, as a living phenomenon, the psychic lies embedded in something that appears to be of a nonpsychic nature. Although we perceive the latter as a psychic datum only, there are sufficient reasons for believing in its objective reality. This reality, so far as it lies outside our body's limits, is mediated to us chiefly by particles of light impinging on the retina of the eye. The organization of these particles produces a picture of the phenomenal world which depends essentially upon the constitution of the apperceiving psyche on the one hand, and upon that of the light medium on the other. The apperceiving consciousness has proved capable of a high degree of development, and constructs instruments with the help of which our range of seeing and hearing has been extended by many octaves. Consequently the postulated reality of the phenomenal world as well as the subjective world of consciousness have undergone an unparalleled expansion. The existence of this remarkable correlation be-

tween consciousness and the phenomenal world, between subjective perception and objectively real processes, i.e., their
energic effects, requires no further proof.

438   As the phenomenal world is an aggregate of processes of
atomic magnitude, it is naturally of the greatest importance to
find out whether, and if so how, the photons (shall we say)
enable us to gain a definite knowledge of the reality underlying
the mediative energy processes. Experience has shown that light
and matter both behave like separate particles and also like
waves. This paradoxical conclusion obliged us to abandon, on
the plane of atomic magnitudes, a causal description of nature
in the ordinary space-time system, and in its place to set up
invisible fields of probability in multidimensional spaces, which
do in fact represent the state of our knowledge at present.
Basic to this abstract scheme of explanation is a conception of
reality that takes account of the uncontrollable effects the observer has upon the system observed, the result being that
reality forfeits something of its objective character and that a
subjective element attaches to the physicist's picture of the
world.[129]

439   The application of statistical laws to processes of atomic
magnitude in physics has a noteworthy correspondence in
psychology, so far as psychology investigates the bases of consciousness by pursuing the conscious processes until they lose
themselves in darkness and unintelligibility, and nothing more
can be seen but effects which have an *organizing* influence on
the contents of consciousness.[130] Investigation of these effects

[129] I owe this formulation to the kind help of Professor W. Pauli.

[130] It may interest the reader to hear the opinion of a physicist on this point.
Professor Pauli, who was good enough to glance through the ms. of this supplement, writes: "As a matter of fact the physicist would expect a psychological
correspondence at this point, because the epistemological situation with regard
to the concepts 'conscious' and 'unconscious' seems to offer a pretty close analogy
to the undermentioned 'complementarity' situation in physics. On the one hand
the unconscious can only be inferred indirectly from its (organizing) effects on
conscious contents. On the other hand every 'observation of the unconscious,'
i.e., every conscious realization of unconscious contents, has an uncontrollable
reactive effect on these same contents (which as we know precludes in principle
the possibility of 'exhausting' the unconscious by making it conscious). Thus the
physicist will conclude *per analogiam* that this uncontrollable reactive effect
of the observing subject on the unconscious limits the objective character of the
latter's reality and lends it at the same time a certain subjectivity. Although the

yields the singular fact that they proceed from an unconscious, i.e., objective, reality which behaves at the same time like a subjective one—in other words, like a consciousness. Hence the reality underlying the unconscious effects includes the observing subject and is therefore constituted in a way that we cannot conceive. It is, at one and the same time, absolute subjectivity and universal truth, for in principle it can be shown to be present everywhere, which certainly cannot be said of conscious contents of a personalistic nature. The elusiveness, capriciousness, haziness, and uniqueness that the lay mind always associates with the idea of the psyche applies only to consciousness, and not to the absolute unconscious. The qualitatively rather than quantitatively definable units with which the unconscious works, namely the archetypes, therefore have a nature that *cannot with certainty be designated as psychic.*

440 Although I have been led by purely psychological considerations to doubt the exclusively psychic nature of the archetypes, psychology sees itself obliged to revise its "only psychic" assumptions in the light of the physical findings too. Physics has demonstrated, as plainly as could be wished, that in the realm of atomic magnitudes an observer is postulated in objective reality, and that only on this condition is a satisfactory scheme of explanation possible. This means that a subjective element attaches to the physicist's world picture, and secondly that a connection necessarily exists between the psyche to be explained and the objective space-time continuum. Since the physical continuum is inconceivable it follows that we can form no picture of its

position of the 'cut' between conscious and unconscious is (at least up to a point) left to the free choice of the 'psychological experimenter,' the *existence* of this 'cut' remains an unavoidable necessity. Accordingly, from the standpoint of the psychologist, the 'observed system' would consist not of physical objects only, but would also include the unconscious, while consciousness would be assigned the role of 'observing medium.' It is undeniable that the development of 'microphysics' has brought the way in which nature is described in this science very much closer to that of the newer psychology: but whereas the former, on account of the basic 'complementarity' situation, is faced with the impossibility of eliminating the effects of the observer by determinable correctives, and has therefore to abandon in principle any objective understanding of physical phenomena, the latter can supplement the purely subjective psychology of consciousness by postulating the existence of an unconscious that possesses a large measure of objective reality."

230

psychic aspect either, which also necessarily exists. Nevertheless, the relative or partial identity of psyche and physical continuum is of the greatest importance theoretically, because it brings with it a tremendous simplification by bridging over the seeming incommensurability between the physical world and the psychic, not of course in any concrete way, but from the physical side by means of mathematical equations, and from the psychological side by means of empirically derived postulates—archetypes—whose content, if any, cannot be represented to the mind. Archetypes, so far as we can observe and experience them at all, manifest themselves only through their ability to *organize* images and ideas, and this is always an unconscious process which cannot be detected until afterwards. By assimilating ideational material whose provenance in the phenomenal world is not to be contested, they become visible and *psychic*. Therefore they are recognized at first only as psychic entities and are conceived as such, with the same right with which we base the physical phenomena of immediate perception on Euclidean space. Only when it comes to explaining psychic phenomena of a minimal degree of clarity are we driven to assume that archetypes must have a nonpsychic aspect. Grounds for such a conclusion are supplied by the phenomena of synchronicity, which are associated with the activity of unconscious operators and have hitherto been regarded, or repudiated, as "telepathy," etc.[131] Scepticism should, however, be levelled only at incorrect theories and not at facts which exist in their own right. No unbiased observer can deny them. Resistance to the recognition of such facts rests principally on the repugnance people feel for an allegedly supernatural faculty tacked on to the psyche, like "clairvoyance." The very diverse and confusing aspects of these phenomena are, so far as I can see at present, completely explicable on the assumption of a psychically relative space-time continuum. As soon as a psychic content crosses the threshold of consciousness, the synchronistic marginal phenomena disappear, time and space resume their accustomed sway, and consciousness is once more isolated in its subjectivity. We have here one of those instances which can best be understood in terms of

131 The physicist Pascual Jordan ("Positivistische Bemerkungen über die parapsychischen Erscheinungen," 14ff.) has already used the idea of relative space to explain telepathic phenomena.

the physicist's idea of "complementarity." When an unconscious content passes over into consciousness its synchronistic manifestation ceases; conversely, synchronistic phenomena can be evoked by putting the subject into an unconscious state (trance). The same relationship of complementarity can be observed just as easily in all those extremely common medical cases in which certain clinical symptoms disappear when the corresponding unconscious contents are made conscious. We also know that a number of psychosomatic phenomena which are otherwise outside the control of the will can be induced by hypnosis, that is, by this same restriction of consciousness. Professor Pauli formulates the physical side of the complementarity relationship here expressed, as follows: "It rests with the free choice of the experimenter (or observer) to decide . . . which insights he will gain and which he will lose; or, to put it in popular language, whether he will measure A and ruin B or ruin A and measure B. It does *not* rest with him, however, to gain only insights and not lose any." This is particularly true of the relation between the physical standpoint and the psychological. Physics determines quantities and their relation to one another; psychology determines qualities without being able to measure quantities. Despite that, both sciences arrive at ideas which come significantly close to one another. The parallelism of psychological and physical explanations has already been pointed out by C. A. Meier in his essay "Moderne Physik—Moderne Psychologie." [132] He says: "Both sciences have, in the course of many years of independent work, amassed observations and systems of thought to match them. Both sciences have come up against certain barriers which . . . display similar basic characteristics. The object to be investigated, and the human investigator with his organs of sense and knowledge and their extensions (measuring instruments and procedures), are indissolubly bound together. That is complementarity in physics as well as in psychology." Between physics and psychology there is in fact "a genuine and authentic relationship of complementarity."

441   Once we can rid ourselves of the highly unscientific pretence that it is merely a question of chance coincidence, we shall see that synchronistic phenomena are not unusual occurrences at

[132] *Die kulturelle Bedeutung der komplexen Psychologie,* p. 362.

all, but are relatively common. This fact is in entire agreement with Rhine's "probability-exceeding" results. The psyche is not a chaos made up of random whims and accidents, but is an objective reality to which the investigator can gain access by the methods of natural science. There are indications that psychic processes stand in some sort of energy relation to the physiological substrate. In so far as they are objective events, they can hardly be interpreted as anything but energy processes,[133] or to put it another way: in spite of the nonmeasurability of psychic processes, the perceptible changes effected by the psyche cannot possibly be understood except as a phenomenon of energy. This places the psychologist in a situation which is highly repugnant to the physicist: the psychologist also talks of energy although he has nothing measurable to manipulate, besides which the concept of energy is a strictly defined mathematical quantity which cannot be applied as such to anything psychic, The formula for kinetic energy, $E = \dfrac{mv^2}{2}$, contains the factors m (mass) and v (velocity), and these would appear to be incommensurable with the nature of the empirical psyche. If psychology nevertheless insists on employing its own concept of energy for the purpose of expressing the activity (ἐνέργεια) of the psyche, it is not of course being used as a mathematical formula, but only as its analogy. But note: the analogy is itself an older intuitive idea from which the concept of physical energy originally developed. The latter rests on earlier applications of an ἐνέργεια not mathematically defined, which can be traced back to the primitive or archaic idea of the "extraordinarily potent." This mana concept is not confined to Melanesia, but can also be found in Indonesia and on the east coast of Africa; and it still echoes in the Latin *numen* and, more faintly, in *genius* (e.g., *genius loci*). The use of the term *libido* in the newer medical psychology has surprising affinities with the primitive mana.[134] This archetypal idea is therefore far from being only primitive, but differs from the physicist's conception of energy by the fact that it is essentially qualitative and not quantitative. In psychology the

133 By this I only mean that psychic phenomena have an energic aspect by virtue of which they can be described as "phenomena." I do not mean that the energic aspect embraces or explains the whole of the psyche.
134 Cf. the first paper in this volume.

exact measurement of quantities is replaced by an approximate
determination of intensities, for which purpose, in strictest contrast to physics, we enlist the function of *feeling* (valuation).
The latter takes the place, in psychology, of concrete measurement in physics. The psychic intensities and their graduated
differences point to quantitative processes which are inaccessible
to direct observation and measurement. While psychological
data are essentially qualitative, they also have a sort of latent
physical energy, since psychic phenomena exhibit a certain
quantitative aspect. Could these quantities be measured the
psyche would be bound to appear as having motion in space,
something to which the energy formula would be applicable.
Therefore, since mass and energy are of the same nature, mass
and velocity would be adequate concepts for characterizing the
psyche so far as it has any observable effects in space: in other
words, it must have an aspect under which it would appear as
mass in motion. If one is unwilling to postulate a pre-established
harmony of physical and psychic events, then they can only be
in a state of interaction. But the latter hypothesis requires a
psyche that touches matter at some point, and, conversely, a
matter with a latent psyche, a postulate not so very far removed
from certain formulations of modern physics (Eddington, Jeans,
and others). In this connection I would remind the reader of the
existence of parapsychic phenomena whose reality value can only
be appreciated by those who have had occasion to satisfy themselves by personal observation.

442   If these reflections are justified, they must have weighty consequences with regard to the nature of the psyche, since as an
objective fact it would then be intimately connected not only
with physiological and biological phenomena but with physical
events too—and, so it would appear, most intimately of all with
those that pertain to the realm of atomic physics. As my remarks
may have made clear, we are concerned first and foremost to
establish certain analogies, and no more than that; the existence
of such analogies does not entitle us to conclude that the connection is already proven. We must, in the present state of our
physical and psychological knowledge, be content with the mere
resemblance to one another of certain basic reflections. The
existing analogies, however, are significant enough in themselves
to warrant the prominence we have given them.

IV

GENERAL ASPECTS OF
DREAM PSYCHOLOGY

ON THE NATURE OF DREAMS

GENERAL ASPECTS OF DREAM PSYCHOLOGY [1]

443   Dreams have a psychic structure which is unlike that of other
contents of consciousness because, so far as we can judge from
their form and meaning, they do not show the continuity of development typical of conscious contents. They do not appear, as
a rule, to be integral components of our conscious psychic life,
but seem rather to be extraneous, apparently accidental occurrences. The reason for this exceptional position of dreams lies
in their peculiar mode of origin: they do not arise, like other
conscious contents, from any clearly discernible, logical and
emotional continuity of experience, but are remnants of a
peculiar psychic activity taking place during sleep. Their mode
of origin is sufficient in itself to isolate dreams from the other
contents of consciousness, and this is still further increased by
the content of the dreams themselves, which contrasts strikingly
with our conscious thinking.

444   An attentive observer, however, will have no difficulty in
discovering that dreams are not entirely cut off from the

1 [First published in English: "The Psychology of Dreams," in *Collected Papers
on Analytical Psychology*, edited by Constance Long (London, 1916; 2nd edn.,
London, 1917, and New York, 1920). The translation was by Dora Hecht from
a ms., which, in much expanded form, was published as "Allgemeine Gesichts-
punkte zur Psychologie des Traumes," in *Über die Energetik der Seele* (Psychologische Abhandlungen, II; Zurich, 1928). It was again expanded in *Über
psychische Energetik und das Wesen der Träume* (Zurich, 1948), and this version
is translated here.—EDITORS.]

continuity of consciousness, for in almost every dream certain details can be found which have their origin in the impressions, thoughts, and moods of the preceding day or days. To that extent a certain continuity does exist, though at first sight it points *backwards*. But anyone sufficiently interested in the dream problem cannot have failed to observe that dreams also have a continuity *forwards*—if such an expression be permitted—since dreams occasionally exert a remarkable influence on the conscious mental life even of persons who cannot be considered superstitious or particularly abnormal. These after-effects consist mostly in more or less distinct alterations of mood.

445   It is probably in consequence of this loose connection with the other contents of consciousness that the recollected dream is so extremely unstable. Many dreams baffle all attempts at reproduction, even immediately after waking; others can be remembered only with doubtful accuracy, and comparatively few can be called really distinct and clearly reproducible. This peculiar behaviour may be explained by considering the characteristics of the various elements combined in a dream. The combination of ideas in dreams is essentially *fantastic;* they are linked together in a sequence which is as a rule quite foreign to our "reality thinking," and in striking contrast to the logical sequence of ideas which we consider to be a special characteristic of conscious mental processes.

446   It is to this characteristic that dreams owe the vulgar epithet "meaningless." But before pronouncing this verdict we should remember that the dream and its context is something that *we* do not understand. With such a verdict, therefore, we would merely be projecting our own lack of understanding upon the object. But that would not prevent dreams from having an inherent meaning of their own.

447   Apart from the efforts that have been made for centuries to extract a prophetic meaning from dreams, Freud's discoveries are the first successful attempt in practice to find their real significance. His work merits the term "scientific" because he has evolved a technique which not only he but many other investigators assert achieves its object, namely the understanding of the meaning of the dream. This meaning is not identical with the fragmentary meanings suggested by the manifest dream-content.

238

448   This is not the place for a critical discussion of Freud's psychology of dreams. I shall try, rather, to give a brief summary of what may be regarded as the more or less established facts of dream psychology today.

449   The first question we must discuss is: what is our justification for attributing to dreams any other significance than the unsatisfying fragmentary meaning suggested by the manifest dream-content? One especially cogent argument in this respect is the fact that Freud discovered the hidden meaning of dreams *empirically* and *not deductively*. A further argument in favour of a possible hidden meaning is obtained by comparing dream-fantasies with other fantasies of the waking state in one and the same individual. It is not difficult to see that waking fantasies have not merely a superficial, concretistic meaning but also a deeper psychological meaning. There is a very old and wide-spread type of fantastic story, of which Aesop's fables are typical examples, that provides a very good illustration of what may be said about the meaning of fantasies in general. For instance, a fantastic tale is told about the doings of a lion and an ass. Taken superficially and concretely, the tale is an impossible phantasm, but the hidden moral meaning is obvious to anyone who reflects upon it. It is characteristic that children are pleased and satisfied with the exoteric meaning of the fable.

450   But by far the best argument for the existence of a hidden meaning in dreams is obtained by conscientiously applying the technical procedure for breaking down the manifest dream-content. This brings us to our second main point, the question of analytic procedure. Here again I desire neither to defend nor to criticize Freud's views and discoveries, but shall confine myself to what seem to me to be firmly established facts. If we start from the fact that a dream is a psychic product, we have not the least reason to suppose that its constitution and function obey laws and purposes other than those applicable to any other psychic product. In accordance with the maxim "Principles are not to be multiplied beyond the necessary," we have to treat the dream, analytically, just like any other psychic product until experience teaches us a better way.

451   We know that every psychic structure, regarded from the causal standpoint, is the result of antecedent psychic contents. We know, furthermore, that every psychic structure, regarded

239

from the final standpoint, has its own peculiar meaning and purpose in the actual psychic process. This criterion must also be applied to dreams. When, therefore, we seek a psychological explanation of a dream, we must first know what were the preceding experiences out of which it is composed. We must trace the antecedents of every element in the dream-picture. Let me give an example: someone dreams that *he is walking down a street—suddenly a child crosses in front of him and is run over by a car.*

452   We reduce the dream-picture to its antecedents with the help of the dreamer's recollections. He recognizes the street as one down which he had walked on the previous day. The child he recognizes as his brother's child, whom he had seen on the previous evening when visiting his brother. The car accident reminds him of an accident that had actually occurred a few days before, but of which he had only read in a newspaper. As we know, most people are satisfied with a reduction of this kind. "Aha," they say, "that's why I had this dream."

453   Obviously this reduction is quite unsatisfying from the scientific point of view. The dreamer had walked down many streets on the previous day; why was this particular one selected? He had read about several accidents; why did he select just this one? The discovery of a single antecedent is by no means sufficient, for a plausible determination of the dream-images results only from the competition of several causes. The collection of additional material proceeds according to the same principle of recollection, which has also been called the method of free association. The result, as can readily be understood, is an accumulation of very diverse and largely heterogeneous material, having apparently nothing in common but the fact of its evident associative connection with the dream-content, otherwise it could never have been reproduced by means of this content.

454   How far the collection of such material should go is an important question from the technical point of view. Since the entire psychic content of a life could ultimately be disclosed from any single starting point, theoretically the whole of a person's previous life-experience might be found in every dream. But we need to collect only just so much material as is absolutely necessary in order to understand the dream's meaning. The limitation of the material is obviously an arbitrary proceed-

ing, in accordance with Kant's principle that to "comprehend" a thing is to "cognize it to the extent necessary for our purpose." [2] For instance, when undertaking a survey of the causes of the French Revolution, we could, in amassing our material, include not only the history of medieval France but also that of Rome and Greece, which certainly would not be "necessary for our purpose," since we can understand the historical genesis of the Revolution just as well from much more limited material. So in collecting the material for a dream we go only so far as seems necessary to us in order to extract from it a valid meaning.

455   Except for the aforesaid arbitrary limitation, the collection of material lies outside the choice of the investigator. The material collected must now be sifted and examined according to principles which are always applied to the examination of historical or any other empirical material. The method is essentially a comparative one, which obviously does not work automatically but is largely dependent on the skill and aim of the investigator.

456   When a psychological fact has to be explained, it must be remembered that psychological data necessitate a twofold point of view, namely that of *causality* and that of *finality*. I use the word finality intentionally, in order to avoid confusion with the concept of teleology. By finality I mean merely the immanent psychological striving for a goal. Instead of "striving for a goal" one could also say "sense of purpose." All psychological phenomena have some such sense of purpose inherent in them, even merely reactive phenomena like emotional reactions. Anger over an insult has its purpose in revenge; the purpose of ostentatious mourning is to arouse the sympathy of others, and so on.

457   Applying the causal point of view to the material associated with the dream, we reduce the manifest dream-content to certain fundamental tendencies or ideas exhibited by the material. These, as one would expect, are of an elementary and general nature. For example, a young man dreams: *"I was standing in a strange garden and picked an apple from a tree. I looked about cautiously, to make sure that no one saw me."*

458   The associated dream-material is a memory of having once, when a boy, plucked a couple of pears surreptitiously from a

_____

2 [Cf. *Introduction to Logic*, p. 55.—EDITORS.]

neighbour's garden. The feeling of bad conscience, which is a prominent feature of the dream, reminds him of a situation experienced on the previous day. He met a young lady in the street—a casual acquaintance—and exchanged a few words with her. At that moment a gentleman passed whom he knew, whereupon he was suddenly seized with a curious feeling of embarrassment, as if he were doing something wrong. He associated the apple with the scene in the Garden of Eden, and also with the fact that he had never really understood why the eating of the forbidden fruit should have had such dire consequences for our first parents. This had always made him feel angry; it seemed to him an unjust act of God, for God had made men as they were, with all their curiosity and greed.

459   Another association was that sometimes his father had punished him for certain things in a way that seemed to him incomprehensible. The worst punishment had been bestowed on him after he was caught secretly watching girls bathing. This led up to the confession that he had recently begun a love-affair with a housemaid but had not yet carried it through to its natural conclusion. On the evening before the dream he had had a rendezvous with her.

460   Reviewing this material, we can see that the dream contains a very transparent reference to the last-named incident. The associative material shows that the apple episode is obviously intended as an erotic scene. For various other reasons, too, it may be considered extremely probable that this experience of the previous day has gone on working in the dream. In the dream the young man plucks the apple of Paradise, which in reality he has not yet plucked. The remainder of the material associated with the dream is concerned with another experience of the previous day, namely the peculiar feeling of bad conscience which seized the dreamer when he was talking to his casual lady acquaintance. This, again, was associated with the fall of man in Paradise, and finally with an erotic misdemeanour of his childhood, for which his father had punished him severely. All these associations are linked together by the idea of *guilt*.

461   We shall first consider this material from the causal standpoint of Freud; in other words, we shall "interpret" the dream, to use Freud's expression. A wish has been left unfulfilled from the day before. In the dream this wish is fulfilled under the

242

symbol of the apple episode. But why is this fulfilment disguised and hidden under a symbolical image instead of being expressed in a clearly sexual thought? Freud would point to the unmistakable element of guilt in this material and say that the morality inculcated into the young man from childhood is bent on repressing such wishes, and to that end brands the natural craving as something painful and incompatible. The repressed painful thought can therefore express itself only "symbolically." As these thoughts are incompatible with the moral content of consciousness, a psychic authority postulated by Freud, called the censor, prevents this wish from passing undisguised into consciousness.

462   Considering a dream from the standpoint of finality, which I contrast with the causal standpoint of Freud, does not—as I would expressely like to emphasize—involve a denial of the dream's causes, but rather a different interpretation of the associative material gathered round the dream. The material facts remain the same, but the criterion by which they are judged is different. The question may be formulated simply as follows: What is the purpose of this dream? What effect is it meant to have? These questions are not arbitrary inasmuch as they can be applied to every psychic activity. Everywhere the question of the "why" and the "wherefore" may be raised, because every organic structure consists of a complicated network of purposive functions, and each of these functions can be resolved into a series of individual facts with a purposive orientation.

463   It is clear that the material added by the dream to the previous day's erotic experience chiefly emphasizes the element of guilt in the erotic act. The same association had already shown itself to be operative in another experience of the previous day, in that meeting with the casual lady acquaintance, when the feeling of a bad conscience was automatically and inexplicably aroused, as if in that instance too the young man was doing something wrong. This feeling also plays a part in the dream and is further intensified by the association of the additional material, the erotic experience of the day before being depicted by the story of the Fall, which was followed by such severe punishment.

464   I maintain that there exists in the dreamer an unconscious propensity or tendency to represent his erotic experiences as

243

guilt. It is characteristic that the dream is followed by the association with the Fall and that the young man had never really grasped why the punishment should have been so drastic. This association throws light on the reasons why he did not think simply: "What I am doing is not right." Obviously he does not know that he might condemn his conduct as morally wrong. This is actually the case. His conscious belief is that his conduct does not matter in the least morally, as all his friends were acting in the same way, besides which he was quite unable on other grounds to understand why such a fuss should be made about it.

465   Now whether this dream should be considered meaningful or meaningless depends on a very important question, namely, whether the standpoint of morality, handed down through the ages, is itself meaningful or meaningless. I do not wish to wander off into a philosophical discussion of this question, but would merely observe that mankind must obviously have had very strong reasons for devising this morality, for otherwise it would be truly incomprehensible why such restraints should be imposed on one of man's strongest desires. If we give this fact its due, we are bound to pronounce the dream to be meaningful, because it shows the young man the necessity of looking at his erotic conduct for once from the standpoint of morality. Primitive tribes have in some respects extremely strict laws concerning sexuality. This proves that sexual morality is a not-to-be-neglected factor in the higher functions of the psyche and deserves to be taken fully into account. In the case in question we should have to say that the young man, hypnotized by his friends' example, has somewhat thoughtlessly given way to his erotic desires, unmindful of the fact that man is a morally responsible being who, voluntarily or involuntarily, submits to the morality that he himself has created.

466   In this dream we can discern a compensating function of the unconscious whereby those thoughts, inclinations, and tendencies which in conscious life are too little valued come spontaneously into action during the sleeping state, when the conscious process is to a large extent eliminated.

467   Here the question might certainly be asked: of what use is this to the dreamer if he does not understand the dream?

468   To this I must remark that understanding is not an exclu-

244

sively intellectual process for, as experience shows, a man may be influenced, and indeed convinced in the most effective way, by innumerable things of which he has no intellectual understanding. I need only remind my readers of the effectiveness of religious symbols.

469   The above example might lead one to suppose that the function of dreams is a distinctly "moral" one. Such it appears to be in this case, but if we recall the formula that dreams contain the subliminal material of a given moment, we cannot speak simply of a "moral" function. For it is worth noting that the dreams of those persons whose actions are morally unassailable bring material to light that might well be described as "immoral" in the ordinary meaning of the term. Thus it is characteristic that St. Augustine was glad that God did not hold him responsible for his dreams. The unconscious is the unknown at any given moment, so it is not surprising that dreams add to the conscious psychological situation of the moment all those aspects which are essential for a totally different point of view. It is evident that this function of dreams amounts to a psychological adjustment, a compensation absolutely necessary for properly balanced action. In a conscious process of reflection it is essential that, so far as possible, we should realize all the aspects and consequences of a problem in order to find the right solution. This process is continued automatically in the more or less unconscious state of sleep, where, as experience seems to show, all those aspects occur to the dreamer (at least by way of allusion) that during the day were insufficiently appreciated or even totally ignored—in other words, were comparatively unconscious.

470   As regards the much discussed *symbolism* of dreams, its evaluation varies according to whether it is considered from the causal or from the final standpoint. The causal approach of Freud starts from a desire or craving, that is, from the repressed dream-wish. This craving is always something comparatively simple and elementary, which can hide itself under manifold disguises. Thus the young man in question could just as well have dreamt that he had to open a door with a key, that he was flying in an aeroplane, kisssing his mother, etc. From this point of view all those things could have the same meaning. Hence it is that the more rigorous adherents of the Freudian school have

245

Diverse [handwritten margin note] cover images for same thing, Sex

come to the point of interpreting—to give a gross example—
pretty well all oblong objects in dreams as phallic symbols and
all round or hollow objects as feminine symbols.

Symbols from [handwritten] finality

471   From the standpoint of finality the images in a dream each
have an intrinsic value of their own. For instance if the young
man, instead of dreaming of the apple scene, had dreamt he
had to open a door with a key, this dream-image would probably have furnished associative material of an essentially different character, which would have supplemented the conscious
situation in a way quite different from the material connected
with the apple scene. From this standpoint, the significance lies
precisely in the diversity of symbolical expressions in the dream
and not in their uniformity of meaning. The causal point of
view tends by its very nature towards uniformity of meaning,
that is, towards a fixed significance of symbols. The final point
of view, on the other hand, perceives in the altered dream-image
the expression of an altered psychological situation. It recognizes no fixed meaning of symbols. From this standpoint, all the
dream-images are important in themselves, each one having a
special significance of its own, to which, indeed, it owes its inclusion in the dream. Keeping to our previous example, we can see
that from the final standpoint the symbol in the dream has more
the value of a parable: it does not conceal, it teaches. The apple
scene vividly recalls the sense of guilt while at the same time
disguising the deed of our first parents.

472   It is clear that we reach very dissimilar interpretations of the
meaning of dreams according to the point of view we adopt. The
question now arises: which is the better or truer interpretation?
After all, for us psychotherapists it is a practical and not merely
a theoretical necessity that we should have *some* interpretation
of the meaning of dreams. If we want to treat our patients we
must for quite practical reasons endeavour to lay hold of any
means that will enable us to educate them effectively. It should
be obvious from the foregoing example that the material associated with the dream has touched on a question calculated to
open the eyes of the young man to many things which till now
he had heedlessly overlooked. But by disregarding these things
he was really overlooking something in himself, for he has a
moral standard and a moral need just like any other man. By
trying to live without taking this fact into account his life was

246

one-sided and incomplete, as if unco-ordinated—with the same consequences for psychic life as a one-sided and incomplete diet would have for the body. In order to educate an individuality to completeness and independence we need to bring to fruition all those functions which have hitherto attained but little conscious development or none at all. And to achieve this aim we must for therapeutic reasons enter into all the unconscious aspects of the contribution made by the dream-material. This makes it abundantly clear that the standpoint of finality is of great importance as an aid to the development of the individual.

473 The causal point of view is obviously more sympathetic to the scientific spirit of our time with its strictly causalistic reasoning. Much may be said for Freud's view as a scientific explanation of dream psychology. But I must dispute its completeness, for the psyche cannot be conceived merely in causal terms but requires also a final view. Only a combination of points of view— which has not yet been achieved in a scientifically satisfactory manner, owing to the enormous difficulties, both practical and theoretical, that still remain to be overcome—can give us a more complete conception of the nature of dreams.

474 I would now like to treat briefly of some further problems of dream psychology which are contingent to a general discussion of dreams. First, as to the *classification of dreams*, I would not put too high a value either on the practical or on the theoretical importance of this question. I investigate yearly some fifteen hundred to two thousand dreams, and on the basis of this experience I can assert that typical dreams do actually exist. But they are not very frequent, and from the final point of view they lose much of the importance which the causal standpoint attaches to them on account of the fixed significance of symbols. It seems to me that the *typical motifs* in dreams are of much greater importance since they permit a comparison with the motifs of mythology. Many of those mythological motifs— in collecting which Frobenius in particular has rendered such signal service—are also found in dreams, often with precisely the same significance. Though I cannot enter into this question more fully here, I would like to emphasize that the comparison of typical dream-motifs with those of mythology suggests the idea—already put forward by Nietzsche—that dream-thinking should be regarded as a phylogenetically older mode of thought.

THE STRUCTURE AND DYNAMICS OF THE PSYCHE

Instead of multiplying examples I can best show what I mean by reference to our specimen dream. It will be remembered that the dream introduced the apple scene as a typical way of representing erotic guilt. The thought abstracted from it would boil down to: "I am doing wrong by acting like this." It is characteristic that dreams never express themselves in this logical, abstract way but always in the language of parable or simile. This is also a characteristic of primitive languages, whose flowery turns of phrase are very striking. If we remember the monuments of ancient literature, we find that what nowadays is expressed by means of abstractions was then expressed mostly by similes. Even a philosopher like Plato did not disdain to express certain fundamental ideas in this way.

475   Just as the body bears the traces of its phylogenetic development, so also does the human mind. Hence there is nothing surprising about the possibility that the figurative language of dreams is a survival from an archaic mode of thought.

476   At the same time the theft of the apple is a typical dream-motif that occurs in many different variations in numerous dreams. It is also a well-known mythological motif, which is found not only in the story of the Garden of Eden but in countless myths and fairytales from all ages and climes. It is one of those universally human symbols which can reappear autochthonously in any one, at any time. Thus dream psychology opens the way to a general comparative psychology from which we may hope to gain the same understanding of the development and structure of the human psyche as comparative anatomy has given us concerning the human body.[3]

477   Dreams, then, convey to us in figurative language—that is, in sensuous, concrete imagery—thoughts, judgments, views, directives, tendencies, which were unconscious either because of repression or through mere lack of realization. Precisely because they are contents of the unconscious, and the dream is a derivative of unconscious processes, it contains a reflection of the unconscious contents. It is not a reflection of unconscious contents in general but only of certain contents, which are linked together associatively and are selected by the conscious situation of the moment. I regard this observation as a very important one in practice. If we want to interpret a dream

[3] [The original 1916 version ends at this point.—EDITORS.]

correctly, we need a thorough knowledge of the conscious situation at that moment, because the dream contains its unconscious complement, that is, the material which the conscious situation has constellated in the unconscious. Without this knowledge it is impossible to interpret a dream correctly, except by a lucky fluke. I would like to illustrate this by an example:

478   A man once came to me for a first consultation. He told me that he was engaged in all sorts of learned pursuits and was also interested in psychoanalysis from a literary point of view. He was in the best of health, he said, and was not to be considered in any sense a patient. He was merely pursuing his psychoanalytic interests. He was very comfortably off and had plenty of time to devote himself to his pursuits. He wanted to make my acquaintance in order to be inducted by me into the theoretical secrets of analysis. He admitted it must be very boring for me to have to do with a normal person, since I must certainly find "mad" people much more interesting. He had written to me a few days before to ask when I could see him. In the course of conversation we soon came to the question of dreams. I thereupon asked him whether he had had a dream the night before he visited me. He affirmed this and told me the following dream: *"I was in a bare room. A sort of nurse received me, and wanted me to sit at a table on which stood a bottle of fermented milk, which I was supposed to drink. I wanted to go to Dr. Jung, but the nurse told me that I was in a hospital and that Dr. Jung had no time to receive me."*

479   It is clear even from the manifest content of the dream that the anticipated visit to me had somehow constellated his unconscious. He gave the following associations: Bare room: "A sort of frosty reception room, as in an official building, or the waiting-room in a hospital. I was never in a hospital as a patient." Nurse: "She looked repulsive, she was cross-eyed. That reminds me of a fortune-teller and palmist whom I once visited to have my fortune told. Once I was sick and had a deaconess as a nurse." Bottle of fermented milk: "Fermented milk is nauseating, I cannot drink it. My wife is always drinking it, and I make fun of her for this because she is obsessed with the idea that one must always be doing something for one's health. I remember I was once in a sanatorium—my nerves were not so good—and there I had to drink fermented milk."

480   At this point I interrupted him with the indiscreet question: had his neurosis entirely disappeared since then? He tried to worm out of it, but finally had to admit that he still had his neurosis, and that actually his wife had for a long time been urging him to consult me. But he certainly didn't feel so nervous that he had to consult me on that account, he was after all not mad, and I treated only mad people. It was merely that he was interested in learning about my psychological theories, etc.

481   From this we can see how the patient has falsified the situation. It suits his fancy to come to me in the guise of a philosopher and psychologist and to allow the fact of his neurosis to recede into the background. But the dream reminds him of it in a very disagreeable way and forces him to tell the truth. He has to swallow this bitter drink. His recollection of the fortune-teller shows us very clearly just how he had imagined my activities. As the dream informs him, he must first submit to treatment before he can get to me.

482   The dream rectifies the situation. It contributes the material that was lacking and thereby improves the patient's attitude. That is the reason we need dream-analysis in our therapy.

483   I do not wish to give the impression that all dreams are as simple as this one, or that they are all of this type. I believe it is true that all dreams are compensatory to the content of consciousness, but certainly not in all dreams is the compensatory function so clear as in this example. Though dreams contribute to the self-regulation of the psyche by automatically bringing up everything that is repressed or neglected or unknown, their compensatory significance is often not immediately apparent because we still have only a very incomplete knowledge of the nature and the needs of the human psyche. There are psychological compensations that seem to be very remote from the problem on hand. In these cases one must always remember that every man, in a sense, represents the whole of humanity and its history. What was possible in the history of mankind at large is also possible on a small scale in every individual. What mankind has needed may eventually be needed by the individual too. It is therefore not surprising that religious compensations play a great role in dreams. That this is increasingly so in our time is a natural consequence of the prevailing materialism of our outlook.

484   Lest it be thought that the compensatory significance of dreams is a new discovery or has simply been "made up" to suit the convenience of interpretation, I shall cite a very old and well-known example which can be found in the fourth chapter of the Book of Daniel (10–16, AV). When Nebuchadnezzar was at the height of his power he had the following dream:

> . . . I saw, and behold a tree in the midst of the earth, and the height thereof was great.
>
> The tree grew, and was strong, and the height thereof reached unto heaven, and the sight thereof to the end of all the earth.
>
> The leaves thereof were fair, and the fruit thereof much, and in it was meat for all: the beasts of the field had shadow under it, and the fowls of the heaven dwelt in the boughs thereof, and all flesh was fed of it.
>
> I saw in the visions of my head upon my bed, and behold, a watcher and an holy one came down from heaven;
>
> He cried aloud, and said thus, Hew down the tree, and cut off his branches, shake off his leaves, and scatter his fruit: let the beasts get away from under it, and the fowls from his branches.
>
> Nevertheless leave the stump of his roots in the earth, even with a band of iron and brass in the tender grass of the field; and let it be wet with the dew of heaven, and let his portion be with the beasts in the grass of the earth:
>
> Let his heart be changed from man's, and let a beast's heart be given unto him; and let seven times pass over him.

485   In the second part of the dream the tree becomes personified, so that it is easy to see that the great tree is the dreaming king himself. Daniel interprets the dream in this sense. Its meaning is obviously an attempt to compensate the king's megalomania which, according to the story, developed into a real psychosis. To interpret the dream-process as compensatory is in my view entirely consistent with the nature of the biological process in general. Freud's view tends in the same direction, since he too ascribes a compensatory role to dreams in so far as they preserve sleep. There are, as Freud has demonstrated, dreams which show how certain external stimuli that would rob the dreamer of sleep are distorted in such a way that they abet the wish to sleep, or rather the desire not to be disturbed. Equally, there are innumerable dreams in which, as Freud was able to show, intrapsychic excitations, such as personal ideas that would be

likely to release powerful affective reactions, are distorted in such a way as to fit in with a dream-context which disguises the painful ideas and makes any strong affective reaction impossible.

486   As against this, we should not overlook the fact that the very dreams which disturb sleep most—and these are not uncommon —have a dramatic structure which aims logically at creating a highly affective situation, and builds it up so efficiently that the affect unquestionably wakes the dreamer. Freud explains these dreams by saying that the censor was no longer able to suppress the painful affect. It seems to me that this explanation fails to do justice to the facts. Dreams which concern themselves in a very disagreeable manner with the painful experiences and activities of daily life and expose just the most disturbing thoughts with the most painful distinctness are known to everyone. It would, in my opinion, be unjustified to speak here of the dream's sleep-preserving, affect-disguising function. One would have to stand reality on its head to see in these dreams a confirmation of Freud's view. The same is true of those cases where repressed sexual fantasies appear undisguised in the manifest dream content.

487   I have therefore come to the conclusion that Freud's view that dreams have an essentially wish-fulfilling and sleep-preserving function is too narrow, even though the basic thought of a compensatory biological function is certainly correct. This compensatory function is concerned only to a limited extent with the sleeping state; its chief significance is rather in relation to conscious life. Dreams, I maintain, are compensatory to the conscious situation of the moment. They preserve sleep whenever possible: that is to say, they function necessarily and automatically under the influence of the sleeping state; but they break through when their function demands it, that is, when the compensatory contents are so intense that they are able to counteract sleep. A compensatory content is especially intense when it has a vital significance for conscious orientation.

488   As far back as 1906 I pointed out the compensatory relation between consciousness and the split-off complexes and also emphasized their purposive character. Flournoy did the same thing independently of me.[4] From these observations the possi-

4 Cf. my "The Psychology of Dementia Praecox." Flournoy, "Automatisme téléologique antisuicide" (1908).

bility of purposive unconscious impulses became evident. It should be emphasized, however, that the final orientation of the unconscious does not run parallel with our conscious intentions. As a rule, the unconscious content contrasts strikingly with the conscious material, particularly when the conscious attitude tends too exclusively in a direction that would threaten the vital needs of the individual. The more one-sided his conscious attitude is, and the further it deviates from the optimum, the greater becomes the possibility that vivid dreams with a strongly contrasting but purposive content will appear as an expression of the self-regulation of the psyche. Just as the body reacts purposively to injuries or infections or any abnormal conditions, so the psychic functions react to unnatural or dangerous disturbances with purposive defence-mechanisms. Among these purposive reactions we must include the dream, since it furnishes the unconscious material constellated in a given conscious situation and supplies it to consciousness in symbolical form. In this material are to be found all those associations which remained unconscious because of their feeble accentuation but which still possess sufficient energy to make themselves perceptible in the sleeping state. Naturally the purposive nature of the dream-content is not immediately discernible from outside without further investigation. An analysis of the manifest dream-content is required before we can get at the really compensatory factors in the latent dream-content. Most of the physical defence-mechanisms are of this non-obvious and, so to speak, indirect nature, and their purposiveness can be recognized only after careful investigation. I need only remind you of the significance of fever or of suppuration processes in an infected wound.

489   The processes of psychic compensation are almost always of a very individual nature, and this makes the task of proving their compensatory character considerably more difficult. Because of this peculiarity, it is often very difficult, especially for the beginner, to see how far a dream-content has a compensatory significance. On the basis of the compensation theory, one would be inclined to assume, for instance, that anyone with a too pessimistic attitude to life must have very cheerful and optimistic dreams. This expectation is true only in the case of someone whose nature allows him to be stimulated and encouraged

253

in this way. But if he has a rather different nature, his dreams will purposively assume a much blacker character than his conscious attitude. They can then follow the principle of like curing like.

490   It is therefore not easy to lay down any special rules for the type of dream-compensation. Its character is always closely bound up with the whole nature of the individual. The possibilities of compensation are without number and inexhaustible, though with increasing experience certain basic features gradually crystallize out.

491   In putting forward a compensation theory I do not wish to assert that this is the only possible theory of dreams or that it completely explains *all* the phenomena of dream-life. The dream is an extraordinarily complicated phenomenon, just as complicated and unfathomable as the phenomena of consciousness. It would be inappropriate to try to understand all conscious phenomena from the standpoint of the wish-fulfilment theory or the theory of instinct, and it is as little likely that dream-phenomena are susceptible of so simple an explanation. Nor should we regard dream-phenomena as merely compensatory and secondary to the contents of consciousness, even though it is commonly supposed that conscious life is of far greater significance for the individual than the unconscious. This view, however, may yet have to be revised, for, as our experience deepens, it will be realized that the function of the unconscious in the life of the psyche has an importance of which we perhaps have still too low an estimate. It is analytical experience, above all, which has discovered to an increasing degree the influences of the unconscious on our conscious psychic life—influences whose existence and significance had till then been overlooked. In my view, which is based on many years of experience and on extensive research, the significance of the unconscious in the total performance of the psyche is probably just as great as that of consciousness. Should this view prove correct, then not only should the function of the unconscious be regarded as compensatory and relative to the content of consciousness, but the content of consciousness would have to be regarded as relative to the momentarily constellated unconscious content. In this case active orientation towards goals and purposes would not be the privilege of consciousness alone but would also be true

of the unconscious, so that it too would be just as capable of taking a finally oriented lead. The dream, accordingly, would then have the value of a positive, guiding idea or of an aim whose vital meaning would be greatly superior to that of the momentarily constellated conscious content. This possibility meets with the approval of the *consensus gentium,* since in the superstitions of all times and races the dream has been regarded as a truth-telling oracle. Making allowances for exaggeration and prejudice, there is always a grain of truth in such widely disseminated views. Maeder has laid energetic stress on the prospective-final significance of dreams as a purposive unconscious function which paves the way for the solution of real conflicts and problems and seeks to portray it with the help of gropingly chosen symbols.[5]

492   I should like to distinguish between the *prospective* function of dreams and their *compensatory* function. The latter means that the unconscious, considered as relative to consciousness, adds to the conscious situation all those elements from the previous day which remained subliminal because of repression or because they were simply too feeble to reach consciousness. This compensation, in the sense of being a self-regulation of the psychic organism, must be called purposive.

493   The prospective function, on the other hand, is an anticipation in the unconscious of future conscious achievements, something like a preliminary exercise or sketch, or a plan roughed out in advance. Its symbolic content sometimes outlines the solution of a conflict, excellent examples of this being given in Maeder. The occurrence of prospective dreams cannot be denied. It would be wrong to call them prophetic, because at bottom they are no more prophetic than a medical diagnosis or a weather forecast. They are merely an anticipatory combination of probabilities which may coincide with the actual behaviour of things but need not necessarily agree in every detail. Only in the latter case can we speak of "prophecy." That the prospective function of dreams is sometimes greatly superior to the combinations we can consciously foresee is not surprising, since a dream results from the fusion of subliminal elements and is thus a combination of all the perceptions, thoughts, and

[5] "Sur le mouvement psychanalytique"; "Über die Funktion des Traumes"; *The Dream Problem.*

feelings which consciousness has not registered because of their feeble accentuation. In addition, dreams can rely on subliminal memory traces that are no longer able to influence consciousness effectively. With regard to prognosis, therefore, dreams are often in a much more favourable position than consciousness.

494   Although the prospective function is, in my view, an essential characteristic of dreams, one would do well not to overestimate this function, for one might easily be led to suppose that the dream is a kind of psychopomp which, because of its superior knowledge, infallibly guides life in the right direction. However much people underestimate the psychological significance of dreams, there is an equally great danger that anyone who is constantly preoccupied with dream-analysis will overestimate the significance of the unconscious for real life. But, judging from all previous experience, we do have a right to assume that the importance of the unconscious is about equal to that of consciousness. Undoubtedly there are conscious attitudes which are surpassed by the unconscious—attitudes so badly adapted to the individual as a whole that the unconscious attitude or constellation is a far better expression of his essential nature. But this is by no means always the case. Very often the dreams contribute only the merest fragments to the conscious attitude, because the latter is on the one hand sufficiently well adapted to reality and on the other satisfies fairly well the nature of the individual. A more or less exclu ve regard for the dream standpoint without considering the conscious situation would be inappropriate in this case and would serve only to confuse and disrupt the conscious performance. Only if there is an obviously unsatisfactory and defective conscious attitude have we a right to allow the unconscious a higher value. The criteria necessary for such a judgment constitute, of course, a delicate problem. It goes without saying that the value of a conscious attitude can never be judged from an exclusively collective standpoint. For this a thorough investigation of the individuality in question is needed, and only from an accurate knowledge of the individual character can it be decided in what respect the conscious attitude is unsatisfactory. When I lay stress on knowledge of individual character I do not mean that the demands of the collective standpoint should be entirely neglected. As we know, the individual is not conditioned by

himself alone but just as much by his collective relationships. When, therefore, the conscious attitude is more or less adequate, the meaning of the dream will be confined simply to its compensatory function. This is the general rule for the normal individual living under normal inner and outer conditions. For these reasons it seems to me that the compensation theory provides the right formula and fits the facts by giving dreams a compensatory function in the self-regulation of the psychic organism.

495   But when the individual deviates from the norm in the sense that his conscious attitude is unadapted both objectively and subjectively, the—under normal conditions—merely compensatory function of the unconscious becomes a guiding, prospective function capable of leading the conscious attitude in a quite different direction which is much better than the previous one, as Maeder has successfully shown in the books I have mentioned. Into this category come dreams of the Nebuchadnezzar type. It is obvious that dreams of this sort are found chiefly in people who are not living on their true level. It is equally obvious that this lack of proportion is very frequent. Hence we have frequent occasion to consider dreams from the standpoint of their prospective value.

496   There is yet another side of dreams to be considered, and one that should certainly not be overlooked. There are many people whose conscious attitude is defective not as regards adaptation to environment but as regards expression of their own character. These are people whose conscious attitude and adaptive performance exceed their capacities as individuals; that is to say, they appear to be better and more valuable than they really are. Their outward success is naturally never paid for out of their individual resources alone, but very largely out of the dynamic reserves generated by collective suggestion. Such people climb above their natural level thanks to the influence of a collective ideal or the lure of some social advantage, or the support offered by society. They have not grown inwardly to the level of their outward eminence, for which reason the unconscious in all these cases has a *negatively compensating, or reductive,* function. It is clear that in these circumstances a reduction or devaluation is just as much a compensatory effort at self-regulation as in other cases, and also that

257

this function may be eminently prospective (witness Nebuchad-
nezzar's dream). We like to associate "prospective" with the idea
of construction, preparation, synthesis. But in order to understand these reductive dreams we must entirely divorce the term
"prospective" from any such idea, for reductive dreams have an
effect that is the very reverse of constructive, preparatory, or
synthetic—it tends rather to disintegrate, to dissolve, to devalue,
even to destroy and demolish. This is naturally not to say that
the assimilation of a reductive content must have an altogether
destructive effect on the individual as a whole; on the contrary,
the effect is often very salutary, in so far as it affects merely his
attitude and not the entire personality. But this secondary effect
does not alter the essential character of such dreams, which bear
a thoroughly reductive and retrospective stamp and for this
reason cannot properly be called prospective. For purposes of
exact qualification it would be better to call them reductive
dreams and the corresponding function a reductive function of
the unconscious although, at bottom, it is still the same compensatory function. We must accustom ourselves to the fact that
the unconscious does not always present the same aspect any
more than the conscious attitude does. It alters its appearance
and its function just as much as the latter—which is another
reason why it is so extremely difficult to form any concrete idea
of the nature of the unconscious.

497   Our knowledge of the reductive function of the unconscious
we owe mainly to the researches of Freud. His dream-interpretation limits itself in essentials to the repressed personal background of the individual and its infantile-sexual aspects.
Subsequent researches then established the bridge to the archaic
elements, to the suprapersonal, historical, phylogenetic functional residues in the unconscious. Today we can safely assert
that the reductive function of dreams constellates material which
consists in the main of repressed infantile-sexual wishes (Freud),
infantile claims to power (Adler), and suprapersonal, archaic
elements of thought, feeling, and instinct. The reproduction of
such elements, with their thoroughly retrospective character,
does more than anything else to undermine effectively a position that is too high, and to reduce the individual to his human
nullity and to his dependence on physiological, historical, and
phylogenetic conditions. Every appearance of false grandeur and

importance melts away before the reductive imagery of the dream, which analyses his conscious attitude with pitiless criticism and brings up devastating material containing a complete inventory of all his most painful weaknesses. One is precluded at the outset from calling such a dream prospective, for everything in it, down to the last detail, is retrospective and can be traced back to a past which the dreamer imagined long since buried. This naturally does not prevent the dream-content from being compensatory to the conscious content and finally oriented, since the reductive tendency may sometimes be of the utmost importance for adaptation. Patients can often feel, quite spontaneously, how the dream-content is related to their conscious situation, and it is felt to be prospective, reductive, or compensatory in accordance with this sensed knowledge. Yet this is not always so, by a long way, and it must be emphasized that in general, particularly at the beginning of an analysis, the patient has an insuperable tendency to interpret the results of the analytical investigation of his material obstinately in terms of his pathogenic attitude.

498   Such cases need the help of the analyst in order to interpret their dreams correctly. This makes it exceedingly important how the analyst judges the conscious psychology of his patient. For dream-analysis is not just the practical application of a method that can be learnt mechanically; it presupposes a familiarity with the whole analytical point of view, and this can only be acquired if the analyst has been analysed himself. The greatest mistake an analyst can make is to assume that his patient has a psychology similar to his own. This projection may hit the mark once, but mostly it remains a mere projection. Everything that is unconscious is projected, and for this reason the analyst should be conscious of at least the most important contents of his unconscious, lest unconscious projections cloud his judgment. Everyone who analyses the dreams of others should constantly bear in mind that there is no simple and generally known theory of psychic phenomena, neither with regard to their nature, nor to their causes, nor to their purpose. We therefore possess no general criterion of judgment. We know that there are all kinds of psychic phenomena, but we know nothing certain about their essential nature. We know only that, though the observation of the psyche from any one isolated standpoint

can yield very valuable results, it can never produce a satisfactory theory from which one could make deductions. The sexual theory and the wish theory, like the power theory, are valuable points of view without, however, doing anything like justice to the profundity and richness of the human psyche. Had we a theory that did, we could then content ourselves with learning a method mechanically. It would then be simply a matter of reading certain signs that stood for fixed contents, and for this it would only be necessary to learn a few semiotic rules by heart. Knowledge and correct assessment of the conscious situation would then be as superfluous as in the performance of a lumbar puncture. The overworked practitioner of our day has learnt to his sorrow that the psyche remains completely refractory to all methods that approach it from a single exclusive standpoint. At present the only thing we know about the contents of the unconscious, apart from the fact that they are subliminal, is that they stand in a compensatory relationship to consciousness and are therefore essentially relative. It is for this reason that knowledge of the conscious situation is necessary if we want to understand dreams.

499   Reductive, prospective, or simply compensatory dreams do not exhaust the possibilities of interpretation. There is a type of dream which could be called simply a *reaction-dream*. One would be inclined to class in this category all those dreams which seem to be nothing more than the reproduction of an experience charged with affect, did not the analysis of such dreams disclose the deeper reason why these experiences are reproduced so faithfully. It turns out that these experiences also have a symbolical side which escaped the dreamer, and only because of this side is the experience reproduced in the dream. These dreams, however, do not belong to the reaction type, but only those in respect of which certain objective events have caused a trauma that is not merely psychic but at the same time a physical lesion of the nervous system. Such cases of severe shock were produced in abundance by the war, and here we may expect a large number of pure reaction-dreams in which the trauma is the determining factor.

500   Although it is certainly very important for the over-all functioning of the psyche that the traumatic content gradually loses its autonomy by frequent repetition and in this way takes

its place again in the psychic hierarchy, a dream of this kind, which is essentially only a reproduction of the trauma, can hardly be called compensatory. Apparently it brings back a split-off, autonomous part of the psyche, but it soon proves that conscious assimilation of the fragment reproduced by the dream does not by any means put an end to the disturbance which determined the dream. The dream calmly goes on "reproducing": that is to say, the content of the trauma, now become autonomous, goes on working and will continue to do so until the traumatic stimulus has exhausted itself. Until that happens, conscious "realization" is useless.

501   In practice it is not easy to decide whether a dream is essentially reactive or is merely reproducing a traumatic situation symbolically. But analysis can decide the question, because in the latter case the reproduction of the traumatic scene ceases at once if the interpretation is correct, whereas reactive reproduction is left undisturbed by dream-analysis.

502   We find similar reactive dreams in pathological physical conditions where, for instance, severe pain influences the course of the dream. But, in my view, it is only in exceptional cases that somatic stimuli are the determining factor. Usually they coalesce completely with the symbolical expression of the unconscious dream-content; in other words, they are used as a means of expression. Not infrequently the dreams show that there is a remarkable inner symbolical connection between an undoubted physical illness and a definite psychic problem, so that the physical disorder appears as a direct mimetic expression of the psychic situation. I mention this curious fact more for the sake of completeness than to lay any particular stress on this problematic phenomenon. It seems to me, however, that a definite connection does exist between physical and psychic disturbances and that its significance is generally underrated, though on the other hand it is boundlessly exaggerated owing to certain tendencies to regard physical disturbances merely as an expression of psychic disturbances, as is particularly the case with Christian Science. Dreams throw very interesting sidelights on the inter-functioning of body and psyche, which is why I raise this question here.

503   Another dream-determinant that deserves mention is telepathy. The authenticity of this phenomenon can no longer be disputed today. It is, of course, very simple to deny its existence

without examining the evidence, but that is an unscientific procedure which is unworthy of notice. I have found by experience that telepathy does in fact influence dreams, as has been asserted since ancient times. Certain people are particularly sensitive in this respect and often have telepathically influenced dreams. But in acknowledging the phenomenon of telepathy I am not giving unqualified assent to the popular theory of action at a distance. The phenomenon undoubtedly exists, but the theory of it does not seem to me so simple. In every case one must consider the possibilities of concordance of associations, of parallel psychic processes [6] which have been shown to play a very great role especially in families, and which also manifest themselves in an identity or far-reaching similarity of attitude. Equally one must take into account the possibility of cryptomnesia, on which special emphasis has been laid by Flournoy.[7] It sometimes causes the most astounding phenomena. Since any kind of subliminal material shows up in dreams, it is not at all surprising that cryptomnesia sometimes appears as a determining factor. I have had frequent occasion to analyse telepathic dreams, among them several whose telepathic significance was still unknown at the moment of analysis. The analysis yielded subjective material, like any other dream-analysis, in consequence of which the dream had a significance that bore on the situation of the dreamer at the moment. It yielded nothing that could have shown that the dream was telepathic. So far I have found no dream in which the telepathic content lay beyond a doubt in the associative material brought up by analysis (i.e., in the latent dream-content). It invariably lay in the manifest dream-content.

504 Usually in the literature of telepathic dreams only those are mentioned where a powerfully affective event is anticipated "telepathically" in space or time, that is to say when the human importance of the event, such as a death, would help to explain the premonition of it or its perception at a distance or at least make it more intelligible. The telepathic dreams I have observed were mostly of this type. A few of them, however, were distinguished by the remarkable fact that the manifest dream-content contained a telepathic statement about something com-

[6] Fürst, "Statistical Investigations . . . on Familial Agreement," pp. 407ff.
[7] *From India to the Planet Mars* and "Nouvelles observations sur un cas de somnambulisme avec glossolalie."

pletely unimportant, for instance the face of an unknown and quite commonplace individual, or a certain arrangement of furniture in indifferent surroundings, or the arrival of an unimportant letter, etc. Naturally when I say "unimportant" I mean only that neither by the usual questioning nor by analysis could I discover any content whose importance would have "justified" the telepathic phenomenon. In such cases one is inclined, more so than in those first mentioned, to think of "chance." But it seems to me, unfortunately, that the hypothesis of chance is always an *asylum ignorantiae*. Certainly no one will deny that very strange chance events do occur, but the fact that one can count with some probability on their repetition excludes their chance nature. I would not, of course, assert that the law behind them is anything "supernatural," but merely something which we cannot get at with our present knowledge. Thus even questionable telepathic contents possess a reality character that mocks all expectations of probability. Although I would not presume to a theoretical opinion on these matters, I nevertheless consider it right to recognize and emphasize their reality. This standpoint brings an enrichment to dream-analysis.[8]

505   As against Freud's view that the dream is essentially a wish-fulfilment, I hold with my friend and collaborator Alphonse Maeder that the dream is a *spontaneous self-portrayal, in symbolic form, of the actual situation in the unconscious.* Our view coincides at this point with the conclusions of Silberer.[9] The agreement with Silberer is the more gratifying in that it came about as the result of mutually independent work.

506   Now this view contradicts Freud's formula only in so far as it declines to make a definite statement about the meaning of dreams. Our formula merely says that the dream is a symbolical representation of an unconscious content. It leaves the question open whether these contents are always wish-fulfilments. Further researches, expressly referred to by Maeder, have shown that the sexual language of dreams is not always to be interpreted in a concretistic way [10]—that it is, in fact, an archaic language which naturally uses all the analogies readiest to hand without their necessarily coinciding with a real sexual content. It is

[8] On the question of telepathy see Rhine, *New Frontiers of the Mind.*
[9] Cf. Silberer's works on "symbol-formation": "Über die Symbolbildung."
[10] At this point we meet with agreement from Adler.

263

therefore unjustifiable to take the sexual language of dreams literally under all circumstances, while other contents are explained as symbolical. But as soon as you take the sexual metaphors as symbols for something unknown, your conception of the nature of dreams at once deepens. Maeder has demonstrated this from a practical example given by Freud.[11] So long as the sexual language of dreams is understood concretistically, there can be only a direct, outward, and concrete solution, or else nothing is done at all—one resigns oneself opportunistically to one's inveterate cowardice or laziness. There is no real conception of, and no attitude to, the problem. But that immediately becomes possible when the concretistic misconception is dropped, that is, when the patient stops taking the unconscious sexual language of the dream literally and interpreting the dream-figures as real persons.

507   Just as we tend to assume that the world is as we see it, we naïvely suppose that people are as we imagine them to be. In this latter case, unfortunately, there is no scientific test that would prove the discrepancy between perception and reality. Although the possibility of gross deception is infinitely greater here than in our perception of the physical world, we still go on naïvely projecting our own psychology into our fellow human beings. In this way everyone creates for himself a series of more or less imaginary relationships based essentially on projection. Among neurotics there are even cases where fantasy projections provide the sole means of human relationship. A person whom I perceive mainly through my projections is an *imago* or, alternatively, a *carrier* of imagos or symbols. All the contents of our unconscious are constantly being projected into our surroundings, and it is only by recognizing certain properties of the objects as projections or imagos that we are able to distinguish them from the real properties of the objects. But if we are not aware that a property of the object is a projection, we cannot do anything else but be naïvely convinced that it really does belong to the object. All human relationships swarm with these projections; anyone who cannot see this in his personal life need only have his attention drawn to the psychology of the press in wartime. *Cum grano salis,* we always see our own

11 Maeder, *The Dream Problem,* pp. 31 ff.

unavowed mistakes in our opponent. Excellent examples of this are to be found in all personal quarrels. Unless we are possessed of an unusual degree of self-awareness we shall never see through our projections but must always succumb to them, because the mind in its natural state presupposes the existence of such projections. It is the natural and given thing for unconscious contents to be projected. In a comparatively primitive person this creates that characteristic relationship to the object which Lévy-Bruhl has fittingly called "mystic identity" or "participation mystique." [12] Thus every normal person of our time, who is not reflective beyond the average, is bound to his environment by a whole system of projections. So long as all goes well, he is totally unaware of the compulsive, i.e., "magical" or "mystical," character of these relationships. But if a paranoid disturbance sets in, then these unconscious relationships turn into so many compulsive ties, decked out, as a rule, with the same unconscious material that formed the content of these projections during the normal state. So long as the libido can use these projections as agreeable and convenient bridges to the world, they will alleviate life in a positive way. But as soon as the libido wants to strike out on another path, and for this purpose begins running back along the previous bridges of projection, they will work as the greatest hindrances it is possible to imagine, for they effectively prevent any real detachment from the former object. We then witness the characteristic phenomenon of a person trying to devalue the former object as much as possible in order to detach his libido from it. But as the previous identity is due to the projection of subjective contents, complete and final detachment can only take place when the imago that mirrored itself in the object is restored, together with its meaning, to the subject. This restoration is achieved through conscious recognition of the projected content, that is, by acknowledging the "symbolic value" of the object.

508   The frequency of such projections is as certain as the fact that they are never seen through. That being so, it is hardly

12 *How Natives Think*, p. 129. It is to be regretted that Lévy-Bruhl expunged this exceedingly apt term from later editions of his books. Probably he succumbed to the attacks of those stupid persons who imagine that "mystic" means their own nonsensical conception of it. [Cf. the original edn., *Les Fonctions mentales*, p. 140.—EDITORS.]

surprising that the naïve person takes it as self-evident from the start that when he dreams of Mr. X this dream-image is identical with the real Mr. X. It is an assumption that is entirely in accord with his ordinary, uncritical conscious attitude, which makes no distinction between the object as such and the idea one has of it. But there is no denying that, looked at critically, the dream-image has only an outward and very limited connection with the object. In reality it is a complex of psychic factors that *has fashioned itself*—albeit under the influence of certain external stimuli—and therefore consists mainly of subjective factors that are peculiar to the subject and often have very little to do with the real object. We understand another person in the same way as we understand, or seek to understand, ourselves. What we do not understand in ourselves we do not understand in the other person either. So there is plenty to ensure that his image will be for the most part subjective. As we know, even an intimate friendship is no guarantee of objective knowledge.

509 Now if one begins, as the Freudian school does, by taking the manifest content of the dream as "unreal" or "symbolical," and explains that though the dream speaks of a church-spire it really means a phallus, then it is only a step to saying that the dream often speaks of sexuality but does not always mean it, and equally, that the dream often speaks of the father but really means the dreamer himself. Our imagos are constituents of our minds, and if our dreams reproduce certain ideas these ideas are primarily *our* ideas, in the structure of which our whole being is interwoven. They are subjective factors, grouping themselves as they do in the dream, and expressing this or that meaning, not for extraneous reasons but from the most intimate promptings of our psyche. The whole dream-work is essentially subjective, and a dream is a theatre in which the dreamer is himself the scene, the player, the prompter, the producer, the author, the public, and the critic. This simple truth forms the basis for a conception of the dream's meaning which I have called *interpretation on the subjective level*. Such an interpretation, as the term implies, conceives all the figures in the dream as personified features of the dreamer's own personality.[13]

13 Several examples of interpretation on the subjective level have been furnished by Maeder. The two kinds of interpretation are discussed in detail in *Two Essays on Analytical Psychology*, pp. 83ff.

510   This view has aroused a considerable amount of resistance. One line of argument appeals to the naïve assumption we have just mentioned, concerning Mr. X. Another argument is based on the question of principle: which is the more important, the "objective level" or the "subjective level"? I can really think of no valid objection to the theoretical probability of a subjective level. But the second problem is considerably more difficult. For just as the image of an object is composed subjectively on the one side, it is conditioned objectively on the other side. When I reproduce it in myself, I am producing something that is determined as much subjectively as objectively. In order to decide which side predominates in any given case, it must first be shown whether the image is reproduced for its subjective or for its objective significance. If, therefore, I dream of a person with whom I am connected by a vital interest, the interpretation on the objective level will certainly be nearer to the truth than the other. But if I dream of a person who is not important to me in reality, then interpretation on the subjective level will be nearer the truth. It is, however, possible—and this happens very frequently in practice—that the dreamer will at once associate this unimportant person with someone with whom he is connected by a strong emotion or affect. Formerly one would have said: the unimportant figure has been thrust forward in the dream intentionally, in order to cover up the painfulness of the other figure. In that case I would follow the path of nature and say: in the dream that highly emotional reminiscence has obviously been replaced by the unimportant figure of Mr. X, hence interpretation on the subjective level would be nearer the truth. To be sure, the substitution achieved by the dream amounts to a repression of the painful reminiscence. But if this reminiscence can be thrust aside so easily it cannot be all that important. The substitution shows that this personal affect allows itself to be depersonalized. I can therefore rise above it and shall not get myself back into the personal, emotional situation again by devaluing the depersonalization achieved by the dream as a mere "repression." I think I am acting more correctly if I regard the replacement of the painful figure by an unimportant one as a depersonalization of the previously personal affect. In this way the affect, or the corresponding sum of libido, has become impersonal, freed from its personal attachment to the object, and

267

I can now shift the previous real conflict on to the subjective plane and try to understand to what extent it is an exclusively subjective conflict. I would like, for clarity's sake, to illustrate this by a short example:

511   I once had a personal conflict with a Mr. A, in the course of which I gradually came to the conclusion that the fault was more on his side than on mine. About this time I had the following dream: *I consulted a lawyer on a certain matter, and to my boundless astonishment he demanded a fee of no less than five thousand francs for the consultation—which I strenuously resisted.*

512   The lawyer was an unimportant reminiscence from my student days. But the student period was important because at that time I got into many arguments and disputes. With a surge of affect, I associated the brusque manner of the lawyer with the personality of Mr. A and also with the continuing conflict. I could now proceed on the objective level and say: Mr. A is hiding behind the lawyer, therefore Mr. A is asking too much of me. He is in the wrong. Shortly before this dream a poor student approached me for a loan of five thousand francs. Thus (by association) Mr. A is a poor student, in need of help and incompetent, because he is at the beginning of his studies. Such a person has no right to make any demands or have any opinions. That, then, would be the wish-fulfilment: my opponent would be gently devalued and pushed aside, and my peace of mind would be preserved. But in reality I woke up at this point with the liveliest affect, furious with the lawyer for his presumption. So I was not in the least calmed by the "wish-fulfilment."

513   Sure enough, behind the lawyer is the unpleasant affair with Mr. A. But it is significant that the dream should dig up that unimportant jurist from my student days. I associate "lawyer" with lawsuit, being in the right, self-righteousness, and hence with that memory from my student days when, right or wrong, I often defended my thesis tenaciously, obstinately, self-righteously, in order at least to win for myself the appearance of superiority by fighting for it. All this, so I feel, has played its part in the dispute with Mr. A. Then I know that he is really myself, that part of me which is unadapted to the present and demands too much, just as I used to do—in other words, squeezes

too much libido out of me. I know then that the dispute with
Mr. A. cannot die because the self-righteous disputant in me
would still like to see it brought to a "rightful" conclusion.

514   This interpretation led to what seemed to me a meaningful
result, whereas interpretation on the objective level was unproductive, since I am not in the least interested in proving
that dreams are wish-fulfilments. If a dream shows me what sort
of mistake I am making, it gives me an opportunity to correct
my attitude, which is always an advantage. Naturally such a result can only be achieved through interpretation on the subjective level.

515   Enlightening as interpretation on the subjective level may
be in such a case, it may be entirely worthless when a vitally
important relationship is the content and cause of the conflict.
Here the dream-figure must be related to the real object. The
criterion can always be discovered from the conscious material,
except in cases where the transference enters into the problem.
The transference can easily cause falsifications of judgment, so
that the analyst may sometimes appear as the absolutely indispensable *deus ex machina* or as an equally indispensable prop for
reality. So far as the patient is concerned he actually is so. It
must be left to the analyst to decide how far he himself is
the patient's real problem. As soon as the objective level of
interpretation starts getting monotonous and unproductive, it
is time to regard the figure of the analyst as a symbol for projected contents that belong to the patient. If the analyst does not
do that, he has only two alternatives: either he can devalue, and
consequently destroy, the transference by reducing it to infantile
wishes, or he can accept its reality and sacrifice himself for the
patient, sometimes in the teeth of the latter's unconscious resistance. This is to the advantage of neither party, and the
analyst invariably comes off worst. But if it is possible to shift
the figure of the analyst on to the subjective level, all the projected contents can be restored to the patient with their original
value. An example of the withdrawal of projections can be
found in my *Two Essays on Analytical Psychology*.[14]

516   It is clear to me that anyone who is not a practising analyst
himself will see no particular point in discussing the relative

14 Concerning projections in the transference, see "Psychology of the Transference."

merits of the "subjective level" and the "objective level." But the more deeply we penetrate into the problem of dreams, the more the technical aspects of practical treatment have to be taken into account. In this regard necessity is indeed the mother of invention, for the analyst must constantly strive to develop his techniques in such a way that they can be of help even in the most difficult cases. We owe it to the difficulties presented by the daily treatment of the sick that we were driven to formulate views which shake the foundations of our everyday beliefs. Although it is a truism to say that an imago is subjective, this statement nevertheless has a somewhat philosophical ring that sounds unpleasant to certain ears. Why this should be so is immediately apparent from what was said above, that the naïve mind at once identifies the imago with the object. Anything that disturbs this assumption has an irritating effect on this class of people. The idea of a subjective level is equally repugnant to them because it disturbs the naïve assumption that conscious contents are identical with objects. As events in wartime [15] have clearly shown, our mentality is distinguished by the shameless naïveté with which we judge our enemy, and in the judgment we pronounce upon him we unwittingly reveal our own defects: we simply accuse our enemy of our own unadmitted faults. We see everything in the other, we criticize and condemn the other, we even want to improve and educate the other. There is no need for me to adduce case material to prove this proposition; the most convincing proof can be found in every newspaper. But it is quite obvious that what happens on a large scale can also happen on a small scale in the individual. Our mentality is still so primitive that only certain functions and areas have outgrown the primary mystic identity with the object. Primitive man has a minimum of self-awareness combined with a maximum of attachment to the object; hence the object can exercise a direct magical compulsion upon him. All primitive magic and religion are based on these magical attachments, which simply consist in the projection of unconscious contents into the object. Self-awareness gradually developed out of this initial state of identity and went hand in hand with the differentiation of subject and object. This differentiation was fol-

[15] The first World War.

270

lowed by the realization that certain qualities which, formerly, were naïvely attributed to the object are in reality subjective contents. Although the men of antiquity no longer believed that they were red cockatoos or brothers to the crocodile, they were still enveloped in magical fantasies. In this respect, it was not until the Age of Enlightenment that any essential advance was made. But as everyone knows, our self-awareness is still a long way behind our actual knowledge. When we allow ourselves to be irritated out of our wits by something, let us not assume that the cause of our irritation lies simply and solely outside us, in the irritating thing or person. In that way we endow them with the power to put us into the state of irritation, and possibly even one of insomnia or indigestion. We then turn round and unhesitatingly condemn the object of offence, while all the time we are raging against an unconscious part of ourselves which is projected into the exasperating object.

517 Such projections are legion. Some of them are favourable, serving as bridges for easing off the libido, some of them are unfavourable, but in practice these are never regarded as obstacles because the unfavourable projections usually settle outside our circle of intimate relationships. To this the neurotic is an exception: consciously or unconsciously, he has such an intensive relationship to his immediate surroundings that he cannot prevent even the unfavourable projections from flowing into the objects closest to him and arousing conflicts. He is therefore compelled—if he wants to be cured—to gain insight into his primitive projections to a far higher degree than the normal person does. It is true that the normal person makes the same projections, but they are better distributed: for the favourable ones the object is close at hand, for the unfavourable ones it is at a distance. It is the same for the primitive: anything strange is hostile and evil. This line of division serves a purpose, which is why the normal person feels under no obligation to make these projections conscious, although they are dangerously illusory. War psychology has made this abundantly clear: everything my country does is good, everything the others do is bad. The centre of all iniquity is invariably found to lie a few miles behind the enemy lines. Because the individual has this same primitive psychology, every attempt to bring these age-old projections to consciousness is felt as irritating. Naturally

one would like to have better relations with one's fellows, but only on the condition that *they* live up to *our* expectations—in other words, that they become willing carriers of our projections. Yet if we make ourselves conscious of these projections, it may easily act as an impediment to our relations with others, for there is then no bridge of illusion across which love and hate can stream off so relievingly, and no way of disposing so simply and satisfactorily of all those alleged virtues that are intended to edify and improve others. In consequence of this obstruction there is a damming up of libido, as a result of which the negative projections become increasingly conscious. The individual is then faced with the task of putting down to his own account all the iniquity, devilry, etc. which he has blandly attributed to others and about which he has been indignant all his life. The irritating thing about this procedure is the conviction, on the one hand, that if everybody acted in this way life would be so much more endurable, and a violent resistance, on the other hand, against applying this principle seriously to oneself. If everybody else did it, how much better the world would be; but to do it oneself—how intolerable!

518   The neurotic is *forced* by his neurosis to take this step, but the normal person is not. Instead, he acts out his psychic disturbances socially and politically, in the form of mass psychoses like wars and revolutions. The real existence of an enemy upon whom one can foist off everything evil is an enormous relief to one's conscience. You can then at least say, without hesitation, who the devil is; you are quite certain that the cause of your misfortune is outside, and not in your own attitude. Once you have accepted the somewhat disagreeable consequences of interpretation on the subjective level, however, the misgiving forces itself on you that it is surely impossible that *all* the bad qualities which irritate you in others should belong to you. By that token the great moralist, the fanatical educationist and world-improver, would be the worst of all. Much could be said about the close proximity of good and evil, and even more about the direct relations between pairs of opposites, but that would lead us too far from our theme.

519   The interpretation on the subjective level should not, of course, be carried to extremes. It is simply a question of a rather more critical examination of what is pertinent and what is not.

Something that strikes me about the object may very well be a real property of that object. But the more subjective and emotional this impression is, the more likely it is that the property will be a projection. Yet here we must make a not unimportant distinction: between the quality actually present in the object, without which a projection could not take place, and the value, significance, or energy of this quality. It is not impossible for a quality to be projected upon the object of which the object shows barely any trace in reality (for instance, the primitive projection of magical qualities into inanimate objects). But it is different with the ordinary projection of traits of character or momentary attitudes. Here it frequently happens that the object offers a hook to the projection, and even lures it out. This is generally the case when the object himself (or herself) is not conscious of the quality in question: in that way it works directly upon the unconscious of the projicient. *For all projections provoke counter-projections* when the object is unconscious of the quality projected upon it by the subject, in the same way that a transference is answered by a counter-transference from the analyst when it projects a content of which he is unconscious but which nevertheless exists in him.[16] The counter-transference is then just as useful and meaningful, or as much of a hindrance, as the transference of the patient, according to whether or not it seeks to establish that better rapport which is essential for the realization of certain unconscious contents. Like the transference, the counter-transference is compulsive, a forcible tie, because it creates a "mystical" or unconscious identity with the object. Against these unconscious ties there are always resistances—conscious resistances if the subject's attitude allows him to give his libido only voluntarily, but not to have it coaxed or forced out of him; unconscious resistances if he likes nothing better than having his libido taken away from him. Thus transference and counter-transference, if their contents remain unconscious, create abnormal and untenable relationships which aim at their own destruction.

520   But even supposing some trace of the projected quality can be found in the object, the projection still has a purely subjective significance in practice and recoils upon the subject, because

16 Cf. "Psychology of the Transference."

it gives an exaggerated value to whatever trace of that quality was present in the object.

521   When the projection corresponds to a quality actually present in the object, the projected content is nevertheless present in the subject too, where it forms a part of the object-imago. The object-imago itself is a psychological entity that is distinct from the actual perception of the object; it is an image existing independently of, and yet based on, all perception,[17] and the relative autonomy of this image remains unconscious so long as it coincides with the actual behaviour of the object. The autonomy of the imago is therefore not recognized by the conscious mind and is unconsciously projected on the object—in other words, it is contaminated with the autonomy of the object. This naturally endows the object with a compelling reality in relation to the subject and gives it an exaggerated value. This value springs from the projection of the imago on the object, from its *a priori* identity with it, with the result that the outer object becomes at the same time an inner one. In this way the outer object can exert, via the unconscious, a direct psychic influence on the subject, since, by virtue of its identity with the imago, it has so to speak a direct hand in the psychic mechanism of the subject. Consequently the object can gain "magical" power over the subject. Excellent examples of this can be found among primitives, who treat their children or any other objects with "souls" exactly as they treat their own psyches. They dare not do anything to them for fear of offending the soul of the child or object. That is why the children are given as little education as possible until the age of puberty, when suddenly a belated education is thrust upon them, often a rather gruesome one (initiation).

522   I have just said that the autonomy of the imago remains unconscious because it is identified with that of the object. The death of the object would, accordingly, be bound to produce remarkable psychological effects, since the object does not disappear completely but goes on existing in intangible form. This is indeed the case. The unconscious imago, which no longer has an object to correspond to it, becomes a ghost and now exerts

17 For the sake of completeness I should mention that no imago comes exclusively from outside. Its specific form is due just as much to the *a priori* psychic disposition, namely the archetype.

influences on the subject which cannot be distinguished in principle from psychic phenomena. The subject's unconscious projections, which canalized unconscious contents into the imago and identified it with the object, outlive the actual loss of the object and play an important part in the life of primitives as well as of all civilized peoples past and present. These phenomena offer striking proof of the autonomous existence of the object-imagos in the unconscious. They are evidently in the unconscious because they have never been consciously differentiated from the object.

523   Every advance, every conceptual achievement of mankind, has been connected with an advance in self-awareness: man differentiated himself from the object and faced Nature as something distinct from her. Any reorientation of psychological attitude will have to follow the same road: it is evident that the identity of the object with the subjective imago gives it a significance which does not properly belong to it but which it has possessed from time immemorial. This identity is the original state of things. For the subject, however, it is a primitive condition, which can last only so long as it does not lead to serious inconvenience. Overvaluation of the object is one of the things most liable to prejudice the development of the subject. An over-accentuated, "magical" object orients the subject's consciousness in the direction of the object and thwarts any attempt at individual differentiation, which would obviously have to set in with the detachment of the imago from the object. The direction of his individual differentiation cannot possibly be maintained if external factors "magically" interfere with the psychic mechanism. The detachment of the imagos that give the objects their exaggerated significance restores to the subject that split-off energy which he urgently needs for his own development.

524   To interpret the dream-imagos on the subjective level has therefore the same meaning for modern man as taking away his ancestral figures and fetishes would have for primitive man, and trying to convince him that his "medicine" is a spiritual force which dwells not in the object but in the human psyche. The primitive feels a legitimate resistance against this heretical assumption, and in the same way modern man feels that it is disagreeable, perhaps even somehow dangerous, to dissolve the

time-honoured and sacrosanct identity between imago and object. The consequences for our psychology, too, can scarcely be
imagined: we would no longer have anybody to rail against,
nobody whom we could make responsible, nobody to instruct,
improve, and punish! On the contrary we would have to begin,
in all things, with ourselves; we would have to demand of ourselves, and of no one else, all the things which we habitually
demand of others. That being so, it is understandable why the
interpretation of dream-imagos on the subjective level is no
light step, particularly as it leads to one-sidednesses and exag-
gerations in one direction or the other.

525   Apart from this purely moral difficulty there are a number
of intellectual obstacles as well. It has often been objected that
interpretation on the subjective level is a philosophical problem
and that the application of this principle verges on a *Weltanschauung* and therefore ceases to be scientific. It does not surprise me that psychology debouches into philosophy, for the
thinking that underlies philosophy is after all a psychic activity
which, as such, is the proper study of psychology. I always think
of psychology as encompassing the whole of the psyche, and that
includes philosophy and theology and many other things besides. For underlying all philosophies and all religions are the
facts of the human soul, which may ultimately be the arbiters of
truth and error.

526   It does not matter greatly to our psychology whether our
problems touch on the one sphere or on the other. We have to
do first and foremost with practical necessities. If the patient's
view of the world becomes a psychological problem, we have
to treat it regardless of whether philosophy pertains to psychology or not. Similarly, religious questions are primarily
psychological questions so far as we are concerned. It is a regrettable defect that present-day medical psychology should, in
general, hold aloof from these problems, and nowhere is this
more apparent than in the treatment of the psychogenic neuroses, which often have a better chance of cure anywhere rather
than in academic medicine. Although I am a doctor myself, and,
on the principle that dog does not eat dog, would have every
reason not to criticize the medical profession, I must nevertheless
confess that doctors are not always the best guardians of the
psychiatric art. I have often found that the medical psychologists

try to practise their art in the routine manner inculcated into them by the peculiar nature of their studies. The study of medicine consists on the one hand in storing up in the mind an enormous number of facts, which are simply memorized without any real knowledge of their foundations, and on the other hand in learning practical skills, which have to be acquired on the principle "Don't think, act!" Thus it is that, of all the professionals, the medical man has the least opportunity of developing the function of *thinking*. So it is no wonder that even psychologically trained doctors have the greatest difficulty in following my reflections, if they follow them at all. They have habituated themselves to handing out prescriptions and mechanically applying methods which they have not thought out themselves. This tendency is the most unsuitable that can be imagined for the practice of medical psychology, for it clings to the skirts of authoritarian theories and techniques and hinders the development of independent thought. I have found that even elementary distinctions, such as those between subjective level and objective level, ego and self, sign and symbol, causality and finality, etc., which are of the utmost importance in practical treatment, overtax their thinking capacities. This may explain their obstinate adherence to views that are out of date and have long been in need of revision. That this is not merely my own subjective opinion is evident from the fanatical one-sidedness and sectarian exclusiveness of certain psychoanalytical groups. Everyone knows that this attitude is a symptom of overcompensated doubt. But then, who applies psychological criteria to himself?

527   The interpretation of dreams as infantile wish-fulfilments or as finalistic "arrangements" subserving an infantile striving for power is much too narrow and fails to do justice to the essential nature of dreams. A dream, like every element in the psychic structure, is a resultant of the total psyche. Hence we may expect to find in dreams everything that has ever been of significance in the life of humanity. Just as human life is not limited to this or that fundamental instinct, but builds itself up from a multiplicity of instincts, needs, desires, and physical and psychic conditions, etc., so the dream cannot be explained by this or that element in it, however beguilingly simple such an explanation may appear to be. We can be certain that it is incorrect, because

no simple theory of instinct will ever be capable of grasping the human psyche, that mighty and mysterious thing, nor, consequently, its exponent, the dream. In order to do anything like justice to dreams, we need an interpretive equipment that must be laboriously fitted together from all branches of the humane sciences.

528   Critics have sometimes accused me outright of "philosophical" or even "theological" tendencies, in the belief that I want to explain everything "philosophically" and that my psychological views are "metaphysical." [18] But I use certain philosophical, religious, and historical material for the exclusive purpose of *illustrating* the psychological facts. If, for instance, I make use of a God-concept or an equally metaphysical concept of energy, I do so because they are images which have been found in the human psyche from the beginning. I find I must emphasize over and over again that neither the moral order, nor the idea of God, nor any religion has dropped into man's lap from outside, straight down from heaven, as it were, but that he contains all this *in nuce* within himself, and for this reason can produce it all out of himself. It is therefore idle to think that nothing but enlightenment is needed to dispel these phantoms. The ideas of the moral order and of God belong to the ineradicable substrate of the human soul. That is why any honest psychology, which is not blinded by the garish conceits of enlightenment, must come to terms with these facts. They cannot be explained away and killed with irony. In physics we can do without a God-image, but in psychology it is a definite fact that has got to be reckoned with, just as we have to reckon with "affect," "instinct," "mother," etc. It is the fault of the everlasting contamination of object and imago that people can make no conceptual distinction between "God" and "God-image," and therefore think that when one speaks of the "God-image" one is speaking of God and offering "theological" explanations. It is not for psychology, as a science, to demand a hypostatization of the God-image. But, the facts being what they are, it does have to reckon with the existence of a God-image. In the same way it reckons with instinct but does not deem itself competent to say what "instinct" really is. The psychological factor thereby

18 By this they mean the theory of archetypes. But is the biological concept of the "pattern of behaviour" also "metaphysical"?

denoted is clear to everyone, just as it is far from clear what that factor is in itself. It is equally clear that the God-image corresponds to a definite complex of psychological facts, and is thus a quantity which we can operate with; but what God is in himself remains a question outside the competence of all psychology. I regret having to repeat such elementary truths.

529   Herewith I have said pretty well all I have to say about the general aspects of dream psychology.[19] I have purposely refrained from going into details; this must be reserved for studies of case material. Our discussion of the general aspects has led us to wider problems which are unavoidable in speaking of dreams. Naturally very much more could be said about the aims of dream-analysis, but since dream-analysis is instrumental to analytical treatment in general, this could only be done if I were to embark on the whole question of therapy. But a thorough-going description of the therapy would require a number of preliminary studies that tackled the problem from different sides. This question is an exceedingly complex one, despite the fact that certain authors outdo one another in simplifications and try to make us believe that the known "roots" of the illness can be extracted with the utmost simplicity. I must warn against all such frivolous undertakings. I would rather see serious minds settling down to discuss, thoroughly and conscientiously, the great problems which analysis has brought in its train. It is really high time academic psychologists came down to earth and wanted to hear about the human psyche as it really is and not merely about laboratory experiments. It is insufferable that professors should forbid their students to have anything to do with analytical psychology, that they should prohibit the use of analytical concepts and accuse our psychology of taking account, in an unscientific manner, of "everyday experiences." I know that psychology in general could derive the greatest benefit from a serious study of the dream problem once it could rid itself of the unjustified lay prejudice that dreams are caused solely by somatic stimuli. This overrating of the somatic factor in psychiatry is one of the basic reasons why psychopathology has made no advances unless directly fertilized by analytical procedures. The dogma that "mental diseases are diseases of the brain" is a hangover from the materialism of the 1870's. It has

19 A few additions will be found in the next paper, written very much later.

become a prejudice which hinders all progress, with nothing to justify it. Even if it were true that all mental diseases are diseases of the brain, that would still be no reason for not investigating the psychic side of the disease. But the prejudice is used to discredit at the outset all attempts in this direction and to strike them dead. Yet the proof that all mental diseases are diseases of the brain has never been furnished and never can be furnished, any more than it can be proved that man thinks or acts as he does because this or that protein has broken down or formed itself in this or that cell. Such a view leads straight to the materialistic gospel: "Man *is* what he eats." Those who think in this way conceive our mental life as anabolic and catabolic processes in the brain-cells. These processes are necessarily thought of merely as laboratory processes of synthesis and disintegration—for to think of them as living processes is totally impossible so long as we cannot think in terms of the life-process itself. But that is how we would have to think of the cell-processes if validity were to be claimed for the materialistic view. In that case we would already have passed beyond materialism, for life can never be thought of as a function of matter, but only as a process existing in and for itself, to which energy and matter are subordinate. Life as a function of matter postulates spontaneous generation, and for proof of that we shall have a very long time to wait. We have no more justification for understanding the psyche as a brain-process than we have for understanding life in general from a one-sided, arbitrarily materialistic point of view that can never be proved, quite apart from the fact that the very attempt to imagine such a thing is crazy in itself and has always engendered craziness whenever it was taken seriously. We have, on the contrary, to consider the psychic process as psychic and not as an organic cell-process. However indignant people may get about "metaphysical phantoms" when cell-processes are explained vitalistically, they nevertheless continue to regard the physical hypothesis as "scientific," although it is no less fantastic. But it fits in with the materialistic prejudice, and therefore every bit of nonsense, provided only that it turns the psychic into the physical, becomes scientifically sacrosanct. Let us hope that the time is not far off when this antiquated relic of ingrained and thoughtless materialism will be eradicated from the minds of our scientists.

ON THE NATURE OF DREAMS [1]

530   Medical psychology differs from all other scientific disciplines in that it has to deal with the most complex problems
without being able to rely on tested rules of procedure, on a
series of verifiable experiments and logically explicable facts.
On the contrary, it is confronted with a mass of shifting irrational happenings, for the psyche is perhaps the most baffling
and unapproachable phenomenon with which the scientific
mind has ever had to deal. Although we must assume that all
psychic phenomena are somehow, in the broadest sense, causally
dependent, it is advisable to remember at this point that causality is in the last analysis no more than a statistical truth.
Therefore we should perhaps do well in certain cases to make
allowance for absolute irrationality even if, on heuristic grounds,
we approach each particular case by inquiring into its causality.
Even then, it is advisable to bear in mind at least one of the
classical distinctions, namely that between *causa efficiens* and
causa finalis. In psychological matters, the question "Why does
it happen?" is not necessarily more productive of results than
the other question "To what purpose does it happen?"

531   Among the many puzzles of medical psychology there is one

1 [First published as "Vom Wesen der Träume," *Ciba-Zeitschrift* (Basel), IX : 99
(July, 1945). Revised and expanded in *Über psychische Energetik und das Wesen
der Träume* (Psychologische Abhandlungen, II; Zurich, 1948).—EDITORS.]

problem-child, the dream. It would be an interesting, as well as difficult, task to examine the dream exclusively in its medical aspects, that is, with regard to the diagnosis and prognosis of pathological conditions. The dream does in fact concern itself with both health and sickness, and since, by virtue of its source in the unconscious, it draws upon a wealth of subliminal perceptions, it can sometimes produce things that are very well worth knowing. This has often proved helpful to me in cases where the differential diagnosis between organic and psychogenic symptoms presented difficulties. For prognosis, too, certain dreams are important.[2] In this field, however, the necessary preliminary studies, such as careful records of case histories and the like, are still lacking. Doctors with psychological training do not as yet make a practice of recording dreams systematically, so as to preserve material which would have a bearing on a subsequent outbreak of severe illness or a lethal issue—in other words, on events which could not be foreseen at the beginning of the record. The investigation of dreams in general is a life-work in itself, and their detailed study requires the co-operation of many workers. I have therefore preferred, in this short review, to deal with the fundamental aspects of dream psychology and interpretation in such a way that those who have no experience in this field can at least get some idea of the problem and the method of inquiry. Anyone who is familiar with the material will probably agree with me that a knowledge of fundamentals is more important than an accumulation of case histories, which still cannot make up for lack of experience.

532   The dream is a fragment of involuntary psychic activity, just conscious enough to be reproducible in the waking state. Of all psychic phenomena the dream presents perhaps the largest number of "irrational" factors. It seems to possess a minimum of that logical coherence and that hierarchy of values shown by the other contents of consciousness, and is therefore less transparent and understandable. Dreams that form logically, morally, or aesthetically satisfying wholes are exceptional. Usually a dream is a strange and disconcerting product distinguished by many "bad qualities," such as lack of logic, questionable morality, uncouth form, and apparent absurdity or nonsense. People are

---

2 Cf. "The Practical Use of Dream-Analysis."

therefore only too glad to dismiss it as stupid, meaningless, and worthless.

533   Every interpretation of a dream is a psychological statement about certain of its contents. This is not without danger, as the dreamer, like most people, usually displays an astonishing sensitiveness to critical remarks, not only if they are wrong, but even more if they are right. Since it is not possible, except under very special conditions, to work out the meaning of a dream without the collaboration of the dreamer, an extraordinary amount of tact is required not to violate his self-respect unnecessarily. For instance, what is one to say when a patient tells a number of indecent dreams and then asks: "Why should *I* have such disgusting dreams?" To this sort of question it is better to give no answer, since an answer is difficult for several reasons, especially for the beginner, and one is very apt under such circumstances to say something clumsy, above all when one thinks one knows what the answer is. So difficult is it to understand a dream that for a long time I have made it a rule, when someone tells me a dream and asks for my opinion, to say first of all to myself: "I have no idea what this dream means." After that I can begin to examine the dream.

534   Here the reader will certainly ask: "Is it worth while in any individual case to look for the meaning of a dream—supposing that dreams have any meaning at all and that this meaning can be proved?"

535   It is easy to prove that an animal is a vertebrate by laying bare the spine. But how does one proceed to lay bare the inner, meaningful structure of a dream? Apparently the dream follows no clearly determined laws or regular modes of behaviour, apart from the well-known "typical" dreams, such as nightmares. Anxiety dreams are not unusual but they are by no means the rule. Also, there are typical dream-motifs known to the layman, such as of flying, climbing stairs or mountains, going about with insufficient clothing, losing your teeth, crowds of people, hotels, railway stations, trains, aeroplanes, automobiles, frightening animals (snakes), etc. These motifs are very common but by no means sufficient to confirm the existence of any system in the organization of a dream.

536   Some people have recurrent dreams. This happens particularly in youth, but the recurrence may continue over several

decades. These are often very impressive dreams which convince one that they "must surely have a meaning." This feeling is justified in so far as one cannot, even taking the most cautious view, avoid the assumption that a definite psychic situation does arise from time to time which causes the dream. But a "psychic situation" is something that, if it can be formulated, is identical with a definite *meaning*—provided, of course, that one does not stubbornly hold to the hypothesis (certainly not proven) that all dreams can be traced back to stomach trouble or sleeping on one's back or the like. Such dreams do indeed tempt one to conjecture some kind of cause. The same is true of so-called typical motifs which repeat themselves frequently in longer series of dreams. Here again it is hard to escape the impression that they mean something.

537   But how do we arrive at a plausible meaning and how can we confirm the rightness of the interpretation? One method—which, however, is not scientific—would be to predict future happenings from the dreams by means of a dream-book and to verify the interpretation by subsequent events, assuming of course that the meaning of dreams lies in their anticipation of the future.

538   Another way to get at the meaning of the dream directly might be to turn to the past and reconstruct former experiences from the occurrence of certain motifs in the dreams. While this is possible to a limited extent, it would have a decisive value only if we could discover in this way something which, though it had actually taken place, had remained unconscious to the dreamer, or at any rate something he would not like to divulge under any circumstances. If neither is the case, then we are dealing simply with memory-images whose appearance in the dream is (a) not denied by anyone, and (b) completely irrelevant so far as a meaningful dream function is concerned, since the dreamer could just as well have supplied the information consciously. This unfortunately exhausts the possible ways of proving the meaning of a dream directly.

539   It is Freud's great achievement to have put dream-interpretation on the right track. Above all, he recognized that no interpretation can be undertaken without the dreamer. The words composing a dream-narrative have not just *one* meaning, but many meanings. If, for instance, someone dreams of a table, we

are still far from knowing what the "table" of the dreamer signifies, although the word "table" sounds unambiguous enough. For the thing we do not know is that this "table" is the very one at which his father sat when he refused the dreamer all further financial help and threw him out of the house as a good-for-nothing. The polished surface of this table stares at him as a symbol of his lamentable worthlessness in his daytime consciousness as well as in his dreams at night. This is what our dreamer understands by "table." Therefore we need the dreamer's help in order to limit the multiple meanings of words to those that are essential and convincing. That the "table" stands as a mortifying landmark in the dreamer's life may be doubted by anyone who was not present. But the dreamer does not doubt it, nor do I. Clearly, dream-interpretation is in the first place an experience which has immediate validity for only two persons.

540   If, therefore, we establish that the "table" in the dream means just that fatal table, with all that this implies, then, although we have not explained the dream, we have at least interpreted one important motif of it; that is, we have recognized the subjective context in which the word "table" is embedded.

541   We arrived at this conclusion by a methodical questioning of the dreamer's own associations. The further procedures to which Freud subjects the dream-contents I have had to reject, for they are too much influenced by the preconceived opinion that dreams are the fulfilment of "repressed wishes." Although there are such dreams, this is far from proving that all dreams are wish-fulfilments, any more than are the thoughts of our conscious psychic life. There is no ground for the assumption that the unconscious processes underlying the dream are more limited and one-sided, in form and content, than conscious processes. One would rather expect that the latter could be limited to known categories, since they usually reflect the regularity or even monotony of the conscious way of life.

542   On the basis of these conclusions and for the purpose of ascertaining the meaning of the dream, I have developed a procedure which I call "taking up the context." This consists in making sure that every shade of meaning which each salient feature of the dream has for the dreamer is determined by the

associations of the dreamer himself. I therefore proceed in the same way as I would in deciphering a difficult text. This method does not always produce an immediately understandable result; often the only thing that emerges, at first, is a hint that looks significant. To give an example: I was working once with a young man who mentioned in his anamnesis that he was happily engaged, and to a girl of "good" family. In his dreams she frequently appeared in very unflattering guise. The context showed that the dreamer's unconscious connected the figure of his bride with all kinds of scandalous stories from quite another source—which was incomprehensible to him and naturally also to me. But, from the constant repetition of such combinations, I had to conclude that, despite his conscious resistance, there existed in him an unconscious tendency to show his bride in this ambiguous light. He told me that if such a thing were true it would be a catastrophe. His acute neurosis had set in a short time after his engagement. Although it was something he could not bear to think about, this suspicion of his bride seemed to me a point of such capital importance that I advised him to instigate some inquiries. These showed the suspicion to be well founded, and the shock of the unpleasant discovery did not kill the patient but, on the contrary, cured him of his neurosis and also of his bride. Thus, although the taking up of the context resulted in an "unthinkable" meaning and hence in an apparently nonsensical interpretation, it proved correct in the light of facts which were subsequently disclosed. This case is of exemplary simplicity, and it is superfluous to point out that only rarely do dreams have so simple a solution.

543   The examination of the context is, to be sure, a simple, almost mechanical piece of work which has only a preparatory significance. But the subsequent production of a readable text, i.e., the actual interpretation of the dream, is as a rule a very exacting task. It needs psychological empathy, ability to coordinate, intuition, knowledge of the world and of men, and above all a special "canniness" which depends on wide understanding as well as on a certain "intelligence du cœur." All these presupposed qualifications, including even the last, are valuable for the art of medical diagnosis in general. No sixth sense is needed to understand dreams. But more is required than routine recipes such as are found in vulgar little dream-

286

books, or which invariably develop under the influence of pre-conceived notions. Stereotyped interpretation of dream-motifs is to be avoided; the only justifiable interpretations are those reached through a painstaking examination of the context. Even if one has great experience in these matters, one is again and again obliged, before each dream, to admit one's ignorance and, renouncing all preconceived ideas, to prepare for something entirely unexpected.

544   Even though dreams refer to a definite attitude of conscious-ness and a definite psychic situation, their roots lie deep in the unfathomably dark recesses of the conscious mind. For want of a more descriptive term we call this unknown background the unconscious. We do not know its nature in and for itself, but we observe certain effects from whose qualities we venture cer-tain conclusions in regard to the nature of the unconscious psyche. Because dreams are the most common and most normal expression of the unconscious psyche, they provide the bulk of the material for its investigation.

545   Since the meaning of most dreams is *not* in accord with the tendencies of the conscious mind but shows peculiar deviations, we must assume that the unconscious, the matrix of dreams, has an independent function. This is what I call the autonomy of the unconscious. The dream not only fails to obey our will but very often stands in flagrant opposition to our conscious inten-tions. The opposition need not always be so marked; sometimes the dream deviates only a little from the conscious attitude and introduces only slight modifications; occasionally it may even coincide with conscious contents and tendencies. When I at-tempted to express this behaviour in a formula, the concept of *compensation* seemed to me the only adequate one, for it alone is capable of summing up all the various ways in which a dream behaves. Compensation must be strictly distinguished from *com-plementation*. The concept of a complement is too narrow and too restricting; it does not suffice to explain the function of dreams, because it designates a relationship in which two things supplement one another more or less mechanically.[3] Compensa-tion, on the other hand, as the term implies, means balancing

3 This is not to deny the principle of *complementarity*. "Compensation" is simply a psychological refinement of this concept.

and comparing different data or points of view so as to produce an adjustment or a rectification.

546   In this regard there are three possibilities. If the conscious attitude to the life situation is in large degree one-sided, then the dream takes the opposite side. If the conscious has a position fairly near the "middle," the dream is satisfied with variations. If the conscious attitude is "correct" (adequate), then the dream coincides with and emphasizes this tendency, though without forfeiting its peculiar autonomy. As one never knows with certainty how to evaluate the conscious situation of a patient, dream-interpretation is naturally impossible without questioning the dreamer. But even if we know the conscious situation we know nothing of the attitude of the unconscious. As the unconscious is the matrix not only of dreams but also of psychogenic symptoms, the question of the attitude of the unconscious is of great practical importance. The unconscious, not caring whether I and those about me feel my attitude to be right, may—so to speak—be of "another mind." This, especially in the case of a neurosis, is not a matter of indifference, as the unconscious is quite capable of bringing about all kinds of unwelcome disturbances "by mistake," often with serious consequences, or of provoking neurotic symptoms. These disturbances are due to lack of harmony between conscious and unconscious. "Normally," as we say, such harmony should be present. The fact is, however, that very frequently it is simply not there, and this is the reason for a vast number of psychogenic misfortunes ranging from severe accidents and illness to harmless slips of the tongue. We owe our knowledge of these relationships to the work of Freud.[4]

547   Although in the great majority of cases compensation aims at establishing a normal psychological balance and thus appears as a kind of self-regulation of the psychic system, one must not forget that under certain circumstances and in certain cases (for instance, in latent psychoses) compensation may lead to a fatal outcome owing to the preponderance of destructive tendencies. The result is suicide or some other abnormal action, apparently preordained in the life-pattern of certain hereditarily tainted individuals.

4 *The Psychopathology of Everyday Life.*

548   In the treatment of neurosis, the task before us is to re-establish an approximate harmony between conscious and unconscious. This, as we know, can be achieved in a variety of ways: from "living a natural life," persuasive reasoning, strengthening the will, to analysis of the unconscious.

549   Because the simpler methods so often fail and the doctor does not know how to go on treating the patient, the compensatory function of dreams offers welcome assistance. I do not mean that the dreams of modern people indicate the appropriate method of healing, as was reported of the incubation-dreams dreamt in the temples of Aesculapius.[5] They do, however, illuminate the patient's situation in a way that can be exceedingly beneficial to health. They bring him memories, insights, experiences, awaken dormant qualities in the personality, and reveal the unconscious element in his relationships. So it seldom happens that anyone who has taken the trouble to work over his dreams with qualified assistance for a longer period of time remains without enrichment and a broadening of his mental horizon. Just because of their compensatory behaviour, a methodical analysis of dreams discloses new points of view and new ways of getting over the dreaded impasse.

550   The term "compensation" naturally gives us only a very general idea of the function of dreams. But if, as happens in long and difficult treatments, the analyst observes a series of dreams often running into hundreds, there gradually forces itself upon him a phenomenon which, in an isolated dream, would remain hidden behind the compensation of the moment. This phenomenon is a kind of developmental process in the personality itself. At first it seems that each compensation is a momentary adjustment of one-sidedness or an equalization of disturbed balance. But with deeper insight and experience, these apparently separate acts of compensation arrange themselves into a kind of plan. They seem to hang together and in the deepest sense to be subordinated to a common goal, so that a long dream-series no longer appears as a senseless string of incoherent and isolated happenings, but resembles the successive steps in a planned and orderly process of development. I have called this unconscious process spontaneously expressing

5 [Cf. Meier, *Antike Inkubation und moderne Psychotherapie.*—EDITORS.]

itself in the symbolism of a long dream-series the individuation process.

551   Here, more than anywhere else in a discussion of dream psychology, illustrative examples would be desirable. Unfortunately, this is quite impossible for technical reasons. I must therefore refer the reader to my book *Psychology and Alchemy*, which contains an investigation into the structure of a dream-series with special reference to the individuation process.

552   The question whether a long series of dreams recorded outside the analytical procedure would likewise reveal a development aiming at individuation is one that cannot be answered at present for lack of the necessary material. The analytical procedure, especially when it includes a systematic dream-analysis, is a "process of quickened maturation," as Stanley Hall once aptly remarked. It is therefore possible that the motifs accompanying the individuation process appear chiefly and predominantly in dream-series recorded under analysis, whereas in "extra-analytical" dream-series they occur only at much greater intervals of time.

553   I have mentioned before that dream-interpretation requires, among other things, specialized knowledge. While I am quite ready to believe that an intelligent layman with some psychological knowledge and experience of life could, with practice, diagnose dream-compensation correctly, I consider it impossible for anyone without knowledge of mythology and folklore and without some understanding of the psychology of primitives and of comparative religion to grasp the essence of the individuation process, which, according to all we know, lies at the base of psychological compensation.

554   Not all dreams are of equal importance. Even primitives distinguish between "little" and "big" dreams, or, as we might say, "insignificant" and "significant" dreams. Looked at more closely, "little" dreams are the nightly fragments of fantasy coming from the subjective and personal sphere, and their meaning is limited to the affairs of everyday. That is why such dreams are easily forgotten, just because their validity is restricted to the day-to-day fluctuations of the psychic balance. Significant dreams, on the other hand, are often remembered for a lifetime, and not infrequently prove to be the richest jewel in the treasure-house of psychic experience. How many people have I

encountered who at the first meeting could not refrain from saying: "I once had a dream!" Sometimes it was the first dream they could ever remember, and one that occurred between the ages of three and five. I have examined many such dreams, and often found in them a peculiarity which distinguishes them from other dreams: they contain symbolical images which we also come across in the mental history of mankind. It is worth noting that the dreamer does not need to have any inkling of the existence of such parallels. This peculiarity is characteristic of dreams of the individuation process, where we find the mythological motifs or mythologems I have designated as archetypes. These are to be understood as specific forms and groups of images which occur not only at all times and in all places but also in individual dreams, fantasies, visions, and delusional ideas. Their frequent appearance in individual case material, as well as their universal distribution, prove that the human psyche is unique and subjective or personal only in part, and for the rest is collective and objective.[6]

555   Thus we speak on the one hand of a *personal* and on the other of a *collective* unconscious, which lies at a deeper level and is further removed from consciousness than the personal unconscious. The "big" or "meaningful" dreams come from this deeper level. They reveal their significance—quite apart from the subjective impression they make—by their plastic form, which often has a poetic force and beauty. Such dreams occur mostly during the critical phases of life, in early youth, puberty, at the onset of middle age (thirty-six to forty), and within sight of death. Their interpretation often involves considerable difficulties, because the material which the dreamer is able to contribute is too meagre. For these archetypal products are no longer concerned with personal experiences but with general ideas, whose chief significance lies in their intrinsic meaning and not in any personal experience and its associations. For example, a young man dreamed of *a great snake that guarded a golden bowl in an underground vault.* To be sure, he had once seen a huge snake in a zoo, but otherwise he could suggest nothing that might have prompted such a dream, except perhaps the reminiscence of fairytales. Judging by this unsatisfactory

6 Cf. "The Psychology of the Unconscious," pp. 63–111.

context the dream, which actually produced a very powerful effect, would have hardly any meaning. But that would not explain its decided emotionality. In such a case we have to go back to mythology, where the combination of snake or dragon with treasure and cave represents an ordeal in the life of the hero. Then it becomes clear that we are dealing with a collective emotion, a typical situation full of affect, which is not primarily a personal experience but becomes one only secondarily. Primarily it is a universally human problem which, because it has been overlooked subjectively, forces itself objectively upon the dreamer's consciousness.[7]

556   A man in middle life still feels young, and age and death lie far ahead of him. At about thirty-six he passes the zenith of life, without being conscious of the meaning of this fact. If he is a man whose whole make-up and nature do not tolerate excessive unconsciousness, then the import of this moment will be forced upon him, perhaps in the form of an archetypal dream. It would be in vain for him to try to understand the dream with the help of a carefully worked out context, for it expresses itself in strange mythological forms that are not familiar to him. The dream uses collective figures because it has to express an eternal human problem that repeats itself endlessly, and not just a disturbance of personal balance.

557   All these moments in the individual's life, when the universal laws of human fate break in upon the purposes, expectations, and opinions of the personal consciousness, are stations along the road of the individuation process. This process is, in effect, the spontaneous realization of the whole man. The ego-conscious personality is only a part of the whole man, and its life does not yet represent his total life. The more he is merely "I," the more he splits himself off from the collective man, of whom he is also a part, and may even find himself in opposition to him. But since everything living strives for wholeness, the inevitable one-sidedness of our conscious life is continually being corrected and compensated by the universal human being in us, whose goal is the ultimate integration of conscious and unconscious, or better, the assimilation of the ego to a wider personality.

[7] Cf. "The Psychology of the Unconscious," chs. 5–7.

558   Such reflections are unavoidable if one wants to understand the meaning of "big" dreams. They employ numerous mythological motifs that characterize the life of the hero, of that greater man who is semi-divine by nature. Here we find the dangerous adventures and ordeals such as occur in initiations. We meet dragons, helpful animals, and demons; also the Wise Old Man, the animal-man, the wishing tree, the hidden treasure, the well, the cave, the walled garden, the transformative processes and substances of alchemy, and so forth—all things which in no way touch the banalities of everyday. The reason for this is that they have to do with the realization of a part of the personality which has not yet come into existence but is still in the process of becoming.

559   How such mythologems get "condensed" in dreams, and how they modify one another, is shown by the picture of the Dream of Nebuchadnezzar (Daniel 4 : 7ff.) [frontispiece]. Although purporting to be no more than a representation of that dream, it has, so to speak, been dreamed over again by the artist, as is immediately apparent if one examines the details more closely. The tree is growing (in a quite unbiblical manner) out of the king's navel: it is therefore the genealogical tree of Christ's ancestors, that grows from the navel of Adam, the tribal father.[8] For this reason it bears in its branches the pelican, who nourishes its young with its blood—a well-known allegory of Christ. Apart from that the pelican, together with the four birds that take the place of the four symbols of the evangelists, form a quincunx, and this quincunx reappears lower down in the stag, another symbol of Christ,[9] with the four animals looking

---

[8] The tree is also an alchemical symbol. Cf. Psychology and Alchemy, pars. 498f., and "The 'Arbor philosophica'."

[9] The stag is an allegory of Christ because legend attributes to it the capacity for self-renewal. Thus Honorius of Autun writes in his Speculum de Mysteriis Ecclesiae (Migne, P.L., vol. 172, col. 847): "They say that the deer, after he has swallowed a serpent, hastens to the water, that by a draught of water he may eject the poison, and then cast his horns and his hair and so take new." In the Saint-Graal (III, pp. 219 and 224), it is related that Christ sometimes appeared to the disciples as a white stag with four lions (= four evangelists). In alchemy, Mercurius is allegorized as the stag (Manget, Bibl. chem., Tab. IX, fig. XIII, and elsewhere) because the stag can renew itself. "Les os du cuer du serf vault moult pour conforter le cuer humain" (Delatte, Textes latins et vieux français relatifs aux Cyranides, p. 346).

expectantly upwards. These two quaternities have the closest connections with alchemical ideas: above the *volatilia,* below the *terrena,* the former traditionally represented as birds, the latter as quadrupeds. Thus not only has the Christian conception of the genealogical tree and of the evangelical quaternity insinuated itself into the picture, but also the alchemical idea of the double quaternity ("superius est sicut quod inferius"). This contamination shows in the most vivid way how individual dreams make use of archetypes. The archetypes are condensed, interwoven, and blended not only with one another (as here), but also with unique individual elements.

560　But if dreams produce such essential compensations, why are they not understandable? I have often been asked this question. The answer must be that the dream is a natural occurrence, and that nature shows no inclination to offer her fruits gratis or according to human expectations. It is often objected that the compensation must be ineffective unless the dream is understood. This is not so certain, however, for many things can be effective without being understood. But there is no doubt that we can enhance its effect considerably by understanding the dream, and this is often necessary because the voice of the unconscious so easily goes unheard. "What nature leaves imperfect is perfected by the art," says an alchemical dictum.

561　Coming now to the form of dreams, we find everything from lightning impressions to endlessly spun out dream-narrative. Nevertheless there are a great many "average" dreams in which a definite structure can be perceived, not unlike that of a drama. For instance, the dream begins with a STATEMENT OF PLACE, such as, "*I was in a street, it was an avenue*" (1), or, "*I was in a large building like a hotel*" (2). Next comes a statement about the PROTAGONISTS, for instance, "*I was walking with my friend X in a city park. At a crossing we suddenly ran into Mrs. Y*" (3), or, "*I was sitting with Father and Mother in a train compartment*" (4), or, "*I was in uniform with many of my comrades*" (5). Statements of time are rarer. I call this phase of the dream the EXPOSITION. It indicates the scene of action, the people involved, and often the initial situation of the dreamer.

562　In the second phase comes the DEVELOPMENT of the plot. For instance: "*I was in a street, it was an avenue. In the distance a car appeared, which approached rapidly. It was being driven*

294

very unsteadily, and I thought the driver must be drunk" (1). Or: *"Mrs. Y seemed to be very excited and wanted to whisper something to me hurriedly, which my friend X was obviously not intended to hear"* (3). The situation is somehow becoming complicated, and a definite tension develops because one does not know what will happen.

563   The third phase brings the CULMINATION or *peripeteia*. Here something decisive happens or something changes completely: *"Suddenly I was in the car and seemed to be myself this drunken driver. Only I was not drunk, but strangely insecure and as if without a steering-wheel. I could no longer control the fast moving car, and crashed into a wall"* (1). Or: *"Suddenly Mrs. Y turned deathly pale and fell to the ground"* (3).

564   The fourth and last phase is the *lysis,* the SOLUTION or RESULT produced by the dream-work. (There are certain dreams in which the fourth phase is lacking, and this can present a special problem, not to be discussed here.) Examples: *"I saw that the front part of the car was smashed. It was a strange car that I did not know. I myself was unhurt. I thought with some uneasiness of my responsibility"* (1). *"We thought Mrs. Y was dead, but it was evidently only a faint. My friend X cried out: 'I must fetch a doctor' "* (3). The last phase shows the final situation, which is at the same time the solution "sought" by the dreamer. In dream 1 a new reflectiveness has supervened after a kind of rudderless confusion, or rather, should supervene, since the dream is compensatory. The upshot of dream 3 is the thought that the help of a competent third person is indicated.

565   The first dreamer was a man who had rather lost his head in difficult family circumstances and did not want to let matters go to extremes. The other dreamer wondered whether he ought to obtain the help of a psychiatrist for his neurosis. Naturally these statements are not an interpretation of the dream, they merely outline the initial situation. This division into four phases can be applied without much difficulty to the majority of dreams met with in practice—an indication that dreams generally have a "dramatic" structure.

566   The essential content of the dream-action, as I have shown above, is a sort of finely attuned compensation of the one-sidedness, errors, deviations, or other shortcomings of the conscious attitude. An hysterical patient of mine, an aristocratic lady who

seemed to herself no end distinguished, met in her dreams a whole series of dirty fishwives and drunken prostitutes. In extreme cases the compensation becomes so menacing that the fear of it results in sleeplessness.

567   Thus the dream may either repudiate the dreamer in a most painful way, or bolster him up morally. The first is likely to happen to people who, like the last-mentioned patient, have too good an opinion of themselves; the second to those whose self-valuation is too low. Occasionally, however, the arrogant person is not simply humiliated in the dream, but is raised to an altogether improbable and absurd eminence, while the all-too-humble individual is just as improbably degraded, in order to "rub it in," as the English say.

568   Many people who know something, but not enough, about dreams and their meaning, and who are impressed by their subtle and apparently intentional compensation, are liable to succumb to the prejudice that the dream actually has a moral purpose, that it warns, rebukes, comforts, foretells the future, etc. If one believes that the unconscious always knows best, one can easily be betrayed into leaving the dreams to take the necessary decisions, and is then disappointed when the dreams become more and more trivial and meaningless. Experience has shown me that a slight knowledge of dream psychology is apt to lead to an overrating of the unconscious which impairs the power of conscious decision. The unconscious functions satisfactorily only when the conscious mind fulfils its tasks to the very limit. A dream may perhaps supply what is then lacking, or it may help us forward where our best efforts have failed. If the unconscious really were superior to consciousness it would be difficult to see wherein the advantage of consciousness lay, or why it should ever have come into being as a necessary element in the scheme of evolution. If it were nothing but a *lusus naturae*, the fact of our conscious awareness of the world and of our own existence would be without meaning. The idea that consciousness is a freak of nature is somehow difficult to digest, and for psychological reasons we should avoid emphasizing it, even if it were correct—which, by the way, we shall luckily never be in a position to prove (any more than we can prove the contrary). It is a question that belongs to the realm of metaphysics, where no criterion of truth exists. However, this is in

296

no way to underestimate the fact that metaphysical views are of the utmost importance for the well-being of the human psyche.

569   In the study of dream psychology we encounter far-reaching philosophical and even religious problems to the understanding of which the phenomenon of dreams has already made decisive contributions. But we cannot boast that we are, at present, in possession of a generally satisfying theory or explanation of this complicated phenomenon. We still know far too little about the nature of the unconscious psyche for that. In this field there is still an infinite amount of patient and unprejudiced work to be done, which no one will begrudge. For the purpose of research is not to imagine that one possesses the theory which alone is right, but, doubting all theories, to approach gradually nearer to the truth.

V

THE PSYCHOLOGICAL FOUNDATIONS
OF BELIEF IN SPIRITS

———

SPIRIT AND LIFE

———

BASIC POSTULATES OF
ANALYTICAL PSYCHOLOGY

———

ANALYTICAL PSYCHOLOGY
AND 'WELTANSCHAUUNG'

———

THE REAL AND THE SURREAL

[The papers in this section present a special problem with regard to the translation of the words *Geist* and *Seele*. In "The Psychological Foundations of Belief in Spirits," the author used *Geist*, as the translated title implies, almost exclusively to designate *a* spirit (ghost, apparition, etc.). In "Spirit and Life," he used it in an equally unequivocal sense to denote *the* spirit, i.e., the spiritual principle in its various definitions. Both here and in "Basic Postulates of Analytical Psychology," however, *Geist* has also the connotation "mind." This makes the translation of *Seele* in this group of papers a problematical matter which may give rise to confusion. Ordinarily *Seele* means "soul," and even in a Jungian context it can sometimes quite legitimately be translated as such. It must nevertheless be remembered that there is no consistent equivalent of *Seele* in English, just as German lacks an unambiguous word for the English "mind." This applies particularly to the use of *Seele* in the essay "Spirit and Life," where "soul" would give entirely the wrong meaning. It has therefore been translated here and in the other papers either as "psyche" or as "mind," and its adjectival form as "psychic" or (less frequently) as "mental," since a consistent use of either term would be misleading. The reader who objects to the one is free to substitute the other in his thoughts. He may then see how easily mind and psyche shade off into each other.

[Those interested in textual criticism will note, in this group of papers, an increasing tendency to replace the concept *Seele* by *Psyche*, until, in "The Real and the Surreal" (1933), *Psyche* alone occupies the field. It appears there as a principle *sui generis*, which has completely ousted the older, ambiguous philosophical concepts of mind, soul, and spirit as the "real" subject of psychology. Cf. Jung, *Psychology and Alchemy*, p. 8, n. 2.—TRANS.]

THE PSYCHOLOGICAL FOUNDATIONS
OF BELIEF IN SPIRITS [1]

570   If we look back into the past history of mankind, we find,
among many other religious convictions, a universal belief in
the existence of phantoms or ethereal beings who dwell in the
neighbourhood of men and who exercise an invisible yet powerful influence upon them. These beings are generally supposed to
be the spirits or souls of the dead. This belief is to be found
among highly civilized peoples as well as among Australian
aborigines, who are still living in the Stone Age. Among Western peoples, however, belief in spirits has been counteracted by
the rationalism and scientific enlightenment of the last one
hundred and fifty years, so that among the majority of educated
people today it has been suppressed along with other metaphysical beliefs.

1 [Originally translated by H. G. and C. F. Baynes from a German ms. and published in *Proceedings of the Society for Psychical Research* (London), XXXI
(1920), having been read at a general meeting of the Society on July 4, 1919.
This translation was republished in *Contributions to Analytical Psychology*
(London and New York, 1928). The German original was first published as "Die
psychologischen Grundlagen des Geisterglaubens," in *Über die Energetik der Seele*
(Psychologische Abhandlungen, II; Zurich, 1928), and was revised and expanded
in *Über psychische Energetik und das Wesen der Träume* (Zurich, 1948). The
latter version is here translated, but the Baynes translation has also been consulted.—EDITORS.]

571   But just as these beliefs are still alive among the masses, so too is the belief in spirits. The "haunted house" has not yet become extinct even in the most enlightened and the most intellectual cities, nor has the peasant ceased to believe in the bewitching of his cattle. On the contrary, in this age of materialism—the inevitable consequence of rationalistic enlightenment—there has been a revival of the belief in spirits, but this time on a higher level. It is not a relapse into the darkness of superstition, but an intense scientific interest, a need to direct the searchlight of truth on to the chaos of dubious facts. The names of Crookes, Myers, Wallace, Zöllner, and many other eminent men symbolize this rebirth and rehabilitation of the belief in spirits. Even if the real nature of their observations be disputed, even if they can be accused of errors and self-deception, these investigators have still earned for themselves the undying moral merit of having thrown the full weight of their authority and of their great scientific name into these endeavours to shed fresh light on the darkness, regardless of all personal fears and considerations. They shrank neither from academic prejudice nor from the derision of the public, and at the very time when the thinking of educated people was more than ever spellbound by materialistic dogmas, they drew attention to phenomena of psychic provenience that seemed to be in complete contradiction to the materialism of their age.

572   These men typify the reaction of the human mind against the materialistic view of the world. Looked at from the historical standpoint, it is not at all surprising that they used the belief in spirits as the most effective weapon against the mere truth of the senses, for belief in spirits has the same functional significance also for primitive man. His utter dependence on circumstances and environment, the manifold distresses and tribulations of his life, surrounded by hostile neighbours, dangerous beasts of prey, and often exposed to the pitiless forces of nature; his keen senses, his cupidity, his uncontrolled emotions —all these things bind him to the physical realities, so that he is in constant danger of adopting a purely materialistic attitude and becoming degenerate. His belief in spirits, or rather, his awareness of a spiritual world, pulls him again and again out of that bondage in which his senses would hold him; it forces on him the certainty of a spiritual reality whose laws he must ob-

serve as carefully and as guardedly as the laws of his physical environment. Primitive man, therefore, really lives in two worlds. Physical reality is at the same time spiritual reality. The physical world is undeniable, and for him the world of spirits has an equally real existence, not just because he thinks so, but because of his naïve awareness of things spiritual. Wherever this naïveté is lost through contact with civilization and its disastrous "enlightenment," he forfeits his dependence on spiritual law and accordingly degenerates. Even Christianity cannot save him from corruption, for a highly developed religion like Christianity demands a highly developed psyche if its beneficial effects are to be felt.

573   For the primitive, the phenomenon of spirits is direct evidence for the reality of a spiritual world. If we inquire what these spirit-phenomena mean to him, and in what they consist, we find that the most frequent phenomenon is the seeing of apparitions, or ghosts. It is generally assumed that the seeing of apparitions is far commoner among primitives than among civilized people, the inference being that this is nothing but superstition, because civilized people do not have such visions unless they are ill. It is quite certain that civilized man makes much less use of the hypothesis of spirits than the primitive, but in my view it is equally certain that psychic phenomena occur no less frequently with civilized people than they do with primitives. The only difference is that where the primitive speaks of ghosts, the European speaks of dreams and fantasies and neurotic symptoms, and attributes less importance to them than the primitive does. I am convinced that if a European had to go through the same exercises and ceremonies which the medicine-man performs in order to make the spirits visible, he would have the same experiences. He would interpret them differently, of course, and devalue them, but this would not alter the facts as such. It is well known that Europeans have very curious psychic experiences if they have to live under primitive conditions for a long time, or if they find themselves in some other unusual psychological situation.

574   One of the most important sources of the primitive belief in spirits is dreams. People very often appear as the actors in dreams, and the primitive readily believes them to be spirits or ghosts. The dream has for him an incomparably higher value

than it has for civilized man. Not only does he talk a great deal about his dreams, he also attributes an extraordinary importance to them, so that it often seems as though he were unable to distinguish between them and reality. To the civilized man dreams as a rule appear valueless, though there are some people who attach great significance to certain dreams on account of their weird and impressive character. This peculiarity lends plausibility to the view that dreams are inspirations. But inspiration implies something that inspires, a spirit or ghost, although this logical inference is not likely to appeal to the modern mind. A good instance of this is the fact that the dead sometimes appear in dreams; the primitive naïvely takes them for revenants.

575   Another source of the belief in spirits is psychogenic diseases, nervous disorders, especially those of an hysterical character, which are not rare among primitives. Since these illnesses stem from psychic conflicts, mostly unconscious, it seems to the primitive that they are caused by certain persons, living or dead, who are in some way connected with his subjective conflict. If the person is dead, it is naturally assumed that his spirit is having an injurious influence. As pathogenic conflicts usually go back to childhood and are connected with memories of the parents, we can understand why the primitive attaches special importance to the spirits of dead relatives. This accounts for the wide incidence of ancestor-worship, which is primarily a protection against the malice of the dead. Anyone who has had experience of nervous illnesses knows how great is the importance of parental influences on patients. Many patients feel persecuted by their parents long after they are dead. The psychological after-effects of the parents are so powerful that many cultures have developed a whole system of ancestor-worship to propitiate them.[2]

576   There can be no doubt that mental illnesses play a signifi-

2 When I was on an expedition to Mount Elgon (East Africa) in 1925-26, one of our water-bearers, a young woman who lived in a neighbouring kraal, fell ill with what looked like a septic abortion with high fever. We were unable to treat her from our meagre medical supplies, so her relatives immediately sent for a *nganga*, a medicine-man. When he arrived, the medicine-man walked round and round the hut in ever-widening circles, snuffing the air. Suddenly he came to a halt on a track that led down from the mountain, and explained that the sick girl was the only daughter of parents who had died young and were now up there in the bamboo forest. Every night they came down to make their daughter ill so that she should die and keep them company. On the instructions

THE PSYCHOLOGICAL FOUNDATIONS OF BELIEF IN SPIRITS

cant part in causing belief in spirits. Among primitive peoples these illnesses, so far as is known, are mostly of a delirious, hallucinatory or catatonic nature, belonging apparently to the broad domain of schizophrenia, an illness which covers the great majority of chronically insane patients. In all ages and all over the world, insane people have been regarded as possessed by evil spirits, and this belief is supported by the patient's own hallucinations. The patients are tormented less by visions than by auditory hallucinations: they hear "voices." Very often these voices are those of relatives or of persons in some way connected with the patient's conflicts. To the naïve mind, the hallucinations naturally appear to be caused by spirits.

577 It is impossible to speak of belief in spirits without at the same time considering the belief in souls. Belief in souls is a correlate of belief in spirits. Since, according to primitive belief, a spirit is usually the ghost of one dead, it must once have been the soul of a living person. This is particularly the case wherever the belief is held that people have only one soul. But this assumption does not prevail everywhere; it is frequently supposed that people have two or more souls, one of which survives death and is immortal. In this case the spirit of the dead is only one of the several souls of the living. It is thus only a part of the total soul—a psychic fragment, so to speak.

578 Belief in souls is therefore a necessary premise for belief in spirits, at least so far as the spirits of the dead are concerned. However, primitives do not believe only in spirits of the dead. There are also elemental demons who are supposed never to have been human souls or soul-parts. This group of spirits must therefore have a different origin.

579 Before going into the psychological grounds for belief in souls I should like to take a quick glance back at the facts already mentioned. I have pointed out three main sources that put the belief in spirits on a solid foundation: the seeing of apparitions, dreams, and pathological disturbances of psychic life. The commonest and most normal of these phenomena is

---

of the medicine-man a "ghost-trap" was then built on the mountain path, in the form of a little hut, and a clay figure of the sick girl was placed inside it together with some food. During the night the ghosts went in there, thinking to be with their daughter. To our boundless astonishment the girl recovered within two days. Was our diagnosis wrong? The puzzle remained unsolved.

the dream, and its great significance for primitive psychology is now widely recognized. What, then, is a dream?

580   A dream is a psychic product originating in the sleeping state without conscious motivation. In a dream, consciousness is not completely extinguished; there is always a small remnant left. In most dreams, for instance, there is still some consciousness of the ego, although it is a very limited and curiously distorted ego known as the dream-ego. It is a mere fragment or shadow of the waking ego. Consciousness exists only when psychic contents are associated with the ego, and the ego is a psychic complex of a particularly solid kind. As sleep is seldom quite dreamless, we may assume that the activity of the ego-complex seldom ceases entirely; its activity is as a rule only restricted by sleep. The psychic contents associated with it in a dream confront the ego in much the same way as do the outward circumstances in real life, so that in dreams we generally find ourselves in situations such as we could not conceive when awake, but which are very like the situations we are confronted with in reality. As in our waking state, real people and things enter our field of vision, so the dream-images enter like another kind of reality into the field of consciousness of the dream-ego. We do not feel as if we were producing the dreams, it is rather as if the dreams came to us. They are not subject to our control but obey their own laws. They are obviously autonomous psychic complexes which form themselves out of their own material. We do not know the source of their motives, and we therefore say that dreams come from the unconscious. In saying this, we assume that there are independent psychic complexes which elude our conscious control and come and go according to their own laws. In our waking life, we imagine we make our own thoughts and can have them when we want them. We also think we know where they come from, and why and to what end we have them. Whenever a thought comes to us against our will, or suddenly vanishes against our will, we feel as if something exceptional or even morbid had happened. The difference between psychic activity in the waking and in the sleeping state seems, therefore, to be an important one. In the waking state the psyche is apparently under the control of the conscious will, but in the sleeping state it produces contents that are strange and incomprehensible, as though they came from another world.

581   The same is true of visions. They are like dreams, only they occur in the waking state. They enter consciousness along with conscious perceptions and are nothing other than the momentary irruption of an unconscious content. The same phenomenon also happens in mental disturbances. Quite out of the blue, apparently, against the background of noises in the environment and sound-waves coming from outside, the ear, excited from within, hears psychic contents that have nothing to do with the immediate concerns of the conscious mind.[3] Besides judgments formed by intellect and feeling from definite premises, opinions and convictions thrust themselves on the patient, apparently deriving from real perceptions but actually from unconscious factors within him. These are delusional ideas.

582   Common to all three types of phenomena is the fact that the psyche is not an indivisible unity but a divisible and more or less divided whole. Although the separate parts are connected with one another, they are relatively independent, so much so that certain parts of the psyche never become associated with the ego at all, or only very rarely. I have called these psychic fragments "autonomous complexes," and I based my theory of complexes on their existence.[4] According to this theory the ego-complex forms the centre characteristic of our psyche. But it is only one among several complexes. The others are more often than not associated with the ego-complex and in this way become conscious, but they can also exist for some time without being associated with it. An excellent and very well known example of this is the conversion of St. Paul. Although the actual moment of conversion often seems quite sudden and unexpected, we know from experience that such a fundamental upheaval always requires a long period of incubation. It is only when this preparation is complete, that is to say when the individual is ripe for conversion, that the new insight breaks through with violent emotion. Saul, as he was then called, had unconsciously been a Christian for a long time, and this would explain his fanatical hatred of the Christians, because fanaticism is always found in those who have to stifle a secret doubt. That is why converts are always the worst fanatics. The vision of Christ on the road to Damascus merely marks the moment when the

3 There are even cases where the voices repeat the patient's thoughts aloud. But these are rather rare.   4 Cf. supra, "A Review of the Complex Theory."

307

unconscious Christ-complex associated itself with Paul's ego. The fact that Christ appeared to him objectively, in the form of a vision, is explained by the circumstance that Saul's Christianity was an unconscious complex which appeared to him in projection, as if it did not belong to him. He could not see himself as a Christian; therefore, from sheer resistance to Christ, he became blind and could only be healed again by a Christian. We know that psychogenic blindness is always an unconscious unwillingness to see, which in Saul's case corresponds with his fanatical resistance to Christianity. This resistance, as we know from the Epistles, was never entirely overcome, and occasionally it broke out in the form of fits which are erroneously explained as epileptic. The fits were a sudden return of the old Saul-complex which had been split off by his conversion just as the Christ-complex was before.

583   For reasons of intellectual morality, we should not explain Paul's conversion on metaphysical grounds, otherwise we should have to explain all similar cases that occur among our patients in the same metaphysical way. This would lead to quite absurd conclusions repugnant to reason and feeling alike.

584   Autonomous complexes appear most clearly in dreams, visions, pathological hallucinations, and delusional ideas. Because the ego is unconscious of them, they always appear first in projected form. In dreams they are represented by other people, in visions they are projected, as it were, into space, just like the voices in insanity when not ascribed to persons in the patient's environment. Ideas of persecution, as we know, are frequently associated with particular persons to whom the patient attributes the peculiarities of his own unconscious complex. He feels these persons as hostile because he is hostile to the unconscious complex, just as Saul resented the Christ-complex he could not acknowledge in himself and persecuted the Christians as its representatives. We see this constantly repeated in everyday life: people unhesitatingly project their own assumptions about others on to the persons concerned and hate or love them accordingly. Since reflection is so troublesome and difficult, they prefer to judge without restraint, not realizing that they are merely projecting and making themselves the victims of a stupid illusion. They take no account of the injustice and uncharitable-

ness of such a procedure, and above all they never consider the serious loss of personality they suffer when, from sheer negligence, they allow themselves the luxury of foisting their own mistakes or merits onto others. It is exceedingly unwise to think that other people are as stupid and inferior as one is oneself, and one should also realize the damage one does by assigning one's own good qualities to moral highwaymen with an eye to the main chance.

585   Spirits, therefore, viewed from the psychological angle, are unconscious autonomous complexes which appear as projections because they have no direct association with the ego.[5]

586   I said earlier on that belief in souls is a necessary correlate of belief in spirits. Whilst spirits are felt to be strange and as not belonging to the ego, this is not true of the soul or souls. The primitive feels the proximity or the influence of a spirit as something uncanny or dangerous, and is greatly relieved when the spirit is banished. Conversely, he feels the loss of a soul as if it were a sickness; indeed, he often attributes serious physical diseases to loss of soul. There are innumerable rites for calling the "soul-bird" back into the sick person. Children may not be struck because their souls might feel insulted and depart. Thus, for the primitive, the soul is something that seems normally to belong to him, but spirits seem to be something that normally should not be near him. He avoids places haunted by spirits, or visits them only with fear, for religious or magical purposes.

587   The plurality of souls indicates a plurality of relatively autonomous complexes that can behave like spirits. The soul-complexes seem to belong to the ego and the loss of them appears pathological. The opposite is true of spirit-complexes: their association with the ego causes illness, and their dissociation from it brings recovery. Accordingly, primitive pathology recognizes two causes of illness: loss of soul, and possession by a spirit. The two theories keep one another more or less balanced. We therefore have to postulate the existence of unconscious complexes that normally belong to the ego, and of those that

[5] This should not be misconstrued as a metaphysical statement. The question of whether spirits exist *in themselves* is far from having been settled. Psychology is not concerned with things as they are "in themselves," but only with what people think about them.

normally should not become associated with it. The former are the soul-complexes, the latter the spirit-complexes.

588   This distinction, common to most primitive beliefs, corresponds exactly to my conception of the unconscious. According to my view, the unconscious falls into two parts which should be sharply distinguished from one another. One of them is the personal unconscious; it includes all those psychic contents which have been forgotten during the course of the individual's life. Traces of them are still preserved in the unconscious, even if all conscious memory of them has been lost. In addition, it contains all subliminal impressions or perceptions which have too little energy to reach consciousness. To these we must add unconscious combinations of ideas that are still too feeble and too indistinct to cross over the threshold. Finally, the personal unconscious contains all psychic contents that are incompatible with the conscious attitude. This comprises a whole group of contents, chiefly those which appear morally, aesthetically, or intellectually inadmissible and are repressed on account of their incompatibility. A man cannot always think and feel the good, the true, and the beautiful, and in trying to keep up an ideal attitude everything that does not fit in with it is automatically repressed. If, as is nearly always the case in a differentiated person, one function, for instance thinking, is especially developed and dominates consciousness, then feeling is thrust into the background and largely falls into the unconscious.

589   The other part of the unconscious is what I call the impersonal or collective unconscious. As the name indicates, its contents are not personal but collective; that is, they do not belong to one individual alone but to a whole group of individuals, and generally to a whole nation, or even to the whole of mankind. These contents are not acquired during the individual's lifetime but are products of innate forms and instincts. Although the child possesses no inborn ideas, it nevertheless has a highly developed brain which functions in a quite definite way. This brain is inherited from its ancestors; it is the deposit of the psychic functioning of the whole human race. The child therefore brings with it an organ ready to function in the same way as it has functioned throughout human history. In the brain the instincts are preformed, and so are the primordial images which have always been the basis of man's thinking—the whole treas-

ure-house of mythological motifs.[6] It is, of course, not easy to prove the existence of the collective unconscious in a normal person, but occasionally mythological ideas are represented in his dreams. These contents can be seen most clearly in cases of mental derangement, especially in schizophrenia, where mythological images often pour out in astonishing variety. Insane people frequently produce combinations of ideas and symbols that could never be accounted for by experiences in their individual lives, but only by the history of the human mind. It is an instance of primitive, mythological thinking, which reproduces its own primordial images, and is not a reproduction of conscious experiences.[7]

590   The personal unconscious, then, contains complexes that belong to the individual and form an intrinsic part of his psychic life. When any complex which ought to be associated with the ego becomes unconscious, either by being repressed or by sinking below the threshold, the individual experiences a sense of loss. Conversely, when a lost complex is made conscious again, for instance through psychotherapeutic treatment, he experiences an increase of power.[8] Many neuroses are cured in this way. But when, on the other hand, a complex of the collective unconscious becomes associated with the ego, i.e., becomes conscious, it is felt as strange, uncanny, and at the same time fascinating. At all events the conscious mind falls under its spell, either feeling it as something pathological, or else being alienated by it from normal life. The association of a collective content with the ego always produces a state of alienation, because something is added to the individual's consciousness which ought really to remain unconscious, that is, separated from the ego. If the content can be removed from consciousness again, the patient will feel relieved and more normal. The irruption

6 By this I do not mean the existing form of the motif but its preconscious, invisible "ground plan." This might be compared to the crystal lattice which is preformed in the crystalline solution. It should not be confused with the variously structured axial system of the individual crystal.

7 Cf. my *Symbols of Transformation;* also Spielrein, "Über den psychischen Inhalt eines Falles von Schizophrenie"; Nelken, "Analytische Beobachtungen über Phantasien eines Schizophrenen"; C. A. Meier, "Spontanmanifestationen des kollektiven Unbewussten."

8 This is not always a pleasant feeling, for the patient was quite content to lose the complex so long as he did not feel the disagreeable consequences of the loss.

of these alien contents is a characteristic symptom marking the onset of many mental illnesses. The patients are seized by weird and monstrous thoughts, the whole world seems changed, people have horrible, distorted faces, and so on.[9]

591   While the contents of the personal unconscious are felt as belonging to one's own psyche, the contents of the collective unconscious seem alien, as if they came from outside. The re-integration of a personal complex has the effect of release and often of healing, whereas the invasion of a complex from the collective unconscious is a very disagreeable and even dangerous phenomenon. The parallel with the primitive belief in souls and spirits is obvious: souls correspond to the autonomous complexes of the personal unconscious, and spirits to those of the collective unconscious. We, from the scientific standpoint, prosaically call the awful beings that dwell in the shadows of the primeval forests "psychic complexes." Yet if we consider the extraordinary role played by the belief in souls and spirits in the history of mankind, we cannot be content with merely establishing the existence of such complexes, but must go rather more deeply into their nature.

592   These complexes can easily be demonstrated by means of the association experiment.[10] The procedure is simple. The experimenter calls out a word to the test-person, and the test-person reacts as quickly as possible with the first word that comes into his mind. The reaction time is measured by a stopwatch. One would expect all simple words to be answered with roughly the same speed, and that only "difficult" words would be followed by a prolonged reaction time. But actually this is not so. There are unexpectedly prolonged reaction times after very simple words, whereas difficult words may be answered quite quickly. Closer investigation shows that prolonged reaction times generally occur when the stimulus-word hits a content with a strong feeling-tone. Besides the prolonged reaction-time there are other

9 Those who are familiar with this material will object that my description is one-sided, because they know that the archetype, the autonomous collective content, does not have only the negative aspect described here. I have merely restricted myself to the common symptomatology that can be found in every text-book of psychiatry, and to the equally common defensive attitude towards anything extraordinary. Naturally the archetype also has a positive numinosity which I have repeatedly mentioned elsewhere.

10 Cf. my *Studies in Word Association.*

characteristic disturbances that cannot be discussed in detail here. The feeling-toned contents generally have to do with things which the test-person would like to keep secret—painful things which he has repressed, some of them being unknown even to the test-person himself. When a stimulus-word hits such a complex, no answer occurs to him at all, or else so many things crowd into his mind that he does not know what answer to give, or he mechanically repeats the stimulus-word, or he gives an answer and then immediately substitutes another, and so forth. When, after completing the experiment, the test-person is asked what answers he gave to the individual words, we find that ordinary reactions are remembered quite well, while words connected with a complex are usually forgotten.

593   These peculiarities plainly reveal the qualities of the autonomous complex. It creates a disturbance in the readiness to react, either inhibiting the answer or causing an undue delay, or it produces an unsuitable reaction, and afterwards often suppresses the memory of the answer. It interferes with the conscious will and disturbs its intentions. That is why we call it autonomous. If we subject a neurotic or insane person to this experiment, we find that the complexes which disturb the reactions are at the same time essential components of the psychic disturbance. They cause not only the disturbances of reaction but also the symptoms. I have seen cases where certain stimulus-words were followed by strange and apparently nonsensical answers, by words that came out of the test-person's mouth quite unexpectedly, as though a strange being had spoken through him. These words belonged to the autonomous complex. When excited by an external stimulus, complexes can produce sudden confusions, or violent affects, depressions, anxiety-states, etc., or they may express themselves in hallucinations. In short, they behave in such a way that the primitive theory of spirits strikes one as being an uncommonly apt formulation for them.

594   We may carry this parallel further. Certain complexes arise on account of painful or distressing experiences in a person's life, experiences of an emotional nature which leave lasting psychic wounds behind them. A bad experience of this sort often crushes valuable qualities in an individual. All these produce unconscious complexes of a personal nature. A primitive would rightly speak of a loss of soul, because certain portions of the

psyche have indeed disappeared. A great many autonomous complexes arise in this way. But there are others that come from quite a different source. While the first source is easily understood, since it concerns the outward life everyone can see, this other source is obscure and difficult to understand because it has to do with perceptions or impressions of the collective unconscious. Usually the individual tries to rationalize these inner perceptions in terms of external causes, but that does not get at the root of the matter. At bottom they are irrational contents of which the individual had never been conscious before, and which he therefore vainly seeks to discover somewhere outside him. The primitive expresses this very aptly when he says that some spirit is interfering with him. So far as I can judge, these experiences occur either when something so devastating happens to the individual that his whole previous attitude to life breaks down, or when for some reason the contents of the collective unconscious accumulate so much energy that they start influencing the conscious mind. In my view this happens when the life of a large social group or of a nation undergoes a profound change of a political, social, or religious nature. Such a change always involves an alteration of the psychological attitude. Incisive changes in history are generally attributed exclusively to external causes. It seems to me, however, that external circumstances often serve merely as occasions for a new attitude to life and the world, long prepared in the unconscious, to become manifest. Social, political, and religious conditions affect the collective unconscious in the sense that all those factors which are suppressed by the prevailing views or attitudes in the life of a society gradually accumulate in the collective unconscious and activate its contents. Certain individuals gifted with particularly strong intuition then become aware of the changes going on in it and translate these changes into communicable ideas. The new ideas spread rapidly because parallel changes have been taking place in the unconscious of other people. There is a general readiness to accept the new ideas, although on the other hand they often meet with violent resistance. New ideas are not just the enemies of the old; they also appear as a rule in an extremely unacceptable form.

595   Whenever contents of the collective unconscious become activated, they have a disturbing effect on the conscious mind,

and confusion ensues. If the activation is due to the collapse of the individual's hopes and expectations, there is a danger that the collective unconscious may take the place of reality. This state would be pathological. If, on the other hand, the activation is the result of psychological processes in the unconscious of the people, the individual may feel threatened or at any rate disoriented, but the resultant state is not pathological, at least so far as the individual is concerned. Nevertheless, the mental state of the people as a whole might well be compared to a psychosis. If the translation of the unconscious into a communicable language proves successful, it has a redeeming effect. The driving forces locked up in the unconscious are canalized into consciousness and form a new source of power, which may, however, unleash a dangerous enthusiasm.[11]

596   Spirits are not under all circumstances dangerous and harmful. They can, when translated into ideas, also have beneficial effects. A well-known example of this transformation of a content of the collective unconscious into communicable language is the miracle of Pentecost. From the point of view of the onlookers, the apostles were in a state of ecstatic intoxication ("These men are full of new wine": Acts 2 : 13). But it was just when they were in this state that they communicated the new teaching which gave expression to the unconscious expectations of the people and spread with astonishing rapidity through the whole Roman Empire.

597   Spirits are complexes of the collective unconscious which appear when the individual loses his adaptation to reality, or which seek to replace the inadequate attitude of a whole people by a new one. They are therefore either pathological fantasies or new but as yet unknown ideas.

598   The psychogenesis of the spirits of the dead seems to me to be more or less as follows. When a person dies, the feelings and emotions that bound his relatives to him lose their application to reality and sink into the unconscious, where they activate a collective content that has a deleterious effect on consciousness. The Bataks and many other primitives therefore say that when a man dies his character deteriorates, so that he is always trying to harm the living in some way. This view is obviously based on

11 This account of the genesis of a collective psyche was written in the spring of 1919. Events since 1933 have amply confirmed it.

the experience that a persistent attachment to the dead makes life seem less worth living, and may even be the cause of psychic illnesses. The harmful effect shows itself in the form of loss of libido, depression, and physical debility. There are also universal reports of these post-mortem phenomena in the form of ghosts and hauntings. They are based in the main on psychic facts which cannot be dismissed out of hand. Very often the fear of superstition—which, strangely enough, is the concomitant of universal enlightenment—is responsible for the hasty suppression of extremely interesting factual reports which are thus lost to science. I have not only found many reports of this kind among my patients, but have also observed a few things myself. But my material is too slender for me to base any verifiable hypothesis on it. Nevertheless, I myself am convinced that ghosts and suchlike have to do with psychic facts of which our academic wisdom refuses to take cognizance, although they appear clearly enough in our dreams.

*

599   In this essay I have sketched out a psychological interpretation of the problem of spirits from the standpoint of our present knowledge of unconscious processes. I have confined myself wholly to the psychological side of the problem, and purposely avoided the question of whether spirits exist in themselves and can give evidence of their existence through material effects. I avoid this question not because I regard it as futile from the start, but because I am not in a position to adduce experiences that would prove it one way or the other. I think the reader will be as conscious as I am that it is extraordinarily difficult to find reliable evidence for the independent existence of spirits, since the usual spiritualistic communications are as a rule nothing but very ordinary products of the personal unconscious.[12] There are, nevertheless, a few exceptions worth mentioning. I would like to call attention to a remarkable case Stewart E. White has described in a number of books. Here the communications have a much profounder content than usual. For instance, a great many archetypal ideas were produced, among them the archetype of the self, so that one might almost think there had been borrowings from my writings. If we discount the possibility

[12] [The rest of this paragraph was added in the 1948 Swiss edition.—EDITORS.]

of conscious plagiarism, I should say that cryptomnesic reproduction is very unlikely. It appears to be a case of genuine,
spontaneous production of a collective archetype. This is not in
itself anything extraordinary, since the archetype of the self is
met with everywhere in mythology as well as in the products of
individual fantasy. The spontaneous irruption of collective
contents whose existence in the unconscious has long been
known to psychology is part of the general tendency of medium-
istic communications to filter the contents of the unconscious
through to consciousness. I have studied a wide range of spiritualistic literature precisely for these tendencies and have come
to the conclusion that in spiritualism we have a spontaneous
attempt of the unconscious to become conscious in a collective
form. The psychotherapeutic endeavours of the so-called spirits
are aimed at the living either directly, or indirectly through
the deceased person, in order to make them more conscious.
Spiritualism as a collective phenomenon thus pursues the
same goals as medical psychology, and in so doing produces, as
in this case, the same basic ideas and images—styling themselves
the "teachings of the spirits"—which are characteristic of the
nature of the collective unconscious. Such things, however
baffling they may be, prove nothing either for or against the
hypothesis of spirits. But it is a very different matter when we
come to proven cases of identity. I shall not commit the fashion-
able stupidity of regarding everything I cannot explain as a
fraud. There are probably very few proofs of this kind which
could stand up to the test of cryptomnesia and, above all, of
extra-sensory perception. Science cannot afford the luxury of
naïveté in these matters. Nevertheless, I would recommend anyone who is interested in the psychology of the unconscious to
read the books of Stewart White.[13] The most interesting to my
mind is *The Unobstructed Universe* (1940). *The Road I Know*
(1942) is also remarkable in that it serves as an admirable introduction to the method of "active imagination" which I have been
using for more than thirty years in the treatment of neurosis, as
a means to bringing unconscious contents to consciousness.[14] In

[13] I am indebted to Dr. Fritz Künkel, of Los Angeles, for drawing my attention to
this author.
[14] For a short description of this method see "The Transcendent Function,"
supra; also "The Relations between the Ego and the Unconscious," ch. III.

all these books you still find the primitive equation: spirit-land = dreamland (the unconscious).

600   These parapsychic phenomena seem to be connected as a rule with the presence of a medium. They are, so far as my experience goes, the exteriorized effects of unconscious complexes. I for one am certainly convinced that they are exteriorizations. I have repeatedly observed the telepathic effects of unconscious complexes, and also a number of parapsychic phenomena. But in all this I see no proof whatever of the existence of real spirits, and until such proof is forthcoming I must regard this whole territory as an appendix of psychology.[15] I think science has to impose this restriction on itself. Yet one should never forget that science is simply a matter of intellect, and that the intellect is only one among several fundamental psychic functions and therefore does not suffice to give a complete picture of the world. For this another function—feeling—is needed too. Feeling often arrives at convictions that are different from those of the intellect, and we cannot always prove that the convictions of feeling are necessarily inferior. We also have subliminal perceptions of the unconscious which are not at the disposal of the intellect and are therefore missing in a purely intellectual picture of the world. So we have every reason to grant our intellect only a limited validity. But when we work with the intellect, we must proceed scientifically and adhere to empirical principles until irrefutable evidence against their validity is forthcoming.

[15] After collecting psychological experiences from many people and many countries for fifty years, I no longer feel as certain as I did in 1919, when I wrote this sentence. To put it bluntly, I doubt whether an exclusively psychological approach can do justice to the phenomena in question. Not only the findings of parapsychology, but my own theoretical reflections, outlined in "On the Nature of the Psyche," have led me to certain postulates which touch on the realm of nuclear physics and the conception of the space-time continuum. This opens up the whole question of the transpsychic reality immediately underlying the psyche.

SPIRIT AND LIFE [1]

601   The connection between spirit and life is one of those problems involving factors of such complexity that we have to be on
our guard lest we ourselves get caught in the net of words in
which we seek to ensnare these great enigmas. For how can we
bring within the orbit of our thought those limitless complexes
of facts which we call "spirit" or "life" unless we clothe them
in verbal concepts, themselves mere counters of the intellect?
The mistrust of verbal concepts, inconvenient as it is, nevertheless seems to me to be very much in place in speaking of fundamentals. "Spirit" and "life" are familiar enough words to us,
very old acquaintances in fact, pawns that for thousands of years
have been pushed back and forth on the thinker's chessboard.
The problem must have begun in the grey dawn of time, when
someone made the bewildering discovery that the living breath
which left the body of the dying man in the last death-rattle
meant more than just air in motion. It can scarcely be an accident that onomatopoeic words like *ruach, ruch, roho* (Hebrew,

1 A lecture delivered to the literary society of Augsburg, October 29, 1926, one
of a series of lectures on the theme "Nature and Spirit." [First published as
"Geist und Leben," *Form und Sinn* (Augsburg), II : 2 (Nov. 1926), which was
translated by H. G. and C. F. Baynes in *Contributions to Analytical Psychology*
(London and New York, 1928). The original version was republished in *Seelenprobleme der Gegenwart* (Psychologische Abhandlungen, II; Zurich, 1931). The
present translation is based on the Baynes version.—EDITORS.]

Arabic, Swahili) mean "spirit" no less clearly than the Greek πνεῦμα and the Latin *spiritus*.

602   Do we know then, for all our familiarity with the verbal concept, what spirit really is? Are we sure that when we use this word we all mean the same thing? Is not the word "spirit" a most perplexingly ambiguous term? The same verbal sign, spirit, is used for an inexpressible, transcendental idea of all-embracing significance; in a more commonplace sense it is synonymous with "mind"; it may connote courage, liveliness, or wit, or it may mean a ghost; it can also represent an unconscious complex that causes spiritualistic phenomena like table-turning, automatic writing, rappings, etc. In a metaphorical sense it may refer to the dominant attitude in a particular social group—the "spirit" that prevails there. Finally, it is used in a material sense, as spirits of wine, spirits of ammonia, and spirituous liquors in general. This is not just a bad joke—it is a part of the venerable heritage of our language, while on the other hand it is a paralysing encumbrance to thought, a tragic obstacle to all who hope to scale the ethereal heights of pure ideas on the ladders of words. When I utter the word "spirit," no matter how accurately I may define the meaning I intend it to convey, the aura of its many other meanings cannot be wholly excluded.

603   We must therefore ask ourselves the fundamental question: What is really meant by the word "spirit" when it is used in connection with the concept "life"? Under no circumstances should it be tacitly assumed that, at bottom, everybody knows just what is meant by "spirit" or "life."

604   Not being a philosopher, but an empiricist, I am inclined in all difficult questions to let experience decide. Where it is impossible to find any tangible basis in experience, I prefer to leave the questions unanswered. It is my aim, therefore, always to reduce abstract concepts to their empirical basis, in order to be moderately sure that I know what I am talking about. I must confess that I know as little what "spirit" may be in itself as I know what "life" is. I know "life" only in the form of a living body; what it might be in and for itself, in an abstract state, other than a mere word, I cannot even darkly guess. Thus instead of "life" I must first speak of the living body, and instead of "spirit" of psychic factors. This does not mean that I want to evade the question as originally put in order to indulge in

reflections on body and mind. On the contrary, I hope the empirical approach will help us to find a real basis for spirit—and not at the expense of life.

605   The concept of the living body brings fewer difficulties to our task of elucidation than does the general concept of life, for the body is a visible and tangible reality that does not elude our grasp. We can easily agree, then, that the body is a self-contained system of material units adapted to the purpose of living and, as such, is a phenomenon of the living being apprehended by our senses. More simply, it is a purposive arrangement of matter that makes a living being possible. To avoid confusion, I must point out that I do not include in my definition of the body proper something which I vaguely characterize as a "living being." This separation of the two things, which I do not propose either to defend or to criticize for the moment, is meant only to indicate that the body cannot be understood as a mere heaping together of inert matter, but must be regarded as a material system ready for life and making life possible, with the proviso that for all its readiness it could not live without the addition of this "living being." For, setting aside the possible significance of "living being," there is lacking to the body by itself something that is necessary to its life, namely the psychic factor. We know this directly from our own experience of ourselves, and indirectly from our experience of our fellow men. We also know it through our scientific study of the higher vertebrates, and, for total lack of evidence to the contrary, we must suppose that some such factor is present in lower organisms and even in plants.

606   Shall we now assume that this "living being" of which I spoke is equivalent to the psychic factor directly experienced by us in human consciousness, and so re-establish the ancient duality of mind and body? Or are there any reasons that would justify the separation of the "living being" from the psyche? In that case the psyche, too, would have to be understood as a purposive system, as an arrangement not merely of matter *ready for life,* but of *living matter* or, more precisely, of *living processes.* I am not at all sure that this view will meet with general acceptance, for we are so accustomed to thinking of mind and body as a living unit that it is difficult for us to conceive of the

psyche merely as an arrangement of life-processes taking place in the body.

607   So far as our experience permits of any inferences at all about the nature of the psyche, it shows the psychic process as a phenomenon dependent on the nervous system. We know with tolerable certainty that disturbance of certain portions of the brain brings about corresponding psychic defects. The spinal cord and the brain consist essentially of interconnections between the sensory and motor tracts, the so-called reflex arcs. What is meant by this I can best show by means of an example. Suppose one touches a hot object with the finger: at once the nerve-endings are stimulated by the heat. This stimulus alters the condition of the whole path of conduction up the spinal cord and thence to the brain. In the spinal cord, the ganglion cells taking up the heat stimulus pass on the change of condition to the neighbouring motor-ganglion cells, which in their turn send out a stimulus to the arm-muscles, thereby causing a sudden contraction of the muscles and a withdrawal of the hand. All this occurs with such rapidity that the conscious perception of pain often comes when the hand has already been withdrawn. The reaction is automatic and is not registered consciously till afterwards. But what happens in the spinal cord is transmitted to the perceiving ego in the form of a record, or image, which one can furnish with names and concepts. On the basis of such a reflex arc, that is, a stimulus moving from without inward, followed by an impulse from within outward, one can form some idea of the processes that lie beneath the mind.

608   Let us now take a less simple example. We hear an indistinct sound the initial effect of which is no more than a stimulus to listen in order to find out what it means. In this case the auditory stimulus releases a whole series of images which associate themselves with the stimulus. They will be partly acoustic images, partly visual images, and partly images of feeling. Here I use the word "image" simply in the sense of a representation. A psychic entity can be a conscious content, that is, it can be represented, only if it has the quality of an image and is thus *representable*. I therefore call all conscious contents images, since they are reflections of processes in the brain.

609   The series of images excited by the auditory stimulus is now suddenly joined by a remembered acoustic image associated with

a visual image: the rattle of a rattlesnake. This is immediately followed by an alarm signal to all the body muscles. The reflex arc is complete, but in this case it differs from the previous one in that a cerebral process, a series of mental images, interposes itself between the sensory stimulus and the motor impulse. The sudden tension of the body now reacts on the heart and blood-vessels and releases processes that are mentally recorded as terror.

610   In this way we can form an idea of the nature of the psyche. It consists of reflected images of simple processes in the brain, and of reproductions of these images in an almost infinite series. These images have the quality of consciousness. The nature of consciousness is a riddle whose solution I do not know. It is possible to say, however, that anything psychic will take on the quality of consciousness if it comes into association with the ego. If there is no such association, it remains unconscious. Forgetfulness shows how often and how easily contents lose their connection with the ego. We could therefore compare consciousness to the beam of a searchlight. Only those objects upon which the cone of light falls enter the field of perception. An object that happens to lie in the darkness has not ceased to exist, it is merely not seen. So what is unconscious to me exists somewhere, in a state which is probably no different from what it is when seen by the ego.

611   Consciousness can therefore be understood as a state of association with the ego. But the critical point is the ego. What do we mean by the ego? For all its appearance of unity, it is obviously a highly composite factor. It is made up of images recorded from the sense-functions that transmit stimuli both from within and from without, and furthermore of an immense accumulation of images of past processes. All these multifarious components need a powerful cohesive force to hold them together, and this we have already recognized as a property of consciousness. Consciousness therefore seems to be the necessary precondition for the ego. Yet without the ego, consciousness is unthinkable. This apparent contradiction may perhaps be resolved by regarding the ego, too, as a reflection not of one but of very many processes and their interplay—in fact, of all those processes and contents that make up ego-consciousness. Their diversity does indeed form a unity, because their relation to consciousness acts as a sort of gravitational force drawing the

various parts together, towards what might be called a virtual centre. For this reason I do not speak simply of *the* ego, but of an *ego-complex,* on the proven assumption that the ego, having a fluctuating composition, is changeable and therefore cannot be simply *the* ego. (Unfortunately, I cannot discuss here the classic ego-changes that are found in mental illnesses and in dreams.)

612 This view of the ego as a composite of psychic elements logically brings us to the question: Is the ego the central image and thus the exclusive representative of the total human being? Are all the contents and functions related to it and does it express them all?

613 We must answer this question in the negative. The ego is a complex that does not comprise the total human being; it has forgotten infinitely more than it knows. It has heard and seen an infinite amount of which it has never become conscious. There are thoughts that spring up beyond the range of consciousness, fully formed and complete, and it knows nothing of them. The ego has scarcely even the vaguest notion of the incredibly important regulative function of the sympathetic nervous system in relation to the internal bodily processes. What the ego comprehends is perhaps the smallest part of what a complete consciousness would have to comprehend.

614 The ego can therefore be only a fragmentary complex. Is it perhaps that peculiar complex whose inner cohesion amounts to consciousness? But is not every cohesion of psychic parts consciousness? It is not altogether clear why the cohesion of a certain part of the sense-functions and a certain part of our memory-material should be consciousness, while the cohesion of other parts of the psyche should not. The complex of seeing, hearing, etc. has a strong and well-organized inner unity. There is no reason to suppose that this unity could not be a consciousness as well. As the case of the deaf and blind Helen Keller shows, the sense of touch and the bodily sensations are sufficient to make consciousness possible, at any rate a consciousness limited to these senses. I therefore think of ego-consciousness as a synthesis of the various "sense-consciousnesses," in which the independence of each separate consciousness is submerged in the unity of the overruling ego.

615 Since ego-consciousness does not embrace all psychic activi-

ties and phenomena, that is, since they are not all recorded there as images, the question naturally arises whether there may not be a cohesion of all psychic activities similar to that of ego-consciousness. This might be conceived as a higher or wider consciousness in which the ego would be seen as an objective content, just as the act of seeing is an object of my consciousness, and, like it, would be fused with other activities of which I am not conscious. Our ego-consciousness might well be enclosed within a more complete consciousness like a smaller circle within a larger.

616 Just as the activities of seeing, hearing, etc. create images of themselves which, when related to the ego, produce a consciousness of the activity in question, so the ego, as I have said, can be understood as an image or reflection of all the activities comprehended by it. We would expect that all psychic activities would produce images of themselves and that this would be their essential nature without which they could not be called "psychic." It is difficult to see why unconscious psychic activities should not have the same faculty of producing images as those that are represented in consciousness. And since man appears to be a living unity in himself, the conclusion would follow that the images of all his psychic activities are united in one total image of the whole man, which if known to him would be regarded as an ego.

617 I could advance no conclusive argument against such an assumption, but it would remain an idle dream so long as it were not needed as an explanatory hypothesis. Yet, even if the possibility of a higher consciousness were needed to explain certain psychic facts, it would still remain a mere hypothesis, since it would far exceed the power of reason to prove the existence of a consciousness other than the one we know. It is always possible that what lies in the darkness beyond our consciousness is totally different from anything the most daring speculation could imagine.

618 I shall return to this question in the course of my exposition. We will put it aside for the time being and turn back to the original question of mind and body. From what has been said, it should be clear that the psyche consists essentially of images. It is a series of images in the truest sense, not an accidental juxtaposition or sequence, but a structure that is throughout

full of meaning and purpose; it is a "picturing" of vital activities. And just as the material of the body that is ready for life has need of the psyche in order to be capable of life, so the psyche presupposes the living body in order that its images may live.

619   Mind and body are presumably a pair of opposites and, as such, the expression of a single entity whose essential nature is not knowable either from its outward, material manifestation or from inner, direct perception. According to an ancient belief, man arose from the coming together of a soul and a body. It would probably be more correct to speak of an unknowable living being, concerning the ultimate nature of which nothing can be said except that it vaguely expresses the quintessence of "life." This living being appears outwardly as the material body, but inwardly as a series of images of the vital activities taking place within it. They are two sides of the same coin, and we cannot rid ourselves of the doubt that perhaps this whole separation of mind and body may finally prove to be merely a device of reason for the purpose of conscious discrimination—an intellectually necessary separation of one and the same fact into two aspects, to which we then illegitimately attribute an independent existence.

620   Science has never been able to grasp the riddle of life either in organic matter or in the mysterious trains of mental imagery; consequently we are still in search of the "living being" whose existence we must postulate somewhere beyond experience. Anyone who knows the abysses of physiology will become dizzy at the thought of them, just as anyone who knows the psyche will be staggered by the thought that this amazing mirror-thing should ever attain anything approaching "knowledge."

621   From this point of view one might easily abandon all hope of discovering anything fundamental about that elusive thing called "spirit." One thing alone seems clear: just as the "living being" is the quintessence of life in the body, so "spirit" is the quintessence of the life of the mind; indeed, the concept "spirit" is often used interchangeably with the concept "mind." Viewed thus, "spirit" exists in the same transliminal realm as "living being," that is, in the same misty state of indistinguishableness. And the doubt as to whether mind and body may not ultimately prove to be the same thing also applies to the apparent contrast

326

between "spirit" and "living being." They too are probably the same thing.

622   But are these quintessential concepts necessary at all? Could we not rest content with the already sufficiently mysterious contrast between mind and body? From the scientific standpoint, we would have to stop here. But there is another standpoint, satisfying to our intellectual conscience, which not only allows but even forces us to go forward and overleap that seemingly impassable boundary. This is the *psychological* standpoint.

623   So far I have based my reflections on the realistic standpoint of scientific thinking, without ever questioning the foundation on which I stood. But in order to explain briefly what I mean by the psychological standpoint, I must show that serious doubt can be cast on the exclusive validity of the realistic standpoint. Let us take as an example what a naïve mind would consider to be the realest thing of all, namely matter. We can make only the dimmest theoretical guesses about the nature of matter, and these guesses are nothing but images created by our minds. The wave-movements or solar emanations which meet my eye are translated by my perception into light. It is my mind, with its store of images, that gives the world colour and sound; and that supremely real and rational certainty which I call "experience" is, in its most simple form, an exceedingly complicated structure of mental images. Thus there is, in a certain sense, nothing that is directly experienced except the mind itself. Everything is mediated through the mind, translated, filtered, allegorized, twisted, even falsified by it. We are so enveloped in a cloud of changing and endlessly shifting images that we might well exclaim with a well-known sceptic: "Nothing is absolutely true— and even that is not quite true." So thick and deceptive is this fog about us that we had to invent the exact sciences in order to catch at least a glimmer of the so-called "real" nature of things. To a naïve-minded person, of course, this almost too vivid world will not seem in the least foggy. But let him delve into the mind of a primitive and compare his picture of the world with that of civilized man. He will then have an inkling of the profound twilight in which we still live.

624   What we know of the world, and what we are immediately aware of in ourselves, are conscious contents that flow from remote, obscure sources. I do not contest the relative validity

327

either of the realistic standpoint, the *esse in re,* or of the idealistic standpoint, the *esse in intellectu solo;* I would only like to unite these extreme opposites by an *esse in anima,* which is the psychological standpoint. We live immediately only in the world of images.

625   If we take this standpoint seriously, peculiar results follow. We find that the validity of psychic facts cannot be subjected either to epistemological criticism or to scientific verification. We can only put the question: Is a conscious content present or not? If it is present, then it is valid in itself. Science can only be invoked when the content claims to be an assertion about something that can be met with in the external world; we can appeal to epistemological criticism only when an unknowable thing is posited as knowable. Let us take an example familiar to everyone. Science has never discovered any "God," epistemological criticism proves the impossibility of knowing God, but the psyche comes forward with the assertion of the experience of God. God is a psychic fact of immediate experience, otherwise there would never have been any talk of God. The fact is valid in itself, requiring no non-psychological proof and inaccessible to any form of non-psychological criticism. It can be the most immediate and hence the most real of experiences, which can be neither ridiculed nor disproved. Only people with a poorly developed sense of fact, or who are obstinately superstitious, could deny this truth. So long as the experience of God does not claim universal validity or assert the absolute existence of God, criticism is impossible; for an irrational fact, such as, for instance, the existence of elephants, cannot be criticized. Nevertheless, the experience of God has general validity inasmuch as almost everyone knows approximately what is meant by the term "experience of God." As a fact occurring with relative frequency it must be recognized by a scientific psychology. Nor can we simply turn our backs on what is decried as superstition. When a person asserts that he has seen ghosts or that he is bewitched, and it means more to him than just talk, then again we are dealing with a fact of experience, and one so general that everyone knows what is meant by "ghost" or by being "bewitched." We can therefore be sure that even in these cases we are confronted with a definite complex of psychic facts which, as such, are just as "real" as the light I see. I do not know how

328

I could prove the existence of the ghost of a dead person in empirical reality, nor can I imagine the logical method whereby I could deduce with certainty the continuance of life after death; but, none the less, I have to reckon with the fact that at all times and in all places the psyche has claimed to experience ghosts. I have to take this into consideration, just as much as the fact that many people flatly deny this subjective experience.

626 After this more general discussion I would now like to come back to the concept of spirit, which we were unable to grasp from our former realistic standpoint. Spirit, like God, denotes an object of psychic experience which cannot be proved to exist in the external world and cannot be understood rationally. This is its meaning if we use the word "spirit" in its best sense. Once we have freed ourselves from the prejudice that we have to refer a concept either to objects of external experience or to *a priori* categories of reason, we can turn our attention and curiosity wholly to that strange and still unknown thing we call "spirit." It is always useful in such cases to take a glance at the probable etymology of the word, because it often happens that a word's history throws a surprising light on the nature of the psychic fact underlying it.

627 In Old High German *Geist*, and in Anglo-Saxon *gāst*, meant a supernatural being in contradistinction to the body. According to Kluge, the fundamental meaning of the word is not quite certain, though there seem to be connections with the Old Norse *geisa*, 'to rage', with the Gothic *us-gaisyan*, 'to be beside oneself', with the Swiss-German *üf-gaistä*, 'to fly into a passion', and with the English *aghast*. These connections are substantiated by other figures of speech. For a person "to be seized with rage" means that something falls on him, sits on him, rides him, he is ridden by the devil, he is possessed, something has got into him, etc. At the pre-psychological stage, and also in poetic language, which owes its power to its vital primitivity, emotions and affects are often personified as daemons. To be in love is to be "struck by Cupid's arrow," or "Eris has thrown the apple of discord," and so on. When we are "beside ourselves with rage" we are obviously no longer identical with ourselves, but are possessed by a daemon or spirit.

628 The primitive atmosphere in which the word "spirit" came to birth exists in us still, though of course on a psychic level

329

somewhere below consciousness. But as modern spiritualism shows, it needs very little to bring that bit of primitive mentality to the surface. If the etymological derivation (which in itself is quite plausible) holds good, then "spirit" in this sense would be the image of a personified affect. For instance, when a person lets himself be carried away by imprudent talk, we say his tongue has run away with him, which is equivalent to saying that his talk has become an independent being that has snatched him up and run off with him. Psychologically we would say: every affect tends to become an autonomous complex, to break away from the hierarchy of consciousness and, if possible, to drag the ego after it. No wonder, then, that the primitive mind sees in this the activity of a strange invisible being, a spirit. Spirit in this case is the reflection of an autonomous affect, which is why the ancients, very appropriately, called the spirits *imagines*, 'images'.

629   Let us now turn to other usages of the concept "spirit." The phrase "he acts in the spirit of his dead father" still has a double meaning, for here the word "spirit" refers as much to the spirit of the dead as to an attitude of mind. Other idioms are "doing something in a new spirit" or "a new spirit is growing up," meaning a renewal of mental attitude. The basic idea is again that of possession by a spirit, which has become, say, the "guiding spirit" of a group. A more sombre note is struck when we say: "An evil spirit reigns in that family."

630   Here we are dealing not with personifications of affects but with visualizations of a whole frame of mind or—to put it psychologically—an attitude. A bad attitude expressed as an evil spirit therefore has, if naïvely conceived, nearly the same psychological function as a personified affect. This may be surprising to many people, since "attitude" is ordinarily understood as taking an attitude towards something, an ego-activity in short, implying purposefulness. However, an attitude or frame of mind is by no means always a product of volition; more often it owes its peculiarity to mental contagion, i.e., to example and the influence of environment. It is a well-known fact that there are people whose bad attitude poisons the atmosphere; their bad example is contagious, they make others nervous by their intolerableness. At school a single mischief-maker can spoil the spirit of a whole class; and conversely, the joyous, innocent disposition of a child can brighten and irradiate the otherwise

dreary atmosphere of a family, which is naturally only possible when the attitude of each individual in it is bettered by the good example. An attitude can also take effect even against the conscious will—"bad company spoils good manners." This is particularly evident in mass-suggestion.

631 The attitude or disposition, then, can thrust itself on consciousness from outside or from inside, like an affect, and can therefore be expressed by the same figures of speech. An attitude seems, at first glance, to be something very much more complicated than an affect. On closer inspection, however, we find that this is not so, because most attitudes are based, consciously or unconsciously, on some kind of *maxim,* which often has the character of a proverb. In some attitudes one can immediately detect the underlying maxim and even discover where it was picked up. Often the attitude is distinguished only by a single word, which as a rule stands for an ideal. Not infrequently, the quintessence of an attitude is neither a maxim nor an ideal but a personality who is revered and emulated.

632 Educators make use of these psychological facts and try to suggest suitable attitudes by means of maxims and ideals, and some of them may indeed remain effective throughout life as permanent guiding principles. They take possession of a person like spirits. On a more primitive level it is the vision of the Master, the shepherd, the *poimen* or *poimandres,* who personifies the guiding principles and concretizes them in a symbolical figure.

633 Here we approach a concept of "spirit" that goes far beyond the animistic frame of reference. Aphorisms and proverbs are as a rule the result of much experience and individual effort, a summing up of insights and conclusions in a few pregnant words. If you subject the Gospel saying "The first shall be last" to a thorough analysis, and try to reconstruct all the experiences that have been distilled into this quintessence of life's wisdom, you cannot but marvel at the fullness and mellowness of the experience behind it. It is an "impressive" saying, which strikes upon the receptive mind with great power, and perhaps retains possession of it for ever. Those sayings or ideals that store up the richest experience of life and the deepest reflection constitute what we call "spirit" in the best sense of the word. When a ruling principle of this kind attains absolute mastery we speak of the

life lived under its guidance as "ruled by the spirit," or as a "spiritual life." The more absolute and compelling the ruling idea, the more it has the nature of an autonomous complex that confronts the ego-consciousness as an unshakable fact.

634   We must not forget, however, that such maxims and ideals, even the best of them, are not magic spells whose power is absolute, but that they gain mastery only under certain conditions, when there is something in us that responds to them, an affect that is ready to seize hold of the proffered form. Only under the stress of emotion can the idea, or whatever the ruling principle may be, become an autonomous complex; without this the idea remains a concept subservient to the arbitrary opinions of the conscious mind, a mere intellectual counter with no compelling power behind it. An idea that is nothing but an intellectual counter can have no influence on life, because in this state it is little more than an empty word. Conversely, once the idea attains the status of an autonomous complex, it works on the individual through his emotions.

635   One should not think of these autonomous attitudes as coming about through conscious volition and conscious choice. When I say that the help of emotion is needed, I could just as well have said that besides the conscious will there must be an unconscious readiness to bring about an autonomous attitude. You cannot, so to speak, *will* to be spiritual. Those principles we can select and strive for always remain within the sphere of our judgment and under our conscious control; hence they can never turn into something that dominates the conscious will. It is far more a matter of fate what principle will rule our attitude.

636   The question will certainly be asked whether for some people their own free will may not be the ruling principle, so that every attitude is intentionally chosen by themselves. I do not believe that anyone reaches or has ever reached this godlike state, but I know that there are many who strive after this ideal because they are possessed by the heroic idea of absolute freedom. In one way or another all men are dependent; all are in some way limited, since none are gods.

637   The truth is that our conscious mind does not express the whole of our human nature; it is and remains only a part. In the introductory section of my lecture I mentioned the possi-

bility that our ego-consciousness is not the only sort of consciousness in our system, but might perhaps be subordinate to a wider consciousness, just as simpler complexes are subordinate to the ego-complex.

638   I would not know how we could ever prove that a consciousness higher or wider than the ego-consciousness exists in us; but, if it does exist, the ego-consciousness must find it acutely disturbing. A simple example will make clear what I mean. Let us imagine that our optical system had a consciousness of its own and was therefore a kind of personality, which we shall call the "eye-personality." This "eye-personality" has, let us say, discovered a beautiful view and is lost in contemplation of it. All of a sudden the auditory system hears the horn of an automobile. This perception remains unconscious to the optical system. From the ego there now follows, again in a way unconscious to the optical system, an order to the muscles to move the body to another position in space. Through this movement the object is suddenly taken away from the eye-consciousness. If the eyes could think, they would naturally come to the conclusion that the light-world was subject to all sorts of obscure disturbances.

639   Something of the sort would be bound to happen if a wider consciousness exists, a consciousness which, as I suggested before, would be an image of the whole man. Are there in fact obscure disturbances of this kind, which no will can control and no purpose deflect? And is there anywhere in us something intangible that might conceivably be the source of such disturbances? To the first question we can answer yes, without more ado. In normal people, not to speak of neurotics, we can easily observe the most obvious interferences and disturbances from another sphere. A mood may suddenly change, a headache comes upon us unawares, the name of a friend we are about to introduce vanishes into thin air, a melody pursues us for a whole day, we want to do something but the energy for it has in some inexplicable way disappeared. We forget what we least wanted to forget, we resign ourselves happily to sleep and sleep is snatched away from us, or we sleep and our slumber is disturbed by fantastic, annoying dreams; spectacles resting on our nose are searched for, the new umbrella is left we know not where. As to the psychology of neurotics, we find ourselves confronted with the most paradoxical disturbances. Amazing pathological

symptoms develop, yet no organ is diseased. Without the least organic disorder the patient's temperature may shoot up to over 105° F., or there may be suffocating states of anxiety without any real foundation, obsessive ideas whose senselessness is apparent even to the patient, skin-rashes that come and go regardless of all reason and all therapy. For each case an explanation can naturally be found, either good or bad, though it entirely fails to explain the next case. Yet there can be no doubt about the existence of the disturbances.

640 Coming now to the second question, the source of the disturbances. We know that medical psychology has put forward the concept of the unconscious, and has demonstrated that these disturbances depend on unconscious processes. It is as though the "eye-personality" had discovered that there must be invisible determining factors as well as visible ones. If the facts do not deceive us, the unconscious processes are far from being unintelligent. The character of automatism and mechanism is lacking to them, even to a striking degree. They are not in the least inferior to the conscious processes in subtlety; on the contrary, they often far surpass our conscious insights.

641 Our imaginary "eye-personality" might doubt that the sudden disturbances of its light-world came from another consciousness. Similarly, we can be sceptical about a wider consciousness, though with no more ground for scepticism than the eye-personality would have. But as we cannot attain to such a state of wider consciousness or understand it, we would do well to call that dark region, from our point of view, the "unconscious," without jumping to the conclusion that it is necessarily unconscious of itself.

642 I have returned at this point in the discussion to my previous hypothesis of a higher consciousness because the problem we are concerned with here, namely the life-ruling power of the spirit, is connected with processes outside ego-consciousness. A little further back I mentioned in passing that an idea which lacks emotional force can never become a life-ruling factor. I also said it was a matter of fate what kind of attitude or "spirit" would develop, in order to emphasize that the conscious mind is not in a position to create an autonomous complex at will. It is not autonomous unless it comes upon us forcibly, and visibly proves its superiority to the conscious will. It, too, is one of

334

those disturbances that arise out of the dark regions. When I said earlier that an idea must evoke a response from the emotions, I meant an unconscious readiness which, because of its affective nature, springs from deeper levels that are quite inaccessible to consciousness. Thus, our conscious reason can never destroy the roots of nervous symptoms; for this emotional processes are needed, which even have the power to influence the sympathetic nervous system. We could equally well say that when the wider consciousness sees fit, a compelling idea is put before the ego-consciousness as an unconditional command. Anyone who is conscious of his guiding principle knows with what indisputable authority it rules his life. But generally consciousness is too preoccupied with the attainment of some beckoning goal to consider the nature of the spirit that determines its course.

643   From the psychological point of view the phenomenon of spirit, like every autonomous complex, appears as an intention of the unconscious superior to, or at least on a par with, the intentions of the ego. If we are to do justice to the essence of the thing we call spirit, we should really speak of a "higher" consciousness rather than of the unconscious, because the concept of spirit is such that we are bound to connect it with the idea of superiority over the ego-consciousness. The superiority of the spirit is not something attributed to it by conscious reflection, but clings to it as an essential quality, as is evident from the records of all ages, from the Holy Scriptures down to Nietzsche's *Zarathustra*. Psychologically, the spirit manifests itself as a personal being, sometimes with visionary clarity; in Christian dogma it is actually the third Person of the Trinity. These facts show that spirit is not always merely a maxim or an idea that can be formulated, but that in its strongest and most immediate manifestations it displays a peculiar life of its own which is felt as an independent being. So long as the spirit can be named and formulated as an intelligible principle or a clear idea, it will certainly not be felt as an independent being. But when the idea or principle involved is inscrutable, when its intentions are obscure in origin and in aim and yet enforce themselves, then the spirit is necessarily felt as an independent being, as a kind of higher consciousness, and its inscrutable, superior nature can no longer be expressed in the concepts of

335

human reason. Our powers of expression then have recourse to other means; they create a *symbol*.

644   By a symbol I do not mean an allegory or a sign, but an image that describes in the best possible way the dimly discerned nature of the spirit. A symbol does not define or explain; it points beyond itself to a meaning that is darkly divined yet still beyond our grasp, and cannot be adequately expressed in the familiar words of our language. Spirit that can be translated into a definite concept is a psychic complex lying within the orbit of our ego-consciousness. It will not bring forth anything, nor will it achieve anything more than we have put into it. But spirit that demands a symbol for its expression is a psychic complex that contains the seeds of incalculable possibilities. The most obvious and best example of this is the effectiveness of the Christian symbols, whose power changed the face of history. If one looks without prejudice at the way the spirit of early Christianity worked on the mind of the average man of the second century, one can only be amazed. But then, no spirit was ever as creative as this. No wonder it was felt to be of godlike superiority.

645   It is this clear feeling of superiority that gives the phenomenon of the spirit its revelatory character and absolute authority —a dangerous quality, to be sure; for what we might perhaps call "higher" consciousness is not always higher from the point of view of our conscious values and often contrasts violently with our accepted ideals. One should, strictly speaking, describe this hypothetical consciousness simply as a "wider" one, so as not to arouse the prejudice that it is necessarily higher in the intellectual or moral sense. There are many spirits, both light and dark. We should, therefore, be prepared to accept the view that spirit is not absolute, but something relative that needs completing and perfecting through life. There are all too many cases of men so possessed by a spirit that the man does not live any more but only the spirit, and in a way that does not bring him a richer and fuller life but only cripples him. I am far from implying that the death of a Christian martyr was a meaningless and purposeless act of destruction—on the contrary, such a death can also mean a fuller life than any other—rather, I refer to the spirit of certain sects which wholly deny life. Naturally the strict Montanist view was in accord with the highest moral demands

of the age, but it destroyed life all the same. What is to become of the spirit when it has exterminated man? I believe, therefore, that a spirit which accords with our highest ideals will find its limits set by life. It is certainly necessary for life, since a mere ego-life, as we well know, is a most inadequate and unsatisfactory thing. Only a life lived in a certain spirit is worth living. It is a remarkable fact that a life lived entirely from the ego is dull not only for the person himself but for all concerned. The fullness of life requires more than just an ego; it needs spirit, that is, an independent, overruling complex, for it seems that this alone is capable of giving vital expression to those psychic potentialities that lie beyond the reach of ego-consciousness.

646   But, just as there is a passion that strives for blind unrestricted life, so there is a passion that would like to sacrifice all life to the spirit because of its superior creative power. This passion turns the spirit into a malignant growth that senselessly destroys human life.

647   Life is a touchstone for the truth of the spirit. Spirit that drags a man away from life, seeking fulfilment only in itself, is a false spirit—though the man too is to blame, since he can choose whether he will give himself up to this spirit or not.

648   Life and spirit are two powers or necessities between which man is placed. Spirit gives meaning to his life, and the possibility of its greatest development. But life is essential to spirit, since its truth is nothing if it cannot live.

BASIC POSTULATES OF ANALYTICAL PSYCHOLOGY [1]

649   It was universally believed in the Middle Ages as well as in the Greco-Roman world that the soul is a substance. Indeed, mankind as a whole has held this belief from its earliest beginnings, and it was left for the second half of the nineteenth century to develop a "psychology without the soul." Under the influence of scientific materialism, everything that could not be seen with the eyes or touched with the hands was held in doubt; such things were even laughed at because of their supposed affinity with metaphysics. Nothing was considered "scientific" or admitted to be true unless it could be perceived by the senses or traced back to physical causes. This radical change of view did not begin with philosophical materialism, for the way was being prepared long before. When the spiritual catastrophe of the Reformation put an end to the Gothic Age, with its impetuous yearning for the heights, its geographical confinement, and its restricted view of the world, the vertical outlook of the European mind was henceforth cut across by the horizontal

1 [First published as "Die Entschleierung der Seele," *Europäische Revue* (Berlin), VII : 2/7 (July 1931), which version was translated by W. S. Dell and Cary F. Baynes as "The Basic Postulates of Analytical Psychology," *Modern Man in Search of a Soul* (London and New York, 1933). The original version was republished, with slight revisions and the title "Das Grundproblem der gegenwärtigen Psychologie," in *Wirklichkeit der Seele* (Psychologische Abhandlungen, IV; Zurich, 1934). The present version is a slight revision of the Dell/Baynes trans.—EDITORS.]

outlook of modern times. Consciousness ceased to grow upward, and grew instead in breadth of view, geographically as well as philosophically. This was the age of the great voyages, of the widening of man's mental horizon by empirical discoveries. Belief in the substantiality of things spiritual yielded more and more to the obtrusive conviction that material things alone have substance, till at last, after nearly four hundred years, the leading European thinkers and investigators came to regard the mind as wholly dependent on matter and material causation.

650 We are certainly not justified in saying that philosophy or natural science has brought about this complete *volte-face*. There were always a fair number of intelligent philosophers and scientists who had enough insight and depth of thought to accept this irrational reversal of standpoint only under protest; a few even resisted it, but they had no following and were powerless against the wave of unreasoning, not to say excitable, surrender to the all-importance of the physical world. Let no one suppose that so radical a change in man's outlook could be brought about by reasoned reflection, for no chain of reasoning can prove or disprove the existence of either mind or matter. Both these concepts, as every intelligent person today can ascertain for himself, are mere symbols that stand for something unknown and unexplored, and this something is postulated or denied according to the temperament of the individual or as the spirit of the age dictates. There is nothing to prevent the speculative intellect from treating the mind as a complicated biochemical phenomenon and at bottom a mere play of electrons, or on the other hand from regarding the unpredictable behaviour of electrons as the sign of mental life even in them.

651 The fact that a metaphysics of the mind was supplanted in the nineteenth century by a metaphysics of matter is, intellectually considered, a mere trick, but from the psychological point of view it is an unexampled revolution in man's outlook. Otherworldliness is converted into matter-of-factness; empirical boundaries are set to every discussion of man's motivations, to his aims and purposes, and even to the assignment of "meaning." The whole invisible inner world seems to have become the visible outer world, and no value exists unless founded on a so-called fact. At least, this is how it appears to the simple mind.

652 It is futile, indeed, to treat this irrational change of opinion

as a question of philosophy. We had better not try to do so, for if we maintain that mental and psychic phenomena arise from the activity of the glands we can be sure of the respect and applause of our contemporaries, whereas if we attempted to explain the break up of atoms in the sun as an emanation of the creative *Weltgeist* we should be looked upon as intellectual cranks. And yet both views are equally logical, equally metaphysical, equally arbitrary and equally symbolic. From the standpoint of epistemology it is just as admissible to derive animals from the human species as man from the animal species. But we know how ill Dacqué [2] fared in his academic career because of his sin against the spirit of the age, which will not let itself be trifled with. It is a religion or, better, a creed which has absolutely no connection with reason, but whose significance lies in the unpleasant fact that it is taken as the absolute measure of all truth and is supposed always to have common sense on its side.

653 The spirit of the age cannot be fitted into the categories of human reason. It is more a bias, an emotional tendency that works upon weaker minds, through the unconscious, with an overwhelming force of suggestion that carries them along with it. To think otherwise than as our contemporaries think is somehow illegitimate and disturbing; it is even indecent, morbid or blasphemous, and therefore socially dangerous for the individual. He is stupidly swimming against the social current. Just as formerly the assumption was unquestionable that everything that exists originates in the creative will of a God who is a spirit, so the nineteenth century discovered the equally unquestionable truth that everything arises from material causes. Today the psyche does not build itself a body, but on the contrary matter, by chemical action, produces the psyche. This reversal of outlook would be ludicrous if it were not one of the unquestioned verities of the spirit of the age. It is the popular way of thinking, and therefore it is decent, reasonable, scientific, and normal. Mind must be thought of as an epiphenomenon of matter. The same conclusion is reached even if we say not "mind" but "psyche," and instead of "matter" speak of "brain," "hormones," "instincts," and "drives." To allow the soul or

2 [Edgar Dacqué (1878–1945) was a geologist who risked (and lost) his reputation by reversing the Darwinian theory of origin of species.—EDITORS.]

psyche a substantiality of its own is repugnant to the spirit of the age, for that would be heresy.

654 We have now discovered that it was an intellectually unjustified presumption on our forefathers' part to assume that man has a soul; that that soul has substance, is of divine nature and therefore immortal; that there is a power inherent within it which builds up the body, sustains its life, heals its ills and enables the soul to live independently of the body; that there are incorporeal spirits with which the soul associates; and that beyond our empirical present there is a spiritual world from which the soul receives knowledge of spiritual things whose origins cannot be discovered in this visible world. But people who are not above the general level of consciousness have not yet discovered that it is just as presumptuous and fantastic to assume that matter produces mind, that apes give rise to human beings, that from the harmonious interplay of the drives of hunger, love, and power Kant's *Critique of Pure Reason* should have emerged, and that all this could not possibly be other than it is.

655 What or who, indeed, is this all-powerful matter? It is the old Creator God over again, stripped this time of his anthropomorphic features and taking the form of a universal concept whose meaning everyone presumes to understand. Consciousness today has grown enormously in breadth and extent, but unfortunately only in the spatial dimension and not in the temporal, otherwise we should have a much more living sense of history. If our consciousness were not of today only, but had historical continuity, we should be reminded of similar transformations of the gods in Greek philosophy, and this might dispose us to be more critical of our present philosophical assumptions. We are, however, effectively prevented from indulging in such reflections by the spirit of the age. History, for it, is a mere arsenal of convenient arguments that enables us, on occasion, to say: "Why, even old Aristotle knew that." This being so, we must ask ourselves how the spirit of the age attains such uncanny power. It is without doubt a psychic phenomenon of the greatest importance—at all events, a prejudice so deeply rooted that until we give it proper consideration we cannot even approach the problem of the psyche.

656 As I have said, the irresistible tendency to explain everything

341

on physical grounds corresponds to the horizontal development of consciousness in the last four centuries, and this horizontal perspective is a reaction against the exclusively vertical perspective of the Gothic Age. It is an ethnopsychological phenomenon, and as such cannot be treated in terms of individual consciousness. Like primitives, we are at first wholly unconscious of our actions, and only discover long afterwards why it was that we acted in a certain way. In the meantime, we content ourselves with all sorts of rationalizations of our behaviour, all of them equally inadequate.

657   If we were conscious of the spirit of the age, we should know why we are so inclined to account for everything on physical grounds; we should know that it is because, up till now, too much was accounted for in terms of spirit. This realization would at once make us critical of our bias. We would say: most likely we are now making exactly the same mistake on the other side. We delude ourselves with the thought that we know much more about matter than about a "metaphysical" mind or spirit, and so we overestimate material causation and believe that it alone affords us a true explanation of life. But matter is just as inscrutable as mind. As to the ultimate things we can know nothing, and only when we admit this do we return to a state of equilibrium. This is in no sense to deny the close connection of psychic happenings with the physiological structure of the brain, with the glands and the body in general. We still remain deeply convinced of the fact that the contents of consciousness are to a large extent determined by our sense-perceptions. We cannot fail to recognize that unalterable characteristics of a physical as well as a psychic nature are unconsciously ingrained in us by heredity, and we are profoundly impressed by the power of the instincts which can inhibit or reinforce or otherwise modify even the most spiritual contents. Indeed, we must admit that as to cause, purpose, and meaning the human psyche, wherever we touch it, is first and foremost a faithful reflection of everything we call material, empirical, and mundane. And finally, in face of all these admissions, we must ask ourselves if the psyche is not after all a secondary manifestation—an epiphenomenon—and completely dependent on the physical substrate. Our practical reasonableness and worldly-mindedness prompt us to say yes to this question, and it is only our doubts as

to the omnipotence of matter that might lead us to examine in a critical way this verdict of science upon the human psyche.

658   The objection has already been raised that this view reduces psychic happenings to a kind of activity of the glands; thoughts are regarded as secretions of the brain, and thus we achieve a psychology without the psyche. From this standpoint, it must be confessed, the psyche does not exist in its own right; it is nothing in itself, but is the mere expression of processes in the physical substrate. That these processes have the quality of consciousness is just an irreducible fact—were it otherwise, so the argument runs, we could not speak of psyche at all; there would be no consciousness, and so we should have nothing to say about anything. Consciousness, therefore, is taken as the *sine qua non* of psychic life, that is to say, as the psyche itself. And so it comes about that all modern "psychologies without the psyche" are psychologies of consciousness, for which an unconscious psychic life simply does not exist.

659   For there is not *one* modern psychology—there are dozens of them. This is curious enough when we remember that there is only one science of mathematics, of geology, zoology, botany, and so forth. But there are so many psychologies that an American university was able to publish a thick volume under the title *Psychologies of 1930*.[3] I believe there are as many psychologies as philosophies, for there is also no single philosophy, but many. I mention this for the reason that philosophy and psychology are linked by indissoluble bonds which are kept in being by the interrelation of their subject-matters. Psychology takes the psyche for its subject, and philosophy—to put it briefly —takes the world. Until recently psychology was a special branch of philosophy, but now we are coming to something which Nietzsche foresaw—the rise of psychology in its own right, so much so that it is even threatening to swallow philosophy. The inner resemblance between the two disciplines consists in this, that both are systems of opinion about objects which cannot be fully experienced and therefore cannot be adequately comprehended by a purely empirical approach. Both fields of study thus encourage speculation, with the result that opinions are formed in such variety and profusion that many heavy volumes are

3 [See Bibliography s.v. "Murchison."—EDITORS.]

needed to contain them all. Neither discipline can do without the other, and the one invariably furnishes the unspoken—and generally unconscious—assumptions of the other.

660   The modern belief in the primacy of physical explanations has led, as already remarked, to a "psychology without the psyche," that is, to the view that the psyche is nothing but a product of biochemical processes. As for a modern, scientific psychology which starts from the spirit as such, there simply is none. No one today would venture to found a scientific psychology on the postulate of a psyche independent of the body. The idea of spirit in and for itself, of a self-contained spiritual world-system, which would be the necessary postulate for the existence of autonomous individual souls, is extremely unpopular with us, to say the least. But here I must remark that, in 1914, I attended at Bedford College, London, a joint session of the Aristotelian Society, the Mind Association, and the British Psychological Society, at which a symposium was held on the question, "Are individual minds contained in God or not?" Should anyone in England dispute the scientific standing of these societies he would not receive a very cordial hearing, for their members include the cream of the British intelligentsia. And perhaps I was the only person in the audience who listened with astonishment to arguments that had the ring of the thirteenth century. This instance may serve to show that the idea of an autonomous spirit whose existence is taken for granted has not died out everywhere in Europe or become a mere fossil left over from the Middle Ages.

661   If we keep this in mind, we can perhaps summon up courage to consider the possibility of a "psychology *with* the psyche"—that is, a theory of the psyche ultimately based on the postulate of an autonomous, spiritual principle. We need not be alarmed at the unpopularity of such an undertaking, for to postulate "spirit" is no more fantastic than to postulate "matter." Since we have literally no idea how the psychic can arise out of the physical, and yet cannot deny the reality of psychic events, we are free to frame our assumptions the other way about for once, and to suppose that the psyche arises from a spiritual principle which is as inaccessible to our understanding as matter. It will certainly not be a modern psychology, for to be modern is to deny such a possibility. For better or worse, therefore, we must

344

turn back to the teachings of our forefathers, for it was they who made such assumptions.

662   The ancient view held that the soul was essentially the life of the body, the life-breath, or a kind of life force which assumed spatial and corporeal form at the moment of conception, or during pregnancy, or at birth, and left the dying body again after the final breath. The soul in itself was a being without extension, and because it existed before taking corporeal form and afterwards as well, it was considered timeless and hence immortal. From the standpoint of modern, scientific psychology, this conception is of course pure illusion. But as it is not our intention to indulge in "metaphysics," even of a modern variety, we will examine this time-honoured notion for once in an unprejudiced way and test its empirical justification.

663   The names people give to their experiences are often very revealing. What is the origin of the word *Seele*? Like the English word *soul*, it comes from the Gothic *saiwala* and the old German *saiwalô*, and these can be connected etymologically with the Greek *aiolos*, 'quick-moving, twinkling, iridescent'. The Greek word *psyche* also means 'butterfly'. *Saiwalô* is related on the other side to the Old Slavonic *sila*, 'strength'. These connections throw light on the original meaning of the word *soul*: it is moving force, that is, life-force.

664   The Latin words *animus*, 'spirit', and *anima*, 'soul', are the same as the Greek *anemos*, 'wind'. The other Greek word for 'wind', *pneuma*, also means 'spirit'. In Gothic we find the same word in *us-anan*, 'to breathe out', and in Latin it is *anhelare*, 'to pant'. In Old High German, *spiritus sanctus* was rendered by *atum*, 'breath'. In Arabic, 'wind' is *rīh*, and *rūh* is 'soul, spirit'. The Greek word *psyche* has similar connections; it is related to *psychein*, 'to breathe', *psychos*, 'cool', *psychros*, 'cold, chill', and *physa*, 'bellows'. These connections show clearly how in Latin, Greek, and Arabic the names given to the soul are related to the notion of moving air, the "cold breath of the spirits." And this is probably the reason why the primitive view also endows the soul with an invisible breath-body.

665   It is quite understandable that, since breath is the sign of life, it should be taken for life, as are also movement and moving force. According to another primitive view the soul is a fire or flame, because warmth is likewise a sign of life. A very curious,

but by no means rare, primitive conception identifies the soul with the name. The name of an individual is his soul, and hence arises the custom of using the ancestor's name to reincarnate the ancestral soul in the new-born child. This means nothing less than that ego-consciousness is recognized as being an expression of the soul. Very often the soul is also identified with the shadow, hence it is a deadly insult to tread on a person's shadow. For the same reason noonday, the ghost-hour of southern latitudes, is considered threatening; one's shadow then grows small, and this means that life is endangered. This conception of the shadow contains an idea which was indicated by the Greeks in the word *synopados,* 'he who follows behind'. They expressed in this way the feeling of an intangible, living presence—the same feeling which led to the belief that the souls of the departed were "shades."

666   These indications may serve to show how primitive man experienced the psyche. To him the psyche appears as the source of life, the prime mover, a ghostlike presence which has objective reality. Therefore the primitive knows how to converse with his soul; it becomes vocal within him because it is not simply he himself and his consciousness. To primitive man the psyche is not, as it is to us, the epitome of all that is subjective and subject to the will; on the contrary, it is something objective, self-subsistent, and living its own life.

667   This way of looking at the matter is empirically justified, for not only on the primitive level, but with civilized man as well, psychic happenings have an objective side. In large measure they are withdrawn from our conscious control. We are unable, for example, to suppress many of our emotions; we cannot change a bad mood into a good one, and we cannot command our dreams to come or go. The most intelligent man may be obsessed at times with thoughts which he cannot drive away even with the greatest effort of will. The mad tricks that memory plays sometimes leave us in helpless amazement, and at any time unexpected fantasies may run through our heads. We believe that we are masters in our own house only because we like to flatter ourselves. In reality we are dependent to a startling degree on the proper functioning of the unconscious psyche, and must trust that it does not fail us. If we study the psychic processes of neurotic persons, it seems perfectly ludicrous that any psy-

chologist could take the psyche as the equivalent of consciousness. And it is well known that the psychic processes of neurotics differ hardly at all from those of so-called normal persons—for what man today is quite sure that he is not neurotic?

668   This being so, we shall do well to admit that there is some justification for the old view of the soul as an objective reality—as something independent, and therefore capricious and dangerous. The further assumption that this being, so mysterious and frightening, is at the same time the source of life is also understandable in the light of psychology. Experience shows us that the sense of the "I"—the ego-consciousness—grows out of unconscious life. The small child has psychic life without any demonstrable ego-consciousness, for which reason the earliest years leave hardly any traces in the memory. Where do all our good and helpful flashes of intelligence come from? What is the source of our enthusiasms, inspirations, and of our heightened feeling of vitality? The primitive senses in the depths of his soul the springs of life; he is deeply impressed by the life-giving activity of his soul, and he therefore believes in everything that affects it—in magical practices of every kind. That is why, for him, the soul is life itself. He does not imagine that he directs it, but feels himself dependent on it in every respect.

669   However preposterous the idea of the immortality of the soul may seem to us, it is nothing extraordinary to the primitive. The soul is, after all, something out of the common. While everything else that exists takes up a certain amount of room, the soul cannot be located in space. We suppose, of course, that our thoughts are in our heads, but when it comes to our feelings we begin to be uncertain; they appear to dwell more in the region of the heart. Our sensations are distributed over the whole body. Our theory is that the seat of consciousness is in the head, but the Pueblo Indians told me that the Americans were mad because they believed their thoughts were in their heads, whereas any sensible man knows that he thinks with his heart. Certain Negro tribes locate their psychic functioning neither in the head nor in the heart, but in the belly.

670   To this uncertainty about the localization of psychic functions another difficulty is added. Psychic contents in general are nonspatial except in the particular realm of sensation. What bulk can we ascribe to thoughts? Are they small, large, long, thin,

heavy, fluid, straight, circular, or what? If we wished to form a living picture of a non-spatial, fourth-dimensional being, we could not do better than to take thought for our model.

671 It would all be so much simpler if only we could deny the existence of the psyche. But here we are with our immediate experiences of something that *is*—something that has taken root in the midst of our measurable, ponderable, three-dimensional reality, that differs mysteriously from this in every respect and in all its parts, and yet reflects it. The psyche could be regarded as a mathematical point and at the same time as a universe of fixed stars. It is small wonder, then, if, to the unsophisticated mind, such a paradoxical being borders on the divine. If it occupies no space, it has no body. Bodies die, but can something invisible and incorporeal disappear? What is more, life and psyche existed for me before I could say "I," and when this "I" disappears, as in sleep or unconsciousness, life and psyche still go on, as our observation of other people and our own dreams inform us. Why should the simple mind deny, in the face of such experiences, that the "soul" lives in a realm beyond the body? I must admit that I can see as little nonsense in this so-called superstition as in the findings of research regarding heredity or the instincts.

672 We can easily understand why higher and even divine knowledge was formerly attributed to the soul if we remember that in ancient cultures, beginning with primitive times, man always resorted to dreams and visions as a source of information. It is a fact that the unconscious contains subliminal perceptions whose scope is nothing less than astounding. In recognition of this fact, primitive societies used dreams and visions as important sources of information. Great and enduring civilizations like those of India and China were built upon this psychological foundation and developed from it a discipline of self-knowledge which they brought to a high pitch of refinement both in philosophy and in practice.

673 A high regard for the unconscious psyche as a source of knowledge is not nearly such a delusion as our Western rationalism likes to suppose. We are inclined to assume that in the last resort all knowledge comes from without. Yet today we know for certain that the unconscious has contents which would bring an immeasurable increase of knowledge if they could only be

made conscious. Modern investigation of animal instinct, for instance in insects, has brought together a rich fund of empirical material which shows that if man sometimes acted as certain insects do he would possess a higher intelligence than at present. It cannot, of course, be proved that insects possess conscious knowledge, but common sense cannot doubt that their unconscious patterns of behaviour are psychic functions. Man's unconscious likewise contains all the patterns of life and behaviour inherited from his ancestors, so that every human child is possessed of a ready-made system of adapted psychic functioning prior to all consciousness. In the conscious life of the adult as well this unconscious, instinctive functioning is continually present and active. In this activity all the functions of the conscious psyche are prefigured. The unconscious perceives, has purposes and intuitions, feels and thinks as does the conscious mind. We find sufficient evidence for this in the field of psychopathology and the investigation of dream-processes. Only in one respect is there an essential difference between the conscious and the unconscious functioning of the psyche. Though consciousness is intensive and concentrated, it is transitory and is trained upon the immediate present and the immediate field of attention; moreover, it has access only to material that represents one individual's experience stretching over a few decades. A wider range of "memory" is an artificial acquisition consisting mostly of printed paper. But matters stand very differently with the unconscious. It is not concentrated and intensive, but shades off into obscurity; it is highly extensive and can juxtapose the most heterogeneous elements in the most paradoxical way. More than this, it contains, besides an indeterminable number of subliminal perceptions, the accumulated deposits from the lives of our ancestors, who by their very existence have contributed to the differentiation of the species. If it were possible to personify the unconscious, we might think of it as a collective human being combining the characteristics of both sexes, transcending youth and age, birth and death, and, from having at its command a human experience of one or two million years, practically immortal. If such a being existed, it would be exalted above all temporal change; the present would mean neither more nor less to it than any year in the hundredth millennium before Christ; it would be a dreamer of age-old dreams and,

owing to its limitless experience, an incomparable prognosti-
cator. It would have lived countless times over again the life of
the individual, the family, the tribe, and the nation, and it would
possess a living sense of the rhythm of growth, flowering, and
decay.

674   Unfortunately—or rather let us say, fortunately—this being
dreams. At least it seems to us as if the collective unconscious,
which appears to us in dreams, had no consciousness of its own
contents, though of course we cannot be sure of this, any more
than we can in the case of insects. The collective unconscious,
moreover, seems to be not a person, but something like an un-
ceasing stream or perhaps ocean of images and figures which
drift into consciousness in our dreams or in abnormal states of
mind.

675   It would be positively grotesque to call this immense system
of experience in the unconscious psyche an illusion, for our
visible and tangible body is itself just such a system. It still carries within it evolutionary traces from primeval times, and it is
certainly a whole that functions purposively—for otherwise we
could not live. It would never occur to anyone to look upon
comparative anatomy or physiology as nonsense, and neither
can we dismiss the investigation of the collective unconscious as
illusion or refuse to recognize it as a valuable source of knowledge.

676   Looked at from the outside, the psyche appears to be essentially a reflection of external happenings—to be not only
occasioned by them, but to have its origin in them. And it also
seems to us, at first, that the unconscious can be explained only
from the outside and from the side of consciousness. It is well
known that Freud has attempted to do this—an undertaking
which could succeed only if the unconscious were actually something that came into being with the existence and consciousness
of the individual. But the truth is that the unconscious is always there beforehand as a system of inherited psychic functioning handed down from primeval times. Consciousness is a
late-born descendant of the unconscious psyche. It would certainly show perversity if we tried to explain the lives of our
ancestors in terms of their late descendants, and it is just as
wrong, in my opinion, to regard the unconscious as a derivative

of consciousness. We are probably nearer the truth if we put it the other way round.

677   This was the standpoint of past ages, which, knowing the untold treasures of experience lying hidden beneath the threshold of the ephemeral individual consciousness, always held the individual soul to be dependent on a spiritual world-system. Not only did they make this hypothesis, they assumed without question that this system was a being with a will and consciousness—was even a person—and they called this being God, the quintessence of reality. He was for them the most real of beings, the first cause, through whom alone the soul could be explained. There is some psychological justification for such an hypothesis, for it is only appropriate that an almost immortal being whose experience is almost eternal should be called, in comparison with man, "divine."

678   In the foregoing I have shown where the problems lie for a psychology that does not appeal to the physical world as a ground of explanation, but rather to a spiritual system whose active principle is neither matter and its qualities nor any state of energy, but God. At this juncture, we might be tempted by the modern brand of nature philosophy to call energy or the *élan vital* God, and thus to blend into one spirit and nature. So long as such an undertaking is restricted to the misty heights of speculative philosophy, no great harm is done. But if we should operate with this idea in the lower realm of practical psychology, where only practical explanations bear any fruit, we should soon find ourselves involved in the most hopeless difficulties. We do not profess a psychology with merely academic pretensions, or seek explanations that have no bearing on life. What we want is a practical psychology which yields approvable results—one which explains things in a way that must be justified by the outcome for the patient. In practical psychotherapy we strive to fit people for life, and we are not free to set up theories which do not concern our patients and may even injure them. Here we come to a question that is sometimes a matter of life and death—the question whether we base our explanations on "physis" or spirit. We must never forget that everything spiritual is illusion from the naturalistic standpoint, and that often the spirit has to deny and overcome an insistent physical fact in order to exist at all. If I recognize only naturalistic values, and

explain everything in physical terms, I shall depreciate, hinder, or even destroy the spiritual development of my patients. And if I hold exclusively to a spiritual interpretation, then I shall misunderstand and do violence to the natural man in his right to exist as a physical being. More than a few suicides in the course of psychotherapeutic treatment are to be laid at the door of such mistakes. Whether energy is God or God is energy concerns me very little, for how, in any case, can I know such things? But to give appropriate psychological explanations—this I must be able to do.

679   The modern psychologist occupies neither the one position nor the other, but finds himself between the two, dangerously committed to "this as well as that"—a situation which seductively opens the way to a shallow opportunism. This is undoubtedly the great danger of the *coincidentia oppositorum*— of intellectual freedom from the opposites. How should anything but a formless and aimless uncertainty result from giving equal value to two contradictory hypotheses? In contrast to this we can readily appreciate the advantage of an explanatory principle that is unequivocal: it allows of a standpoint that can serve as a point of reference. Undoubtedly we are confronted here with a very difficult problem. We must be able to appeal to an explanatory principle founded on reality, and yet it is no longer possible for the modern psychologist to take his stand exclusively on the physical aspect of reality once he has given the spiritual aspect its due. Nor will he be able to put weight on the latter alone, for he cannot ignore the relative validity of the physical aspect. To what, then, can he appeal?

680   The following reflections are my way of attempting to solve this problem. The conflict between nature and spirit is itself a reflection of the paradox of psychic life. This reveals a physical and a spiritual aspect which appear a contradiction because, ultimately, we do not understand the nature of psychic life itself. Whenever, with our human understanding, we want to make a statement about something which in the last analysis we have not grasped and cannot grasp, then we must, if we are honest, be willing to contradict ourselves, we must pull this something into its antithetical parts in order to be able to deal with it at all. The conflict between the physical and the spiritual aspects only shows that psychic life is in the last analysis an

incomprehensible "something." Without a doubt it is our only immediate experience. All that I experience is psychic. Even physical pain is a psychic image which I experience; my sense-impressions—for all that they force upon me a world of impenetrable objects occupying space—are psychic images, and these alone constitute my immediate experience, for they alone are the immediate objects of my consciousness. My own psyche even transforms and falsifies reality, and it does this to such a degree that I must resort to artificial means to determine what things are like apart from myself. Then I discover that a sound is a vibration of air of such and such a frequency, or that a colour is a wave of light of such and such a length. We are in truth so wrapped about by psychic images that we cannot penetrate at all to the essence of things external to ourselves. All our knowledge consists of the stuff of the psyche which, because it alone is immediate, is superlatively real. Here, then, is a reality to which the psychologist can appeal—namely, psychic reality.

681   If we try to penetrate more deeply into the meaning of this concept, it seems to us that certain psychic contents or images are derived from a "material" environment to which our bodies belong, while others, which are in no way less real, seem to come from a "spiritual" source which appears to be very different from the physical environment. Whether I picture to myself the car I wish to buy or try to imagine the state in which the soul of my dead father now is—whether it is an external fact or a thought that concerns me—both happenings are psychic reality. The only difference is that one psychic happening refers to the physical world, and the other to the spiritual world. If I shift my concept of reality on to the plane of the psyche—where alone it is valid—this puts an end to the conflict between mind and matter, spirit and nature, as contradictory explanatory principles. Each becomes a mere designation for the particular source of the psychic contents that crowd into my field of consciousness. If a fire burns me I do not question the reality of the fire, whereas if I am beset by the fear that a ghost will appear, I take refuge behind the thought that it is only an illusion. But just as the fire is the psychic image of a physical process whose nature is ultimately unknown, so my fear of the ghost is a psychic image from a spiritual source; it is just as real as the fire, for my fear is

as real as the pain caused by the fire. As for the spiritual process that underlies my fear of the ghost, it is as unknown to me as the ultimate nature of matter. And just as it never occurs to me to account for the nature of fire except by the concepts of chemistry and physics, so I would never think of trying to explain my fear of ghosts except in terms of spiritual processes.

682   The fact that all immediate experience is psychic and that immediate reality can only be psychic explains why it is that primitive man puts spirits and magical influences on the same plane as physical events. He has not yet torn his original experience into antithetical parts. In his world, spirit and matter still interpenetrate each other, and his gods still wander through forest and field. He is like a child, only half born, still enclosed in his own psyche as in a dream, in a world not yet distorted by the difficulties of understanding that beset a dawning intelligence. When this aboriginal world fell apart into spirit and nature, the West rescued nature for itself. It was prone by temperament to a belief in nature, and only became the more entangled in it with every painful effort to make itself spiritual. The East, on the other hand, took spirit for its own, and by explaining away matter as mere illusion—Maya—continued to dream in Asiatic filth and misery. But since there is only *one* earth and *one* mankind, East and West cannot rend humanity into two different halves. Psychic reality still exists in its original oneness, and awaits man's advance to a level of consciousness where he no longer believes in the one part and denies the other, but recognizes both as constituent elements of one psyche.

683   We could well point to the idea of psychic reality as the most important achievement of modern psychology if it were recognized as such. It seems to me only a question of time for this idea to be generally accepted. It must be accepted in the end, for it alone enables us to understand the manifestations of the psyche in all their variety and uniqueness. Without this idea it is unavoidable that we should explain our psychic experiences in a way that does violence to a good half of them, while with it we can give its due to that side of psychic life which expresses itself in superstition and mythology, religion and philosophy. And this aspect of the psyche is not to be undervalued. Truth that appeals to the testimony of the senses may satisfy reason, but it offers nothing that stirs our feelings and expresses them

by giving a meaning to human life. Yet it is most often feeling that is decisive in matters of good and evil, and if feeling does not come to the aid of reason, the latter is usually powerless. Did reason and good intentions save us from the World War, or have they ever saved us from any other catastrophic stupidity? Have any of the great spiritual and social revolutions sprung from reason—for instance, the transformation of the Greco-Roman world into the age of feudalism, or the explosive spread of Islam?

684   As a physician I am of course not directly concerned with these epochal questions; my duties lie with people who are ill. Medicine has until recently gone on the supposition that illness should be treated and cured by itself; yet voices are now heard which declare this view to be wrong, and demand the treatment of the sick person and not of the sickness. The same demand is forced upon us in the treatment of psychic suffering. More and more we turn our attention from the visible illness and direct it upon the man as a whole. We have come to understand that psychic suffering is not a definitely localized, sharply delimited phenomenon, but rather the symptom of a wrong attitude assumed by the total personality. We can therefore never hope for a thorough cure from a treatment restricted to the illness itself, but only from a treatment of the personality as a whole.

685   I am reminded of a case which is very instructive in this respect. It concerns a highly intelligent young man who had worked out a detailed analysis of his own neurosis after a thorough study of the medical literature. He brought me his findings in the form of a precise and admirably written monograph, fit for publication, and asked me to read the manuscript and to tell him why he was still not cured, although he ought to have been, according to his scientific judgment. After reading his monograph I was forced to admit that, if it were only a question of insight into the causal structure of a neurosis, he should in all truth have been cured. Since he was not, I supposed this must be due to the fact that his attitude to life was somehow fundamentally wrong, though certainly his symptoms did not betray it. During his anamnesis I had been struck by his remark that he often spent his winters at St. Moritz or Nice. I therefore asked him who actually paid for these holidays, and it thereupon came out that a poor school-teacher who loved him almost

starved herself to indulge this young man in his visits to pleas-
ure-resorts. His want of conscience was the cause of his neurosis,
and this also explains why all his scientific insight availed him
nothing. His fundamental error lay in his moral attitude. He
found my way of looking at it shockingly unscientific, for morals
have nothing to do with science. He thought that he could
scientifically unthink the immorality which he himself, at bottom, could not stomach. He would not even admit that any
conflict existed, because his mistress gave him the money of her
own free will.

686   We can think what we like about this scientifically, but the
fact remains that the great majority of civilized persons simply
cannot tolerate such behaviour. The moral attitude is a real
factor with which the psychologist must reckon if he is not to
commit the gravest errors. He must also remember that certain
religious convictions not founded on reason are a vital necessity
for many people. Again, there are psychic realities which can
cause or cure diseases. How often have I heard a patient exclaim: "If only I knew that my life had some meaning and
purpose, there would be no need of all this trouble with my
nerves!" Whether the patient is rich or poor, has family and
social position or not, alters nothing, for outer circumstances
are far from giving his life a meaning. It is much more a question of his quite irrational need for what we call a spiritual life,
and this he cannot obtain from universities, libraries, or even
from churches. He cannot accept what these have to offer because it touches only his head but does not stir his heart. In such
cases the physician's recognition of the spiritual factors in their
true light is vitally important, and the patient's unconscious
comes to the aid of this vital need by producing dreams whose
content is essentially religious. Not to recognize the spiritual
source of such contents means faulty treatment and failure.

687   General conceptions of a spiritual nature are indispensable
constituents of psychic life. We can point them out among all
peoples who possess some measure of articulated consciousness.
Their relative absence or their denial by a civilized people is
therefore to be regarded as a sign of degeneration. Whereas, in
its development up to the present, psychology has considered
psychic processes mainly in the light of their physical causation,
the future task of psychology will be the investigation of their

spiritual determinants. But the natural history of the mind is no further advanced today than was natural science in the thirteenth century. We are only just beginning to take scientific note of our spiritual experiences.

688   If modern psychology can boast of having removed any of the veils which hid the psyche from us, it is only that one which had concealed from the investigator the psyche's biological aspect. We may compare the present situation to the state of medicine in the sixteenth century, when people began to study anatomy but had not as yet the faintest idea of physiology. So, too, the spiritual aspect of the psyche is known to us only in a very fragmentary way. We have learnt that there are spiritual processes of transformation in the psyche which underlie, for example, the well-known initiation rites of primitive peoples and the states induced by the practice of yoga. But we have not yet succeeded in determining their particular laws. We only know that many of the neuroses arise from a disturbance of these processes. Psychological research has not drawn aside all the many veils from the human psyche; it remains as unapproachable and obscure as all the deep secrets of life. We can only speak of what we have tried to do, and what we hope to do in the future, in the way of attempting a solution of the great riddle.

ANALYTICAL PSYCHOLOGY
AND 'WELTANSCHAUUNG' [1]

689   The German expression *Weltanschauung* is scarcely translatable into another language. This tells us at once that the word must have a peculiar psychological character. It expresses not only a conception of the world—this meaning could be translated without much difficulty—but also the way in which one views the world. The word "philosophy" implies something similar, but restricted to the intellectual sphere, whereas *Weltanschauung* embraces all sorts of attitudes to the world, including the philosophical. Thus there is an aesthetic, a religious, an idealistic, a realistic, a romantic, a practical *Weltanschauung*, to mention only a few possibilities. In this sense a *Weltanschauung* has much in common with an attitude. Accordingly, we could define *Weltanschauung* as an attitude that has been formulated into concepts.

690   Now what is to be understood by attitude? Attitude is a psychological term designating a particular arrangement of psychic contents oriented towards a goal or directed by some kind of

1 [A lecture delivered in Karlsruhe, 1927. It was translated from the original ms. by H. G. and C. F. Baynes and first published under the present title in *Contributions to Analytical Psychology* (London and New York, 1928). The original version was subsequently revised, enlarged, and published as "Analytische Psychologie und Weltanschauung," *Seelenprobleme der Gegenwart* (Psychologische Abhandlungen, III; Zurich, 1931). The present translation is of the latter, but the Baynes version has been consulted.—EDITORS.]

ruling principle. If we compare our psychic contents to an army, and the various forms of attitude to military dispositions, then attention, for example, would be represented by a concentrated force standing to arms, surrounded by reconnoitring parties. As soon as the strength and position of the enemy are known, the disposition changes: the army begins to move in the direction of a given objective. In precisely the same way the psychic attitude changes. During the state of attention the dominant idea is alertness; one's own thoughts are suppressed as much as possible, along with other subjective contents. But in going over to an active attitude, subjective contents appear in consciousness—purposive ideas and impulses to act. And just as an army has a commander and a general staff, so the psychic attitude has a general guiding idea which is reinforced by a wide assortment of experiences, principles, affects of all kinds, etc.

691   That is to say, no human action is entirely simple—an isolated reaction, as it were, to a single stimulus. Each of our actions and reactions is influenced by complicated psychic factors. To use the military analogy again, we might compare these processes with the situation at general headquarters. To the man in the ranks it might seem that the army retreated simply because it was attacked, or that an attack was launched because the enemy had been located. Our conscious mind is always disposed to play the role of the common soldier and to believe in the simplicity of its actions. But, in reality, battle was given at this particular place and this particular moment because of a general plan of attack, which for days before had been marshalling the common soldier to this point. Again, this general plan is not simply a reaction to reconnaissance reports, but results from the creative initiative of the commander. Furthermore, it is conditioned by the action of the enemy, and also perhaps by wholly unmilitary, political considerations of which the common soldier is quite unaware. These last factors are of a very complex nature and lie far outside the understanding of the common soldier, though they may be only too clear to the commander of the army. But even to him certain factors are unknown, such as his own personal psychology and its complicated assumptions. Thus the army stands under a simple and unified command, but this command is a result of the coordinated operation of infinitely complex factors.

692   Psychic action takes place on a similarly complicated basis. However simple an impulse appears to be, every nuance of its particular character, its strength and direction, its course, its timing, its aim, all depend on special psychic conditions, in other words, on an attitude; and the attitude in turn consists of a constellation of contents so numerous that they cannot be counted. The ego is the army commander; its reflections and decisions, its reasons and doubts, its intentions and expectations are the general staff, and its dependence on outside factors is the dependence of the commander on the well-nigh incalculable influences emanating from general headquarters and from the dark machinations of politics in the background.

693   I hope we shall not overload our analogy if we now include within it the relation of man to the world. The individual ego could be conceived as the commander of a small army in the struggle with his environment—a war not infrequently on two fronts, before him the struggle for existence, in the rear the struggle against his own rebellious instinctual nature. Even to those of us who are not pessimists our existence feels more like a struggle than anything else. The state of peace is a desideratum, and when a man has found peace with himself and the world it is indeed a noteworthy event. Hence, in order to meet the more or less chronic state of war, we need a carefully organized attitude; and should some superman achieve enduring mental peace his attitude would need a still higher degree of detailed preparation if his peace is to have even a modest duration. It is much easier for the mind to live in a state of movement, in a continuous up and down of events, than in a balanced state of permanency, for in the latter state—however lofty and perfect it may be—one is threatened with suffocation and unbearable ennui. So we are not deluding ourselves if we assume that peaceful states of mind, that is, moods without conflict, serene, deliberate, and well-balanced, so far as they are lasting, depend on specially well-developed attitudes.

694   You may perhaps be surprised that I prefer the word "attitude" to *Weltanschauung*. In using the concept of attitude, I have simply left it an open question whether this depends on a conscious or unconscious *Weltanschauung*. One can be one's own army commander and engage successfully in the struggle for existence both without and within, and even achieve a rela-

tively secure condition of peace, without possessing a conscious *Weltanschauung,* but one cannot do this without an attitude. We can only speak of a *Weltanschauung* when a person has at least made a serious attempt to formulate his attitude in conceptual or concrete form, so that it becomes clear to him why and to what purpose he acts and lives as he does.

695　But what is the use of a *Weltanschauung,* you may ask, if one can get on perfectly well without it? You might just as well ask why have consciousness if one can do without it! For what, after all, is a *Weltanschauung* but a widened or deepened consciousness? The reason why consciousness exists, and why there is an urge to widen and deepen it, is very simple: without consciousness things go less well. This is obviously the reason why Mother Nature deigned to produce consciousness, that most remarkable of all nature's curiosities. Even the well-nigh unconscious primitive can adapt and assert himself, but only in his primitive world, and that is why under other conditions he falls victim to countless dangers which we on a higher level of consciousness can avoid without effort. True, a higher consciousness is exposed to dangers undreamt of by the primitive, but the fact remains that the conscious man has conquered the earth and not the unconscious one. Whether in the last analysis, and from a superhuman point of view, this is an advantage or a calamity we are not in a position to decide.

696　Consciousness determines *Weltanschauung.* All conscious awareness of motives and intentions is a *Weltanschauung* in the bud; every increase in experience and knowledge is a step in the development of a *Weltanschauung.* And with the picture that the thinking man fashions of the world he also changes himself. The man whose sun still moves round the earth is essentially different from the man whose earth is a satellite of the sun. Giordano Bruno's reflections on infinity were not in vain: they represent one of the most important beginnings of modern consciousness. The man whose cosmos hangs in the empyrean is different from one whose mind is illuminated by Kepler's vision. The man who is still dubious about the sum of twice two is different from the thinker for whom nothing is less doubtful than the *a priori* truths of mathematics. In short, it is not a matter of indifference what sort of *Weltanschauung* we possess, since not only do we create a picture of the world, but this picture retroactively changes us.

697   The conception we form of the world is our picture of what we call world. And it is in accordance with this picture that we orient ourselves and adapt to reality. As I have said, this does not happen consciously. Nearly always a forceful decision is needed to tear the mind away from the pressing concerns of the moment and to direct it to the general problem of attitude. If we do not do this, we naturally remain unconscious of our attitude, and in that case we have no *Weltanschauung,* but merely an unconscious attitude. If no account is taken of our motives and intentions they remain unconscious; that is, everything seems very simple, as though it just happened like that. But in reality complicated processes are at work in the background, using motives and intentions whose subtlety leaves nothing to be desired. For this reason there are many scientists who avoid having a *Weltanschauung* because this is supposed not to be scientific. It has obviously not dawned on these people what they are really doing. For what actually happens is this: by deliberately leaving themselves in the dark as to their guiding ideas they cling to a lower, more primitive level of consciousness than would correspond to their true capacities. Criticism and scepticism are not always a sign of intelligence— often they are just the reverse, especially when used by someone as a cloak to hide his lack of *Weltanschauung.* Very often it is a moral rather than an intellectual deficiency. For you cannot see the world without seeing yourself, and as a man sees the world, so he sees himself, and for this considerable courage is needed. Hence it is always fatal to have no *Weltanschauung.*

698   To have a *Weltanschauung* means to create a picture of the world and of oneself, to know what the world is and who I am. Taken literally, this would be too much. No one can know what the world is, just as little as can he know himself. But, *cum grano salis,* it means the best possible knowledge—a knowledge that esteems wisdom and abhors unfounded assumptions, arbitrary assertions, and didactic opinions. Such knowledge seeks the well-founded hypothesis, without forgetting that all knowledge is limited and subject to error.

699   If the picture we create of the world did not have a retroactive effect on us, we could be content with any sort of beautiful or diverting sham. But such self-deception recoils on us,

making us unreal, foolish, and ineffectual. Because we are tilting at a false picture of the world, we are overcome by the superior power of reality. In this way we learn from experience how important it is to have a well-based and carefully constructed *Weltanschauung*.

700   A *Weltanschauung* is a hypothesis and not an article of faith. The world changes its face—*tempora mutantur et nos mutamur in illis*—for we can grasp the world only as a psychic image in ourselves, and it is not always easy to decide, when the image changes, whether the world or ourselves have changed, or both. The picture of the world can change at any time, just as our conception of ourselves changes. Every new discovery, every new thought, can put a new face on the world. We must be prepared for this, else we suddenly find ourselves in an antiquated world, itself a relic of lower levels of consciousness. We shall all be as good as dead one day, but in the interests of life we should postpone this moment as long as possible, and this we can only do by never allowing our picture of the world to become rigid. Every new thought must be tested to see whether or not it adds something to our *Weltanschauung*.

*

701   If I now set out to discuss the relation between analytical psychology and *Weltanschauung*, I do so from the standpoint I have just elaborated, namely, "Do the findings of analytical psychology add something new to our *Weltanschauung,* or not?" In order to deal with this question effectively, we must first consider the essentials of analytical psychology. What I mean by this term is a special trend in psychology which is mainly concerned with complex psychic phenomena, in contrast to physiological or experimental psychology, which strives to reduce complex phenomena as far as possible to their elements. The term "analytical" derives from the fact that this branch of psychology developed out of the original Freudian psychoanalysis. Freud identified psychoanalysis with his theory of sex and repression, and thereby riveted it to a doctrinaire framework. For this reason I avoid the expression "psychoanalysis" when I am discussing other than merely technical matters.

702   Freudian psychoanalysis consists essentially in a technique for bringing back to consciousness so-called repressed contents

that have become unconscious. This technique is a therapeutic method designed to treat and to cure neuroses. In the light of this method, it seems as if the neuroses came into existence because disagreeable memories and tendencies—so-called incompatible contents—were repressed from consciousness and made unconscious by a sort of moral resentment due to educational influences. From this point of view unconscious psychic activity, or what we call the unconscious, appears chiefly as a receptacle of all those contents that are antipathetic to consciousness, as well as of all forgotten impressions. On the other hand, one cannot close one's eyes to the fact that these same incompatible contents derive from unconscious instincts, which means that the unconscious is not just a receptacle but is the matrix of the very things that the conscious mind would like to be rid of. We can go a step further and say that the unconscious actually creates *new* contents. Everything that the human mind has ever created sprang from contents which, in the last analysis, existed once as unconscious seeds. While Freud lays special emphasis on the first aspect, I have stressed the latter, without denying the first. Although it is a not unimportant fact that man evades everything unpleasant, and therefore gladly forgets whatever does not suit him, it nevertheless seems to me far more important to find out what really constitutes the *positive* activity of the unconscious. From this point of view the unconscious appears as the totality of all psychic contents *in statu nascendi*. This positive function of the unconscious is, in the main, merely disturbed by repressions, and this disturbance of its natural activity is perhaps the most important source of the so-called psychogenic illnesses. The unconscious is best understood if we regard it as a natural organ with its own specific creative energy. If as a result of repressions its products can find no outlet in consciousness, a sort of blockage ensues, an unnatural inhibition of a purposive function, just as if the bile, the natural product of the function of the liver, were impeded in its discharge into the bowel. As a result of the repression, wrong psychic outlets are found. Like bile seeping into the blood, the repressed content infiltrates into other psychic and physiological spheres. In hysteria it is chiefly the physiological functions that are disturbed; in other neuroses, such as phobias, obsessions, and compulsion neuroses, it is chiefly the psychic functions, including dreams. Just as the activity of the repressed contents can be demonstrated in the physical symptoms of hysteria and in the psychic symptoms of other neuroses (and also psychoses), so it can in dreams. The dream in itself is a normal function which can be disturbed by blockages like any other function. The Freudian theory of dreams considers, and even explains, the dream from this angle alone, as though it were nothing but a symptom. Other fields of activity are, as we know, treated by psychoanalysis in the same way—works of art, for instance. But here the weakness of the theory becomes painfully evident, since a work of art is clearly not a symptom but a genuine creation. A creative achievement can only be understood on its own merits. If it is taken as a pathological misunderstanding and explained in the same terms as a neurosis, the attempted explanation soon begins to assume a curiously bedraggled air.

703   The same is true of the dream. It is a typical product of the unconscious, and is merely deformed and distorted by repression. Hence any explanation that interprets it as a mere symptom of repression will go very wide of the mark.

704   Let us confine ourselves for the moment to the conclusions to be drawn from Freud's psychoanalysis. In Freudian theory, man appears as a creature of instinct who, in various ways, comes into conflict with the law, with moral precepts, and with his own insights, and who is consequently compelled to repress certain instincts either wholly or in part. The aim of the method is to bring these instinctual contents to consciousness and make repression unnecessary by conscious correction. The menace entailed by their liberation is countered by the explanation that they are nothing but infantile wish-fantasies, which can still be suppressed, though in a wiser way. It is also assumed that they can be "sublimated," to use the technical term, by which is meant a sort of bending of them to a suitable form of adaptation. But if anyone believes this can be done at will he is sadly mistaken—only absolute necessity can effectively inhibit a natural instinct. When there is no need and no inexorable necessity, the "sublimation" is merely a self-deception, a new and somewhat more subtle form of repression.

705   Does this theory and this conception of man contain anything valuable for our *Weltanschauung*? I hardly think so. It is the well-known rationalistic materialism of the late nineteenth

century, which is the guiding principle of the interpretive psychology underlying Freud's psychoanalysis. From it can come no other picture of the world, and therefore no other attitude to the world. But we must not forget that only in rare instances is an attitude influenced by theories. A far more effective influence is that of feeling. True, a dry theoretical presentation cannot reach the feelings. I could read you a detailed statistical report on prisons and you would go to sleep. But if I took you through a prison, or through a lunatic asylum, you would certainly not go to sleep. You would be profoundly impressed. Was it any theory that made the Buddha what he was? No, it was the sight of old age, sickness, and death that burned into his soul.

706   Thus the partly one-sided, partly erroneous concepts of psychoanalysis really tell us very little. But if we look into the psychoanalysis of actual cases of neurosis and see what devastation the so-called repressions have wrought, what destruction has resulted from a disregard of elementary instinctual processes, then we receive—to put it mildly—a lasting impression. There is no form of human tragedy that does not in some measure proceed from this conflict between the ego and the unconscious. Anyone who has ever seen the horror of a prison, an insane asylum, or a hospital will surely experience, from the impression these things make upon him, a profound enrichment of his *Weltanschauung*. And he will be no less deeply impressed if he looks into the abyss of human suffering behind a neurosis. How often I have heard: "But that is terrible! Who could ever have believed such things were possible!" And there's no gainsaying that one really does receive a tremendous impression of the power of the unconscious when one tries, with the necessary conscientiousness and thoroughness, to investigate the structure of a neurosis. It is also rewarding to show someone the slums of London, and anyone who has seen them has seen a great deal more than one who has not. But all that is nothing more than a shock, and the question "What is to be done about it?" still remains unanswered.

707   Psychoanalysis has removed the veil from facts that were known only to a few, and has even made an effort to deal with them. But has it any new attitude to them? Has the deep impression produced lasting and fruitful results? Has it altered our picture of the world and thus added to our *Weltanschauung*?

The *Weltanschauung* of psychoanalysis is a rationalistic materialism, the *Weltanschauung* of an essentially practical science—and this view we feel to be inadequate. When we trace a poem of Goethe's to his mother-complex, when we seek to explain Napoleon as a case of masculine protest, or St. Francis as a case of sexual repression, a sense of profound dissatisfaction comes over us. The explanation is insufficient and does not do justice to the reality and meaning of things. What becomes of beauty, greatness, and holiness? These are vital realities without which human existence would be superlatively stupid. What is the right answer to the problem of terrible sufferings and conflicts? The true answer should strike a chord that at least reminds us of the magnitude of the suffering. But the merely reasonable, practical attitude of the rationalist, however desirable it may be in other respects, ignores the real meaning of suffering. It is simply set aside and explained away as irrelevant. It was a great noise about nothing. Much may fall into this category, but not everything.

708   The mistake, as I have said, lies in the circumstance that psychoanalysis has a scientific but purely rationalistic conception of the unconscious. When we speak of instincts we imagine that we are talking about something known, but in reality we are talking about something unknown. As a matter of fact, all we know is that effects come to us from the dark sphere of the psyche which somehow or other must be assimilated into consciousness if devastating disturbances of other functions are to be avoided. It is quite impossible to say offhand what the nature of these effects is, whether they originate in sexuality, the power instinct, or some other instinct. They have as many meanings and facets as the unconscious itself.

709   I have already pointed out that although the unconscious is a receptacle for everything that is forgotten, past, and repressed, it is also the sphere in which all subliminal processes take place. It contains sense-perceptions that are still too weak to reach consciousness, and, furthermore, is the matrix out of which the whole psychic future grows. Thus, just as a person can repress a disquieting wish and thereby cause its energy to contaminate other functions, so he can shut out a new idea that is alien to him so that its energy flows off into other functions and disturbs them. I have seen many cases where abnormal sexual

367

fantasies disappeared, suddenly and completely, the moment a new idea or content became conscious, or when a migraine suddenly vanished when the patient became aware of an unconscious poem. Just as sexuality can express itself inappropriately in fantasies, so creative fantasy can express itself inappropriately in sexuality. As Voltaire once remarked: "En étymologie n'importe quoi peut désigner n'importe quoi"— and we must say the same thing of the unconscious. At any rate we can never know beforehand what is what. With regard to the unconscious we merely have the gift of being wise after the event; it is quite impossible to know anything about the true state of things. Every conclusion in this respect is an admitted "as if."

710   Under these circumstances the unconscious seems like a great X, concerning which the only thing indisputably known is that important effects proceed from it. A glance at the world religions shows us just how important these effects are historically. And a glance at the suffering of modern man shows us the same thing—we merely express ourselves somewhat differently. Three hundred years ago a woman was said to be possessed of the devil, now we say she has a hysteria. Formerly a sufferer was said to be bewitched, now the trouble is called a neurotic dyspepsia. The facts are the same; only the previous explanation, psychologically speaking, is almost exact, whereas our rationalistic description of symptoms is really without content. For if I say that someone is possessed by an evil spirit, I imply that the possessed person is not legitimately ill but suffers from some invisible psychic influence which he is quite unable to control. This invisible something is an autonomous complex, an unconscious content beyond the reach of the conscious will. When one analyses the psychology of a neurosis one discovers a complex, a content of the unconscious, that does not behave as other contents do, coming or going at our command, but obeys its own laws, in other words it is independent or, as we say, autonomous. It behaves exactly like a goblin that is always eluding our grasp. And when the complex is made conscious—which is the aim of analysis—the patient will exclaim with relief: "So that's what the trouble was!" Apparently something has been gained: the symptoms disappear, the complex is, as we say, resolved. We can exclaim with Goethe: "Be off with you, you've been ex-

368

plained away!" but with Goethe we must go on to add: "For all our wisdom, Tegel still is haunted." [2] The true state of affairs is now for the first time revealed. We become aware that this complex would never have existed at all had not our nature lent it a secret driving power. I will explain what I mean by an example:

711   A patient suffers from nervous stomach symptoms that consist in painful contractions resembling hunger. Analysis shows an infantile longing for the mother, a so-called mother-complex. The symptoms disappear with this new-won insight, but there remains a longing which refuses to be assuaged by the explanation that it was "nothing but an infantile mother-complex." What was before a sort of physical hunger and a physical pain now becomes psychic hunger and psychic pain. One longs for something and yet knows that it would be quite wrong to mistake it for the mother. But the ever-present, unappeasable longing remains, and the solution of this problem is considerably more difficult than the reduction of the neurosis to a mother-complex. The longing is an insistent demand, an aching inner emptiness, which can be forgotten from time to time but never overcome by strength of will. It always returns. At first one does not know where it comes from or what the patient is really longing for. A good deal can be conjectured, but all that can be said with certainty is that over and above the mother-complex something unconscious voices this demand independently of consciousness and continues to raise its voice despite all criticism. This something I have called an autonomous complex. It is the source of that driving power which originally sustained the infantile claim on the mother and thus caused the neurosis, for an adult consciousness was bound to discountenance such a childish demand and repress it as incompatible.

712   All infantile complexes ultimately resolve themselves into autonomous contents of the unconscious. The primitive mind has always felt these contents to be strange and incomprehensible and, personifying them as spirits, demons, and gods, has sought to fulfil their demands by sacred and magical rites. Recognizing correctly that this hunger or thirst can be stilled neither by food nor by drink nor by returning to the mother's

2 *Faust*, Part I, trans. by Wayne, p. 178.

womb, the primitive mind created images of invisible, jealous, and exacting beings, more potent and more dangerous than man, denizens of an invisible world, yet so interfused with visible reality that there are spirits who dwell even in the cooking-pots. Spirits and magic are almost the sole causes of illness among primitives. The autonomous contents are projected by the primitive upon these supernatural beings. Our world, on the other hand, is freed of demons to the last trace, but the autonomous contents and their demands have remained. They express themselves partly in religion, but the more the religion is rationalized and watered down—an almost unavoidable fate—the more intricate and mysterious become the ways by which the contents of the unconscious contrive to reach us. One of the commonest ways is neurosis, which is the last thing one would expect. A neurosis is usually considered to be something inferior, a *quantité négligeable* from the medical point of view. This is a great mistake, as we have seen. For behind the neurosis are hidden those powerful psychic influences which underlie our mental attitude and its guiding principles. Rationalistic materialism, an attitude that does not seem at all suspect, is really a psychological countermove to mysticism—*that* is the secret antagonist who has to be combatted. Materialism and mysticism are a psychological pair of opposites, just like atheism and theism. They are hostile brothers, two different methods of grappling with these powerful influences from the unconscious, the one by denying, the other by recognizing them.

713   If, therefore, I had to name the most essential thing that analytical psychology can add to our *Weltanschauung*, I should say it is the recognition that there exist certain unconscious contents which make demands that cannot be denied, or send forth influences with which the conscious mind must come to terms, whether it will or no.

714   You would no doubt find my remarks somewhat unsatisfactory if I left that "something" which I described as an autonomous content in this indefinite state and made no attempt to tell you what our psychology has discovered empirically about these contents.

715   If, as psychoanalysis assumes, a definitive and satisfactory answer can be given, as for example that the original infantile dependence on the mother is the cause of the longing, then this

recognition should also provide a solution. And in some cases the infantile dependence does in fact disappear when the patient has recognized it sufficiently. But one must not infer that this is true in all cases. In every case something remains unresolved; sometimes it is apparently so little that the case is, for all practical purposes, finished; but again, it may be so much that neither the patient nor the analyst is satisfied with the result, and it seems as though nothing had been accomplished. Moreover, I have treated many patients who were conscious of the cause of their complexes down to the last detail, without having been helped in any essential way by this insight.

716 A causal explanation may be relatively satisfactory from a scientific point of view, but psychologically there is still something unsatisfying about it, because we still do not know anything about the purpose of that driving power at the root of the complex—the meaning of the longing, for example—nor what is to be done about it. If I already know that an epidemic of typhoid comes from infected drinking water, this is still not sufficient to stop the pollution of the water-supply. A satisfactory answer is given only when we know *what* it is that maintained the infantile dependence into adult life, and what it is aiming at.

717 If the human mind came into the world as a complete *tabula rasa* these problems would not exist, for there would then be nothing in the mind that it had not acquired or that had not been implanted in it. But there are many things in the human psyche that were never acquired by the individual, for the human mind is not born a *tabula rasa,* nor is every man provided with a wholly new and unique brain. He is born with a brain that is the result of development in an endlessly long chain of ancestors. This brain is produced in each embryo in all its differentiated perfection, and when it starts functioning it will unfailingly produce the same results that have been produced innumerable times before in the ancestral line. The whole anatomy of man is an inherited system identical with the ancestral constitution, which will unfailingly function in the same way as before. Consequently, the possibility that anything new and essentially different will be produced becomes increasingly small. All those factors, therefore, which were essential to our near and remote ancestors will also be essential to us, since

they are embedded in the inherited organic system. They are even necessities which make themselves felt as needs.

718   Do not fear that I shall speak to you of inherited ideas. Far from it. The autonomous contents of the unconscious, or, as I have called them, dominants, are not inherited ideas but inherited possibilities, not to say compelling necessities, for reproducing the images and ideas by which these dominants have always been expressed. Of course every region of the earth and every epoch has its own distinctive language, and this can be endlessly varied. It matters little if the mythological hero conquers now a dragon, now a fish or some other monster; the fundamental motif remains the same, and that is the common property of mankind, not the ephemeral formulations of different regions and epochs.

719   Thus man is born with a complicated psychic disposition that is anything but a *tabula rasa*. Even the boldest fantasies have their limits determined by our psychic inheritance, and through the veil of even the wildest fantasy we can still glimpse the dominants that were inherent in the human mind from the very beginning. It seems very remarkable to us when we discover that insane people develop fantasies that can be found in almost identical form among primitives. But it would be remarkable if it were otherwise.

720   I have called the sphere of our psychic heritage the collective unconscious. The contents of consciousness are all acquired individually. If the human psyche consisted simply and solely of consciousness, there would be nothing psychic that had not arisen in the course of the individual's life. In that case we would seek in vain for any prior conditions or influences behind a simple parental complex. With the reduction to father and mother the last word would be said, for they are the figures that first influenced the conscious psyche to the exclusion of all else. But actually the contents of consciousness did not come into existence simply through the influence of the environment; they were also influenced and arranged by our psychic inheritance, the collective unconscious. Naturally the image of the individual mother is impressive, but its peculiar impressiveness is due to the fact that it is blended with an unconscious aptitude or inborn image which is the result of the symbiotic relationship of mother and child that has existed from eternity. Where the

372

individual mother fails in this or that respect, a loss is felt, and this amounts to a demand of the collective mother-image for fulfilment. An instinct has been balked, so to speak. This very often gives rise to neurotic disturbances, or at any rate to peculiarities of character. If the collective unconscious did not exist, everything could be achieved by education; one could reduce a human being to a psychic machine with impunity, or transform him into an ideal. But strict limits are set to any such enterprise, because the dominants of the unconscious make almost irresistible demands for fulfilment.

721   So if, in the case of the patient with the stomach-neurosis, I were asked to name what it is in the unconscious, over and above the personal mother-complex, that keeps alive an indefinable but agonizing longing, the answer is: it is the collective image of the mother, not of the personal mother, but of the mother in her universal aspect.

722   But why should this collective image arouse such longing? It is not very easy to answer this question. Yet if we could get a clear idea of the nature and meaning of this collective image, which I have called the archetype, then its effects could readily be understood.

723   In order to explain this, I should use the following argument. The mother-child relationship is certainly the deepest and most poignant one we know; in fact, for some time the child is, so to speak, a part of the mother's body. Later it is part of the psychic atmosphere of the mother for several years, and in this way everything original in the child is indissolubly blended with the mother-image. This is true not only for the individual, but still more in a historical sense. It is the absolute experience of our species, an organic truth as unequivocal as the relation of the sexes to one another. Thus there is inherent in the archetype, in the collectively inherited mother-image, the same extraordinary intensity of relationship which instinctively impels the child to cling to its mother. With the passing of the years, the man grows naturally away from the mother—provided, of course, that he is no longer in a condition of almost animal-like primitivity and has attained some degree of consciousness and culture—but he does not outgrow the archetype in the same natural way. If he is merely instinctive, his life will run on without choice, since freedom of will always presupposes consciousness.

It will proceed according to unconscious laws, and there will be no deviation from the archetype. But, if consciousness is at all effective, conscious contents will always be overvalued to the detriment of the unconscious, and from this comes the illusion that in separating from the mother nothing has happened except that one has ceased to be the child of this individual woman. Consciousness only recognizes contents that are individually acquired; hence it recognizes only the individual mother and does not know that she is at the same time the carrier and representative of the archetype, of the "eternal" mother. Separation from the mother is sufficient only if the archetype is included, and the same is true of separation from the father.

724   The development of consciousness and of free will naturally brings with it the possibility of deviating from the archetype and hence from instinct. Once the deviation sets in a dissociation between conscious and unconscious ensues, and then the activity of the unconscious begins. This is usually felt as very unpleasant, for it takes the form of an inner, unconscious fixation which expresses itself only symptomatically, that is, indirectly. Situations then develop in which it seems as though one were still not freed from the mother.

725   The primitive mind, while not understanding this dilemma, felt it all the more keenly and accordingly instituted highly important rites between childhood and adulthood, puberty-rites and initiation ceremonies, for the quite unmistakable purpose of effecting the separation from the parents by magical means. This institution would be entirely superfluous if the relation to the parents were not felt to be equally magical. But "magical" means everything where unconscious influences are at work. The purpose of these rites, however, is not only separation from the parents, but induction into the adult state. There must be no more longing backward glances at childhood, and for this it is necessary that the claims of the injured archetype should be met. This is done by substituting for the intimate relationship with the parents another relationship, namely that with the clan or tribe. The infliction of certain marks on the body, such as circumcision and scars, is intended to serve this end, as also the mystical instruction which the young man receives during

374

his initiation. Often these initiations have a decidedly cruel character.

726   This is the way the primitive, for reasons unknown to him, attempts to fulfil the claims of the archetype. A simple parting from the parents is not sufficient; there must be a drastic ceremony that looks very like sacrifice to the powers which might hold the young man back. This shows us at a glance the power of the archetype: it forces the primitive to act against nature so that he shall not become her victim. This is indeed the beginning of all culture, the inevitable result of consciousness and of the possibility of deviating from unconscious law.

727   Our world has long been estranged to these things, though this does not mean that nature has forfeited any of her power over us. We have merely learnt to undervalue that power. But we find ourselves at something of a loss when we come to the question, what should be our way of dealing with the effects of unconscious contents? For us it can no longer be a matter of primitive rites; that would be an artificial and futile regression. If you put the question to me, I too would be at a loss for an answer. I can only say this much, that for years I have observed in many of my patients the ways they instinctively select in order to meet the demands of the unconscious. It would far exceed the limits of a lecture if I were to report on these observations. I must refer you to the literature in which this question is thoroughly discussed.[3]

728   If, in this lecture, I have helped you to recognize that the powers which men have always projected into space as gods, and worshipped with sacrifices, are still alive and active in our own unconscious psyche, I shall be content. This recognition should suffice to show that the manifold religious practices and beliefs which, from the earliest times, have played such an enormous role in history cannot be traced back to the whimsical fancies and opinions of individuals, but owe their existence far more to the influence of unconscious powers which we cannot neglect without disturbing the psychic balance. The example I gave of the mother-complex is naturally only one among many. The archetype of the mother is a single instance that could be

3 [*Two Essays on Analytical Psychology; Psychology and Alchemy*, Part I; "A Study in the Process of Individuation"; "Concerning Mandala Symbolism."— EDITORS.]

supplemented by a number of other archetypes. This multiplicity of unconscious dominants helps to explain the diversity of religious ideas.

729   All these factors are still active in our psyche; only the expression and evaluation of them have been superseded, not their actual existence and effectiveness. The fact that we can now understand them as psychic quantities is a new formulation, a new expression, which may enable us to discover a new way of relating to the powers of the unconscious. I believe this possibility to be of immense significance, because the collective unconscious is in no sense an obscure corner of the mind, but the mighty deposit of ancestral experience accumulated over millions of years, the echo of prehistoric happenings to which each century adds an infinitesimally small amount of variation and differentiation. Because the collective unconscious is, in the last analysis, a deposit of world-processes embedded in the structure of the brain and the sympathetic nervous system, it constitutes in its totality a sort of timeless and eternal world-image which counterbalances our conscious, momentary picture of the world. It means nothing less than another world, a mirror-world if you will. But, unlike a mirror-image, the unconscious image possesses an energy peculiar to itself, independent of consciousness. By virtue of this energy it can produce powerful effects which do not appear on the surface but influence us all the more powerfully from within. These influences remain invisible to anyone who fails to subject his momentary picture of the world to adequate criticism, and who therefore remains hidden from himself. That the world has an inside as well as an outside, that it is not only outwardly visible but acts upon us in a timeless present, from the deepest and apparently most subjective recesses of the psyche—this I hold to be an insight which, even though it be ancient wisdom, deserves to be evaluated as a new factor in building a *Weltanschauung*.

*

730   Analytical psychology is not a *Weltanschauung* but a science, and as such it provides the building-material or the implements with which a *Weltanschauung* can be built up or torn down, or else reconstructed. There are many people today who think they can smell a *Weltanschauung* in analytical psychol-

ogy. I wish I were one of them, for then I should be spared the pains of investigation and doubt, and could tell you clearly and simply the way that leads to Paradise. Unfortunately we are still a long way from that. I merely conduct an experiment in *Weltanschauung* when I try to make clear to myself the meaning and scope of what is happening today. But this experimentation is, in a sense, a way, for when all is said and done, our own existence is an experiment of nature, an attempt at a new synthesis.[4]

731   A science can never be a *Weltanschauung* but merely the tool with which to make one. Whether we take this tool in hand or not depends on the sort of *Weltanschauung* we already have. For no one is without a *Weltanschauung* of some sort. Even in an extreme case, he will at least have the *Weltanschauung* that education and environment have forced on him. If this tells him, to quote Goethe, that "the highest joy of man should be the growth of personality," he will unhesitatingly seize upon science and its conclusions, and with this as a tool will build himself a *Weltanschauung*—to his own edification. But if his hereditary convictions tell him that science is not a tool but an end in itself, he will follow the watchword that has become more and more prevalent during the last one hundred and fifty years and has proved to be the decisive one in practice. Here and there single individuals have desperately resisted it, for to their way of thinking the meaning of life culminates in the perfection of the human personality and not in the differentiation of techniques, which inevitably leads to an extremely one-sided development of a single instinct, for instance the instinct for knowledge. If science is an end in itself, man's *raison d'être* lies in being a mere intellect. If art is an end in itself, then his sole value lies in the imaginative faculty, and the intellect is consigned to the lumber-room. If making money is an end in itself, both science and art can quietly shut up shop. No one can deny that our modern consciousness, in pursuing these mutually exclusive ends, has become hopelessly fragmented. The consequence is that people are trained to develop one quality only; they become tools themselves.

732   In the last one hundred and fifty years we have witnessed

4 [The remaining paragraphs were added in the 1931 Swiss edn.—EDITORS.]

a plethora of *Weltanschauungen*—a proof that the whole idea of a *Weltanschauung* has been discredited, for the more difficult an illness is to treat, the more the remedies multiply, and the more remedies there are, the more disreputable each one becomes. It seems as if a *Weltanschauung* were now an obsolete phenomenon.

733   One can hardly imagine that this development is a mere accident, a regrettable and senseless aberration, for something that is good and valuable in itself does not usually disappear from sight in this suspicious manner. There must have been something meretricious and objectionable about it to begin with. We must therefore ask ourselves: what is wrong with all *Weltanschauungen*?

734   It seems to me that the fatal error of every *Weltanschauung* so far has been that it claims to be an objectively valid truth, and ultimately a kind of scientific evidence of this truth. This would lead to the insufferable conclusion that, for instance, the same God must help the Germans, the French, the English, the Turks, and the heathen—in short, everybody against everybody else. Our modern consciousness, with its broader grasp of world-events, has recoiled in horror from such a monstrosity, only to put in its place various philosophical substitutes. But these in turn laid claims to being objectively valid truths. That discredited them, and so we arrive at the differentiated fragmentation of consciousness with its highly undesirable consequences.

735   The basic error of every *Weltanschauung* is its remarkable tendency to pretend to be the truth of things themselves, whereas actually it is only a name which we give to things. Would any scientist argue whether the name of the planet Neptune befits the nature of this heavenly body and whether, therefore, it is the only "right" name? Of course not—and that is why science is superior, because it deals only in working hypotheses. In the fairytale you can blast Rumpelstiltskin to fragments if you call him by his right name. The tribal chief hides his true name and gives himself an exoteric name for daily use, so that nobody can put a spell on him. When the Egyptian Pharaohs were laid in the tomb, the true names of the gods were imparted to them in word and image, so that they could compel the gods to do their bidding. For the Cabalists the possession of the true name

378

of God meant absolute magic power. To sum up: for the primitive mind the thing itself is posited by the name. "What he says, is" runs the old saying about Ptah.

736   This piece of unconscious primitivity is the bane of every *Weltanschauung*. Just as astronomers have no means of knowing whether the inhabitants of Neptune have complained about the wrong naming of their planet, so we may safely assume that it is all one to the world what we think about it. But that does not mean that we need stop thinking. And indeed we do not; science lives on, as the heir to *Weltanschauungen* fallen into decay. It is only man who is impoverished by this change of status. In a *Weltanschauung* of the old style he had naïvely substituted his mind for things; he could regard his own face as the face of the world, see himself in the likeness of God—a glory that was not paid for too dearly even with everlasting damnation. But in science he does not think of himself, he thinks only of the world, of the object; he has put himself aside and sacrificed his personality to the objective spirit of research. That is why the spirit of science is ethically superior to a *Weltanschauung* of the old style.

737   Nevertheless, we are beginning to feel the consequences of this atrophy of the human personality. Everywhere one hears the cry for a *Weltanschauung;* everyone asks the meaning of life and the world. There have been numerous attempts in our time to put the clock back and to indulge in a *Weltanschauung* of the old style—to wit, theosophy, or, as it is more palatably called, anthroposophy. But if we do not want to develop backwards, a new *Weltanschauung* will have to abandon the superstition of its objective validity and admit that it is only a picture which we paint to please our minds, and not a magical name with which we can conjure up real things. A *Weltanschauung* is made not for the world, but for ourselves. If we do not fashion for ourselves a picture of the world, we do not see ourselves either, who are the faithful reflections of that world. Only when mirrored in our picture of the world can we see ourselves in the round. Only in our creative acts do we step forth into the light and see ourselves whole and complete. Never shall we put any face on the world other than our own, and we have to do this precisely in order to find ourselves. For higher than science or art as an end in itself stands man, the creator of his instruments.

Nowhere are we closer to the sublime secret of all origination than in the recognition of our own selves, whom we always think we know already. Yet we know the immensities of space better than we know our own depths, where—even though we do not understand it—we can listen directly to the throb of creation itself.

738   In this sense analytical psychology offers us new possibilities. It calls our attention to the existence of fantasy-images that spring from the dark background of the psyche and throw light on the processes going on in the unconscious. The contents of the collective unconscious are, as I have pointed out, the results of the psychic functioning of our whole ancestry; in their totality, they compose a natural world-image, the condensation of millions of years of human experience. These images are mythological and therefore symbolical, for they express the harmony of the experiencing subject with the object experienced. All mythology and all revelation come from this matrix of experience, and all our future ideas about the world and man will come from it likewise. Nevertheless, it would be a misunderstanding to suppose that the fantasy-images of the unconscious can be used directly, like a revelation. They are only the raw material, which, in order to acquire a meaning, has first to be translated into the language of the present. If this is successful, then the world as we perceive it is reunited with the primordial experience of mankind by the symbol of a *Weltanschauung;* the historical, universal man in us joins hands with the newborn, individual man. This is an experience which comes very close to that of the primitive, who symbolically unites himself with the totem-ancestor by partaking of the ritual feast.

739   Seen in this light, analytical psychology is a reaction against the exaggerated rationalization of consciousness which, seeking to control nature, isolates itself from her and so robs man of his own natural history. He finds himself transplanted into a limited present, consisting of the short span between birth and death. The limitation creates a feeling that he is a haphazard creature without meaning, and it is this feeling that prevents him from living his life with the intensity it demands if it is to be enjoyed to the full. Life becomes stale and is no longer the exponent of the complete man. That is why so much unlived life falls into the unconscious. People live as though they were

walking in shoes too small for them. That quality of eternity which is so characteristic of the life of primitive man is entirely lacking. Hemmed round by rationalistic walls, we are cut off from the eternity of nature. Analytical psychology seeks to break through these walls by digging up again the fantasy-images of the unconscious which our rationalism has rejected. These images lie beyond the walls; they are part of the nature *in us,* which apparently lies buried in our past and against which we have barricaded ourselves behind the walls of reason. Analytical psychology tries to resolve the resultant conflict not by going "back to Nature" with Rousseau, but by holding on to the level of reason we have successfully reached, and by enriching consciousness with a knowledge of man's psychic foundations.

740   Everyone who has achieved this break-through always describes it as overwhelming. But he will not be able to enjoy this impression for long, because the question immediately arises of how the new-won knowledge is to be assimilated. What lies on this side of the walls proves to be irreconcilable with what lies outside. This opens up the whole problem of translation into contemporary language, and perhaps the creation of a new language altogether. Thus we come back to the question of *Weltanschauung*—a *Weltanschauung* that will help us to get into harmony with the historical man in us, in such a way that the deeper chords in him are not drowned by the shrill strains of rationalism, and the precious light of individual consciousness is not extinguished in the infinite darknesses of the natural psyche. But no sooner do we touch this question than we have to leave the realm of science behind us, for now we need the creative resolve to entrust our life to this or that hypothesis. In other words, this is where the ethical problem begins, without which a *Weltanschauung* is inconceivable.

741   I think I have made it clear enough in the present discussion that analytical psychology, though not in itself a *Weltanschauung,* can still make an important contribution to the building of one.

THE REAL AND THE SURREAL [1]

742   I know nothing of a "super-reality." Reality contains everything I can know, for everything that acts upon me is real and
actual. If it does not act upon me, then I notice nothing and
can, therefore, know nothing about it. Hence I can make statements only about real things, but not about things that are
unreal, or surreal, or subreal. Unless, of course, it should occur
to someone to limit the concept of reality in such a way that
the attribute "real" applied only to a particular segment of the
world's reality. This restriction to the so-called material or concrete reality of objects perceived by the senses is a product of a
particular way of thinking—the thinking that underlies "sound
common sense" and our ordinary use of language. It operates
on the celebrated principle "Nihil est in intellectu quod non
antea fuerit in sensu," regardless of the fact that there are very
many things in the mind which did not derive from the data of
the senses. According to this view, everything is "real" which
comes, or seems to come, directly or indirectly from the world
revealed by the senses.

743   This limited picture of the world is a reflection of the one-
sidedness of Western man, which is often very unjustly laid at
the door of the Greek intellect. Restriction to *material* reality
carves an exceedingly large chunk out of reality as a whole, but

1 [Originally published as "Wirklichkeit und Überwirklichkeit," *Querschnitt*
(Berlin), XII : 12 (Dec. 1933).—EDITORS.]

it nevertheless remains a fragment only, and all round it is a dark penumbra which one would have to call unreal or surreal. This narrow perspective is alien to the Eastern view of the world, which therefore has no need of any philosophical conception of super-reality. Our arbitrarily delimited reality is continually menaced by the "supersensual," the "supernatural," the "superhuman," and a whole lot more besides. Eastern reality includes all this as a matter of course. For us the zone of disturbance already begins with the concept of the "psychic." In our reality the psychic cannot be anything except an effect at third hand, produced originally by physical causes; a "secretion of the brain," or something equally savoury. At the same time, this appendage of the material world is credited with the power to pull itself up by its own bootstraps, so to speak; and not only to fathom the secrets of the physical world, but also, in the form of "mind," to know itself. All this, without its being granted anything more than an indirect reality.

744   Is a thought "real"? Probably—to this way of thinking—only in so far as it refers to something that can be perceived by the senses. If it does not, it is considered "unreal," "fanciful," "fantastic," etc., and is thus declared nonexistent. This happens all the time in practice, despite the fact that it is a philosophical monstrosity. The thought *was* and *is*, even though it refers to no tangible reality; it even has an effect, otherwise no one would have noticed it. But because the little word "is"—to our way of thinking—refers to something material, the "unreal" thought must be content to exist in a nebulous super-reality, which in practice means the same thing as unreality. And yet the thought may have left undeniable traces of its reality behind it; we may, perhaps, have speculated with it, and thereby made a painful hole in our bank balance.

745   Our practical conception of reality would therefore seem to be in need of revision. So true is this that even popular literature is beginning to include all sorts of "super"-concepts in its mental horizon. I have every sympathy with this, for there is something really not quite right about the way we look at the world. Far too little in theory, and almost never in practice, do we remember that consciousness has no direct relation to any material objects. We perceive nothing but images, transmitted to us indirectly by a complicated nervous apparatus. Between the

nerve-endings of the sense-organs and the image that appears in consciousness, there is interpolated an unconscious process which transforms the physical fact of light, for example, into the psychic image "light." But for this complicated and unconscious process of transformation consciousness could not perceive anything material.

746   The consequence of this is, that what appears to us as immediate reality consists of carefully processed images, and that, furthermore, we live immediately only in a world of images. In order to determine, even approximately, the real nature of material things we need the elaborate apparatus and complicated procedures of chemistry and physics. These disciplines are really tools which help the human intellect to cast a glance behind the deceptive veil of images into a non-psychic world.

747   Far, therefore, from being a material world, this is a psychic world, which allows us to make only indirect and hypothetical inferences about the real nature of matter. The psychic alone has immediate reality, and this includes all forms of the psychic, even "unreal" ideas and thoughts which refer to nothing "external." We may call them "imagination" or "delusion," but that does not detract in any way from their effectiveness. Indeed, there is no "real" thought that cannot, at times, be thrust aside by an "unreal" one, thus proving that the latter is stronger and more effective than the former. Greater than all physical dangers are the tremendous effects of delusional ideas, which are yet denied all reality by our world-blinded consciousness. Our much vaunted reason and our boundlessly overestimated will are sometimes utterly powerless in the face of "unreal" thoughts. The world-powers that rule over all mankind, for good or ill, are unconscious psychic factors, and it is they that bring consciousness into being and hence create the *sine qua non* for the existence of any world at all. We are steeped in a world that was created by our own psyche.

748   From this we can judge the magnitude of the error which our Western consciousness commits when it allows the psyche only a reality derived from physical causes. The East is wiser, for it finds the essence of all things grounded in the psyche. Between the unknown essences of spirit and matter stands the reality of the psychic—psychic reality, the only reality we can experience immediately.

VI

THE STAGES OF LIFE

THE SOUL AND DEATH

THE STAGES OF LIFE [1]

749   To discuss the problems connected with the stages of human development is an exacting task, for it means nothing less than unfolding a picture of psychic life in its entirety from the cradle to the grave. Within the framework of a lecture such a task can be carried out only on the broadest lines, and it must be well understood that no attempt will be made to describe the normal psychic occurrences within the various stages. We shall restrict ourselves, rather, to certain "problems," that is, to things that are difficult, questionable, or ambiguous; in a word, to questions which allow of more than one answer—and, moreover, answers that are always open to doubt. For this reason there will be much to which we must add a question-mark in our thoughts. Worse still, there will be some things we must accept on faith, while now and then we must even indulge in speculations.

750   If psychic life consisted only of self-evident matters of fact—which on a primitive level is still the case—we could content

1 [Originally published as "Die seelischen Probleme der menschlichen Altersstufen," *Neue Zürcher Zeitung*, March 14 and 16, 1930. Revised and largely rewritten, it was republished as "Die Lebenswende," *Seelenprobleme der Gegenwart* (Psychologische Abhandlungen, III; Zurich, 1931), which version was translated by W. S. Dell and Cary F. Baynes as "The Stages of Life," *Modern Man in Search of a Soul* (London and New York, 1933). The present translation is based on this.–EDITORS.]

ourselves with a sturdy empiricism. The psychic life of civilized man, however, is full of problems; we cannot even think of it except in terms of problems. Our psychic processes are made up to a large extent of reflections, doubts, experiments, all of which are almost completely foreign to the unconscious, instinctive mind of primitive man. It is the growth of consciousness which we must thank for the existence of problems; they are the Danaän gift of civilization. It is just man's turning away from instinct—his opposing himself to instinct—that creates consciousness. Instinct is nature and seeks to perpetuate nature, whereas consciousness can only seek culture or its denial. Even when we turn back to nature, inspired by a Rousseauesque longing, we "cultivate" nature. As long as we are still submerged in nature we are unconscious, and we live in the security of instinct which knows no problems. Everything in us that still belongs to nature shrinks away from a problem, for its name is doubt, and wherever doubt holds sway there is uncertainty and the possibility of divergent ways. And where several ways seem possible, there we have turned away from the certain guidance of instinct and are handed over to fear. For consciousness is now called upon to do that which nature has always done for her children—namely, to give a certain, unquestionable, and unequivocal decision. And here we are beset by an all-too-human fear that consciousness—our Promethean conquest—may in the end not be able to serve us as well as nature.

751   Problems thus draw us into an orphaned and isolated state where we are abandoned by nature and are driven to consciousness. There is no other way open to us; we are forced to resort to conscious decisions and solutions where formerly we trusted ourselves to natural happenings. Every problem, therefore, brings the possibility of a widening of consciousness, but also the necessity of saying goodbye to childlike unconsciousness and trust in nature. This necessity is a psychic fact of such importance that it constitutes one of the most essential symbolic teachings of the Christian religion. It is the sacrifice of the merely natural man, of the unconscious, ingenuous being whose tragic career began with the eating of the apple in Paradise. The biblical fall of man presents the dawn of consciousness as a curse. And as a matter of fact it is in this light that we first look upon every problem that forces us to greater consciousness

388

and separates us even further from the paradise of unconscious childhood. Every one of us gladly turns away from his problems; if possible, they must not be mentioned, or, better still, their existence is denied. We wish to make our lives simple, certain, and smooth, and for that reason problems are taboo. We want to have certainties and no doubts—results and no experiments— without even seeing that certainties can arise only through doubt and results only through experiment. The artful denial of a problem will not produce conviction; on the contrary, a wider and higher consciousness is required to give us the certainty and clarity we need.

752   This introduction, long as it is, seemed to me necessary in order to make clear the nature of our subject. When we must deal with problems, we instinctively resist trying the way that leads through obscurity and darkness. We wish to hear only of unequivocal results, and completely forget that these results can only be brought about when we have ventured into and emerged again from the darkness. But to penetrate the darkness we must summon all the powers of enlightenment that consciousness can offer; as I have already said, we must even indulge in speculations. For in treating the problems of psychic life we perpetually stumble upon questions of principle belonging to the private domains of the most heterogeneous branches of knowledge. We disturb and anger the theologian no less than the philosopher, the physician no less than the educator; we even grope about in the field of the biologist and of the historian. This extravagant behaviour is due not to arrogance but to the circumstance that man's psyche is a unique combination of factors which are at the same time the special subjects of far-reaching lines of research. For it is out of himself and out of his peculiar constitution that man has produced his sciences. They are *symptoms* of his psyche.

753   If, therefore, we ask ourselves the unavoidable question, "Why does man, in obvious contrast to the animal world, have problems at all?" we run into that inextricable tangle of thoughts which many thousands of incisive minds have woven in the course of the centuries. I shall not perform the labours of a Sisyphus upon this masterpiece of confusion, but will try to present quite simply my contribution toward man's attempt to answer this basic question.

754   There are no problems without consciousness. We must therefore put the question in another way and ask, "How does consciousness arise in the first place?" Nobody can say with certainty; but we can observe small children in the process of becoming conscious. Every parent can see it if he pays attention. And what we see is this: when the child recognizes someone or something—when he "knows" a person or a thing—then we feel that the child has consciousness. That, no doubt, is also why in Paradise it was the tree of knowledge which bore such fateful fruit.

755   But what is recognition or "knowledge" in this sense? We speak of "knowing" something when we succeed in linking a new perception to an already existing context, in such a way that we hold in consciousness not only the perception but parts of this context as well. "Knowing" is based, therefore, upon the perceived connection between psychic contents. We can have no knowledge of a content that is not connected with anything, and we cannot even be conscious of it should our consciousness still be on this low initial level. Accordingly the first stage of consciousness which we can observe consists in the mere connection between two or more psychic contents. At this level, consciousness is merely sporadic, being limited to the perception of a few connections, and the content is not remembered later on. It is a fact that in the early years of life there is no continuous memory; at most there are islands of consciousness which are like single lamps or lighted objects in the far-flung darkness. But these islands of memory are not the same as those earliest connections which are merely perceived; they contain a new, very important series of contents belonging to the perceiving subject himself, the so-called ego. This series, like the initial series of contents, is at first merely perceived, and for this reason the child logically begins by speaking of itself objectively, in the third person. Only later, when the ego-contents—the so-called ego-complex—have acquired an energy of their own (very likely as a result of training and practice) does the feeling of subjectivity or "I-ness" arise. This may well be the moment when the child begins to speak of itself in the first person. The continuity of memory probably begins at this stage. Essentially, therefore, it would be a continuity of ego-memories.

756   In the childish stage of consciousness there are as yet no prob-

lems; nothing depends upon the subject, for the child itself is still wholly dependent on its parents. It is as though it were not yet completely born, but were still enclosed in the psychic atmosphere of its parents. Psychic birth, and with it the conscious differentiation from the parents, normally takes place only at puberty, with the eruption of sexuality. The physiological change is attended by a psychic revolution. For the various bodily manifestations give such an emphasis to the ego that it often asserts itself without stint or moderation. This is sometimes called "the unbearable age".

757 Until this period is reached the psychic life of the individual is governed largely by instinct, and few or no problems arise. Even when external limitations oppose his subjective impulses, these restraints do not put the individual at variance with himself. He submits to them or circumvents them, remaining quite at one with himself. He does not yet know the state of inner tension induced by a problem. This state only arises when what was an external limitation becomes an inner one; when one impulse is opposed by another. In psychological language we would say: the problematical state, the inner division with oneself, arises when, side by side with the series of ego-contents, a second series of equal intensity comes into being. This second series, because of its energy value, has a functional significance equal to that of the ego-complex; we might call it another, second ego which can on occasion even wrest the leadership from the first. This produces the division with oneself, the state that betokens a problem.

758 To recapitulate what we have said: the first stage of consciousness, consisting in merely recognizing or "knowing," is an anarchic or chaotic state. The second, that of the developed ego-complex, is monarchic or monistic. The third brings another step forward in consciousness, and consists in an awareness of the divided, or dualistic, state.

759 And here we come to our real theme—the problem of the stages of life. First of all we must deal with the period of youth. It extends roughly from the years just after puberty to middle life, which itself begins between the thirty-fifth and fortieth year.

760 I might well be asked why I begin with the second stage, as though there were no problems connected with childhood. The

391

complex psychic life of the child is, of course, a problem of the first magnitude to parents, educators, and doctors, but when normal the child has no real problems of its own. It is only the adult human being who can have doubts about himself and be at variance with himself.

761   We are all familiar with the sources of the problems that arise in the period of youth. For most people it is the demands of life which harshly put an end to the dream of childhood. If the individual is sufficiently well prepared, the transition to a profession or career can take place smoothly. But if he clings to illusions that are contrary to reality, then problems will surely arise. No one can take the step into life without making certain assumptions, and occasionally these assumptions are false—that is, they do not fit the conditions into which one is thrown. Often it is a question of exaggerated expectations, underestimation of difficulties, unjustified optimism, or a negative attitude. One could compile quite a list of the false assumptions that give rise to the first conscious problems.

762   But it is not always the contradiction between subjective assumptions and external facts that gives rise to problems; it may just as often be inner, psychic difficulties. They may exist even when things run smoothly in the outside world. Very often it is the disturbance of psychic equilibrium caused by the sexual instinct; equally often it is the feeling of inferiority which springs from an unbearable sensitivity. These inner conflicts may exist even when adaptation to the outer world has been achieved without apparent effort. It even seems as if young people who have had a hard struggle for existence are spared inner problems, while those who for some reason or other have no difficulty with adaptation run into problems of sex or conflicts arising from a sense of inferiority.

763   People whose own temperaments offer problems are often neurotic, but it would be a serious misunderstanding to confuse the existence of problems with neurosis. There is a marked difference between the two in that the neurotic is ill because he is unconscious of his problems, while the person with a difficult temperament suffers from his conscious problems without being ill.

764   If we try to extract the common and essential factors from the almost inexhaustible variety of individual problems found

in the period of youth, we meet in all cases with one particular feature: a more or less patent clinging to the childhood level of consciousness, a resistance to the fateful forces in and around us which would involve us in the world. Something in us wishes to remain a child, to be unconscious or, at most, conscious only of the ego; to reject everything strange, or else subject it to our will; to do nothing, or else indulge our own craving for pleasure or power. In all this there is something of the inertia of matter; it is a persistence in the previous state whose range of consciousness is smaller, narrower, and more egoistic than that of the dualistic phase. For here the individual is faced with the necessity of recognizing and accepting what is different and strange as a part of his own life, as a kind of "also-I."

765   The essential feature of the dualistic phase is the widening of the horizon of life, and it is this that is so vigorously resisted. To be sure, this expansion—or diastole, as Goethe called it—had started long before this. It begins at birth, when the child abandons the narrow confinement of the mother's body; and from then on it steadily increases until it reaches a climax in the problematical state, when the individual begins to struggle against it.

766   What would happen to him if he simply changed himself into that foreign-seeming "also-I" and allowed the earlier ego to vanish into the past? We might suppose this to be a quite practical course. The very aim of religious education, from the exhortation to put off the old Adam right back to the rebirth rituals of primitive races, is to transform the human being into the new, future man, and to allow the old to die away.

767   Psychology teaches us that, in a certain sense, there is nothing in the psyche that is old; nothing that can really, finally die away. Even Paul was left with a thorn in the flesh. Whoever protects himself against what is new and strange and regresses to the past falls into the same neurotic condition as the man who identifies himself with the new and runs away from the past. The only difference is that the one has estranged himself from the past and the other from the future. In principle both are doing the same thing: they are reinforcing their narrow range of consciousness instead of shattering it in the tension of opposites and building up a state of wider and higher conⁿ sciousness.

768   This outcome would be ideal if it could be brought about in the second stage of life—but there's the rub. For one thing, nature cares nothing whatsoever about a higher level of consciousness; quite the contrary. And then society does not value these feats of the psyche very highly; its prizes are always given for achievement and not for personality, the latter being rewarded for the most part posthumously. These facts compel us towards a particular solution: we are forced to limit ourselves to the attainable, and to differentiate particular aptitudes in which the socially effective individual discovers his true self.

769   Achievement, usefulness and so forth are the ideals that seem to point the way out of the confusions of the problematical state. They are the lodestars that guide us in the adventure of broadening and consolidating our physical existence; they help us to strike our roots in the world, but they cannot guide us in the development of that wider consciousness to which we give the name of culture. In the period of youth, however, this course is the normal one and in all circumstances preferable to merely tossing about in a welter of problems.

770   The dilemma is often solved, therefore, in this way: whatever is given to us by the past is adapted to the possibilities and demands of the future. We limit ourselves to the attainable, and this means renouncing all our other psychic potentialities. One man loses a valuable piece of his past, another a valuable piece of his future. Everyone can call to mind friends or schoolmates who were promising and idealistic youngsters, but who, when we meet them again years later, seem to have grown dry and cramped in a narrow mould. These are examples of the solution mentioned above.

771   The serious problems in life, however, are never fully solved. If ever they should appear to be so it is a sure sign that something has been lost. The meaning and purpose of a problem seem to lie not in its solution but in our working at it incessantly. This alone preserves us from stultification and petrifaction. So also the solution of the problems of youth by restricting ourselves to the attainable is only temporarily valid and not lasting in a deeper sense. Of course, to win for oneself a place in society and to transform one's nature so that it is more or less fitted to this kind of existence is in all cases a considerable achievement. It is a fight waged within oneself as well as out-

side, comparable to the struggle of the child for an ego. That struggle is for the most part unobserved because it happens in the dark; but when we see how stubbornly childish illusions and assumptions and egoistic habits are still clung to in later years we can gain some idea of the energies that were needed to form them. And so it is with the ideals, convictions, guiding ideas and attitudes which in the period of youth lead us out into life, for which we struggle, suffer, and win victories: they grow together with our own being, we apparently change into them, we seek to perpetuate them indefinitely and as a matter of course, just as the young person asserts his ego in spite of the world and often in spite of himself.

772   The nearer we approach to the middle of life, and the better we have succeeded in entrenching ourselves in our personal attitudes and social positions, the more it appears as if we had discovered the right course and the right ideals and principles of behaviour. For this reason we suppose them to be eternally valid, and make a virtue of unchangeably clinging to them. We overlook the essential fact that the social goal is attained only at the cost of a diminution of personality. Many—far too many— aspects of life which should also have been experienced lie in the lumber-room among dusty memories; but sometimes, too, they are glowing coals under grey ashes.

773   Statistics show a rise in the frequency of mental depressions in men about forty. In women the neurotic difficulties generally begin somewhat earlier. We see that in this phase of life—between thirty-five and forty—an important change in the human psyche is in preparation. At first it is not a conscious and striking change; it is rather a matter of indirect signs of a change which seems to take its rise in the unconscious. Often it is something like a slow change in a person's character; in another case certain traits may come to light which had disappeared since childhood; or again, one's previous inclinations and interests begin to weaken and others take their place. Conversely —and this happens very frequently—one's cherished convictions and principles, especially the moral ones, begin to harden and to grow increasingly rigid until, somewhere around the age of fifty, a period of intolerance and fanaticism is reached. It is as if the existence of these principles were endangered and it were therefore necessary to emphasize them all the more.

774   The wine of youth does not always clear with advancing years; sometimes it grows turbid. All the phenomena mentioned above can best be seen in rather one-sided people, turning up sometimes sooner and sometimes later. Their appearance, it seems to me, is often delayed by the fact that the parents of the person in question are still alive. It is then as if the period of youth were being unduly drawn out. I have seen this especially in the case of men whose fathers were long-lived. The death of the father then has the effect of a precipitate and almost catastrophic ripening.

775   I know of a pious man who was a churchwarden and who, from the age of forty onward, showed a growing and finally unbearable intolerance in matters of morality and religion. At the same time his moods grew visibly worse. At last he was nothing more than a darkly lowering pillar of the Church. In this way he got along until the age of fifty-five, when suddenly, sitting up in bed in the middle of the night, he said to his wife: "Now at last I've got it! I'm just a plain rascal." Nor did this realization remain without results. He spent his declining years in riotous living and squandered a goodly part of his fortune. Obviously quite a likable fellow, capable of both extremes!

776   The very frequent neurotic disturbances of adult years all have one thing in common: they want to carry the psychology of the youthful phase over the threshold of the so-called years of discretion. Who does not know those touching old gentlemen who must always warm up the dish of their student days, who can fan the flame of life only by reminiscences of their heroic youth, but who, for the rest, are stuck in a hopelessly wooden Philistinism? As a rule, to be sure, they have this one merit which it would be wrong to undervalue: they are not neurotic, but only boring and stereotyped. The neurotic is rather a person who can never have things as he would like them in the present, and who can therefore never enjoy the past either.

777   As formerly the neurotic could not escape from childhood, so now he cannot part with his youth. He shrinks from the grey thoughts of approaching age, and, feeling the prospect before him unbearable, is always straining to look behind him. Just as the childish person shrinks back from the unknown in the world and in human existence, so the grown man shrinks back from the second half of life. It is as if unknown and dangerous tasks

396

awaited him, or as if he were threatened with sacrifices and losses which he does not wish to accept, or as if his life up to now seemed to him so fair and precious that he could not relinquish it.

778 Is it perhaps at bottom the fear of death? That does not seem to me very probable, because as a rule death is still far in the distance and therefore somewhat abstract. Experience shows us, rather, that the basic cause of all the difficulties of this transition is to be found in a deep-seated and peculiar change within the psyche. In order to characterize it I must take for comparison the daily course of the sun—but a sun that is endowed with human feeling and man's limited consciousness. In the morning it rises from the nocturnal sea of unconsciousness and looks upon the wide, bright world which lies before it in an expanse that steadily widens the higher it climbs in the firmament. In this extension of its field of action caused by its own rising, the sun will discover its significance; it will see the attainment of the greatest possible height, and the widest possible dissemination of its blessings, as its goal. In this conviction the sun pursues its course to the unforeseen zenith—unforeseen, because its career is unique and individual, and the culminating point could not be calculated in advance. At the stroke of noon the descent begins. And the descent means the reversal of all the ideals and values that were cherished in the morning. The sun falls into contradiction with itself. It is as though it should draw in its rays instead of emitting them. Light and warmth decline and are at last extinguished.

779 All comparisons are lame, but this simile is at least not lamer than others. A French aphorism sums it up with cynical resignation: *Si jeunesse savait, si vieillesse pouvait.*

780 Fortunately we are not rising and setting suns, for then it would fare badly with our cultural values. But there is something sunlike within us, and to speak of the morning and spring, of the evening and autumn of life is not mere sentimental jargon. We thus give expression to psychological truths and, even more, to physiological facts, for the reversal of the sun at noon changes even bodily characteristics. Especially among southern races one can observe that older women develop deep, rough voices, incipient moustaches, rather hard features and other masculine traits. On the other hand the masculine physique is

toned down by feminine features, such as adiposity and softer facial expressions.

781   There is an interesting report in the ethnological literature about an Indian warrior chief to whom in middle life the Great Spirit appeared in a dream. The spirit announced to him that from then on he must sit among the women and children, wear women's clothes, and eat the food of women. He obeyed the dream without suffering a loss of prestige. This vision is a true expression of the psychic revolution of life's noon, of the beginning of life's decline. Man's values, and even his body, do tend to change into their opposites.

782   We might compare masculinity and femininity and their psychic components to a definite store of substances of which, in the first half of life, unequal use is made. A man consumes his large supply of masculine substance and has left over only the smaller amount of feminine substance, which must now be put to use. Conversely, the woman allows her hitherto unused supply of masculinity to become active.

783   This change is even more noticeable in the psychic realm than in the physical. How often it happens that a man of forty-five or fifty winds up his business, and the wife then dons the trousers and opens a little shop where he perhaps performs the duties of a handyman. There are many women who only awaken to social responsibility and to social consciousness after their fortieth year. In modern business life, especially in America, nervous breakdowns in the forties are a very common occurrence. If one examines the victims one finds that what has broken down is the masculine style of life which held the field up to now, and that what is left over is an effeminate man. Contrariwise, one can observe women in these self-same business spheres who have developed in the second half of life an uncommonly masculine tough-mindedness which thrusts the feelings and the heart aside. Very often these changes are accompanied by all sorts of catastrophes in marriage, for it is not hard to imagine what will happen when the husband discovers his tender feelings and the wife her sharpness of mind.

784   The worst of it all is that intelligent and cultivated people live their lives without even knowing of the possibility of such transformations. Wholly unprepared, they embark upon the second half of life. Or are there perhaps colleges for forty-year-

olds which prepare them for their coming life and its demands as the ordinary colleges introduce our young people to a knowledge of the world? No, thoroughly unprepared we take the step into the afternoon of life; worse still, we take this step with the false assumption that our truths and ideals will serve us as hitherto. But we cannot live the afternoon of life according to the programme of life's morning; for what was great in the morning will be little at evening, and what in the morning was true will at evening have become a lie. I have given psychological treatment to too many people of advancing years, and have looked too often into the secret chambers of their souls, not to be moved by this fundamental truth.

785   Ageing people should know that their lives are not mounting and expanding, but that an inexorable inner process enforces the contraction of life. For a young person it is almost a sin, or at least a danger, to be too preoccupied with himself; but for the ageing person it is a duty and a necessity to devote serious attention to himself. After having lavished its light upon the world, the sun withdraws its rays in order to illuminate itself. Instead of doing likewise, many old people prefer to be hypochondriacs, niggards, pedants, applauders of the past or else eternal adolescents—all lamentable substitutes for the illumination of the self, but inevitable consequences of the delusion that the second half of life must be governed by the principles of the first.

786   I said just now that we have no schools for forty-year-olds. That is not quite true. Our religions were always such schools in the past, but how many people regard them like that today? How many of us older ones have been brought up in such a school and really prepared for the second half of life, for old age, death and eternity?

787   A human being would certainly not grow to be seventy or eighty years old if this longevity had no meaning for the species. The afternoon of human life must also have a significance of its own and cannot be merely a pitiful appendage to life's morning. The significance of the morning undoubtedly lies in the development of the individual, our entrenchment in the outer world, the propagation of our kind, and the care of our children. This is the obvious purpose of nature. But when this purpose has been attained—and more than attained—shall the

399

earning of money, the extension of conquests, and the expansion of life go steadily on beyond the bounds of all reason and sense? Whoever carries over into the afternoon the law of the morning, or the natural aim, must pay for it with damage to his soul, just as surely as a growing youth who tries to carry over his childish egoism into adult life must pay for this mistake with social failure. Money-making, social achievement, family and posterity are nothing but plain nature, not culture. Culture lies outside the purpose of nature. Could by any chance culture be the meaning and purpose of the second half of life?

788   In primitive tribes we observe that the old people are almost always the guardians of the mysteries and the laws, and it is in these that the cultural heritage of the tribe is expressed. How does the matter stand with us? Where is the wisdom of our old people, where are their precious secrets and their visions? For the most part our old people try to compete with the young. In the United States it is almost an ideal for a father to be the brother of his sons, and for the mother to be if possible the younger sister of her daughter.

789   I do not know how much of this confusion is a reaction against an earlier exaggeration of the dignity of age, and how much is to be charged to false ideals. These undoubtedly exist, and the goal of those who hold them lies behind, and not ahead. Therefore they are always striving to turn back. We have to grant these people that it is hard to see what other goal the second half of life can offer than the well-known aims of the first. Expansion of life, usefulness, efficiency, the cutting of a figure in society, the shrewd steering of offspring into suitable marriages and good positions—are not these purposes enough? Unfortunately not enough meaning and purpose for those who see in the approach of old age a mere diminution of life and can feel their earlier ideals only as something faded and worn out. Of course, if these persons had filled up the beaker of life earlier and emptied it to the lees, they would feel quite differently about everything now; they would have kept nothing back, everything that wanted to catch fire would have been consumed, and the quiet of old age would be very welcome to them. But we must not forget that only a very few people are artists in life; that the art of life is the most distinguished and rarest of all the arts. Who ever succeeded in draining the whole cup with grace?

So for many people all too much unlived life remains over—
sometimes potentialities which they could never have lived with
the best of wills, so that they approach the threshold of old age
with unsatisfied demands which inevitably turn their glances
backward.

790   It is particularly fatal for such people to look back. For them
a prospect and a goal in the future are absolutely necessary.
That is why all great religions hold out the promise of a life
beyond, of a supramundane goal which makes it possible for
mortal man to live the second half of life with as much purpose
and aim as the first. For the man of today the expansion of life
and its culmination are plausible goals, but the idea of life after
death seems to him questionable or beyond belief. Life's cessation, that is, death, can only be accepted as a reasonable goal
either when existence is so wretched that we are only too glad
for it to end, or when we are convinced that the sun strives to
its setting "to illuminate distant races" with the same logical
consistency it showed in rising to the zenith. But to believe has
become such a difficult art today that it is beyond the capacity
of most people, particularly the educated part of humanity.
They have become too accustomed to the thought that, with
regard to immortality and such questions, there are innumerable contradictory opinions and no convincing proofs. And
since "science" is the catchword that seems to carry the weight
of absolute conviction in the temporary world, we ask for
"scientific" proofs. But educated people who can think know
very well that proof of this kind is a philosophical impossibility.
We simply cannot know anything whatever about such things.

791   May I remark that for the same reasons we cannot know,
either, whether something *does* happen to a person after death?
No answer of any kind is permissible, either for or against. We
simply have no definite scientific knowledge about it one way
or the other, and are therefore in the same position as when
we ask whether the planet Mars is inhabited or not. And the
inhabitants of Mars, if there are any, are certainly not concerned whether we affirm or deny their existence. They may
exist or they may not. And that is how it stands with so-called
immortality—with which we may shelve the problem.

792   But here my medical conscience awakens and urges me to say
a word which has an important bearing on this question. I

have observed that a life directed to an aim is in general better, richer, and healthier than an aimless one, and that it is better to go forwards with the stream of time than backwards against it. To the psychotherapist an old man who cannot bid farewell to life appears as feeble and sickly as a young man who is unable to embrace it. And as a matter of fact, it is in many cases a question of the selfsame childish greediness, the same fear, the same defiance and wilfulness, in the one as in the other. As a doctor I am convinced that it is hygienic—if I may use the word—to discover in death a goal towards which one can strive, and that shrinking away from it is something unhealthy and abnormal which robs the second half of life of its purpose. I therefore consider that all religions with a supramundane goal are eminently reasonable from the point of view of psychic hygiene. When I live in a house which I know will fall about my head within the next two weeks, all my vital functions will be impaired by this thought; but if on the contrary I feel myself to be safe, I can dwell there in a normal and comfortable way. From the standpoint of psychotherapy it would therefore be desirable to think of death as only a transition, as part of a life process whose extent and duration are beyond our knowledge.

793   In spite of the fact that the majority of people do not know why the body needs salt, everyone demands it nonetheless because of an instinctive need. It is the same with the things of the psyche. By far the greater portion of mankind have from time immemorial felt the need of believing in a continuance of life. The demands of therapy, therefore, do not lead us into any bypaths but down the middle of the highway trodden by humanity. For this reason we are thinking correctly, and in harmony with life, even though we do not understand what we think.

794   Do we ever understand what we think? We only understand that kind of thinking which is a mere equation, from which nothing comes out but what we have put in. That is the working of the intellect. But besides that there is a thinking in primordial images, in symbols which are older than the historical man, which are inborn in him from the earliest times, and, eternally living, outlasting all generations, still make up the groundwork of the human psyche. It is only possible to live the

fullest life when we are in harmony with these symbols; wisdom is a return to them. It is a question neither of belief nor of knowledge, but of the agreement of our thinking with the primordial images of the unconscious. They are the unthinkable matrices of all our thoughts, no matter what our conscious mind may cogitate. One of these primordial thoughts is the idea of life after death. Science and these primordial images are incommensurables. They are irrational data, *a priori* conditions of the imagination which are simply there, and whose purpose and justification science can only investigate *a posteriori,* much as it investigates a function like that of the thyroid gland. Before the nineteenth century the thyroid was regarded as a meaningless organ merely because it was not understood. It would be equally shortsighted of us today to call the primordial images senseless. For me these images are something like psychic organs, and I treat them with the very greatest respect. It happens sometimes that I must say to an older patient: "Your picture of God or your idea of immortality is atrophied, consequently your psychic metabolism is out of gear." The ancient *athanasias pharmakon,* the medicine of immortality, is more profound and meaningful than we supposed.

795 In conclusion I would like to come back for a moment to the comparison with the sun. The one hundred and eighty degrees of the arc of life are divisible into four parts. The first quarter, lying to the east, is childhood, that state in which we are a problem for others but are not yet conscious of any problems of our own. Conscious problems fill out the second and third quarters; while in the last, in extreme old age, we descend again into that condition where, regardless of our state of consciousness, we once more become something of a problem for others. Childhood and extreme old age are, of course, utterly different, and yet they have one thing in common: submersion in unconscious psychic happenings. Since the mind of a child grows out of the unconscious its psychic processes, though not easily accessible, are not as difficult to discern as those of a very old person who is sinking again into the unconscious, and who progressively vanishes within it. Childhood and old age are the stages of life without any conscious problems, for which reason I have not taken them into consideration here.

THE SOUL AND DEATH [1]

796   I have often been asked what I believe about death, that un-
problematical ending of individual existence. Death is known
to us simply as the end. It is the period, often placed before the
close of the sentence and followed only by memories or after-
effects in others. For the person concerned, however, the sand
has run out of the glass; the rolling stone has come to rest.
When death confronts us, life always seems like a downward
flow or like a clock that has been wound up and whose eventual
"running down" is taken for granted. We are never more convinced of this "running down" than when a human life comes
to its end before our eyes, and the question of the meaning and
worth of life never becomes more urgent or more agonizing
than when we see the final breath leave a body which a moment
before was living. How different does the meaning of life seem
to us when we see a young person striving for distant goals and
shaping the future, and compare this with an incurable invalid,
or with an old man who is sinking reluctantly and impotently

---

[1] [Originally published as "Seele und Tod," *Europäische Revue* (Berlin), X
(April 1934) and republished in *Wirklichkeit der Seele* (Psychologische Abhandlungen, IV; Zurich, 1934). A shortened version appeared as "Von der Psychologie
des Sterbens," *Münchner Neueste Nachrichten*, No. 269 (Oct. 2, 1935). The
present version is a slight revision of a translation by Eugene H. Henley in
Spring (Analytical Psychology Club, New York), 1945, to whom grateful acknowledgment is made.—EDITORS.]

into the grave! Youth—we should like to think—has purpose, future, meaning, and value, whereas the coming to an end is only a meaningless cessation. If a young man is afraid of the world, of life and the future, then everyone finds it regrettable, senseless, neurotic; he is considered a cowardly shirker. But when an ageing person secretly shudders and is even mortally afraid at the thought that his reasonable expectation of life now amounts to only so and so many years, then we are painfully reminded of certain feelings within our own breast; we look away and turn the conversation to some other topic. The optimism with which we judge the young man fails us here. Naturally we have a stock of suitable banalities about life which we occasionally hand out to the other fellow, such as "everyone must die sometime," "you can't live forever," etc. But when one is alone and it is night and so dark and still that one hears nothing and sees nothing but the thoughts which add and subtract the years, and the long row of those disagreeable facts which remorselessly indicate how far the hand of the clock has moved forward, and the slow, irresistible approach of the wall of darkness which will eventually engulf everything I love, possess, wish for, hope for, and strive for, then all our profundities about life slink off to some undiscoverable hiding-place, and fear envelops the sleepless one like a smothering blanket.

797 Many young people have at bottom a panic fear of life (though at the same time they intensely desire it), and an even greater number of the ageing have the same fear of death. Indeed, I have known those people who most feared life when they were young to suffer later just as much from the fear of death. When they are young one says they have infantile resistances against the normal demands of life; one should really say the same thing when they are old, for they are likewise afraid of one of life's normal demands. We are so convinced that death is simply the end of a process that it does not ordinarily occur to us to conceive of death as a goal and a fulfilment, as we do without hesitation the aims and purposes of youthful life in its ascendance.

798 Life is an energy-process. Like every energy-process, it is in principle irreversible and is therefore directed towards a goal. That goal is a state of rest. In the long run everything that

405

happens is, as it were, no more than the initial disturbance of a perpetual state of rest which forever attempts to re-establish itself. Life is teleology *par excellence;* it is the intrinsic striving towards a goal, and the living organism is a system of directed aims which seek to fulfil themselves. The end of every process is its goal. All energy-flow is like a runner who strives with the greatest effort and the utmost expenditure of strength to reach his goal. Youthful longing for the world and for life, for the attainment of high hopes and distant goals, is life's obvious teleological urge which at once changes into fear of life, neurotic resistances, depressions, and phobias if at some point it remains caught in the past, or shrinks from risks without which the unseen goal cannot be attained. With the attainment of maturity and at the zenith of biological existence, life's drive towards a goal in no wise halts. With the same intensity and irresistibility with which it strove upward before middle age, life now descends; for the goal no longer lies on the summit, but in the valley where the ascent began. The curve of life is like the parabola of a projectile which, disturbed from its initial state of rest, rises and then returns to a state of repose.

799   The psychological curve of life, however, refuses to conform to this law of nature. Sometimes the lack of accord begins early in the ascent. The projectile ascends biologically, but psychologically it lags behind. We straggle behind our years, hugging our childhood as if we could not tear ourselves away. We stop the hands of the clock and imagine that time will stand still. When after some delay we finally reach the summit, there again, psychologically, we settle down to rest, and although we can see ourselves sliding down the other side, we cling, if only with longing backward glances, to the peak once attained. Just as, earlier, fear was a deterrent to life, so now it stands in the way of death. We may even admit that fear of life held us back on the upward slope, but just because of this delay we claim all the more right to hold fast to the summit we have now reached. Though it may be obvious that in spite of all our resistances (now so deeply regretted) life has reasserted itself, yet we pay no attention and keep on trying to make it stand still. Our psychology then loses its natural basis. Consciousness stays up in the air, while the curve of the parabola sinks downward with ever-increasing speed.

800   Natural life is the nourishing soil of the soul. Anyone who
fails to go along with life remains suspended, stiff and rigid in
midair. That is why so many people get wooden in old age;
they look back and cling to the past with a secret fear of death
in their hearts. They withdraw from the life-process, at least
psychologically, and consequently remain fixed like nostalgic
pillars of salt, with vivid recollections of youth but no living
relation to the present. From the middle of life onward, only he
remains vitally alive who is ready to *die with life*. For in the
secret hour of life's midday the parabola is reversed, death is
born. The second half of life does not signify ascent, unfolding,
increase, exuberance, but death, since the end is its goal. The
negation of life's fulfilment is synonymous with the refusal to
accept its ending. Both mean not wanting to live, and not
wanting to live is identical with not wanting to die. Waxing
and waning make one curve.

801   Whenever possible our consciousness refuses to accommodate
itself to this undeniable truth. Ordinarily we cling to our past
and remain stuck in the illusion of youthfulness. Being old is
highly unpopular. Nobody seems to consider that not being
able to grow old is just as absurd as not being able to outgrow child's-size shoes. A still infantile man of thirty is surely to
be deplored, but a youthful septuagenarian—isn't that delight-
ful? And yet both are perverse, lacking in style, psychological
monstrosities. A young man who does not fight and conquer has
missed the best part of his youth, and an old man who does not
know how to listen to the secrets of the brooks, as they tumble
down from the peaks to the valleys, makes no sense; he is a
spiritual mummy who is nothing but a rigid relic of the past.
He stands apart from life, mechanically repeating himself to the
last triviality.

802   Our relative longevity, substantiated by present-day statistics,
is a product of civilization. It is quite exceptional for primitive
people to reach old age. For instance, when I visited the primitive tribes of East Africa, I saw very few men with white hair
who might have been over sixty. But they were really old, they
seemed to have always been old, so fully had they assimilated
their age. They were exactly what they were in every respect.
We are forever only more or less than we actually are. It is as
if our consciousness had somehow slipped from its natural

407

foundations and no longer knew how to get along on nature's timing. It seems as though we were suffering from a hybris of consciousness which fools us into believing that one's time of life is a mere illusion which can be altered according to one's desire. (One asks oneself where our consciousness gets its ability to be so contrary to nature and what such arbitrariness might signify.)

803   Like a projectile flying to its goal, life ends in death. Even its ascent and its zenith are only steps and means to this goal. This paradoxical formula is no more than a logical deduction from the fact that life strives towards a goal and is determined by an aim. I do not believe that I am guilty here of playing with syllogisms. We grant goal and purpose to the ascent of life, why not to the descent? The birth of a human being is pregnant with meaning, why not death? For twenty years and more the growing man is being prepared for the complete unfolding of his individual nature, why should not the older man prepare himself twenty years and more for his death? Of course, with the zenith one has obviously reached something, one is it and has it. But what is attained with death?

804   At this point, just when it might be expected, I do not want suddenly to pull a belief out of my pocket and invite my reader to do what nobody can do—that is, believe something. I must confess that I myself could never do it either. Therefore I shall certainly not assert now that one must believe death to be a second birth leading to survival beyond the grave. But I can at least mention that the *consensus gentium* has decided views about death, unmistakably expressed in all the great religions of the world. One might even say that the majority of these religions are complicated systems of preparation for death, so much so that life, in agreement with my paradoxical formula, actually has no significance except as a preparation for the ultimate goal of death. In both the greatest living religions, Christianity and Buddhism, the meaning of existence is consummated in its end.

805   Since the Age of Enlightenment a point of view has developed concerning the nature of religion which, although it is a typically rationalistic misconception, deserves mention because it is so widely disseminated. According to this view, all religions are something like philosophical systems, and like them are

concocted out of the head. At some time someone is supposed to have invented a God and sundry dogmas and to have led humanity around by the nose with this "wish-fulfilling" fantasy. But this opinion is contradicted by the psychological fact that the head is a particularly inadequate organ when it comes to thinking up religious symbols. They do not come from the head at all, but from some other place, perhaps the heart; certainly from a deep psychic level very little resembling consciousness, which is always only the top layer. That is why religious symbols have a distinctly "revelatory" character; they are usually spontaneous products of unconscious psychic activity. They are anything rather than thought up; on the contrary, in the course of the millennia, they have developed, plant-like, as natural manifestations of the human psyche. Even today we can see in individuals the spontaneous genesis of genuine and valid religious symbols, springing from the unconscious like flowers of a strange species, while consciousness stands aside perplexed, not knowing what to make of such creations. It can be ascertained without too much difficulty that in form and content these individual symbols arise from the same unconscious mind or "spirit" (or whatever it may be called) as the great religions of mankind. At all events experience shows that religions are in no sense conscious constructions, but that they arise from the natural life of the unconscious psyche and somehow give adequate expression to it. This explains their universal distribution and their enormous influence on humanity throughout history, which would be incomprehensible if religious symbols were not at the very least truths of man's psychological nature.

806   I know that very many people have difficulties with the word "psychological." To put these critics at ease, I should like to add that no one knows what "psyche" is, and one knows just as little how far into nature "psyche" extends. A psychological truth is therefore just as good and respectable a thing as a physical truth, which limits itself to matter as the former does to the psyche.

807   The *consensus gentium* that expresses itself through the religions is, as we saw, in sympathy with my paradoxical formula. Hence it would seem to be more in accord with the collective psyche of humanity to regard death as the fulfilment of life's meaning and as its goal in the truest sense, instead of a mere

meaningless cessation. Anyone who cherishes a rationalistic opinion on this score has isolated himself psychologically and stands opposed to his own basic human nature.

808   This last sentence contains a fundamental truth about all neuroses, for nervous disorders consist primarily in an alienation from one's instincts, a splitting off of consciousness from certain basic facts of the psyche. Hence rationalistic opinions come unexpectedly close to neurotic symptoms. Like these, they consist of distorted thinking, which takes the place of psychologically correct thinking. The latter kind of thinking always retains its connection with the heart, with the depths of the psyche, the tap-root. For, enlightenment or no enlightenment, consciousness or no consciousness, nature prepares itself for death. If we could observe and register the thoughts of a young person when he has time and leisure for day-dreaming, we would discover that, aside from a few memory-images, his fantasies are mainly concerned with the future. As a matter of fact, most fantasies consist of anticipations. They are for the most part preparatory acts, or even psychic exercises for dealing with certain future realities. If we could make the same experiment with an ageing person—without his knowledge, of course— we would naturally find, owing to his tendency to look backwards, a greater number of memory-images than with a younger person, but we would also find a surprisingly large number of anticipations, including those of death. Thoughts of death pile up to an astonishing degree as the years increase. Willynilly, the ageing person prepares himself for death. That is why I think that nature herself is already preparing for the end. Objectively it is a matter of indifference what the individual consciousness may think about it. But subjectively it makes an enormous difference whether consciousness keeps in step with the psyche or whether it clings to opinions of which the heart knows nothing. It is just as neurotic in old age not to focus upon the goal of death as it is in youth to repress fantasies which have to do with the future.

809   In my rather long psychological experience I have observed a great many people whose unconscious psychic activity I was able to follow into the immediate presence of death. As a rule the approaching end was indicated by those symbols which, in normal life also, proclaim changes of psychological condition—

rebirth symbols such as changes of locality, journeys, and the like. I have frequently been able to trace back for over a year, in a dream-series, the indications of approaching death, even in cases where such thoughts were not prompted by the outward situation. Dying, therefore, has its onset long before actual death. Moreover, this often shows itself in peculiar changes of personality which may precede death by quite a long time. On the whole, I was astonished to see how little ado the unconscious psyche makes of death. It would seem as though death were something relatively unimportant, or perhaps our psyche does not bother about what happens to the individual. But it seems that the unconscious is all the more interested in *how* one dies; that is, whether the attitude of consciousness is adjusted to dying or not. For example, I once had to treat a woman of sixty-two. She was still hearty, and moderately intelligent. It was not for want of brains that she was unable to understand her dreams. It was unfortunately only too clear that she did not *want* to understand them. Her dreams were very plain, but also very disagreeable. She had got it fixed in her head that she was a faultless mother to her children, but the children did not share this view at all, and the dreams too displayed a conviction very much to the contrary. I was obliged to break off the treatment after some weeks of fruitless effort because I had to leave for military service (it was during the war). In the meantime the patient was smitten with an incurable disease, leading after a few months to a moribund condition which might bring about the end at any moment. Most of the time she was in a sort of delirious or somnambulistic state, and in this curious mental condition she spontaneously resumed the analytical work. She spoke of her dreams again and acknowledged to herself everything that she had previously denied to me with the greatest vehemence, and a lot more besides. This self-analytic work continued daily for several hours, for about six weeks. At the end of this period she had calmed herself, just like a patient during normal treatment, and then she died.

810   From this and numerous other experiences of the kind I must conclude that our psyche is at least not indifferent to the dying of the individual. The urge, so often seen in those who are dying, to set to rights whatever is still wrong might point in the same direction.

811 How these experiences are ultimately to be interpreted is a problem that exceeds the competence of an empirical science and goes beyond our intellectual capacities, for in order to reach a final conclusion one must necessarily have had the actual experience of death. This event unfortunately puts the observer in a position that makes it impossible for him to give an objective account of his experiences and of the conclusions resulting therefrom.

812 Consciousness moves within narrow confines, within the brief span of time between its beginning and its end, and shortened by about a third by periods of sleep. The life of the body lasts somewhat longer; it always begins earlier and, very often, it ceases later than consciousness. Beginning and end are unavoidable aspects of all processes. Yet on closer examination it is extremely difficult to see where one process ends and another begins, since events and processes, beginnings and endings, merge into each other and form, strictly speaking, an indivisible continuum. We divide the processes from one another for the sake of discrimination and understanding, knowing full well that at bottom every division is arbitrary and conventional. This procedure in no way infringes the continuum of the world process, for "beginning" and "end" are primarily necessities of conscious cognition. We may establish with reasonable certainty that an individual consciousness as it relates to ourselves has come to an end. But whether this means that the continuity of the psychic process is also interrupted remains doubtful, since the psyche's attachment to the brain can be affirmed with far less certitude today than it could fifty years ago. Psychology must first digest certain parapsychological facts, which it has hardly begun to do as yet.

813 The unconscious psyche appears to possess qualities which throw a most peculiar light on its relation to space and time. I am thinking of those spatial and temporal telepathic phenomena which, as we know, are much easier to ignore than to explain. In this regard science, with a few praiseworthy exceptions, has so far taken the easier path of ignoring them. I must confess, however, that the so-called telepathic faculties of the psyche have caused me many a headache, for the catchword "telepathy" is very far from explaining anything. The limitation of consciousness in space and time is such an overwhelming

412

reality that every occasion when this fundamental truth is broken through must rank as an event of the highest theoretical significance, for it would prove that the space-time barrier can be annulled. The annulling factor would then be the psyche, since space-time would attach to it at most as a relative and conditioned quality. Under certain conditions it could even break through the barriers of space and time precisely because of a quality essential to it, that is, its relatively trans-spatial and trans-temporal nature. This possible transcendence of space-time, for which it seems to me there is a good deal of evidence, is of such incalculable import that it should spur the spirit of research to the greatest effort. Our present development of consciousness is, however, so backward that in general we still lack the scientific and intellectual equipment for adequately evaluating the facts of telepathy so far as they have bearing on the nature of the psyche. I have referred to this group of phenomena merely in order to point out that the psyche's attachment to the brain, i.e., its space-time limitation, is no longer as self-evident and incontrovertible as we have hitherto been led to believe.

814   Anyone who has the least knowledge of the parapsychological material which already exists and has been thoroughly verified will know that so-called telepathic phenomena are undeniable facts. An objective and critical survey of the available data would establish that perceptions occur as if in part there were no space, in part no time. Naturally, one cannot draw from this the metaphysical conclusion that in the world of things as they are "in themselves" there is neither space nor time, and that the space-time category is therefore a web into which the human mind has woven itself as into a nebulous illusion. Space and time are not only the most immediate certainties for us, they are also obvious empirically, since everything observable happens as though it occurred in space and time. In the face of this overwhelming certainty it is understandable that reason should have the greatest difficulty in granting validity to the peculiar nature of telepathic phenomena. But anyone who does justice to the facts cannot but admit that their apparent space-timelessness is their most essential quality. In the last analysis, our naïve perception and immediate certainty are, strictly speaking, no more than evidence of a psychological *a priori* form of percep-

tion which simply rules out any other form. The fact that we are totally unable to imagine a form of existence without space and time by no means proves that such an existence is in itself impossible. And therefore, just as we cannot draw, from an appearance of space-timelessness, any absolute conclusion about a space-timeless form of existence, so we are not entitled to conclude from the apparent space-time quality of our perception that there is no form of existence *without* space and time. It is not only permissible to doubt the absolute validity of space-time perception; it is, in view of the available facts, even imperative to do so. The hypothetical possibility that the psyche touches on a form of existence outside space and time presents a scientific question-mark that merits serious consideration for a long time to come. The ideas and doubts of theoretical physicists in our own day should prompt a cautious mood in psychologists too; for, philosophically considered, what do we mean by the "limitedness of space" if not a relativization of the space category? Something similar might easily happen to the category of time (and to that of causality as well).[2] Doubts about these matters are more warranted today than ever before.

815   The nature of the psyche reaches into obscurities far beyond the scope of our understanding. It contains as many riddles as the universe with its galactic systems, before whose majestic configurations only a mind lacking in imagination can fail to admit its own insufficiency. This extreme uncertainty of human comprehension makes the intellectualistic hubbub not only ridiculous, but also deplorably dull. If, therefore, from the needs of his own heart, or in accordance with the ancient lessons of human wisdom, or out of respect for the psychological fact that "telepathic" perceptions occur, anyone should draw the conclusion that the psyche, in its deepest reaches, participates in a form of existence beyond space and time, and thus partakes of what is inadequately and symbolically described as "eternity" —then critical reason could counter with no other argument than the "non liquet" of science. Furthermore, he would have the inestimable advantage of conforming to a bias of the human psyche which has existed from time immemorial and is universal. Anyone who does not draw this conclusion, whether

2 [Cf. the final paper in this volume.—EDITORS.]

from scepticism or rebellion against tradition, from lack of courage or inadequate psychological experience or thoughtless ignorance, stands very little chance, statistically, of becoming a pioneer of the mind, but has instead the indubitable certainty of coming into conflict with the truths of his blood. Now whether these are in the last resort absolute truths or not we shall never be able to determine. It suffices that they are present in us as a "bias," and we know to our cost what it means to come into unthinking conflict with these truths. It means the same thing as the conscious denial of the instincts—uprootedness, disorientation, meaninglessness, and whatever else these symptoms of inferiority may be called. One of the most fatal of the sociological and psychological errors in which our time is so fruitful is the supposition that something can become entirely different all in a moment; for instance, that man can radically change his nature, or that some formula or truth might be found which would represent an entirely new beginning. Any essential change, or even a slight improvement, has always been a miracle. Deviation from the truths of the blood begets neurotic restlessness, and we have had about enough of that these days. Restlessness begets meaninglessness, and the lack of meaning in life is a soul-sickness whose full extent and full import our age has not as yet begun to comprehend.

VII

SYNCHRONICITY: AN ACAUSAL
CONNECTING PRINCIPLE

[Translated from "Synchronizität als ein Prinzip akausaler Zusammenhänge," which, together with a monograph by Professor W. Pauli entitled "Der Einfluss archetypischer Vorstellungen auf die Bildung naturwissenschaftlicher Theorien bei Kepler," formed the volume *Naturerklärung und Psyche* (Studien aus dem C. G. Jung-Institut, IV; Zurich, 1952). This volume was translated, with revisions, as *The Interpretation of Nature and the Psyche* (New York [Bollingen Series LI] and London, 1955). The monograph by Professor Jung is here republished with further revisions of a minor nature.

[The brief essay "On Synchronicity" printed in the appendix to Part VII, infra, was an earlier (1951) and more popular version of the present work. Here it replaces a brief "Résumé" written by the author for the 1955 version of the monograph.—EDITORS.]

FOREWORD

816   In writing this paper I have, so to speak, made good a promise which for many years I lacked the courage to fulfil. The difficulties of the problem and its presentation seemed to me too great; too great the intellectual responsibility without which such a subject cannot be tackled; too inadequate, in the long run, my scientific training. If I have now conquered my hesitation and at last come to grips with my theme, it is chiefly because my experiences of the phenomenon of synchronicity have multiplied themselves over decades, while on the other hand my researches into the history of symbols, and of the fish symbol in particular, brought the problem ever closer to me, and finally because I have been alluding to the existence of this phenomenon on and off in my writings for twenty years without discussing it any further. I would like to put a temporary end to this unsatisfactory state of affairs by trying to give a consistent account of everything I have to say on this subject. I hope it will not be construed as presumption on my part if I make uncommon demands on the open-mindedness and goodwill of the reader. Not only is he expected to plunge into regions of human experience which are dark, dubious, and hedged about with prejudice, but the intellectual difficulties are such as the treatment and elucidation of so abstract a subject must inevitably entail. As anyone can see for himself after reading a

419

few pages, there can be no question of a complete description and explanation of these complicated phenomena, but only an attempt to broach the problem in such a way as to reveal some of its manifold aspects and connections, and to open up a very obscure field which is philosophically of the greatest importance. As a psychiatrist and psychotherapist I have often come up against the phenomena in question and could convince myself how much these inner experiences meant to my patients. In most cases they were things which people do not talk about for fear of exposing themselves to thoughtless ridicule. I was amazed to see how many people have had experiences of this kind and how carefully the secret was guarded. So my interest in this problem has a human as well as a scientific foundation.

817   In the performance of my work I had the support of a number of friends who are mentioned in the text. Here I would like to express my particular thanks to Dr. Liliane Frey-Rohn, for her help with the astrological material.

1. EXPOSITION

818   The discoveries of modern physics have, as we know, brought about a significant change in our scientific picture of the world, in that they have shattered the absolute validity of natural law and made it relative. Natural laws are *statistical* truths, which means that they are completely valid only when we are dealing with macrophysical quantities. In the realm of very small quantities prediction becomes uncertain, if not impossible, because very small quantities no longer behave in accordance with the known natural laws.

819   The philosophical principle that underlies our conception of natural law is *causality*. But if the connection between cause and effect turns out to be only statistically valid and only relatively true, then the causal principle is only of relative use for explaining natural processes and therefore presupposes the existence of one or more other factors which would be necessary for an explanation. This is as much as to say that the connection of events may in certain circumstances be other than causal, and requires another principle of explanation.[1]

820   We shall naturally look round in vain in the macrophysical world for acausal events, for the simple reason that we cannot imagine events that are connected non-causally and are capable

1 [Other than, or supplementary to, the laws of chance.—Editors.]

of a non-causal explanation. But that does not mean that such events do not exist. Their existence—or at least their possibility —follows logically from the premise of statistical truth.

821   The experimental method of inquiry aims at establishing regular events which can be repeated. Consequently, unique or rare events are ruled out of account. Moreover, the experiment imposes limiting conditions on nature, for its aim is to force her to give answers to questions devised by man. Every answer of nature is therefore more or less influenced by the kind of questions asked, and the result is always a hybrid product. The so-called "scientific view of the world" based on this can hardly be anything more than a psychologically biased partial view which misses out all those by no means unimportant aspects that cannot be grasped statistically. But, to grasp these unique or rare events at all, we seem to be dependent on equally "unique" and individual descriptions. This would result in a chaotic collection of curiosities, rather like those old natural history cabinets where one finds, cheek by jowl with fossils and anatomical monsters in bottles, the horn of a unicorn, a mandragora manikin, and a dried mermaid. The descriptive sciences, and above all biology in the widest sense, are familiar with these "unique" specimens, and in their case only *one* example of an organism, no matter how unbelievable it may be, is needed to establish its existence. At any rate numerous observers will be able to convince themselves, on the evidence of their own eyes, that such a creature does in fact exist. But where we are dealing with ephemeral events which leave no demonstrable traces behind them except fragmentary memories in people's minds, then a single witness no longer suffices, nor would several witnesses be enough to make a unique event appear absolutely credible. One has only to think of the notorious unreliability of eye-witness accounts. In these circumstances we are faced with the necessity of finding out whether the apparently unique event is really unique in our recorded experience, or whether the same or similar events are not to be found elsewhere. Here the *consensus omnium* plays a very important role psychologically, though empirically it is somewhat doubtful, for only in exceptional cases does the *consensus omnium* prove to be of value in establishing facts. The empiricist will not leave it out of account, but will do better not to rely on it. Absolutely unique and ephem-

eral events whose existence we have no means of either denying or proving can never be the object of empirical science; rare events might very well be, provided that there was a sufficient number of reliable individual observations. The so-called *possibility* of such events is of no importance whatever, for the criterion of what is possible in any age is derived from that age's rationalistic assumptions. There are no "absolute" natural laws to whose authority one can appeal in support of one's prejudices. The most that can fairly be demanded is that the number of individual observations shall be as high as possible. If this number, statistically considered, falls within the limits of chance expectation, then it has been statistically proved that it was a question of chance; but no *explanation* has thereby been furnished. There has merely been an exception to the rule. When, for instance, the number of symptoms indicating a complex falls below the probable number of disturbances to be expected during the association experiment, this is no justification for assuming that no complex exists. But that did not prevent the reaction disturbances from being regarded earlier as pure chance.[2]

822   Although, in biology especially, we move in a sphere where causal explanations often seem very unsatisfactory—indeed, well-nigh impossible—we shall not concern ourselves here with the problems of biology, but rather with the question whether there may not be some general field where acausal events not only are possible but are found to be actual facts.

823   Now, there is in our experience an immeasurably wide field whose extent forms, as it were, the counterbalance to the domain of causality. This is the world of chance, where a chance event seems causally unconnected with the coinciding fact. So we shall have to examine the nature and the whole idea of chance a little more closely. Chance, we say, must obviously be susceptible of some causal explanation and is only called "chance" or "coincidence" because its causality has not yet been discovered. Since we have an inveterate conviction of the absolute validity of causal law, we regard this explanation of chance as being quite adequate. But if the causal principle is only relatively valid, then it follows that even though in the vast majority of

2 [Cf. Jung, *Studies in Word Association.*—EDITORS.]

cases an apparently chance series can be causally explained, there must still remain a number of cases which do not show any causal connection. We are therefore faced with the task of sifting chance events and separating the acausal ones from those that can be causally explained. It stands to reason that the number of causally explicable events will far exceed those suspected of acausality, for which reason a superficial or prejudiced observer may easily overlook the relatively rare acausal phenomena. As soon as we come to deal with the problem of chance the need for a statistical evaluation of the events in question forces itself upon us.

824   It is not possible to sift the empirical material without a criterion of distinction. How are we to recognize acausal combinations of events, since it is obviously impossible to examine all chance happenings for their causality? The answer to this is that acausal events may be expected most readily where, on closer reflection, a causal connection appears to be inconceivable. As an example I would cite the "duplication of cases" which is a phenomenon well known to every doctor. Occasionally there is a trebling or even more, so that Kammerer[3] can speak of a "law of series," of which he gives a number of excellent examples. In the majority of such cases there is not even the remotest probability of a causal connection between the coinciding events. When for instance I am faced with the fact that my tram ticket bears the same number as the theatre ticket which I buy immediately afterwards, and I receive that same evening a telephone call during which the same number is mentioned again as a telephone number, then a causal connection between these events seems to me improbable in the extreme, although it is obvious that each must have its own causality. I know, on the other hand, that chance happenings have a tendency to fall into aperiodic groupings—necessarily so, because otherwise there would be only a periodic or regular arrangement of events which would by definition exclude chance.

825   Kammerer holds that though "runs"[4] or successions of chance events are not subject to the operation of a common cause,[5] i.e., are acausal, they are nevertheless an expression of

3 Paul Kammerer, *Das Gesetz der Serie.*   4 Ibid., p. 130.
5 Pp. 36, 93f., 102f.

inertia—the property of persistence.[6] The simultaneity of a "run of the same thing side by side" he explains as "imitation." [7] Here he contradicts himself, for the run of chance has not been "removed outside the realm of the explicable," [8] but, as we would expect, is included within it and is consequently reducible, if not to a common cause, then at least to several causes. His concepts of seriality, imitation, attraction, and inertia belong to a causally conceived view of the world and tell us no more than that the run of chance corresponds to statistical and mathematical probability.[9] Kammerer's factual material contains nothing but runs of chance whose only "law" is probability; in other words, there is no apparent reason why he should look behind them for anything else. But for some obscure reason he does look behind them for something more than mere probability warrants—for a *law of seriality* which he would like to introduce as a principle coexistent with causality and finality. This tendency, as I have said, is in no way justified by his material. I can only explain this obvious contradiction by supposing that he had a dim but fascinated intuition of an acausal arrangement and combination of events, probably because, like all thoughtful and sensitive natures, he could not escape the peculiar impression which runs of chance usually make on us, and therefore, in accordance with his scientific disposition, took the bold step of postulating an acausal seriality on the basis of empirical material that lay within the limits of probability. Unfortunately he did not attempt a quantitative evaluation of seriality. Such an undertaking would undoubtedly have thrown up questions that are difficult to answer. The investigation of individual cases serves well enough for the purpose of general orientation, but only quantitative evaluation or the statistical method promises results in dealing with chance.

826   Chance groupings or series seem, at least to our present way

[6] "The law of series is an expression of the inertia of the objects involved in its repetitions (i.e., producing the series). The far greater inertia of a complex of objects and forces (as compared to that of a single object or force) explains the persistence of an identical constellation and the emergence, connected therewith, of repetitions over long periods of time" (p. 117).   [7] P. 130.   [8] P. 94.

[9] [The term "probability" therefore refers to the probability on a chance hypothesis (Null Hypothesis). This is the sense in which the term is most often used in this paper.—EDITORS.]

of thinking, to be meaningless, and to fall as a general rule within the limits of probability. There are, however, incidents whose "chancefulness" seems open to doubt. To mention but one example out of many, I noted the following on April 1, 1949: Today is Friday. We have fish for lunch. Somebody happens to mention the custom of making an "April fish" of someone. That same morning I made a note of an inscription which read: "Est homo totus medius *piscis* ab imo." In the afternoon a former patient of mine, whom I had not seen for months, showed me some extremely impressive pictures of fish which she had painted in the meantime. In the evening I was shown a piece of embroidery with fish-like sea-monsters in it. On the morning of April 2 another patient, whom I had not seen for many years, told me a dream in which she stood on the shore of a lake and saw a large fish that swam straight towards her and landed at her feet. I was at this time engaged on a study of the fish symbol in history. Only one of the persons mentioned here knew anything about it.

827   The suspicion that this must be a case of *meaningful coincidence,* i.e., an acausal connection, is very natural. I must own that this run of events made a considerable impression on me. It seemed to me to have a certain numinous quality.[10] In such circumstances we are inclined to say, "That cannot be mere chance," without knowing what exactly we are saying. Kammerer would no doubt have reminded me of his "seriality." The strength of an impression, however, proves nothing against the fortuitous coincidence of all these fishes. It is, admittedly, exceedingly odd that the fish theme recurs no less than six times within twenty-four hours. But one must remember that fish on Friday is the usual thing, and on April 1 one might very easily think of the April fish. I had at that time been working on the fish symbol for several months. Fishes frequently occur as symbols of unconscious contents. So there is no possible justification for seeing in this anything but a chance grouping. Runs or

[10] The numinosity of a series of chance happenings grows in proportion to the number of its terms. Unconscious—probably archetypal—contents are thereby constellated, which then give rise to the impression that the series has been "caused" by these contents. Since we cannot conceive how this could be possible without recourse to positively magical categories, we generally let it go at the bare impression.

series which are composed of quite ordinary occurrences must for the present be regarded as fortuitous.[11] However wide their range may be, they must be ruled out as acausal connections. It is, therefore, generally assumed that all coincidences are lucky hits and do not require an acausal interpretation.[12] This assumption can, and indeed must, be regarded as true so long as proof is lacking that their incidence exceeds the limits of probability. Should this proof be forthcoming, however, it would prove at the same time that there are genuinely non-causal combinations of events for whose explanation we should have to postulate a factor incommensurable with causality. We should then have to assume that events in general are related to one another on the one hand as causal chains, and on the other hand by a kind of *meaningful cross-connection*.

828   Here I should like to draw attention to a treatise of Schopenhauer's, "On the Apparent Design in the Fate of the Individual," [13] which originally stood godfather to the views I am now developing. It deals with the "simultaneity of the causally unconnected, which we call 'chance'." [14] Schopenhauer illustrates this simultaneity by a geographical analogy, where the parallels represent the cross-connection between the meridians, which are thought of as causal chains.[15]

[11] As a pendant to what I have said above, I should like to mention that I wrote these lines sitting by the lake. Just as I had finished this sentence, I walked over to the sea-wall and there lay a dead fish, about a foot long, apparently uninjured. No fish had been there the previous evening. (Presumably it had been pulled out of the water by a bird of prey or a cat.) The fish was the seventh in the series.

[12] We find ourselves in something of a quandary when it comes to making up our minds about the phenomenon which Stekel calls the "compulsion of the name." What he means by this is the sometimes quite grotesque coincidence between a man's name and his peculiarities or profession. For instance Herr Gross (Mr. Grand) suffers from delusions of grandeur, Herr Kleiner (Mr. Small) has an inferiority complex. The Altmann sisters marry men twenty years older than themselves. Herr Feist (Mr. Stout) is the Food Minister, Herr Rosstäuscher (Mr. Horsetrader) is a lawyer, Herr Kalberer (Mr. Calver) is an obstetrician, Herr Freud (joy) champions the pleasure-principle, Herr Adler (eagle) the will-to-power, Herr Jung (young) the idea of rebirth, and so on. Are these the whimsicalities of chance, or the suggestive effects of the name, as Stekel seems to suggest, or are they "meaningful coincidences"? ("Die Verpflichtung des Namens," 110ff.)

[13] *Parerga und Paralipomena*, I, ed. by von Koeber. [Cf. the trans. by David Irvine, to which reference is made for convenience, though not quoted here.]

[14] Ibid., p. 40. [Irvine, p. 41.]   [15] P. 39. [Irvine, pp. 39f.]

THE STRUCTURE AND DYNAMICS OF THE PSYCHE

All the events in a man's life would accordingly stand in two fundamentally different kinds of connection: firstly, in the objective,
causal connection of the natural process; secondly, in a subjective
connection which exists only in relation to the individual who experiences it, and which is thus as subjective as his own dreams.
. . . That both kinds of connection exist simultaneously, and the
selfsame event, although a link in two totally different chains, nevertheless falls into place in both, so that the fate of one individual
invariably fits the fate of the other, and each is the hero of his own
drama while simultaneously figuring in a drama foreign to him—
this is something that surpasses our powers of comprehension, and
can only be conceived as possible by virtue of the most wonderful
pre-established harmony.[16]

In his view "the subject of the great dream of life . . . is but
one," [17] the transcendental Will, the *prima causa*, from which
all causal chains radiate like meridian lines from the poles and,
because of the circular parallels, stand to one another in a
meaningful relationship of simultaneity.[18] Schopenhauer believed in the absolute determinism of the natural process and
furthermore in a first cause. There is nothing to warrant either
assumption. The first cause is a philosophical mythologem
which is only credible when it appears in the form of the old
paradox Ἑν τὸ πᾶν, as unity and multiplicity at once. The idea
that the simultaneous points in the causal chains, or meridians,
represent meaningful coincidences would only hold water if the
first cause really were a unity. But if it were a multiplicity, which
is just as likely, then Schopenhauer's whole explanation col-
lapses, quite apart from the fact, which we have only recently
realized, that natural law possesses a merely statistical validity
and thus keeps the door open to indeterminism. Neither philosophical reflection nor experience can provide any evidence for
the regular occurrence of these two kinds of connection, in which
the same thing is both subject and object. Schopenhauer thought
and wrote at a time when causality held sovereign sway as a
category *a priori* and had therefore to be dragged in to explain
meaningful coincidences. But, as we have seen, it can do this
with some degree of probability only if we have recourse to the

16 P. 45. [Irvine, pp. 49f.]
17 P. 46. [Irvine, p. 50.]
18 Hence my term "synchronicity."

other, equally arbitrary assumption of the unity of the first cause. It then follows as a *necessity* that every point on a given meridian stands in a relationship of meaningful coincidence to every other point on the same degree of latitude. This conclusion, however, goes far beyond the bounds of what is empirically possible, for it credits meaningful coincidences with occurring so regularly and systematically that their verification would be either unnecessary or the simplest thing in the world. Schopenhauer's examples carry as much or as little conviction as all the others. Nevertheless, it is to his credit that he saw the problem and understood that there are no facile *ad hoc* explanations. Since this problem is concerned with the foundations of our epistemology, he derived it in accordance with the general trend of his philosophy from a transcendental premise, from the Will which creates life and being on all levels, and which modulates each of these levels in such a way that they are not only in harmony with their synchronous parallels but also prepare and arrange future events in the form of Fate or Providence.

829   In contrast to Schopenhauer's accustomed pessimism, this utterance has an almost friendly and optimistic tone which we can hardly sympathize with today. One of the most problematical and momentous centuries the world has ever known separates us from that still medievalistic age when the philosophizing mind believed it could make assertions beyond what could be empirically proved. It was an age of large views, which did not cry halt and think that the limits of nature had been reached just where the scientific road-builders had come to a temporary stop. Thus Schopenhauer, with true philosophical vision, opened up a field for reflection whose peculiar phenomenology he was not equipped to understand, though he outlined it more or less correctly. He recognized that with their *omina* and *praesagia* astrology and the various intuitive methods of interpreting fate have a common denominator which he sought to discover by means of "transcendental speculation." He recognized, equally rightly, that it was a problem of principle of the first order, unlike all those before and after him who operated with futile conceptions of some kind of energy transmission, or conveniently dismissed the whole thing as nonsense in order to

avoid a too difficult task.[19] Schopenhauer's attempt is the more remarkable in that it was made at a time when the tremendous advance of the natural sciences had convinced everybody that causality alone could be considered the final principle of explanation. Instead of ignoring all those experiences which refuse to bow down to the sovereign rule of causality, he tried, as we have seen, to fit them into his deterministic view of the world. In so doing, he forced concepts like prefiguration, correspondence, and pre-established harmony, which as a universal order coexisting with the causal one have always underlain man's explanations of nature, into the causal scheme, probably because he felt—and rightly—that the scientific view of the world based on natural law, though he did not doubt its validity, nevertheless lacked something which played a considerable role in the classical and medieval view (as it also does in the intuitive feelings of modern man).

830   The mass of facts collected by Gurney, Myers, and Podmore [20] inspired three other investigators—Dariex,[21] Richet,[22] and Flammarion [23]— to tackle the problem in terms of a probability calculus. Dariex found a probability of 1 : 4,114,545 for telepathic precognitions of death, which means that the explanation of such a warning as due to "chance" is more than four million times more improbable than explaining it as a "telepathic," or acausal, meaningful coincidence. The astronomer Flammarion reckoned a probability of no less than 1 : 804,622,222 for a particularly well-observed instance of "phantasms of the living." [24] He was also the first to link up other suspicious happenings with the general interest in phenomena connected with death. Thus he relates [25] that, while writing his book on the atmosphere, he was just at the chapter on wind-force when a sudden gust of wind swept all his papers off the table and blew them out of the window. He also cites, as an example of triple coincidence, the edifying story of

19 Here I must make an exception of Kant, whose treatise "Dreams of a Spirit-Seer, Illustrated by Dreams of Metaphysics" pointed the way for Schopenhauer.
20 Edmund Gurney, Frederic W. H. Myers, and Frank Podmore, *Phantasms of the Living.*   21 Xavier Dariex, "Le Hazard et la télépathie."
22 Charles Richet, "Relations de diverses expériences sur transmission mentale, la lucidité, et autres phénomènes non explicable par les données scientifiques actuelles."   23 Camille Flammarion, *The Unknown,* pp. 191ff.
24 Ibid., p. 202.   25 Pp. 192f.

Monsieur de Fortgibu and the plum-pudding.[26] The fact that he mentions these coincidences at all in connection with the problem of telepathy shows that Flammarion had a distinct intuition, albeit an unconscious one, of a far more comprehensive principle.

831 The writer Wilhelm von Scholz [27] has collected a number of stories showing the strange ways in which lost or stolen objects come back to their owners. Among other things, he tells the story of a mother who took a photograph of her small son in the Black Forest. She left the film to be developed in Strassburg. But, owing to the outbreak of war, she was unable to fetch it and gave it up for lost. In 1916 she bought a film in Frankfurt in order to take a photograph of her daughter, who had been born in the meantime. When the film was developed it was found to be doubly exposed: the picture underneath was the photograph she had taken of her son in 1914! The old film had not been developed and had somehow got into circulation again among the new films. The author comes to the understandable conclusion that everything points to the "mutual attraction of related objects," or an "elective affinity." He suspects that these happenings are arranged as if they were the dream of a "greater and more comprehensive consciousness, which is unknowable."

832 The problem of chance has been approached from the psychological angle by Herbert Silberer.[28] He shows that apparently meaningful coincidences are partly unconscious arrangements, and partly unconscious, arbitrary interpretations. He takes no account either of parapsychic phenomena or of synchronicity, and theoretically he does not go much beyond the causalism of Schopenhauer. Apart from its valuable psychological criticism of our methods of evaluating chance, Silberer's

---

[26] Pp. 194ff. A certain M. Deschamps, when a boy in Orléans, was once given a piece of plum-pudding by a M. de Fortgibu. Ten years later he discovered another plum-pudding in a Paris restaurant, and asked if he could have a piece. It turned out, however, that the plum-pudding was already ordered—by M. de Fortgibu. Many years afterwards M. Deschamps was invited to partake of a plum-pudding as a special rarity. While he was eating it he remarked that the only thing lacking was M. de Fortgibu. At that moment the door opened and an old, old man in the last stages of disorientation walked in: M. de Fortgibu, who had got hold of the wrong address and burst in on the party by mistake.

[27] *Der Zufall: Eine Vorform des Schicksals.*

[28] *Der Zufall und die Koboldstreiche des Unbewussten.*

study contains no reference to the occurrence of meaningful coincidences as here understood.

833   Decisive evidence for the existence of acausal combinations of events has been furnished, with adequate scientific safeguards, only very recently, mainly through the experiments of J. B. Rhine and his fellow-workers,[29] who have not, however, recognized the far-reaching conclusions that must be drawn from their findings. Up to the present no critical argument that cannot be refuted has been brought against these experiments. The experiment consists, in principle, in an experimenter turning up, one after another, a series of numbered cards bearing simple geometrical patterns. At the same time the subject, separated by a screen from the experimenter, is given the task of guessing the signs as they are turned up. A pack of twenty-five cards is used, each five of which carry the same sign. Five cards are marked with a star, five with a square, five with a circle, five with wavy lines, and five with a cross. The experimenter naturally does not know the order in which the pack is arranged, nor has the subject any opportunity of seeing the cards. Many of the experiments were negative, since the result did not exceed the probability of five chance hits. In the case of certain subjects, however, some results were distinctly above probability. The first series of experiments consisted in each subject trying to guess the cards 800 times. The average result showed 6.5 hits for 25 cards, which is 1.5 more than the chance probability of 5 hits. The probability of there being a chance deviation of 1.5 from the number 5 works out at 1 : 250,000. This proportion shows that the probability of a chance deviation is not exactly high, since it is to be expected only once in 250,000 cases. The results vary according to the specific gift of the individual subject. One young man, who in numerous experiments scored an average of 10 hits for every 25 cards (double the probable number), once guessed all 25 cards correctly, which

---

[29] J. B. Rhine, *Extra-Sensory Perception* and *New Frontiers of the Mind.* J. G. Pratt, J. B. Rhine, C. E. Stuart, B. M. Smith, and J. A. Greenwood, *Extra-Sensory Perception after Sixty Years.* A general survey of the findings in Rhine, *The Reach of the Mind,* and also in the valuable book by G. N. M. Tyrrell, *The Personality of Man.* A short résumé in Rhine, "An Introduction to the Work of Extra-Sensory Perception." S. G. Soal and F. Bateman, *Modern Experiments in Telepathy.*

gives a probability of 1 : 298,023,223,876,953,125. The possibility of the pack being shuffled in some arbitrary way is guarded against by an apparatus which shuffles the cards automatically, independently of the experimenter.

834   After the first series of experiments the spatial distance between the experimenter and the subject was increased, in one case to 250 miles. The average result of numerous experiments amounted here to 10.1 hits for 25 cards. In another series of experiments, when experimenter and subject were in the same room, the score was 11.4 for 25; when the subject was in the next room, 9.7 for 25; when two rooms away, 12.0 for 25. Rhine mentions the experiments of F. L. Usher and E. L. Burt, which were conducted with positive results over a distance of 960 miles.[30] With the aid of synchronized watches experiments were also conducted between Durham, North Carolina, and Zagreb, Yugoslavia, about 4,000 miles, with equally positive results.[31]

835   The fact that distance has no effect in principle shows that the thing in question cannot be a phenomenon of force or energy, for otherwise the distance to be overcome and the diffusion in space would cause a diminution of the effect, and it is more than probable that the score would fall proportionately to the square of the distance. Since this is obviously not the case, we have no alternative but to assume that distance is psychically variable, and may in certain circumstances be reduced to vanishing point by a psychic condition.

836   Even more remarkable is the fact that *time* is not in principle a prohibiting factor either; that is to say, the scanning of a series of cards to be turned up in the future produces a score that exceeds chance probability. The results of Rhine's time experiment show a probability of 1 : 400,000, which means a considerable probability of there being some factor independent of time. They point, in other words, to a psychic relativity of time, since the experiment was concerned with perceptions of events which had not yet occurred. In these circumstances the time factor seems to have been eliminated by a psychic function or psychic condition which is also capable of abolishing the spatial factor. If, in the spatial experiments, we were obliged to admit that energy does not decrease with distance, then the

30 *The Reach of the Mind* (1954 edn.), p. 48.
31 Rhine and Betty M. Humphrey, "A Transoceanic ESP Experiment."

time experiments make it completely impossible for us even to think of there being any energy relationship between the perception and the future event. We must give up at the outset all explanations in terms of energy, which amounts to saying that events of this kind cannot be considered from the point of view of causality, for causality presupposes the existence of space and time in so far as all observations are ultimately based upon bodies in motion.

837   Among Rhine's experiments we must also mention the experiments with dice. The subject has the task of throwing the dice (which is done by an apparatus), and at the same time he has to wish that one number (say 3) will turn up as many times as possible. The results of this so-called PK (psychokinetic) experiment were positive, the more so the more dice were used at one time.[32] If space and time prove to be psychically relative, then the moving body must possess, or be subject to, a corresponding relativity.

838   One consistent experience in all these experiments is the fact that the number of hits scored tends to sink after the first attempt, and the results then become negative. But if, for some inner or outer reason, there is a freshening of interest on the subject's part, the score rises again. Lack of interest and boredom are negative factors; enthusiasm, positive expectation, hope, and belief in the possibility of ESP make for good results and seem to be the real conditions which determine whether there are going to be any results at all. In this connection it is interesting to note that the well-known English medium, Mrs. Eileen J. Garrett, achieved bad results in the Rhine experiments because, as she herself admits, she was unable to summon up any feeling for the "soulless" test-cards.

839   These few hints may suffice to give the reader at least a superficial idea of these experiments. The above-mentioned book by G. N. M. Tyrrell, late president of the Society for Psychical Research, contains an excellent summing-up of all experiences in this field. Its author himself rendered great service to ESP research. From the physicist's side the ESP experiments have been evaluated in a positive sense by Robert A.

32 *The Reach of the Mind*, pp. 75ff.

McConnell in an article entitled "ESP—Fact or Fancy?" [33]

840   As is only to be expected, every conceivable kind of attempt has been made to explain away these results, which seem to border on the miraculous and frankly impossible. But all such attempts come to grief on the facts, and the facts refuse so far to be argued out of existence. Rhine's experiments confront us with the fact that there are events which are related to one another experimentally, and in this case *meaningfully*, without there being any possibility of proving that this relation is a causal one, since the "transmission" exhibits none of the known properties of energy. There is therefore good reason to doubt whether it is a question of transmission at all. The time experiments rule out any such thing in principle, for it would be absurd to suppose that a situation which does not yet exist and will only occur in the future could transmit itself as a phenomenon of energy to a receiver in the present.[34] It seems more likely that scientific explanation will have to begin with a criticism of our concepts of space and time on the one hand, and with the unconscious on the other. As I have said, it is impossible, with our present resources, to explain ESP, or the fact of meaningful coincidence, as a phenomenon of energy. This makes an end of the causal explanation as well, for "effect" cannot be understood as anything except a phenomenon of energy. Therefore it cannot be a question of cause and effect, but of a falling together in time, a kind of simultaneity. Because of this quality of simultaneity, I have picked on the term "synchronicity" to designate a hypothetical factor equal in rank to causality as a principle of explanation. In my essay "On the Nature of the Psyche," [35] I defined synchronicity as a psychically conditioned relativity of space and time. Rhine's experiments show that in relation to the psyche space and time are, so to speak, "elastic" and can apparently be reduced almost to vanishing point, as though they were dependent on psychic conditions and did not exist in themselves but were only "postulated" by the conscious mind. In man's original view of the world, as we

[33] Professor Pauli was kind enough to draw my attention to this paper, which appeared in 1949.

[34] Kammerer has dealt, not altogether convincingly, with the question of the "countereffect of the succeeding state on the preceding one" (cf. *Das Gesetz der Serie*, pp. 131f.).   [35] Cf. above, par. 440.

find it among primitives, space and time have a very precarious existence. They become "fixed" concepts only in the course of his mental development, thanks largely to the introduction of measurement. In themselves, space and time consist of *nothing*. They are hypostatized concepts born of the discriminating activity of the conscious mind, and they form the indispensable co-ordinates for describing the behaviour of bodies in motion. They are, therefore, essentially psychic in origin, which is probably the reason that impelled Kant to regard them as *a priori* categories. But if space and time are only apparently properties of bodies in motion and are created by the intellectual needs of the observer, then their relativization by psychic conditions is no longer a matter for astonishment but is brought within the bounds of possibility. This possibility presents itself when the psyche observes, not external bodies, but *itself*. That is precisely what happens in Rhine's experiments: the subject's answer is not the result of his observing the physical cards, it is a product of pure imagination, of "chance" ideas which reveal the structure of that which produces them, namely the unconscious. Here I will only point out that it is the decisive factors in the unconscious psyche, the archetypes, which constitute the structure of the collective unconscious. The latter represents a psyche that is identical in all individuals. It cannot be directly perceived or "represented," in contrast to the perceptible psychic phenomena, and on account of its "irrepresentable" nature I have called it "psychoid."

841   The archetypes are formal factors responsible for the organization of unconscious psychic processes: they are "patterns of behaviour." At the same time they have a "specific charge" and develop numinous effects which express themselves as *affects*. The affect produces a partial *abaissement du niveau mental*, for although it raises a particular content to a supernormal degree of luminosity, it does so by withdrawing so much energy from other possible contents of consciousness that they become darkened and eventually unconscious. Owing to the restriction of consciousness produced by the affect so long as it lasts, there is a corresponding lowering of orientation which in its turn gives the unconscious a favourable opportunity to slip into the space vacated. Thus we regularly find that unexpected or otherwise inhibited unconscious contents break through and find expres-

sion in the affect. Such contents are very often of an inferior or primitive nature and thus betray their archetypal origin. As I shall show further on, certain phenomena of simultaneity or synchronicity seem to be bound up with the archetypes. That is the reason why I mention the archetypes here.

842   The extraordinary spatial orientation of animals may also point to the psychic relativity of space and time. The puzzling time-orientation of the palolo worm, for instance, whose tail-segments, loaded with sexual products, always appear on the surface of the sea the day before the last quarter of the moon in October and November,[36] might be mentioned in this connection. One of the causes suggested is the acceleration of the earth owing to the gravitational pull of the moon at this time. But, for astronomical reasons, this explanation cannot possibly be right.[37] The relation which undoubtedly exists between the human menstruation period and the course of the moon is connected with the latter only numerically and does not really coincide with it. Nor has it been proved that it ever did.

*

843   The problem of synchronicity has puzzled me for a long time, ever since the middle twenties,[38] when I was investigating the phenomena of the collective unconscious and kept on coming across connections which I simply could not explain as chance groupings or "runs." What I found were "coincidences" which were connected so meaningfully that their "chance" concurrence would represent a degree of improbability that would have to be expressed by an astronomical figure. By way

36 To be more accurate, the swarming begins a little before and ends a little after this day, when the swarming is at its height. The months vary according to location. The palolo worm, or wawo, of Amboina is said to appear at full moon in March. (A. F. Krämer, *Über den Bau der Korallenriffe.*)

37 Fritz Dahns, "Das Schwärmen des Palolo."

38 Even before that time certain doubts had arisen in me as to the unlimited applicability of the causal principle in psychology. In the foreword to the 1st edn. of *Collected Papers on Analytical Psychology,* I had written (p. ix): "Causality is only one principle and psychology essentially cannot be exhausted by causal methods only, because the mind [= psyche] lives by aims as well." Psychic finality rests on a "pre-existent" meaning which becomes problematical only when it is an unconscious arrangement. In that case we have to suppose a "knowledge" prior to all consciousness. Hans Driesch comes to the same conclusion (*Die "Seele" als elementarer Naturfaktor,* pp. 8off.).

of example, I shall mention an incident from my own observation. A young woman I was treating had, at a critical moment, a dream in which she was given a golden scarab. While she was telling me this dream I sat with my back to the closed window. Suddenly I heard a noise behind me, like a gentle tapping. I turned round and saw a flying insect knocking against the window-pane from outside. I opened the window and caught the creature in the air as it flew in. It was the nearest analogy to a golden scarab that one finds in our latitudes, a scarabaeid beetle, the common rose-chafer (*Cetonia aurata*), which contrary to its usual habits had evidently felt an urge to get into a dark room at this particular moment. I must admit that nothing like it ever happened to me before or since, and that the dream of the patient has remained unique in my experience.[38a]

844   I should like to mention another case that is typical of a certain category of events. The wife of one of my patients, a man in his fifties, once told me in conversation that, at the deaths of her mother and her grandmother, a number of birds gathered outside the windows of the death-chamber. I had heard similar stories from other people. When her husband's treatment was nearing its end, his neurosis having been cleared up, he developed some apparently quite innocuous symptoms which seemed to me, however, to be those of heart-disease. I sent him along to a specialist, who after examining him told me in writing that he could find no cause for anxiety. On the way back from this consultation (with the medical report in his pocket) my patient collapsed in the street. As he was brought home dying, his wife was already in a great state of anxiety because, soon after her husband had gone to the doctor, a whole flock of birds alighted on their house. She naturally remembered the similar incidents that had happened at the death of her own relatives, and feared the worst.

845   Although I was personally acquainted with the people concerned and know very well that the facts here reported are true, I do not imagine for a moment that this will induce anybody who is determined to regard such things as pure "chance" to change his mind. My sole object in relating these two incidents

[38a] [The case is discussed more fully below, par. 982.—EDITORS.]

438

is simply to give some indication of how meaningful coincidences usually present themselves in practical life. The meaningful connection is obvious enough in the first case in view of the approximate identity of the chief objects (the scarab and the beetle); but in the second case the death and the flock of birds seem to be incommensurable with one another. If one considers, however, that in the Babylonian Hades the souls wore a "feather dress," and that in ancient Egypt the *ba*, or soul, was thought of as a bird,[39] it is not too far-fetched to suppose that there may be some archetypal symbolism at work. Had such an incident occurred in a dream, that interpretation would be justified by the comparative psychological material. There also seems to be an archetypal foundation to the first case. It was an extraordinarily difficult case to treat, and up to the time of the dream little or no progress had been made. I should explain that the main reason for this was my patient's animus, which was steeped in Cartesian philosophy and clung so rigidly to its own idea of reality that the efforts of three doctors—I was the third—had not been able to weaken it. Evidently something quite irrational was needed which was beyond my powers to produce. The dream alone was enough to disturb ever so slightly the rationalistic attitude of my patient. But when the "scarab" came flying in through the window in actual fact, her natural being could burst through the armour of her animus possession and the process of transformation could at last begin to move. Any essential change of attitude signifies a psychic renewal which is usually accompanied by symbols of rebirth in the patient's dreams and fantasies. The scarab is a classic example of a rebirth symbol. The ancient Egyptian Book of What Is in the Netherworld describes how the dead sun-god changes himself at the tenth station into Khepri, the scarab, and then, at the twelfth station, mounts the barge which carries the rejuvenated sun-god into the morning sky. The only difficulty here is that with educated people cryptomnesia often cannot be ruled out with certainty (although my patient did not happen to know this symbol). But this does not alter the fact that the psychologist is continually coming up against cases where the emergence of

---

[39] In Homer the souls of the dead "twitter." [*Odyssey*, Book XI.—EDITORS.]

symbolic parallels [40] cannot be explained without the hypothesis of the collective unconscious.

846   Meaningful coincidences—which are to be distinguished from meaningless chance groupings [41]—therefore seem to rest on an archetypal foundation. At least all the cases in my experience —and there is a large number of them—show this characteristic. What that means I have already indicated above.[42] Although anyone with my experience in this field can easily recognize their archetypal character, he will find it difficult to link them up with the psychic conditions in Rhine's experiments, because the latter contain no direct evidence of any constellation of the archetype. Nor is the emotional situation the same as in my examples. Nevertheless, it must be remembered that with Rhine the first series of experiments generally produced the best results, which then quickly fell off. But when it was possible to arouse a new interest in the essentially rather boring experiment, the results improved again. It follows from this that the emotional factor plays an important role. Affectivity, however, rests to a large extent on the instincts, whose formal aspect is the archetype.

847   There is yet another psychological analogy between my two cases and the Rhine experiments, though it is not quite so obvious. These apparently quite different situations have as their common characteristic an element of "impossibility." The patient with the scarab found herself in an "impossible" situation because the treatment had got stuck and there seemed to be no way out of the impasse. In such situations, if they are serious enough, archetypal dreams are likely to occur which point out a possible line of advance one would never have thought of oneself. It is this kind of situation that constellates the archetype with the greatest regularity. In certain cases the psychotherapist therefore sees himself obliged to discover the

40 Naturally these can only be verified when the doctor himself has the necessary knowledge of symbology.

41 [Statistical analysis is designed to separate out groupings (termed dispersions) due to random activity from significant dispersions in which causes may be looked for. On Professor Jung's hypothesis, however, dispersions due to chance can be subdivided into meaningful and meaningless. The meaningful dispersions due to chance are made meaningful by the activation of the psychoid archetype.—EDITORS.]

42 Cf. par. 841; also "On the Nature of the Psyche," par. 404f.

rationally insoluble problem towards which the patient's unconscious is steering. Once this is found, the deeper layers of the
unconscious, the primordial images, are activated and the transformation of the personality can get under way.

848   In the second case there was the half-unconscious fear and
the threat of a lethal end with no possibility of an adequate
recognition of the situation. In Rhine's experiment it is the
"impossibility" of the task that ultimately fixes the subject's
attention on the processes going on inside him, and thus gives
the unconscious a chance to manifest itself. The questions set
by the ESP experiment have an emotional effect right from the
start, since they postulate something unknowable as being potentially knowable and in that way take the possibility of a
miracle seriously into account. This, regardless of the subject's
scepticism, immediately appeals to his unconscious readiness to
witness a miracle, and to the hope, latent in all men, that such
a thing may yet be possible. Primitive superstition lies just
below the surface of even the most toughminded individuals,
and it is precisely those who most fight against it who are the
first to succumb to its suggestive effects. When therefore a
serious experiment with all the authority of science behind it
touches this readiness, it will inevitably give rise to an emotion
which either accepts or rejects it with a good deal of affectivity.
At all events an affective expectation is present in one form or
another even though it may be denied.

849   Here I would like to call attention to a possible misunderstanding which may be occasioned by the term "synchronicity."
I chose this term because the simultaneous occurrence of two
meaningfully but not causally connected events seemed to me
an essential criterion. I am therefore using the general concept
of synchronicity in the special sense of a coincidence in time
of two or more causally unrelated events which have the same
or a similar meaning, in contrast to "synchronism," which
simply means the simultaneous occurrence of two events.

850   Synchronicity therefore means the simultaneous occurrence
of a certain psychic state with one or more external events
which appear as meaningful parallels to the momentary subjective state—and, in certain cases, vice versa. My two examples
illustrate this in different ways. In the case of the scarab the
simultaneity is immediately obvious, but not in the second

example. It is true that the flock of birds occasioned a vague fear, but that can be explained causally. The wife of my patient was certainly not conscious beforehand of any fear that could be compared with my own apprehensions, for the symptoms (pains in the throat) were not of a kind to make the layman suspect anything bad. The unconscious, however, often knows more than the conscious, and it seems to me possible that the woman's unconscious had already got wind of the danger. If, therefore, we rule out a conscious psychic content such as the idea of deadly danger, there is an obvious simultaneity between the flock of birds, in its traditional meaning, and the death of the husband. The psychic state, if we disregard the possible but still not demonstrable excitation of the unconscious, appears to be dependent on the external event. The woman's psyche is nevertheless involved in so far as the birds settled on her house and were observed by her. For this reason it seems to me probable that her unconscious was in fact constellated. The flock of birds has, as such, a traditional mantic significance.[43] This is also apparent in the woman's own interpretation, and it therefore looks as if the birds represented an unconscious premonition of death. The physicians of the Romantic Age would probably have talked of "sympathy" or "magnetism." But, as I have said, such phenomena cannot be explained causally unless one permits oneself the most fantastic *ad hoc* hypotheses.

851 The interpretation of the birds as an omen is, as we have seen, based on two earlier coincidences of a similar kind. It did not yet exist at the time of the grandmother's death. There the coincidence was represented only by the death and the gathering of the birds. Both then and at the mother's death the coincidence was obvious, but in the third case it could only be verified when the dying man was brought into the house.

852 I mention these complications because they have an important bearing on the concept of synchronicity. Let us take another

---

[43] A literary example is "The Cranes of Ibycus." [A poem by Schiller (1798), inspired by the story of the Greek poet murdered by robbers who were brought to justice through the appearance of a swarm of cranes. As cranes had also flown over the scene of the crime, the murderers cried out at the sight and so betrayed themselves.—EDITORS.] Similarly, when a flock of chattering magpies settles on a house it is supposed to mean death, and so on. Cf. also the significance of auguries.

example: An acquaintance of mine saw and experienced in a dream the sudden death of a friend, with all the characteristic details. The dreamer was in Europe at the time and the friend in America. The death was confirmed next morning by telegram, and ten days later a letter confirmed the details. Comparison of European time with American time showed that the death occurred at least an hour before the dream. The dreamer had gone to bed late and not slept until about one o'clock. The dream occurred at approximately two in the morning. The dream experience is *not synchronous* with the death. Experiences of this kind frequently take place a little before or after the critical event. J. W. Dunne [44] mentions a particularly instructive dream he had in the spring of 1902, when serving in the Boer War. He seemed to be standing on a volcanic mountain. It was an island, which he had dreamed about before and knew was threatened by a catastrophic volcanic eruption (like Krakatoa). Terrified, he wanted to save the four thousand inhabitants. He tried to get the French officials on the neighbouring island to mobilize all available shipping for the rescue work. Here the dream began to develop the typical nightmare motifs of hurrying, chasing, and not arriving on time, and all the while there hovered before his mind the words: "Four thousand people will be killed unless——" A few days later Dunne received with his mail a copy of the *Daily Telegraph,* and his eye fell on the following headlines:

VOLCANO DISASTER
IN MARTINIQUE

Town Swept Away

AN AVALANCHE OF FLAME

*Probable Loss of Over
40,000 Lives*

853   The dream did not take place at the moment of the actual catastrophe, but only when the paper was already on its way to

44 *An Experiment with Time* (2nd edn.), pp. 34ff.

him with the news. While reading it, he misread 40,000 as 4,000. The mistake became fixed as a paramnesia, so that whenever he told the dream he invariably said 4,000 instead of 40,000. Not until fifteen years later, when he copied out the article, did he discover his mistake. His unconscious knowledge had made the same mistake in reading as himself.

854   The fact that he dreamed this shortly before the news reached him is something that happens fairly frequently. We often dream about people from whom we receive a letter by the next post. I have ascertained on several occasions that at the moment when the dream occurred the letter was already lying in the post-office of the addressee. I can also confirm, from my own experience, the reading mistake. During the Christmas of 1918 I was much occupied with Orphism, and in particular with the Orphic fragment in Malalas, where the Primordial Light is described as the "trinitarian Metis, Phanes, Ericepaeus." I consistently read Ericapaeus instead of Ericepaeus, as in the text. (Actually both readings occur.) This misreading became fixed as a paramnesia, and later I always remembered the name as Ericapaeus and only discovered thirty years afterward that Malalas' text has Ericepaeus. Just at this time one of my patients, whom I had not seen for a month and who knew nothing of my studies, had a dream in which an unknown man handed her a piece of paper, and on it was written a "Latin" hymn to a god called *Ericipaeus*. The dreamer was able to write this hymn down upon waking. The language it was written in was a peculiar mixture of Latin, French, and Italian. The lady had an elementary knowledge of Latin, knew a bit more Italian, and spoke French fluently. The name "Ericipaeus" was completely unknown to her, which is not surprising as she had no knowledge of the classics. Our two towns were about fifty miles apart, and there had been no communication between us for a month. Oddly enough, the variant of the name affected the very same vowel which I too had misread (*a* instead of *e*), but her unconscious misread it another way (*i* instead of *e*). I can only suppose that she unconsciously "read" not my mistake but the text in which the Latin transliteration "Ericepaeus" occurs, and was evidently put off her stroke by my misreading.

855   Synchronistic events rest on the *simultaneous occurrence of two different psychic states*. One of them is the normal, probable

state (i.e., the one that is causally explicable), and the other, the critical experience, is the one that cannot be derived causally from the first. In the case of sudden death the critical experience cannot be recognized immediately as "extra-sensory perception" but can only be verified as such afterwards. Yet even in the case of the "scarab" what is immediately experienced is a psychic state or psychic image which differs from the dream image only because it can be verified immediately. In the case of the flock of birds there was in the woman an unconscious excitation or fear which was certainly conscious *to me* and caused me to send the patient to a heart specialist. In all these cases, whether it is a question of spatial or of temporal ESP, we find a simultaneity of the normal or ordinary state with another state or experience which is not causally derivable from it, and whose objective existence can only be verified afterwards. This definition must be borne in mind particularly when it is a question of future events. They are evidently not *synchronous* but are *synchronistic,* since they are experienced as psychic images *in the present,* as though the objective event already existed. An unexpected content which is directly or indirectly connected with some objective external event coincides with the ordinary psychic state: this is what I call synchronicity, and I maintain that we are dealing with exactly the same category of events whether their objectivity appears separated from my consciousness in space or in time. This view is confirmed by Rhine's results in so far as they were not influenced by changes in space or time. Space and time, the conceptual co-ordinates of bodies in motion, are probably at bottom one and the same (which is why we speak of a long or short "space of time"), and Philo Judaeus said long ago that "the extension of heavenly motion is time." [45] Synchronicity in space can equally well be conceived as perception in time, but remarkably enough it is not so easy to understand synchronicity in time as spatial, for we cannot imagine any space in which future events are objectively present and could be experienced as such through a reduction of this spatial distance. But since experience has shown that under certain conditions space and time can be reduced almost to zero, causality disappears along with them, because causality is bound up with

---

[45] *De opificio mundi,* 26. ("Διάστημα τῆς τοῦ οὐρανοῦ κινήσεώς ἐστι ὁ χρόνος.")

the existence of space and time and physical changes, and consists essentially in the succession of cause and effect. For this reason synchronistic phenomena cannot in principle be associated with any conceptions of causality. Hence the interconnection of meaningfully coincident factors must necessarily be thought of as acausal.

856   Here, for want of a demonstrable cause, we are all too likely to fall into the temptation of positing a *transcendental* one. But a "cause" can only be a demonstrable quantity. A "transcendental cause" is a contradiction in terms, because anything transcendental cannot by definition be demonstrated. If we don't want to risk the hypothesis of acausality, then the only alternative is to explain synchronistic phenomena as mere chance, which brings us into conflict with Rhine's ESP discoveries and other well-attested facts reported in the literature of parapsychology. Or else we are driven to the kind of reflections I described above, and must subject our basic principles of explanation to the criticism that space and time are constants in any given system only when they are measured without regard to psychic conditions. That is what regularly happens in scientific experiments. But when an event is observed without experimental restrictions, the observer can easily be influenced by an emotional state which alters space and time by "contraction." Every emotional state produces an alteration of consciousness which Janet called *abaissement du niveau mental;* that is to say there is a certain narrowing of consciousness and a corresponding strengthening of the unconscious which, particularly in the case of strong affects, is noticeable even to the layman. The tone of the unconscious is heightened, thereby creating a gradient for the unconscious to flow towards the conscious. The conscious then comes under the influence of unconscious instinctual impulses and contents. These are as a rule complexes whose ultimate basis is the archetype, the "instinctual pattern." The unconscious also contains subliminal perceptions (as well as forgotten memory-images that cannot be reproduced at the moment, and perhaps not at all). Among the subliminal contents we must distinguish perceptions from what I would call an inexplicable "knowledge" or "immediate existence." Whereas the perceptions can be related to possible or probable sense stimuli below the threshold of consciousness, either the "knowl-

446

edge" or "immediate existence" of unconscious images has no
recognizable basis, or else we find recognizable causal connections with certain already existing, and often archetypal, contents. These images, whether rooted in an already existing basis
or not, stand in an analogous or equivalent (i.e., meaningful)
relationship to objective occurrences which have no recognizable or even conceivable causal relationship with them. How
could an event remote in space and time produce a corresponding psychic image when the transmission of energy necessary
for this is not even thinkable? However incomprehensible it
may appear, we are finally compelled to assume that there is in
the unconscious something like an *a priori* knowledge or an
"immediacy" of events which lacks any causal basis. At any rate
our conception of causality is incapable of explaining the facts.

857   In view of this complicated situation it may be worth while
to recapitulate the argument discussed above, and this can best
be done with the aid of our examples. In Rhine's experiment
I made the assumption that, owing to the tense expectation or
emotional state of the subject, an already existing, correct, but
unconscious image of the result enables his conscious mind to
score a more than chance number of hits. The scarab dream is
a conscious representation arising from an unconscious, already
existing image of the situation that will occur on the following
day, i.e., the recounting of the dream and the appearance of the
rose-chafer. The wife of the patient who died had an unconscious knowledge of the impending death. The flock of birds
evoked the corresponding memory-images and consequently her
fear. Similarly, the almost simultaneous dream of the violent
death of the friend arose from an already existing unconscious
knowledge of it.

858   In all these cases and others like them there seems to be an
a priori, causally inexplicable knowledge of a situation which
at the time is unknowable. Synchronicity therefore consists of
two factors: *a*) An unconscious image comes into consciousness
either directly (i.e., literally) or indirectly (symbolized or suggested) in the form of a dream, idea, or premonition. *b*) An
objective situation coincides with this content. The one is as
puzzling as the other. How does the unconscious image arise,
and how the coincidence? I understand only too well why people prefer to doubt the reality of these things. Here I will only

pose the question. Later in the course of this study I will try to give an answer.

859   As regards the role which affects play in the occurrence of synchronistic events, I should perhaps mention that this is by no means a new idea but was already known to Avicenna and Albertus Magnus. On the subject of magic, Albertus Magnus writes:

> I discovered an instructive account [of magic] in Avicenna's *Liber sextus naturalium,* which says that a certain power [46] to alter things indwells in the human soul and subordinates the other things to her, particularly when she is swept into a great excess of love or hate or the like.[47] When therefore the soul of a man falls into a great excess of any passion, it can be proved by experiment that it [the excess] binds things [magically] and alters them in the way it wants,[48] and for a long time I did not believe it, but after I had read the nigromantic books and others of the kind on signs and magic, I found that the emotionality [49] of the human soul is the chief cause of all these things, whether because, on account of her great emotion, she alters her bodily substance and the other things towards which she strives, or because, on account of her dignity, the other, lower things are subject to her, or because the appropriate hour or astrological situation or another power coincides with so inordinate an emotion, and we [in consequence] believe that what this power does is then done by the soul.[50] . . . Whoever would learn the secret of doing and undoing these things must know that everyone can influence everything magically if he falls into a great excess . . . and he must do it at that hour when the excess befalls him, and operate with the things which the soul prescribes. For the soul is then so desirous of the matter she would accomplish that of her own accord she seizes on the more significant and better astrological hour which also rules over the things suited to that matter. . . . Thus it is the soul who desires a thing more intensely, who makes things more effective and more like what comes forth. . . . Such is the manner of production with everything the soul intensely desires. Everything she does with that aim in view possesses motive power and efficacy for what the soul desires.[51]

46 "virtus"

47 "quando ipsa fertur in magnum amoris excessum aut odii aut alicuius talium."

48 "fertur in grandem excessum alicuius passionis invenitur experimento manifesto quod ipse ligat res et alterat ad idem quod desiderat"   49 "affectio"

50 "cum tali affectione exterminata concurrat hora conveniens aut ordo coelestis aut alia virtus, quae quodvis faciet, illud reputavimus tunc animam facere."

51 *De mirabilibus mundi* (1485?).

860   This text shows clearly that synchronistic ("magical") happenings are regarded as being dependent on affects. Naturally Albertus Magnus, in accordance with the spirit of his age, explains this by postulating a magical faculty in the soul, without considering that the psychic process itself is just as much "arranged" as the coinciding image which anticipates the external physical process. This image originates in the unconscious and therefore belongs to those "cogitationes quae sunt a nobis independentes," which, in the opinion of Arnold Geulincx, are prompted by God and do not spring from our own thinking.[52] Goethe thinks of synchronistic events in the same "magical" way. Thus he says, in his conversations with Eckermann: "We all have certain electric and magnetic powers within us and ourselves exercise an attractive and repelling force, according as we come into touch with something like or unlike." [53]

861   After these general considerations let us return to the problem of the empirical basis of synchronicity. The main difficulty here is to procure empirical material from which we can draw reasonably certain conclusions, and unfortunately this difficulty is not an easy one to solve. The experiences in question are not ready to hand. We must therefore look in the obscurest corners and summon up courage to shock the prejudices of our age if we want to broaden the basis of our understanding of nature. When Galileo discovered the moons of Jupiter with his telescope he immediately came into head-on collision with the prejudices of his learned contemporaries. Nobody knew what a telescope was and what it could do. Never before had anyone talked of the moons of Jupiter. Naturally every age thinks that all ages before it were prejudiced, and today we think this more than ever and are just as wrong as all previous ages that thought so. How often have we not seen the truth condemned! It is sad but unfortunately true that man learns nothing from history. This melancholy fact will present us with the greatest difficulties as soon as we set about collecting empirical material that would throw a little light on this dark subject, for we shall be quite certain to find it where all the authorities have assured us that nothing is to be found.

52 *Metaphysica vera,* Part III, "Secunda scientia," in *Opera philosophica,* ed. by Land, II, pp. 187f.

53 *Eckermann's Conversations with Goethe,* trans. by Moon, pp. 514f. (modified)

862   Reports of remarkable isolated cases, however well authenticated, are unprofitable and lead at most to their reporter being regarded as a credulous person. Even the careful recording and verification of a large number of such cases, as in the work of Gurney, Myers, and Podmore,[54] have made next to no impression on the scientific world. The great majority of "professional" psychologists and psychiatrists seem to be completely ignorant of these researches.[55]

*

863   The results of the ESP and PK experiments have provided a statistical basis for evaluating the phenomenon of synchronicity, and at the same time have pointed out the important part played by the psychic factor. This fact prompted me to ask whether it would not be possible to find a method which would on the one hand demonstrate the existence of synchronicity and, on the other hand, disclose psychic contents which would at least give us a clue to the nature of the psychic factor involved. I asked myself, in other words, whether there were not a method which would yield measurable results and at the same time give us an insight into the psychic background of synchronicity. That there are certain essential psychic conditions for synchronistic phenomena we have already seen from the ESP experiments, although the latter are in the nature of the case restricted to the fact of coincidence and only stress its psychic background without illuminating it any further. I had known for a long time that there were intuitive or "mantic" methods which start with the psychic factor and take the existence of synchronicity as self-evident. I therefore turned my attention first of all to the intuitive technique for *grasping the total situation* which is so characteristic of China, namely the *I Ching* or *Book of Changes*.[56] Unlike the Greek-trained Western mind, the Chinese mind does not aim at grasping details for their own sake, but at a view which sees the detail as part of a whole. For obvious

54 See p. 430, supra.

55 Recently Pascual Jordan has put up an excellent case for the scientific investigation of spatial clairvoyance ("Positivistische Bemerkungen über die parapsychischen Erscheinungen"). I would also draw attention to his *Verdrängung und Komplementarität,* concerning the relations between microphysics and the psychology of the unconscious.

56 Trans. by Cary F. Baynes from the Richard Wilhelm translation.

reasons, a cognitive operation of this kind is impossible to the unaided intellect. Judgment must therefore rely much more on the irrational functions of consciousness, that is on sensation (the "sens du réel") and intuition (perception by means of subliminal contents). The *I Ching,* which we can well call the experimental foundation of classical Chinese philosophy, is one of the oldest known methods for grasping a situation as a whole and thus placing the details against a cosmic background—the interplay of Yin and Yang.

864　This grasping of the whole is obviously the aim of science as well, but it is a goal that necessarily lies very far off because science, whenever possible, proceeds experimentally and in all cases statistically. Experiment, however, consists in asking a definite question which excludes as far as possible anything disturbing and irrelevant. It makes conditions, imposes them on Nature, and in this way forces her to give an answer to a question devised by man. She is prevented from answering out of the fullness of her possibilities since these possibilities are restricted as far as practicable. For this purpose there is created in the laboratory a situation which is artificially restricted to the question and which compels Nature to give an unequivocal answer. The workings of Nature in her unrestricted wholeness are completely excluded. If we want to know what these workings are, we need a method of inquiry which imposes the fewest possible conditions, or if possible no conditions at all, and then leaves Nature to answer out of her fullness.

865　In the laboratory experiment, the known and established procedure forms the stable factor in the statistical compilation and comparison of the results. In the intuitive or "mantic" experiment-with-the-whole, on the other hand, there is no need of any question which imposes conditions and restricts the wholeness of the natural process. It is given every possible chance to express itself. In the *I Ching* the coins fall just as happens to suit them.[57] From the point of view of an observer, an unknown question is followed by a rationally unintelligible answer. Thus far the conditions for a total reaction are positively ideal. The disadvantage, however, leaps to the eye: in contrast to the scientific experiment one does not know what

[57] If the experiment is made with the traditional yarrow stalks, the division of the forty-nine stalks represents the chance factor.

has happened. To overcome this drawback, two Chinese sages, King Wên and the Duke of Chou, in the twelfth century before our era, basing themselves on the hypothesis of the unity of nature, sought to explain the simultaneous occurrence of a psychic state with a physical process as *an equivalence of meaning*. In other words, they supposed that the same living reality was expressing itself in the psychic state as in the physical. But, in order to verify such an hypothesis, *some* limiting condition was needed in this apparently limitless experiment, namely a definite form of physical procedure, a method or technique which forced nature to answer in even and odd numbers. These, as representatives of Yin and Yang, are found both in the unconscious and in nature in the characteristic form of opposites, as the "mother" and "father" of everything that happens, and they therefore form the *tertium comparationis* between the psychic inner world and the physical outer world. Thus the two sages devised a method by which an inner state could be represented as an outer one and vice versa. This naturally presupposes an intuitive knowledge of the meaning of each oracle figure. The *I Ching*, therefore, consists of a collection of sixty-four interpretations in which the meaning of each of the possible Yin-Yang combinations is worked out. These interpretations formulate the inner unconscious knowledge that corresponds to the state of consciousness at the moment, and this psychological situation coincides with the chance results of the method, that is, with the odd and even numbers resulting from the fall of the coins or the division of the yarrow stalks.[58]

866   The method, like all divinatory or intuitive techniques, is based on an acausal or synchronistic connective principle.[59] In practice, as any unprejudiced person will admit, many obvious cases of synchronicity occur during the experiment, which could be rationally and somewhat arbitrarily explained away as mere projections. But if one assumes that they really are what they

---

[58] See below.

[59] I first used this term in my memorial address for Richard Wilhelm (delivered May 10, 1930, in Munich). The address later appeared as an appendix to *The Secret of the Golden Flower*, where I said: "The science of the *I Ching* is not based on the causality principle, but on a principle (hitherto unnamed because not met with among us) which I have tentatively called the *synchronistic* principle" (p. 142).

appear to be, then they can only be meaningful coincidences for which, as far as we know, there is no causal explanation. The method consists either in dividing the forty-nine yarrow stalks into two heaps at random and counting off the heaps by threes and fives, or in throwing three coins six times, each line of the hexagram being determined by the value of obverse and reverse (heads 3, tails 2).[60] The experiment is based on a triadic principle (two trigrams) and contains sixty-four mutations, each corresponding to a psychic situation. These are discussed at length in the text and appended commentaries. There is also a Western method of very ancient origin [61] which is based on the same general principle as the *I Ching,* the only difference being that in the West this principle is not triadic but, significantly enough, tetradic, and the result is not a hexagram built up of Yang and Yin lines but sixteen figures composed of odd and even numbers. Twelve of them are arranged, according to certain rules, in the astrological houses. The experiment is based on 4 × 4 lines consisting of a random number of points which the questioner marks in the sand or on paper from right to left.[62] In true Occidental fashion the combination of all these factors goes into considerably more detail than the *I Ching.* Here too there are any amount of meaningful coincidences, but they are as a rule harder to understand and therefore less obvious than in the latter. In the Western method, which was known since the thirteenth century as the *Ars Geomantica* or the Art of Punctation [63] and enjoyed a widespread vogue, there are no real commentaries, since its use was only mantic and never philosophical like that of the *I Ching.*

867   Though the results of both procedures point in the desired direction, they do not provide any basis for a statistical evaluation. I have, therefore, looked round for another intuitive technique and have hit on astrology, which, at least in its modern form, claims to give a more or less total picture of the individual's character. There is no lack of commentaries here; indeed,

---

60 *I Ching,* I, pp. 392f.

61 Mentioned by Isidore of Seville in his *Liber etymologiarum,* VIII, ix, 13.

62 Grains of corn or dice can also be used.

63 The best account is to be found in Robert Fludd (1574–1637), *De arte geomantica.* Cf. Lynn Thorndike, *A History of Magic and Experimental Science,* II, p. 110.

we find a bewildering profusion of them—a sure sign that interpretation is neither simple nor certain. The meaningful coincidence we are looking for is immediately apparent in astrology, since the astronomical data are said by astrologers to correspond to individual traits of character; from the remotest times the various planets, houses, zodiacal signs, and aspects have all had meanings that serve as a basis for a character study or for an interpretation of a given situation. It is always possible to object that the result does not agree with our psychological knowledge of the situation or character in question, and it is difficult to refute the assertion that knowledge of character is a highly subjective affair, because in characterology there are no infallible or even reliable signs that can be in any way measured or calculated—an objection that also applies to graphology, although in practice it enjoys widespread recognition.

868   This criticism, together with the absence of reliable criteria for determining traits of character, makes the meaningful coincidence of horoscope structure and individual character postulated by astrology seem inapplicable for the purpose here under discussion. If, therefore, we want astrology to tell us anything about the acausal connection of events, we must discard this uncertain diagnosis of character and put in its place an absolutely certain and indubitable fact. One such fact is the marriage connection between two persons.[64]

869   Since antiquity, the main traditional astrological and alchemical correspondence to marriage has been the *coniunctio Solis* (☉) *et Lunae* (☾), the *coniunctio Lunae et Lunae,* and the conjunction of the moon with the ascendent.[65] There are others, but these do not come within the main traditional

[64] Other obvious facts would be murder and suicide. Statistics are to be found in Herbert von Kloeckler (*Astrologie als Erfahrungswissenschaft,* pp. 232ff. and 26off.), but unfortunately they fail to give comparisons with normal average values and cannot be used for our purpose. On the other hand, Paul Flambart (*Preuves et bases de l'astrologie scientifique,* pp. 79ff.) shows a graph of statistics on the ascendents of 123 outstandingly intelligent people. Definite accumulations occur at the corners of the airy trigon (♊, ♎, ♒). This result was confirmed by a further 300 cases.

[65] This view dates back to Ptolemy: "Apponit [Ptolemaeus] autem tres gradus concordiae: Primus cum Sol in viro, et Sol vel Luna in femina, aut Luna in utrisque, fuerint in locis se respicientibus trigono, vel hexagono aspectu. Secundus cum in viro Luna, in uxore Sol eodem modo disponuntur. Tertius si cum hoc

stream. The ascendent-descendent axis was introduced into the tradition because it has long been regarded as having a particularly important influence on the personality.[66] As I shall refer later to the conjunction and opposition of Mars (♂) and Venus (♀), I may say here that these are related to marriage only because the conjunction or opposition of these two planets points to a love relationship, and this may or may not produce a marriage. So far as my experiment is concerned, we have to investigate the coincident aspects ☉ ☾, ☾ ☾, and ☾ *Asc.* in the horoscopes of married pairs in relation to those of unmarried pairs. It will, further, be of interest to compare the relation of the above aspects to those of the aspects which belong only in a minor degree to the main traditional stream. No belief in astrology is needed to carry out such an investigation, only the birth-dates, an astronomical almanac, and a table of logarithms for working out the horoscope.

---

alter alterum recipiat." (Ptolemy postulates three degrees of harmony. The first is when the sun in the man's [horoscope], and the sun or moon in the woman's, or the moon in both, are in their respective places in a trine or sextile aspect. The second degree is when the moon in a man's [horoscope] and the sun in a woman's are constellated in the same way. The third degree is when the one is receptive to the other.) On the same page, Cardan quotes Ptolemy (*De iudiciis astrorum*): "Omnino vero constantes et diurni convictus permanent quando in utriusque conjugis genitura luminaria contigerit configurata esse concorditer" (Generally speaking, their life together will be long and constant when in the horoscopes of both partners the luminaries [sun and moon] are harmoniously constellated). Ptolemy regards the conjunction of a masculine moon with a feminine sun as particularly favourable for marriage.—Jerome Cardan, *Commentaria in Ptolemaeum de astrorum iudiciis*, Book IV (in his *Opera omnia*, V, p. 332).

66 The practising astrologer can hardly suppress a smile here, because for him these correspondences are absolutely self-evident, a classic example being Goethe's connection with Christiane Vulpius: ☉ 5⁰ ♍ ♂ ☾ 7⁰ ♍.

I should perhaps add a few explanatory words for those readers who do not feel at home with the ancient art and technique of astrology. Its basis is the horoscope, a circular arrangement of sun, moon, and planets according to their relative positions in the signs of the zodiac at the moment of an individual's birth. There are three main positions, viz., those of sun (☉), moon (☾), and the so-called ascendent (*Asc.*); the last has the greatest importance for the interpretation of a nativity: the *Asc.* represents the degree of the zodiacal sign rising over the eastern horizon at the moment of birth. The horoscope consists of 12 so-called "houses," sectors of 30° each. Astrological tradition ascribes different qualities to them as it does to the various "aspects," i.e., angular relations of the planets and the *luminaria* (sun ☉ and moon ☾), and to the zodiacal signs.

870   As the above three mantic procedures show, the method best adapted to the nature of chance is the numerical method. Since the remotest times men have used numbers to establish meaningful coincidences, that is, coincidences that can be interpreted. There is something peculiar, one might even say mysterious, about numbers. They have never been entirely robbed of their numinous aura. If, so a text-book of mathematics tells us, a group of objects is deprived of every single one of its properties or characteristics, there still remains, at the end, its *number*, which seems to indicate that number is something irreducible. (I am not concerned here with the logic of this mathematical argument, but only with its psychology!) The sequence of natural numbers turns out to be unexpectedly more than a mere stringing together of identical units: it contains the whole of mathematics and everything yet to be discovered in this field. Number, therefore, is in one sense an unpredictable entity. Although I would not care to undertake to say anything illuminating about the inner relation between two such apparently incommensurable things as number and synchronicity, I cannot refrain from pointing out that not only were they always brought into connection with one another, but that both possess numinosity and mystery as their common characteristics. Number has invariably been used to characterize some numinous object, and all numbers from 1 to 9 are "sacred," just as 10, 12, 13, 14, 28, 32, and 40 have a special significance. The most elementary quality about an object is whether it is one or many. Number helps more than anything else to bring order into the chaos of appearances. It is the predestined instrument for creating order, or for apprehending an already existing, but still unknown, regular arrangement or "orderedness." It may well be the most primitive element of order in the human mind, seeing that the numbers 1 to 4 occur with the greatest frequency and have the widest incidence. In other words, primitive patterns of order are mostly triads or tetrads. That numbers have an archetypal foundation is not, by the way, a conjecture of mine but of certain mathematicians, as we shall see in due course. Hence it is not such an audacious conclusion after all if we define number psychologically as an *archetype of order* which has become conscious.[67] Remarkably enough, the psychic

[67] Cf. "On the Psychology of Eastern Meditation," par. 942.

images of wholeness which are spontaneously produced by the unconscious, the symbols of the self in mandala form, also have a mathematical structure. They are as a rule quaternities (or their multiples).[68] These structures not only express order, they also create it. That is why they generally appear in times of psychic disorientation in order to compensate a chaotic state or as formulations of numinous experiences. It must be emphasized yet again that they are not inventions of the conscious mind but are spontaneous products of the unconscious, as has been sufficiently shown by experience. Naturally the conscious mind can imitate these patterns of order, but such imitations do not prove that the originals are conscious inventions. From this it follows irrefutably that the unconscious uses number as an ordering factor.

871   It is generally believed that numbers were *invented* or thought out by man, and are therefore nothing but concepts of quantities, containing nothing that was not previously put into them by the human intellect. But it is equally possible that numbers were *found* or discovered. In that case they are not only concepts but something more—autonomous entities which somehow contain more than just quantities. Unlike concepts, they are based not on any psychic conditions but on the quality of being themselves, on a "so-ness" that cannot be expressed by an intellectual concept. Under these conditions they might easily be endowed with qualities that have still to be discovered. I must confess that I incline to the view that numbers were as much found as invented, and that in consequence they possess a relative autonomy analogous to that of the archetypes. They would then have, in common with the latter, the quality of being pre-existent to consciousness, and hence, on occasion, of conditioning it rather than being conditioned by it. The archetypes too, as *a priori* forms of representation, are as much found as invented: they are *discovered* inasmuch as one did not know of their unconscious autonomous existence, and *invented* inasmuch as their presence was inferred from analogous conceptual structures. Accordingly it would seem that natural numbers have an archetypal character. If that is so, then not only would certain numbers and combinations of numbers have a relation

68 Cf. "A Study in the Process of Individuation" and "Concerning Mandala Symbolism."

to and an effect on certain archetypes, but the reverse would also be true. The first case is equivalent to number magic, but the second is equivalent to inquiring whether numbers, in conjunction with the combination of archetypes found in astrology, would show a tendency to behave in a special way.

2. AN ASTROLOGICAL EXPERIMENT

872   As I have already said, we need two different facts, one of which represents the astrological constellation, and the other the married state.

873   The material to be examined, namely a quantity of marriage horoscopes, was obtained from friendly donors in Zurich, London, Rome, and Vienna. Originally the material had been put together for purely astrological purposes, some of it many years ago, so that those who gathered the material knew of no connection between its collection and the aim of the present study, a fact which I stress because it might be objected that the material was specially selected with that aim in view. This was not so; the sample was a random one. The horoscopes, or rather the birth data, were piled up in chronological order just as the post brought them in. When the horoscopes of 180 married pairs had come in, there was a pause in the collection, during which the 360 horoscopes were worked out. This first batch was used to conduct a pilot investigation, as I wanted to test out the methods to be employed.

874   Since the material had been collected originally in order to test the empirical foundations of this intuitive method, a few more general remarks may not be out of place concerning the considerations which prompted the collection of the material.

875   Marriage is a well-characterized fact, though its psychological

459

aspect shows every conceivable sort of variation. According to the astrological view, it is precisely this aspect of marriage that expresses itself most markedly in the horoscopes. The possibility that the individuals characterized by the horoscopes married one another, so to say, by accident will necessarily recede into the background; all external factors seem capable of astrological evaluation, but only inasmuch as they are represented psychologically. Owing to the very large number of characterological variations, we would hardly expect marriage to be characterized by only *one* astrological configuration; rather, if astrological assumptions are at all correct, there will be several configurations that point to a predisposition in the choice of a marriage partner. In this connection I must call the reader's attention to the well-known correspondence between the sun-spot periods and the mortality curve. The connecting link appears to be the disturbances of the earth's magnetic field, which in their turn are due to fluctuations in the proton radiation from the sun. These fluctuations also have an influence on "radio weather" by disturbing the ionosphere that reflects the radio waves.[1] Investigation of these disturbances seems to indicate that the conjunctions, oppositions, and quartile aspects of the planets play a considerable part in increasing the proton radiation and thus causing electromagnetic storms. On the other hand, the astrologically favourable trine and sextile aspects have been reported to produce uniform radio weather.

876   These observations give us an unexpected glimpse into a possible causal basis for astrology. At all events, this is certainly true of Kepler's weather astrology. But it is also possible that, over and above the already established physiological effects of proton radiation, psychic effects can occur which would rob astrological statements of their chance nature and bring them within range of a causal explanation. Although nobody knows what the validity of a nativity horoscope rests on, it is just conceivable that there is a causal connection between the planetary aspects and the psycho-physiological disposition. One would therefore do well not to regard the results of astrological observation as synchronistic phenomena, but to take them as

[1] For a comprehensive account of this, see Max Knoll, "Transformations of Science in Our Age," in *Man and Time*.

possibly causal in origin. For, wherever a cause is even remotely thinkable, synchronicity becomes an exceedingly doubtful proposition.

877   For the present, at any rate, we have insufficient grounds for believing that the astrological results are more than mere chance, or that statistics involving large numbers yield a statistically significant result.[2] As large-scale studies are lacking, I decided to investigate the empirical basis of astrology, using a large number of horoscopes of married pairs just to see what kind of figures would turn up.

Pilot Investigation

878   With the first batch assembled, I turned first to the conjunctions (☌) and oppositions (☍) of sun and moon,[3] two aspects

Male

Female		☉	☾	♂	♀	Asc.	Desc.
	☉	☌ ☍	☌ ☍	☌ ☍	☍ ☌	☌	☌
	☾	☌ ☍	☌ ☍	☍ ☌	☌ ☍	☌	☌
	♂	☍ ☌	☌ ☍	☌ ☍	☌ ☍	☌	☌
	♀	☌ ☍	☍ ☌	☌ ☍	☍ ☌	☌	☌
	Asc.	☌	☌	☌	☌	☌	☌
	Desc.	☌	☌	☌	☌		

☌ = conjunction   ☍ = opposition

FIG. 1

2 Cf. the statistical results in K. E. Krafft and others, *Le Premier Traité d'astrobiologie*, pp. 23ff. and passim.

3 Although the quartile, trine and sextile aspects and the relations to the Medium and Imum Coeli ought really to be considered, I have omitted them here so as not to make the exposition unduly complicated. The main point is not *what* marriage aspects are, but whether they can be detected in the horoscope.

regarded in astrology as being about equally strong (though in opposite senses), i.e., as signifying intensive relations between the heavenly bodies. Together with the ♂, ♀, *Asc.*, and *Desc.* conjunctions and oppositions, they yield fifty different aspects.[4]

879   The reasons why I chose these combinations will be clear to the reader from my remarks on the astrological traditions in the previous chapter. I have only to add here that, of the conjunctions and oppositions, those of Mars and Venus are far less important than the rest, as will readily be appreciated from the following consideration: the relation of Mars to Venus can reveal a love relation, but a marriage is not always a love relation and a love relation is not always a marriage. My aim in including the conjunction and opposition of Mars and Venus was therefore to compare them with the other conjunctions and oppositions.

880   These fifty aspects were first studied for 180 married couples. It is clear that these 180 men and 180 women can also be paired off into unmarried couples. In fact, since any one of the 180 men could be paired off with any one of the 179 women to whom he was not married, it is clear that we can investigate $180 \times 179 = 32,220$ unmarried pairs within the group of 180 marriages. This was done (cf. Table I), and the aspect analysis for these unmarried pairs was compared with that for the married pairs. For all calculations, an orbit of 8° either way was assumed, clockwise and anticlockwise, not only inside the sign but extending beyond it. Later, additional marriages were added to the original batch, so that, in all, 483 marriages, or 966 horoscopes, were examined. As the following account shows, the testing and the tabulation of results were carried out in batches.

881   To begin with, what interested me most was, of course, the question of probability: were the maximum results that we obtained "significant" figures or not?—that is, were they improbable or not? Calculations undertaken by a mathematician showed unmistakably that the average frequency of 10% in the first batch and subsequently in all three batches is far from representing a significant figure. Its probability is much too great; in other words, there is no ground for assuming that our

[4] Fig. 1 (p. 461) sets out clearly the 50 different aspects as they actually occurred in the 180 married pairs.

maximum frequencies are more than mere dispersions due to chance.

Analysis of First Batch

882　First we counted all the conjunctions and oppositions between ☉ ☾ ♂ ♀ *Asc.* and *Desc.* for the 180 married and the 32,220 unmarried pairs. The results are shown in Table I, where it will be observed that the aspects are arranged by frequency of their occurrence in the married and unmarried pairs.

883　Clearly, the frequencies of occurrence shown in columns 2 and 4 of Table I for observed occurrences of the aspects in married and unmarried pairs respectively are not immediately comparable, since the first are occurrences in 180 pairs and the second in 32,220 pairs.[5] In column 5, therefore, we show the figures in column 4 multiplied by the factor $\frac{180}{32,220}$. If the right side (unmarried pairs) $= 1$, then we get the following proportion: $18 : 8.40 = 2.14 : 1$. In Table II, these proportions are arranged according to frequency.

884　To a statistician, these numbers cannot be used to confirm anything, and so are valueless, because they are chance dispersions. But on psychological grounds I have discarded the idea that we are dealing with *mere* chance numbers. In a total picture of natural events, it is just as important to consider the exceptions to the rule as the averages. This is the fallacy of the statistical picture: it is one-sided, inasmuch as it represents only the average aspect of reality and excludes the total picture. The statistical view of the world is a mere abstraction and therefore incomplete and even fallacious, particularly so when it deals with man's psychology. Inasmuch as chance maxima and minima occur, they are *facts* whose nature I set out to explore.

[5] [In this way a rough control group is obtained. It will, however, be appreciated that it is derived from a much larger number of pairs than the married pairs: 32,220 as compared with 180. This leads to the possibility of showing the chance nature of the 180 pairs. On the hypothesis that all the figures are due to chance, we would expect a far greater accuracy in the greater number and consequently a much smaller range in the figures. This is so, for the range in the 180 married pairs is $18 - 2 = 16$, whereas in the 180 unmarried pairs we get $9.6 - 7.4 = 2.2$. —Editors.]

TABLE I

Aspect			Observed Occurrences for 180 Married Pairs		Observed Occurrences for 32,220 Unmarried Pairs	Calculated Frequency for 180 Unmarried Pairs	
Fem.		Masc.	Actual Occurrences	Percentage Occurrences		Actual Frequency	Frequency Percentage
Moon	☌	Sun	18	10.0%	1506	8.4	4.7
Asc.	☌	Venus	15	8.3%	1411	7.9	4.4
Moon	☌	Asc.	14	7.7%	1485	8.3	4.6
Moon	☍	Sun	13	7.2%	1438	8.0	4.4
Moon	☌	Moon	13	7.2%	1479	8.3	4.6
Venus	☍	Moon	13	7.2%	1526	8.5	4.7
Mars	☌	Moon	13	7.2%	1548	8.6	4.8
Mars	☌	Mars	13	7.2%	1711	9.6	5.3
Mars	☌	Asc.	12	6.6%	1467	8.2	4.6
Sun	☌	Mars	12	6.6%	1485	8.3	4.6
Venus	☌	Asc.	11	6.1%	1409	7.9	4.4
Sun	☌	Asc.	11	6.1%	1413	7.9	4.4
Mars	☌	Desc.	11	6.1%	1471	8.2	4.6
Desc.	☌	Venus	11	6.1%	1470	8.2	4.6
Venus	☌	Desc.	11	6.1%	1526	8.5	4.7
Moon	☍	Mars	10	5.5%	1540	8.6	4.8
Venus	☍	Venus	9	5.0%	1415	7.9	4.4
Venus	☌	Mars	9	5.0%	1498	8.4	4.7
Venus	☌	Sun	9	5.0%	1526	8.5	4.7
Moon	☌	Mars	9	5.0%	1539	8.6	4.8
Sun	☌	Desc.	9	5.0%	1556	8.7	4.8
Asc.	☌	Asc.	9	5.0%	1595	8.9	4.9
Desc.	☌	Sun	8	4.3%	1398	7.8	4.3
Venus	☍	Sun	8	4.3%	1485	8.3	4.6
Sun	☌	Moon	8	4.3%	1508	8.4	4.7

TABLE I (continued)

Fem.	Aspect	Masc.	Observed Occurrences for 180 Married Pairs		Observed Occurrences for 32,220 Unmarried Pairs	Calculated Frequency for 180 Unmarried Pairs	
			Actual Occurrences	Percentage Occurrences		Actual Frequency	Frequency Percentage
Sun	☌	Venus	8	4.3%	1502	8.4	4.7
Sun	☌	Mars	8	4.3%	1516	8.5	4.7
Mars	☌	Sun	8	4.3%	1516	8.5	4.7
Mars	☌	Venus	8	4.3%	1520	8.5	4.7
Venus	☌	Mars	8	4.3%	1531	8.6	4.8
Asc.	☌	Moon	8	4.3%	1541	8.6	4.8
Moon	☌	Moon	8	4.3%	1548	8.6	4.8
Desc.	☌	Moon	8	4.3%	1543	8.6	4.8
Asc.	☌	Mars	8	4.3%	1625	9.1	5.0
Moon	☌	Venus	7	3.8%	1481	8.3	4.6
Mars	☌	Venus	7	3.8%	1521	8.5	4.7
Moon	☌	Desc.	7	3.8%	1539	8.6	4.8
Mars	☌	Moon	7	3.8%	1540	8.6	4.8
Asc.	☌	Desc.	6	3.3%	1328	7.4	4.1
Desc.	☌	Mars	6	3.3%	1433	8.0	4.4
Venus	☌	Moon	6	3.3%	1436	8.0	4.4
Asc.	☌	Sun	6	3.3%	1587	8.9	4.9
Mars	☌	Sun	6	3.3%	1575	8.8	4.9
Moon	☌	Venus	6	3.3%	1576	8.8	4.9
Venus	☌	Venus	5	2.7%	1497	8.4	4.7
Sun	☌	Moon	5	2.7%	1530	8.6	4.8
Sun	☌	Venus	4	2.2%	1490	8.3	4.6
Mars	☌	Mars	3	1.6%	1440	8.0	4.4
Sun	☌	Sun	2	1.1%	1480	8.3	4.6
Sun	☌	Sun	2	1.1%	1482	8.3	4.6

TABLE II

Fem.	Aspect	Masc.	Proportion of Aspect Frequencies for Married Pairs	Fem.	Aspect	Masc.	Proportion of Aspect Frequencies for Married Pairs
Moon	☌	Sun	2.14	Sun	☍	Venus	0.95
Asc.	☌	Venus	1.89	Sun	☍	Mars	0.94
Moon	☌	Asc.	1.68	Mars	☍	Sun	0.94
Moon	☍	Sun	1.61	Mars	☌	Venus	0.94
Moon	☌	Moon	1.57	Venus	☍	Mars	0.94
Venus	☍	Moon	1.53	Asc.	☌	Moon	0.93
Mars	☌	Moon	1.50	Moon	☍	Moon	0.93
Mars	☌	Asc.	1.46	Desc.	☌	Moon	0.92
Sun	☌	Mars	1.44	Asc.	☌	Mars	0.88
Venus	☌	Asc.	1.39	Moon	☌	Venus	0.85
Sun	☌	Asc.	1.39	Mars	☍	Venus	0.82
Mars	☌	Mars	1.36	Moon	☌	Desc.	0.81
Mars	☌	Desc.	1.34	Asc.	☌	Desc.	0.81
Desc.	☌	Venus	1.34	Mars	☍	Moon	0.81
Venus	☌	Desc.	1.29	Desc.	☌	Mars	0.75
Moon	☍	Mars	1.16	Venus	☌	Moon	0.75
Venus	☍	Venus	1.14	Asc.	☌	Sun	0.68
Venus	☌	Mars	1.07	Mars	☌	Sun	0.68
Venus	☌	Sun	1.06	Moon	☍	Venus	0.68
Moon	☌	Mars	1.05	Venus	☌	Venus	0.60
Sun	☌	Desc.	1.04	Sun	☍	Moon	0.59
Desc.	☌	Sun	1.02	Sun	☌	Venus	0.48
Asc.	☌	Asc.	1.01	Mars	☍	Mars	0.37
Venus	☍	Sun	0.96	Sun	☌	Sun	0.24
Sun	☌	Moon	0.95	Sun	☍	Sun	0.24

885   What strikes us in Table II is the unequal distribution of the frequency values. The top seven and bottom six aspects both show a fairly strong dispersion, while the middle values tend to cluster round the proportion 1 : 1. I shall come back to this peculiar distribution with the help of a special graph (Fig. 2).

886   An interesting point is the confirmation of the traditional astrological and alchemical correspondence between marriage and the moon-sun aspects:

> (fem.) moon ☌ (masc.) sun 2.14 : 1
> (fem.) moon ☍ (masc.) sun 1.61 : 1

whereas there is no evidence of any emphasis on the Venus-Mars aspects.

887   Of the fifty possible aspects, the result shows that for the married pairs there are fifteen such configurations whose frequency is well above the proportion 1 : 1. The highest value is found in the aforementioned moon-sun conjunction, and the two next-highest figures—1.89 : 1 and 1.68 : 1—correspond to the conjunctions between (fem.) *Asc.* and (masc.) Venus, or (fem.) moon and (masc.) *Asc.*, thus apparently confirming the traditional significance of the ascendent.

888   Of these fifteen aspects, a moon aspect occurs four times for women, whereas only six moon aspects are distributed among the thirty-five other possible values. The mean proportional value of all moon aspects amounts to 1.24 : 1. The average value of the four just cited in the table amounts to 1.74 : 1, as compared with 1.24 : 1 for all moon aspects. The moon seems to be less emphasized for men than for women.

889   For men the corresponding role is played not by the sun but by the *Asc.-Desc.* axis. In the first fifteen aspects of Table II, these aspects occur six times for men and only twice for women. In the former case they have an average value of 1.42 : 1, as compared with 1.22 : 1 for all masculine aspects between *Asc.* or *Desc.* on the one hand and one of the four heavenly bodies on the other.

890   Figures 2 and 3 give a graphic representation of the values listed in Figure 1 from the point of view of the dispersion of aspects.

891   This arrangement enables us not only to visualize the dispersions in the frequency of occurrence of the different aspects but also to make a rapid estimate of the mean number of occurrences per aspect, using the median as an estimator. Whereas, in order to get the arithmetic mean, we have to total the aspect frequencies and divide by the number of aspects, the median

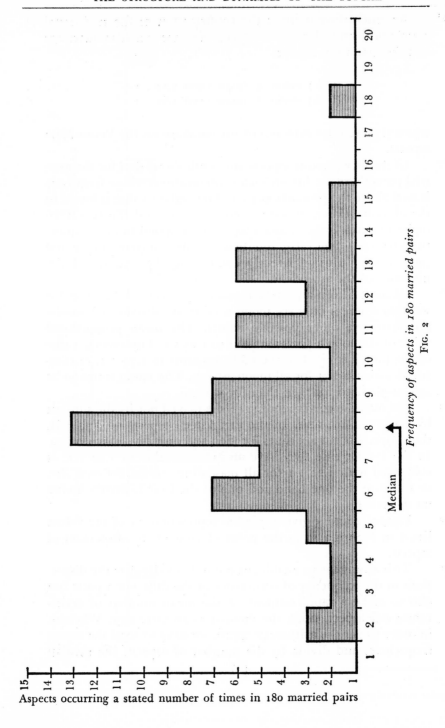

Median

Frequency of aspects in 180 married pairs

FIG. 2

Aspects occurring a stated number of times in 180 married pairs

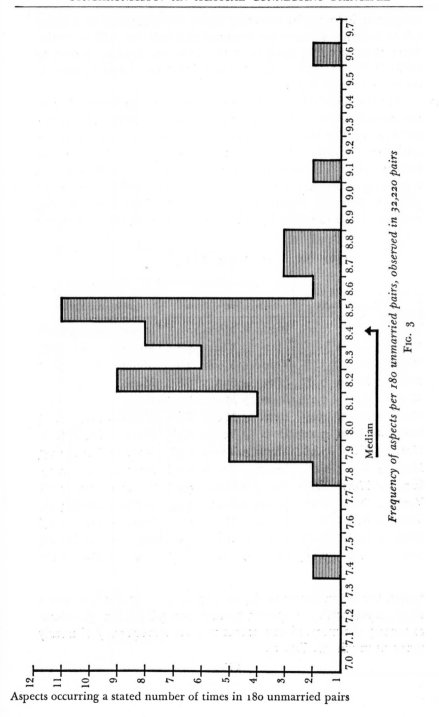

Aspects occurring a stated number of times in 180 unmarried pairs

Frequency of aspects per 180 unmarried pairs, observed in 32,220 pairs

FIG. 3

Median

THE STRUCTURE AND DYNAMICS OF THE PSYCHE

frequency is found by counting down the histogram to a point where half the squares are counted and half are still to count. Since there are fifty squares in this case, the median is seen to be 8.0, since 25 squares do not exceed this value and 25 squares do exceed it (cf. Fig. 2).

892   For the married pairs the median amounts to 8 cases, but in the combinations of unmarried persons it is more, namely 8.4 (cf. Fig. 3). For the unmarried the median coincides with the arithmetic mean—both amount to 8.4—whereas the median for the married is lower than the corresponding mean value of 8.4, which is due to the presence of lower values for the married pairs. A glance at Figure 2 will show that there is a wide dispersion of values which contrasts strikingly with those clustered

TABLE III

First Batch		Second Batch		Both Batches	
180 Married Pairs		220 Married Pairs		400 Married Pairs	
Moon ☌ Sun	10.0%	Moon ☌ Moon	10.9%	Moon ☌ Moon	9.2%
Asc. ☌ Venus	9.4%	Mars ☍ Venus	7.7%	Moon ☍ Sun	7.0%
Moon ☌ Asc.	7.7%	Venus ☌ Moon	7.2%	Moon ☌ Sun	7.0%
Moon ☌ Moon	7.2%	Moon ☍ Sun	6.8%	Mars ☌ Mars	6.2%
Moon ☍ Sun	7.2%	Moon ☍ Mars	6.8%	Desc. ☌ Venus	6.2%
Mars ☌ Moon	7.2%	Desc. ☌ Mars	6.8%	Moon ☍ Mars	6.2%
Venus ☍ Moon	7.2%	Desc. ☌ Venus	6.3%	Mars ☌ Moon	6.0%
Mars ☌ Mars	7.2%	Moon ☍ Venus	6.3%	Mars ☍ Venus	5.7%
Mars ☌ Asc.	6.6%	Venus ☌ Venus	6.3%	Moon ☌ Asc.	5.7%
Sun ☌ Mars	6.6%	Sun ☍ Mars	5.9%	Venus ☌ Desc.	5.7%
Venus ☌ Desc.	6.1%	Venus ☌ Desc.	5.4%	Venus ☌ Moon	5.5%
Venus ☌ Asc.	6.1%	Venus ☌ Mars	5.4%	Desc. ☌ Mars	5.2%
Mars ☌ Desc.	6.1%	Sun ☌ Moon	5.4%	Asc. ☌ Venus	5.2%
Sun ☌ Asc.	6.1%	Sun ☌ Sun	5.4%	Sun ☍ Mars	5.2%

round the mean figure of 8.4 in Figure 3. Here there is not a single aspect with a frequency greater than 9.6 (cf. Fig. 3), whereas among the married one aspect reaches a frequency of nearly twice as much (cf. Fig. 2).

Comparison of All Batches

893　　On the supposition that the dispersion apparent in Figure 2 was due to chance I investigated a larger number of marriage horoscopes, four hundred in all (or eight hundred individual horoscopes). The results of this additional material are shown in Table III and set against the 180 cases already discussed, though I have here confined myself to the maximal numbers that clearly exceed the median. Figures are given in percentages.

894　　The 180 married couples in the first column show the results of the first collection, while the 220 in the second column were collected more than a year later. The second column not only differs from the first in its aspects, but shows a marked sinking of the frequency values. The only exception is the top number, representing the classical ☽ ☌ ☽. It takes the place of the equally classical ☽ ☌ ☉ in the first column. Of the fourteen aspects in the first column only four come up again in the second, but of these no less than three are moon aspects, and this is in accord with astrological expectations. The absence of correspondence between the aspects of the first and second columns indicates a great inequality of material, i.e., there is a wide dispersion. One can see this in the aggregate figures for the 400 married pairs: as a result of the evening out of the dispersion they all show a marked decrease. These proportions are brought out still more clearly in Table IV.

TABLE IV

Frequency in %	☽ ☌ ☉	☽ ☌ ☽	☽ ☍ ☉	Average
180 Married Pairs	10.0	7.2	7.2	8.1
220 Married Pairs	4.5	10.9	6.8	7.4
180 + 220 = 400 Married Pairs	7.0	9.2	7.0	7.7
83 Additional Married Pairs	7.2	4.8	4.8	5.6
83 + 400 = 483 Married Pairs	7.2	8.4	6.6	7.4

895　　This table shows the frequency figures for the three constellations that occur most often: two lunar conjunctions and one lunar opposition. The highest average frequency, that for the

471

original 180 marriages, is 8.1%; for the 220 collected and worked out later the average maximum drops to 7.4%; and for the 83 marriages that were added still later the average amounts to only 5.6%. In the original batches of 180 and 220 the maxima still lie with the same aspects, but in the last batch of 83 the maxima lie with different aspects, namely *Asc.* ☌ ☾, ☉ ☌ ♀, ☉ ☌ ♂, and *Asc.* ☌ *Asc.* The average maximum for these four aspects is 8.7%. This high figure exceeds our highest average of 8.1% for the first batch of 180, which only proves how fortuitous our "favourable" initial results were. Nevertheless it is worth pointing out that, amusingly enough, the maximum of 9.6% [6] lies with the *Asc.* ☌ ☾ aspect, that is to say, with another lunar aspect which is supposed to be particularly characteristic of marriage—a *lusus naturae,* no doubt, but a very queer one, since according to tradition the ascendent or "horoscopus," together with sun and moon, forms the trinity that determines fate and character. Had one wanted to falsify the statistical findings so as to bring them into line with tradition one could not have done it more successfully.

896   Table V gives the maximal frequencies for unmarried pairs.

TABLE V

Maximal Frequency in % for

1. 300 pairs combined at random 7.3
2. 325 pairs chosen by lot 6.5
3. 400 pairs chosen by lot 6.2
4. 32,220 pairs 5.3

The first result was obtained by my co-worker, Dr. Liliane Frey-Rohn, putting the men's horoscopes on one side and the women's on the other, and then combining each of the pairs that happened to lie on top. Care was naturally taken that a real married pair was not accidentally combined. The resultant frequency of 7.3 is pretty high in comparison with the much more probable maximal figure for the 32,220 unmarried pairs, which is only 5.3. This first result seemed to me somewhat

6 [I.e., 8 in 83.—EDITORS.]

suspicious.[7] I therefore suggested that we should not combine the pairs ourselves, but should proceed in the following way: 325 men's horoscopes were numbered, the numbers were written on separate slips, thrown into a pot, and mixed up. Then a person who knew nothing of astrology and psychology and even less of these investigations was invited to draw the slips one by one out of the pot, without looking at them. The numbers were each combined with the topmost on the pile of women's horoscopes, care being again taken that married pairs did not accidentally come together. In this way 325 artificial pairs were obtained. The resultant 6.5 is rather nearer to probability. Still more probable is the result obtained for the 400 unmarried pairs. Even so, this figure (6.2) is still too high.

*

897   The somewhat curious behaviour of our figures led to a further experiment whose results I mention here with all the necessary reserve, though it seems to me to throw some light on the statistical variations. It was made with three people whose psychological status was accurately known. The experiment consisted in taking 400 marriage horoscopes at random and providing 200 of them with numbers. Twenty of these were then drawn by lot by the subject. These twenty married pairs were

[7] How subtle these things can be is shown by the following incident: Recently it fell to my colleague to make the table arrangement for a number of people who were invited to dinner. She did this with care and discretion. But at the last moment an esteemed guest, a man, unexpectedly turned up who had at all costs to be suitably placed. The table arrangement was all upset, and a new one had to be hastily devised. There was no time for elaborate reflection. As we sat down to table, the following astrological picture manifested itself in the immediate vicinity of the guest:

LADY	LADY	GUEST	LADY
☾ in ♌	☉ in ♓	☉ in ♉	☉ in ♓
LADY	LADY	GENTLEMAN	LADY
☉ in ♌	☾ in ♓	☾ in ♉	☾ in ♓

Four ☉ ☾ marriages had arisen. My colleague, of course, had a thorough knowledge of astrological marriage aspects, and she was also acquainted with the horoscopes of the people in question. But the speed with which the new table arrangement had to be made left her no opportunity for reflection, so that the unconscious had a free hand in secretly arranging the "marriages."

473

examined statistically for our fifty marriage characteristics. The first subject was a woman patient who, at the time of the experiment, found herself in a state of intense emotional excitement. It proved that of twenty Mars aspects no less than ten were emphasized, with a frequency of 15.0; of the moon aspects nine, with a frequency of 10.0; and of the sun aspects nine, with a frequency of 14.0. The classical significance of Mars lies in his emotionality, in this case supported by the masculine sun. As compared with our general results there is a predominance of the Mars aspects, which fully agrees with the psychic state of the subject.

898   The second subject was a woman patient whose main problem was to realize and assert her personality in the face of her self-suppressive tendencies. In this case the axial aspects (*Asc. Desc.*), which are supposed to be characteristic of the personality, came up twelve times with a frequency of 20.0, and the moon aspects with a frequency of 18.0. This result, astrologically considered, was in full agreement with the subject's actual problems.

899   The third subject was a woman with strong inner oppositions whose union and reconciliation constituted her main problem. The moon aspects came up fourteen times with a frequency of 20.0, the sun aspects twelve times with a frequency of 15.0, and the axial aspects nine times with a frequency of 14.0. The classical *coniunctio Solis et Lunae* as the symbol of the union of opposites is clearly emphasized.

900   In all these cases the selection by lot of marriage horoscopes proves to have been influenced, and this fits in with our experience of the *I Ching* and other mantic procedures. Although all these figures lie well within the limits of probability and cannot therefore be regarded as anything more than chance, their variation, which each time corresponds surprisingly well with the psychic state of the subject, still gives one food for thought. The psychic state was characterized as a situation in which insight and decision come up against the insurmountable barrier of an unconscious opposed to the will. This relative defeat of the powers of the conscious mind constellates the moderating archetype, which appears in the first case as Mars, the emotional *maleficus,* in the second case as the equilibrating axial system that strengthens the personality, and in the third

case as the *hieros gamos* or *coniunctio* of supreme opposites.[8] The psychic and physical event (namely, the subject's problems and choice of horoscope) correspond, it would seem, to the nature of the archetype in the background and could therefore represent a synchronistic phenomenon.

*

901   Inasmuch as I am not very well up in the higher mathematics, and had therefore to rely on the help of a professional, I asked Professor Markus Fierz, of Basel, to calculate the probability of my maximal numbers.[9] This he very kindly did, and using the Poisson distribution he arrived at a probability of approximately 1 : 10,000. Later, on checking the calculation, he found an error whose correction raised the probability to 1 : 1500.[10] From this it is clear that although our best results—☽ ☌ ☉ and ☽ ☌ ☽—are fairly improbable in practice, they are theoretically so probable that there is little justification for regarding the immediate results of our statistics as anything more than chance. If for instance there is a 1 : 1500 probability of my getting the telephone connection I want, I shall probably prefer, instead of waiting on the off-chance for a telephone conversation, to write a letter. Our investigation shows that not only do the frequency values approximate to the average with the greatest number of married pairs, but that any chance pairings produce similar statistical proportions. From the scientific point of view the result of our investigation is in some respects not encouraging for astrology, as everything seems to indicate that in the case of large numbers the differences between the frequency values for the marriage aspects of married and unmarried persons disappear altogether. Thus, from the scientific point of view, there is little hope of proving that astrological correspondence is something that conforms to law. At the same

8 Cf. the nuptials of sun and moon in alchemy: *Psychology and Alchemy*, index, s.v. "sun and moon."

9 [See the appendix to this chapter.—EDITORS.]

10 Professor Fierz wishes to correct this sentence as follows: "Later on he called my attention to the fact that the sequence of the 3 aspects does not matter. As there are 6 possible sequences, we have to multiply our probability by 6, which gives 1 : 1500." To this I reply that I never suggested anything of the kind! The sequence, i.e., the way in which the 3 conjunctions follow each other, has no importance at all.

time, it is not so easy to counter the astrologer's objection that my statistical method is too arbitrary and too clumsy to evaluate correctly the numerous psychological and astrological aspects of marriage.

902   So the essential thing that remains over from our astrological statistics is the fact that the first batch of 180 marriage horoscopes shows a distinct maximum of 18 for ☾ ☌ ☉ and the second batch of 220 a maximum of 24 for ☾ ☌ ☾. These two aspects have long been mentioned in the old literature as marriage characteristics, and they therefore represent the oldest tradition. The third batch of 83 yields, as we have said, a maximum of 8 for ☾ ☌ *Asc.* These batches have probabilities of about 1 : 1000, 1 : 10,000, and 1 : 50 respectively. I should like to illustrate what has happened here by means of an example:

You take three matchboxes, put 1,000 black ants in the first, 10,000 in the second and 50 in the third, together with one white ant in each, shut the boxes, and bore a hole in each of them, small enough to allow only one ant to crawl through at a time. The first ant to come out of each of the three boxes is always the white one.

903   The chances of this actually happening are extremely improbable. Even in the first two cases, the probability works out at 1 : 1000 × 10,000, which means that such a coincidence is to be expected only in one case out of 10,000,000. It is improbable that it would ever happen in anyone's experience. Yet in my statistical investigation it happened that precisely the three conjunctions stressed by astrological tradition came together in the most improbable way.

904   For the sake of accuracy, however, it should be pointed out that it is not the *same* white ant that is the first to appear each time. That is to say, although there is always a lunar conjunction and always a "classical" one of decisive significance, they are nevertheless different conjunctions, because each time the moon is associated with a different partner. These are of course the three main components of the horoscope, namely the ascendent, or rising degree of a zodiacal sign, which characterizes the moment, the moon, which characterizes the day, and the sun, which characterizes the month of birth. Hence, if we consider only the first two batches, we must assume two white ants

476

for each box. This correction raises the probability of the coinciding lunar conjunctions to 1 : 2,500,000. If we take the third batch as well, the coincidence of the three classical moon aspects has a probability of 1 : 62,500,000. The first proportion is significant even when taken by itself, for it shows that the coincidence is a very improbable one. But the coincidence with the third lunar conjunction is so remarkable that it looks like a deliberate arrangement in favour of astrology. If, therefore, the result of our experiment should be found to have a significant—i.e., more than merely chance—probability, the case for astrology would be proved in the most satisfactory way. If, on the contrary, the figures actually fall within the limits of chance probability, they do not support the astrological claim, they merely *imitate* accidentally the ideal answer to astrological expectation. It is nothing but a chance result from the statistical point of view, yet it is *meaningful* on account of the fact that it looks as if it validated this expectation. It is just what I call a synchronistic phenomenon. The statistically significant statement only concerns regularly occurring events, and if considered as axiomatic, it simply abolishes all exceptions to the rule. It produces a merely average picture of natural events, but not a *true* picture of the world as it is. Yet the exceptions—and my results are exceptions and most improbable ones at that—are just as important as the rules. Statistics would not even make sense without the exceptions. There is no rule that is true under all circumstances, for this is the real and not a statistical world. Because the statistical method shows only the average aspects, it creates an artificial and predominantly conceptual picture of reality. That is why we need a complementary principle for a complete description and explanation of nature.

905   If we now consider the results of Rhine's experiments, and particularly the fact that they depend in large measure on the subject's active interest,[11] we can regard what happened in our case as a synchronistic phenomenon. The statistical material shows that a practically as well as theoretically improbable chance combination occurred which coincides in the most remarkable way with traditional astrological expectations. That

11 Cf. G. Schmiedler, "Personality Correlates of ESP as Shown by Rorschach Studies." The author points out that those who accept the possibility of ESP get results above expectation, whereas those who reject it get negative results.

such a coincidence should occur at all is so improbable and so incredible that nobody could have dared to predict anything like it. It really does look as if the statistical material had been manipulated and arranged so as to give the appearance of a positive result. The necessary emotional and archetypal conditions for a synchronistic phenomenon were already given, since it is obvious that both my co-worker and myself had a lively interest in the outcome of the experiment, and apart from that the question of synchronicity had been engaging my attention for many years. What seems in fact to have happened—and seems often to have happened, bearing in mind the long astrological tradition—is that we got a result which has presumably turned up many times before in history. Had the astrologers (with but few exceptions) concerned themselves more with statistics and questioned the justice of their interpretations in a scientific spirit, they would have discovered long ago that their statements rested on a precarious foundation. But I imagine that in their case too, as with me, a secret, mutual connivance existed between the material and the psychic state of the astrologer. This correspondence is simply *there* like any other agreeable or annoying accident, and it seems doubtful to me whether it can be proved scientifically to be anything more than that.[12] One may be fooled by coincidence, but one has to have a very thick skin not to be impressed by the fact that, out of fifty possibilities, three times precisely those turned up as maxima which are regarded by tradition as typical.

906   As though to make this startling result even more impressive, we found that use had been made of unconscious deception. On first working out the statistics I was put off the trail by a number of errors which I fortunately discovered in time. After overcoming this difficulty I then forgot to mention, in the Swiss edition of this book, that the ant comparison, if applied to our experiment, only fits if respectively two or three white ants are assumed each time. This considerably reduces the improbability of our results. Then, at the eleventh hour, Professor Fierz, on

---

[12] As my statistics show, the result becomes blurred with larger figures. So it is very probable that if more material were collected it would no longer produce a similar result. We have therefore to be content with this apparently unique *lusus naturae*, though its uniqueness in no way prejudices the facts.

checking his probability calculations yet again, found that he had been deceived by the factor 5. The improbability of our results was again reduced, though without reaching a degree which one could have described as probable. *The errors all tend to exaggerate the results in a way favourable to astrology,* and add most suspiciously to the impression of an artificial or fraudulent arrangement of the facts, which was so mortifying to those concerned that they would probably have preferred to keep silent about it.

907   I know, however, from long experience of these things that spontaneous synchronistic phenomena draw the observer, by hook or by crook, into what is happening and occasionally make him an accessory to the deed. That is the danger inherent in all parapsychological experiments. The dependence of ESP on an emotional factor in the experimenter and subject is a case in point. I therefore consider it a scientific duty to give as complete an account as possible of the result and to show how not only the statistical material, but the psychic processes of the interested parties, were affected by the synchronistic arrangement. Although, warned by previous experience, I was cautious enough to submit my original account (in the Swiss edition) to four competent persons, among them two mathematicians, I allowed myself to be lulled into a sense of security too soon.

908   The corrections made here do not in any way alter the fact that the maximal frequencies lie with the three classical lunar aspects.

909   In order to assure myself of the chance nature of the result, I undertook one more statistical experiment. I broke up the original and fortuitous chronological order and the equally fortuitous division into three batches by mixing the first 150 marriages with the last 150, taking the latter in reverse order; that is to say, I put the first marriage on top of the last, and then the second on top of the last but one, and so on. Then I divided the 300 marriages into three batches of a hundred. The result was as follows:

	1st Batch	2nd Batch	3rd Batch
Maximum	No Aspects 11%	☉ ☌ ♂ 11% ☽ ☌ ☽ 11%	☽ ☌ *Asc.* 12%

910   The result of the first batch is amusing in so far as only fifteen of the 300 marriages have none of the fifty selected aspects in common. The second batch yields two maxima, of which the second again represents a classical conjunction. The third batch yields a maximum for ☽ ☌ *Asc.,* which we already know as the third "classical" conjunction. The total result shows that another chance arrangement of the marriages can easily produce a result that deviates from the earlier total, but still does not quite prevent the classical conjunctions from turning up.

*

911   The result of our experiment tallies with our experience of mantic procedures. One has the impression that these methods, and others like them, create favourable conditions for the occurrence of meaningful coincidences. It is quite true that the verification of synchronistic phenomena is a difficult and sometimes impossible task. Rhine's achievement in demonstrating, with the help of unexceptionable material, the coincidence of a psychic state with a corresponding objective process must therefore be rated all the higher. Despite the fact that the statistical method is in general highly unsuited to do justice to unusual events, Rhine's experiments have nevertheless withstood the ruinous influence of statistics. Their results must therefore be taken into account in any assessment of synchronistic phenomena.

912   In view of the levelling influence which the statistical method has on the quantitative determination of synchronicity, we must ask how it was that Rhine succeeded in obtaining positive results. I maintain that he would never have got the results he did if he had carried out his experiments with a single subject,[13] or only a few. He needed a constant renewal of interest, an emotion with its characteristic *abaissement mental,* which tips the scales in favour of the unconscious. Only in this way can space and time be relativized to a certain extent, thereby reducing the chances of a causal process. What then happens is a kind of *creatio ex nihilo,* an act of creation that is not causally explicable. The mantic procedures owe their effectiveness to

13 By which I mean a subject chosen at random, and not one with specific gifts.

this same connection with emotionality: by touching an unconscious aptitude they stimulate interest, curiosity, expectation, hope, and fear, and consequently evoke a corresponding preponderance of the unconscious. The effective (numinous) agents in the unconscious are the archetypes. By far the greatest number of spontaneous synchronistic phenomena that I have had occasion to observe and analyse can easily be shown to have a direct connection with an archetype. This, in itself, is an irrepresentable, psychoid factor [14] of the collective unconscious. The latter cannot be localized, since either it is complete in principle in every individual or is found to be the same everywhere. You can never say with certainty whether what appears to be going on in the collective unconscious of a single individual is not also happening in other individuals or organisms or things or situations. When, for instance, the vision arose in ,Swedenborg's mind of a fire in Stockholm, there was a real fire raging there at the same time, without there being any demonstrable or even thinkable connection between the two.[15] I certainly would not like to undertake to prove the archetypal connection in this case. I would only point to the fact that in Swedenborg's biography there are certain things which throw a remarkable light on his psychic state. We must assume that there was a lowering of the threshold of consciousness which gave him access to "absolute knowledge." The fire in Stockholm was, in a sense, burning in him too. For the unconscious psyche space and time seem to be relative; that is to say, knowledge finds itself in a space-time continuum in which space is no longer space, nor time time. If, therefore, the unconscious should develop or maintain a potential in the direction of consciousness, it is then possible for parallel events to be perceived or "known."

913   Compared with Rhine's work the great disadvantage of my astrological statistics lies in the fact that the entire experiment was carried out on only one subject, myself. I did not experiment with a variety of subjects; rather, it was the varied material that challenged *my* interest. I was thus in the position of a subject who is at first enthusiastic, but afterwards cools off on

14 Cf. "On the Nature of the Psyche," pars. 417f.
15 This case is well authenticated. See report in Kant's "Dreams of a Spirit-Seer, Illustrated by Dreams of Metaphysics."

becoming habituated to the ESP experiment. The results therefore deteriorated with the growing number of experiments, which in this case corresponded to the exposition of the material in batches, so that the accumulation of larger numbers only blurred the "favourable" initial result. Equally my final experiment showed that the discarding of the original order and the division of the horoscopes into arbitrary batches produce, as might be expected, a different picture, though its significance is not altogether clear.

914   Rhine's rules are to be recommended wherever (as in medicine) very large numbers are not involved. The interest and expectancy of the investigator might well be accompanied synchronistically by surprisingly favourable results to begin with, despite every precaution. These will be interpreted as "miracles" only by persons insufficiently acquainted with the statistical character of natural law.[16]

*

915   If—and it seems plausible—the meaningful coincidence or "cross-connection" of events cannot be explained causally, then the connecting principle must lie in the *equal significance* of parallel events; in other words, their *tertium comparationis* is *meaning*. We are so accustomed to regard meaning as a psychic process or content that it never enters our heads to suppose that it could also exist outside the psyche. But we do know at least enough about the psyche not to attribute to it any magical power, and still less can we attribute any magical power to the conscious mind. If, therefore, we entertain the hypothesis that one and the same (transcendental) meaning might manifest itself simultaneously in the human psyche and in the arrangement of an external and independent event, we at once come into conflict with the conventional scientific and epistemological views. We have to remind ourselves over and over again of the merely statistical validity of natural laws and of the effect of the statistical method in eliminating all unusual occurrences, if we want to lend an ear to such an hypothesis. The great difficulty is that we have absolutely no scientific means of proving the existence of an *objective* meaning which is not just a psychic

16 Cf. the interesting reflections of G. Spencer Brown: "De la recherche psychique considérée comme un test de la théorie des probabilités."

product. We are, however, driven to some such assumption if we are not to regress to a *magical causality* and ascribe to the psyche a power that far exceeds its empirical range of action. In that case we should have to suppose, if we don't want to let causality go, either that Swedenborg's unconscious staged the Stockholm fire, or conversely that the objective event activated in some quite inconceivable manner the corresponding images in Swedenborg's brain. In either case we come up against the unanswerable question of transmission discussed earlier. It is of course entirely a matter of subjective opinion which hypothesis is felt to make more sense. Nor does tradition help us much in choosing between magical causality and transcendental meaning, because on the one hand the primitive mentality has always explained synchronicity as magical causality right down to our own day, and on the other hand philosophy assumed a secret correspondence or meaningful connection between natural events until well into the eighteenth century. I prefer the latter hypothesis because it does not, like the first, conflict with the empirical concept of causality, and can count as a principle *sui generis*. That obliges us, not indeed to correct the principles of natural explanation as hitherto understood, but at least to add to their number, an operation which only the most cogent reasons could justify. I believe, however, that the hints I have given in the foregoing constitute an argument that needs thorough consideration. Psychology, of all the sciences, cannot in the long run afford to overlook such experiences. These things are too important for an understanding of the unconscious, quite apart from their philosophical implications.

APPENDIX TO CHAPTER 2

[The following notes have been compiled by the Editors on the basis of Professor Fierz's mathematical argument, of which he kindly furnished a précis. These represent his latest thoughts on the topic. These data are presented here for the benefit of readers with a special interest in mathematics or statistics who want to know how the figures in the text were arrived at.

Since an orbit of 8° was taken as the basis of Professor Jung's calculations for the estimation of conjunctions and oppositions (cf. par. 880), it follows that, for a particular relation between two heavenly bodies to be called a conjunction (e.g., sun ☌ moon), one of them must lie within an arc of 16°. (Since the only concern was to test the character of the distribution, an arc of 15° was taken for convenience.)

Now, all positions on a circle of 360° are equally probable. So the probability α that the heavenly body will lie on an arc of 15° is

$$\alpha = \frac{15}{360} = \frac{1}{24} \tag{1}$$

This probability α holds for every aspect.

Let n be the number of particular aspects that will occur in N married pairs if the probability that it will occur in one married pair be α.

Applying the binomial distribution, we get:

$$W_n = \frac{N!}{n!(N-n)!} \, \alpha^n (1-\alpha)^{N-n} \tag{2}$$

In order to obtain a numerical evaluation of W_n, (2) can be simplified. This results in an error, which, however, is not important. The simplification can be arrived at by replacing (2) by the Poisson distribution:

$$P_n = \frac{1}{n!} x^n \cdot e^{-x}$$

This approximation is valid if α may be regarded as very small in comparison with 1, while x is finite.

Upon the basis of these considerations the following numerical results can be arrived at:

(a) The probability of ☾ ☌ ☉, ☾ ☌ ☾, and ☾ ☌ *Asc.* turning up simultaneously is:

$$\alpha^3 = \left(\frac{1}{24}\right)^3 \sim \frac{1}{10,000}$$

(b) The probability P for the maximal figures in the three batches is:

1. 18 aspects in 180 married pairs, $P = 1 : 1,000$
2. 24 aspects in 220 married pairs, $P = 1 : 10,000$
3. 8 aspects in 83 married pairs, $P = 1 : 50$.

—Editors]

3. FORERUNNERS OF THE IDEA OF SYNCHRONICITY

916   The causality principle asserts that the connection between cause and effect is a necessary one. The synchronicity principle asserts that the terms of a meaningful coincidence are connected by *simultaneity* and *meaning*. So if we assume that the ESP experiments and numerous other observations are established facts, we must conclude that besides the connection between cause and effect there is another factor in nature which expresses itself in the arrangement of events and appears to us as meaning. Although meaning is an anthropomorphic interpretation it nevertheless forms the indispensable criterion of synchronicity. What that factor which appears to us as "meaning" may be in itself we have no possibility of knowing. As an hypothesis, however, it is not quite so impossible as may appear at first sight. We must remember that the rationalistic attitude of the West is not the only possible one and is not all-embracing, but is in many ways a prejudice and a bias that ought perhaps to be corrected. The very much older civilization of the Chinese has always thought differently from us in this respect, and we have to go back to Heraclitus if we want to find something similar in our civilization, at least where philosophy is concerned. Only in astrology, alchemy, and the mantic procedures do we find no differences of principle between our attitude and the Chinese. That is why alchemy developed along parallel lines in East and

485

West and why in both spheres it strove towards the same goal with more or less identical ideas.[1]

917   In Chinese philosophy one of the oldest and most central ideas is that of Tao, which the Jesuits translated as "God." But that is correct only for the Western way of thinking. Other translations, such as "Providence" and the like, are mere makeshifts. Richard Wilhelm brilliantly interprets it as "meaning." [2] The concept of Tao pervades the whole philosophical thought of China. Causality occupies this paramount position with us, but it acquired its importance only in the course of the last two centuries, thanks to the levelling influence of the statistical method on the one hand and the unparalleled success of the natural sciences on the other, which brought the metaphysical view of the world into disrepute.

918   Lao-tzu gives the following description of Tao in his celebrated *Tao Teh Ching:* [3]

> There is something formless yet complete
> That existed before heaven and earth.
>   How still! how empty!
> Dependent on nothing, unchanging,
> All pervading, unfailing.
> One may think of it as the mother of all things under heaven.
> I do not know its name,
> But I call it "Meaning."
> If I had to give it a name, I should call it "The Great."
>   [Ch. XXV.]

919   Tao "covers the ten thousand things like a garment but does not claim to be master over them"(Ch. XXXIV). Lao-tzu describes it as "Nothing," [4] by which he means, says Wilhelm, only its "contrast with the world of reality." Lao-tzu describes its nature as follows:

[1] Cf. my *Psychology and Alchemy*, p. 343, and "The Spirit Mercurius" (Swiss edn., p. 115). Also the doctrine of *chen-yen* in Wei Po-yang ("An Ancient Chinese Treatise on Alchemy Entitled Ts'an T'ung Ch'i,") and in Chuang-tzu.

[2] Wilhelm and Jung, *The Secret of the Golden Flower*, p. 94, and Wilhelm, *Chinesische Lebensweisheit*.

[3] [Quotations from Arthur Waley's *The Way and Its Power*, with occasional slight changes to fit Wilhelm's reading.—TRANS.]

[4] Tao is the contingent, which Andreas Speiser defines as "pure nothing" ("Über die Freiheit").

> We put thirty spokes together and call it a wheel;
> But it is on the space where there is nothing that the utility of
>   the wheel depends.
> We turn clay to make a vessel;
> But it is on the space where there is nothing that the utility of
>   the vessel depends.
> We pierce doors and windows to make a house;
> And it is on these spaces where there is nothing that the utility of
>   the house depends.
> Therefore just as we take advantage of what is, we should rec-
>   ognize the utility of what is not. [Ch. XI.]

920   "Nothing" is evidently "meaning" or "purpose," and it is only called Nothing because it does not appear in the world of the senses, but is only its organizer.[5] Lao-tzu says:

> Because the eye gazes but can catch no glimpse of it,
> It is called elusive.
> Because the ear listens but cannot hear it,
> It is called the rarefied.
> Because the hand feels for it but cannot find it,
> It is called the infinitesimal. . . .
> These are called the shapeless shapes,
> Forms without form,
> Vague semblances.
> Go towards them, and you can see no front;
> Go after them, and you see no rear. [Ch. XIV.]

921   Wilhelm describes it as "a borderline conception lying at the extreme edge of the world of appearances." In it, the opposites "cancel out in non-discrimination," but are still potentially present. "These seeds," he continues, "point to something that corresponds firstly to *the visible,* i.e., something in the nature of an image; secondly to *the audible,* i.e., something in the nature of words; thirdly to *extension in space,* i.e., something with a form. But these three things are not clearly distinguished and definable, they are a non-spatial and non-temporal unity, having no above and below or front and back." As the *Tao Teh Ching* says:

[5] Wilhelm, *Chinesische Lebensweisheit,* p. 15: "The relation between meaning (Tao) and reality cannot be conceived under the category of cause and effect."

Incommensurable, impalpable,
Yet latent in it are forms;
Impalpable, incommensurable,
Yet within it are entities.
Shadowy it is and dim. [Ch. XXI.]

922   Reality, thinks Wilhelm, is conceptually knowable because according to the Chinese view there is in all things a latent "rationality." [6] This is the basic idea underlying meaningful coincidence: it is possible because both sides have the same meaning. Where meaning prevails, order results:

Tao is eternal, but has no name;
The Uncarved Block, though seemingly of small account,
Is greater than anything under heaven.
If the kings and barons would but possess themselves of it,
The ten thousand creatures would flock to do them homage;
Heaven and earth would conspire
To send Sweet Dew;
Without law or compulsion men would dwell in harmony.
[Ch. XXXII.]

Tao never does;
Yet through it all things are done. [Ch. XXXVII.]

Heaven's net is wide;
Coarse are the meshes, yet nothing slips through. [Ch. LXXIII.]

923   Chuang-tzu (a contemporary of Plato's) says of the psychological premises on which Tao is based: "The state in which ego and non-ego are no longer opposed is called the pivot of Tao." [7] It sounds almost like a criticism of our scientific view of the world when he remarks that "Tao is obscured when you fix your eye on little segments of existence only," [8] or "Limitations are not originally grounded in the meaning of life. Originally words had no fixed meanings. Differences only arose through looking at things subjectively." [9] The sages of old, says Chuang-tzu, "took as their starting-point a state when the existence of things had not yet begun. That is indeed the ex-

6 Ibid., p. 19.
7 *Das wahre Buch vom südlichen Blütenland,* trans. by R. Wilhelm, II, 3.
8 Ibid., II, 3.   9 II, 7.

treme limit beyond which you cannot go. The next assumption was that though things existed they had not yet begun to be separated. The next, that though things were separated in a sense, affirmation and negation had not yet begun. When affirmation and negation came into being, Tao faded. After Tao faded, then came one-sided attachments." [10] "Outward hearing should not penetrate further than the ear; the intellect should not seek to lead a separate existence, thus the soul can become empty and absorb the whole world. It is Tao that fills this emptiness." If you have insight, says Chuang-tzu, "you use your inner eye, your inner ear, to pierce to the heart of things, and have no need of intellectual knowledge." [11] This is obviously an allusion to the absolute knowledge of the unconscious, and to the presence in the microcosm of macrocosmic events.

924   This Taoistic view is typical of Chinese thinking. It is, whenever possible, *a thinking in terms of the whole,* a point also brought out by Marcel Granet,[12] the eminent authority on Chinese psychology. This peculiarity can be seen in ordinary conversation with the Chinese: what seems to us a perfectly straightforward, precise question about some detail evokes from the Chinese thinker an unexpectedly elaborate answer, as though one had asked him for a blade of grass and got a whole meadow in return. With us details are important for their own sakes; for the Oriental mind they always complete a total picture. In this totality, as in primitive or in our own medieval, pre-scientific psychology (still very much alive!), are included things which seem to be connected with one another only "by chance," by a coincidence whose meaningfulness appears altogether arbitrary. This is where the theory of *correspondentia* [13] comes in, which was propounded by the natural philosophers of the Middle Ages, and particularly the classical idea of the *sympathy of all things.*[14] Hippocrates says:

10 II, 5.   11 IV, 1.

12 *La Pensée chinoise;* also Lily Abegg, *The Mind of East Asia.* The latter gives an excellent account of the synchronistic mentality of the Chinese.

13 Professor W. Pauli kindly calls my attention to the fact that Niels Bohr used "correspondence" as a mediating term between the representation of the discontinuum (particle) and the continuum (wave). Originally (1913–18) he called it the "principle of correspondence," but later (1927) it was formulated as the "argument of correspondence."   14 "συμπάθεια τῶν ὅλων."

There is one common flow, one common breathing, all things are in sympathy. The whole organism and each one of its parts are working in conjunction for the same purpose . . . the great principle extends to the extremest part, and from the extremest part it returns to the great principle, to the one nature, being and not-being.[15]

The universal principle is found even in the smallest particle, which therefore corresponds to the whole.

925   In this connection there is an interesting idea in Philo (25 B.C.–A.D. 42):

God, being minded to unite in intimate and loving fellowship the beginning and end of created things, made heaven the beginning and man the end, the one the most perfect of imperishable objects of sense, the other the noblest of things earthborn and perishable, being, in very truth, a miniature heaven. He bears about within himself, like holy images, endowments of nature that correspond to the constellations. . . . For since the corruptible and the incorruptible are by nature contrary the one to the other, God assigned the fairest of each sort to the beginning and the end, heaven (as I have said) to the beginning, and man to the end.[16]

926   Here the great principle [17] or beginning, heaven, is infused into man the microcosm, who reflects the star-like natures and thus, as the smallest part and end of the work of Creation, contains the whole.

927   According to Theophrastus (371–288 B.C.) the suprasensuous and the sensuous are joined by a bond of community. This bond cannot be mathematics, so must presumably be God.[18] Similarly in Plotinus the individual souls born of the one World Soul are related to one another by sympathy or antipathy, regardless of distance.[19] Similar views are to be found in Pico della Mirandola:

15 *De alimento*, a tract ascribed to Hippocrates. (Trans. by John Precope in *Hippocrates on Diet and Hygiene*, p. 174, modified.) "Σύρροια μία, συμπνοία μία, πάντα συμπαθέα κατὰ μὲν οὐλομελίην πάντα κατὰ μέρος δὲ τὰ ἐν ἑκάστῳ μέρει μερέα πρὸς τὸ ἔργον . . . ἀρχὴ μεγάλη ἐς ἔσχατον μέρος ἀφικνέεται, ἐξ ἐσχάτου μέρεος εἰς ἀρχὴν μεγάλην ἀφικνέεται, μία φύσις εἶναι καὶ μὴ εἶναι."
16 *De opificio mundi*, 82 (trans. by F. H. Colson and G. H. Whitaker, I, p. 67).
17 "ἀρχὴ μεγάλη"
18 Eduard Zeller, *Die Philosophie der Griechen*, II, part ii, p. 654.
19 *Enneads*, IV, 3, 8 and 4, 32 (in A. C. H. Drews, *Plotin und der Untergang der antiken Weltanschauung*, p. 179).

Firstly there is the unity in things whereby each thing is at one with itself, consists of itself, and coheres with itself. Secondly there is the unity whereby one creature is united with the others and all parts of the world constitute one world. The third and most important (unity) is that whereby the whole universe is one with its Creator, as an army with its commander.[20]

By this threefold unity Pico means a simple unity which, like the Trinity, has three aspects; "a unity distinguished by a three-fold character, yet in such a way as not to depart from the simplicity of unity." [21] For him the world is *one* being, a visible God, in which everything is naturally arranged from the very beginning like the parts of a living organism. The world appears as the *corpus mysticum* of God, just as the Church is the *corpus mysticum* of Christ, or as a well-disciplined army can be called a sword in the hand of the commander. The view that all things are arranged according to God's will is one that leaves little room for causality. Just as in a living body the different parts work in harmony and are meaningfully adjusted to one another, so events in the world stand in a meaningful relationship which cannot be derived from any immanent causality. The reason for this is that in either case the behaviour of the parts depends on a central control which is supraordinate to them.

928　　In his treatise *De hominis dignitate* Pico says: "The Father implanted in man at birth seeds of all kinds and the germs of original life." [22] Just as God is the "copula" of the world, so, within the created world, is man. "Let us make man in our image, who is not a fourth world or anything like a new nature, but is rather the fusion and synthesis of three worlds (the supra-celestial, the celestial, and the sublunary)." [23] In body and spirit

---

20 *Heptaplus*, VI, prooem., in *Opera omnia*, pp. 40f. ("Est enim primum ea in rebus unitas, qua unumquodque sibi est unum sibique constat atque cohaeret. Est ea secundo, per quam altera alteri creatura unitur, et per quam demum omnes mundi partes unus sunt mundus. Tertia atque omnium principalissima est, qua totum universum cum suo opifice quasi exercitus cum suo duce est unum.")
21 "unitas ita ternario distincta, ut ab unitatis simplicitate non discedat."
22 *Opera omnia*, p. 315. ("Nascenti homini omnifaria semina et origenae vitae germina indidit pater.")
23 *Heptaplus*, V, vi, in ibid., p. 38. ("Faciamus hominem ad imaginem nostram, qui non tam quartus est mundus, quasi nova aliqua natura, quam trium (mundus supercoelestis, coelestis, sublunaris) complexus et colligatio."

man is "the little God of the world," the microcosm.[24] Like God, therefore, man is a centre of events, and all things revolve about him.[25] This thought, so utterly strange to the modern mind, dominated man's picture of the world until a few generations ago, when natural science proved man's subordination to nature and his extreme dependence on causes. The idea of a correlation between events and meaning (now assigned exclusively to man) was banished to such a remote and benighted region that the intellect lost track of it altogether. Schopenhauer remembered it somewhat belatedly after it had formed one of the chief items in Leibniz's scientific explanations.

929   By virtue of his microcosmic nature man is a son of the firmament or macrocosm. "I am a star travelling together with you," the initiate confesses in the Mithraic liturgy.[26] In alchemy the microcosmos has the same significance as the *rotundum,* a favourite symbol since the time of Zosimos of Panopolis, which was also known as the Monad.

930   The idea that the inner and outer man together form the whole, the οὐλομελίη of Hippocrates, a microcosm or smallest part wherein the "great principle" is undividedly present, also characterizes the thought of Agrippa von Nettesheim. He says:

It is the unanimous consent of all Platonists, that as in the archetypal World, all things are in all; so also in this corporeal world, all things are in all, albeit in different ways, according to the receptive nature of each. Thus the Elements are not only in these inferiour bodies, but also in the Heavens, in Stars, in Divels, in Angels, and lastly in God, the maker, and archetype of all things.[27]

24 "God . . . placed man in the centre [of the world] after his image and the similitude of forms" ("Deus . . . hominem in medio [mundi] statuit ad imaginem suam et similitudinem formarum").
25 Pico's doctrine is a typical example of the medieval correspondence theory. A good account of cosmological and astrological correspondence is to be found in Alfons Rosenberg, *Zeichen am Himmel: Das Weltbild der Astrologie.*
26 Albrecht Dieterich, *Eine Mithrasliturgie,* p. 9.
27 Henricus Cornelius Agrippa von Nettesheim, *De occulta philosophia Libri tres,* I, viii, p. 12. Trans. by "J. F." as *Three Books of Occult Philosophy* (1651 edn.), p. 20; republished under the editorship of W. F. Whitehead, p. 55. [Quotations from the J. F. translation have been slightly modified.—Trans.] ("Est Platonicorum omnium unanimis sententia quemadmodum i ı archetypo mundo omnia sunt in omnibus, ita etiam in hoc corporeo mundo, omnia in omnibus esse, modis tamen diversis, pro natura videlicet suscipientium: sic et elementa non solum sunt in istis inferioribus, sed in coelis, in stellis, in daemonibus, in angelis, in ipso denique omnium opifice et archetypo.")

The ancients had said: "All things are full of gods." [28] These gods were "divine powers which are diffused in things." [29] Zoroaster had called them "divine allurements," [30] and Synesius "symbolic inticements." [31] This latter interpretation comes very close indeed to the idea of archetypal projections in modern psychology, although from the time of Synesius until quite recently there was no epistemological criticism, let alone the newest form of it, namely psychological criticism. Agrippa shares with the Platonists the view that "there is in the lower beings a certain virtue through which they agree in large measure with the higher," and that as a result the animals are connected with the "divine bodies" (i.e., the stars) and exert an influence on them.[32] Here he quotes Virgil: "I for my part do not believe that they [the rooks] are endowed with divine spirit or with a foreknowledge of things greater than the oracle." [33]

931   Agrippa is thus suggesting that there is an inborn "knowledge" or "perception" in living organisms, an idea which recurs in our own day in Hans Driesch.[34] Whether we like it or not, we find ourselves in this embarrassing position as soon as we begin seriously to reflect on the teleological processes in biology or to investigate the compensatory function of the unconscious, not to speak of trying to explain the phenomenon of synchronicity. Final causes, twist them how we will, postulate a *foreknowledge of some kind*. It is certainly not a knowledge that could be connected with the ego, and hence not a conscious knowledge as we know it, but rather a self-subsistent "unconscious" knowledge which I would prefer to call "absolute knowledge." It is not cognition but, as Leibniz so excellently calls it,

---

28 "Omna plena diis esse."   29 "virtutes divinae in rebus diffusae"
30 "divinae illices"
31 "symbolicae illecebrae." [In J. F. original edn., p. 32; Whitehead edn., p. 69.— Trans.] Agrippa is basing himself here on the Marsilio Ficino translation (*Auctores Platonici*, II, v⁰). In Synesius (*Opuscula*, ed. by Nicolaus Terzaghi, p. 148), the text of Περὶ ἐνυπνίων III B has τὸ θελγόμενον, from θέλγειν, "to excite, charm, enchant."
32 *De occulta philosophia*, I, iv, p. 69. (J. F. edn., p. 117; Whitehead edn., p. 169.) Similarly in Paracelsus.
33 "Haud equidem credo, quia sit divinius illis
    Ingenium aut rerum fato prudentia maior."
            —*Georgics*, I, 415f.
34 *Die "Seele" als elementarer Naturfaktor*, pp. 80, 82.

a "perceiving" which consists—or to be more cautious, seems to consist—of images, of subjectless "simulacra." These postulated images are presumably the same as my archetypes, which can be shown to be formal factors in spontaneous fantasy products. Expressed in modern language, the microcosm which contains "the images of all creation" would be the collective unconscious.[35] By the *spiritus mundi,* the *ligamentum animae et corporis,* the *quinta essentia,*[36] which he shares with the alchemists, Agrippa probably means what we would call the unconscious. The spirit that "penetrates all things," or shapes all things, is the World Soul: "The soul of the world therefore is a certain only thing, filling all things, bestowing all things, binding, and knitting together all things, that it might make one frame of the world. . . ."[37] Those things in which this spirit is particularly powerful therefore have a tendency to "beget their like,"[38] in other words, to produce correspondences or meaningful coincidences.[39] Agrippa gives a long list of these correspondences, based on the numbers 1 to 12.[40] A similar but more alchemical table of correspondences can be found in a treatise of Aegidius de Vadis.[41] Of these I would only mention the *scala unitatis,* because it is especially interesting from the point of

[35] Cf. "On the Nature of the Psyche," pars. 392f.

[36] Agrippa says of this (op. cit., I, xiv, p. 29; J. F. edn., p. 33; Whitehead edn., p. 70): "That which we call the quintessence: because it is not from the four Elements, but a certain fifth thing, having its being above, and besides them." ("Quoddam quintum super illa [elementa] aut praeter illa subsistens.")

[37] II, lvii, p. 203 (J. F. edn., p. 331): "Est itaque anima mundi, vita quaedam unica replens, omnia perfundens, omnia colligens et connectens, ut unam reddat totius mundi machinam. . . ."

[38] Ibid.: ". . . potentius perfectiusque agunt, tum etiam promptius generant sibi simile."

[39] The zoologist A. C. Hardy reaches similar conclusions: "Perhaps our ideas on evolution may be altered if something akin to telepathy—unconscious no doubt—were found to be a factor in moulding the patterns of behaviour among members of a species. If there was such a non-conscious group-behaviour plan, distributed between, and linking, the individuals of the race, we might find ourselves coming back to something like those ideas of subconscious racial memory of Samuel Butler, but on a group rather than an individual basis." "The Scientific Evidence for Extra-Sensory Perception," in *Discovery,* X, 328, quoted by Soal, q.v.

[40] Op. cit., II, iv–xiv.

[41] "Dialogus inter naturam et filium philosophiae." *Theatrum chemicum,* II (1602), p. 123.

view of the history of symbols: "Yod [the first letter of the tetragrammaton, the divine name]—anima mundi—sol—lapis philosophorum—cor—Lucifer."[42] I must content myself with saying that this is an attempt to set up a hierarchy of archetypes, and that tendencies in this direction can be shown to exist in the unconscious.[43]

932   Agrippa was an older contemporary of Theophrastus Paracelsus and is known to have had a considerable influence on him.[44] So it is not surprising if the thinking of Paracelsus proves to be steeped in the idea of correspondence. He says:

> If a man will be a philosopher without going astray, he must lay the foundations of his philosophy by making heaven and earth a microcosm, and not be wrong by a hair's breadth. Therefore he who will lay the foundations of medicine must also guard against the slightest error, and must make from the microcosm the revolution of heaven and earth, so that the philosopher does not find anything in heaven and earth which he does not also find in man, and the physician does not find anything in man which heaven and earth do not have. And these two differ only in outward form, and yet the form on both sides is understood as pertaining to one thing.[45]

The *Paragranum*[46] has some pointed psychological remarks to make about physicians:

> For this reason, [we assume] not four, but one arcanum, which is, however, four-square, like a tower facing the four winds. And as little as a tower may lack a corner, so little may the physician lack one of the parts. . . . At the same [time he] knows how the world is symbolized [by] an egg in its shell, and how a chick with all its substance lies hidden within it. Thus everything in the world and in man must lie hidden in the physician. And just as the hens, by their brooding, transform the world prefigured in the shell into a chick, so Alchemy brings to maturity the philosophical arcana lying in the

---

[42] Cited in Agrippa, op. cit., II, iv, p. 104 (J. F. edn., p. 176).
[43] Cf. Aniela Jaffé, "Bilder und Symbole aus E. T. A. Hoffmann's Märchen 'Der goldene Topf,'" and Marie-Louise von Franz, "Die Passio Perpetuae."
[44] Cf. my "Paracelsus as a Spiritual Phenomenon" (Swiss edn., pp. 47ff.).
[45] *Das Buch Paragranum*, ed. by Franz Strunz, pp. 35f. Much the same in *Labyrinthus medicorum*, in the *Sämtliche Werke*, ed. Sudhoff, XI, pp. 204ff.
[46] Strunz edn., p. 34.

physician. . . . Herein lies the error of those who do not understand the physician aright.[47]

What this means for alchemy I have shown in some detail in my
Psychology and Alchemy.

933   Johannes Kepler thought in much the same way. He says in
his *Tertius interveniens* (1610): [48]

> This [viz., a geometrical principle underlying the physical world] is
> also, according to the doctrine of Aristotle, the strongest tie that
> links the lower world to the heavens and unifies it therewith so that
> all its forms are governed from on high; for in this lower world, that
> is to say the globe of the earth, there is inherent a spiritual nature,
> capable of *Geometria,* which *ex instinctu creatoris, sine ratio-
> cinatione* comes to life and stimulates itself into a use of its forces
> through the geometrical and harmonious combination of the heav-
> enly rays of light. Whether all plants and animals as well as the
> globe of the earth have this faculty in themselves I cannot say. But
> it is not an unbelievable thing. . . . For, in all these things [e.g., in
> the fact that flowers have a definite colour, form, and number of
> petals] there is at work the *instinctus divinus, rationis particeps,* and
> not at all man's own intelligence. That man, too, through his soul
> and its lower faculties, has a like affinity to the heavens as has the
> soil of the earth can be tested and proven in many ways.[49]

934   Concerning the astrological "Character," i.e., astrological
synchronicity, Kepler says:

> This *Character* is received, not into the body, which is much too
> inappropriate for this, but into the soul's own nature, which behaves
> like a point (for which reason it can also be transformed into the
> point of the *confluxus radiorum*). This [nature of the soul] not only
> partakes of their reason (on account of which we human beings are
> called reasonable above other living creatures) but also has another,
> innate reason [enabling it] to apprehend instantaneously, without
> long learning, the *Geometriam* in the *radiis* as well as in the *vocibus,*
> that is to say, in *Musica.*[50]

[47] Similar ideas in Jakob Böhme, *The Signature of All Things,* trans. by John
Ellistone, p. 10: "Man has indeed the forms of all the three worlds in him, for
he is a complete image of God, or of the Being of all beings. . . ." (*Signatura
rerum,* I, 7.)
[48] *Opera omnia,* ed. by C. Frisch, I, pp. 605ff.
[49] Ibid., No. 64.   [50] No. 65.

Thirdly, another marvellous thing is that the nature which receives this *Characterem* also induces a certain correspondence *in constellationibus coelestibus* in its relatives. When a mother is great with child and the natural time of delivery is near, nature selects for the birth a day and hour which correspond, on account of the heavens [scil., from an astrological point of view], to the nativity of the mother's brother or father, and this *non qualitative, sed astronomice et quantitative.*[51]

Fourthly, so well does each nature know not only its *characterem coelestem* but also the celestial *configurationes* and courses of every day that, whenever a planet moves *de praesenti* into its *characteris ascendentem* or *loca praecipua*, especially into the *Natalitia*,[52] it responds to this and is affected and stimulated thereby in various ways.[53]

935   Kepler supposes that the secret of the marvellous correspondence is to be found in the *earth,* because the earth is animated by an *anima telluris,* for whose existence he adduces a number of proofs. Among these are: the constant temperature below the surface of the earth; the peculiar power of the earth-soul to produce metals, minerals, and fossils, namely the *facultas formatrix,* which is similar to that of the womb and can bring forth in the bowels of the earth shapes that are otherwise found only outside —ships, fishes, kings, popes, monks, soldiers, etc.; [54] further the practice of geometry, for it produces the five geometrical bodies and the six-cornered figures in crystals. The *anima telluris* has all this from an original impulse, independent of the reflection and ratiocination of man.[55]

936   The seat of astrological synchronicity is not in the planets but in the earth; [56] not in matter, but in the *anima telluris.*

51 No. 67.

52 ["in die Natalitia" = "into those [positions presiding] at birth," if "in die" is construed as German. The *Gesammelte Werke*, ed. by M. Caspar and F. Hammer, IV, p. 211, has "in die Natalitio" = "in the day of birth," the words "in die" being construed as Latin.—TRANS.]   53 No. 68.

54 See the dreams mentioned below.

55 Kepler, *Opera*, ed. by Frisch, V, p. 254; cf. also II, pp. 270f. and VI, pp. 178f. ". . . formatrix facultas est in visceribus terrae, quae feminae praegnantis more occurrentes foris res humanas veluti eas videret, in fissibilibus lapidibus exprimit, ut militum, monachorum, pontificum, regum et quidquid in ore hominum est. . . ."

56 ". . . quod scl. principatus causae in terra sedeat, non in planetis ipsis." Ibid., II, p. 642.

Therefore every kind of natural or living power in bodies has a certain "divine similitude." [57]

*

937   Such was the intellectual background when Gottfried Wilhelm von Leibniz (1646–1716) appeared with his idea of *pre-established harmony,* that is, an absolute synchronism of psychic and physical events. This theory finally petered out in the concept of "psychophysical parallelism." Leibniz's pre-established harmony and the above-mentioned idea of Schopenhauer's, that the unity of the primal cause produces a simultaneity and interrelationship of events not in themselves causally connected, are at bottom only a repetition of the old peripatetic view, with a modern deterministic colouring in the case of Schopenhauer and a partial replacement of causality by an antecedent order in the case of Leibniz. For him God is the creator of order. He compares soul and body to two synchronized clocks [58] and uses

[57] ". . . ut omne genus naturalium vel animalium facultatum in corporibus Dei quandam gerat similitudinem." Ibid. I am indebted to Dr. Liliane Frey-Rohn and Dr. Marie-Louise von Franz for this reference to Kepler.

[58] G. W. Leibniz, "Second Explanation of the System of the Communication between Substances" (*The Philosophical Works of Leibniz,* trans. by. G. M. Duncan, pp. 90–91): "From the beginning God has made each of these two substances of such a nature that merely by following its own peculiar laws, received with its being, it nevertheless accords with the other, just as if there were a mutual influence or as if God always put his hand thereto in addition to his general co-operation."

As Professor Pauli has kindly pointed out, it is possible that Leibniz took his idea of the synchronized clocks from the Flemish philosopher Arnold Geulincx (1625–99). In his *Metaphysica vera,* Part III, there is a note to "Octava scientia" (p. 195), which says (p. 296): ". . . horologium voluntatis nostrae quadret cum horologio motus in corpore" (the clock of our will is synchronized with the clock of our physical movement). Another note (p. 297) explains: "Voluntas nostra nullum habet influxum, causalitatem, determinationem aut efficaciam quamcunque in motum . . . cum cogitationes nostras bene excutimus, nullam apud nos invenimus ideam seu notionem determinationis. . . . Restat igitur Deus solus primus motor et solus motor, quia et ita motum ordinat atque disponit et ita simul voluntati nostrae licet libere moderatur, ut eodem temporis momento conspiret et voluntas nostra ad projiciendum v.g. pedes inter ambulandum, et simul ipsa illa pedum projectio seu ambulatio." (Our will has no influence, no causative or determinative power, and no effect of any kind on our movement. . . . If we examine our thoughts carefully, we find in ourselves no idea or concept of determination. . . . There remains, therefore, only God as the prime

the same simile to express the relations of the monads or entelechies with one another. Although the monads cannot influence one another directly because, as he says, they "have no windows" [59] (relative abolition of causality!), they are so constituted that they are always in accord without having knowledge of one another. He conceives each monad to be a "little world" or "active indivisible mirror." [60] Not only is man a microcosm enclosing the whole in himself, but every entelechy or monad is in effect such a microcosm. Each "simple substance" has connections "which express all the others." It is "a perpetual living mirror of the universe." [61] He calls the monads of living organisms "souls": "the soul follows its own laws, and the body its own likewise, and they accord by virtue of the harmony pre-established among all substances, since they are all representations of one and the same universe." [62] This clearly expresses the idea that man is a microcosm. "Souls in general," says Leibniz, "are the living mirrors or images of the universe of created things." He distinguishes between minds on the one hand, which are "images of the Divinity . . . capable of knowing the system of the universe, and of imitating something of it by architectonic patterns, each mind being as it were a little

---

mover and only mover, because he arranges and orders movement and freely co-ordinates it with our will, so that our will wishes simultaneously to throw the feet forward into walking, and simultaneously the forward movement and the walking take place.) A note to "Nona scientia" adds (p. 298): "Mens nostra . . . penitus independens est ab illo (scl. corpore) . . . omnia quae de corpore scimus jam praevie quasi ante nostram cognitionem esse in corpore. Ut illa quodam modo nos in corpore legamus, non vero inscribamus, quod Deo proprium est." (Our mind . . . is totally independent of the body . . . everything we know about the body is already in the body, before our thought. So that we can, as it were, read ourselves in our body, but not imprint ourselves on it. Only God can do that.) This idea anticipates Leibniz' clock comparison.

[59] *Monadology*, § 7: "Monads have no windows, by which anything could come in or go out. . . . Thus neither substance nor accident can enter a monad from without."

[60] Rejoinder to the remarks in Bayle's Dictionary, from the *Kleinere philosophische Schriften*, XI, p. 105.

[61] *Monadology*, § 56 (Morris edn., p. 12): "Now this connection or adaptation of all created things with each, and of each with all the rest, means that each simple substance has relations which express all the others, and that consequently it is a perpetual living mirror of the universe." [62] Ibid., § 78 (p. 17).

divinity in its own department," [63] and bodies on the other hand, which "act according to the laws of efficient causes by motions," while the souls act "according to the laws of final causes by appetitions, ends, and means." [64] In the monad or soul alterations take place whose cause is the "appetition." [65] "The passing state, which involves and represents a plurality within the unity or simple substance, is nothing other than what is called perception," says Leibniz.[66] Perception is the "inner state of the monad representing external things," and it must be distinguished from conscious apperception. "For perception is unconscious." [67] Herein lay the great mistake of the Cartesians, "that they took no account of perceptions which are not apperceived." [68] The perceptive faculty of the monad corresponds to the *knowledge*, and its appetitive faculty to the *will*, that is in God.[69]

938   It is clear from these quotations that besides the causal connection Leibniz postulates a complete pre-established parallelism of events both inside and outside the monad. The synchronicity principle thus becomes the absolute rule in all cases where an inner event occurs simultaneously with an outside one. As against this, however, it must be borne in mind that the synchronistic phenomena which can be verified empirically, far from constituting a rule, are so exceptional that most people doubt their existence. They certainly occur much more frequently in reality than one thinks or can prove, but we still do not know whether they occur so frequently and so regularly in any field of experience that we could speak of them as conforming to law.[70] We only know that there must be an under-

[63] § 83 (p. 18); cf. *Theodicy*, § 147 (trans. by E. M. Huggard, pp. 215f.).
[64] *Monadology*, § 79 (Morris edn., p. 17).   [65] Ibid., § 15 (p. 5).
[66] § 14 (pp. 4f.).
[67] *Principles of Nature and of Grace, Founded on Reason*, § 4 (Morris edn., p. 22).
[68] *Monadology*, § 14 (p. 5). Cf. also Dr. Marie-Louise von Franz's paper on the dream of Descartes in *Zeitlose Dokumente der Seele*.
[69] *Monadology*, § 48 (p. 11); *Theodicy*, § 149.
[70] I must again stress the possibility that the relation between body and soul may yet be understood as a synchronistic one. Should this conjecture ever be proved, my present view that synchronicity is a relatively rare phenomenon would have to be corrected. Cf. C. A. Meier's observations in *Zeitgemässe Probleme der Traumforschung*, p. 22.

lying principle which might possibly explain all such (related) phenomena.

939   The primitive as well as the classical and medieval views of nature postulate the existence of some such principle alongside causality. Even in Leibniz, causality is neither the only view nor the predominant one. Then, in the course of the eighteenth century, it became the exclusive principle of natural science. With the rise of the physical sciences in the nineteenth century the correspondence theory vanished completely from the surface, and the magical world of earlier ages seemed to have disappeared once and for all until, towards the end of the century, the founders of the Society for Psychical Research indirectly opened up the whole question again through their investigation of telepathic phenomena.

940   The medieval attitude of mind I have described above underlies all the magical and mantic procedures which have played an important part in man's life since the remotest times. The medieval mind would regard Rhine's laboratory-arranged experiments as magical performances, whose effect for this reason would not seem so very astonishing. It was interpreted as a "transmission of energy," which is still commonly the case today, although, as I have said, it is not possible to form any empirically verifiable conception of the transmitting medium.

941   I need hardly point out that for the primitive mind synchronicity is a self-evident fact; consequently at this stage there is no such thing as chance. No accident, no illness, no death is ever fortuitous or attributable to "natural" causes. Everything is somehow due to magical influence. The crocodile that catches a man while he is bathing has been sent by a magician; illness is caused by some spirit or other; the snake that was seen by the grave of somebody's mother is obviously her soul; etc. On the primitive level, of course, synchronicity does not appear as an idea by itself, but as "magical" causality. This is an early form of our classical idea of causality, while the development of Chinese philosophy produced from the significance of the magical the "concept" of Tao, of meaningful coincidence, but no causality-based science.

942   Synchronicity postulates a meaning which is *a priori* in relation to human consciousness and apparently exists outside

man.[71] Such an assumption is found above all in the philosophy of Plato, which takes for granted the existence of transcendental images or models of empirical things, the εἴδη (forms, species), whose reflections (εἴδωλα) we see in the phenomenal world. This assumption not only presented no difficulty to earlier centuries but was on the contrary perfectly self-evident. The idea of an *a priori* meaning may also be found in the older mathematics, as in the mathematician Jacobi's paraphrase of Schiller's poem "Archimedes and His Pupil." He praises the calculation of the orbit of Uranus and closes with the lines:

> What you behold in the cosmos is only the light of God's glory;
> In the Olympian host Number eternally reigns.

943   The great mathematician Gauss is the putative author of the saying: "God arithmetizes." [72]

944   The idea of synchronicity and of a self-subsistent meaning, which forms the basis of classical Chinese thinking and of the naïve views of the Middle Ages, seems to us an archaic assumption that ought at all costs to be avoided. Though the West has done everything possible to discard this antiquated hypothesis, it has not quite succeeded. Certain mantic procedures seem to have died out, but astrology, which in our own day has attained an eminence never known before, remains very much alive. Nor has the determinism of a scientific epoch been able to extinguish altogether the persuasive power of the synchronicity principle. For in the last resort it is not so much a question of superstition as of a truth which remained hidden for so long only because it had less to do with the physical side of events than with their psychic aspects. It was modern psychology and parapsychology which proved that causality does not explain a certain class of

---

[71] In view of the possibility that synchronicity is not only a psychophysical phenomenon but might also occur without the participation of the human psyche, I should like to point out that in this case we should have to speak not of *meaning* but of equivalence or conformity.

[72] "ὁ θεὸς ἀριθμητίζει." But in a letter of 1830 Gauss says: "We must in all humility admit that if number is *merely* a product of our mind, space has a reality outside our mind." (Leopold Kronecker, *Über den Zahlenbegriff*, in his *Werke*, III, p. 252.) Hermann Weyl likewise takes number as a product of reason. ("Wissenschaft als symbolische Konstruktion des Menschen," p. 375). Markus Fierz, on the other hand, inclines more to the Platonic idea. ("Zur physikalischen Erkenntnis," p. 434.)

events and that in this case we have to consider a formal factor, namely synchronicity, as a principle of explanation.

945   For those who are interested in psychology I should like to mention here that the peculiar idea of a self-subsistent meaning is suggested in dreams. Once when this idea was being discussed in my circle somebody remarked: "The geometrical square does not occur in nature except in crystals." A lady who had been present had the following dream that night: *In the garden there was a large sandpit in which layers of rubbish had been deposited. In one of these layers she discovered thin, slaty plates of green serpentine. One of them had black squares on it, arranged concentrically. The black was not painted on, but was ingrained in the stone, like the markings in an agate. Similar marks were found on two or three other plates, which Mr. A (a slight acquaintance) then took away from her.*[73] Another dream-motif of the same kind is the following: *The dreamer was in a wild mountain region where he found contiguous layers of triassic rock. He loosened the slabs and discovered to his boundless astonishment that they had human heads on them in low relief.* This dream was repeated several times at long intervals.[74] Another time the dreamer *was travelling through the Siberian tundra and found an animal he had long been looking for. It was a more than lifesize cock, made of what looked like thin, colourless glass. But it was alive and had just sprung by chance from a microscopic unicellular organism which had the power to turn into all sorts of animals (not otherwise found in the tundra) or even into objects of human use, of whatever size. The next moment each of these chance forms vanished without trace.* Here is another dream of the same type: *The dreamer was walking in a wooded mountain region. At the top of a steep slope he came to a ridge of rock honeycombed with holes, and there he found a little brown man of the same colour as the iron oxide with which the rock was coated.*[75] *The little man was busily*

---

[73] According to the rules of dream interpretation this Mr. A would represent the animus, who, as a personification of the unconscious, takes back the designs because the conscious mind has no use for them and regards them only as *lusus naturae.*

[74] The recurrence of the dream expresses the persistent attempt of the unconscious to bring the dream content before the conscious mind.

[75] An Anthroparion or "metallic man."

*engaged in hollowing out a cave, at the back of which a cluster
of columns could be seen in the living rock. On the top of each
column was a dark brown human head with large eyes, carved
with great care out of some very hard stone, like lignite. The
little man freed this formation from the amorphous conglomerate surrounding it. The dreamer could hardly believe his eyes
at first, but then had to admit that the columns were continued
far back into the living rock and must therefore have come into
existence without the help of man. He reflected that the rock
was at least half a million years old and that the artefact could
not possibly have been made by human hands.[76]*

946   These dreams seem to point to the presence of a formal factor in nature. They describe not just a *lusus naturae,* but the
meaningful coincidence of an absolutely natural product with
a human idea apparently independent of it. This is what the
dreams are obviously saying,[77] and what they are trying to bring
nearer to consciousness through repetition.

[76] Cf. Kepler's ideas quoted above.

[77] Those who find the dreams unintelligible will probably suspect them of harbouring quite a different meaning which is more in accord with their preconceived opinions. One can indulge in wishful thinking about dreams just as one
can about anything else. For my part I prefer to keep as close to the dream
statement as possible, and to try to formulate it in accordance with its manifest
meaning. If it proves impossible to relate this meaning to the conscious situation
of the dreamer, then I frankly admit that I do not understand the dream, but I
take good care not to juggle it into line with some preconceived theory.

4. CONCLUSION

947   I do not regard these statements as in any way a final proof of my views, but simply as a conclusion from empirical premises which I would like to submit to the consideration of my reader. From the material before us I can derive no other hypothesis that would adequately explain the facts (including the ESP experiments). I am only too conscious that synchronicity is a highly abstract and "irrepresentable" quantity. It ascribes to the moving body a certain psychoid property which, like space, time, and causality, forms a criterion of its behaviour. We must completely give up the idea of the psyche's being somehow connected with the brain, and remember instead the "meaning-ful" or "intelligent" behaviour of the lower organisms, which are without a brain. Here we find ourselves much closer to the formal factor which, as I have said, has nothing to do with brain activity.

948   If that is so, then we must ask ourselves whether the relation of soul and body can be considered from this angle, that is to say whether the co-ordination of psychic and physical processes in a living organism can be understood as a synchronistic phenomenon rather than as a causal relation. Both Geulincx and Leibniz regarded the co-ordination of the psychic and the physical as an act of God, of some principle standing outside empirical nature. The assumption of a causal relation between psyche

and physis leads on the other hand to conclusions which it is difficult to square with experience: either there are physical processes which cause psychic happenings, or there is a pre-existent psyche which organizes matter. In the first case it is hard to see how chemical processes can ever produce psychic processes, and in the second case one wonders how an immaterial psyche could ever set matter in motion. It is not necessary to think of Leibniz's pre-established harmony or anything of that kind, which would have to be absolute and would manifest itself in a universal correspondence and sympathy, rather like the meaningful coincidence of time-points lying on the same degree of latitude in Schopenhauer. The synchronicity principle possesses properties that may help to clear up the body-soul problem. Above all it is the fact of causeless order, or rather, of meaningful orderedness, that may throw light on psychophysical parallelism. The "absolute knowledge" which is characteristic of synchronistic phenomena, a knowledge not mediated by the sense organs, supports the hypothesis of a self-subsistent meaning, or even expresses its existence. Such a form of existence can only be transcendental, since, as the knowledge of future or spatially distant events shows, it is contained in a psychically relative space and time, that is to say in an irrepresentable space-time continuum.

949   It may be worth our while to examine more closely, from this point of view, certain experiences which seem to indicate the existence of psychic processes in what are commonly held to be unconscious states. Here I am thinking chiefly of the remarkable observations made during deep syncopes resulting from acute brain injuries. Contrary to all expectations, a severe head injury is not always followed by a corresponding loss of consciousness. To the observer, the wounded man seems apathetic, "in a trance," and not conscious of anything. Subjectively, however, consciousness is by no means extinguished. Sensory communication with the outside world is in a large measure restricted, but is not always completely cut off, although the noise of battle, for instance, may suddenly give way to a "solemn" silence. In this state there is sometimes a very distinct and impressive sensation or hallucination of levitation, the wounded man seeming to rise into the air in the same position he was in at the moment he was wounded. If he was wounded standing up, he rises in a

standing position, if lying down, he rises in a lying position, if sitting, he rises in a sitting position. Occasionally his surroundings seem to rise with him—for instance the whole bunker in which he finds himself at the moment. The height of the levitation may be anything from eighteen inches to several yards. All feeling of weight is lost. In a few cases the wounded think they are making swimming movements with their arms. If there is any perception of their surroundings at all, it seems to be mostly imaginary, i.e., composed of memory images. During levitation the mood is predominantly euphoric. " 'Buoyant, solemn, heavenly, serene, relaxed, blissful, expectant, exciting' are the words used to describe it. . . . There are various kinds of 'ascension experiences.' "[1] Jantz and Beringer rightly point out that the wounded can be roused from their syncope by remarkably small stimuli, for instance if they are addressed by name or touched, whereas the most terrific bombardment has no effect.

950   Much the same thing can be observed in deep comas resulting from other causes. I would like to give an example from my own medical experience. A woman patient, whose reliability and truthfulness I have no reason to doubt, told me that her first birth was very difficult. After thirty hours of fruitless labour the doctor considered that a forceps delivery was indicated. This was carried out under light narcosis. She was badly torn and suffered great loss of blood. When the doctor, her mother, and her husband had gone, and everything was cleared up, the nurse wanted to eat, and the patient saw her turn round at the door and ask, "Do you want anything before I go to supper?" She tried to answer, but couldn't. She had the feeling that she was sinking through the bed into a bottomless void. She saw the nurse hurry to the bedside and seize her hand in order to take her pulse. From the way she moved her fingers to and fro the patient thought it must be almost imperceptible. Yet she herself felt quite all right, and was slightly amused at the nurse's alarm. She was not in the least frightened. That was the last she could remember for a long time. The next thing she was aware of was that, without feeling her body and its position, she was *looking down* from a point in the ceiling and could see everything going on in the room below her: she saw herself lying in the bed,

[1] Hubert Jantz and Kurt Beringer, "Das Syndrom des Schwebeerlebnisses unmittelbar nach Kopfverletzungen," 202.

deadly pale, with closed eyes. Beside her stood the nurse. The doctor paced up and down the room excitedly, and it seemed to her that he had lost his head and didn't know what to do. Her relatives crowded to the door. Her mother and her husband came in and looked at her with frightened faces. She told herself it was too stupid of them to think she was going to die, for she would certainly come round again. All this time she knew that behind her was a glorious, park-like landscape shining in the brightest colours, and in particular an emerald green meadow with short grass, which sloped gently upwards beyond a wrought-iron gate leading into the park. It was spring, and little gay flowers such as she had never seen before were scattered about in the grass. The whole demesne sparkled in the sunlight, and all the colours were of an indescribable splendour. The sloping meadow was flanked on both sides by dark green trees. It gave her the impression of a clearing in the forest, never yet trodden by the foot of man. "I knew that this was the entrance to another world, and that if I turned round to gaze at the picture directly, I should feel tempted to go in at the gate, and thus step out of life." She did not actually *see* this landscape, as her back was turned to it, but she *knew* it was there. She felt there was nothing to stop her from entering in through the gate. She only knew that she would turn back to her body and would not die. That was why she found the agitation of the doctor and the distress of her relatives stupid and out of place.

951 The next thing that happened was that she awoke from her coma and saw the nurse bending over her in bed. She was told that she had been unconscious for about half an hour. The next day, some fifteen hours later, when she felt a little stronger, she made a remark to the nurse about the incompetent and "hysterical" behaviour of the doctor during her coma. The nurse energetically denied this criticism in the belief that the patient had been completely unconscious at the time and could therefore have known nothing of the scene. Only when she described in full detail what had happened during the coma was the nurse obliged to admit that the patient had perceived the events exactly as they happened in reality.

952 One might conjecture that this was simply a psychogenic twilight state in which a split-off part of consciousness still continued to function. The patient, however, had never been hys-

terical and had suffered a genuine heart collapse followed by syncope due to cerebral anaemia, as all the outward and evidently alarming symptoms indicated. She really was in a coma and ought to have had a complete psychic black-out and been altogether incapable of clear observation and sound judgment. The remarkable thing was that it was not an immediate perception of the situation through indirect or unconscious observation, but she saw the whole situation from *above,* as though "her eyes were in the ceiling," as she put it.

953   Indeed, it is not easy to explain how such unusually intense psychic processes can take place, and be remembered, in a state of severe collapse, and how the patient could observe actual events in concrete detail with closed eyes. One would expect such obvious cerebral anaemia to militate against or prevent the occurrence of highly complex psychic processes of that kind.

954   Sir Auckland Geddes presented a very similar case before the Royal Society of Medicine on February 26, 1927, though here the ESP went very much further. During a state of collapse the patient noted the splitting off of an integral consciousness from his bodily consciousness, the latter gradually resolving itself into its organ components. The other consciousness possessed verifiable ESP.[2]

955   These experiences seem to show that in swoon states, where by all human standards there is every guarantee that conscious activity and sense perception are suspended, consciousness, reproducible ideas, acts of judgment, and perceptions can still continue to exist. The accompanying feeling of levitation, alteration of the angle of vision, and extinction of hearing and of coenaesthetic perceptions indicate a shift in the localization of consciousness, a sort of separation from the body, or from the cerebral cortex or cerebrum which is conjectured to be the seat of conscious phenomena. If we are correct in this assumption, then we must ask ourselves whether there is some other nervous substrate in us, apart from the cerebrum, that can think and perceive, or whether the psychic processes that go on in us during loss of consciousness are synchronistic phenomena, i.e., events which have no causal connection with organic processes. This last possibility cannot be rejected out of hand in view of

[2] Cf. G. N. M. Tyrrell's report in *The Personality of Man,* pp. 197f. There is another case of this kind on pp. 199f.

the existence of ESP, i.e., of perceptions independent of space and time which cannot be explained as processes in the biological substrate. Where sense perceptions are impossible from the start, it can hardly be a question of anything but synchronicity. But where there are spatial and temporal conditions which would make perception and apperception possible in principle, and only the activity of consciousness, or the cortical function, is extinguished, and where, as in our example, a conscious phenomenon like perception and judgment nevertheless occurs, then the question of a nervous substrate might well be considered. It is well nigh axiomatic that conscious processes are tied to the cerebrum, and that the lower centres contain nothing but chains of reflexes which in themselves are unconscious. This is particularly true of the sympathetic system. Hence the insects, which have no cerebrospinal nervous system at all, but only a double chain of ganglia, are regarded as reflex automata.

956 This view has recently been challenged by the researches which von Frisch, of Graz, made into the life of bees. It turns out that bees not only tell their comrades, by means of a peculiar sort of dance, that they have found a feeding-place, but that they also indicate its direction and distance, thus enabling the beginners to fly to it directly.[3] This kind of message is no different in principle from information conveyed by a human being. In the latter case we would certainly regard such behaviour as a conscious and intentional act and can hardly imagine how anyone could prove in a court of law that it had taken place unconsciously. We could, at a pinch, admit on the basis of psychiatric experiences that objective information can in exceptional cases be communicated in a twilight state, but would expressly deny that communications of this kind are normally unconscious. Nevertheless it would be possible to suppose that in bees the process is unconscious. But that would not help to solve the problem, because we are still faced with the fact that the ganglionic system apparently achieves exactly the same result as our cerebral cortex. Nor is there any proof that bees are unconscious.

957 Thus we are driven to the conclusion that a nervous substrate like the sympathetic system, which is absolutely different

3 Karl von Frisch, *The Dancing Bees,* trans. by Dora Ilse, pp. 112ff.

from the cerebrospinal system in point of origin and function, can evidently produce thoughts and perceptions just as easily as the latter. What then are we to think of the sympathetic system in vertebrates? Can it also produce or transmit specifically psychic processes? Von Frisch's observations prove the existence of transcerebral thought and perception. One must bear this possibility in mind if we want to account for the existence of some form of consciousness during an unconscious coma. During a coma the sympathetic system is not paralysed and could therefore be considered as a possible carrier of psychic functions. If that is so, then one must ask whether the normal state of unconsciousness in sleep, and the potentially conscious dreams it contains, can be regarded in the same light—whether, in other words, dreams are produced not so much by the activity of the sleeping cortex, as by the unsleeping sympathetic system, and are therefore of a transcerebral nature.

958   Outside the realm of psychophysical parallelism, which we cannot at present pretend to understand, synchronicity is not a phenomenon whose regularity it is at all easy to demonstrate. One is as much impressed by the disharmony of things as one is surprised by their occasional harmony. In contrast to the idea of a pre-established harmony, the synchronistic factor merely stipulates the existence of an intellectually necessary principle which could be added as a fourth to the recognized triad of space, time, and causality. These factors are necessary but not absolute—most psychic contents are non-spatial, time and causality are psychically relative—and in the same way the synchronistic factor proves to be only conditionally valid. But unlike causality, which reigns despotically over the whole picture of the macrophysical world and whose universal rule is shattered only in certain lower orders of magnitude, synchronicity is a phenomenon that seems to be primarily connected with psychic conditions, that is to say with processes in the unconscious. Synchronistic phenomena are found to occur—experimentally— with some degree of regularity and frequency in the intuitive, "magical" procedures, where they are subjectively convincing but are extremely difficult to verify objectively and cannot be statistically evaluated (at least at present).

959   On the organic level it might be possible to regard biological morphogenesis in the light of the synchronistic factor. Professor

A. M. Dalcq (of Brussels) understands form, despite its tie with matter, as a "continuity that is supraordinate to the living organism." [4] Sir James Jeans reckons radioactive decay among the causeless events which, as we have seen, include synchronicity. He says: "Radioactive break-up appeared to be an effect without a cause, and suggested that the ultimate laws of nature were not even causal." [5] This highly paradoxical formula, coming from the pen of a physicist, is typical of the intellectual dilemma with which radioactive decay confronts us. It, or rather the phenomenon of "half-life," appears as an instance of acausal orderedness—a conception which also includes synchronicity and to which I shall revert below.

960   Synchronicity is not a philosophical view but an empirical concept which postulates an intellectually necessary principle. This cannot be called either materialism or metaphysics. No serious investigator would assert that the nature of what is observed to exist, and of that which observes, namely the psyche, are known and recognized quantities. If the latest conclusions of science are coming nearer and nearer to a unitary idea of being, characterized by space and time on the one hand and by causality and synchronicity on the other, that has nothing to do with materialism. Rather it seems to show that there is some possibility of getting rid of the incommensurability between the observed and the observer. The result, in that case, would be a unity of being which would have to be expressed in terms of a new conceptual language—a "neutral language," as W. Pauli once called it.

961   Space, time, and causality, the triad of classical physics, would then be supplemented by the synchronicity factor and become a tetrad, a *quaternio* which makes possible a whole judgment:

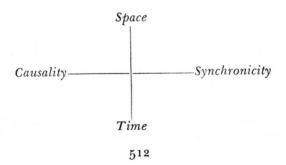

962   Here synchronicity is to the three other principles as the one-dimensionality of time [6] is to the three-dimensionality of space, or as the recalcitrant "Fourth" in the *Timaeus*, which, Plato says, can only be added "by force" to the other three.[7] Just as the introduction of time as the fourth dimension in modern physics postulates an irrepresentable space-time continuum, so the idea of synchronicity with its inherent quality of meaning produces a picture of the world so irrepresentable as to be completely baffling.[8] The advantage, however, of adding this concept is that it makes possible a view which includes the psychoid factor in our description and knowledge of nature—that is, an *a priori* meaning or "equivalence." The problem that runs like a red thread through the speculations of alchemists for fifteen hundred years thus repeats and solves itself, the so-called axiom of Maria the Jewess (or Copt): "Out of the Third comes the One as the Fourth." [9] This cryptic observation confirms what I said above, that in principle new points of view are not as a rule discovered in territory that is already known, but in out-of-the-way places that may even be avoided because of their bad name. The old dream of the alchemists, the transmutation of chemical elements, this much-derided idea, has become a reality in our own day, and its symbolism, which was no less an object of ridicule, has turned out to be a veritable gold-mine for the psychology of the unconscious. Their dilemma of three and four, which began with the story that serves as a setting for the *Timaeus* and extends all the way to the Cabiri scene in *Faust*, Part II, is recognized by a sixteenth-century alchemist, Gerhard Dorn, as the decision between the Christian Trinity and the *serpens quadricornutus*, the four-horned serpent who is the Devil. As though in anticipation of things to come he anathematizes the pagan quaternity which was ordinarily so beloved of the alche-

---

[4] "La Morphogénèse dans la cadre de la biologie générale." Cf. above, the similar conclusion reached by the zoologist A. C. Hardy.

[5] *Physics and Philosophy*, p. 127; cf. also p. 151.

[6] I am not counting P. A. M. Dirac's multi-dimensionality of time.

[7] Cf. my "Psychological Approach to the Dogma of the Trinity."

[8] Sir James Jeans (*Physics and Philosophy*, p. 215) thinks it possible "that the springs of events in this substratum include our own mental activities, so that the future course of events may depend in part on these mental activities." The causalism of this argument does not seem to me altogether tenable.

[9] "ἐκ τοῦ τρίτου τὸ ἓν τέταρτον." Cf. *Psychology and Alchemy*, p. 23.

mists, on the ground that it arose from the binarius (the number 2) and is thus something material, feminine, and devilish.[10] Dr. von Franz has demonstrated this emergence of trinitarian thinking in the *Parable* of Bernard of Treviso, in Khunrath's *Amphitheatrum,* in Michael Maier, and in the anonymous author of the *Aquarium sapientum.*[11] W. Pauli calls attention to the polemical writings of Kepler and of Robert Fludd, in which Fludd's correspondence theory was the loser and had to make room for Kepler's theory of three principles.[12] The decision in favour of freedom, which in certain respects ran counter to the alchemical tradition, was followed by a scientific epoch that knew nothing of correspondence and clung with passionate insistence to a triadic view of the world—a continuation of the trinitarian type of thinking—which described and explained everything in terms of space, time, and causality.

963   The revolution brought about by the discovery of radioactivity has considerably modified the classical views of physics. So great is the change of standpoint that we have to revise the classical schema I made use of above. As I was able, thanks to the friendly interest which Professor Pauli evinced in my work, to discuss these questions of principle with a professional physicist who could at the same time appreciate my psychological arguments, I am in a position to put forward a suggestion that takes modern physics into account. Pauli suggested replacing the opposition of space and time in the classical schema by (conservation of) energy and the space-time continuum. This suggestion led me to a closer definition of the other pair of opposites—causality and synchronicity—with a view to establishing some kind of connection between these two heterogeneous concepts. We finally agreed on the following *quaternio:*

Indestructible Energy

Constant Connection through Effect (Causality)	*Inconstant Connection through Contingence, Equivalence, or "Meaning" (Synchronicity)*

Space-Time Continuum

[10] "De tenebris contra naturam," in *Theatrum chemicum,* I (1602), pp. 518ff.
[11] Marie-Louise von Franz, "Die Parabel von der Fontina des Grafen von Tarvis."
[12] See Pauli's contribution in *The Interpretation of Nature and the Psyche.*

964   This schema satisfies on the one hand the postulates of modern physics, and on the other hand those of psychology. The psychological point of view needs clarifying. A causalistic explanation of synchronicity seems out of the question for the reasons given above. It consists essentially of "chance" equivalences. Their *tertium comparationis* rests on the psychoid factors I call archetypes. These are *indefinite,* that is to say they can be known and determined only approximately. Although associated with causal processes, or "carried" by them, they continually go beyond their frame of reference, an infringement to which I would give the name "transgressiveness," because the archetypes are not found exclusively in the psychic sphere, but can occur just as much in circumstances that are not psychic (equivalence of an outward physical process with a psychic one). Archetypal equivalences are *contingent* to causal determination, that is to say there exist between them and the causal processes no relations that conform to law. They seem, therefore, to represent a special instance of randomness or chance, or of that "random state" which "runs through time in a way that fully conforms to law," as Andreas Speiser says.[13] It is an initial state which is "not governed by mechanistic law" but is the precondition of law, the chance substrate on which law is based. If we consider synchronicity or the archetypes as the contingent, then the latter takes on the specific aspect of a modality that has the functional significance of a world-constituting factor. The archetype represents *psychic probability,* portraying ordinary instinctual events in the form of *types.* It is a special psychic instance of probability in general, which "is made up of the laws of chance and lays down rules for nature just as the laws of mechanics do." [14] We must agree with Speiser that although in the realm of pure intellect the contingent is "a formless substance," it reveals itself to psychic introspection—so far as inward perception can grasp it at all—as an image, or rather a type which underlies not only the psychic equivalences but, remarkably enough, the psychophysical equivalences too.

965   It is difficult to divest conceptual language of its causalistic colouring. Thus the word "underlying," despite its causalistic connotation, does not refer to anything causal, but simply to an

13 *Über die Freiheit,* 4f.   14 Ibid., p. 6.

existing quality, an irreducible contingency which is "Just-So." The meaningful coincidence or equivalence of a psychic and a physical state that have no causal relationship to one another means, in general terms, that it is a modality without a cause, an "acausal orderedness." The question now arises whether our definition of synchronicity with reference to the equivalence of psychic and physical processes is capable of expansion, or rather, requires expansion. This requirement seems to force itself on us when we consider the above, wider conception of synchronicity as an "acausal orderedness." Into this category come all "acts of creation," *a priori* factors such as the properties of natural numbers, the discontinuities of modern physics, etc. Consequently we would have to include constant and experimentally reproducible phenomena within the scope of our expanded concept, though this does not seem to accord with the nature of the phenomena included in synchronicity narrowly understood. The latter are mostly individual cases which cannot be repeated experimentally. This is not of course altogether true, as Rhine's experiments show and numerous other experiences with clairvoyant individuals. These facts prove that even in individual cases which have no common denominator and rank as "curiosities" there are certain regularities and therefore constant factors, from which we must conclude that our narrower conception of synchronicity is probably too narrow and really needs expanding. I incline in fact to the view that synchronicity in the narrow sense is only a particular instance of general acausal orderedness—that, namely, of the equivalence of psychic and physical processes where the observer is in the fortunate position of being able to recognize the *tertium comparationis*. But as soon as he perceives the archetypal background he is tempted to trace the mutual assimilation of independent psychic and physical processes back to a (causal) effect of the archetype, and thus to overlook the fact that they are merely contingent. This danger is avoided if one regards synchronicity as a special instance of general acausal orderedness. In this way we also avoid multiplying our principles of explanation illegitimately, for the archetype *is* the introspectively recognizable form of *a priori* psychic orderedness. If an external synchronistic process now associates itself with it, it falls into the same basic pattern—in other words, it too is "ordered." This form of orderedness differs from that of the properties of natural numbers or the discontinuities of physics in that the latter have existed from eternity and occur regularly, whereas the forms of psychic orderedness are *acts of creation in time*. That, incidentally, is precisely why I have stressed the element of time as being characteristic of these phenomena and called them *synchronistic*.

966   The modern discovery of discontinuity (e.g., the orderedness of energy quanta, of radium decay, etc.) has put an end to the sovereign rule of causality and thus to the triad of principles. The territory lost by the latter belonged earlier to the sphere of correspondence and sympathy, concepts which reached their greatest development in Leibniz's idea of pre-established harmony. Schopenhauer knew far too little about the empirical foundations of correspondence to realize how hopeless his causalistic attempt at explanation was. Today, thanks to the ESP experiments, we have a great deal of empirical material at our disposal. We can form some conception of its reliability when we learn from G. E. Hutchinson [15] that the ESP experiments conducted by S. G. Soal and K. M. Goldney have a probability of $1 : 10^{35}$, this being equivalent to the number of molecules in 250,000 tons of water. There are relatively few experiments in the field of the natural sciences whose results come anywhere near so high a degree of certainty. The exaggerated scepticism in regard to ESP is really without a shred of justification. The main reason for it is simply the ignorance which nowadays, unfortunately, seems to be the inevitable accompaniment of specialism and screens off the necessarily limited horizon of specialist studies from all higher and wider points of view in the most undesirable way. How often have we not found that the so-called "superstitions" contain a core of truth that is well worth knowing! It may well be that the originally magical significance of the word "wish," which is still preserved in "wishing-rod" (divining rod, or magic wand) and expresses not just wishing in the sense of desire but a magical action,[16] and

15 S. G. Soal, "Science and Telepathy," p. 6.
16 Jacob Grimm, *Teutonic Mythology*, trans. by J. S. Stallybrass, I, p. 137. Wish-objects are magic implements forged by dwarfs, such as Odin's spear Gungnir, Thor's hammer Mjollnir, and Freya's sword (II, p. 870). Wishing is "gotes kraft" (divine power). "Got hât an sie den wunsch geleit und der wünschelruoten hort"

the traditional belief in the efficacy of prayer, are both based on the experience of concomitant synchronistic phenomena.

967   Synchronicity is no more baffling or mysterious than the discontinuities of physics. It is only the ingrained belief in the sovereign power of causality that creates intellectual difficulties and makes it appear unthinkable that causeless events exist or could ever occur. But if they do, then we must regard them as *creative acts,* as the continuous creation [17] of a pattern that exists from all eternity, repeats itself sporadically, and is not derivable from any known antecedents. We must of course guard against thinking of every event whose cause is unknown as "causeless." This, as I have already stressed, is admissible only when a cause is not even thinkable. But thinkability is itself an idea that needs the most rigorous criticism. Had the atom [18] corresponded to the original philosophical conception of it, its fissionability would be unthinkable. But once it proves to be a measurable quantity, its non-fissionability becomes unthinkable. Meaningful coincidences are thinkable as pure chance. But the more they multiply and the greater and more exact the

---

(God has bestowed the wish on her and the treasure of [*or:* found by] the wishing-rod). "Beschoenen mit wunsches gewalte" (to make beautiful with the power of the wish) (IV, p. 1329). "Wish" = Sanskrit *manoratha,* literally, "car of the mind" or of the psyche, i.e., wish, desire, fancy. (A. A. Macdonell, *A Practical Sanskrit Dictionary,* s.v.)

17 Continuous creation is to be thought of not only as a series of successive acts of creation, but also as the eternal presence of the *one* creative act, in the sense that God "was always the Father and always generated the Son" (Origen, *De principiis,* I, 2, 3), or that he is the "eternal Creator of minds" (Augustine, *Confessions,* XI, 31, trans. F. J. Sheed, p. 232). God is contained in his own creation, "nor does he stand in need of his own works, as if he had place in them where he might abide; but endures in his own eternity, where he abides and creates whatever pleases him, both in heaven and earth" (Augustine, on Ps. 113 : 14, in *Expositions on the Book of Psalms*). What happens successively in time is simultaneous in the mind of God: "An immutable order binds mutable things into a pattern, and in this order things which are not simultaneous in time exist simultaneously outside time" (Prosper of Aquitaine, *Sententiae ex Augustino delibatae,* XLI [Migne, *P.L.,* LI, col. 433]). "Temporal succession is without time in the eternal wisdom of God" (LVII [Migne, col. 455]). Before the Creation there was no time—time only began with created things: "Rather did time arise from the created than the created from time" (CCLXXX [Migne, col. 468]). "There was no time before time, but time was created together with the world" (Anon., *De triplici habitaculo,* VI [Migne, *P.L.,* XL, col. 995]).

18 [From ἄτομος, 'indivisible, that cannot be cut.'—TRANS.]

correspondence is, the more their probability sinks and their unthinkability increases, until they can no longer be regarded as pure chance but, for lack of a causal explanation, have to be thought of as meaningful arrangements. As I have already said, however, their "inexplicability" is not due to the fact that the cause is unknown, but to the fact that a cause is not even thinkable in intellectual terms. This is necessarily the case when space and time lose their meaning or have become relative, for under those circumstances a causality which presupposes space and time for its continuance can no longer be said to exist and becomes altogether unthinkable.

968   For these reasons it seems to me necessary to introduce, alongside space, time, and causality, a category which not only enables us to understand synchronistic phenomena as a special class of natural events, but also takes the contingent partly as a universal factor existing from all eternity, and partly as the sum of countless individual acts of creation occurring in time.

ON SYNCHRONICITY [1]

969   It might seem appropriate to begin my exposition by defin-
ing the concept with which it deals. But I would rather approach
the subject the other way and first give you a brief description of
the facts which the concept of synchronicity is intended to cover.
As its etymology shows, this term has something to do with time
or, to be more accurate, with a kind of simultaneity. Instead of
simultaneity we could also use the concept of a *meaningful coincidence* of two or more events, where something other than the
probability of chance is involved. A statistical—that is, a probable—concurrence of events, such as the "duplication of cases"
found in hospitals, falls within the category of chance. Groupings of this kind can consist of any number of terms and still
remain within the framework of the probable and rationally
possible. Thus, for instance, someone chances to notice the
number on his street-car ticket. On arriving home he receives a telephone call during which the same number is men-

1 [Originally given as a lecture, "Über Synchronizität," at the 1951 Eranos conference, Ascona, Switzerland, and published in the *Eranos-Jahrbuch 1951* (Zurich,
1952). The present translation was published in *Man and Time* (Papers from the
Eranos Yearbooks, 3; New York and London, 1957); it is republished with minor
revisions. The essay was, in the main, drawn from the preceding monograph.
—Editors.]

tioned. In the evening he buys a theatre ticket that again has the same number. The three events form a chance grouping that, although not likely to occur often, nevertheless lies well within the framework of probability owing to the frequency of each of its terms. I would like to recount from my own experience the following chance grouping, made up of no fewer than six terms:

970   On April 1, 1949, I made a note in the morning of an inscription containing a figure that was half man and half fish. There was fish for lunch. Somebody mentioned the custom of making an "April fish" of someone. In the afternoon, a former patient of mine, whom I had not seen for months, showed me some impressive pictures of fish. In the evening, I was shown a piece of embroidery with sea monsters and fishes in it. The next morning, I saw a former patient, who was visiting me for the first time in ten years. She had dreamed of a large fish the night before. A few months later, when I was using this series for a larger work and had just finished writing it down, I walked over to a spot by the lake in front of the house, where I had already been several times that morning. This time a fish a foot long lay on the sea-wall. Since no one else was present, I have no idea how the fish could have got there.

971   When coincidences pile up in this way one cannot help being impressed by them—for the greater the number of terms in such a series, or the more unusual its character, the more improbable it becomes. For reasons that I have mentioned elsewhere and will not discuss now, I assume that this was a chance grouping. It must be admitted, though, that it is more improbable than a mere duplication.

972   In the above-mentioned case of the street-car ticket, I said that the observer "chanced" to notice the number and retain it in his memory, which ordinarily he would never have done. This formed the basis for the series of chance events, but I do not know what caused him to notice the number. It seems to me that in judging such a series a factor of uncertainty enters in at this point and requires attention. I have observed something similar in other cases, without, however, being able to draw any reliable conclusions. But it is sometimes difficult to avoid the impression that there is a sort of foreknowledge of the coming series of events. This feeling becomes irresistible when, as so frequently

happens, one thinks one is about to meet an old friend in the street, only to find to one's disappointment that it is a stranger. On turning the next corner one then runs into him in person. Cases of this kind occur in every conceivable form and by no means infrequently, but after the first momentary astonishment they are as a rule quickly forgotten.

973   Now, the more the foreseen details of an event pile up, the more definite is the impression of an existing foreknowledge, and the more improbable does chance become. I remember the story of a student friend whose father had promised him a trip to Spain if he passed his final examinations satisfactorily. My friend thereupon dreamed that he was walking through a Spanish city. The street led to a square, where there was a Gothic cathedral. He then turned right, around a corner, into another street. There he was met by an elegant carriage drawn by two cream-coloured horses. Then he woke up. He told us about the dream as we were sitting round a table drinking beer. Shortly afterward, having successfully passed his examinations, he went to Spain, and there, in one of the streets, he recognized the city of his dream. He found the square and the cathedral, which exactly corresponded to the dream-image. He wanted to go straight to the cathedral, but then remembered that in the dream he had turned right, at the corner, into another street. He was curious to find out whether his dream would be corroborated further. Hardly had he turned the corner when he saw in reality the carriage with the two cream-coloured horses.

974   The *sentiment du déjà-vu* is based, as I have found in a number of cases, on a foreknowledge in dreams, but we saw that this foreknowledge can also occur in the waking state. In such cases mere chance becomes highly improbable because the coincidence is known in advance. It thus loses its chance character not only psychologically and subjectively, but objectively too, since the accumulation of details that coincide immeasurably increases the improbability of chance as a determining factor. (For correct precognitions of death, Dariex and Flammarion have computed probabilities ranging from 1 in 4,000,000 to 1 in 8,000,-000.) [2] So in these cases it would be incongruous to speak of "chance" happenings. It is rather a question of meaningful coin-

2 [For documentation, see supra, par. 830.—EDITORS.]

cidences. Usually they are explained by precognition—in other words, foreknowledge. People also talk of clairvoyance, telepathy, etc., without, however, being able to explain what these faculties consist of or what means of transmission they use in order to render events distant in space and time accessible to our perception. All these ideas are mere names; they are not scientific concepts which could be taken as statements of principle, for no one has yet succeeded in constructing a causal bridge between the elements making up a meaningful coincidence.

975   Great credit is due to J. B. Rhine for having established a reliable basis for work in the vast field of these phenomena by his experiments in extrasensory perception, or ESP. He used a pack of 25 cards divided into 5 groups of 5, each with its special sign (star, square, circle, cross, two wavy lines). The experiment was carried out as follows. In each series of experiments the pack is laid out 800 times, in such a way that the subject cannot see the cards. He is then asked to guess the cards as they are turned up. The probability of a correct answer is 1 in 5. The result, computed from very high figures, showed an average of 6.5 hits. The probability of a chance deviation of 1.5 amounts to only 1 in 250,000. Some individuals scored more than twice the probable number of hits. On one occasion all 25 cards were guessed correctly, which gives a probability of 1 in 298,023,223,-876,953,125. The spatial distance between experimenter and subject was increased from a few yards to about 4,000 miles, with no effect on the result.

976   A second type of experiment consisted in asking the subject to guess a series of cards that was still to be laid out in the near or more distant future. The time factor was increased from a few minutes to two weeks. The result of these experiments showed a probability of 1 in 400,000.

977   In a third type of experiment, the subject had to try to influence the fall of mechanically thrown dice by wishing for a certain number. The results of this so-called psychokinetic (PK) experiment were the more positive the more dice were used at a time.

978   The result of the spatial experiment proves with tolerable certainty that the psyche can, to some extent, eliminate the space factor. The time experiment proves that the time factor (at any

rate, in the dimension of the future) can become psychically relative. The experiment with dice proves that moving bodies, too, can be influenced psychically—a result that could have been predicted from the psychic relativity of space and time.

979   The energy postulate shows itself to be inapplicable to the Rhine experiments, and thus rules out all ideas about the transmission of force. Equally, the law of causality does not hold—a fact that I pointed out thirty years ago. For we cannot conceive how a future event could bring about an event in the present. Since for the time being there is no possibility whatever of a causal explanation, we must assume provisionally that improbable accidents of an acausal nature—that is, meaningful coincidences—have entered the picture.

980   In considering these remarkable results we must take into account a fact discovered by Rhine, namely that in each series of experiments the first attempts yielded a better result than the later ones. The falling off in the number of hits scored was connected with the mood of the subject. An initial mood of faith and optimism makes for good results. Scepticism and resistance have the opposite effect, that is, they create an unfavourable disposition. As the energic, and hence also the causal, approach to these experiments has shown itself to be inapplicable, it follows that the affective factor has the significance simply of a *condition* which makes it possible for the phenomenon to occur, though it need not. According to Rhine's results, we may nevertheless expect 6.5 hits instead of only 5. But it cannot be predicted in advance when the hit will come. Could we do so, we would be dealing with a law, and this would contradict the entire nature of the phenomenon. It has, as said, the improbable character of a "lucky hit" or accident that occurs with a more than merely probable frequency and is as a rule dependent on a certain state of affectivity.

981   This observation has been thoroughly confirmed, and it suggests that the psychic factor which modifies or even eliminates the principles underlying the physicist's picture of the world is connected with the affective state of the subject. Although the phenomenology of the ESP and PK experiments could be considerably enriched by further experiments of the kind described above, deeper investigation of its bases will have to concern itself with the nature of the affectivity involved. I have there-

fore directed my attention to certain observations and experiences which, I can fairly say, have forced themselves upon me during the course of my long medical practice. They have to do with spontaneous, meaningful coincidences of so high a degree of improbability as to appear flatly unbelievable. I shall therefore describe to you only one case of this kind, simply to give an example characteristic of a whole category of phenomena. It makes no difference whether you refuse to believe this particular case or whether you dispose of it with an *ad hoc* explanation. I could tell you a great many such stories, which are in principle no more surprising or incredible than the irrefutable results arrived at by Rhine, and you would soon see that almost every case calls for its own explanation. But the causal explanation, the only possible one from the standpoint of natural science, breaks down owing to the psychic relativization of space and time, which together form the indispensable premises for the cause-and-effect relationship.

982   My example concerns a young woman patient who, in spite of efforts made on both sides, proved to be psychologically inaccessible. The difficulty lay in the fact that she always knew better about everything. Her excellent education had provided her with a weapon ideally suited to this purpose, namely a highly polished Cartesian rationalism with an impeccably "geometrical" [3] idea of reality. After several fruitless attempts to sweeten her rationalism with a somewhat more human understanding, I had to confine myself to the hope that something unexpected and irrational would turn up, something that would burst the intellectual retort into which she had sealed herself. Well, I was sitting opposite her one day, with my back to the window, listening to her flow of rhetoric. She had had an impressive dream the night before, in which someone had given her a golden scarab— a costly piece of jewellery. While she was still telling me this dream, I heard something behind me gently tapping on the window. I turned round and saw that it was a fairly large flying insect that was knocking against the window-pane from outside in the obvious effort to get into the dark room. This seemed to me very strange. I opened the window immediately and caught the insect in the air as it flew in. It was a scarabaeid beetle, or

3 [Descartes demonstrated his propositions by the "Geometrical Method."— EDITORS.]

common rose-chafer (*Cetonia aurata*), whose gold-green colour most nearly resembles that of a golden scarab. I handed the beetle to my patient with the words, "Here is your scarab." This experience punctured the desired hole in her rationalism and broke the ice of her intellectual resistance. The treatment could now be continued with satisfactory results.

983   This story is meant only as a paradigm of the innumerable cases of meaningful coincidence that have been observed not only by me but by many others, and recorded in large collections. They include everything that goes by the name of clairvoyance, telepathy, etc., from Swedenborg's well-attested vision of the great fire in Stockholm to the recent report by Air Marshal Sir Victor Goddard about the dream of an unknown officer, which predicted the subsequent accident to Goddard's plane.[4]

984   All the phenomena I have mentioned can be grouped under three categories:

1. The coincidence of a psychic state in the observer with a simultaneous, objective, external event that corresponds to the psychic state or content (e.g., the scarab), where there is no evidence of a causal connection between the psychic state and the external event, and where, considering the psychic relativity of space and time, such a connection is not even conceivable.

2. The coincidence of a psychic state with a corresponding (more or less simultaneous) external event taking place outside the observer's field of perception, i.e., at a distance, and only verifiable afterward (e.g., the Stockholm fire).

3. The coincidence of a psychic state with a corresponding, not yet existent future event that is distant in time and can likewise only be verified afterward.

985   In groups 2 and 3 the coinciding events are not yet present in the observer's field of perception, but have been anticipated in time in so far as they can only be verified afterward. For this reason I call such events *synchronistic,* which is not to be confused with *synchronous.*

986   Our survey of this wide field of experience would be incomplete if we failed to take into account the so-called mantic methods. Manticism lays claim, if not actually to producing synchronistic events, then at least to making them serve its ends.

4 [This case was the subject of an English film, *The Night My Number Came Up.*—EDITORS.]

An example of this is the oracle method of the *I Ching*, which Dr. Hellmut Wilhelm has described in detail.[5] The *I Ching* presupposes that there is a synchronistic correspondence between the psychic state of the questioner and the answering hexagram. The hexagram is formed either by the random division of the 49 yarrow stalks or by the equally random throw of three coins. The result of this method is, incontestably, very interesting, but so far as I can see it does not provide any tool for an objective determination of the facts, that is to say a statistical evaluation, since the psychic state in question is much too indefinite and indefinable. The same holds true of the geomantic experiment, which is based on similar principles.

987   We are in a somewhat more favourable situation when we turn to the astrological method, as it presupposes a meaningful coincidence of planetary aspects and positions with the character or the existing psychic state of the questioner. In the light of the most recent astrophysical research, astrological correspondence is probably not a matter of synchronicity but, very largely, of a causal relationship. As Professor Max Knoll has demonstrated,[6] the solar proton radiation is influenced to such a degree by planetary conjunctions, oppositions, and quartile aspects that the appearance of magnetic storms can be predicted with a fair amount of probability. Relationships can be established between the curve of the earth's magnetic disturbances and the mortality rate that confirm the unfavourable influence of conjunctions, oppositions, and quartile aspects and the favourable influence of trine and sextile aspects. So it is probably a question here of a causal relationship, i.e., of a natural law that excludes synchronicity or restricts it. At the same time, the zodiacal qualification of the houses, which plays a large part in the horoscope, creates a complication in that the astrological zodiac, although agreeing with the calendar, does not coincide with the actual constellations themselves. These have shifted their positions by almost a whole platonic month as a result of the precession of the equinoxes since the time when the springpoint was in zero Aries, about the beginning of our era. Therefore, anyone born in Aries today (according to the calendar) is

5 ["The Concept of Time in the Book of Changes," originally a lecture at the 1951 Eranos conference.—EDITORS.]
6 ["Transformations of Science in Our Age," ibid.]

actually born in Pisces. It is simply that his birth took place at a time which, for approximately 2,000 years, has been called "Aries." Astrology presupposes that this time has a determining quality. It is possible that this quality, like the disturbances in the earth's magnetic field, is connected with the seasonal fluctuations to which solar proton radiation is subject. It is therefore not beyond the realm of possibility that the zodiacal positions may also represent a causal factor.

988   Although the psychological interpretation of horoscopes is still a very uncertain matter, there is nevertheless some prospect today of a causal explanation in conformity with natural law. Consequently, we are no longer justified in describing astrology as a mantic method. Astrology is in the process of becoming a science. But as there are still large areas of uncertainty, I decided some time ago to make a test and find out how far an accepted astrological tradition would stand up to statistical investigation. For this purpose it was necessary to select a definite and indisputable fact. My choice fell on marriage. Since antiquity, the traditional belief in regard to marriage has been that there is a conjunction of sun and moon in the horoscope of the marriage partners, that is, ☉ (sun) with an orbit of 8 degrees in the case of one partner, in ☌ (conjunction) with ☽ (moon) in the case of the other. A second, equally old, tradition takes ☽ ☌ ☽ as another marriage characteristic. Of like importance are the conjunctions of the ascendent (*Asc.*) with the large luminaries.

989   Together with my co-worker, Mrs. Liliane Frey-Rohn, I first proceeded to collect 180 marriages, that is to say, 360 horoscopes,[7] and compared the 50 most important aspects that might possibly be characteristic of marriage, namely the conjunctions and oppositions of ☉ ☽ ♂ (Mars) ♀ (Venus) *Asc.* and *Desc.* This resulted in a maximum of 10 per cent for ☉ ☌ ☽. As Professor Markus Fierz, of Basel, who kindly went to the trouble of computing the probability of my result, informed me, my figure has a probability of 1 : 10,000. The opinion of several mathematical physicists whom I consulted about the significance of this figure is divided: some find it considerable, others find it of question-

[7] This material stemmed from different sources. They were simply horoscopes of married people. There was no selection of any kind. We took at random all the marriage horoscopes we could lay hands on.

able value. Our figure is inconclusive inasmuch as a total of 360 horoscopes is far too small from a statistical point of view.

990   While the aspects of these 180 marriages were being worked out statistically, our collection was enlarged, and when we had collected 220 more marriages, this batch was subjected to separate investigation. As on the first occasion, the material was evaluated just as it came in. It was not selected from any special point of view and was drawn from the most varied sources. Evaluation of this second batch yielded a maximum figure of 10.9 per cent for ☽ ☌ ☽ . The probability of this figure is also about 1 : 10,000.

991   Finally, 83 more marriages arrived, and these in turn were investigated separately. The result was a maximum figure of 9.6 per cent for ☽ ☌ *Asc.* The probability of this figure is approximately 1 : 3,000.[8]

992   One is immediately struck by the fact that the conjunctions are all *moon conjunctions,* which is in accord with astrological expectations. But the strange thing is that what has turned up here are the three basic positions of the horoscope, ☉ ☽ and *Asc.* The probability of a concurrence of ☉ ☌ ☽ and ☽ ☌ ☽ amounts to 1 : 100,000,000. The concurrence of the three moon conjunctions with ☉ ☽ *Asc.* has a probability of 1 : 3 × 10^{11}; in other words, the improbability of its being due to mere chance is so enormous that we are forced to take into account the existence of some factor responsible for it. The three batches were so small that little or no theoretical significance can be attached to the individual probabilities of 1 : 10,000 and 1 : 3,000. Their concurrence, however, is so improbable that one cannot help assuming the existence of an impelling factor that produced this result.

993   The possibility of there being a scientifically valid connection between astrological data and proton radiation cannot be held responsible for this, since the individual probabilities of 1 : 10,000 and 1 : 3,000 are too great for us to be able, with any degree of certainty, to view our result as other than mere chance. Besides, the maxima cancel each other out as soon as one divides up the marriages into a larger number of batches. It would require hundreds of thousands of marriage horoscopes to establish

8 [These and the following figures were later revised by Professor Fierz and considerably reduced. See supra, pars. 901ff.—EDITORS.]

the statistical regularity of occurrences like the sun, moon, and ascendent conjunctions, and even then the result would be questionable. That anything so improbable as the turning up of the three classical moon conjunctions should occur at all, however, can only be explained either as the result of an intentional or unintentional fraud, or else as precisely such a meaningful coincidence, that is, as synchronicity.

994   Although I was obliged to express doubt, earlier, about the mantic character of astrology, I am now forced as a result of my astrological experiment to recognize it again. The chance arrangement of the marriage horoscopes, which were simply piled on top of one another as they came in from the most diverse sources, and the equally fortuitous way they were divided into three unequal batches, suited the sanguine expectations of the research workers and produced an over-all picture that could scarcely have been improved upon from the standpoint of the astrological hypothesis. The success of the experiment is entirely in accord with Rhine's ESP results, which were also favorably affected by expectation, hope, and faith. However, there was no definite expectation of any one result. Our selection of 50 aspects is proof of this. After we got the result of the first batch, a slight expectation did exist that the $\odot \, \delta \, \mathbb{C}$ would be confirmed. But we were disappointed. The second time, we made up a larger batch from the newly added horoscopes in order to increase the element of certainty. But the result was $\mathbb{C} \, \delta \, \mathbb{C}$. With the third batch, there was only a faint expectation that $\mathbb{C} \, \delta \, \mathbb{C}$ would be confirmed, but again this was not the case.

995   What happened in this case was admittedly a curiosity, apparently a unique instance of meaningful coincidence. If one is impressed by such things, one could call it a minor miracle. Today, however, we are obliged to view the miraculous in a somewhat different light. The Rhine experiments have demonstrated that space and time, and hence causality, are factors that can be eliminated, with the result that acausal phenomena, otherwise called miracles, appear possible. All natural phenomena of this kind are unique and exceedingly curious combinations of chance, held together by the common meaning of their parts to form an unmistakable whole. Although meaningful coincidences are infinitely varied in their phenomenology, as acausal events they nevertheless form an element that is part

of the scientific picture of the world. Causality is the way we explain the link between two successive events. Synchronicity designates the parallelism of time and meaning between psychic and psychophysical events, which scientific knowledge so far has been unable to reduce to a common principle. The term explains nothing, it simply formulates the occurrence of meaningful coincidences which, in themselves, are chance happenings, but are so improbable that we must assume them to be based on some kind of principle, or on some property of the empirical world. No reciprocal causal connection can be shown to obtain between parallel events, which is just what gives them their chance character. The only recognizable and demonstrable link between them is a common meaning, or equivalence. The old theory of correspondence was based on the experience of such connections—a theory that reached its culminating point and also its provisional end in Leibniz' idea of pre-established harmony, and was then replaced by causality. Synchronicity is a modern differentiation of the obsolete concept of correspondence, sympathy, and harmony. It is based not on philosophical assumptions but on empirical experience and experimentation.

996   Synchronistic phenomena prove the simultaneous occurrence of meaningful equivalences in heterogeneous, causally unrelated processes; in other words, they prove that a content perceived by an observer can, at the same time, be represented by an outside event, without any causal connection. From this it follows either that the psyche cannot be localized in space, or that space is relative to the psyche. The same applies to the temporal determination of the psyche and the psychic relativity of time. I do not need to emphasize that the verification of these findings must have far-reaching consequences.

997   In the short space of a lecture I cannot, unfortunately, do more than give a very cursory sketch of the vast problem of synchronicity. For those of you who would care to go into this question more deeply, I would mention that a more extensive work of mine is soon to appear under the title "Synchronicity: An Acausal Connecting Principle." It will be published together with a work by Professor W. Pauli in a book called *The Interpretation of Nature and the Psyche.*[9]

9 [See the foregoing.—EDITORS.]

BIBLIOGRAPHY

BIBLIOGRAPHY

ABEGG, LILY. *The Mind of East Asia.* London and New York, 1952.

AEGIDIUS DE VADIS. "Dialogus inter naturam et filium philosophiae." See *Theatrum chemicum,* iv.

AGRIPPA VON NETTESHEIM, HEINRICH (HENRICUS) CORNELIUS. *De occulta philosophia libri tres.* Cologne, 1533. For translation, see: *Three Books of Occult Philosophy.* Translated by "J. F." London, 1651. Republished (Book I only) as: *The Occult Philosophy or Magic.* Edited by Willis F. Whitehead. Chicago, 1898.

ALBERTUS MAGNUS. *De mirabilibus mundi.* Incunabulum, undated, in the Zentralbibliothek, Zurich. (There is an ed. printed at Cologne, 1485.)

ALVERDES, FRIEDRICH. "Die Wirksamkeit von Archetypen in den Instinkthandlungen der Tiere," *Zoologischer Anzeiger* (Leipzig), CXIX: 9/10 (1937), 225–36.

ANONYMOUS. *De triplici habitaculo.* See MIGNE, *P.L.,* vol. 40, cols. 991–98.

ARTIS AURIFERAE quam chemiam vocant . . . Basileae [Basel], [1593]. 2 vols.
> Contents quoted in this volume:
> VOLUME I
> i Aurora consurgens, quae dicitur Aurea hora [pp. 185–246]
> VOLUME II
> ii Morienus Romanus: Sermo de transmutatione metallica [Liber de compositione Alchemiae] (pp. 7–54).

AUGUSTINE, SAINT. *Confessions.* Translated by Francis Joseph Sheed. London and New York, 1951.

——. *Expositions on the Book of Psalms.* Translated by J. Tweed, T. Scratton, and others. (Library of the Fathers of the Holy Catholic Church.) Oxford, 1847–57. 6 vols.

"Aurora consurgens." See *Artis auriferae,* i.

BASTIAN, ADOLF. *Ethnische Elementargedanken in der Lehre vom Menschen.* Berlin, 1895. 2 parts.

BASTIAN, ADOLF. *Der Mensch in der Geschichte.* Leipzig, 1860. 3 vols.

BERGER, HANS. *Über die körperlichen Äusserungen psychischer Zustände.* Jena, 1904.

BINSWANGER, LUDWIG. "On the Psycho-galvanic Phenomenon in Association Experiments." In: JUNG, *Studies in Word-Association,* q.v. (pp. 446–530).

BLEULER, EUGEN. *Naturgeschichte der Seele und ihres Bewusstwerdens.* Berlin, 1921.

———. *Die Psychoide als Prinzip der organischen Entwicklung.* Berlin, 1925.

BÖHME, JAKOB. *De signatura rerum.* Amsterdam, 1635. For translation, see: *The Signature of All Things.* Translated by John Ellistone, edited by Clifford Bax. (Everyman's Library.) London and New York, 1912.

BOLTZMANN, LUDWIG. *Populäre Schriften.* Leipzig, 1905.

BROWN, G. SPENCER. "De la recherche psychique considérée comme un test de la théorie des probabilités," *Revue métapsychique* (Paris), no. 29–30 (May–Aug. 1954), 87–96.

BUSEMANN, ADOLF. *Die Einheit der Psychologie.* Stuttgart, 1948.

BUSSE, LUDWIG. *Geist und Körper, Seele und Leib.* Leipzig, 1903.

BUTLER, SAMUEL. *Hudibras.* Edited by A. R. Waller. Cambridge, 1905.

CARDAN, JEROME (Hieronymus Cardanus). *Commentaria in Ptolemaeum De astrorum judiciis.* In: *Opera omnia.* Lyons, 1663. 10 vols. (V, 93–368.)

CARPENTER, WILLIAM B. *Principles of Mental Physiology.* London, 1874; 4th edn., 1876.

CHAMBERLAIN, HOUSTON STEWART. *Goethe.* Munich, 1912.

CODRINGTON, ROBERT HENRY. *The Melanesians.* Oxford, 1891.

COOMARASWAMY, ANANDA K. "Rgveda 10.90.1 áty atisthad daśangulám," *Journal of American Oriental Society* (Boston, Mass.), LVI (1946), 145–61.

CRAWLEY, ALFRED ERNEST. *The Idea of the Soul.* London, 1909.

CUMONT, FRANZ. *Textes et monuments figurés relatifs aux mystères de Mithra*. Brussels, 1894–99. 2 vols.

DAHNS, FRITZ. "Das Schwärmen des Palolo," *Der Naturforscher* (Berlin), VIII (1932), 379–82.

DALCQ, A. M. "La Morphogenèse dans la cadre de la biologie générale," *Verhandlungen der Schweizerischen naturforschenden Gesellschaft* (129th Annual Meeting at Lausanne; pub. at Aarau), 1949, 37–72.

DARIEX, XAVIER. "Le Hazard et la télépathie," *Annales des sciences psychiques* (Paris), I (1891), 295–304.

DELATTE, LOUIS. *Textes latins et vieux français relatifs aux Cyranides*. (Bibliothèque de la faculté de philosophie et de lettres de l'Université de Liège, fasc. 93.) Liège and Paris, 1942.

DESSOIR, MAX. *Geschichte der neueren deutschen Psychologie*. 2nd edn., Berlin, 1902. 2 vols.

"De triplici habitaculo." See ANONYMOUS.

DIETERICH, ALBRECHT. *Eine Mithrasliturgie*. Leipzig, 1903; 2nd edn., 1910.

DILTHEY, WILHELM. *Gesammelte Schriften*. Leipzig, 1923–36. 12 vols.

DORN, GERHARD. See *Theatrum chemicum*, i–iii.

DREWS, A. C. H. *Plotin und der Untergang der antiken Weltanschauung*. Jena, 1907.

DRIESCH, HANS. *Philosophie des Organischen*. Leipzig, 1909. 2 vols. 2nd edn., Leipzig, 1921. 1 vol. For translation, see: *The Science and Philosophy of the Organism*. 2nd edn., London, 1929.

———. *Die "Seele" als elementarer Naturfaktor*. Leipzig, 1903.

DUNNE, JOHN WILLIAM. *An Experiment with Time*. London, 1927; 2nd edn., New York, 1938.

ECKERMANN, J. P. *Conversations with Goethe*. Translated by R. O. Moon. London [1951].

EISLER, ROBERT. *Weltenmantel und Himmelszelt*. Munich, 1910. 2 vols.

ERMAN, ADOLF. *Life in Ancient Egypt*. Translated by H. M. Tirard. London, 1894.

FECHNER, GUSTAV THEODOR. *Elemente der Psychophysik*. 2nd edn., Leipzig, 1889. 2 vols.

FIERZ, MARKUS. "Zur physikalischen Erkenntnis," *Eranos-Jahrbuch 1948* (Zurich, 1949), 433–460.

FLAMBART, PAUL. *Preuves et bases de l'astrologie scientifique*. Paris, 1921.

FLAMMARION, CAMILLE. *The Unknown*. London and New York, 1900.

FLOURNOY, THÉODORE. "Automatisme téléologique antisuicide," *Archives de psychologie de la Suisse romande* (Geneva), VII (1908), 113–37.

———. *From India to the Planet Mars*. Translated by D. B. Vermilye. New York and London, 1900. (Orig.: *Des Indes à la Planète Mars; Étude sur un cas de somnambulisme avec glossolalie*. Paris and Geneva, 3rd edn., 1900.)

———. "Nouvelles observations sur un cas de somnambulisme avec glossolalie," *Archives de psychologie de la Suisse romande* (Geneva), I (1901, pub. 1902), 102–255.

FLUDD, ROBERT. [*De arte geomantica.*] "Animae intellectualis scientia seu De geomantia." In: *Fasciculus geomanticus, in quo varia variorum opera geomantica*. Verona, 1687.

FRANZ, MARIE-LOUISE VON. "Die Parabel von der Fontina des Grafen von Tarvis." Unpublished.

———. "Die Passio Perpetuae." In: C. G. JUNG. *Aion*. Zurich, 1951.

———. "Der Traum des Descartes." In: *Zeitlose Dokumente der Seele*. (Studien aus dem C. G. Jung Institut, 3.) Zurich, 1952.

FREUD, SIGMUND. *Introductory Lectures on Psycho-Analysis*. Translated by Joan Riviere. London, 1922.

———. *The Psychopathology of Everyday Life*. Translated by A. A. Brill. New York and London, 1914.

———. *Sammlung kleiner Schriften zur Neurosenlehre*. Vienna, 1906–22. 5 vols. (Mostly translated in: *Collected Papers of Sigmund Freud*, Vols. I–IV. London, 1924–25.)

———. "The Unconscious." *Papers on Metapsychology*. In: The Standard Edition of the Complete Psychological Works, 14. Translated by James Strachey et al. London, 1957. (Pp. 159–215.)

538

FRISCH, KARL VON. *The Dancing Bees.* Translated by Dora Ilse. New York and London, 1954.

FROBENIUS, LEO. *Das Zeitalter des Sonnengottes.* Berlin, 1904.

FUNK, PHILIPP. *Ignatius von Loyola.* (Die Klassiker der Religion, 6.) Berlin, 1913.

FÜRST, EMMA. "Statistical Investigations on Word-Associations and on Familial Agreement in Reaction Type among Uneducated Persons." In JUNG, *Studies in Word-Association,* q.v. (Pp. 407–45.)

GATSCHET, ALBERT SAMUEL. "The Klamath Indians of South-Western Oregon." In: *Contributions to North American Ethnology,* Vol. II. (Miscellaneous Documents of the House of Representatives for the First Session of the 51st Congress, 1889–90; United States Department of the Interior, U.S. Geographical and Geological Survey of the Rocky Mountain Region, 44.) Washington, 1890–91. 2 vols.

GEULINCX, ARNOLD. *Opera philosophica.* Edited by J. P. N. Land. The Hague, 1891–99. 3 vols. (Vol. II: *Metaphysica vera.*)

GOBLET D'ALMELLAS, EUGÈNE, COUNT. *The Migration of Symbols.* With an introduction by Sir G. Birdwood. Westminster, 1894.

GOETHE, J. W. VON. *Faust, Part One.* Translated by Philip Wayne. Harmondsworth, 1949.

GONZALES, LOYS (Ludovicus Gonsalvus). *The Testament of Ignatius Loyola, being Sundry Acts of our Father Ignatius, . . . taken down from the Saint's own lips by Luis Gonzales.* Translated by E. M. Rix. London, 1900.

GRANET, MARCEL. *La Pensée chinoise.* Paris, 1934.

GRIMM, JACOB. *Teutonic Mythology.* Translated by J. S. Stallybrass. London, 1883–88. 4 vols.

GROT, NICOLAS VON. "Die Begriffe der Seele und der psychischen Energie in der Psychologie," *Archiv für systematische Philosophie* (Berlin), IV (1898), 257–335.

GURNEY, EDMUND; MYERS, FREDERIC W. H.; and PODMORE, FRANK. *Phantasms of the Living.* London, 1886. 2 vols.

HARDY, A. C. See: "The Scientific Evidence for Extra-Sensory Perception," in Report of the British Association Meeting at Newcastle, 31 Aug.–7 Sept., 1949, *Discovery* (London), X (1949), 348.

HARTMANN, CARL ROBERT EDUARD VON. *Philosophie des Unbewuss-ten.* Leipzig, 1869. For translation, see: *Philosophy of the Unconscious.* (English and Foreign Philosophical Library, vols. 25–27.) Translated by W. C. Coupland. London, 1884. 3 vols.

———. *Die Weltanschauung der modernen Physik.* Leipzig, 1909.

HERBERT OF CHERBURY, EDWARD, BARON. *De veritate* [originally published 1624]. Translated by Meyrick H. Carré. (University of Bristol Studies, 6.) Bristol, 1937.

HETHERWICK, ALEXANDER. "Some Animistic Beliefs among the Yaos of Central Africa," *Journal of the Royal Anthropological Institute* (London), XXXII (1902), 89–95.

HIPPOCRATES (ascribed to). *De alimento.* In: *Hippocrates on Diet and Hygiene.* Translated by John Precope. London, 1952.

HIPPOLYTUS. *Elenchos.* In: *Hippolytus' Werke,* Vol. III. Edited by Paul Wendland. (Griechische Christliche Schriftsteller.) Leipzig, 1916. For translation, see: *Philosophumena: or, The Refutation of All Heresies.* Translated by Francis Legge. (Translations of Christian Literature.) London and New York, 1921. 2 vols.

HONORIUS OF AUTUN. *Speculum de Mysteriis Ecclesiae.* See MIGNE, *P.L.,* vol. 172, cols. 313–1108.

[HORAPOLLO NILIACUS.] *The Hieroglyphics of Horapollo.* Translated and edited by George Boas. (Bollingen Series XXIII.) New York, 1950.

HUBERT, HENRI, and MAUSS, MARCEL. *Mélanges d'histoire des religions.* (Travaux de l'Année sociologique.) Paris, 1909.

I Ching. The German translation by Richard Wilhelm, rendered into English by Cary F. Baynes. New York (Bollingen Series XIX), 1950; London, 1951. 2 vols.

IGNATIUS OF ANTIOCH, SAINT. *Epistle to the Ephesians.* In: *The Apostolic Fathers.* Translated by Kirsopp Lake. (Loeb Classical Library.) London and New York, 1914. 2 vols. (Vol. I, pp. 173–97.)

IRENAEUS, SAINT. *Contra* [or *Adversus*] *haereses libri quinque.* See MIGNE, *P.G.,* vol. 7, cols. 433–1224. For translation, see: *The Writings of Irenaeus.* Translated by Alexander Roberts and W. H. Rambaut. Vol. I. (Ante-Nicene Christian Library, 5.) Edinburgh, 1868.

ISIDORE OF SEVILLE, SAINT. *Liber etymologiarum.* See MIGNE, *P.L.*, vol. 82, cols. 73–728.

JAFFÉ, ANIELA. "Bilder und Symbole aus E. T. A. Hoffmanns Märchen 'Der Goldene Topf'." In: C. G. JUNG. *Gestaltungen des Unbewussten.* Zurich, 1950.

JAMES, WILLIAM. "Frederic Myers' Service to Psychology," *Proceedings of the Society for Psychical Research* (London), XVII (1901; pub. 1903), 13–23.

———. *Principles of Psychology.* New York, 1890. 2 vols.

———. *The Varieties of Religious Experience.* London, 1902.

JANET, PIERRE. *L'Automatisme psychologique.* Paris, 1889.

———. *Les Névroses.* Paris, 1909.

JANTZ, HUBERT, and BERINGER, KURT. "Das Syndrom des Schwebeerlebnisses unmittelbar nach Kopfverletzungen," *Der Nervenarzt* (Berlin), XVII (1944), 197–206.

JEANS, JAMES. *Physics and Philosophy.* Cambridge, 1942.

JERUSALEM, WILHELM. *Lehrbuch der Psychologie.* 3rd edn., Vienna and Leipzig, 1902.

JORDAN, PASCUAL. "Positivistische Bemerkungen über die parapsychischen Erscheinungen," *Zentralblatt für Psychotherapie* (Leipzig), IX (1936), 3–17.

———. *Verdrängung und Komplementarität.* Hamburg, 1947.

JUNG, CARL GUSTAV.* "The Aims of Psychotherapy." In: *The Practice of Psychotherapy.* (Collected Works, 16.) 1954.

———. "The 'Arbor philosophica.'" In: *Alchemical Studies.* (Collected Works, 13.*) (Alternate source: "Der philosophische Baum," in JUNG, *Von dem Wurzeln des Bewusstseins,* Zurich, 1954.)

———. "The Association Method." In: *Experimental Researches.* (Collected Works, 2.*) (Alternate source: *Collected Papers on Analytical Psychology,* q.v.)

———. *Collected Papers on Analytical Psychology.* Edited by Constance Long, translated by various hands. London, 1916; 2nd edn., London, 1917, New York, 1920.

* For details of the *Collected Works of C. G. Jung* (especially volumes yet unpublished, listed here without date) see the end of this volume.

JUNG, CARL GUSTAV. Commentary to *The Secret of the Golden Flower*. See WILHELM, RICHARD.

———. "The Concept of the Collective Unconscious." In: *The Archetypes and the Collective Unconscious*. (Collected Works, 9, i.) 1959.

———. "Concerning Mandala Symbolism." In: ibid.

———. "On the Psychology of Eastern Meditation." In: *Psychology and Religion: West and East*. (Collected Works, 11.) 1958.

———. "Paracelsus as a Spiritual Phenomenon." In: *Alchemical Studies*. (Collected Works, 13.*) (Alternate source: "Paracelsus als geistige Erscheinung," *Paracelsica*, Zurich, 1942.)

———. "The Phenomenology of the Spirit in Fairytales." In: *The Archetypes and the Collective Unconscious*. (Collected Works, 9, i.) 1959.

———. "The Practical Use of Dream-Analysis." In: *The Practice of Psychotherapy*. (Collected Works, 16.) 1954.

———. *Psychiatric Studies*. (Collected Works, 1.) 1957.

———. "A Psychological Approach to the Dogma of the Trinity." In: *Psychology and Religion: West and East*. (Collected Works, 11.) 1958.

———. *Psychological Types*. (Collected Works, 6.*) (Alternate source: Translation by H. G. Baynes, London and New York, 1923.)

———. *Psychology and Alchemy*. (Collected Works, 12.) 1953.

———. "The Psychology of Dementia Praecox." In: *Psychogenesis in Mental Disease*. (Collected Works, 3.) 1960.

———. "Psychology of the Transference." In: *The Practice of Psychotherapy*. (Collected Works, 16.) 1954.

———. "The Psychology of the Unconscious." In: *Two Essays on Analytical Psychology*, q.v.

———. "The Relations between the Ego and the Unconscious." In: ibid.

———. "The Spirit Mercurius." In: *Alchemical Studies*. (Collected Works, 13.*)

* For details of the *Collected Works of C. G. Jung* (especially volumes yet unpublished, listed here without date) see the end of this volume.

———. *Studies in Word Association.* In: *Experimental Researches.* (Collected Works, 2.*) (Alternate source: *Studies in Word-Association* . . . under the direction of C. G. Jung. Translated by M. D. Eder. London, 1918; New York, 1919.)

———. "A Study in the Process of Individuation." In: *The Archetypes and the Collective Unconscious.* (Collected Works, 9, i.) 1959.

———. *Symbols of Transformation.* (Collected Works, 5.) 1956.

———. "The Theory of Psychoanalysis." In: *Freud and Psychoanalysis.* (Collected Works, 4.*) (Alternate sources: *The Theory of Psychoanalysis,* Nervous and Mental Disease Monograph Series, 19, New York, 1915. Also: *Versuch einer Darstellung der psychoanalytischen Theorie,* Zurich, 1954.)

———. *Two Essays on Analytical Psychology.* (Collected Works, 7.) 1953.

———. *Von den Wurzeln des Bewusstseins.* Zurich, 1954.

———. See also PETERSON; RICKSHER.

KAMMERER, PAUL. *Das Gesetz der Serie.* Stuttgart and Berlin, 1919.

KANT, IMMANUEL. *Werke.* Edited by Ernst Cassirer. Berlin, 1912–22. 11 vols. (*Anthropologie,* VIII, pp. 2–228; *Logik,* VIII, pp. 325–452; *Träume eines Geistersehers,* II, pp. 331–90.)

———. *Dreams of a Spirit-Seer, Illustrated by Dreams of Metaphysics.* Translated by Emanuel F. Goerwitz. London, 1900.

———. *Introduction to Logic.* Translated by Thomas Kingsmill Abbott. London, 1885.

KATZ, DAVID. *Animals and Men.* Translated by Hannah Steinberg and Arthur Summerfield. London (Penguin Books), 1953.

KEPLER, JOHANNES. *Gesammelte Werke.* Edited by Max Caspar and others. Munich, 1937ff. (Vol. IV: *Kleinere Schriften (1602–1611).* Edited by Max Caspar and Franz Hammer. 1941.)

[———.] *Joannis Kepleri astronomi Opera omnia.* Edited by C. Frisch. Frankfurt and Erlangen, 1858–71. 8 vols.

KERNER VON MARILAUN, ANTON. *The Natural History of Plants.*

* For details of the *Collected Works* of C. G. *Jung* (especially volumes yet unpublished, listed here without date) see the end of this volume.

Translated by F. W. Oliver and others. London, 1902. 2 vols.

KHUNRATH, HEINRICH. *Amphitheatrum sapientiae aeternae solius verae.* Hanau, 1604.

———. *Von hylealischen . . . Chaos.* Magdeburg, 1597.

KLOECKLER, HERBERT VON. *Astrologie als Erfahrungswissenschaft.* Leipzig, 1927.

KNOLL, MAX. "Transformations of Science in Our Age." In *Man and Time,* q.v.

KOCH-GRÜNBERG, THEODOR. *Südamerikanische Felszeichnungen.* Berlin, 1907.

KRAFFT, K. E.; BUDAI, E.; and FERRIÈRE, A. *Le Premier Traité d'astro-biologie.* Paris, 1939.

KRÄMER, AUGUSTIN FRIEDRICH. *Über den Bau der Korallenriffe.* Kiel and Leipzig, 1897.

KRONECKER, LEOPOLD. *Werke.* Leipzig, 1895–1930. 5 vols.

KÜLPE, OSWALD. *Einleitung in die Philosophie.* 7th edn., Leipzig, 1915.

———. *Outlines of Psychology.* Translated by Edward Bradford Titchener. London and New York, 1895.

LEHMANN, ALFRED. *Die körperlichen Äusserungen psychischer Zustände.* Translated (into German) by F. Bendixen. Leipzig, 1899–1905. 3 vols.

LEHMANN, FRIEDRICH RUDOLF. *Mana, der Begriff des "ausserordentlich Wirkungsvollen" bei Südseevölkern.* Leipzig, 1922.

LEIBNIZ, GOTTFRIED WILHELM. *Kleinere philosophische Schriften.* Edited by R. Habs. Leipzig, 1883. 3 vols.

———. *Philosophical Writings.* Selected and translated by Mary Morris. (Everyman's Library.) London and New York, 1934. (*Monadology,* pp. 3–20; *Principles of Nature and of Grace, founded on Reason,* pp. 21–31.)

[———.] *The Philosophical Works of Leibniz; a Selection.* Translated by G. M. Duncan. New Haven, 1890.

———. *Theodicy.* Translated by E. M. Huggard. Edited by Austin Farrer. London, 1951 [1952].

LÉVY-BRUHL, LUCIEN. *How Natives Think.* Translated by Lilian A. Clare. London, 1926. (Orig.: *Les Fonctions mentales dans les sociétés inférieures.* Paris, 1912.)

LEWES, GEORGE HENRY. *Problems of Life and Mind.* London, 1874 [1873]–79. 5 vols. (Vol. II, *The Physical Basis of Mind*, 1877.)

"Liber de compositione Alchemiae." See *Artis auriferae*, ii.

LIPPS, THEODOR. "Der Begriff des Unbewussten." In: [*Report of*] *Third International Congress for Psychology*, Munich, 4–7 August 1896. Munich, 1897.

——. *Grundtatsachen des Seelenlebens.* Bonn, 1912.

——. *Leitfaden der Psychologie.* Leipzig, 1903; 2nd edn., 1906.

LOVEJOY, ARTHUR O. "The Fundamental Concept of the Primitive Philosophy," *The Monist* (Chicago), XVI (1906), 357–82.

LUMHOLTZ, CARL. *Unknown Mexico.* London, 1903.

MCCONNELL, ROBERT A. "E.S.P.—Fact or Fancy?" *Scientific Monthly* (Lancaster, Pennsylvania), LXIX: 2 (1949), 121–25.

MACDONELL, A. A. *A Practical Sanskrit Dictionary.* London, 1924.

MCGEE, W. J. "The Siouan Indians—A Preliminary Sketch." In: *Fifteenth Report of the U.S. Bureau of Ethnology for 1893–94.* Washington, 1897. (Pp. 153–204.)

MACNICOL, NICOL (ed.). *Hindu Scriptures.* (Everyman's Library.) London and New York, 1938.

MAEDER, ALPHONSE. *Heilung und Entwicklung im Seelenleben.* Zurich, 1918.

——. "Régulation psychique et guérison," *Archives suisses de neurologie et de psychiatrie* (Zurich), XVI (1925), 198–224.

——. "Sur le mouvement psychanalytique: un point de vue nouveau en psychologie," *L'Année psychologique* (Paris), XVIII (1912), 389–418.

——. "Über die Funktion des Traumes," *Jahrbuch für psychoanalytische und psychopathologische Forschungen* (Leipzig and Vienna), IV (1912), 692–707.

——. *The Dream Problem.* Translated by Frank Mead Hallack and Smith Ely Jelliffe. (Nervous and Mental Disease Monograph Series, 20.) New York, 1916. (Orig.: "Über das Traumproblem,"

Jahrbuch für psychoanalytische und psychopathologische For-schungen (Leipzig and Vienna), V (1913), 647–86.)

Man and Time. (Papers from the Eranos Yearbooks, 3.) Translated by Ralph Manheim and R. F. C. Hull. New York (Bollingen Series XXX) and London, 1957.

MANGET, JOANNES JACOBUS (ed.). *Bibliotheca chemica curiosa*. Geneva, 1702. 2 vols.

MANNHARDT, WILHELM. *Wald- und Feldkulte*. 2nd edn., Berlin, 1904–5. 2 vols.

MARAIS, EUGÈNE NIELEN. *The Soul of the White Ant*. Translated (from the Afrikaans) by Winifred de Kok. London, 1937.

MARSILIO FICINO. *Auctores platonici*. Venice, 1497.

MEIER, CARL ALFRED. *Antike Inkubation und moderne Psychotherapie*. Zurich, 1949.

———. "Moderne Physik—Moderne Psychologie." In: *Die kulturelle Bedeutung der komplexen Psychologie*. (Festschrift zum 60. Geburtstag von C. G. Jung.) Berlin, 1935.

———. "Spontanmanifestationen des kollektiven Unbewussten," *Zentralblatt für Psychotherapie* (Leipzig), XI (1939), 284–303.

———. *Zeitgemässe Probleme der Traumforschung*. (Eidgenössische Technische Hochschule: Kultur- und Staatswissenschaftliche Schriften, 75.) Zurich, 1950.

MERINGER, R. "Wörter und Sachen," *Indogermanische Forschungen* (Strassburg), XVI (1904), 101–196.

MIGNE, JACQUES PAUL (ed.). *Patrologiae cursus completus*. [*P.L.*] Latin series. Paris, 1844–64. 221 vols. [*P.G.*] Greek series. Paris, 1857–66. 166 vols. [These works are cited as "MIGNE, *P.L.*" and "MIGNE, *P.G.*" respectively. References are to columns, not to pages.]

MORGAN, CONWAY LLOYD. *Habit and Instinct*. London, 1896.

MURCHISON, C. (ed.). *Psychologies of 1930*. (International University Series in Psychology.) Worcester, Mass., 1930.

MYERS, FREDERIC W. H. "The Subliminal Consciousness," *Proceedings of the Society for Psychical Research* (London), VII (1892), 298–355.

MYLIUS, JOHANN DANIEL. *Philosophia reformata.* Frankfurt, 1622.

NELKEN, JAN. "Analytische Beobachtungen über Phantasien eines Schizophrenen," *Jahrbuch für psychoanalytische und psycho-pathologische Forschungen* (Leipzig), IV (1912), 504–62.

NIETZSCHE, FRIEDRICH WILHELM. *Thus Spake Zarathustra.* Translated by Thomas Common, revised by Oscar Levy and John L. Beevers. London, 1932.

NUNBERG, H. "On the Physical Accompaniments of Association Processes." In: *Studies in Word-Association* . . . under the direction of C. G. Jung. Translated by M. D. Eder. London, 1918; New York, 1919. (Pp. 531–60.)

ORANDUS, EIRENAEUS. *Nicholas Flammel: His Exposition of the Hieroglyphicall Figures, etc.* London, 1624.

ORIGEN. *De principiis.* See MIGNE, *P.G.,* vol. 11, cols. 115–414. For translation, see: *On First Principles.* Translated by G. W. Butterworth. London, 1936.

——. *In Jeremiam homiliae.* See MIGNE, *P.G.,* vol. 13, cols. 255–544.

OSTWALD, (FRIEDRICH) WILHELM. *Die Philosophie der Werte.* Leipzig, 1913.

PARACELSUS (Theophrastus Bombastes of Hohenheim). *Das Buch Paragranum.* Edited by Franz Strunz. Leipzig, 1903.

——. *De vita longa.* Edited by Adam von Bodenstein. Basel, 1562.

——. *Sämtliche Werke.* Edited by Karl Sudhoff and Wilhelm Matthiessen. Munich and Berlin, 1922–35. 15 vols.

——. *Erster [–Zehender] Theil der Bücher und Schrifften . . . Philippi Theophrasti Bombast von Hohenheim, Paracelsi genannt.* Edited by Johannes Huser. Basel, 1589–91. 10 vols.

PAULI, W. "The Influence of Archetypal Ideas on the Scientific Theories of Kepler." Translated by Priscilla Silz. In: *The Interpretation of Nature and the Psyche.* New York (Bollingen Series LI) and London, 1955.

PAULUS, JEAN. *Le Problème de l'hallucination et l'évolution de la psychologie d'Esquirol à Pierre Janet.* (Bibliothèque de la Faculté de Philosophie et de Lettres de l'Université de Liège, fasc. 91.) Liège and Paris, 1941.

547

PECHUËL-LOESCHE, EDUARD. *Volkskunde von Loango.* Stuttgart, 1907.

PETERSON, FREDERICK, and JUNG, C. G. "Psycho-physical Investigations with the Galvanometer and Pneumograph in Normal and Insane Individuals," *Brain* (London), XXX (1907), 153–218.

PHILO JUDAEUS. *De opificio mundi.* In: [*Works*]. Translated by F. H. Colson and G. H. Whitaker. (Loeb Classical Library.) New York and London, 1929– . 12 vols. [I, 2–137.)

PICAVET, FRANÇOIS. *Essais sur l'histoire générale et comparée des théologies et des philosophies médiévales.* Paris, 1913.

PICO DELLA MIRANDOLA. *Opera omnia.* Basel, 1557.

PITRA, JEAN BAPTISTE. *Analecta sacra et classica Spicilegio Solesmensi parata.* Paris and Rome, 1876–91. 8 vols.

PLOTINUS. *The Enneads.* Translated by Stephen Mackenna. 2nd edn., revised by B. S. Page. London, 1956.

PRATT, J. G.; RHINE, J. B.; STUART, C. E.; SMITH, B. M.; and GREENWOOD, J. A. *Extra-Sensory Perception after Sixty Years.* New York, 1940.

PREUSS, K. T. "Der Ursprung der Religion und Kunst," *Globus* (Brunswick), LXXXVI (1904), 321–92 passim; LXXXVII (1905), 333–419 passim.

PROSPER OF AQUITAINE. *Sententiae ex Augustino delibatae.* See MIGNE, *P.L.*, vol. 51, cols. 427–496.

PTOLEMAEUS (Ptolemy). See CARDAN, JEROME.

REID, THOMAS. *Essays on the Active Powers of Man.* Edinburgh, 1788.

RHINE, J. B. *Extra-Sensory Perception.* Boston, 1934.

——. "An Introduction to the Work of Extra-Sensory Perception," *Transactions of the New York Academy of Sciences* (New York), Ser. II, XII (1950), 164–68.

——. *New Frontiers of the Mind.* New York and London, 1937.

——. *The Reach of the Mind.* London, 1948. Reprinted Harmondsworth (Penguin Books), 1954.

—— and HUMPHREY, BETTY M. "A Transoceanic ESP Experiment," *Journal of Parapsychology* (Durham, North Carolina), VI (1942), 52–74.

RICHET, CHARLES. "Relations de diverses expériences sur transmission mentale, la lucidité, et autres phénomènes non explicable par les données scientifiques actuelles," *Proceedings of the Society for Psychical Research* (London), V (1888), 18–168.

RICKSHER, C., and JUNG, C. G. "Further Investigations on the Galvanic Phenomenon," *Journal of Abnormal and Social Psychology* (Albany, N. Y.), II (1907), 189–217.

RIPLEY, SIR GEORGE. *Opera omnia chemica.* Cassel, 1649.

RIVERS, W. H. R. "Instinct and the Unconscious," *British Journal of Psychology* (Cambridge), X (1919–20), 1–7.

RÖHR, J. "Das Wesen des Mana," *Anthropos* (Salzburg), XIV–XV (1919–20), 97–124.

ROSENBERG, ALFONS. *Zeichen am Himmel: Das Weltbild der Astrologie.* Zurich, 1949.

ROSENCREUTZ, CHRISTIAN. *Chymische Hochzeit.* Strasbourg, 1616.

Saint-Graal. Edited by Eugène Hucher. Le Mans, 1878. 3 vols.

SCHILLER, FRIEDRICH. *On the Aesthetic Education of Man.* Translated by Reginald Snell. London, 1954.

——. "The Cranes of Ibycus." In: *The Poems.* Translated by E. P. Arnold-Forster. London, 1901. (Pp. 158–63.)

SCHMIEDLER, G. R. "Personality Correlates of ESP as Shown by Rorschach Studies," *Journal of Parapsychology* (Durham, North Carolina), XIII (1949), 23–31.

SCHOLZ, WILHELM VON. *Der Zufall: eine Vorform des Schicksals.* Stuttgart, 1924.

SCHOPENHAUER, ARTHUR. *Parerga und Paralipomena.* Edited by R. von Koeber. Berlin, 1891. 2 vols.

——. *Transcendent Speculations on the Apparent Design in the Fate of the Individual.* Translated by David Irvine. London, 1913.

SCHULTZE, FRITZ. *Psychologie der Naturvölker.* Leipzig, 1900; another edn., 1925.

SELIGMANN, CHARLES GABRIEL. *The Melanesians of British New Guinea.* Cambridge, 1910.

SIEBECK, HERMANN. *Geschichte der Psychologie.* Gotha, 1880–84. 2 parts.

SILBERER, HERBERT. *Problems of Mysticism and Its Symbolism.* Translated by Smith Ely Jelliffe. New York, 1917.

———. "Über die Symbolbildung," *Jahrbuch für psychoanalytische und psychopathologische Forschungen* (Vienna and Leipzig), III (1911), 661–723; IV (1912), 607–83.

———. *Der Zufall und die Koboldstreiche des Unbewussten.* (Schriften zur Seelenkunde und Erziehungskunst, 3.) Bern and Leipzig, 1921.

SOAL, S. G. "Science and Telepathy," *Enquiry* (London), I:2 (1948), 5–7.

———. "The Scientific Evidence for Extra-Sensory Perception," *Discovery* (London), X (1949), 373–77.

——— and BATEMAN, F. *Modern Experiments in Telepathy.* London, 1954.

SÖDERBLOM, NATHAN. *Das Werden des Gottesglaubens.* Leipzig, 1926.

SPEISER, ANDREAS. *Über die Freiheit.* (Basler Universitätsreden, 28.) Basel, 1950.

SPENCER, BALDWIN, and GILLEN, F. J. *The Northern Tribes of Central Australia.* London, 1904.

SPIELREIN, S. "Über den psychischen Inhalt eines Falles von Schizophrenie," *Jahrbuch für psychoanalytische und psychopathologische Forschungen* (Vienna and Leipzig), III (1911), 329–400.

SPINOZA, BENEDICT. *Ethics.* Translated by Andrew Boyle. (Everyman's Library.) London and New York, 1934.

Spirit and Nature. (Papers from the Eranos Yearbooks, 1.) Translated by Ralph Manheim and R. F. C. Hull. New York (Bollingen Series XXX), 1954; London, 1955.

STEKEL, WILHELM. "Die Verpflichtung des Namens," *Zeitschrift für Psychotherapie und medizinische Psychologie* (Stuttgart), III (1911), 110ff.

STERN, L. WILLIAM. *Über Psychologie der individuellen Differenzen.*

550

(Schriften der Gesellschaft für psychologische Forschung, 12.) Leipzig, 1900.

SYNESIUS. *Opuscula.* Edited by Nicolaus Terzaghi. (Scriptores Graeci et Latini.) Rome, 1949.

SZONDI, LIPOT. *Experimentelle Triebdiagnostik.* Bonn, 1947–49. 2 vols.

———. *Triebpathologie.* Bern, 1952.

Tao Teh Ching. See WALEY.

THEATRUM CHEMICUM. Ursel and Strasbourg, 1602–61. 6 vols. (Vols. 1–3, Ursel, 1602; etc.)

Contents quoted in this volume:

VOLUME I
 i Dorn: Speculativae philosophiae [pp. 255–310]
 ii Dorn: Philosophia meditativa [pp. 450–72]
 iii Dorn: De tenebris contra naturam et vita brevi [pp. 518–35]

VOLUME II
 iv Aegidius de Vadis: Dialogus inter naturam et filium philosophiae [pp. 95–123]

THORNDIKE, LYNN. *A History of Magic and Experimental Science.* New York, 1929–41. 6 vols.

TYLOR, EDWARD B. *Primitive Culture.* 3rd edn., London, 1891. 2 vols.

TYRRELL, G. N. M. *The Personality of Man.* London, 1947.

VERAGUTH, OTTO. *Das psycho-galvanische Reflexphänomen.* Berlin, 1909.

VILLA, GUIDO. *Einleitung in die Psychologie der Gegenwart.* (Translated from Italian.) Leipzig, 1902.

VIRGIL. [*Works*]. Translated by H. Rushton Fairclough. (Loeb Classical Library.) London and New York, 1929. 2 vols.

VISCHER, FRIEDRICH THEODOR. *Auch Einer.* Stuttgart and Leipzig, 1884. 2 vols.

WALEY, ARTHUR (trans.). *The Way and Its Power.* London, 1934.

WARNECKE, J. *Die Religion der Batak.* Leipzig, 1909.

[WEI PO-YANG.] "An Ancient Chinese Treatise on Alchemy entitled Ts'an T'ung Ch'i" (translated by Lu-chiang Wu), *Isis* (Bruges), XVIII (1932), 210–89.

WEYL, HERMANN. "Wissenschaft als symbolische Konstruktion des Menschen," *Eranos-Jahrbuch 1948* (Zurich, 1949), 375–439.

WHITE, STEWART EDWARD. *The Road I Know.* New York, 1942; London, 1951.

——. *The Unobstructed Universe.* New York, 1940; London, 1949.

WILHELM, HELLMUT. "The Concept of Time in the Book of Changes." In *Man and Time,* q.v.

WILHELM, RICHARD. *Chinesische Lebensweisheit.* Darmstadt, 1922.

—— (trans.). *The Secret of the Golden Flower.* With a commentary and a memorial by C. G. Jung. London and New York, 1931.

——. *Das wahre Buch vom südlichen Blütenland.* Jena, 1912.

——. See also *I Ching.*

WOLF, CHRISTIAN VON. *Psychologia empirica.* Frankfurt and Leipzig, 1732.

——. *Vernünftige Gedanken von Gott, der Welt, und der Seele des Menschen.* 1719.

WUNDT, WILHELM. *Grundzüge der physiologischen Psychologie.* 5th edn., Leipzig, 1902–3. 3 vols.

——. *Outlines of Psychology.* Translated by Charles Hubbard Judd. Leipzig, 1902.

——. *Völkerpsychologie.* Leipzig, 1911–23. 10 vols.

ZELLER, EDUARD. *Die Philosophie der Griechen in ihrer geschichtlichen Entwicklung dargestellt.* Tübingen, 1856. 3 vols.

INDEX

INDEX

A

abaissement du niveau mental, 77, 235, 436, 446, 480
Abegg, Lily, 489*n*
Abelard, Pierre, 5*n*, 196
abstraction, 5
acausal events, *see* events
actions: instinctive, 130; symptomatic, 34, 77; volitional, 172
activity: drive to, 117, 118; psychic, waking and sleeping, 306
Acts of the Apostles, 315
Adam, 293; old, 393
adaptation, 23, 34*ff*; and direction, 35; harmonious, 39; need of continuous, 73; to outer world, 392; psychological, libido and, 32; stages towards achievement, 32
adhista, 154, 209
Adler, Alfred, 10*n*, 24, 50, 258, 263*n*
adiposity, 398
adolescents, eternal, 399
adult state, induction into, 374
Aegidius de Vadis, 494
aeroplanes, dream-motif, 283
Aesculapius, 289
Aesop, 239
affect(s): archetypes and, 436; and attitude, 330*ff*; displacement of, 10; disproportionate, 130; dulling of, 26; enrichment of, 82; impulsive, 131; personified, 329*f*; and synchronicity, 448*f*; tends to become autonomous complex, 330; value-estimation of, 14; violent, 313

affectivity: and ESP experiments, 524; and the instincts, 440; in unconscious, 172
affinity, elective, 431
Africa, 233; East, 407
afternoon of life, 399*f*; *see also* second half of life
age: dignity of, 400; physiological and psychological, 119; *see also* old, the; old age
ageing, the: and contraction of life, 399; and preparation for death, 410; *see also* old, the; old age
"aghast," 329
agriculture: libido and, 43; origin of, 43
Agrippa von Nettesheim, Henricus Cornelius, 195, 492*f*, 495
aiolos, 345
air, moving, and soul, 345
Albertus Magnus, 196, 448*f*
alchemy, 46*f*, 190*ff*, 485, 495; microcosmos in, 492; and three/four, 513; transformation in, 293
alertness, 359
Algonquins, 61
alienation, 311
"all-or-none reaction," 129*f*, 131, 135, 137, 181, 187
allurements, divine, 493
"also-I," 393
Alverdes, Friedrich, 138*n*
ambition, inordinate, 116
Amboina, 437*n*
Amenophis IV, 49
amoeba, 152
America; death of friend in, 443; *see also* United States

Berger, Hans, 14*n*
Bergson, Henri, 30, 132, 137
Bernard of Treviso, 514
bewitchment, 368; of cattle, 302
Bible, *see names of individual books*
bile, 364
binarius, 514
Binswanger, Ludwig, 14*n*
biochemical processes, psyche and, 344
biology: causality in, 423; energic standpoint and, 16; and the psyche, 114*ff;* and the "unique," 422
bird(s), 293, 294; flock seen at death, 438*f,* 442, 445, 447; as redeemer figure, 111; *see also* weaver-bird
birth, 345; psychic, 391
Bleuler, Eugen, 176*f,* 188*n*
blindness: peripheral, 143; psychogenic, 308
blockage: dreams and, 365; of unconscious, 364
blue (colour), representing spirit, 211
body: correspondence with psychic organism, 152; living, concept of, 320*f;* inner/subtle/breath-, 194; and mind, duality, 321; —, two aspects of single fact, 326; and psyche, co-functioning, 261, 321, 342; separation of consciousness from, 509
body markings, 374
body-soul problem, 506; *see also* body and mind
Boer War, 443
Böhme, Jakob, 495*n*
Bohr, Niels, 489*n*
Boltzmann, Ludwig, 26
"Book of What Is in the Netherworld," 439
boredom: in analysis, 74; and telepathic experiments, 434
bowl, golden, 291
brain, 340, 505; at birth, 371; child's, 53, 310; disturbance of, and psychic defects, 322; injuries to,

506; mental diseases and, 279*f;* and psyche, 115, 412; psychic as secretion of, 383; and reflex arcs, 322; thought as secretion of, 343
brain psychology, 8, 16
breakdowns, nervous, in forties, 398
break-up, radioactive, *see* radioactive decay
breath, 319, 345; breath-body, 345
British Psychological Society, 344
brothers, hostile, 370
Brown, G. Spencer, 482
Bruno, Giordano, 361
Buddha, 366
Buddhists/Buddhism, 68*f;* and death, 408; *see also* Zen
bull, of Mithras, 155
Burckhardt, Jakob, 133*n*
Burt, E. L., 433
Busemann, Adolf, 177*n*
Busse, Ludwig, 7 & *n,* 17, 18
Butler, Samuel (1612–80), 34
Butler, Samuel (1835–1902), 494*n*
butterfly, 345

C

Cabalists, 378
cabinets, natural history, 422
candle, 156
Cardan, Jerome, 455*n*
cards, for ESP experiments, 432, 523
career, transition to, 392
Carnot's law, 25
Carpenter, W. B., 179*n*
Cartesians, and perception, 500; *see also* Descartes
Carus, C. G., 102, 167, 169, 170, 171
Catholic, and collective unconscious, 156
cattle, bewitching of, 302
cauda pavonis, see peacock's tail
causa efficiens/causa finalis, 281
causality, 421*ff,* 445*f,* 486, 491, 501, 511, 530; and behaviour, 22; and finality, 4*ff,* 22*ff,* 241, *see also* finality; magical, 483, 501; and ob-

tivity of, 200; return of complex to, 311; secondary, 174; semiotic contents, 175; and sense-functions, 175*f*, 342; shift in localization of, 509; *sine qua non* of psychic life, 343; in sleep, 143; splitting off of, 410, 508; subliminal, 167*n*, 185*n;* symptomatic contents, 175; total, impossible, 119; transitoriness of, 349; unconscious as fringe of, 185; and *Weltanschauung,* 361; why it exists, 361
consensus gentium: and death, 408; and religion, 409
consensus omnium, 422
constancy, principle of, 18
constellation, 94, 95; of the archetype, 440
constellations, celestial, 152
constitution, and psyche, 107*ff*
contagion, mental, attitude and, 330
context, taking up, 285*f*
contingent, the, 515, 519
continuum, 412; *see also* space-time continuum
contraction, 446
conversion: of St. Paul, *see* Paul, St.; sudden, 307
convictions, hardening of, 395
Coomaraswamy, Ananda, 198*n*
co-ordinates, conceptual, 445
co-ordination, of psychic and physical processes, 505
Corpus Hermeticum, 136*n*
corpus mysticum, 491
correspondence(s), 430, 494, 497, 517; argument/principle/theory of, 489*n*, 492*n*, 495, 501, 514, 531; astrological, 527
correspondentia, 489
cortex, cerebral, 509, 510; dreams and, 511
cortical function, extinction of, 510
counteraction, of unconscious, 79*f*
counter-transference, 273
cranes, 442*n*
craving, in dreams, 245

Crawley, Ernest, 48*n*
creatio ex nihilo, 480
creation: acts of, 516, 517, 518; continuous, 517
creative: achievements, 365; acts, *see* creation, acts of; instinct, 118; products, in unconscious, 11*n*
creativity: and sexuality, 118, 368; and unconscious, 70, 157
criticism, 362
crocodile, 501
Crookes, Sir William, 302
cross, *see* quaternity
cross-connection, meaningful, 427, 482
crowds, dream-motif, 283
crown, 112
cryptomnesia, 148, 151, 262, 317, 439
crystals, 108, 311*n*, 503
culmination, of dream, 295
culture, 394; beginning of, 375; consciousness and, 388; individual, 60; natural, 42; and nature, 400; reflection and, 116*ff; see also* work
Cumont, Franz, 197
Cupid's arrow, 329
cure, analysis not a, 72, 73

D

Dacqué, Edgar, 340
dagger, 76
Dahns, Fritz, 437*n*
Dakota Indians, 61
Dalcq, A. M., 512
Damascus, 307
damnation, everlasting, 379
dance/dancing, 42*f*, 202; of bees, 510; buffalo-, 44
dangers, 155
Daniel, Book of, 80, 251
Dariex, Xavier, 430, 522
dark night of the soul, 225
Darwin, Charles, 23
day-dreaming, 410; *see also* fantasies
dead: appearance in dreams, 304; deterioration of character in the,

181*f;* transcendent, an artificial product, 76; —, contents, 90; —, how produced, 77; meaning, 68*f*, 73
Funk, Philipp, 198*n*
Furies, 99
Fürst, Emma, 111
future, psychic, 367

G

gain, lust for, 116
Galileo, 449
ganglia: in insects, 510; ganglion cells, 322
garden, walled, 293
Garrett, Eileen J., 434
Gatschet, Albert Samuel, 49
Gauss, Karl Friedrich, 502
Geddes, Sir Auckland, 509
Geist/gāst, 300, 329
Gelaria, 65*n*
generation, spontaneous, 280
Genesis, Book of, 147
genius, 233
geomantic experiment, 527
geometria, 496
geometry, 497
Germany, 170, 225
"getting stuck," 440
Geulincx, Arnold, 449, 498*n*, 505
ghost(s), 303, 316, 328; fear of, 353*f;* unconscious imago as, 274
ghost-trap, 305*n*
Gilgamesh Epic, 101
Gillen, F. J., 44*n*, 48*n*, 62*n*, 63*n*
glands, 340, 342, 343; hormone-producing, 115; instincts and, 180; *see also* thyroid gland
globes, luminous, 199
globus hystericus, 146
Gnosticism, 54, 190*n*
goal: life and, 405*f*, 408; of second half of life, 400; social, 395; supramundane, 401; *see also* death
Goblet d'Almellas, Eugène, Count, 111

God: bacchantic, 170; bond of sensuous and suprasensuous, 490; Cabalists, and name of, 378*f;* concept of, 278; contradictoriness of, 55; creator/ and creation, 341, 518*n;* energy as, 352; experience of, 328; always Father, 518*n;* and God-image, 278*f;* idea of, and *mana,* 65; and imperfect creation, 54; individual minds and, 344; invention of, 409; knowledge and will in, 500; as psychic fact, 328; as spirit/spirit of, 54, 170, 340; and Sun, Elgonyi view, 154, 209; world as visible/world-system as, 351, 491
God-image, 278*f*
Goddard, Air Marshal Sir Victor, 526
gods: all things full of, 493; complexes as, 369; as libido analogues, 49; names of, 378; transformations of, Greek, 341
Goethe, Johann Wolfgang von, 37, 60, 89, 187*n*, 212, 368*f*, 377, 393, 449, 455*n*, 513; mother-complex of, 367
gold, 199
Gold Coast [Ghana], 62
Golden Age, 210
Goldney, K. M., 517
Gonzales, Loys, 199
good and evil, 272
Gothic Age, 338, 342
Gottesminne, 20
Granet, Marcel, 489
graphology, 454
Great Mother, 153; *see also* mother; mother-image
Greco-Roman world, 338, 355
greed, 116
Greek intellect, and one-sidedness, 382
Greeks, and the soul, 345
Grimm, Jacob, 517*n*
Grot, Nicolas von, 7, 8, 15
Guillaume de Conches, 196
guilt, 242*ff*, 248

loss, sense of, and repression of complex, 311
lost objects, return to owners, 431
Lovejoy, Arthur O., 61*n*, 62*n*, 64
lower organisms, "meaningful" behaviour of, 505
Lucifer, 495
Luke, Gospel of, 194*n*
lumen, 191; *naturae,* 192
Lumholtz, Carl, 63
luminosity(-ies), 189*ff,* 199, 436
lysis, 295

M

McConnell, Robert A., 434*f*
Macdonell, A. A., 518*n*
McGee, W. J., 61*n*
machine, life and use of, 42
macrocosm, 492
Maeder, Alphonse, 10*n,* 15*n,* 255, 257, 263*f*
magic, 46, 61*ff,* 270, 448, 501; "mother of science," 46; number, 458; among primitives, 137, 157, 347, 369, 370, 374; sympathetic, 149; *see also* ceremonies
magna mater, 156
magnetic field, earth's, 460, 527*f*
magnetism, 442
magpies, 442*n*
Maier, Michael, 514
Malagasy, 64
Malalas, John, 444
Malaya, 63
Malebranche, Nicolas, 136
man: brown, dream of, 503*f;* centre of events, 492; civilized, psychic life of, 388; Cosmic, *see* Purusha; effeminate, 398; First, 199; and heaven, affinity, 490, 495, 496; inner, 194; metallic, 503*n;* new, 393; synthesis of three worlds, 491; universal and individual, 380; wounded, 506; *see also* mass man; medieval man; microcosm

mana, 28*n,* 63*f,* 65, 137*n,* 155, 158, 209, 233; personality, 156
mandala, 199, 213, 227*f,* 457
Manichaeism, 190*n*
Manget, J. J., 293*n*
manitu, 61*f*
Mannhardt, Wilhelm, 43*n,* 44*n*
"mantic" methods/procedures, 450, 451, 453, 456, 474, 480, 485, 501, 502, 525*f,* 530
Maoris, 64
Marais, E. N., 180*n*
Maria the Jewess, 513
marriage: catastrophes in, 398; connections, 454*ff;* horoscopes, 459*ff,* 528*f; see also* aspects, astrological
martyr, Christian, 336
Mars, 401, 455, 461, 474, 528
Mary, the Virgin, 151, 156
Masai, 64
masculine protest, 367
masculinity, 119, 397*f*
Mass, the, 149
mass, energy and, 20*n*
mass man, 208*f,* 219, 220
Master, 331
mater ecclesia, 156
materialism, 280, 302, 338, 365*f,* 367, 370, 512; reaction against, 302
mathematics, 456, 490, 502
matter: inscrutable, 342; latent psyche in, 234; mind and, 339; nature of, 327, 384; and psyche, relation, 215, 234; as psychic category, 120; and spirit, 216
Matthew, Gospel of, 193*n*
maturity, 406; need of education in, 60
Mauss, Marcel, 28*n,* 122
maxim, 331
maya, 354
Mayer, Robert, 65*n*
Mazdaznan, 49
meaning, 339, 482, 485*ff,* 487*ff;* criterion of synchronicity, 485; equivalence of, 452, 531; self-subsistent, dreams and, 503; Tao as, 486

number(s) (*cont.*):
dence of, 424, 520*f;* invented or
found, 457; properties of, 516,
517; "sacred," 456; and synchronicity, 456
numen, 191, 233
numinosity, 186, 191, 456; of archetype, 205*f,* 209, 312; of series of
chance happenings, 426*n*
numinosum, 104
Nunberg, H., 14*n*
nurse, 249

O

object: death of, 274; -imago, 274;
mischievousness of, 97; overvaluation of, 275; projection and, 273;
and subject, primitive confusion,
154; *see also* subject and object;
subjective level
observer: in physics, 215, 229; and
observed, incommensurability, 512
obsessions, 131, 364; *see also* ideas,
obsessive
Occam's razor, 186
Odin, 517*n*
oki, 61
old, the/old age: extreme, 403; "getting wooden" in, 407; and libido
in dance, 44; among primitives,
400, 407; purpose of, 399*ff*
omen, 442
one-sidedness, 122*f,* 124, 207, 276,
377, 396; of conscious life/con-
sciousness, 292; —, compensation
for, 73; implied by direction, 71,
79; of science, 220; of Western
man, 382
opposites: pairs of, 272; —, and
libido, 32*f;* problem of, 125; tension of, 393; —, in child, 52*f;* —, in
God, 55; —, and progress of culture,
59; and transcendental function,
90; union of, 203, 207, 474; see
also *complexio oppositorum;* conflict; INSTANCES: atheism/theism,

370; light/dark, 203; materialism/
mysticism, 370; mind/body, 326;
nature/spirit, 51; physical/spirit-
ual passion, 212; right/left, 203;
spirit/instinct, 207*f;* upper/lower,
203; Yin/Yang, 452
opposition(s), astrological, 461*ff*
optimism, 526; unjustified, 392
Orandus, Eirenaeus, 197*n*
order: archetype of, 456; in fantasy,
203; God as creator of, 498; number and, 456
orderedness, acausal, 512, 516
organic systems, production of, 181
organological standpoint, 177
Origen, 222*n,* 518*n*
Orphism, 444
Osiris, 155
Ostwald, (Friedrich) Wilhelm, 6*n,*
12*n*
Otto, Rudolf, 104
outlooks, horizontal and vertical,
339, 342

P

pain: and dreams, 261; perception
of, 322; a psychic image, 353
pain-pleasure reaction, 123
painting, 82, 86, 202
Palau, 64
palladium, 49
palolo worm, 437
pan-psychism, 16
Papa, 156
parable, language of, 248
Paracelsus, 191, 192, 193*ff,* 493*n,* 495
Paradise, 388, 390
parallelism: pre-established, 500; of
psychic processes, 262; psychophysical, 17, 498, 506, 511; *see also*
harmony
parallels, symbolic, 440
paramnesia, 444
parapraxes, 101
parapsychic phenomena, 205*n,* 234,
318

planets, 454; seven, 197
plants, 321
Plato, 30, 156, 502; and archetypes, 135; cave myth, 213*n;* "Fourth" in *Timaeus,* 513; parables of, 248
Platonists, 493
play-instinct, 117
pleasure. craving for, 393; Freud and, 50
Plotinus, 490
plum-pudding, 431*n*
pneuma/πνεῦμα, 320, 345
Podmore, F., 430*n,* 450
poimandres/poimen, 331
political changes, and psychology, 314
polytheism, extermination of, 49
Ponape, 64
pontifex maximus, 156
possession, 98; and hysteria, 368; and insanity, 305
possibility, criterion of, 423
potentialities, psychic, loss of, 394
power: craving for, 393; infantile claims to, 258, 260; instinct, 367; psychotherapy and increase of, 311
"powers," suprapersonal, subjection to, 50
Pratt, J. G., et al., 432*n*
prayer, 518
precognition, *see* foreknowledge
predicates, value, 94
prefiguration, 430
pregnancy, 345
Press, the, in wartime, 264
prestige, psychology of, 50
Preuss, K. T., 42*n,* 65
primitives, 354, 361; and autonomous psychic contents, 369; and belief in souls/spirits, 302*ff,* 305, 309; and canalization of libido, 44*f;* and claims of archetype, 375; conceptions of libido, 61*ff;* dissociability in, 104; and dreams, 49*n,* 303; and evocation of unconscious, 78; hunger among, 116; in-stincts in, 134; intuition among, 137; live in two worlds, 303; and loss of soul, 313; and magic, 46; matter and spirit among, 120; mental illnesses in, 305; and meta-phor, 147; and myths, 38, 153; and object, 270, 274; old people among, 400; and the psyche, 346; psychology of, 50; quasi-neurosis of, 50; seldom reach old age, 407; and sexuality, 244; and space and time, 436; symbol and, 25; and synchronicity, 50; and uncon-scious, 157; world-picture of, 327; *see also* initiation; magic
Prince, Morton, 96
principle(s): guiding, 335; harden-ing of, 395; triad of, 517; univer-sal, 490
probability, 228*f,* 425, 528*f;* calculus, 430; psychic, archetypes as, 515
problems, 388*ff;* and consciousness, 390; purpose of, 394
process(es): and instincts, 180; psychic, 166, 207
Proclus, 137
prognosis, dreams and, 282
progression: and development, 37; energic view, 38*f;* and extraver-sion, 40; of libido, 32*ff;* means to regression, 40; origin of, 39
projectile, 406, 408
projection(s), 207, 264*f,* 271, 308, 370, 452; of analyst's psychology, 259; archetypal, 493; in child, on to parents, 53; and counter-pro-jections, 273; favourable and un-favourable, 271; negative, 272; in neurotics, 264; of primitive psyche, 121; withdrawal of, 269
proof, demand for, 401
prophecy, in dreams, 255
Prosper of Aquitaine, 518*n*
protagonists, in dream, 294
Protestant/Protestantism, 59, 156
Proteus anguinus, 152
proton radiation, 460, 527, 528

523, 526; and dreams, 261*f;* and unconscious complexes, 318

telescope, 168, 449

temperament, difficult, 392

temperature, 334, 497

tension: bodily, 322; problems and, 391; *see also* energy-tension; opposites

terrena, 294

terror, 323

tetrad, 456, 512

tetradic principle, in astrology, 453

tetragrammaton, 495

Theatrum chemicum, 192*n,* 193*n,* 494*n,* 514*n*

Theophrastus, 490

theosophy, 49, 59, 379

thinking: apotropaic, 99; control of, 306; directed, 27; distorted, 410; dream-, 247; faculty of, 123; function, and adaptation, 34; medical man and, 277; primitive, 311; and primordial images, 402*f;* and recognition, 141; trinitarian type, 514; and understanding, 402; wishful, and dreams, 504*n; see also* thought

Thor, 517*n*

Thorndike, Lynn, 196*n,* 453*n*

thought(s): extra-conscious, 324; non-spatial, 347*f;* reality of, 383; seat of, 347; as secretions of brain, 343; transcerebral, 511; unreal and real, 384; *see also* thinking

thought-deprivation, 13

thought-transference, 151

three and four, dilemma of, 513

threshold, 310; lower and upper, 176; psychological, 166*n,* 176

throat, lump in, 145*f*

thyroid gland, 403

Timaeus, 513; *see also* Plato

time, 511; in association experiments, 13; and creation, 518*n;* as fourth dimension, 512; multi-dimensionality of, 513*n;* one-dimensionality of, 512; psychic in origin, 436; psychic relativity of, 433, 531;

probably same as space, 445; in Rhine's experiments, 433; statements of, in dream, 294; symbolism, 197*f;* and synchronistic phenomena, 445, 517; symbolism, 197*f; see also* space; space-time

Tobi, 64

Tobit, Book of, 101

tondi, 64

tongue, slips of, *see* speech, lapses of

Torres Strait, tribesmen of, 62

totem, 49; -ancestor, 380

touch, magic, 43

trains, dream-motif, 283

trance, 232, 506

transference, 74, 269, 273; erotic character of, 74

transformation: alchemical, 293; energic, 41; of physical into psychic, 384; psychic, in middle life, 398; spiritual processes of, 357

transgressiveness, of archetypes, 515

transmission, 435, 524

transmutation of elements, *see* elements

transpsychic reality, underlying psyche, 318*n*

trauma, 98, 260*f*

travel, urge to, 117

treasure: hard to attain, 112, 194; hero and, 292; hidden, 293

tree: as alchemical symbol, 293*n;* of knowledge, 390; in Nebuchadnezzar's dream, *frontisp.,* 251, 293; wishing, 293

triad, 456, 517

triadic: fantasy-formations, 203; principle, in *I Ching,* 453; view of world, 514

tribe, 374

trigrams, 453

Trinity, 156, 335, 491, 513; astrological, 472; Nicholas of Flüe's version of, 211

truth(s): of the blood, 415; identification with one-sided, 219; psychological, 409; statistical, 421*f;* and *Weltanschauungen,* 378

Venus, 455, 461, 528
Veraguth, Otto, 14*n*, 95
verbal concepts, mistrust of, 319
vertebrates: aquatic, 152; higher, 321; sympathetic system in, 511
view, day-time and night-time, 219
Villa, Guido, 164*n*
violet (colour), representing archetype, 211, 212
Virgil, 493
Vischer, F. T., 97
vision: of sun-tube, 151; of Trinity, 211; *see also* Ezekiel; Nicholas of Flüe; Swedenborg
vitalism, 28
vitality, heightened feeling of, 347
vituperation, 103
voice(s): deepening of, in women, 397; heard by insane, 305, 308; inner, 83; "other," 83, 88*f*
volatilia, 294
volcano, 443
volition, 142; and attitude, 332; presupposes choosing subject, 183; *see also* will
Voltaire, 368
voyages, great, 339
Vulpius, Christine, 455*n*

W

Wachandi, 42*f*, 45
Wagner, Richard, 80
wakan, 63
wakonda, 61
walen/wälzen, 43
Waley, Arthur, 486*n*
Wallace, A. R., 302
wand, magic, 517
war: and judgment of enemy, 270; psychology of, 271; and reaction-dreams, 260; World, reason and, 355; *see also* atom-bomb; Boer War
Warnecke, J., 64*n*
water, in alchemy, 191
wawo, 437*n*

weather, radio, 460
weaver-bird, 226
wedding, sacred, see *hieros gamos*
Wei Po-yang, 486*n*
well, 293
Weltanschauung, 276, 358*ff*; and attitude, 360*f*; claims to truth, 378; determined by consciousness, 361; purpose of, 361; what is wrong with?, 378
Wên, King, 452
wheat, 155
West, the, and nature, 354
Weyl, Hermann, 502
wheels, 198
White, Stewart Edward, 316, 317
whole, grasping of the, 451
wholeness, 292; conscious, 225*n*; preconscious, 225; psychic, 175; —, images of, 457; unconscious, 211
Wilhelm, Hellmut, 527
Wilhelm, Richard, 452*n*, 486, 487, 488
will, 181*ff*, 498-9*n*; and attitude, 332; biological motivation of, 183; as factor determining behaviour, 118*f*; free or determined, 119; freedom of, and consciousness, 373; and function, 182; and instinct, 132, 134, 200; primitives and, 45; in Schopenhauer, 170; subordination to self, 224; supremacy of, 96; transcendental, 428, 429; in unconscious, 172; unconscious acts of, 173, 174
William of Auvergne, 196
wind, sun-phallus and, 150*f*
wind-force, 430
Wisdom of Solomon, 191
wise old man, 293
"wish," 517
wish-fantasies, 365
wish-fulfilment, 268, 277, 285; religion as, 409; theory, 254, 260, 263
wishing-rod, 517
wish-objects, 517*n*
witches/wizards, 155

witnesses, 422
Wolf, Christian von, 161, 165
woman, and moon, 154
women: masculinity in, 398; neurotic difficulties in, 395; physical
change in older, 397; psychic
change in older, 398
wong, 62
words: fantasied, 83; magic of, 109;
spellbinding, 170
work: culture and, 41; energy and,
41*f*
world: created by psyche, 384; Eastern view of, 383; man's relation
to, 360; material and psychic, 384;
picture of, 361*ff;* as psychic image,
363; scientific view of, 422
World Essence, 191
world-image, 376, 380
world-soul, 190, 196, 490, 494; see also
anima mundi
wounded man, 506
wounds: head and brain, 506*f;*
psychic, 313; *see also* trauma
writing: automatic, 84, 121, 320;
mistakes in, 13
Wundt, Wilhelm, 3*n,* 4*n,* 6 & *n,* 16,
22, 23, 101, 164*ff,* 172, 173

Y

Yang and Yin, 451, 452
Yaos, 62
yaris, 64
yarrow stalks, 451*n,* 452, 453, 527
yod, 495
yoga, 357
youth, 405; period of, 391*ff;* unwillingness to part with, 396
yucca moth, 132, 137

Z

Zacharias, Book of, 197
Zagreb, 433
Zarathustra (Nietzsche's), 80, 122,
335
Zeller, Eduard, 490*n*
Zen Buddhists/Buddhism, 68, 225
zodiac, 197, 527; signs of, 454, 455*n*
zogo, 62
Zöllner, J. K. F., 302
Zoroaster, 493
Zorobabel, 197
Zosimos of Panopolis, 492

THE COLLECTED WORKS OF

C. G. JUNG

THE PUBLICATION of the first complete collected edition, in English, of the works of C. G. Jung has been undertaken by Routledge and Kegan Paul, Ltd., in England and by the Bollingen Foundation through Pantheon Books, Inc., in the United States. The edition contains revised versions of works previously published, such as *Psychology of the Unconscious*, which is now entitled *Symbols of Transformation;* works originally written in English, such as "Psychology and Religion"; works not previously translated, such as *Aion;* and, in general, new translations of the major body of Professor Jung's writings. The author has supervised the textual revision, which in some cases is extensive. Sir Herbert Read, Dr. Michael Fordham, and Dr. Gerhard Adler compose the Editorial Committee; the translator is R. F. C. Hull.

Every volume of the Collected Works contains material that either has not previously been published in English or is being newly published in revised form. In addition to *Aion,* the following volumes will, entirely or in large part, be new to English readers: *Psychiatric Studies; Archetypes and the Collective Unconscious; Alchemical Studies; Mysterium Coniunctionis; The Spirit in Man, Art, and Literature;* and *The Practice of Psychotherapy.*

The volumes are not being published in strictly consecutive order; but, generally speaking, works of which translations are lacking or unavailable are given precedence. The price of the volumes varies according to size; they are sold separately, and may also be obtained on standing order. Several of the volumes are extensively illustrated. Each volume contains an index and, in most cases, a bibliography; the final volumes will contain a complete bibliography of Professor Jung's writings and a general index of the entire edition. Subsequent works of the author's will be added in due course.

*1. PSYCHIATRIC STUDIES
    On the Psychology and Pathology of So-Called Occult Phenomena
    On Hysterical Misreading
    Cryptomnesia   *(continued)*
* Published 1957.

* To be published 1960.

* Published 1956.

* Published 1959.

*12. PSYCHOLOGY AND ALCHEMY   *Illustrated*

Introduction to the Religious and Psychological Problems of Alchemy
Individual Dream Symbolism in Relation to Alchemy
Religious Ideas in Alchemy
Epilogue

13. ALCHEMICAL STUDIES   *Illustrated*

Commentary on "The Secret of the Golden Flower"
The Spirit Mercurius
Some Observations on the Visions of Zosimos
Paracelsus as a Spiritual Phenomenon
The "Arbor philosophica"

14. MYSTERIUM CONIUNCTIONIS

The Components of the *Coniunctio*
The Paradox
The Personification of Opposites: Introduction; Sol; Sulphur; Luna;
    Sal; Rex; Regina; Adam and Eve
The Conjunction

15. THE SPIRIT IN MAN, ART, AND LITERATURE

Paracelsus
Paracelsus the Physician
Sigmund Freud: A Cultural Phenomenon
Sigmund Freud: An Obituary
Richard Wilhelm: An Obituary
Psychology and Literature
On the Relation of Analytical Psychology to the Poetic Art
Picasso
"Ulysses"

†16. THE PRACTICE OF PSYCHOTHERAPY   *Illustrated*

GENERAL PROBLEMS OF PSYCHOTHERAPY
Principles of Practical Psychotherapy
What Is Psychotherapy?
Some Aspects of Modern Psychotherapy
Aims of Modern Psychotherapy
Problems of Modern Psychotherapy
Psychotherapy and a Philosophy of Life   (*continued*)

* Published 1953.   † Published 1954.